www.wadsworth.com

wadsworth.com is the World Wide Web site for
Wadsworth Publishing Company and is your direct
source to dozens of online resources.

At *wadsworth.com* you can find out about supplements,
demonstration software, and student resources. You can
also send e-mail to many of our authors and preview new
publications and exciting new technologies.

wadsworth.com
Changing the way the world learns®

SOCIAL AND PERSONAL ETHICS

FIFTH EDITION

William H. Shaw
San Jose State University

2005

THOMSON
★
WADSWORTH

Australia • Canada • Mexico • Singapore • Spain • United Kingdom • United States

Publisher: Holly J. Allen
Philosophy Editor: Steve Wainwright
Assistant Editors: Lee McCracken, Anna Lustig
Editorial Assistant: Barbara Hillaker
Marketing Manager: Worth Hawes
Advertising Project Managers: Bryan Vann, Vicky Wan
Composition Buyer: Ben Schroeter
Print/Media Buyer: Doreen Suruki

Permissions Editor: Stephanie Lee
Production Service: Greg Hubit Bookworks
Copy Editor: Debra Priest
Cover Designer: Yvo Riezebos
Cover Image: Palo Alto Photography/Veer
Compositor: International Typesetting and
    Composition
Printer: Webcom

Printed in Canada
1 2 3 4 5 6 7   08 07 06 05 04

For more information about our products, contact us at:
Thomson Learning Academic Resource Center
1-800-423-0563

For permission to use material from this text, contact us by:
Web: http://www.thomsonrights.com

Library of Congress Control Number: 2003116254

ISBN: 0-534-64024-9

Wadsworth/Thomson Learning
10 Davis Drive
Belmont, CA 94002-3098
USA

Asia
Thomson Learning
5 Shenton Way #01-01
UIC Building
Singapore 068808

Australia/New Zealand
Thomson Learning
102 Dodds Street
Southbank, Victoria 3006
Australia

Canada
Nelson
1120 Birchmount Road
Toronto, Ontario M1K 5G4
Canada

Europe/Middle East/Africa
Thomson Learning
High Holborn House
50/51 Bedford Row
London WC1R 4LR
United Kingdom

Latin America
Thomson Learning
Seneca, 53
Colonia Polanco
11560 Mexico D.F.
Mexico

Spain/Portugal
Paraninfo
Calle Magallanes, 25
28015 Madrid, Spain

CONTENTS

Shaded type indicates material new to this edition.

6. Animals and Environmental Ethics

7. Pornography and Sexual Morality

8. Liberty, Paternalism, and Freedom of Expression

9. The Responsibilities of Citizens

10. Gun Control

11. Punishment and the Death Penalty

PREFACE

MOST ETHICS COURSES these days, especially at the introductory level, put significant emphasis on contemporary moral issues and problems of applied ethics. *Social and Personal Ethics* is designed for use in such a course. As the book enters its fifth edition, readers familiar with earlier versions of it will notice striking changes while at the same time, I hope, also appreciating that *Social and Personal Ethics* has retained its distinctive philosophical and pedagogical strengths.

Changes in This Edition

Highlighting this fifth edition are four new chapter topics—on ethical relativism, on the responsibilities of citizens, on war and terrorism, and on ethics in business. Overall, *Social and Personal Ethics* contains twenty-four new essays. These include discussions of current issues like date rape, gay rights, corporate downsizing, terrorism, civil disobedience, international sweatshops, gun control, and the ethics of advertising, to name a few, as well as new perspectives on familiar issues like abortion and euthanasia. The book also incorporates two recent and highly relevant Supreme Court decisions: one on executing mentally retarded criminals, the other on affirmative action in higher education. Fresh material appears in all but three of the book's fifteen chapters; several existing chapters have been reorganized, and the sequence of topics in the book has been rearranged. I have touched up the introductory essays and improved the editing or pedagogical apparatus of a number of the previous readings in order to increase their accessibility and to ensure their continued relevance to undergraduate ethics courses.

The Readings

Because *Social and Personal Ethics* covers a broad range of moral topics and offers a large and diverse collection of articles that lend themselves well to classroom discussion, it should appeal to instructors of various philosophical persuasions. But this fact should not obscure the book's organizational and pedagogical coherence. I have tried to avoid offering simply a grab bag of intriguing essays. The readings of each section are designed to work well together, so that there is a dialogue among the writers in each chapter. In addition, the ordering of the various chapters and the thematic connections among them make intellectual sense. Taken together with the links between Part I and Part II (see below), these features make for a textbook with about as much unity and coherence as one can expect in this field.

For *Social and Personal Ethics* I have sought essays that are philosophically intelligent yet interesting and accessible to undergraduates and fun to teach. The book reprints a number of "classics," whose classroom effectiveness is well established, but it also includes many recent, previously unanthologized essays. The majority of these are by eminent philosophers, but other selections represent important contributions by less well-known philosophers or by other writers with whom philosophy instructors may be unacquainted. As before, the essays are prefaced by short introductions with study questions to guide students in their reading, and they are followed by questions for review and discussion.

Ethics: Theoretical and Applied

Social and Personal Ethics begins with two essays that discuss the nature of morality and acquaint students with the major theories and concepts of ethics. The first essay provides an economical introduction to the relationship between law and morality and between religion and morality, to ethical relativism, to the distinguishing features of moral standards, to the nature of conscience and personal values, and to the potential conflict between morality and self-interest, among other topics. The second essay is a critical overview of egoism, utilitarianism, and Kant's ethics, along with Ross's non-consequentialism and rights-based approaches to ethics.

These essays are followed by James Rachels's chapter on cultural relativism, an issue of great interest to undergraduates and a necessary discussion topic in any introductory level ethics course. The final chapter of Part I contains substantial but carefully edited extracts from the works of Aristotle, Kant, and Mill. Themes from these giants of moral philosophy echo throughout the rest of the book.

Depending on instructors' philosophical perspectives and teaching goals, they can use Part I in different ways. They can, of course, work through it systematically. But it is also possible to focus on only some of this material—for example, assigning the first two essays only as recommended reading or, alternatively, spending time on them but skipping the historical essays. Some instructors may wish to begin with Rachels's essay, then move on to the applied topics of Part II, before turning at the end of the course to a discussion of rival normative theories and more general questions in moral philosophy.

Despite its division into two parts, *Social and Personal Ethics* does not divorce moral theory from the philosophical discussion of applied ethical issues. Questions of ethical theory and of the alternative normative directions that are open to us surface throughout Part II. A number of the essays on applied ethics adopt an approach explicitly derived from one or other of the classic theories—for example, Rosalind Hursthouse's virtue-oriented approach to abortion, Nicholas Dixon's utilitarian analysis of gun control, or Robert Van Wyk's Kantian approach to world hunger. Other essays implicitly or explicitly address the tension between the rival theoretical perspectives discussed in Part I—Michael Phillips's essay on manipulative advertising is one example—while yet other "applied" essays raise important theoretical issues, such as the nature of rights, the meaning of liberty and autonomy, the extensiveness of moral obligation, the characteristics of moral reasoning, and the scope and requirements of justice.

Ethics: Social and Personal

Many moral philosophers today see ethics as more properly concerned with character, moral education, vices, and virtues than with rules, rights, and public policy. This perspective makes itself felt in Part II. Hursthouse's essay on abortion and Mike Martin's discussion of adultery are good examples. And the radical environmentalism of J. Baird Callicott challenges many of the normally unarticulated assumptions of contemporary rule-oriented moral theory. Questions of personal value and individual choice also appear throughout Part II—for example, in the essays by Richard Brandt and John Hardwig on choosing death, in Mylan Engel's advocacy of vegetarianism, in R. M. Hare's discussion of loyalty and obedience in war, and in Michael Davis's essay on whistleblowing.

Questions of personal ethics (that is, of personal values and individual moral choice) constantly intermingle with questions of social ethics (that is, the assessment of social norms, public policy, and the institutional rules of morality). One sees this commingling particularly clearly in the sections on sexuality, on abortion and euthanasia, and on liberty and paternalism, but it is true of almost every chapter in the book. Because questions of personal conduct and social policy intertwine in practice, they can and should be taught side by side, and the articles chosen for this collection generally discuss personal or social questions or both without drawing sharp lines between them. Some authors may lean toward a virtue-based approach to ethics and others toward a rule-based approach, but the essays themselves do not require endorsement of one perspective over the other; nor do they presuppose an incompatibility between the two.

Acknowledgments

I am grateful for the assistance of the following reviewers, whose thoughtful suggestions and useful criticisms helped shape this book: Susan Armstrong, Humboldt State University; James Baillie, University of Portland; Joseph Betz, Villanova University; Claudia Card, University of Wisconsin; Ann Davis, University of Colorado, Boulder; Debra DeBruin, University of Illinois, Chicago; James Dreier, Brown University; Randolph Feezell, Crieghton University; Sterling Harwood, San Jose City College; Daniel M. Hausman, University of Wisconsin at Madison; John Himelright, Hartnell College; Robert Hollinger, Iowa State University of Science and Technology; Michael LeBuffe, Texas A&M University; Judith Little, State University of New York College at Potsdam; Scott C. Lowe, Bloomsburg University; Heidi Malm, Loyola University, Chicago; Don Marietta, Florida Atlantic University; Andrew McLaughlin, City University of New York; John McLaughlin, Elmira College; Peter Murphy, Utah State University; Lucia Palmer, University of Delaware; Robert E. Reuman, Colby College; Barbara C. Scholz, San Jose State University; Jerome Shaffer, University of Connecticut; Ed Sherline, University of Wyoming; Laurie Shrage, California State Polytechnic University; Caroline J. Simon, Hope College; Sharon Sytsma, Northern Illinois University; Barbara Tucker, Trident Technical College; Gary Varner, Texas A&M University; and Rebecca Whisnant, University of Dayton.

PART I

ETHICAL THEORY

1

AN INTRODUCTION TO ETHICS

The Nature of Morality

IN AN AWARD-WINNING TELEVISION DRAMA, police captain Frank Furillo firmly believes that the two toughs just brought in by his officers are guilty of the rape-murder of a nun earlier that morning inside the parish church. But the evidence is only circumstantial. As word of the crime spreads, the community is aghast and angry. From all sides—the press, local citizens, city hall, the police commissioner—pressure mounts on Furillo and his department for a speedy resolution of the matter. Outside the Hill Street station, a mob grows frenzied, hoping to get their hands on the two young men and administer street justice to them. Someone in the mob has even taken a shot at the suspects inside the police station!

The police, however, have only enough evidence to arraign the suspects on the relatively minor charge of being in possession of goods stolen from the church. Furillo and his colleagues could demand high bail, thus keeping the defendants in custody while the police try to turn up evidence that will convict the men of murder. In a surprise move at the arraignment, the district attorney, acting in conjunction with Furillo, declines to ask the judge for bail. The men are free to go. But they and their outraged public defender,

Joyce Davenport, know that their lives will be worthless once they hit the streets: Community members have sworn to avenge the much-loved sister if the police are unable to do their job. To remain in police custody, and thus safe, their only choice is to confess to murder. So the two men confess.

Davenport argues passionately but unsuccessfully against what she considers to be a police-state tactic. Anyone in that circumstance, guilty or innocent, would confess. It is an affront to the very idea of the rule of law, she contends: police coercion by way of mob pressure. No system of justice can permit such conduct from its public officials. Yet the confession allows the police to locate the murder weapon, thus bringing independent confirmation of the culprits' guilt. Furillo's tactic, nevertheless, does not rest easily on his own conscience, and the teleplay closes with him entering the church confessional later that night: "Forgive me, Father, for I have sinned. . . ."

Furillo is understandably worried about whether he did the morally right thing. His action was successful, and it was for a good cause. But does the end always justify the means? Did the police and district attorney behave in a way that accords with due process and the rights of defendants? Should community pressure influence one's professional decisions? Did Furillo act in accordance with some principle that he could defend publicly? In a tough and controversial situation like this, the issue does not concern the moral sincerity of either Furillo or Davenport. Both can be assumed to want to do what is right, but what exactly is the morally justified thing to do? How are we to judge Furillo's tactics?

These are difficult questions. Your answers will depend on the moral principles you accept. Moral principles provide the confirmatory standards for our moral judgments, and any defensible moral judgment must be supportable by a sound moral principle. But what are the appropriate principles to rely on when making moral judgments? Philosophers have given different answers to this question, and the second introductory essay will examine their answers. But first we must look more generally at the nature of morality: what moral standards are, where they come from, and how they fit into our lives. In particular, this essay discusses the following:

- The meaning of ethics
- What distinguishes moral standards from nonmoral standards, such as etiquette, law, and professional codes of conduct
- The relationship between morality and religion
- The doctrine of ethical relativism and its difficulties
- What it means to have moral principles, the nature of conscience, and the relationship between morality and self-interest
- The place of values and ideals in an individual's life

Ethics

"The word *ethics* comes from the Greek word *ethos*, meaning character or custom," writes philosophy professor Robert C. Solomon.[1] Today we use the word *ethos* to refer to the distinguishing disposition, character, or attitude of a specific people, culture, or group (as in, for example, "the American ethos" or "the business ethos"). According to Solomon, the etymology of *ethics* suggests its basic concerns: (1) individual character, including what it means to be "a good person," and (2) the social rules that govern and limit our conduct, especially the ultimate rules concerning right and wrong, which we call *morality*.

Philosophers generally distinguish ethics from morality. "Morality" refers to a person or group's standards of right and wrong or good and bad, and "ethics" refers to the study and assessment of those standards. Thus, when we reflect critically on our own moral standards or the moral values of the society around us, we are beginning to do ethics. Few people, however, would distinguish a person's "morals" from his or her "ethics," and almost everyone uses "ethical" and "moral" interchangeably to describe people we consider good and actions we consider right, and "unethical" and "immoral" to designate bad people and wrong actions. This essay follows that common usage.

Moral Versus Nonmoral Standards

Moral questions differ from other kinds of questions. Whether your office computer can download a copyrighted album from the Web is a factual question, not a moral question. On the other hand, whether you should download the album is a moral question. When we answer a moral question or make a moral judgment, we appeal to moral standards. These standards differ from other kinds of standards.

Wearing shorts to a formal dinner party is boorish behavior. Murdering the King's English with double negatives violates the basic conventions of proper language usage. Photographing the finish of a horse race with low-speed film is poor photographic technique. In each case a standard is violated—fashion, grammatical, artistic— but the violation does not pose a serious threat to human well-being.

Moral standards are different because they concern behavior that is of serious consequence to human welfare, that can profoundly injure or benefit people.[2] The conventional moral norms against lying, stealing, and murdering deal with actions that can hurt people. And the moral principle that human beings should be treated with dignity and respect uplifts the human personality. Whether products are healthful or harmful, work conditions safe or dangerous, personnel procedures biased or fair, privacy respected or invaded are also matters that seriously affect human well-being. The standards that govern our conduct in these areas are moral standards.

A second characteristic follows from the first. Moral standards take priority over other standards, including self-interest. Something that morality condemns—for instance, the burglary of your neighbor's home—cannot be justified on the nonmoral grounds that it would be a thrill to do it or that it would pay off handsomely. We take moral standards to be more important than other considerations in guiding our actions.

A third characteristic of moral standards is that their soundness depends on the adequacy of the reasons that support or justify them. For the most part, fashion standards are set by clothing designers, merchandisers, and consumers; grammatical standards by grammarians and students of language; technical standards by practitioners and experts in the field. Legislators make laws, boards of directors make organizational policy, and licensing boards establish standards for professionals. In these cases, some authoritative body is the ultimate validating source of the standards and thus can change the standards if it wishes. Moral standards are not made by such bodies, although they are often endorsed or rejected by them. More precisely, the validity of moral standards depends not on authoritative fiat but rather on the quality of the arguments or the reasoning that supports them. Exactly what constitutes adequate grounds or justification for a moral standard is a debated question, which, as we shall see, underlies disagreement among philosophers over which specific moral principles are best.

Although these three characteristics set moral standards apart from others, it is useful to discuss more specifically how morality differs from three things with which it is sometimes confused: etiquette, law, and professional codes of ethics.

Morality and etiquette

Etiquette refers to the norms of correct conduct in polite society or, more generally, to any special code of social behavior or courtesy. In our society, for example, it is considered bad etiquette to chew with your mouth open or to pick your nose when talking to someone; it is considered good etiquette to say "please" when requesting and "thank you" when receiving and to hold a door open for someone entering immediately behind you. Good business etiquette, to take another example, typically calls for writing follow-up letters after meetings, returning phone calls, and dressing appropriately. It is commonplace to judge people's manners as "good" or "bad" and the conduct that reflects them as "right" or "wrong." "Good," "bad," "right," and "wrong" here simply mean socially appropriate or socially inappropriate. In these contexts, such words express judgments about manners, not ethics.

So-called rules of etiquette that you might learn in an etiquette book are prescriptions for socially acceptable behavior. If you want to fit in, get along with others, and be thought well of by them, you should observe common rules of etiquette. If you violate the rules, then you're rightly considered ill-mannered, impolite, or even uncivilized—but not necessarily immoral.

Scrupulous observance of rules of etiquette does not make one moral. In fact, it can camouflage moral issues. A few decades ago in some parts of the United States, it was thought bad manners for blacks and whites to eat together. Those who obeyed the convention and were thus judged well mannered certainly had no grounds for feeling moral. The only way to dramatize the injustice underlying this practice was to violate the rule and be judged ill-mannered. For those in the civil rights movement of the 1960s, being considered boorish was a small price to pay for exposing the unequal treatment and human degradation that underlay this rule of etiquette.

Morality and law

People sometimes confuse legality and morality, but they are different things. On one hand, breaking the law is not always or necessarily immoral. On the other hand, the legality of an action does not guarantee that it is morally right. Let's consider these points further.

1. An action can be illegal but morally right. For example, helping a Jewish family to hide from the Nazis was against German law in 1939, but it would have been a morally admirable thing to have done. Of course, the Nazi regime was vicious and evil. By contrast, in a democratic society with a basically just legal order, the fact that something is illegal provides a moral consideration against doing it. For example, one moral reason for not burning trash in your back yard is that it violates an ordinance that your community has voted in favor of. Some philosophers believe that sometimes the illegality of an action can make it morally wrong, even if the action would otherwise have been morally acceptable. But even if they are right about this, the fact that something is illegal does not trump all other moral considerations. Nonconformity to law is not always immoral, even in a democratic society. There can be circumstances where, all things considered, violating the law is morally permissible, perhaps even morally required.

Probably no one in the modern era has expressed this point more eloquently than Dr. Martin Luther King, Jr. Confined in the Birmingham, Alabama, city jail on charges of parading without a permit, King penned his now famous "Letter from Birmingham Jail" to eight of his fellow clergymen who had published a statement attacking King's unauthorized protest of racial segregation as unwise and untimely. King wrote:

> All segregation statutes are unjust because segregation distorts the soul and damages the per-

sonality. It gives the segregator a false sense of superiority and the segregated a false sense of inferiority. Segregation, to use the terminology of the Jewish philosopher Martin Buber, substitutes an "I-it" relationship for an "I-thou" relationship and ends up relegating persons to the status of things. Hence segregation is not only politically, economically, and sociologically unsound, it is morally wrong and sinful. . . . Thus it is that I can urge men to obey the 1954 decision of the Supreme Court,* for it is morally right; and I can urge them to disobey segregation ordinances, for they are morally wrong.[3]

2. An action that is legal can be morally wrong. For example, it may have been perfectly legal for the chairman of a profitable company to lay off 125 workers and use three-quarters of the money saved to boost his pay and that of the company's other top manager,[4] but the morality of his doing so is open to debate.

Or, to take another example, suppose that you're driving to work one day and see an accident victim sitting on the side of the road, clearly in shock and needing medical assistance. Because you know first aid and are in no great hurry to get to your destination, you could easily stop and assist the person. Legally speaking, though, you are not obligated to stop and render aid. Under common law, the prudent thing would be to drive on, because by stopping you would bind yourself to use reasonable care and thus incur legal liability if you fail to do so and the victim thereby suffers injury. Many states have enacted so-called Good Samaritan laws to provide immunity from damages to those rendering aid (except for gross negligence or serious misconduct). But in most states the law does not oblige people to give such aid or even to call an ambulance. Moral theorists would agree, however, that if you sped away without rendering aid or even calling for help, your action might be perfectly legal but would be morally suspect.

---

*In *Brown v. Board of Education of Topeka* (1954), the Supreme Court struck down the half-century-old "separate but equal doctrine," which permitted racially segregated schools as long as comparable quality was maintained.

Regardless of the law, such conduct would almost certainly be wrong.

What then may we say about the relationship between law and morality? To a significant extent, law codifies a society's customs, ideals, norms, and moral values. Changes in law tend to reflect changes in what a society takes to be right and wrong, but sometimes changes in the law can alter people's ideas about the rightness or wrongness of conduct. However, even if a society's laws are sensible and morally sound, it is a mistake to see them as sufficient to establish the moral standards that should guide us. The law cannot cover the wide variety of possible individual and group conduct, and in many situations it is too blunt an instrument to provide adequate moral guidance. The law generally prohibits egregious affronts to a society's moral standards and in that sense is the "floor" of moral conduct, but breaches of moral conduct can slip through cracks in that floor.

Professional codes

Somewhere between etiquette and law lie *professional codes of ethics*. These are the rules that are supposed to govern the conduct of members of a given profession. Generally speaking, the members of a profession are understood to have agreed to abide by those rules as a condition of their engaging in that profession. Violation of the professional code may result in the disapproval of one's professional peers and, in serious cases, loss of one's license to practice that profession. Sometimes these codes are unwritten and are part of the common understanding of members of a profession—for example, that professors should not date their students. In other instances, these codes or portions of them may be written down by an authoritative body so they may be better taught and more efficiently enforced.

These written rules are sometimes so vague and general as to be of little value, and often they amount to little more than self-promotion by the professional organization. In other cases—for example with attorneys—professional codes can be very specific and detailed. It is difficult to generalize about the content of professional codes of ethics, however, because they frequently involve a mix of purely moral rules (for example, client confidentiality), of professional etiquette (for example, the billing of services to other professionals), and of restrictions intended to benefit the group's economic interests (for example, limitations on price competition).

Given their nature, professional codes of ethics are neither a complete nor a completely reliable guide to one's moral obligations. First, not all the rules of a professional code are purely moral in character, and even when they are, the fact that a rule is officially enshrined as part of the code of a profession does not guarantee that it is a sound moral principle. As a professional, you must take seriously the injunctions of your profession, but you still have the responsibility to critically assess those rules for yourself.

Where do moral standards come from?

So far you have seen how moral standards are different from various nonmoral standards, but you probably wonder about the source of those moral standards. Most, if not all, people have certain moral principles or a moral code that they explicitly or implicitly accept. Because the moral principles of different people in the same society overlap, at least in part, we can also talk about the moral code of a society, meaning the moral standards shared by its members. How do we come to have certain moral principles and not others? Obviously, many things influence us in the moral principles we accept: our early upbringing, the behavior of those around us, the explicit and implicit standards of our culture, our own experiences, and our critical reflections on those experiences.

For philosophers, though, the important question is not how in fact we came to have the particular principles we have. The philosophical issue is whether the principles we have can be justified. Do we simply take for granted the values of those around us? Or, like Martin Luther King, Jr., are we able to think independently about moral matters? By analogy, we pick up our nonmoral beliefs from all sorts of sources: books, conversations with friends, movies, experiences we've had. The philosopher's concern is not so much with how we actually got the beliefs we have, but whether or to what extent those beliefs—for example, that women are more emotional than men or that telekinesis is possible—can withstand critical scrutiny. Likewise, ethical theories attempt to justify moral standards and ethical beliefs. The second introductory essay examines some of the major theories of normative ethics. That is, it looks at what some of the major thinkers in human history have argued are the best justified standards of right and wrong.

But first we need to consider the relationship between morality and religion on the one hand and that between morality and society on the other. Some people maintain that morality just boils down to religion. Others have argued for the doctrine of *ethical relativism,* which says that right and wrong are only a function of what a particular society takes to be right and wrong. Both these views are mistaken.

Religion and Morality

Any religion provides its believers with a world view, part of which involves certain moral instructions, values, and commitments. The Jewish and Christian traditions, to name just two, offer a view of humans as unique products of a divine intervention that has endowed them with consciousness and an ability to love. Both these traditions posit creatures who stand midway between nature and spirit. On one hand, we are finite and bound to earth, not only capable of wrongdoing but born morally flawed (original sin). On the other, we can transcend nature and realize infinite possibilities.

Primarily because of the influence of Western religion, many Americans and others view themselves as beings with a supernatural destiny, as possessing a life after death, as being immortal. One's purpose in life is found in serving and loving God.

For the Christian, the way to serve and love God is by emulating the life of Jesus of Nazareth. In the life of Jesus, Christians find an expression of the highest virtue—love. They love when they perform selfless acts, develop a keen social conscience, and realize that human beings are creatures of God and therefore intrinsically worthwhile. For the Jew, one serves and loves God chiefly through expressions of justice and righteousness. Jews also develop a sense of honor derived from a commitment to truth, humility, fidelity, and kindness. This commitment hones their sense of responsibility to family and community.

Religion, then, involves not only a formal system of worship but also prescriptions for social relationships. One example is the mandate "Do unto others as you would have them do unto you." Termed the "Golden Rule," this injunction represents one of humankind's highest moral ideals and can be found in essence in all the great religions of the world:

- Good people proceed while considering that what is best for others is best for themselves. (*Hitopadesa,* Hinduism)
- Thou shalt love thy neighbor as thyself. (*Leviticus* 19:18, Judaism)
- Therefore all things whatsoever ye would that men should do to you, do ye even so to them. (*Matthew* 7:12, Christianity)
- Hurt not others with that which pains yourself. (*Udanavarga* 5:18, Buddhism)
- What you do not want done to yourself, do not do to others. (*Analects* 15:23, Confucianism)
- No one of you is a believer until he loves for his brother what he loves for himself. (*Traditions,* Islam)

Although inspiring, such religious ideals are very general and can be difficult to translate into precise policy injunctions. Religious bodies, nevertheless, occasionally articulate positions on more specific political, educational, economic, and medical issues, which help mold public opinion on matters as diverse as abortion, euthanasia, nuclear weapons, and national defense.

Morality needn't rest on religion

Many people believe that morality must be based on religion, either in the sense that without religion people would have no incentive to be moral or in the sense that only religion can provide moral guidance. Others contend that morality is based on the commands of God. None of these claims is convincing.

First, although a desire to avoid hell and to go to heaven may prompt some of us to act morally, this is not the only reason or even the most common reason that people behave morally. Often we act morally out of habit or simply because that is the kind of person we are. It would just not occur to most of us to swipe an elderly woman's purse. And if the idea did occur to us, we wouldn't do it because such an act simply doesn't fit with our personal standards or with our concept of ourselves. We are often motivated to do what is morally right out of concern for others or just because it is right. In addition, the approval of our peers, the need to appease our conscience, and the desire to avoid earthly punishment may all motivate us to act morally. Furthermore, atheists generally live lives as moral and upright as those of believers.

Second, the moral instructions of the world's great religions are general and imprecise: They do not relieve us of the necessity to engage in moral reasoning ourselves. For example, the Bible says, "Thou shalt not kill." Yet Christians disagree among themselves over the morality of fighting in wars, of capital punishment, of killing in self-defense, of slaughtering animals, of abortion and euthanasia, and of allowing foreigners to die from famine because we have not provided them with as much food as we might have. The Bible does not give unambiguous answers to these moral problems. So even believers must engage in moral philosophy if they are to have intelligent answers. On the other hand, there are lots of reasons for believing that, say, a cold-blooded murder motivated by greed is immoral; you do not have to believe in a religion to figure that out.

Third, although some theologians have advocated the *divine command theory*—that if some-

thing is wrong (like killing an innocent person for fun), then the only reason it is wrong is that God commands us not to do it—many theologians and certainly most philosophers would reject this view. They would contend that if God commands human beings not to do something, like commit rape, it is because God sees that rape is wrong, but it is not God's forbidding rape that makes it wrong. The fact that rape is wrong is independent of God's decrees.

Most believers think not only that God gives us moral instructions or rules but also that God has moral reasons for giving them to us. According to the divine command theory, this would make no sense. In this view, there is no reason that something is right or wrong, other than the fact that it is God's will. All believers, of course, believe that God is good and that He commands us to do what is right and forbids us to do what is wrong. But this doesn't mean, say critics of the divine command theory, that God's saying so makes a thing wrong, any more than your mother's telling you not to steal makes it wrong to steal.

All this is simply to argue that morality is not necessarily based on religion in any of these three senses. That religion influences the moral standards and values of most of us is beyond doubt. But given that religions differ in their moral principles and that even members of the same faith often disagree among themselves on moral matters, practically speaking you cannot justify a moral principle simply by appealing to religion—for that will only persuade those who already agree with your particular interpretation of your particular religion. Besides, most religions hold that human reason is capable of understanding what is right and wrong, so it is human reason to which you will have to appeal in order to support your ethical principle.

Ethical Relativism

Some people do not believe that morality boils down to religion but rather that it is just a function of what a particular society happens to believe. This view is called *ethical relativism,* the theory that what is right is determined by what a culture or society says is right. What is right in one place may be wrong in another, because the only criterion for distinguishing right from wrong—and so the only ethical standard for judging an action—is the moral system of the society in which the act occurs.

Abortion, for example, is condemned as immoral in Catholic Ireland but is practiced as a morally neutral form of birth control in Japan. According to the ethical relativist, then, abortion is wrong in Ireland but morally permissible in Japan. The relativist is not saying merely that the Irish believe abortion is abominable and the Japanese do not; that is acknowledged by everyone. Rather, the ethical relativist contends that abortion is immoral in Ireland because the Irish believe it to be immoral and that it is morally permissible in Japan because the Japanese believe it to be so. Thus, for the ethical relativist there is no absolute ethical standard independent of cultural context, no criteria of right and wrong by which to judge other than those of particular societies. In short, what morality requires is relative to society.

Those who endorse ethical relativism point to the apparent diversity of human values and the multiformity of moral codes to support their case. From our own cultural perspective, some seemingly immoral moralities have been adopted; polygamy, pedophilia, stealing, slavery, infanticide, and cannibalism have all been tolerated or even encouraged by the moral system of one society or another. In light of this fact, the ethical relativist believes that there can be no nonethnocentric standard by which to judge actions.

Some thinkers believe that the moral differences between societies are smaller and less significant than they appear. They contend that variations in moral standards reflect differing factual beliefs and differing circumstances rather than fundamental differences in values. But suppose they are wrong about this matter. The relativist's conclusion still does not follow. As Allan Bloom writes, "The fact that there have been different opinions about good and bad in different times and places in no way proves that none is true or superior to others. To say that it does so prove is as absurd as to say that the diversity of points of view expressed in a college bull session proves there is no truth."[5] Disagreement in ethical matters does not imply that all opinions are equally correct.

Moreover, ethical relativism has some unpleasant implications. First, it undermines any moral criticism of the practices of other societies as long as their actions conform to their own standards. We cannot say that slavery in a slave society like that of the American South 150 years ago was immoral and unjust as long as that society held it to be morally permissible.

Second, and closely related, is the fact that for the relativist there is no such thing as ethical progress. Although moralities may change, they cannot get better or worse. Thus, we cannot say that our moral standards today are any more enlightened than they were in the Middle Ages.

Third, it makes no sense from the relativist's point of view for people to criticize principles or practices accepted by their own society. People can be censured for not living up to their society's moral code, but that is all. The moral code itself cannot be criticized because whatever a society takes to be right really is right for it. Reformers who identify injustices in their society and campaign against them are only encouraging people to be immoral—that is, to depart from the moral standards of their society—unless or until the majority of the society agrees with the reformers. The minority can never be right in moral matters; to be right it must become the majority.

The ethical relativist is right to emphasize that in viewing other cultures we should keep an open mind and not simply dismiss alien social practices on the basis of our own cultural prejudices. But the relativist's theory of morality doesn't hold up. The more carefully we examine it, the less plausible it becomes. There is no good reason for saying that the majority view on moral issues is automatically right, and the belief that it is automatically right has unacceptable consequences.

Having Moral Principles

Most people at some time in their lives pause to reflect on what moral principles they have or should have and on what moral standards are the best justified. When a person accepts a moral principle, when that principle is part of his or her personal moral code, then naturally the person believes the principle is important and well justified. But there is more to moral principles than that, as the philosopher Richard Brandt (1910–1997) emphasized. When a principle is part of a person's moral code, that person is strongly motivated toward the conduct required by the principle and against behavior that conflicts with that principle. The person will tend to feel guilty when his or her own conduct violates that principle and to disapprove of others whose behavior conflicts with it. Likewise, the person will tend to hold in esteem those whose conduct shows an abundance of the motivation required by the principle.[6]

Other philosophers have, in different ways, reinforced Brandt's point. To accept a moral principle is not a purely intellectual act like accepting a scientific hypothesis or a mathematical theorem. Rather, it also involves a desire to follow that principle for its own sake, the likelihood of feeling guilty about not doing so, and a tendency to evaluate the conduct of others according to the principle in question. We would find it very strange, for example, if Sally claimed to be morally opposed to cruelty to animals yet abused her own pets and felt no inclination to protest when some ruffians down the street lit a cat on fire.

Conscience

People can, and unfortunately sometimes do, go against their moral principles. But we would doubt that they sincerely held the principle in question if violating it did not bother their conscience. We have all felt the pangs of conscience, but what exactly is conscience and how reliable a guide is it? Our conscience, of course, is not literally a little voice inside of us. To oversimplify a complex story in developmental psychology, our conscience evolved as we internalized the moral instructions of the parents or other authority figures who raised us as children.

When you were very young, you were probably told to tell the truth and to return something you filched to its proper owner. If you were caught lying or being dishonest, you were probably punished—scolded, spanked, sent to bed without dinner, denied a privilege. On the other hand, truth telling and kindness to your siblings were probably rewarded—with approval, praise, maybe even hugs or candy. Seeking reward and avoiding punishment motivate small children to do what is expected of them. Gradually, children come to internalize those parental commands. Thus, they feel vaguely that their parents know what they are doing even when the parents are not around. When children do something forbidden, they experience the same feelings as when scolded by their parents—the first stirrings of guilt. By the same token, even in the absence of explicit parental reward, children feel a sense of self-approval about having done what they were supposed to have done.

As we grow older, of course, our motivations are not so simple and our self-understanding is greater. We are able to reflect on and understand the moral lessons we were taught, as well as to refine and modify those principles. As adults we are morally independent agents. Yet however much our conscience has evolved and however much our adult moral code differs from the moral perspective of our childhood, those pangs of guilt we occasionally feel still stem from that early internalization of parental demands.

The limits of conscience

How reliable a guide is conscience? People often say, "Follow your conscience" or "You should never go against your conscience," but not only is such advice not very helpful, it may sometimes be bad advice. First, when we are genuinely perplexed over what we ought to do, we are trying to figure out what our conscience ought to be saying to us. When it is not possible to do both, should we keep our promise to a colleague or come to the aid of an old friend? To be told that we should follow our conscience is no help at all.

Second, it may not always be good for us to follow our conscience. It all depends on what our conscience says. Our conscience might reflect moral motivations that cannot withstand critical scrutiny. Consider an episode in Chapter 16 of Mark Twain's *The Adventures of Huckleberry Finn*. Huck has taken off down the Mississippi on a raft with his friend, the runaway slave Jim. But as they get nearer to the place where Jim will become legally free, Huck starts feeling guilty about helping him run away:

> It hadn't ever come to me before, what this thing was that I was doing. But now it did; and it stayed with me, and scorched me more and more. I tried to make out to myself that *I* warn't to blame, because *I* didn't run Jim off from his rightful owner; but it warn't no use, conscience up and says, every time: "But you knowed he was running for his freedom, and you could a paddled ashore and told somebody." That was so—I couldn't get around that, no way. That was where it pinched. Conscience says to me: "What had poor Miss Watson done to you, that you could see her nigger go off right under your eyes and never say one single word? What did that poor old woman do to you, that you could treat her so mean? . . ." I got to feeling so mean and miserable I most wished I was dead.

Here Huck is feeling guilty about doing what we would all agree is the morally right thing to do. But Huck is only a boy, and his pangs of conscience reflect the principles that he has picked up uncritically from the slave-owning society around him. Unable to think independently about matters of right and wrong, Huck in the end decides to disregard his conscience. He follows his instincts and sticks by his friend Jim.

The point here is not that you should ignore your conscience but that the voice of conscience is itself something that can be critically examined. A pang of conscience is like a warning. When you feel one, you should definitely stop and reflect

on the rightness of what you are doing. On the other hand, you cannot justify your actions simply by saying you were following your conscience. Terrible crimes have been committed in the name of conscience.

Moral principles and self-interest

Sometimes doing what you believe would be morally right and doing what would best satisfy your own interests may be two different things. Imagine that you are in your car hurrying home along a quiet road, trying hard to get there in time to see the kickoff of an important football game. You pass an acquaintance who is having car trouble. He doesn't recognize you. As a dedicated fan, you would much prefer to keep on going than to stop and help him, thus missing at least part of the game. You might rationalize that someone else will eventually come along and help him if you don't, but deep down you know that you really ought to stop. On the other hand, self-interest seems to say, "Keep going."

Consider another example.[7] You have applied for a new job, and if you land it, it will be an enormous break for you: It is exactly the kind of position you want and have been trying to get for some time. It pays well and will settle you into a desirable career for the rest of your life. The competition has come down to just you and one other person, and you believe correctly that she has a slight edge on you. Now imagine that you could spread a nasty rumor about her that would guarantee she wouldn't get the job and that you could do this in a way that wouldn't come back to you. Presumably, circulating this lie would violate your moral code; on the other hand, doing it would clearly be to your benefit.

Some people argue that moral action and self-interest can never really be in conflict, and some philosophers have gone to great lengths to try to prove this, but they are almost certainly mistaken. They maintain that if you do the wrong thing, then you will be caught, your conscience will bother you, or in some way "what goes around comes around," so that your misdeed will come back to haunt you. This is often correct. But unfortunately—viewed just in terms of personal self-interest—sometimes doing what you know to be wrong may pay off. People sometimes get away with their wrongdoings, and if their conscience bothers them at all, it may not bother them that much. To believe otherwise not only is wishful thinking but also shows a lack of understanding of morality.

Morality serves to restrain our purely self-interested desires so we can all live together. The moral standards of a society provide the basic guidelines for cooperative social existence and allow conflicts to be resolved by appeal to shared principles of justification. If our interests never came into conflict—that is, if it were never advantageous for one person to deceive or cheat another—then there would be little need for morality. We would already be in heaven. Both a system of law that punishes people for hurting others and a system of morality that encourages people to refrain from pursuing their self-interest at great expense to others help to make social existence possible.

Usually, following our moral principles is in our best interest. But notice one thing. If you do the right thing only because you think it will pay off, you are not really motivated by moral concerns. Having a moral principle involves having a desire to follow the principle for its own sake—just because it is the right thing to do. If you only do the right thing because you believe it will pay off, you might just as easily not do it if it looks as if it is not going to pay off.

In addition, there is no guarantee that moral behavior will always pay off in strictly selfish terms. As argued earlier, there will be exceptions. From the moral point of view, you ought to stop and help your acquaintance and you shouldn't lie about competitors. From the selfish point of view, you should do exactly the opposite. Should you follow your self-interest or your moral principles? There's no final answer to this question. From the moral point of view, you should, of course, follow your moral principles. But from the selfish point of view, you should look out solely for Number One.

Which option you choose will depend on the strength of your self-interested or self-regarding desires in comparison with the strength of your other-regarding desires (that is, your moral motivations and your concern for others). In other words, your choice will depend on the kind of person you are, which depends in large part on how you were raised. A selfish person will pass by the acquaintance in distress and will spread the rumor, whereas a person who has a stronger concern for others, or a stronger desire to do what is right just because it is right, will not.

Although it may be impossible to prove to selfish people that they should not do the thing that best advances their self-interest (because, if they are selfish, that is all they care about), there are considerations that suggest it is not in a person's overall self-interest to be a selfish person. People who are exclusively concerned with their own interests tend to have less happy and less satisfying lives than those whose desires extend beyond themselves. This is sometimes called the *paradox of hedonism*. Individuals who care only about their own happiness will generally be less happy than those who care about others. Moreover, people often find greater satisfaction in a life lived according to moral principle, and in being the kind of person that entails, than in a life devoted solely to immediate self-interest. Thus, or so many philosophers have argued, people have self-interested reasons not to be so self-interested. How do selfish people make themselves less so? Not overnight, obviously. But by involving themselves in the concerns and cares of others, they can in time come to care sincerely about those people.

Morality and Personal Values

Some philosophers distinguish between morality in a narrow sense and morality in a broad sense. In a narrow sense, morality is the moral code of an individual or a society (insofar as the moral codes of the individuals making up that society overlap). Although the principles that make up our code may not be explicitly formulated, as laws are, they do guide us in our conduct. They function as internal monitors of our own behavior and as a basis for assessing the action of others. Morality in the narrow sense concerns the principles that do or should regulate people's conduct and relations with others. These principles can be debated, however. (Take, for example, John Stuart Mill's contention that society ought not to interfere with people's liberty when their actions affect only themselves.) And a large part of moral philosophy involves assessing rival moral principles. This discussion is part of the ongoing development in our moral culture. What is at stake are the basic standards that ought to govern our behavior—that is, the basic framework or ground rules that make coexistence possible. If there were not already fairly widespread agreement about these principles, our social order would not be possible.

But in addition we can talk about our morality in a broader sense, meaning not just the principles of conduct that we embrace but also the values, ideals, and aspirations that shape our lives. Many different ways of living our lives would meet our basic moral obligations. The type of life each of us seeks to live reflects our individual values—whether following a profession, devoting ourselves to community service, raising a family, seeking solitude, pursuing scientific truth, striving for athletic excellence, amassing political power, cultivating glamorous people as friends, or some combination of these and many other possible ways of living. The life that each of us forges and the way we understand that life are part of our morality in the broad sense of the term.

It is important to bear this in mind throughout your study of applied ethics. Although the usual concern is with the principles that ought to govern conduct in certain situations—for example, whether a hiring officer may take the race of applicants into account, whether euthanasia is immoral, or whether surrogate parenting contracts should be permitted—the moral choices you make in your own life will also reflect your other values and ideals—or in other words, the kind of person you are striving to be.

The decisions you make and much of the way you shape your life will depend not just on your moral code but also on the understanding you have of yourself in certain roles and relationships. Your morality—in the sense of your ideals, values, and aspirations—involves, among other things, your understanding of human nature, tradition, and society; of one's proper relationship to the natural environment; and of an individual's place in the cosmos. Professionals in various fields, for example, are invariably guided not just by rules but also by their understanding of what being a professional involves. And a businessperson's conception of the ideal or model relationship to have with clients will greatly influence his or her day-to-day conduct.

There is more to living a morally good life, of course, than being good at your job, as Aristotle (384–322 B.C.E.) argued long ago. He underscored the necessity of trying to achieve virtue or excellence, not just in some particular field of endeavor but as a human being. Aristotle thought that things have functions. The function of a piano, for instance, is to make certain sounds, and a piano that performs this function well is a good or excellent piano. Likewise, we have an idea of what it is for a person to be an excellent athlete, an excellent manager, or an excellent professor—it is to do well the types of things that athletes, managers, or professors are supposed to do.

But Aristotle also thought that, just as there was an ideal of excellence for any particular craft or occupation, similarly there must be an excellence that we can achieve simply as human beings. That is, he thought that we can live our lives as a whole in such a way that they can be judged not just as excellent in this respect or in that occupation, but as excellent, period. Aristotle thought that only when we develop our truly human capacities sufficiently to achieve this human excellence would we have lives blessed with happiness. Philosophers since Aristotle's time have been skeptical of his apparent belief that this human excellence would come in just one form, but many would underscore the importance of developing our various potential capacities and striving to achieve a kind of excellence in our lives. How we understand this excellence is a function of our values, ideals, and world view—our morality in a broad sense.

NOTES

1. Robert C. Solomon, *Morality and the Good Life* (New York: McGraw-Hill, 1984), 3.
2. On the characteristics of moral standards, see Manuel G. Velasquez, *Business Ethics,* 5th ed. (Englewood Cliffs, N.J.: Prentice-Hall, 2001), 9–11.
3. Martin Luther King, Jr., "Letter from Birmingham Jail," in *Why We Can't Wait* (New York: Harper & Row, 1963), 85.
4. *Newsweek,* May 26, 1997, 54.
5. Allan Bloom, *The Closing of the American Mind* (New York: Simon & Schuster, 1987), 39.
6. Richard B. Brandt, *A Theory of the Good and the Right* (New York: Oxford University Press, 1979), 165–170.
7. Baruch Brody, *Beginning Philosophy* (Englewood Cliffs, N.J.: Prentice-Hall, 1977), 33.

Normative Theories of Ethics

LIKE CAPTAIN FRANK FURILLO in our earlier example, we may sometimes be faced with the problem of deciding what is the right thing to do. How do we go about deciding? Is there a single "right way" to answer moral questions? The scientific method tells us what steps to take if we seek to answer a scientific question, but there is no comparable "moral method" for engaging moral questions. Moral principles are the basis for making moral judgments, but the use of these principles is not a mechanical process in which one cranks in data and out pops an automatic moral judgment. Rather, the principles provide a conceptual framework that guides us in making moral decisions. Careful thought and open-minded reflection are always necessary to work from one's moral principles to a considered moral judgment.

But what are the appropriate principles to rely on when making moral judgments? The truth is that there is no consensus among people who have studied ethics and reflected on these matters. Different theories exist as to the proper standards of right and wrong. As the British philosopher Bernard Williams put it, we are heirs to a rich and complex ethical tradition, in which a variety of different moral principles and ethical considerations intertwine and sometimes compete.[1]

This essay discusses the normative perspectives and rival ethical principles that are our heritage. After distinguishing between what are called consequentialist and nonconsequentialist normative theories, it looks in detail at several ethical approaches, discussing their pros and cons:

- Egoism, both as an ethical theory and as a psychological theory
- Utilitarianism, the theory that the morally right action is the one that achieves the greatest total amount of happiness for everyone concerned
- Kant's ethics, with his categorical imperative and his emphasis on moral motivation and respect for persons
- Other nonconsequentialist normative themes: duties, moral rights, and prima facie principles

Consequentialist and Nonconsequentialist Theories

In ethics, *normative theories* propose some principle or principles for distinguishing right actions from wrong actions. These theories can, for convenience, be divided into two kinds: consequentialist and nonconsequentialist.

Many philosophers have argued that the moral rightness of an action is determined solely by its results. If its consequences are good, then the act is right; if they are bad, the act is wrong. Moral theorists who adopt this approach are therefore called *consequentialists*. They determine what is right by weighing the ratio of good to bad that an action will produce. The right act is the one that produces (or will probably produce) at least as great a ratio of good to evil as any other course of action.

One question that arises here is, Consequences for whom? Should one consider the consequences only for oneself? Or the consequences for everyone affected? The two most important consequentialist theories, *egoism* and *utilitarianism,* are distinguished by their different answers to this question. Egoism advocates individual self-interest as its guiding principle; utilitarianism holds that one must take into account everyone affected by the action. But both theories agree that rightness and wrongness are solely a function of an action's results.

In contrast, *nonconsequentialist* (or *deontological*) theories contend that right and wrong are determined by more than the likely consequences of an action. Nonconsequentialists do not necessarily deny that consequences are morally significant, but they believe that other factors are also relevant to the moral assessment of an action. For example, a nonconsequentialist would hold that for Kevin to break his promise to Cindy is wrong not simply because it has bad results (Cindy's hurt feelings, Kevin's damaged reputation, and so on) but because of the inherent character of the act itself. Even if more good than bad were to come from Kevin's breaking the promise, a nonconsequentialist might still view it as wrong. What matters is the nature of the act in question, not just its results. This concept will become clearer later in the essay as we examine some specific nonconsequentialist principles and theories.

Egoism

The view that identifies morality with self-interest is referred to as *egoism*. Egoism contends that an act is morally right if and only if it best promotes the individual's long-term interests. Egoists use their best long-term advantage as the standard for measuring an action's rightness. If an action produces or will probably produce for the individual a greater ratio of good to evil in the long run than any other alternative, then that action is the right one to perform. The individual should take that course to be moral.

Moral philosophers distinguish between two kinds of egoism: personal and impersonal. Personal egoists claim they should pursue their own best long-term interests, but they do not say what others should do. Impersonal egoists claim that everyone should follow his or her best long-term interests.

Misconceptions about egoism

Several misconceptions haunt both versions of egoism. One is that egoists do only what they like, that they believe in "eat, drink, and be merry." Not so. Undergoing unpleasant, even painful experience meshes with egoism, provided such temporary sacrifice is necessary for the advancement of our long-term interests.

Another misconception is that all egoists endorse *hedonism,* the view that only pleasure (or happiness) is of intrinsic value, the only good in life worth pursuing. Although some egoists are hedonistic—as was the ancient Greek philosopher Epicurus (341–270 B.C.E.)—other egoists have a broader view of what constitutes self-interest. They identify the good with knowledge, power, or what some modern psychologists call self-actualization. Egoists may, in fact, hold any theory of what is good.

A final but very important misconception is that egoists cannot act honestly, be gracious and helpful, or otherwise promote other people's interests. Egoism, however, requires us to do whatever will best further our own interests, and doing this sometimes requires us to advance the interests of others. In particular, egoism tells us to benefit others when we expect that doing so will be reciprocated or when the act will bring us pleasure or in some way promote our own good.

For example, egoism might discourage a shop-keeper from trying to cheat customers because it is likely to hurt business in the long run. Or egoism might recommend to the chairman of the board that she hire as a vice president her nephew, who is not the best candidate for the job but whom the chairman is very fond of. Hiring the nephew might bring her more satisfaction than any other course of action, even if the nephew doesn't perform his job as well as someone else might.

Psychological egoism

Egoism does not preach that we should never assist others but rather that we have no basic moral duty to do so. The only moral obligation we have is to ourselves. Although you and I are not required to act in the interests of others, we should if that is the best way to promote our own self-interest. In short: Always look out for Number One.

Proponents of the ethical theory of egoism generally attempt to derive their basic moral principle from the alleged fact that human beings are by nature selfish creatures. According to this doctrine, termed *psychological egoism*, people are, as a matter of fact, so constructed that they must behave selfishly. Psychological egoism asserts that all actions are in fact selfishly motivated and that truly unselfish actions are therefore impossible. Even such apparently self-sacrificial acts as giving up your own life to save the lives of your children or blowing the whistle on your organization's misdeeds at great personal expense are, according to psychological egoism, done to satisfy the person's own self-interested desires. For example, the parent may seek to perpetuate the family line or to avoid guilt, and the worker may be after fame or revenge.

Problems with egoism

Although egoism as an ethical doctrine has always had its adherents, the theory is open to very strong objections. And it is safe to say that few, if any, philosophers today would advocate it. Consider these objections:

1. Psychological egoism is not a sound theory. Of course, self-interest motivates all of us to some extent, and we all know of situations in which someone pretended to be acting altruistically or morally but was really motivated only by self-interest. The theory of psychological egoism contends, however, that self-interest is the only thing that ever motivates anyone.

This claim seems open to many counterexamples. Take the actual case of a man who, while driving a company truck, spotted smoke coming from inside a parked car and a child trying to escape from the vehicle. The man quickly made a U-turn, drove over to the burning vehicle, and found a one-year-old girl trapped in the back seat, restrained by a seat belt. Flames raged in the front seat as heavy smoke billowed from the car. Disregarding his own safety, the man entered the car and removed the infant, who authorities said otherwise would have died from the poisonous fumes and the flames.

Or take a more mundane example. It's Saturday, and you feel like having a beer with a couple of pals and watching the ball game. On the other hand, you believe you ought to take your two children to the zoo, as you had earlier suggested to them you might. Going to the zoo would bring them a lot of pleasure—and besides, you haven't done much with them recently. Of course, you love your children and it will bring you some pleasure to go to the zoo with them, but—let's face it—they've been cranky lately and you'd prefer to watch the ball game. Nonetheless, you feel an obligation and so you go to the zoo.

These appear to be cases in which people are acting for reasons that are not self-interested. Of course, the reasons that lead you to take your children to the zoo—a sense of obligation, a desire to promote their happiness—are your reasons, but that by itself does not make them self-interested reasons. Still less does it show that you are selfish. Anything that you do is a result of your desires, but that fact doesn't establish what the believer in psychological egoism claims—namely, that the only desires you have, or the only desires that ultimately move you, are self-interested desires.

Psychological egoists (that is, advocates of the theory of psychological egoism) will claim that deep down both the heroic man who saved the girl and the unheroic parent who took the children to the zoo were really motivated by self-interest in some way or another. Maybe the hero was hoping to win praise or the parent to advance his or her own pleasure by enhancing the children's affection for the parent. Or maybe some other self-interested consideration motivated them. Psychological egoists can always claim that some yet-to-be-identified subconscious egoistic motivation is the main impulse behind any action.

At this point, though, the psychological egoists' claims sound a little far-fetched, and we may suspect them of trying to make their theory true by definition. Whatever example we come up with, they will simply claim that the person is really motivated by self-interest. One may well wonder how scientific this theory is, or how much content it has, when both the hero and the coward, both the parent who goes to the zoo and the parent who stays home, are equally selfish in their motivations.

A defender of egoism as an ethical doctrine could concede that people are not fully egoistic by nature and yet continue to insist that people morally ought to pursue only their own interests. Yet without the doctrine of psychological egoism, the ethical thesis of egoism becomes less attractive. Other types of ethical principles are possible. We all care about ourselves, but how much sense does it make to see self-interest as the basis of right and wrong? Do we really want to say that someone acting altruistically is behaving immorally?

2. Ethical egoism is not really a moral theory at all. Many critics of egoism as an ethical standard contend that it misunderstands the nature and point of morality: to restrain our purely self-interested desires so we can all live together. If our interests never came into conflict—that is, if it were never advantageous for one person to deceive or cheat another—then we would have no need of morality. The moral standards of a society provide the basic guidelines for cooperative social existence and allow us to resolve conflicts by appeal to shared principles of justification.

It is difficult to see how ethical egoism could perform this function. In a society of egoists, people might publicly agree to follow certain rules so their lives would run more smoothly. But it would be a very unstable world, because people would not hesitate to break the rules if they thought they could get away with it. Nor can egoism provide a means for settling conflicts and disputes, because it simply tells each party to do whatever is necessary to promote effectively his or her interests.

Many moral theorists maintain that moral principles apply equally to the conduct of all persons and that their application requires us to be objective and impartial. Moral agents are seen as those who, despite their own involvement in an issue, can be reasonably disinterested and objective—those who try to see all sides of an issue without being committed to the interests of a particular individual or group, including themselves. If we accept this attitude of detachment and impartiality as at least part of what it means to take a moral point of view, then we must look for it in any proposed moral principle.

Those who make egoism their moral standard are anything but objective, for they seek to guide themselves by their own best interests, regardless of the issue or circumstances. They do not even attempt to be impartial, except insofar as impartiality furthers their own interests. And, according to their theory, any third party offering advice should simply represent his or her own interest.

3. Ethical egoism ignores blatant wrongs. The most common objection to egoism as an ethical doctrine is that by reducing everything to the standard of best long-term self-interest, egoism takes no stand against seemingly outrageous acts like stealing, murder, racial and sexual discrimination, deliberately false advertising, and wanton pollution. All such actions are morally neutral until the test of self-interest is applied.

Of course, the defender of egoism might argue that this objection begs the question by assuming that such acts are immoral and then repudiating egoism on this basis when, in fact, their morality is the very issue that moral principles such as egoism are meant to resolve. Still, egoism must respond to the widely observed human desire to be fair or just, a desire that at least sometimes seems stronger than competing selfish desires. A moral principle that allows the possibility of murder in the cause of self-interest offends our basic intuitions about right and wrong.

Utilitarianism

Utilitarianism is the moral doctrine that we should always act to produce the greatest possible balance of good over bad for everyone affected by our action. By "good," utilitarians understand happiness or pleasure. Thus, the greatest happiness of all constitutes the standard that determines whether an action is right or wrong. Although the basic theme of utilitarianism is present in the writings of many earlier thinkers, Jeremy Bentham (1748–1832) and John Stuart Mill (1806–1873) were the first to develop the theory explicitly and in detail. Both Bentham and Mill were philosophers with a strong interest in legal and social reform. They used the utilitarian standard to evaluate and criticize the social and political institutions of their day—for example, the prison system. As a result, utilitarianism has long been associated with social improvement.

Bentham viewed a community as no more than the individual persons who compose it. The interests of the community are simply the sum of the interests of its members. An action promotes the interests of an individual when it adds to the individual's pleasure or diminishes the person's pain. Correspondingly, an action augments the happiness of a community only insofar as it increases the total amount of individual happiness. In this

way, Bentham argued for the utilitarian principle that actions are right if they promote the greatest human welfare, wrong if they do not.

For Bentham, pleasure and pain are merely types of sensations. He offered a "hedonic calculus" of six criteria for evaluating pleasure and pain exclusively by their quantitative differences—in particular, by their intensity and duration. This calculus, he believed, makes possible an objective determination of the morality of anyone's conduct, individual or collective, on any occasion.

Bentham rejected any distinctions based on quality of pleasure except insofar as they might indicate differences in quantity. Thus, if equal amounts of pleasure are involved, throwing darts is as good as writing poetry and baking a cake as good as composing a symphony; reading Stephen King is of no less value than reading Shakespeare. Although he himself was an intelligent, cultivated man, Bentham maintained there is nothing intrinsically better about cultivated and intellectual pleasures than about crude and prosaic ones. The only issue is which yields the greater amount of enjoyment.

John Stuart Mill thought Bentham's concept of pleasure was too simple. He viewed human beings as having elevated faculties that allow them to pursue various kinds of pleasure. The pleasures of the intellect and imagination, in particular, have a higher value than those of mere physical sensation. Thus, for Mill the utility principle allows consideration of the relative quality of pleasure and pain, not just their intensity and duration.

Although Bentham and Mill had different conceptions of pleasure, both men equated pleasure and happiness and considered pleasure the ultimate value. In this sense they are hedonists: Pleasure, in their view, is the one thing that is intrinsically good or worthwhile. Anything that is good is good only because it brings about pleasure (or happiness), directly or indirectly. Take education, for example. The learning process itself might be pleasurable to us; reflecting on or working with what we have learned might bring us satisfaction at some later time; or by making possible a career and life that we could not have had otherwise, education might bring us happiness indirectly. In contrast, critics of Bentham and Mill contend that things other than happiness are also inherently good—for example, knowledge, friendship, and aesthetic satisfaction. The implication is that these things are valuable even if they do not lead to happiness.

Some moral theorists have modified utilitarianism so that it aims at other consequences in addition to happiness. Other utilitarians, wary of trying to compare one person's happiness with another's, have interpreted their theory as requiring us not to maximize happiness but rather to maximize the satisfaction of people's desires or preferences. The focus here will be utilitarianism in its standard form, in which the good to be aimed at is human happiness or welfare. But what will be said about standard or classical utilitarianism applies, with the appropriate modifications, to other versions as well.

Although this essay will also consider another form of utilitarianism, known as *rule utilitarianism*, utilitarianism in its most basic version, often called *act utilitarianism*, states that we must ask ourselves what the consequences of a particular act in a particular situation will be for all those affected. If its consequences bring more total good than those of any alternative course of action, then this action is the right one and the one we should perform. Thus a utilitarian could defend Frank Furillo's decision not to request bail, thereby coercing a confession from the suspects.

Six points about utilitarianism

Before evaluating utilitarianism, one should understand some points that might lead to confusion and misapplication. First, when deciding which action will produce the greatest happiness, we must consider unhappiness or pain as well as happiness. Suppose, for example, that an action produces eight units of happiness and four units of unhappiness. Its net worth is four units of happiness. Suppose also that an opposed action produces ten units of happiness and seven units of unhappiness; its net worth is three units. In this case we should choose the first action over the second. In the event that both lead not to happiness but to unhappiness, and there is no third option, we should choose the one that brings fewer units of unhappiness.

Second, actions affect people to different degrees. Your playing the radio loudly might enhance two persons' pleasure a little, cause significant discomfort to two others, and leave a fifth person indifferent. The utilitarian theory is not that each person votes on the basis of his or her pleasure or pain, with the majority ruling, but rather that we add up the various pleasures and pains, however large or small, and go with the action that brings about the greatest net amount of happiness.

Third, because utilitarians evaluate actions according to their consequences, and actions produce different results in different circumstances, almost anything might in principle be morally right in some particular circumstance. For example, although breaking a promise generally produces unhappiness, there can be circumstances in which, on balance, more happiness would be produced by breaking a promise than by keeping it. In those circumstances, utilitarianism would require us to break the promise.

Fourth, utilitarians wish to maximize happiness not simply immediately but in the long run as well. All the indirect ramifications of an act have to be taken into account. Lying might seem a good way out of a tough situation, but if and when the people we deceive find out, not only will they be unhappy, but our reputation and our relationships with them will be damaged. This is a serious risk that a utilitarian cannot ignore.

Fifth, utilitarians acknowledge that we often do not know with certainty what the future consequences of our actions will be. Accordingly, we must act so that the expected or likely happiness is as great as possible. If I take my friend's money, without his knowledge, and buy lottery tickets with it, there is a chance that we will end up millionaires and that my action will have maximized happiness all around. But the odds are definitely against it; the most likely result is loss of money (and probably of a friendship, too). Therefore, no utilitarian could justify gambling with purloined funds on the grounds that it might maximize happiness.

Sometimes it is difficult to determine the likely results of alternative actions, and no modern utilitarian really believes that we can assign precise units of happiness and unhappiness to people. But as Mill reminds us, we really do have quite a lot of experience as to what typically makes people happy or unhappy. In any case, as utilitarians our duty is to strive to maximize total happiness, even when it may seem difficult to know what action is likely to promote it effectively.

Finally, when choosing among possible actions, utilitarianism does not require us to disregard our own pleasure. Nor should we give it added weight. Rather, our own pleasure and pain enter into the calculus equally with the pleasures and pains of others. Even if we are sincere in our utilitarianism, we must guard against the possibility of being biased in our calculations when our own interests are at stake. For this reason, and because it would be time-consuming to do a utilitarian calculation before every action, utilitarians encourage us to rely on rules of thumb in ordinary moral circumstances. We can make it a rule of thumb, for example, to tell the truth and keep our promises, rather than to calculate possible pleasures and pains in every routine case, because we know that in general telling the truth and keeping promises result in more happiness than lying and breaking promises.

Critical inquiries of utilitarianism

1. Is utilitarianism really workable? Utilitarianism instructs us to maximize happiness, but in hard cases we may be very uncertain about the likely results of the alternative courses of action open to us. Furthermore, comparing your level of happiness or unhappiness with mine is at best tricky, at worst impossible—and when many people are involved, the matter may get hopelessly complex. Even if we assume that it is possible to make comparisons and to calculate the various possible results of each course of action that a person might take (and the odds of each happening), is it realistic to expect people to take the time to make those calculations and, if they do, to make them accurately? Some critics of act utilitarianism have contended that teaching people to follow the basic utilitarian principle would not in fact promote happiness because of the difficulties in applying utilitarianism accurately.

2. Are some actions wrong, even if they produce good? Like egoism, utilitarianism focuses on the results of an action, not on the character of the action itself. For utilitarians, no action is in itself objectionable. It is objectionable only when it leads to a lesser amount of total good than could otherwise have been brought about. Critics of utilitarianism, in contrast, contend that some actions can be immoral and thus are things we must not do, even if doing them would maximize happiness

Suppose a dying woman has asked you to promise to send the $25,000 under her bed to her nephew in another part of the country. She dies without anyone else's knowing of the money or of the promise that you made. Now suppose, too, that you know the nephew is a spendthrift and a drunkard and, were the money delivered to him, it would be wasted in a week of outrageous partying. On the other hand, a very fine orphanage in your town needs such a sum to improve and expand its recreational facilities, something that would provide happiness to many children for years to come. It seems clear that on utilitarian grounds you should give the money to the orphanage, because this action would result in more total happiness.

Many people would balk at this conclusion, contending that it would be wrong to break your promise, even if doing so would bring about more good than keeping it. Having made a promise, you have an obligation to keep it, and a deathbed promise is particularly serious. Furthermore, the deceased woman had a right to do with her money as she wished; it is not for you to decide how to spend it. Likewise, having been bequeathed the money, the nephew has a right to it, regardless of how wisely or foolishly he might spend it. Defenders of utilitarianism, however, would insist that promoting happiness is all that really matters and warn you not to be blinded by moral prejudice.

Critics of utilitarianism, on the other hand, maintain that utilitarianism is morally blind in not just permitting, but requiring, immoral actions in order to maximize happiness. Philosopher Richard Brandt states the case against act utilitarianism this way:

> Act-utilitarianism . . . implies that if you have employed a boy to mow your lawn and he has finished the job and asks for his pay, you should pay him what you promised only if you cannot find a better use for your money. . . . It implies that if your father is ill and has no prospect of good in his life, and maintaining him is a drain on the energy and enjoyments of others, then, if you can end his life without provoking any public scandal or setting a bad example, it is your positive duty to take matters into your own hands and bring his life to a close.[2]

In the same vein, ethicist A. C. Ewing concludes that "[act] utilitarian principles, logically carried out, would result in far more cheating, lying, and unfair action than any good man would tolerate."[3]

Defenders of act utilitarianism would reply that these charges are exaggerated. Although it is theoretically possible, for example, that not paying the boy for his work might maximize happiness, this is extremely unlikely. Utilitarians contend that only in very unusual circumstances will pursuit of the good conflict with our ordinary ideas of right and wrong, and in those cases—like the deathbed promise—we should put aside those ordinary ideas. The anti-utilitarian replies that the theoretical possibility that utilitarianism may require immoral conduct shows it to be an unsatisfactory moral theory.

3. Is utilitarianism unjust? Utilitarianism concerns itself with the sum total of happiness produced, not with how that happiness is distributed. If policy X brings two units of happiness to each

of five people and policy Y brings nine units of happiness to one person, one unit each to two others, and none to the remaining two, then Y is to be preferred (eleven units of happiness versus ten), even though it distributes that happiness very unequally.

Worse still from the critic's point of view, utilitarianism may even require that some people's happiness be sacrificed in order to achieve the greatest overall amount of happiness. Sometimes the general utility can be served only at the expense of a single individual or group, but to do so would be unjust.

Consider the Dan River experiment, a part of the long-running controversy over the cause of brown lung disease. Claiming that the disease is caused by the inhalation of microscopic fibers in cotton dust, textile unions fought for years for tough regulations to protect their workers. The Occupational Safety and Health Administration (OSHA) responded by proposing cotton dust standards, which would require many firms to install expensive new equipment. A few months before the deadline for installing the equipment, officials at Dan River textile plants in Virginia asked the state to waive the requirements for a time so the company could conduct an experiment to determine the precise cause of brown lung disease. Both the state and the Department of Labor allowed the extension. In response, the Amalgamated Clothing and Textile Workers Union asked OSHA to stop the proposed project, charging, "It is simply unconscionable to allow hundreds of cotton mill workers to continue to face a high risk of developing brown lung disease."[4]

Suppose that the Dan River project does expose workers to a high risk of contracting lung disease. If so, then a small group of individuals—633 textile workers at ten locations in Danville, Virginia—are being compelled to carry the burden of isolating the cause of brown lung. Is this just?

Although their critics would say no, utilitarians would respond that it is just if the experiment maximizes the total good of society. Does it? If the project succeeds in identifying the exact cause of the disease, then thousands of textile workers across the country and perhaps around the world will benefit. Researchers might also discover a more economical way to ensure worker safety, which in turn would yield a consumer benefit: more economical textiles than the ones produced if the industry installs expensive new equipment. Certainly, utilitarians would introduce the potential negative impact on workers at Dan River, but merely as one effect among many others. After the interests of all affected parties are equally weighed, if extending the deadline would likely yield the greatest net utility, then doing so is just—despite the fact that workers may be injured. (This sketch is not intended to justify the project or to foreclose a fuller utilitarian analysis of the case but merely to illustrate generally the utilitarian approach.)

Kant's Ethics

Most of us find the ideal of promoting human happiness and well-being an attractive one. As a result, we admire greatly people like Mother Teresa (1910–1997), who devoted her life to working with the poor. Despite the attractiveness of this ideal, many moral philosophers are critical of utilitarianism—particularly because, like egoism, it reduces all morality to a concern with consequences. Although nonconsequentialist normative theories vary significantly, adopting different approaches and stressing different themes, the writings of the preeminent German philosopher Immanuel Kant (1724–1804) provide an excellent example of a thoroughly nonconsequentialist approach to ethics. Perhaps few thinkers today would endorse Kant's theory on every point, but his work has greatly influenced subsequent philosophers and has helped shape our general moral culture.

Kant sought moral principles that do not rest on contingencies and that define actions as inherently right or wrong apart from any particular circumstances. He believed that moral rules can, in principle, be known as a result of reason alone and are not based on observation (as are, for example,

scientific judgments). In contrast to utilitarianism and other consequentialist doctrines, Kant's ethical theory holds that we do not have to know anything about the likely results of, say, my telling a lie to my boss in order to know that it is immoral. "The basis of obligation," Kant wrote, "must not be sought in human nature, [nor] in the circumstances of the world." Rather it is *a priori*, by which he meant that moral reasoning is not based on factual knowledge and that reason by itself can reveal the basic principles of morality.

Good will

The first essay mentioned Good Samaritan laws, which shield from lawsuits those rendering emergency aid. Such laws, in effect, give legal protection to the humanitarian impulse behind emergency interventions. They formally recognize that the interventionist's heart was in the right place, that the person's intention was irreproachable. And because the person acted from right intention, he or she should not be held liable for any inadvertent harm except in cases of extreme negligence. The widely observable human tendency to introduce a person's intentions in assigning blame or praise is a good springboard for engaging Kant's ethics.

Nothing, said Kant, is good in itself except a good will. This does not mean that intelligence, courage, self-control, health, happiness, and other things are not good and desirable. But Kant believed that their goodness depends on the will that makes use of them. Intelligence, for instance, is not good when used by an evil person.

By *will* Kant meant the uniquely human capacity to act from principle. Contained in the notion of good will is the concept of duty: Only when we act from duty does our action have moral worth. When we act only out of feeling, inclination, or self-interest, our actions—although they may be otherwise identical with ones that spring from the sense of duty—have no true moral worth.

Suppose that you're a clerk in a small stop-and-go store. Late one night a customer pays for his five-dollar purchase with a twenty-dollar bill, which you mistake for a ten. It's only after the customer leaves that you realize you short-changed him. You race out the front door and find him lingering by a vending machine. You give him the ten dollars with your apologies, and he thanks you profusely.

Can we say with certainty that you acted from a good will? Not necessarily. You may have acted from a desire to promote business or to avoid legal entanglement. If so, you would have acted in accordance with, but not from, duty. Your apparently virtuous gesture just happened to coincide with duty. According to Kant, if you do not will the action from a sense of your duty to be fair and honest, your action lacks moral worth. Actions have true moral worth only when they spring from a recognition of duty and a choice to discharge it.

But then what determines our duty? How do we know what morality requires of us? Kant answered these questions by formulating what he called the "categorical imperative." This extraordinarily significant moral concept is the linchpin of Kant's ethics.

The categorical imperative

We have seen that egoists and utilitarians allow factual circumstances or empirical data to determine moral judgments. In contrast, Kant believed that reason alone can yield a moral law. We need not rely on empirical evidence relating to consequences and to similar situations. Just as we know, seemingly through reason alone, such abstract truths as "Every change must have a cause," so we can arrive at absolute moral truth through nonempirical reasoning. And we can thereby discover our duty.

For Kant, an absolute moral truth must be logically consistent, free from internal contradiction. For example, it is a contradiction to say that an effect does not have a cause. Kant aimed to ensure that his absolute moral law would avoid such contradictions. If he could formulate such a rule, he maintained, everyone would be obliged to follow it without exception.

Kant believed that there is just one command (imperative) that is categorical—that is necessarily binding on all rational agents, regardless of any other considerations. From this one categorical imperative, this universal command, we can derive all commands of duty. Kant's *categorical imperative* says that we should always act in such a way that we can will the maxim of our action to become a universal law. So Kant's answer to the question "What determines whether an act is right?" is that an act is morally right if and only if we can will it to become a universal law of conduct.

The obvious and crucial question that arises here is, "When are we justified in saying that the maxim of our action can become a universal law of conduct?"

By *maxim*, Kant meant the subjective principle of an action, the principle (or rule) that people formulate in determining their conduct. For example, suppose building contractor Martin promises to install a sprinkler system in a project but is willing to break that promise to suit his purposes. His maxim can be expressed this way: "I'll make promises that I'll break whenever keeping them no longer suits my purposes." This is the subjective principle, the maxim, that directs his action.

Kant insisted that the morality of any maxim depends on whether we can logically will it to become a universal law. Could Martin's maxim be universally acted on? That depends on whether the maxim as law would involve a contradiction. The maxim "I'll make promises that I'll break whenever keeping them no longer suits my purposes" could not be universally acted on because it involves a contradiction of will. On the one hand, Martin is willing that it be possible to make promises and have them honored. On the other, if everyone intended to break promises when they so desired, then promises would not be honored in the first place, because it is in the nature of promises that they be believed. A law that allowed promise breaking would contradict the very nature of a promise. Similarly, a law that allowed lying would contradict the very nature of serious communication, for the activity of serious communication (as opposed to joking) requires that participants intend to speak the truth. I cannot, without contradiction, will both serious conversation and lying. In contrast, there is no problem, Kant thinks, in willing promise keeping or truth telling to be universal laws.

Consider, as another example, Kant's account of a man who, in despair after suffering a series of major setbacks, contemplates suicide. While still rational, the man asks whether it would be contrary to his duty to take his own life. Could the maxim of his action become a universal law of nature? Kant thinks not:

> His maxim is: From self-love I adopt it as a principle to shorten my life when its longer duration is likely to bring more evil than satisfaction. It is asked then simply whether this principle founded on self-love can become a universal law of nature. Now we see at once that a system of nature of which it should be a law to destroy life by means of the very feeling whose special nature it is to impel to the improvement of life would contradict itself, and therefore could not exist as a system of nature; hence that maxim cannot possibly exist as a universal law of nature, and consequently would be wholly inconsistent with the supreme principle of all duty.[5]

When Kant insists that a moral rule be consistently universalizable, he is saying that moral rules prescribe categorically, not hypothetically. A hypothetical prescription tells us what to do if we desire a particular outcome. Thus, "If I want people to like me, I should be nice to them" and "If you want to go to medical school, you must take biology" are hypothetical imperatives. They tell us what we must do on the assumption that we have some particular goal. If that is what we want, then this is what we must do. On the other hand, if we don't want to go to medical school, then the command to take biology does not apply to us. In contrast, Kant's imperative is categorical—it commands unconditionally. That is, it is necessarily binding on everyone, regardless of his or her specific goals or desires, regardless of consequences. A categorical imperative takes the form of "Do this" or "Don't do that"—no ifs, ands, or buts.

Universal Acceptability. There is another way of looking at the categorical imperative. Each person, through his or her own acts of will, legislates the moral law. The moral rules that we obey are not imposed on us from the outside. They are self-imposed and self-recognized, fully internalized principles. The sense of duty that we obey comes from within; it is an expression of our own higher selves.

Thus, moral beings give themselves the moral law and accept its demands on themselves. But that is not to say we can prescribe anything we want, for we are bound by reason and its demands. Because reason is the same for all rational beings, we all give ourselves the same moral law. In other words, when you answer the question "What should I do?" you must consider what all rational beings should do. If the moral law is valid for you, it must be valid for all other rational beings.

To see whether a rule or principle is a moral law, we can thus ask if what the rule commands would be acceptable to all rational beings acting rationally. In considering lying, theft, or murder, for example, you must consider the act not only from your own viewpoint but from the perspective of the person lied to, robbed, or murdered. Presumably, rational beings do not want to be lied to, robbed, or murdered. The test of the morality of a rule, then, is not whether people in fact accept it but whether all rational beings thinking rationally would accept it regardless of whether they are the doers or the receivers of the actions. This is an important moral insight, and most philosophers see it as implicit in Kant's discussion of the categorical imperative, even though Kant (whose writings are difficult to understand) did not make the point in this form.

The principle of universal acceptability has important applications. Suppose a man advocates a hiring policy that discriminates against women. For this rule to be universally acceptable, the man would have to be willing to accept it if he were a woman, something he would presumably be unwilling to do. Or suppose the manufacturer of a product decides to market it even though the manufacturer knows that the product is unsafe when used in a certain common way and that consumers are ignorant of this fact. Applying the universal acceptability principle, the company's decision makers would have to be willing to advocate marketing the product even if they were themselves in the position of uninformed consumers. Presumably they would be unwilling to do this. So the rule that would allow the product to be marketed would fail the test of universal acceptability.

Humanity as an End, Never Merely as a Means. In addition to the principle of universal acceptability, Kant explicitly offered another, very famous way of formulating the core idea of his categorical imperative. According to this formulation, rational creatures should always treat other rational creatures as ends in themselves and never as only means to ends. This formulation underscores Kant's belief that every human being has an inherent worth resulting from the sheer possession of rationality. We must always act in a way that respects this humanity in others and in ourselves.

As rational beings, humans would act inconsistently if they did not treat everyone else the way they themselves would want to be treated. Here we see shades of the Golden Rule. Indeed, Kant's moral philosophy can be viewed as a profound reconsideration of this basic nonconsequentialist principle. Because rational beings recognize their own inner worth, they would never wish to be used as entities possessing worth only as means to an end.

Thus, when brokers encourage unnecessary buying and selling of stocks in order to reap a commission (a practice called churning), they are treating their clients simply as a means and not respecting them as persons, as ends in themselves. Likewise, Kant would object to using patients as subjects in a medical experiment without their consent. Even though great social benefit might result, the researchers would intentionally be using the patients solely as a means to the researchers' own goals and thus failing to respect the patients' basic humanity.

Kant maintained, as explained first, that an action is morally right if and only if we can will it to be a universal law. We now have two ways of reformulating his categorical imperative that may be easier to grasp and apply:

First reformulation: An action is only right if the agent would be willing to be so treated were the positions of the parties reversed.

Second reformulation: One must always act so as to treat other people as ends in themselves.

Critical inquiries of Kant's ethics

1. What has moral worth? According to Kant, the clerk who returns the ten dollars to the customer is doing the right thing. But if his action is motivated by self-interest (perhaps he wants to get a reputation for honesty), then it does not have moral worth. That seems plausible. But Kant also held that if the clerk does the right thing out of instinct, habit, or sympathy for the other person, then the act still does not have moral worth. Only if it is done out of a sense of duty does the clerk's action have moral value. Many moral theorists have felt that Kant was too severe on this point. Do we really want to say that giving money to famine relief efforts has no moral worth if one is emotionally moved to do so by pictures of starving children rather than by a sense of duty? We might, to the contrary, find a person with strong human sympathies no less worthy or admirable than the person who gives solely out of an abstract sense of duty.

2. Is the categorical imperative an adequate test of right? Kant said that a moral rule must function without exception. Critics wonder why the prohibition against such actions as lying, breaking a promise, committing suicide, and so on must be exceptionless. They say that Kant failed to distinguish between saying that a person should not except himself or herself from a rule and that the rule itself has no exceptions.

If stealing is wrong, it's wrong for me as well as for you. "Stealing is wrong, except if I do it" is not universalizable, for then stealing would be right for all to do, which contradicts the assertion that stealing is wrong. But just because no one may make of oneself an exception to a rule, it does not follow that the rule itself has no exceptions.

Suppose, for example, that we decide that stealing is sometimes right, perhaps in the case of a person who is starving. Thus the rule becomes "Never steal except when starving." This rule seems just as universalizable as "Never steal." The phrase "except . . ." can be viewed not as justifying a violation of the rule but as building a qualification into it. Critics in effect are asking why a qualified rule is not just as good as an unqualified one. If it is, then we no longer need to state rules in the simple, direct, unqualified manner that Kant did.

In fairness to Kant, it could be argued that his universalization formula can be interpreted flexibly enough to meet commonsense objections. For example, perhaps we could universalize the principle that individuals should steal rather than starve to death or that it is permissible to take one's own life to extinguish unspeakable pain. And yet to qualify the rules against stealing, lying, and taking one's life seems to invite a non-Kantian analysis to justify the exceptions. One could, it seems, universalize more than one moral rule in a given situation: "Do not lie unless a life is at stake" versus "Lying is wrong unless necessary to avoid the suffering of innocent people." If so, then the categorical imperative would supply at best a necessary, but not a sufficient, test of right. But once we start choosing among various alternative rules, then we are adopting an approach to ethics that Kant would have rejected.

3. What does it mean to treat people as means? Kant's mandate that individuals must always be considered as ends in themselves and never merely as means expresses our sense of the intrinsic value of the human spirit and has profound moral appeal. Yet it is not always clear when people are being treated as ends and when merely as means.

For example, Kant believed that prostitution is immoral because, by selling their sexual services, prostitutes allow themselves to be treated as means. Prostitutes, however, are not the only ones to sell their services. Anyone who works for a wage does so. Does that mean that we are all being treated immorally, because our employers are presumably hiring us as a means to advance their own ends? Presumably not, because we freely agreed to do the work. But then the prostitute might have freely chosen that line of work too.

Other Nonconsequentialist Perspectives

For Kant, the categorical imperative provides the basic test of right and wrong, and he is resolutely nonconsequentialist in his application of it. You know now what he would say about the case of the deathbed promise: The maxim permitting you to break your promise cannot be universalized, and hence it would be immoral of you to give the money to the orphanage, despite the happiness that doing so would bring. But nonconsequentialists are not necessarily Kantians, and several different nonutilitarian moral concerns emerged in the discussion of the deathbed promise.

Critics of act utilitarianism believe that it is faulty for maintaining that we have one and only one moral duty. A utilitarian might follow various principles as rules of thumb, but they are only calculation substitutes. All that matters morally to utilitarians is the maximization of happiness. Yet this idea, many philosophers think, fails to do justice to the richness and complexity of our moral lives.

Prima facie principles

One influential philosopher who argued this way was the British scholar W. D. Ross (1877–1971).[6] Ross rejected utilitarianism as too simple and as untrue to the way we ordinarily think about morality and about our moral obligations. We see ourselves, Ross and like-minded thinkers contend, as being under various moral duties that cannot be reduced to the single obligation to maximize happiness. Often these obligations grow out of special relationships into which we enter or out of determinate roles that we undertake. Our lives are intertwined with other people's in particular ways, and we have, as a result, certain specific moral obligations.

For example, as a professor, Rodriguez is obligated to assist her students in the learning process and to evaluate their work in a fair and educationally productive way—obligations to the specific people in her classroom that she does not have to other people. As a spouse, Rodriguez must maintain a certain emotional and sexual fidelity to her partner. As a parent, she must provide for the individual human beings who are her children. As a friend to Smith, she may have a moral responsibility to help him out in a time of crisis. Having borrowed money from Chang, Rodriguez is morally obligated to pay it back. Thus, different relationships and different circumstances generate a variety of specific moral obligations.

In addition, we have moral duties that do not arise from our unique interactions and relationships with other people. For example, we ought to treat all people fairly, do what we can to remedy injustices, and make an effort to promote human welfare generally. The latter obligation is important, but for a nonconsequentialist like Ross it is only one among various obligations that people have.

At any given time, we are likely to be under more than one obligation, and sometimes these obligations can conflict. That is, we may have an obligation to do *A* and an obligation to do *B*, where it is not possible for us to do both *A* and *B*. For example, I promise to meet a friend on an urgent matter, and now, as I am hurrying there, I pass an injured person who is obviously in need of assistance. Stopping to aid the person will make it impossible for me to fulfill my promise. What should I do? For moral philosophers like Ross, there is no single answer for all cases. What I ought to do will depend on the circumstances and relative importance of the conflicting obligations. I have an obligation to keep my prom-

ise, and I have an obligation to assist people in distress. What I must decide is which of these obligations is, in the given circumstance, the more important. I must weigh the moral significance of the promise against the comparative moral urgency of assisting the injured person.

Ross and many contemporary philosophers believe that all (or at least most) of our moral obligations are prima facie ones. A *prima facie obligation* is an obligation that can be overridden by a more important obligation. For instance, we take the keeping of promises seriously, but almost everyone would agree that in some circumstances—for example, when a life is at stake—it would be not only morally permissible, but morally required, to break a promise. Our obligation to keep a promise is a real one, and if there is no conflicting obligation, then we must keep the promise. But that obligation is not absolute or categorical; it could in principle be outweighed by a more stringent moral obligation. The idea that our obligations are prima facie is foreign to Kant's way of looking at things.

Consider an example that Kant himself discussed.[7] Imagine that a murderer comes to your door, wanting to know where your friend is so that he can kill her. Your friend is in fact hiding in your bedroom closet. Most people would probably agree that your obligation to your friend overrides your general obligation to tell the truth and that the right thing to do would be to lie to the murderer to throw him off your friend's trail. Although you have a genuine obligation to tell the truth, it is a prima facie obligation, one that other moral considerations can outweigh. Kant disagreed. He maintained that you must always tell the truth—that is, in all circumstances and without exception. For him, telling the truth is an absolute or categorical obligation, not a prima facie one.

Ross thought that our various prima facie obligations could be divided into seven basic types: duties of fidelity (that is, to respect explicit and implicit promises), duties of reparation (for previous wrongful acts), duties of gratitude, duties of justice, duties of beneficence (that is, to make the condition of others better), duties of self-improvement, and duties not to injure others.[8] Unlike utilitarianism, Ross's ethical perspective is pluralistic in recognizing a variety of genuine obligations. But contrary to Kant, Ross does not see these obligations as absolute and exceptionless. On both points, Ross contended that his view of morality more closely fits with our actual moral experience and the way we view our moral obligations.

Ross also saw himself as siding with common-sense morality in maintaining that our prima facie obligations are obvious. He believed that the basic principles of duty are as self-evident as the simplest rules of arithmetic and that any person who has reached the age of reason can discern that it is wrong to lie, to break promises, and to injure people needlessly. However, what we should do, all things considered, when two or more prima facie obligations conflict is often difficult to judge. In deciding what to do in any concrete situation, Ross thought, we are always "taking a moral risk."[9] Even after the fullest reflection, judgments about which of these self-evident rules should govern our conduct are only "more or less probable opinions which are not logically justified conclusions from the general principles that are recognised as self-evident."[10]

Assisting others

Nonconsequentialists believe that utilitarianism presents too simple a picture of our moral world. In addition, they worry that utilitarianism risks making us all slaves to the maximization of total happiness. Stop and think about it: Isn't there something that you could be doing—for instance, volunteering at the local hospital or orphanage, collecting money for Third World development, helping the homeless—that would do more for the general good than what you are doing now or are planning to do tonight or tomorrow? Sure, working with the homeless might not bring you quite as much pleasure as what you would otherwise be doing, but if it would nonetheless maximize total happiness, then you are morally

required to do it. However, by following this reasoning, you could end up working around the clock, sacrificing yourself for the greater good. This notion seems mistaken.

Most nonutilitarian philosophers, like Ross, believe that we have some obligation to promote the general welfare, but they typically view this obligation as less stringent than, for example, the obligation not to injure people. They see us as having a much stronger obligation to refrain from violating people's rights than to promote their happiness or well-being.

Many moral philosophers draw a related distinction between actions that are morally required and charitable or *supererogatory* actions—that is, actions that it would be good to do but not immoral not to do. Act utilitarianism does not make this distinction. While we admire Mother Teresa and Albert Schweitzer for devoting their lives to doing good works among the poor, we see them as acting above and beyond the call of duty. We do not expect so much from ordinary people. Yet people who are not moral heroes or who fall short of sainthood may nonetheless be living morally satisfactory lives.

Nonutilitarian theorists see the distinction between morally obligatory actions and supererogatory actions not so much as a realistic concession to human weakness but as a necessary demarcation if we are to avoid becoming enslaved to the maximization of the general welfare. The idea here is that each of us should have a sphere in which to pursue our own plans and goals, to carve out a distinctive life plan. These plans and goals are limited by various moral obligations, in particular by other people's rights, but the demands of morality are not all-encompassing.

Moral rights

What, then, are rights, and what rights do people have? Broadly defined, a *right* is an entitlement to act or have others act in a certain way. The connection between rights and duties is that, generally speaking, if you have a right to do something, then someone else has a correlative duty to act in a certain way. For example, if you claim a right to drive, you mean that you are entitled to drive or that others should—that is, have a duty to—permit you to drive. Your right to drive under certain conditions is derived from our legal system and is thus considered a *legal right.*

In addition to rights that are derived from some specific legal system, we also have *moral rights.* Some of these moral rights derive from special relationships, roles, or circumstances in which we happen to be. For example, if Tom has an obligation to return Bob's car to him on Saturday morning, then Bob has a right to have Tom return his car. If I have agreed to water your plants while you are on vacation, you have a right to expect me to look after them in your absence. As a student, you have a right to be graded fairly, and so on.

Even more important are rights that do not rest on special relationships, roles, or situations. For example, the rights to life, free speech, and unhampered religious affiliation are widely accepted, not just as the entitlements of some specific political or legal system but as fundamental moral rights. More controversial, but often championed as moral rights, are the rights to medical care, decent housing, education, and work. Moral rights that are not the result of particular roles, special relationships, or specific circumstances are called *human rights.* They have several important characteristics.

First, human rights are universal. For instance, if the right to life is a human right, as most of us believe it is, then everyone, everywhere, and at all times, has that right. In contrast, there is nothing universal about your right that I keep my promise to help you move or about my right to drive 65 miles per hour on certain roads.

Second, and closely related, human rights are equal rights. If the right to free speech is a human right, then everyone has this right equally. No one has a greater right to free speech than anyone else. In contrast, your daughter has a greater right than do the daughters of other people to your emotional and financial support.

Third, human rights are not transferable, nor can they be relinquished. If we have a funda-mental human right, we cannot give, lend, or sell it to someone else. That is what is meant in the Declaration of Independence when certain rights—namely, life, liberty, and the pursuit of happiness—are described as "inalienable." By comparison, legal rights can be renounced or transferred, as when one party sells another a house or a business.

Fourth, human rights are natural rights, not in the sense that they can be derived from a study of human nature, but in the sense that they do not depend on human institutions the way legal rights do. If people have human rights, they have them simply because they are human beings. They do not have them because they live under a certain legal system. Human rights rest on the assumption that people have certain basic moral entitlements simply because they are human beings. No authoritative body assigns us human rights. The law may attempt to protect human rights, to make them safe and explicit through codification, but law is not their source.

Rights, and in particular human rights, can be divided into two broad categories: negative rights and positive rights. *Negative rights* reflect the vital interests that human beings have in being free from outside interference. The rights guaranteed in the Bill of Rights—freedom of speech, assembly, religion, and so on—fall within this category, as do the rights to freedom from injury and to privacy. Correlating with these are duties that we all have not to interfere with others' pursuit of these interests and activities. *Positive rights* reflect the vital interests that human beings have in receiving certain benefits. They are rights to have others provide us with certain goods, services, or opportunities. Today, positive rights often are taken to include the rights to education, medical care, a decent neighborhood, equal job opportunity, comparable pay, and so on. Correlating with these are positive duties for appropriate parties to assist individuals in their pursuit of these interests.

Thus a child's right to education implies not just that no one should interfere with the child's education but also that the necessary resources for that education ought to be provided. In the case of some positive rights—for example, the right to a decent standard of living, as proclaimed by the United Nations' 1948 Human Rights Charter—who exactly has the duty to provide the goods and services required to fulfill those rights is unclear. Also, interpreting a right as negative or positive is sometimes controversial. For example, is my right to liberty simply the right not to be interfered with as I live my own life, or does it also imply a duty to provide me with the means to make the exercise of that liberty meaningful?

The significance of positing moral rights is that they provide grounds for making moral judgments that differ radically from utilitarianism's grounds. Once moral rights are asserted, the locus of moral judgment becomes the individual, not society. For example, if every potential human research subject has a moral right to be fully informed about the nature of a medical experiment and the moral right to decide freely for himself or herself whether to participate, then it is wrong to violate these rights—even if, by so doing, medical science and the common good would be served. Again, if workers have a right to compensation equal to what others receive for doing comparable work, then they cannot be paid less on the grounds that doing so will maximize total well-being. And if everyone has a right to equal consideration for a job regardless of color or sex, then sex and color cannot be introduced merely because so doing will result in greater net utility.

Utilitarianism, in effect, treats all such entitlements as subordinate to the general welfare. Thus individuals are entitled to act in a certain way and entitled to have others allow or aid them to so act only insofar as acknowledging this right or entitlement achieves the greatest good. The assertion of moral rights, therefore, decisively sets nonconsequentialists apart from utilitarians.

Critical inquiries of nonconsequentialism

1. How well justified are these nonconsequentialist principles and moral rights? Ross maintained that we have immediate intuitive knowledge of the basic prima facie moral principles, and indeed

it would seem absurd to try to deny that it is wrong to cause needless suffering or that making a promise imposes some obligation to keep it. Only someone the moral equivalent of colorblind could fail to see the truth of these statements; to reject them would seem as preposterous as denying some obvious fact of arithmetic—for example, that $12 + 4 = 16$. Likewise, it appears obvious—indeed, as Thomas Jefferson wrote, "self-evident"—that human beings have certain basic and inalienable rights, unconditional rights that do not depend on the decrees of any particular government.

Yet we must be careful. What seems obvious, even self-evident, to one culture or at one time in human history may turn out to be not only not self-evident but actually false. That the earth is flat and that heavier objects fall faster than lighter ones were two "truths" taken as obvious in former centuries. Likewise, the inferiority of women and of various nonwhite races was long taken for granted; this supposed fact was so obvious that it was hardly even commented on. The idea that people have a right to practice a religion that the majority "knows" to be false—or, indeed, to practice no religion whatsoever—would have seemed morally scandalous to many of our forebears and is still not embraced in all countries today. Today, many vegetarians eschew meat eating on moral grounds and contend that future generations will consider our treatment of animals, factory farming in particular, to be as morally benighted as slavery. So what seems obvious, self-evident, or simple common sense may not be the most reliable guide to morally sound principles.

2. Can nonconsequentialists satisfactorily handle conflicting rights and principles? People today disagree among themselves about the correctness of certain moral principles. Claims of right, as we have seen, are often controversial. For example, do employees have a moral right to their jobs—an entitlement to be fired only with just cause? To some of us, it may seem obvious that they do; to others, perhaps not. And how are we to settle various conflicting claims of right? Jones, for instance, claims a right to her property, which she has acquired honestly through her labors; that is, she claims a right to do with it as she wishes. Smith is ill and claims adequate medical care as a human right. Because he cannot afford the care himself, acknowledging his right will probably involve taxing people like Jones and thus limiting their property rights.

To sum up these two points: First, even the deliverances of moral common sense have to be examined critically; and second, nonconsequentialists should not rest content until they find a way of resolving disputes among conflicting prima facie principles or rights. This is not to suggest that nonconsequentialists cannot find deeper and theoretically more satisfactory ways of grounding moral claims and of handling disputes between them. The point to be underscored here is simply the necessity of doing so.

Utilitarianism Once More

Until now, the discussion of utilitarianism has focused on its most classic and straightforward form, called act utilitarianism. According to *act utilitarianism,* we have one and only one moral obligation—the maximization of happiness for everyone concerned—and every action is to be judged according to how well it lives up to this standard. But a different utilitarian approach, called rule utilitarianism, is relevant to the discussion of the moral concerns characteristic of nonconsequentialism—in particular, relevant to the nonconsequentialist's criticisms of act utilitarianism. The rule utilitarian would, in fact, agree with many of these criticisms. (Rule utilitarianism has been formulated in different ways, but this discussion follows the version defended by Richard Brandt.)

Rule utilitarianism maintains that the utilitarian standard should be applied not to individual actions but to moral codes as a whole. The rule utilitarian asks what moral code (that is, what set of moral rules) a society should adopt in order to maximize happiness. The principles that make up that code would then be the basis for distin-guishing right actions from wrong actions. As Brandt explains:

> A rule-utilitarian thinks that right actions are the kind permitted by the moral code optimal for the society of which the agent is a member. An optimal code is one designed to maximize welfare or what is good (thus, utility). This leaves open the possibility that a particular right act by itself may not maximize benefit. . . . On the rule-utilitarian view, then, to find what is morally right or wrong we need to find which actions would be permitted by a moral system that is "optimal" for the agent's society.[11]

The "optimal" moral code does not refer to the set of rules that would do the most good if everyone conformed to them all the time. The meaning is more complex. The optimal moral code must take into account what rules can reasonably be taught and obeyed, as well as the costs of inculcating those rules in people. Recall that if a principle or rule is part of a person's moral code, then it will influence the person's behavior. The person will tend to follow that principle, to feel guilty when he or she does not follow it, and to disapprove of others who fail to conform to it. Rule utilitarians must consider not just the benefits of having people motivated to act in certain ways but also the cost of instilling those motivations in them. As Brandt writes:

> The more intense and widespread an aversion to a certain sort of behavior, the less frequent the behavior is apt to be. But the more intense and widespread, the greater the cost of teaching the rule and keeping it alive, the greater the burden on the individual, and so on.[12]

Thus, the optimality of a moral code encompasses both the benefits of reduced objectionable behavior and the long-term costs. Perfect compliance is not a realistic goal. "Like the law," Brandt continues, "the optimal moral code normally will not produce 100 percent compliance with all its rules; that would be too costly."[13]

Elements of the rule-utilitarian approach were clearly suggested by Mill himself, although he did not draw the distinction between act and rule utilitarianism. According to the rule-utilitarian perspective, we should apply the utilitarian standard only to the assessment of alternative moral codes; we should not try to apply it to individual actions. We should seek, that is, to determine the specific set of principles that would in fact best promote total happiness for a society. Those are the rules we should promulgate, instill in ourselves, and teach to the next generation.

What will the optimal code look like?

Rule utilitarians such as Brandt argue strenuously that the ideal or optimal moral code for a society will not be the single act-utilitarian command to maximize happiness. They contend that teaching people that their only obligation is to maximize happiness would not in fact maximize happiness.

First, people will make mistakes if they always try to promote total happiness. Second, if all of us were act utilitarians, such practices as keeping promises and telling the truth would be rather shaky, because we would expect others to keep promises or tell the truth only when they believed that doing so would maximize happiness. Third, the act-utilitarian principle is too demanding, because it seems to imply that each person should continually be striving to promote total well-being.

For these reasons, rule utilitarians believe that more happiness will come from instilling in people a pluralistic moral code, one with a number of different principles. By analogy, imagine a traffic system with just one rule: Drive your car in a way that maximizes happiness. Such a system would be counterproductive; we do much better in terms of total human well-being to have a variety of traffic regulations—for example, obey stop signs, yield to the right, and pass only on the left. In such a pluralistic system we cannot justify cruising through a red light with the argument that doing so maximizes total happiness by getting us home more quickly.

The principles of the optimal code would presumably be prima facie in Ross's sense—that is, capable of being overridden by other principles. Different principles would also have different moral weights. It would make sense, for example, to instill in people an aversion to killing that is stronger than the aversion to telling white lies. In addition, the ideal code would acknowledge moral rights. Teaching people to respect moral rights maximizes human welfare in the long run.

The rules of the optimal code provide the sole basis for determining right and wrong. An action is not necessarily wrong if it fails to maximize happiness; it is wrong only if it conflicts with the ideal moral code. Rule utilitarianism thus gets around many of the problems that plague act utilitarianism. At the same time, it provides a plausible basis for deciding which moral principles and rights we should acknowledge and how much weight we should attach to them. We try to determine those principles and rights that, generally adhered to, would best promote human happiness.

Still, rule utilitarianism has its critics. There are two common objections. First, act utilitarians maintain that a utilitarian who cares about happiness should be willing to violate rules in order to maximize happiness. Why make a fetish out of the rules?

Second, nonconsequentialists, although presumably viewing rule utilitarianism more favorably than act utilitarianism, still balk at seeing moral principles determined by their consequences. They contend, in particular, that rule utilitarians ultimately subordinate rights to utilitarian calculation and therefore fail to treat rights as fundamental and independent moral factors.

Conclusion

Theoretical controversies permeate the subject of ethics, and as we have seen, philosophers have proposed rival ways of understanding right and wrong. These philosophical differences of perspective, emphasis, and theory are significant and can have profound practical consequences. This essay has surveyed some of these issues, but obviously it cannot settle all of the questions that divide moral philosophers. Fortunately, however, many problems of applied ethics can be intelligently discussed and even resolved by people whose fundamental moral theories differ (or who have not yet worked out their own moral ideas in some systematic way).

In the abstract, it might seem impossible for people to reach agreement on controversial ethical issues, given that ethical theories differ so much and that people themselves place moral value on different things. Yet in practice moral problems are rarely so intractable that open-minded and thoughtful people cannot, by discussing matters calmly, rationally, and thoroughly, make significant progress toward resolving them. Moral judgments should be logical, should be based on facts, and should appeal to sound moral principles. Bearing this in mind can often help, especially when various people are discussing an issue and proposing rival answers.

First, in any moral discussion, make sure participants agree about the relevant facts. Often moral disputes hinge not on matters of moral principle but on differing assessments of what the facts of the situation are, what alternatives are open, and what the probable results of different courses of action will be. For instance, the directors of an international firm might acrimoniously dispute the moral permissibility of a new overseas investment. The conflict might appear to involve some fundamental clash of moral principles and perspectives and yet, in fact, be the result of some underlying disagreement about what effects the proposed investment will have on the lives of the local population. Until this factual disagreement is acknowledged and dealt with, little is likely to be resolved.

Second, once there is general agreement on factual matters, try to spell out the moral principles to which different people are, at least implicitly, appealing. Seeking to determine these principles will often help people clarify their own thinking enough to reach a solution. Sometimes they will agree on what moral principles are relevant and yet disagree over

how to balance them. But identifying this discrepancy can itself be useful. Bear in mind, too, that skepticism is in order when someone's moral stance on an issue appears to rest simply on a hunch or intuition and cannot be related to some more general moral principle. As moral decision makers, we are seeking not just an answer to a moral issue but an answer that can be publicly defended. And the public defense of a moral judgment usually requires an appeal to general principle. By analogy, judges do not hand down judgments based simply on what strikes them as fair in a particular case. They must relate their decisions to general legal principles or statutes.

A reluctance to defend our moral decisions in public is almost always a warning sign. If we are unwilling to account for our actions publicly, chances are that we are doing something we cannot really justify morally. In addition, Kant's point that we must be willing to universalize our moral judgments is relevant here. We cannot sincerely endorse a principle if we are not willing to see it applied generally. Unfortunately, we occasionally do make judgments—for example, that Alfred's being late to work is a satisfactory reason for firing him—that rest on a principle we would be unwilling to apply to our own situations. Hence, the moral relevance of the familiar question: "How would you like it if . . . ?" Looking at an issue from the other person's point of view can cure moral myopia.[14]

NOTES

1. Bernard Williams, *Ethics and the Limits of Philosophy* (Cambridge, Mass.: Harvard University Press, 1985), 16.

2. Richard B. Brandt, "Toward a Credible Form of Utilitarianism," in Hector-Neri Castañeda and George Nakhnikian, eds., *Morality and the Language of Conduct* (Detroit: Wayne State University Press, 1963), 109–110.

3. A. C. Ewing, *Ethics* (New York: Free Press, 1965), 40.

4. Molly Moore, "Did the Experts Really Approve the 'Brown Lung' Experiment?" *The Washington Post National Weekly Edition*, June 4, 1984, 31.

5. Immanuel Kant, *The Foundations of the Metaphysics of Morals,* trans. T. K. Abbott. See p. 58 of this volume.

6. See, in particular, W. D. Ross, *The Right and the Good* (London: Oxford University Press, 1930).

7. Immanuel Kant, *Practical Philosophy,* ed. M. J. Gregor (Cambridge: Cambridge University Press, 1996), 611–615.

8. Ross, *The Right and the Good,* 21.

9. Ibid., 30.

10. Ibid., 31.

11. Richard B. Brandt, "The Real and Alleged Problems of Utilitarianism," *The Hastings Center Report* (April 1983), 38.

12. Ibid., 42.

13. Ibid., 42.

14. This and the previous essay draw on material from William H. Shaw and Vincent Barry, *Moral Issues in Business,* 9th ed. (Belmont, CA: Wadsworth Publishing Co., 2004). I am grateful to Vince for permitting me to use our joint work here.

ETHICAL RELATIVISM

The Challenge of Cultural Relativism

JAMES RACHELS

Cultural relativism (also known as ethical or moral relativism) is the doctrine that there are no universal, cross-cultural moral standards; rather, right and wrong are determined by what a particular culture or society says is right or wrong. In this essay, the late James Rachels, professor of philosophy at the University of Alabama-Birmingham and the author of several books and numerous essays on ethics, critically examines cultural relativism. After spelling out the theory's basic tenets and explaining why many thinkers have been attracted to it, he rebuts the main argument for cultural relativism and goes on to argue that the theory has unacceptable implications. Rachels then discusses the values that different societies share and why there is often less ethical disagreement between societies than initially appears to be the case. After explaining how cross-cultural moral criticism can sometimes by justified, he concludes by explaining what we can learn from cultural relativism.

Study Questions

1. What is cultural relativism?
2. What is the Cultural Differences Argument, and on what ground does Rachels criticize it?
3. Rachels argues that cultural relativism has three unacceptable consequences. What are they?
4. How does the example of the Eskimos support Rachels's point that there is often less ethical disagreement between societies than there appears to be?
5. What examples does Rachels give of values that all cultures share?
6. What are the two positive lessons that we can learn from cultural relativism?

From James Rachels, The Elements of Moral Philosophy, *4th ed. (New York: McGraw Hill, 2003).*
Reprinted by permission of The McGraw-Hill Companies.

Morality differs in every society, and is a convenient term for socially approved habits.

RUTH BENEDICT, *Patterns of Culture* (1934)

1. How Different Cultures Have Different Moral Codes

DARIUS, A KING OF ANCIENT PERSIA, was intrigued by the variety of cultures he encountered in his travels. He had found, for example, that the Callatians (a tribe of Indians) customarily ate the bodies of their dead fathers. The Greeks, of course, did not do that—the Greeks practiced cremation and regarded the funeral pyre as the natural and fitting way to dispose of the dead. Darius thought that a sophisticated understanding of the world must include an appreciation of such differences between cultures. One day, to teach this lesson, he summoned some Greeks who happened to be present at his court and asked them what they would take to eat the bodies of their dead fathers. They were shocked, as Darius knew they would be, and replied that no amount of money could persuade them to do such a thing. Then Darius called in some Callatians, and while the Greeks listened asked them what they would take to burn their dead fathers' bodies. The Callatians were horrified and told Darius not even to mention such a dreadful thing.

This story, recounted by Herodotus in his *History,* illustrates a recurring theme in the literature of social science: Different cultures have different moral codes. What is thought right within one group may be utterly abhorrent to the members of another group, and vice versa. Should we eat the bodies of the dead or burn them? If you were a Greek, one answer would seem obviously correct; but if you were a Callatian, the opposite would seem equally certain.

It is easy to give additional examples of the same kind. Consider the Eskimos (of which the largest group is the Inuit). They are a remote and inaccessible people. Numbering only about 25,000,

they live in small, isolated settlements scattered mostly along the northern fringes of North America and Greenland. Until the beginning of the 20th century, the outside world knew little about them. Then explorers began to bring back strange tales.

Eskimo customs turned out to be very different from our own. The men often had more than one wife, and they would share their wives with guests, lending them for the night as a sign of hospitality. Moreover, within a community a dominant male might demand and get regular sexual access to other men's wives. The women however, were free to break these arrangements simply by leaving their husbands and taking up with new partners—free, that is, so long as their former husbands chose not to make trouble. All in all, the Eskimo practice was a volatile scheme that bore little resemblance to what we call marriage.

But it was not only their marriage and sexual practices that were different. The Eskimos also seemed to have less regard for human life. Infanticide, for example, was common. Knud Rasmussen, one of the most famous early explorers, reported that he met one woman who had borne 20 children but had killed 10 of them at birth. Female babies, he found, were especially liable to be destroyed, and this was permitted simply at the parents' discretion, with no social stigma attached to it. Old people also, when they became too feeble to contribute to the family, were left out in the snow to die. So there seemed to be, in this society, remarkably little respect for life.

To the general public, these were disturbing revelations. Our own way of living seems so natural and right that for many of us it is hard to conceive of others living so differently. And when we do hear of such things, we tend immediately to categorize the other peoples as "backward" or "primitive."

But to anthropologists, there was nothing particularly surprising about the Eskimos. Since the time of Herodotus, enlightened observers have been accustomed to the idea that conceptions of right and wrong differ from culture to culture. If we assume that our ethical ideas will be shared by all peoples at all times, we are merely naive.

2. Cultural Relativism

To many thinkers, this observation—"Different cultures have different moral codes"—has seemed to be the key to understanding morality. The idea of universal truth in ethics, they say, is a myth. The customs of different societies are all that exist. These customs cannot be said to be "correct" or "incorrect," for that implies we have an independent standard of right and wrong by which they may be judged. But there is no such independent standard; every standard is culture-bound. The great pioneering sociologist William Graham Sumner, writing in 1906, put it like this:

> The "right" way is the way which the ancestors used and which has been handed down. The tradition is its own warrant. It is not held subject to verification by experience. The notion of right is in the folkways. It is not outside of them, of independent origin, and brought to test them. In the folkways, whatever is, is right. This is because they are traditional, and therefore contain in themselves the authority of the ancestral ghosts. When we come to the folkways we are at the end of our analysis.

This line of thought has probably persuaded more people to be skeptical about ethics than any other single thing. Cultural Relativism, as it has been called, challenges our ordinary belief in the objectivity and universality of moral truth. It says, in effect, that there is no such thing as universal truth in ethics; there are only the various cultural codes, and nothing more. Moreover, our own code has no special status; it is merely one among many. As we shall see, this basic idea is really a compound of

several different thoughts. It is important to separate the various elements of the theory because, on analysis, some parts turn out to be correct, while others seem to be mistaken. As a beginning, we may distinguish the following claims, all of which have been made by cultural relativists:

1. Different societies have different moral codes.
2. The moral code of a society determines what is right within that society; that is, if the moral code of a society says that a certain action is right, then that action *is* right, at least within that society.
3. There is no objective standard that can be used to judge one society's code better than another's.
4. The moral code of our own society has no special status; it is merely one among many.
5. There is no "universal truth" in ethics; that is, there are no moral truths that hold for all peoples at all times.
6. It is mere arrogance for us to try to judge the conduct of other peoples. We should adopt an attitude of tolerance toward the practices of other cultures.

Although it may seem that these six propositions go naturally together, they are independent of one another, in the sense that some of them might be false even if others are true. In what follows, we will try to identify what is correct in Cultural Relativism, but we will also be concerned to expose what is mistaken about it.

3. The Cultural Differences Argument

Cultural Relativism is a theory about the nature of morality. At first blush it seems quite plausible. However, like all such theories, it may be evaluated by subjecting it to rational analysis; and when we analyze Cultural Relativism, we find that it is not so plausible as it first appears to be.

The first thing we need to notice is that at the heart of Cultural Relativism there is a certain *form of argument*. The strategy used by cultural relativists is to argue from facts about the differences between cultural outlooks to a conclusion about the status of morality. Thus we are invited to accept this reasoning:

(1) The Greeks believed it was wrong to eat the dead, whereas the Callatians believed it was right to eat the dead.

(2) Therefore, eating the dead is neither objectively right nor objectively wrong. It is merely a matter of opinion that varies from culture to culture.

Or, alternatively:

(1) The Eskimos see nothing wrong with infanticide, whereas Americans believe infanticide is immoral.

(2) Therefore, infanticide is neither objectively right nor objectively wrong. It is merely a matter of opinion, which varies from culture to culture.

Clearly, these arguments are variations of one fundamental idea. They are both special cases of a more general argument, which says:

(1) Different cultures have different moral codes.

(2) Therefore, there is no objective "truth" in morality. Right and wrong are only matters of opinion, and opinions vary from culture to culture.

We may call this the Cultural Differences Argument. To many people, it is persuasive. But from a logical point of view, is it sound?

It is not sound. The trouble is that the conclusion does not follow from the premise—that is, even if the premise is true, the conclusion still might be false. The premise concerns what people *believe*—in some societies, people believe one thing; in other societies, people believe differently. The conclusion, however, concerns what *really is the case*. The trouble is that this sort of conclusion does not follow logically from this sort of premise.

Consider again the example of the Greeks and Callatians. The Greeks believed it was wrong to eat the dead; the Callatians believed it was right. Does it follow, *from the mere fact that they disagreed*, that there is no objective truth in the matter? No, it does not follow; for it could be that the practice was objectively right (or wrong) and that one or the other of them was simply mistaken.

To make the point clearer, consider a different matter. In some societies, people believe the earth is flat. In other societies, such as our own, people believe the earth is (roughly) spherical. Does it follow, from the mere fact that people disagree, that there is no "objective truth" in geography? Of course not; we would never draw such a conclusion because we realize that, in their beliefs about the world, the members of some societies might simply be wrong. There is no reason to think that if the world is round everyone must know it. Similarly, there is no reason to think that if there is moral truth everyone must know it. The fundamental mistake in the Cultural Differences Argument is that it attempts to derive a substantive conclusion about a subject from the mere fact that people disagree about it.

This is a simple point of logic, and it is important not to misunderstand it. We are not saying (not yet, anyway) that the conclusion of the argument is false. That is still an open question. The logical point is just that the conclusion does not *follow from* the premise. This is important, because in order to determine whether the conclusion is true, we need arguments in its support. Cultural Relativism proposes this argument, but unfortunately the argument turns out to be fallacious. So it proves nothing.

4. The Consequences of Taking Cultural Relativism Seriously

Even if the Cultural Differences Argument is invalid, Cultural Relativism might still be true. What would it be like if it were true?

In the passage quoted above, William Graham Sumner summarizes the essence of Cultural Relativism. He says that there is no measure of right and wrong other than the standards of one's society: "The notion of right is in the folkways. It is not outside of them, of independent origin, and brought to test them. In the folkways, whatever is, is right." Suppose we took this seriously. What would be some of the consequences?

1. We could no longer say that the customs of other societies are morally inferior to our own. This, of course, is one of the main points stressed by Cultural Relativism. We would have to stop condemning other societies merely because they are "different." So long as we concentrate on certain examples, such as the funerary practices of the Greeks and Callatians, this may seem to be a sophisticated, enlightened attitude.

However, we would also be stopped from criticizing other, less benign practices. Suppose a society waged war on its neighbors for the purpose of taking slaves. Or suppose a society was violently anti-Semitic and its leaders set out to destroy the Jews. Cultural Relativism would preclude us from saying that either of these practices was wrong. (We would not even be able to say that a society tolerant of Jews is *better* than the anti-Semitic society, for that would imply some sort of transcultural standard of comparison.) The failure to condemn *these* practices does not seem enlightened; on the contrary, slavery and anti-Semitism seem wrong wherever they occur. Nevertheless, if we took Cultural Relativism seriously, we would have to regard these social practices as immune from criticism.

2. We could decide whether actions are right or wrong just by consulting the standards of our society. Cultural Relativism suggests a simple test for determining what is right and what is wrong: All one need do is ask whether the action is in accordance with the code of one's society. Suppose in 1975 a resident of South Africa was wondering whether his country's policy of apartheid—a rigidly racist system—was morally correct. All he

has to do is ask whether this policy conformed to his society's moral code. If it did, there would have been nothing to worry about, at least from a moral point of view.

This implication of Cultural Relativism is disturbing because few of us think that our society's code is perfect—we can think of all sorts of ways in which it might be improved. Yet Cultural Relativism not only forbids us from criticizing the codes of *other* societies; it also stops us from criticizing our own. After all, if right and wrong are relative to culture, this must be true for our own culture just as much as for other cultures.

3. The idea of moral progress is called into doubt. Usually, we think that at least some social changes are for the better. (Although, of course, other changes may be for the worse.) Throughout most of Western history the place of women in society was narrowly circumscribed. They could not own property; they could not vote or hold political office; and generally they were under the almost absolute control of their husbands. Recently much of this has changed, and most people think of it as progress.

But if Cultural Relativism is correct, can we legitimately think of this as progress? Progress means replacing a way of doing things with a better way. But by what standard do we judge the new ways as better? If the old ways were in accordance with the social standards of their time, then Cultural Relativism would say it is a mistake to judge them by the standards of a different time. Eighteenth-century society was a different society from the one we have now. To say that we have made progress implies a judgment that present-day society is better, and that is just the sort of transcultural judgment that, according to Cultural Relativism, is impossible.

Our idea of social *reform* will also have to be reconsidered. Reformers such as Martin Luther King, Jr., have sought to change their societies for the better. Within the constraints imposed by Cultural Relativism, there is one way this might be done. If a society is not living up to its own ideals, the reformer may be regarded as acting for the best; the ideals of the society are the standard by which we judge his or her proposals as worthwhile. But no one may challenge the ideals themselves, for those ideals are by definition correct. According to Cultural Relativism, then, the idea of social reform makes sense only in this limited way.

These three consequences of Cultural Relativism have led many thinkers to reject it as implausible on its face. It does make sense, they say, to condemn some practices, such as slavery and anti-Semitism, wherever they occur. It makes sense to think that our own society has made some moral progress, while admitting that it is still imperfect and in need of reform. Because Cultural Relativism implies that these judgments make no sense, the argument goes, it cannot be right.

5. Why There Is Less Disagreement Than It Seems

The original impetus for Cultural Relativism comes from the observation that cultures differ dramatically in their views of right and wrong. But just how much do they differ? It is true that there are differences. However, it is easy to overestimate the extent of those differences. Often, when we examine what seems to be a dramatic difference, we find that the cultures do not differ nearly as much as it appears.

Consider a culture in which people believe it is wrong to eat cows. This may even be a poor culture, in which there is not enough food; still, the cows are not to be touched. Such a society would appear to have values very different from our own. But does it? We have not yet asked *why* these people will not eat cows. Suppose it is because they believe that after death the souls of humans inhabit the bodies of animals, especially cows, so that a cow may be someone's grandmother. Now shall we say that their values are different from ours? No; the difference lies elsewhere. The difference is in our belief systems, not in our values. We agree that we shouldn't eat Grandma; we simply disagree about whether the cow is (or could be) Grandma.

The point is that many factors work together to produce the customs of a society. The society's values are only one of them. Other matters, such as the religious and factual beliefs held by its members, and the physical circumstances in which they must live, are also important. We cannot conclude, then, merely because customs differ, that there is a disagreement about values. The difference in customs may be attributable to some other aspect of social life. Thus there may be less disagreement about values than there appears to be.

Consider again the Eskimos, who often kill perfectly normal infants, especially girls. We do not approve of such things; in our society, a parent who killed a baby would be locked up. Thus there appears to be a great difference in the values of our two cultures. But suppose we ask why the Eskimos do this. The explanation is not that they have less affection for their children or less respect for human life. An Eskimo family will always protect its babies if conditions permit. But they live in a harsh environment, where food is in short supply. A fundamental postulate of Eskimo thought is: "Life is hard, and the margin of safety small." A family may want to nourish its babies but be unable to do so.

As in many "primitive" societies, Eskimo mothers will nurse their infants over a much longer period of time than mothers in our culture. The child will take nourishment from its mother's breast for four years, perhaps even longer. So even in the best of times there are limits to the number of infants that one mother can sustain. Moreover, the Eskimos are a nomadic people—unable to farm, they must move about in search of food. Infants must be carried, and a mother can carry only one baby in her parka as she travels and goes about her outdoor work. Other family members help however they can.

Infant girls are more readily disposed of because, first, in this society the males are the primary food providers—they are the hunters, following the traditional division of labor—and it is obviously important to maintain a sufficient number of food providers. But there is an important second reason as well. Because the hunters suffer a high casualty rate, the adult men who die prematurely far outnumber the women who die early. Thus if male and female infants survived in equal numbers, the female adult population would greatly outnumber the male adult population. Examining the available statistics, one writer concluded that "were it not for female infanticide . . . there would be approximately one-and-a-half times as many females in the average Eskimo local group as there are food-producing males."

So among the Eskimos, infanticide does not signal a fundamentally different attitude toward children. Instead, it is a recognition that drastic measures are sometimes needed to ensure the family's survival. Even then, however, killing the baby is not the first option considered. Adoption is common; childless couples are especially happy to take a more fertile couple's "surplus." Killing is only the last resort. I emphasize this in order to show that the raw data of the anthropologists can be misleading; it can make the differences in values between cultures appear greater than they are. The Eskimos' values are not all that different from our values. It is only that life forces upon them choices that we do not have to make.

6. How All Cultures Have Some Values in Common

It should not be surprising that, despite appearances, the Eskimos are protective of their children. How could it be otherwise? How could a group survive that did not value its young? It is easy to see that, in fact, all cultural groups must protect their infants. Babies are helpless and cannot survive if they are not given extensive care for a period of years. Therefore, if a group did not care for its young, the young would not survive, and the older members of the group would not be replaced. After a while the group would die out. This means that any cultural group that continues to exist must care for its young. Infants that are not cared for must be the exception rather than the rule.

Similar reasoning shows that other values must be more or less universal. Imagine what it would be like for a society to place no value at all on truth telling. When one person spoke to another, there would be no presumption that she was telling the truth, for she could just as easily be speaking falsely. Within that society, there would be no reason to pay attention to what anyone says. (I ask you what time it is, and you say "Four o'clock." But there is no presumption that you are speaking truly; you could just as easily have said the first thing that came into your head. So I have no reason to pay attention to your answer. In fact, there was no point in my asking you in the first place.) Communication would then be extremely difficult, if not impossible. And because complex societies cannot exist without communication among their members, society would become impossible. It follows that in any complex society there must be a presumption in favor of truthfulness. There may of course be exceptions to this rule: There may be situations in which it is thought to be permissible to lie. Nevertheless, these will be exceptions to a rule that *is* in force in the society.

Here is one further example of the same type. Could a society exist in which there was no prohibition on murder? What would this be like? Suppose people were free to kill other people at will, and no one thought there was anything wrong with it. In such a "society," no one could feel safe. Everyone would have to be constantly on guard. People who wanted to survive would have to avoid other people as much as possible. This would inevitably result in individuals trying to become as self-sufficient as possible—after all, associating with others would be dangerous. Society on any large scale would collapse. Of course, people might band together in smaller groups with others that they could trust not to harm them. But notice what this means: They would be forming smaller societies that did acknowledge a rule against murder. The prohibition of murder, then, is a necessary feature of all societies.

There is a general theoretical point here, namely, that *there are some moral rules that all societies must have in common, because those rules are necessary for society to exist.* The rules against lying and murder are two examples. And in fact, we do find these rules in force in all viable cultures. Cultures may differ in what they regard as legitimate exceptions to the rules, but this disagreement exists against a background of agreement on the larger issues. Therefore, it is a mistake to overestimate the amount of difference between cultures. Not every moral rule can vary from society to society.

7. Judging a Cultural Practice to Be Undesirable

In 1996, a 17-year-old girl named Fauziya Kassindja arrived at Newark International Airport and asked for asylum. She had fled her native country of Togo, a small west African nation, to escape what people there call "excision." Excision is a permanently disfiguring procedure that is sometimes called "female circumcision," although it bears little resemblance to the Jewish practice. More commonly, at least in Western newspapers, it is referred to as "female genital mutilation."

According to the World Health Organization, the practice is widespread in 26 African nations, and two million girls each year are "excised." In some instances, excision is part of an elaborate tribal ritual, performed in small traditional villages, and girls look forward to it because it signals their acceptance into the adult world. In other instances, the practice is carried out by families living in cities on young women who desperately resist.

Fauziya Kassindja was the youngest of five daughters in a devoutly Muslim family. Her father, who owned a successful trucking business, was opposed to excision, and he was able to defy the tradition because of his wealth. His first four daughters were married without being mutilated. But when Fauziya was 16, he suddenly died. Fauziya then came under the authority of his father, who arranged a marriage for her and prepared to have her excised. Fauziya was terrified, and her mother and oldest sister helped her to escape. Her mother, left without resources, eventually had to formally apologize and submit to the authority of the patriarch she had offended.

Meanwhile, in America, Fauziya was imprisoned for two years while the authorities decided what to do with her. She was finally granted asylum, but not before she became the center of a controversy about how we should regard the cultural practices of other peoples. A series of articles in the *New York Times* encouraged the idea that excision is a barbaric practice that should be condemned. Other observers were reluctant to be so judgmental—live and let live, they said; after all, our culture probably seems just as strange to them.

Suppose we are inclined to say that excision is bad. Would we merely be imposing the standards of our own culture? If Cultural Relativism is correct, that is all we can do, for there is no culture-neutral moral standard to which we may appeal. But is that true?

Is there a culture-neutral standard of right and wrong?

There is, of course, a lot that can be said against excision. Excision is painful and it results in the permanent loss of sexual pleasure. Its short-term effects include hemorrhage, tetanus, and septicemia. Sometimes the woman dies. Long-term effects include chronic infection, scars that hinder walking, and continuing pain.

Why, then, has it become a widespread social practice? It is not easy to say. Excision has no apparent social benefits. Unlike Eskimo infanticide, it is not necessary for the group's survival. Nor is it a matter of religion. Excision is practiced by groups with various religions, including Islam and Christianity, neither of which commend it.

Nevertheless, a number of reasons are given in its defense. Women who are incapable of sexual pleasure are said to be less likely to be promiscuous; thus there will be fewer unwanted pregnancies in unmarried women. Moreover, wives for whom sex is only a duty are less likely to be unfaithful to their husbands; and because they will not be thinking about sex, they will be more attentive to the needs of their husbands and children. Husbands, for their part, are said to enjoy sex more with wives who have been excised. (The women's own lack of enjoyment is said to be unimportant.) Men will not want unexcised women, as they are unclean and immature. And above all, it has been done since antiquity, and we may not change the ancient ways.

It would be easy, and perhaps a bit arrogant, to ridicule these arguments. But we may notice an important feature of this whole line of reasoning: It attempts to justify excision by showing that excision is beneficial—men, women, and their families are said to be better off when women are excised. Thus we might approach this reasoning, and excision itself, by asking whether this is true: Is excision, on the whole, helpful or harmful?

In fact, this is a standard that might reasonably be used in thinking about any social practice whatever: We may ask *whether the practice promotes or hinders the welfare of the people whose lives are affected by it*. And, as a corollary, we may ask if there is an alternative set of social arrangements that would do a better job of promoting their welfare. If so, we may conclude that the existing practice is deficient.

But this looks like just the sort of independent moral standard that Cultural Relativism says cannot exist. It is a single standard that may be brought to bear in judging the practices of any culture, at any time, including our own. Of course, people will not usually see this principle as being "brought in from the outside" to judge them, because, like the rules against lying and homicide, the welfare of its members is a value internal to all viable cultures.

Why, despite all this, thoughtful people may nevertheless be reluctant to criticize other cultures

Although they are personally horrified by excision, many thoughtful people are reluctant to say it is wrong, for at least three reasons.

First, there is an understandable nervousness about "interfering in the social customs of other peoples." Europeans and their cultural descendents in America have a shabby history of destroying native cultures in the name of Christianity and Enlightenment. Recoiling from this record, some people refuse to make any negative judgments about other cultures, especially cultures that resemble those that have been wronged in the past. We should notice, however, that there is a difference between (a) judging a cultural practice to be deficient, and (b) thinking that we should announce the fact, conduct a campaign, apply diplomatic pressure, or send in the army. The first is just a matter of trying to see the world clearly, from a moral point of view. The second is another matter altogether. Sometimes it may be right to "do something about it," but often it will not be.

People also feel, rightly enough, that they should be tolerant of other cultures. Tolerance is, no doubt, a virtue—a tolerant person is willing to live in peaceful cooperation with those who see things differently. But there is nothing in the nature of tolerance that requires you to say that all beliefs, all religions, and all social practices are equally admirable. On the contrary, if you did not think that some were better than others, there would be nothing for you to tolerate.

Finally, people may be reluctant to judge because they do not want to express contempt for the society being criticized. But again, this is misguided: To condemn a particular practice is not to say that the culture is on the whole contemptible or that it is generally inferior to any other culture, including one's own. It could have many admirable features. In fact, we should expect this to be true of most human societies—they are mixes of good and bad practices. Excision happens to be one of the bad ones.

8. What Can Be Learned from Cultural Relativism

At the outset, I said that we were going to identify both what is right and what is wrong in Cultural Relativism. But I have dwelled on its mistakes: I have said that it rests on an invalid argument, that it has consequences that make it implausible on its face, and that the extent of moral disagreement is far less than it implies. This all adds up to a pretty thorough repudiation of the theory. Nevertheless, it is still a very appealing idea, and the reader may have the feeling that all this is a little unfair. The theory must have something going for it, or else why has it been so influential? In fact, I think there is something right about Cultural Relativism, and now I want to say what that is. There are two lessons we should learn from the theory, even if we ultimately reject it.

First, Cultural Relativism warns us, quite rightly, about the danger of assuming that all our preferences are based on some absolute rational standard. They are not. Many (but not all) of our practices are merely peculiar to our society, and it is easy to lose sight of that fact. In reminding us of it, the theory does a service.

Funerary practices are one example. The Callatians, according to Herodotus, were "men who eat their fathers"—a shocking idea, to us at least. But eating the flesh of the dead could be understood as a sign of respect. It could be taken as a symbolic act that says: we wish this person's spirit to dwell within us. Perhaps this was the understanding of the Callatians. On such a way of thinking, burying the dead could be seen as an act of rejection, and burning the corpse as positively scornful. If this is hard to imagine, then we may need to have our imaginations stretched. Of course we may feel a visceral repugnance at the idea of eating human flesh in any circumstances. But what of it? This repugnance may be, as the relativists say, only a matter of what is customary in our particular society.

There are many other matters that we tend to think of in terms of objective right and wrong that are really nothing more than social conventions. We could make a long list. Should women cover their breasts? A publicly exposed breast is scandalous in our society, whereas in other cultures it is unremarkable. Objectively speaking, it is neither right nor wrong—there is no objective reason why either custom is better. Cultural Relativism begins with the valuable insight that many of our practices are like this; they are only cultural products. Then it goes wrong by inferring that, because some practices are like this, all must be.

The second lesson has to do with keeping an open mind. In the course of growing up, each of us has acquired some strong feelings: We have learned to think of some types of conduct as acceptable, and others we have learned to reject. Occasionally, we may find those feelings challenged. For example, we may have been taught that homosexuality is immoral, and we may feel quite uncomfortable around gay people and see them as alien and "different." Now someone suggests that this may be a mere prejudice; that there is nothing evil about homosexuality; that gay people are just people, like anyone else, who happen, through no choice of their own, to be attracted to others of the same sex. But because we feel so strongly about the matter, we may find it hard to take this seriously. Even after we listen to the arguments, we may still have the unshakable feeling that homosexuals must, somehow, be an unsavory lot.

Cultural Relativism, by stressing that our moral views can reflect the prejudices of our society, provides an antidote for this kind of dogmatism. When he tells the story of the Greeks and Callatians, Herodotus adds:

> For if anyone, no matter who, were given the opportunity of choosing from amongst all the nations of the world the set of beliefs which he thought best, he would inevitably, after careful

consideration of their relative merits, choose that of his own country. Everyone without exception believes his own native customs, and the religion he was brought up in, to be the best.

Realizing this can result in our having more open minds. We can come to understand that our feelings are not necessarily perceptions of the truth—they may be nothing more than the result of cultural conditioning. Thus when we hear it suggested that some element of our social code is *not* really the best, and we find ourselves instinctively resisting the suggestion, we might stop and remember this. Then we may be more open to discovering the truth, whatever that might be.

We can understand the appeal of Cultural Relativism, then, even though the theory has serious shortcomings. It is an attractive theory because it is based on a genuine insight, that many of the practices and attitudes we think so natural are really only cultural products. Moreover, keeping this thought firmly in view is important if we want to avoid arrogance and have open minds. These are important points, not to be taken lightly. But we can accept these points without going on to accept the whole theory.

Review and Discussion Questions

1. Would you agree that societies sometimes differ in their moral values and principles? Have you ever been in or seen a situation in which the ethical values of different cultures were in conflict? If so, was the conflict somehow resolved?

2. If societies differ in their ethical standards, how important are these differences—that is, are the moral differences between societies minor and superficial or deep and fundamental?

3. Are there certain values or moral principles that all societies share? If so, what are they? Is a moral value or ethical principle justified by the fact that all societies share it?

4. Why do you think so many people have been attracted to cultural relativism as an ethical theory?

5. If an ethical relativist visits another country, should he or she follow its ethical norms if they differ from those back home?

6. Rachels implies that ethical relativists should tolerate alien cultural values. But what if tolerating the practices of other cultures is not one of the values of the ethical relativist's own culture?

7. Do you agree with Rachels that cultural relativism has unacceptable implications?

8. Rachels identifies six propositions that cultural relativists believe. Examine each of them: Is it true, partially true, or totally false? Explain your answers.

9. Can one say that female genital mutilation is wrong even if the society in question accepts the practice, or would such a judgment be culturally biased? Can there be objective or culturally neutral standards by which to judge the moral rules of different societies?

THREE RIVAL ETHICAL PERSPECTIVES

Happiness, Function, and Virtue

ARISTOTLE

Aristotle was born in 384 B.C.E. in a town near Macedonia. When he was seventeen years old, he went to Athens and studied with Plato for twenty years. When Plato died, Aristotle left Athens and became a tutor to Alexander, the young heir to the Macedonian throne, who was later to become known as Alexander the Great. In 334 B.C.E. Aristotle returned to Athens and founded his own school, the Lyceum. When Alexander died in 323, there was strong anti-Macedonian feeling in Athens, and Aristotle left the city. He died the next year at the age of sixty-two.

Aristotle studied and wrote about an astonishing range of subjects. His knowledge was encyclopedic and deep. No one person has ever founded and advanced so many fields of learning. Aristotle wrote separate treatises on physics, biology, logic, psychology, rhetoric, metaphysics, aesthetics, literary criticism, and political science. In the Middle Ages, Aristotle was known simply as the Philosopher.

Nicomachean Ethics, from which the following reading selection is drawn, is a classic in the history of philosophy. Thought to have been named after Aristotle's son, *Nicomachean Ethics* appears to have been prepared as a series of lectures. In them Aristotle argues that the good for human beings is happiness and that happiness consists in their fulfilling their function as human beings. He then goes on to describe the nature of virtue, which he sees as a mean between excess and deficiency.

Study Questions

1. What are some of the ordinary views of good or happiness that people have? What does Aristotle have to say about them?
2. Why is happiness the supreme or highest good?

From Nicomachean Ethics, *translated by James E. C. Welldon. Subheadings added.*

3. What is the function of human beings?

4. What is the connection between function and happiness? What other factors influence human happiness?

5. What is Aristotle's theory of virtue as a mean?

Book I: Happiness

All human activities aim at some good

EVERY ART AND EVERY SCIENTIFIC INQUIRY, and similarly every action and purpose, may be said to aim at some good. Hence the good has been well defined as that at which all things aim. But it is clear that there is a difference in ends; for the ends are sometimes activities, and sometimes results beyond the mere activities. Where there are ends beyond the action, the results are naturally superior to the action.

As there are various actions, arts, and sciences, it follows that the ends are also various. Thus health is the end of the medical art, a ship of shipbuilding, victory of strategy, and wealth of economics. It often happens that a number of such arts or sciences combine for a single enterprise, as the art of making bridles and all such other arts as furnish the implements of horsemanship combine for horsemanship, and horsemanship and every military action for strategy; and in the same way, other arts or sciences combine for others. In all these cases, the ends of the master arts or sciences, whatever they may be, are more desirable than those of the subordinate arts or sciences, as it is for the sake of the former that the latter are pursued. . . .

If it is true that in the sphere of action there is some end which we wish for its own sake, and for the sake of which we wish everything else, and if we do not desire everything for the sake of something else (for, if that is so, the process will go on *ad infinitum,* and our desire will be idle and futile), clearly this end will be good and the supreme good. Does it not follow then that the knowledge of this good is of great importance for the conduct of life? Like archers who have a mark at which to aim, shall we not have a better chance

of attaining what we want? If this is so, we must endeavor to comprehend, at least in outline, what this good is. . . .

Ethics is not an exact science

This then is the object at which the present inquiry aims. . . . But our statement of the case will be adequate, if it be made with all such clearness as the subject-matter admits; for it would be as wrong to expect the same degree of accuracy in all reasonings. . . . Things noble and just . . . exhibit so great a diversity and uncertainty that they are sometimes thought to have only a conventional, and not a natural, existence. There is the same sort of uncertainty in regard to good things, as it often happens that injuries result from them; thus there have been cases in which people were ruined by wealth, or again by courage. As our subjects then and our premises are of this nature, we must be content to indicate the truth roughly and in outline; and as our subjects and premises are true generally *but not universally,* we must be content to arrive at conclusions which are only generally true. It is right to receive the particular statements which are made in the same spirit; for an educated person will expect accuracy in each subject only so far as the nature of the subject allows. . . .

Everybody is competent to judge the subjects which he understands, and is a good judge of them. It follows that in particular subjects it is a person of special education, and in general a person of universal education, who is a good judge. Hence the young are not proper students of political science,* as they have no experience of the actions of life which form the premises and

*Political science as Aristotle understands it includes moral philosophy.—ED.

subjects of the reasonings. Also it may be added that from their tendency to follow their emotions they will not study the subject to any purpose or profit, as its end is not knowledge but action. It makes no difference whether a person is young in years or youthful in character; for the defect of which I speak is not one of time, but is due to the emotional character of his life and pursuits. Knowledge is as useless to such a person as it is to an intemperate person. But where the desires and actions of people are regulated by reason the knowledge of these subjects will be extremely valuable.

But having said so much by way of preface as to the students of [the subject], the spirit in which it should be studied, and the object which we set before ourselves, let us resume our argument.

Different conceptions of happiness

As every science and undertaking aims at some good, what is in our view . . . the highest of all practical goods? As to its name there is, I may say, a general agreement. The masses and the cultured classes agree in calling it happiness, and conceive that "to live well" or "to do well" is the same thing as "to be happy." But as to what happiness is they do not agree, nor do the masses give the same account of it as the philosophers. The former take it to be something visible and palpable, such as pleasure, wealth, or honor; different people, however, give different definitions of it, and often even the same man gives different definitions at different times. When he is ill, it is health, when he is poor, it is wealth; if he is conscious of his own ignorance, he envies people who use grand language above his own comprehension. . . .

Men's conception of the good or of happiness may be read in the lives they lead. Ordinary or vulgar people conceive it to be a pleasure, and accordingly choose a life of enjoyment. For there are, we may say, three conspicuous types of life, the sensual, the political, and, thirdly, the life of thought. Now the mass of men present an absolutely slavish appearance, choosing the life of brute beasts, but they have ground for so doing because so many persons in authority share the tastes of Sardanapalus.* Cultivated and energetic people, on the other hand, identify happiness with honor, as honor is the general end of political life. But this seems too superficial an idea for our present purpose; for honor depends more upon the people who pay it than upon the person to whom it is paid, and the good we feel is something which is proper to a man himself and cannot be easily taken away from him. Men too appear to seek honor in order to be assured of their own goodness. Accordingly, they seek it at the hands of the sage and of those who know them well, and they seek it on the ground of their virtue; clearly then, in their judgment at any rate, virtue is better than honor. Perhaps then we might look on virtue rather than honor as the end of political life. Yet even this idea appears not quite complete; for a man may possess virtue and yet be asleep or inactive throughout life, and not only so, but he may experience the greatest calamities and misfortunes. Yet no one would call such a life a life of happiness, unless he were maintaining a paradox. . . . The third life is the life of thought, which we will discuss later.†

The life of money making is a life of constraint; and wealth is obviously not the good of which we are in quest; for it is useful merely as a means to something else. It would be more reasonable to take the things mentioned before—sensual pleasure, honor, and virtue—as ends than wealth, since they are things desired on their own account. Yet these too are evidently not ends, although much argument has been employed to show that they are. . . .

Characteristics of the good

But leaving this subject for the present, let us revert to the good of which we are in quest and

---

* A half-legendary ruler whose name to the Greeks stood for extreme luxury and extravagance.—ED.

† In Book X of *Nicomachean Ethics*.—ED.

consider what it may be. For it seems different in different activities or arts; it is one thing in medicine, another in strategy, and so on. What is the good in each of these instances? It is presumably that for the sake of which all else is done. In medicine this is health, in strategy victory, in architecture a house, and so on. In every activity and undertaking it is the end, since it is for the sake of the end that all people do whatever else they do. If then there is an end for all our activity, this will be the good to be accomplished; and if there are several such ends, it will be these.

Our argument has arrived by a different path at the same point as before; but we must endeavor to make it still plainer. Since there are more ends than one, and some of these ends—for example, wealth, flutes, and instruments generally—we desire as means to something else, it is evident that not all are final ends. But the highest good is clearly something final. Hence if there is only one final end, this will be the object of which we are in search; and if there are more than one, it will be the most final. We call that which is sought after for its own sake more final than that which is sought after as a means to something else; we call that which is never desired as a means to something else more final than things that are desired both for themselves and as means to something else. Therefore, we call absolutely final that which is always desired for itself and never as a means to something else. Now happiness more than anything else answers to this description. For happiness we always desire for its own sake and never as a means to something else, whereas honor, pleasure, intelligence, and every virtue we desire partly for their own sakes (for we should desire them independently of what might result from them), but partly also as means to happiness, because we suppose they will prove instruments of happiness. Happiness, on the other hand, nobody desires for the sake of these things, nor indeed as a means to anything else at all. . . .

The function of man

Perhaps, however, it seems a commonplace to say that happiness is the supreme good; what is wanted is to define its nature a little more clearly. The best way of arriving at such a definition will probably be to ascertain the function of man. For, as with a flute player, a sculptor, or any artist, or in fact anybody who has a special function or activity, his goodness and excellence seem to lie in his function, so it would seem to be with man, if indeed he has a special function. Can it be said that, while a carpenter and a cobbler have special functions and activities, man, unlike them, is naturally functionless? Or, as the eye, the hand, the foot, and similarly each part of the body has a special function, so may man be regarded as having a special function apart from all these? What, then, can this function be? It is not life; for life is apparently something that man shares with plants; and we are looking for something peculiar to him. We must exclude therefore the life of nutrition and growth. There is next what may be called the life of sensation. But this too, apparently, is shared by man with horses, cattle, and all other animals. There remains what I may call the active life of the rational part of man's being. . . .

The function of man then is activity of soul in accordance with reason, or not apart from reason. Now, the function of a man of a certain kind, and of a man who is good of that kind—for example, of a harpist and a good harpist—are in our view the same in kind. This is true of all people of all kinds without exception, the superior excellence being only an addition to the function; for it is the function of a harpist to play the harp, and of a good harpist to play the harp well. This being so, if we define the function of man as a kind of life, and this life as an activity of the soul or a course of action in accordance with reason, and if the function of a good man is such activity of a good and noble kind, and if everything is well done when it is done in accordance with its proper excellence, it follows that the good of man is activity of soul in accordance with virtue, or, if there are more virtues than one, in accordance with the best and most complete virtue. But we must add the words "in a complete life." For as one swallow or one day does not make a spring, so one day or a short time does not make a man blessed or happy. . . .

Human happiness

Still it is clear that happiness requires the addition of external goods; for it is impossible, or at least difficult, to do noble deeds with no outside means. For many things can be done only through the aid of friends or wealth or political power; and there are some things the lack of which spoils our felicity, such as good birth, wholesome children, and personal beauty. For a man who is extremely ugly in appearance or low born or solitary and childless can hardly be happy; perhaps still less so, if he has exceedingly bad children or friends, or has had good children or friends and lost them by death. As we said, then, happiness seems to need prosperity of this kind in addition to virtue. For this reason some persons identify happiness with good fortune, though others do so with virtue. . . .

It is reasonable then not to call an ox or a horse or any other animal happy; for none of them is capable of sharing in this activity. For the same reason no child can be happy, since the youth of a child keeps him for the time being from such activity; if a child is ever called happy, the ground of felicitation is his promise, rather than his actual performance. For happiness demands, as we said, a complete virtue and a complete life. And there are all sorts of changes and chances in life, and the most prosperous of men may in his old age fall into extreme calamities, as Priam did in the heroic legends.* And a person who has experienced such chances and died a miserable death, nobody calls happy. . . .

Now the events of chance are numerous and of different magnitudes. Small pieces of good for-

*The disastrous fate of Priam, King of Troy, was part of the well-known Homeric tales.—ED.

tune or the reverse do not turn the scale of life in any way, but great and numerous events make life happier if they turn out well, since they naturally give it beauty and the use of them may be noble and good. If, on the other hand, they turn out badly, they mar and mutilate happiness by causing pain and hindrances to many activities. Still, even in these circumstances, nobility shines out when a person bears with calmness the weight of accumulated misfortunes, not from insensibility but from dignity and greatness of spirit.

Then if activities determine the quality of life, as we said, no happy man can become miserable; for he will never do what is hateful and mean. For our idea of the truly good and wise man is that he bears all the chances of life with dignity and always does what is best in the circumstances, as a good general makes the best use of the forces at his command in war, or a good cobbler makes the best shoe with the leather given him, and so on through the whole series of the arts. If this is so, the happy man can never become miserable. I do not say that he will be fortunate if he meets such chances of life as Priam. Yet he will not be variable or constantly changing, for he will not be moved from his happiness easily or by ordinary misfortunes, but only by great and numerous ones; nor after them will he quickly regain his happiness. If he regains it at all, it will be only over a long and complete period of time and after great and notable achievement.

We may safely then define a happy man as one who is active in accord with perfect virtue and adequately furnished with external goods, not for some chance period of time but for his whole lifetime. . . .

Inasmuch as happiness is an activity of soul in accordance with complete or perfect virtue, it is necessary to consider virtue, as this will perhaps be the best way of studying happiness. . . .

Book II: Virtue

Virtue and habit

Virtue is twofold, partly intellectual and partly moral, and intellectual virtue is originated and fostered mainly by teaching; it demands therefore experience and time. Moral virtue on the other hand is the outcome of habit. . . . From this fact it is clear that moral virtue is not implanted in us by nature; for nothing that exists by nature can be transformed by habit. It is neither by nature then nor in defiance of nature that virtues grow in us. Nature gives us the capacity to receive them, and that capacity is perfected by habit. . . .

It is by playing the harp that both good and bad harpists are produced; and the case of builders and others is similar, for it is by building well that they become good builders and by building badly that they become bad builders. If it were not so, there would be no need of anybody to teach them; they would all be born good or bad in their several crafts. The case of the virtues is the same. It is by our actions in dealings between man and man that we become either just or unjust. It is by our actions in the face of danger and by our training ourselves to fear or to courage that we become either cowardly or courageous. It is much the same with our appetites and angry passions. People become temperate and gentle, others licentious and passionate, by behaving in one or the other way in particular circumstances. In a word, moral states are the results of activities like the states themselves. It is our duty therefore to keep a certain character in our activities, since our moral states depend on the differences in our activities. So the difference between one and another training in habits in our childhood is not a light matter, but important, or rather, all-important.

Virtues and the mean

Our present study is not, like other studies, purely theoretical in intention; for the object of our inquiry is not to know what virtue is but how to become good, and that is the sole benefit of it. We must, therefore, consider the right way of performing actions, for it is acts, as we have said, that determine the character of the resulting moral states. . . .

The first point to be observed is that in the matters we are now considering deficiency and excess are both fatal. It is so, we see, in questions of health and strength. . . . Too much or too little gymnastic exercise is fatal to strength. Similarly, too much or too little meat and drink is fatal to health, whereas a suitable amount produces, increases, and sustains it. It is the same with temperance, courage, and other moral virtues. A person who avoids and is afraid of everything and faces nothing becomes a coward; a person who is not afraid of anything but is ready to face everything becomes foolhardy. Similarly, he who enjoys every pleasure and abstains from none is licentious; he who refuses all pleasures, like a boor, is an insensible sort of person. For temperance and courage are destroyed by excess and deficiency but preserved by the mean. . . .

Every art then does its work well, if it regards the mean and judges the works it produces by the mean. For this reason we often say of successful works of art that it is impossible to take anything from them or to add anything to them, which implies that excess or deficiency is fatal to excellence but that the mean state ensures it. Good artists too, as we say, have an eye to the mean in their works. Now virtue, like Nature herself, is more accurate and better than any art; virtue, therefore, will aim at the mean. I speak of moral virtue, since it is moral virtue which is concerned with emotions and actions, and it is in these we have excess and deficiency and the mean. Thus it is possible to go too far, or not far enough in fear, pride, desire, anger, pity, and pleasure and pain generally, and the excess and the deficiency are alike wrong; but to feel these emotions at the right times, for the right objects, towards the right persons, for the right motives, and in the right manner, is the mean or the best good, which signifies virtue. Similarly, there may be excess, deficiency, or the mean, in acts. Virtue is concerned with both emotions and actions, wherein excess is an error and deficiency a fault, while the mean is successful and praised, and success and praise are both characteristics of virtue.

It appears then that virtue is a kind of mean because it aims at the mean. . . .

But not every action or every emotion admits of a mean. There are some whose very name implies wickedness, as, for example, malice, shamelessness, and envy among the emotions, and adultery, theft, and murder among the actions. All these and others like them are marked as intrinsically wicked, not merely the excesses or deficiencies of them. It is never possible then to be right in them; they are always sinful. . . .

Practical advice

We have now sufficiently shown that moral virtue is a mean, and in what sense it is so; that it is a mean as lying between two vices, a vice of excess on the one side, and a vice of deficiency on the other, and as aiming at the mean in emotion and action.

That is why it is so hard to be good; for it is always hard to find the mean in anything. . . . Anybody can get angry—that is easy—and anybody can give or spend money, but to give it to the right person, to give the right amount of it, at the right time, for the right cause and in the right way, this is not what anybody can do, nor is it easy. That is why goodness is rare and praiseworthy and noble. One then who aims at a mean must begin by departing from the extreme that is more contrary to the mean . . . , for of the two extremes one is more wrong than the other. As it is difficult to hit the mean exactly, we should take the second best course, as the saying is, and choose the lesser of two evils. This we shall best do in the way described, that is, steering clear of the evil which is further from the mean. We must also note the weaknesses to which we are ourselves particularly prone, since different natures tend in different ways; and we may ascertain what our tendency is by observing our feelings of pleasure and pain. Then we must drag ourselves away towards the opposite extreme; for by pulling ourselves as far as possible from what is wrong we shall arrive at the mean, as we do when we pull a crooked stick straight.

In all cases we must especially be on our guard against the pleasant, or pleasure, for we are not impartial judges of pleasure.

In *Nicomachean Ethics,* Aristotle went on to work out the means, excesses, and deficiencies for various virtues. The following table summarizes Aristotle's discussion of some of these virtues:

Type of Feeling or Action	Vice (Excess)	Virtue (Mean)	Vice (Deficit)
Fear	Too much fear (i.e., cowardice)	Right amount of fear (i.e., courage)	Too little fear (i.e., foolhardiness)
Confidence	Too much confidence (i.e., recklessness)	Right amount of confidence (i.e., courage)	Too little confidence (i.e., cowardice)
Pleasure	Licentiousness/ self-indulgence	Temperance/ self-control	No name for this state, but it might be called "insensibility"
Giving money	Extravagance	Generosity	Stinginess
Large-scale giving	Vulgarity	Magnificence	Being cheap
Claiming honors	Vanity	Pride	Humility
Anger	Irascibility/ short-temperedness	Good temper	Too little anger ("inirascibility"/apathy)
Retribution for wrongdoing	Injustice	Justice	Injustice
Social intercourse	Obsequiousness	Friendliness	Surliness
Giving amusement	Buffoonery	Wittiness	Boorishness

Review and Discussion Questions

1. Aristotle believed that ethics is not an exact science and that young people are not proper students of ethics. Why? Are you persuaded by his reasoning?

2. Why did Aristotle believe that happiness is the supreme good? Do you agree?

3. What were Aristotle's reasons for rejecting the view that the pursuit of honor or wealth constitutes the good or happy life?

4. What did Aristotle mean when he talked about our function as human beings? Can you state his viewpoint in your own words?

5. What is the relationship between virtue and habit? How do we come to be virtuous?

6. Discuss Aristotle's theory of virtue with regard to the specific virtues given in the table on the previous page.

Good Will, Duty, and the Categorical Imperative

IMMANUEL KANT

Immanuel Kant was born in Königsberg in East Prussia in 1724. He spent his whole life there, eventually becoming a professor at the local university. He remained a bachelor and was reported to have been so regular in his habits that neighbors set their clocks by his afternoon walks. He died at eighty, by which time he had left a lasting mark on the world of philosophy. Today he is considered one of the greatest philosophers of all time.

Kant's ethical theory has been enormously influential. This excerpt from his classic work *The Foundations of the Metaphysics of Morals* presents Kant's account of moral duty. For an action to have moral worth, for it to reflect a good will, Kant stressed that the action must be undertaken for duty's sake—and not for some other reason, such as fear of being caught and punished. Ethics is based on reason alone, Kant thought, and not— as it was for Aristotle—on human nature. The imperatives of morality are, in his famous terminology, not hypothetical but categorical. That is, the moral duty that binds us is unconditional, universally valid, and necessary.

Kant formulated his basic test of right and wrong, his famous categorical imperative, in different ways. But the core idea is that an action is right if and only if we can will it to become a universal law of conduct. That is, we must never perform an action unless we can consistently will that the maxim or principle governing it be one that everyone can follow. Consider, for example, making a promise that you know you cannot keep. Kant believed that it is impossible to will the maxim "Make promises that you know you cannot keep" as a universal law, because if everyone were to act on this maxim, the institution of promising would be impossible. An alternative formulation of the categorical imperative Kant offered is that one should always treat human beings as ends in themselves, never as means alone.

From The Foundations of the Metaphysics of Morals, *translated by T. K. Abbott. Subheadings added.*

Study Questions

1. Why is a good will the only thing that is good without qualification?
2. When does an action have moral worth?
3. What is the difference between a hypothetical imperative and a categorical imperative?
4. What is the second formulation of the categorical imperative?
5. What did Kant mean by the "kingdom of ends"?

The Good Will

NOTHING CAN POSSIBLY BE CONCEIVED in the world, or even out of it, which can be called good, without qualification, except a Good Will. Intelligence, wit, judgment, and the other *talents* of the mind, however they may be named, or courage, resolution, perseverance, as qualities of temperament, are undoubtedly good and desirable in many respects; but these gifts of nature may also become extremely bad and mischievous if the will which is to make use of them, and which, therefore, constitutes what is called *character,* is not good. It is the same with the *gifts of fortune*. Power, riches, honour, even health, and the general well-being and contentment with one's condition which is called *happiness,* inspire pride, and often presumption, if there is not a good will to correct the influence of these on the mind, and with this also to rectify the whole principle of acting, and adapt it to its end. The sight of a being who is not adorned with a single feature of a pure and good will, enjoying unbroken prosperity, can never give pleasure to an impartial rational spectator. Thus a good will appears to constitute the indispensable condition even of being worthy of happiness.

There are even some qualities which are of service to this good will itself, and may facilitate its action, yet which have no intrinsic unconditional value, but always presuppose a good will, and this qualifies the esteem that we justly have for them, and does not permit us to regard them as absolutely good. Moderation in the affections and passions, self-control, and calm deliberation are not only good in many respects, but even seem to constitute part of the intrinsic worth of the person; but they are far from deserving to be called good without qualification, although they have been so unconditionally praised by the ancients. For without the principles of a good will, they may become extremely bad; and the coolness of a villain not only makes him far more dangerous, but also directly makes him more abominable in our eyes than he would have been without it.

A good will is good not because of what it performs or effects, not by its aptness for the attainment of some proposed end, but simply by virtue of the volition, that is, it is good in itself, and considered by itself is to be esteemed much higher than all that can be brought about by it in favour of any inclination, nay, even of the sum-total of all inclinations. Even if it should happen that, owing to special disfavour of fortune, or the niggardly provision of a stepmotherly nature, this will should wholly lack power to accomplish its purpose, if with its greatest efforts it should yet achieve nothing, and there should remain only the good will (not, to be sure, a mere wish, but the summoning of all means in our power), then, like a jewel, it would still shine by its own light, as a thing which has its whole value in itself. Its usefulness or fruitlessness can neither add to nor take away anything from this value. It would be, as it were, only the setting to enable us to handle it the more conveniently in common commerce, or to attract to it the attention of those who are not yet connoisseurs, but not to recommend it to true connoisseurs, or to determine its value. . . .

Moral Worth

It is always a matter of duty that a dealer should not overcharge an inexperienced purchaser; and wherever there is much commerce the prudent tradesman does not overcharge, but keeps a fixed price for everyone, so that a child buys of him as well as any other. Men are thus *honestly* served; but this is not enough to make us believe that the tradesman has so acted from duty and from principles of honesty: his own advantage required it; it is out of the question in this case to suppose that he might besides have a direct inclination in favour of the buyers, so that, as it were, from love he should give no advantage to one over another. Accordingly the action was done neither from duty nor from direct inclination, but merely with a selfish view.

On the other hand, it is a duty to maintain one's life; and, in addition, everyone has also a direct inclination to do so. But on this account the often anxious care which most men take for it has no intrinsic worth. . . . They preserve their life *as duty requires,* no doubt, but not *because duty requires.* On the other hand, if adversity and hopeless sorrow have completely taken away the relish for life; if the unfortunate one, strong in mind, indignant at his fate rather than desponding or dejected, wishes for death, and yet preserves his life without loving it—not from inclination or fear, but from duty—then his maxim has a moral worth.

To be beneficent when we can is a duty; and besides this, there are many minds so sympathetically constituted that, without any other motive of vanity or self-interest, they find a pleasure in spreading joy around them, and can take delight in the satisfaction of others so far as it is their own work. But I maintain that in such a case an action of this kind, however proper, however amiable it may be, has nevertheless no true moral worth, but is on a level with other inclinations, *e.g.* the inclination to honour, which, if it is happily directed to that which is in fact of public utility and accordant with duty, and consequently honourable, deserves praise and encouragement, but not esteem. For the maxim lacks the moral import, namely, that such actions be done *from duty,* not from inclination. Put the case that the mind of that philanthropist was clouded by sorrow of his own, extinguishing all sympathy

with the lot of others, and that while he still has the power to benefit others in distress, he is not touched by their trouble because he is absorbed with his own; and now suppose that he tears himself out of this dead insensibility, and performs the action without any inclination to it, but simply from duty, then first has his action its genuine moral worth. Further still; if nature has put little sympathy in the heart of this or that man; if he, supposed to be an upright man, is by temperament cold and indifferent to the sufferings of others, perhaps because in respect of his own he is provided with the special gift of patience and fortitude, and supposes, or even requires, that others should have the same—and such a man would certainly not be the meanest product of nature—but if nature had not specially framed him for a philanthropist, would he not still find in himself a source from whence to give himself a far higher worth than that of a good-natured temperament could be? Unquestionably. It is just in this that the moral worth of the character is brought out which is incomparably the highest of all, namely, that he is beneficent, not from inclination, but from duty. . . .

An action done from duty derives its moral worth, *not from the purpose* which is to be attained by it, but from the maxim by which it is determined and therefore does not depend on the realization of the object of the action, but merely on the *principle of volition* by which the action has taken place, without regard to any object of desire. . . . Moral worth . . . cannot lie anywhere but in the *principle of the will*. . . . An action done from duty must wholly exclude the influence of inclination, and with it every object of the will, so that nothing remains which can determine the will except objectively the *law* and subjectively *pure respect* for this practical law, and consequently the maxim that I should follow this law even to the thwarting of all my inclinations.

Thus the moral worth of an action does not lie in the effect expected from it, nor in any principle of action which requires to borrow its motive from this expected effect. For all these effects—agreeableness of one's condition, and even the promotion of the happiness of others—could have been also brought about by other causes, so that for this there would have been no need of the will of a rational being; whereas it is in this alone that the supreme and unconditional good can be found. The pre-eminent good which we call moral can therefore consist in nothing else than *the conception of law* in itself, *which certainly is only possible in a rational being,* in so far as this conception, and not the expected effect, determines the will. . . .

The Supreme Principle of Morality: The Categorical Imperative

But what sort of law can that be, the conception of which must determine the will, even without paying any regard to the effect expected from it, in order that this will may be called good absolutely and without qualification? As I have deprived the will of every impulse which could arise to it from obedience to any law, there remains nothing but the universal conformity of its actions to law in general, which alone is to serve the will as a principle, *i.e.* I am never to act otherwise than so *that I could also will that my maxim should become a universal law.* Here, now, it is the simple conformity to law in general, without assuming any particular law applicable to certain actions, that serves the will as its principle, and must so serve it, if duty is not to be a vain delusion and a chimerical notion. The common reason of men in its practical judgments perfectly coincides with this, and always has in view the principle here suggested. Let the question be, for example: May I when in distress make a promise with the intention not to keep it? I readily distinguish here between the two significations which the question may have: Whether it is prudent, or whether it is right, to make a false promise? The former may undoubtedly often be the case. I see clearly indeed that it is not enough to extricate myself from a present difficulty by means of this subterfuge, but it must be well considered whether there may not hereafter spring from this

lie much greater inconvenience than that from which I now free myself, and as, with all my supposed *cunning,* the consequences cannot be so easily foreseen but that credit once lost may be much more injurious to me than any mischief which I seek to avoid at present, it should be considered whether it would not be more *prudent* to act herein according to a universal maxim, and to make it a habit to promise nothing except with the intention of keeping it. But it is soon clear to me that such a maxim will still only be based on the fear of consequences. Now it is a wholly different thing to be truthful from duty, and to be so from apprehension of injurious consequences. In the first case, the very notion of the action already implies a law for me; in the second case, I must first look about elsewhere to see what results may be combined with it which would affect myself. For to deviate from the principle of duty is beyond all doubt wicked; but to be unfaithful to my maxim of prudence may often be very advantageous to me, although to abide by it is certainly safer. The shortest way, however, and an unerring one, to discover the answer to this question whether a lying promise is consistent with duty, is to ask myself, Should I be content that my maxim (to extricate myself from difficulty by a false promise) should hold good as a universal law, for myself as well as for others? and should I be able to say to myself, "Every one may make a deceitful promise when he finds himself in a difficulty from which he cannot otherwise extricate himself"? Then I presently become aware that while I can will the lie, I can by no means will that lying should be a universal law. For with such a law there would be no promises at all, since it would be in vain to allege my intention in regard to my future actions to those who would not believe this allegation, or if they overhastily did so, would pay me back in my own coin. Hence my maxim, as soon as it should be made a universal law, would necessarily destroy itself.

I do not, therefore, need any far-reaching penetration to discern what I have to do in order that my will may be morally good. Inexperienced in the course of the world, incapable of being prepared for all its contingencies, I only ask myself: Canst thou also will that thy maxim should be a universal law? If not, then it must be rejected, and that not because of a disadvantage accruing from myself or even to others, but because it cannot enter as a principle into a possible universal legislation, and reason extorts from me immediate respect for such legislation. I do not indeed as yet *discern* on what this respect is based (this the philosopher may inquire), but at least I understand this, that it is an estimation of the worth which far outweighs all worth of what is recommended by inclination, and that the necessity of acting from *pure* respect for the practical law is what constitutes duty, to which every other motive must give place, because it is the condition of a will being good *in itself,* and the worth of such a will is above everything.

Thus, then, without quitting the moral knowledge of common human reason, we have arrived at its principle. And although, no doubt, common men do not conceive it in such an abstract and universal form, yet they always have it really before their eyes, and use it as the standard of their decision. . . .

Imperatives: Hypothetical and Categorical

Everything in nature works according to laws. Rational beings alone have the faculty of acting according *to the conception of laws,* that is according to principles, *i.e.* have a *will.* Since the deduction of actions from principles requires *reason,* the will is nothing but practical reason. If reason infallibly determines the will, then the actions of such a being which are recognized as objectively necessary are subjectively necessary also, *i.e.* the will is a faculty to choose *that only* which reason independent of inclination recognizes as practically necessary, *i.e.* as good. But if reason of itself does not sufficiently determine the will, if the latter is subject also to subjective conditions (particular impulses) which do not always coincide

with the objective conditions; in a word, if the will does not *in itself* completely accord with reason (which is actually the case with men), then the actions which objectively are recognized as necessary are subjectively contingent, and the determination of such a will according to objective laws is *obligation,* that is to say, the relation of the objective laws to a will that is not thoroughly good is conceived as the determination of the will of a rational being by principles of reason, but which the will from its nature does not of necessity follow.

The conception of an objective principle, in so far as it is obligatory for a will, is called a command (of reason), and the formula of the command is called an Imperative. . . .

Now all *imperatives* command either *hypothetically* or *categorically.* The former represent the practical necessity of a possible action as means to something else that is willed (or at least which one might possibly will). The categorical imperative would be that which represented an action as necessary of itself without reference to another end, *i.e.,* as objectively necessary. . . .

If now the action is good only as a means *to something else,* then the imperative is *hypothetical;* if it is conceived as good *in itself* and consequently as being necessarily the principle of a will which of itself conforms to reason, then it is *categorical.* . . .

When I conceive a hypothetical imperative, in general I do not know beforehand what it will contain until I am given the condition. But when I conceive a categorical imperative, I know at once what it contains. For as the imperative contains besides the law only the necessity that the maxims shall conform to this law, while the law contains no conditions restricting it, there remains nothing but the general statement that the maxim of the action should conform to a universal law, and it is this conformity alone that the imperative properly represents as necessary.

There is therefore but one categorical imperative, namely, this: *Act only on that maxim whereby thou canst at the same time will that it should become a universal law.*

Now if all imperatives of duty can be deduced from this one imperative as from their principle, then, although it should remain undecided whether what is called duty is not merely a vain notion, yet at least we shall be able to show what we understand by it and what this notion means.

Since the universality of the law according to which effects are produced constitutes what is properly called *nature* in the most general sense (as to form), that is the existence of things so far as it is determined by general laws, the imperative of duty may be expressed thus: *Act as if the maxim of thy action were to become by thy will a universal law of nature.*

Four Illustrations

We shall now enumerate a few duties, adopting the usual division of them into duties to ourselves and to others, and into perfect and imperfect duties.

1. A man reduced to despair by a series of misfortunes feels wearied of life, but is still so far in possession of his reason that he can ask himself whether it would not be contrary to his duty to himself to take his own life. Now he inquires whether the maxim of his action could become a universal law of nature. His maxim is: From self-love I adopt it as a principle to shorten my life when its longer duration is likely to bring more evil than satisfaction. It is asked then simply whether this principle founded on self-love can become a universal law of nature. Now we see at once that a system of nature of which it should be a law to destroy life by means of the very feeling whose special nature it is to impel to the improvement of life would contradict itself, and therefore could not exist as a system of nature; hence that maxim cannot possibly exist as a universal law of nature, and consequently would be wholly inconsistent with the supreme principle of all duty.

2. Another finds himself forced by necessity to borrow money. He knows that he will not be able to repay it, but sees also that nothing will be lent to him, unless he promises stoutly to repay it in a definite time. He desires to make this promise, but he has still so much conscience as to ask himself: Is it not unlawful and inconsistent with duty to get out of a difficulty in this way? Suppose, however, that he resolves to do so, then the maxim of his action would be expressed thus: When I think myself in want of money, I will borrow money and promise to repay it, although I know that I never can do so. Now this principle of self-love or of one's own advantage may perhaps be consistent with my whole future welfare; but the question now is, Is it right? I change then the suggestion of self-love into a universal law, and state the question thus: How would it be if my maxim were a universal law? Then I see at once that it could never hold as a universal law of nature, but would necessarily contradict itself. For supposing it to be a universal law that everyone when he thinks himself in a difficulty should be able to promise whatever he pleases, with the purpose of not keeping his promise, the promise itself would become impossible, as well as the end that one might have in view in it, since no one would consider that anything was promised to him, but would ridicule all such statements as vain pretences.

3. A third finds in himself a talent which with the help of some culture might make him a useful man in many respects. But he finds himself in comfortable circumstances, and prefers to indulge in pleasure rather than to take pains in enlarging and improving his happy natural capacities. He asks, however, whether his maxim of neglect of his natural gifts,

besides agreeing with his inclination to indulgence, agrees also with what is called duty. He sees then that a system of nature could indeed subsist with such a universal law although men (like the South Sea islanders) should let their talents rest, and resolve to devote their lives merely to idleness, amusement, and propagation of their species—in a word, to enjoyment; but he cannot possibly *will* that this should be a universal law of nature, or be implanted in us as such by a natural instinct. For, as a rational being, he necessarily wills that his faculties be developed, since they serve him, and have been given him, for all sorts of possible purposes.

4. A fourth, who is in prosperity, while he sees that others have to contend with great wretchedness and that he could help them, thinks: What concern is it of mine? Let everyone be as happy as Heaven pleases, or as he can make himself; I will take nothing from him nor even envy him, only I do not wish to contribute anything to his welfare or to his assistance in distress! Now no doubt if such a mode of thinking were a universal law, the human race might very well subsist, and doubtless even better than in a state in which everyone talks of sympathy and good-will, or even takes care occasionally to put it into practice, but, on the other side, also cheats when he can, betrays the rights of men, or otherwise violates them. But although it is possible that a universal law of nature might exist in accordance with that maxim, it is impossible to *will* that such a principle should have the universal validity of a law of nature. For a will which resolved this would contradict itself, inasmuch as many cases might occur in which one would have need of the love and sympathy of others, and in which, by

such a law of nature, sprung from his own will, he would deprive himself of all hope of the aid he desires. . . .

Second Formulation of the Categorical Imperative: Humanity as an End in Itself

The will is conceived as a faculty of determining oneself to action *in accordance with the conception of certain laws*. And such a faculty can be found only in rational beings. . . .

Now I say: man and generally any rational being exists as an end in himself, *not merely as a means* to be arbitrarily used by this or that will, but in all his actions, whether they concern himself or other rational beings, must be always regarded at the same time as an end. All objects of the inclinations have only a conditional worth; for if the inclinations and the wants founded on them did not exist, then their object would be without value. But the inclinations themselves being sources of want are so far from having an absolute worth for which they should be desired, that, on the contrary, it must be the universal wish of every rational being to be wholly free from them. Thus the worth of any object which is *to be acquired* by our action is always conditional. Beings whose existence depends not on our will but on nature's, have nevertheless, if they are nonrational beings, only a relative value as means, and are therefore called *things;* rational beings, on the contrary, are called *persons,* because their very nature points them out as ends in themselves, that is as something which must not be used merely as means, and so far therefore restricts freedom of action (and is an object of respect). These, therefore, are not merely subjective ends whose existence has a worth *for us* as an effect of our action, but *objective ends,* that is things whose existence is an end in itself: an end moreover for which no other can be substituted, which they should subserve *merely* as means, for otherwise nothing whatever would possess *absolute worth;* but if all worth were conditioned and therefore contingent, then there would be no supreme practical principle of reason whatever.

If then there is a supreme practical principle or, in respect of the human will, a categorical imperative, it must be one which, being drawn from the conception of that which is necessarily an end for everyone because it is *an end in itself*, constitutes an *objective* principle of will, and can therefore serve as a universal practical law. The foundation of this principle is: *rational nature exists as an end in itself*. Man necessarily conceives his own existence as being so: so far then this is a *subjective* principle of human actions. But every other rational being regards its existence similarly, just on the same rational principle that holds for me: so that it is at the same time an objective principle, from which as a supreme practical law all laws of the will must be capable of being deduced. Accordingly the practical imperative will be as follows: *So act as to treat humanity, whether in thine own person or in that of any other, in every case as an end withal, never as means only.* . . .

Looking back now on all previous attempts to discover the principle of morality, we need not wonder why they all failed. It was seen that man was bound to laws by duty, but it was not observed that the laws to which he is subject are *only those of his own giving*, though at the same time they are *universal*, and that he is only bound to act in conformity with his own will; a will, however, which is designed by nature to give universal laws. . . .

The Kingdom of Ends

The conception of every rational being as one which must consider itself as giving in all the maxims of its will universal laws, so as to judge itself and its actions from this point of view—this conception leads to another which depends on it and is very fruitful, namely, that of a *kingdom of ends*.

By a *kingdom* I understand the union of different rational beings in a system by common laws. Now since it is by laws that ends are determined as regards their universal validity, hence, if we abstract from the personal differences of rational beings, and likewise from all the content of their private ends, we shall be able to conceive all ends combined in a systematic whole (including both rational beings as ends in themselves, and also the special ends which each may propose to himself), that is to say, we can conceive a kingdom of ends, which on the preceding principles is possible.

For all rational beings come under the *law* that each of them must treat itself and all others *never merely as means*, but in every case *at the same time as ends in themselves*. Hence results a systematic union of rational beings by common objective laws, *i.e.*, a kingdom which may be called a kingdom of ends, since what these laws have in view is just the relation of these beings to one another as ends and means.

Review and Discussion Questions

1. Consider the case of the philanthropist who lacks sympathy for others. Was Kant correct to maintain that an action has moral worth only if it is done from a sense of duty (and not from inclination)?

2. How exactly does a hypothetical imperative differ from a categorical imperative? Can there really be an imperative that is more than hypothetical?

3. Explain how each of Kant's four examples illustrates the categorical imperative. Do you see any problems with Kant's reasoning?

4. Kant believed that we should always treat people as ends in themselves, never as a means only. What exactly does this imply? How can one square this duty with normal, day-to-day business activity—for example, buying a ticket to a movie?

5. How do you see Kant's approach as differing from that of Aristotle?

Utilitarianism

JOHN STUART MILL

John Stuart Mill (1806–1873) was a leading exponent of utilitarian moral philosophy and probably the most important British philosopher of the nineteenth century. He was educated at home by his father, learning Greek at the age of three and Latin at eight. He was something of a prodigy and as a young man was an active crusader for the utilitarian cause. His autobiography describes very movingly his education and youthful activities and the mental breakdown he suffered when he was twenty years old. Around the time of his recovery, he began a friendship with Harriet Taylor, who became his lifelong companion and intellectual collaborator. Their relationship was viewed as unorthodox, if not scandalous, because Taylor was married. In fact, she continued to live with her husband until his death twenty years later, at which time she and Mill married. Mill spent much of his life working for the East India Company, where he began as a clerk at the age of seventeen and eventually became a company director. He was elected to Parliament in 1865.

Utilitarianism is the moral theory that right and wrong are a function of the consequences of our actions. It holds that we should act so as to produce the greatest possible balance of good over bad for everyone affected by our actions. By "good," utilitarians like Mill understand happiness or pleasure. Mill, however, modified the earlier utilitarian theory of Bentham by arguing that the "higher" pleasures of the intellect are of greater value than other pleasures. This excerpt from Mill's classic work *Utilitarianism* explains the utilitarian principle, defends it against various objections, and argues that happiness is the only thing of intrinsic value. The final section presents a slightly more complicated view of right and wrong and discusses the relationship between utility, on the one hand, and rights and justice, on the other.

Study Questions

1. What is Mill's initial statement of the utilitarian principle?
2. What is Mill's test for distinguishing higher pleasures from lower pleasures?
3. How did Mill answer the objection that utilitarianism is too demanding because it requires us always to act in a way that promotes the general interests of society?
4. What is Mill's proof of the principle of utility? How did he try to establish that the only thing people desire is happiness?
5. What is Mill's final definition of right and wrong, and how does it differ from his initial statement of the utilitarian doctrine?
6. What is the relationship between utility and justice?

From John Stuart Mill, Utilitarianism *(1861).*

Chapter I: General Remarks

THERE ARE FEW CIRCUMSTANCES among those which make up the present condition of human knowledge, more unlike what might have been expected, or more significant of the backward state in which speculation on the most important subjects still lingers, than the little progress which has been made in the decision of the controversy respecting the criterion of right and wrong. . . .

On the present occasion, I shall . . . attempt to contribute something towards the understanding and appreciation of the Utilitarian or Happiness theory, and towards such proof as it is susceptible of. It is evident that this cannot be proof in the ordinary and popular meaning of the term. Questions of ultimate ends are not amenable to direct proof. . . . We are not, however, to infer that its acceptance or rejection must depend on blind impulse, or arbitrary choice. There is a larger meaning of the word proof. . . . Considerations may be presented capable of determining the intellect either to give or withhold its assent to the doctrine; and this is equivalent to proof. . . .

Chapter II: What Utilitarianism Is

. . . The creed which accepts as the foundation of morals, Utility, or the Greatest Happiness Principle, holds that actions are right in proportion as they tend to promote happiness, wrong as they tend to produce the reverse of happiness. By happiness is intended pleasure, and the absence of pain; by unhappiness, pain, and the privation of pleasure. . . . Pleasure, and freedom from pain, are the only things desirable as ends; and . . . all desirable things (which are as numerous in the utilitarian as in any other scheme) are desirable either for the pleasure inherent in themselves, or as means to the promotion of pleasure and the prevention of pain.

Now, such a theory of life excites in many minds, and among them in some of the most estimable in feeling and purpose, inveterate dislike. To suppose that life has (as they express it) no higher end than pleasure—no better and nobler object of desire and pursuit—they designate as utterly mean and grovelling; as a doctrine worthy only of swine, to whom the followers of Epicurus were, at a very early period, contemptuously likened. . . .

When thus attacked, the Epicureans have always answered, that it is not they, but their accusers, who represent human nature in a degrading light; since the accusation supposes human beings to be capable of no pleasures except those of which swine are capable. . . . The comparison of the Epicurean life to that of beasts is felt as degrading, precisely because a beast's pleasures do not satisfy a human being's conceptions of happiness. Human beings have faculties more elevated than the animal appetites, and when once made conscious of them, do not regard anything as happiness which does not include their gratification. . . . It is quite compatible with the principle of utility to recognize the fact, that some *kinds* of pleasure are more desirable and more valuable than others. It would be absurd that while, in estimating all other things, quality is considered as well as quantity, the estimation of pleasures should be supposed to depend on quantity alone.

If I am asked, what I mean by difference of quality in pleasures, or what makes one pleasure more valuable than another, merely as a pleasure, except its being greater in amount, there is but one possible answer. Of two pleasures, if there be one to which all or almost all who have experience of both give a decided preference, irrespective of any feeling of moral obligation to prefer it, that is the more desirable pleasure. If one of the two is, by those who are competently acquainted with both, placed so far above the other that they prefer it, even though knowing it to be attended with a greater amount of discontent, and would not resign it for any quantity of the other pleasure which their nature is capable of, we are justified in ascribing to the preferred enjoyment a superiority in quality, so far outweighing quantity as to render it, in comparison, of small account.

Now it is an unquestionable fact that those who are equally acquainted with and equally capable of appreciating and enjoying, both, do give a most marked preference to the manner of existence which employs their higher faculties. Few human creatures would consent to be changed into any of the lower animals, for a promise of the fullest allowance of a beast's pleasures; no intelligent human being would consent to be a fool, no instructed person would be an ignoramus, no person of feeling and conscience would be selfish and base, even though they should be persuaded that the fool, the dunce, or the rascal is better satisfied with his lot than they are with theirs. They would not resign what they possess more than he, for the most complete satisfaction of all the desires which they have in common with him. If they ever fancy they would, it is only in cases of unhappiness so extreme, that to escape from it they would exchange their lot for almost any other, however undesirable in their own eyes. A being of higher faculties requires more to make him happy, is capable probably of more acute suffering, and is certainly accessible to it at more points, than one of an inferior type; but in spite of these liabilities, he can never really wish to sink into what he feels to be a lower grade of existence. . . . Whoever supposes that this preference takes place at a sacrifice of happiness—that the superior being, in anything like the equal circumstances, is not happier than the inferior—confounds the two very different ideas, of happiness, and content. It is indisputable that the being whose capacities of enjoyment are low, has the greatest chance of having them fully satisfied; and a highly-endowed being will always feel that any happiness which he can look for, as the world is constituted, is imperfect. But he can learn to bear its imperfections, if they are at all bearable; and they will not make him envy the being who is indeed unconscious of the imperfections, but only because he feels not at all the good which those imperfections qualify. It is better to be a human being dissatisfied than a pig satisfied; better to be Socrates dissatisfied than a fool satisfied. And if the fool, or the pig, is of a different opinion, it is because they only know their own side of the question. The other party to the comparison knows both sides. . . .

From this verdict of the only competent judges, I apprehend there can be no appeal. On a question which is the best worth having of two pleasures, or which of two modes of existence is the most grateful to the feelings, apart from its moral attributes and from its consequences, the judgment of those who are qualified by knowledge of both, or, if they differ, that of the majority among them, must be admitted as final. . . . There is no other tribunal to be referred to even on the question of quantity. What means are there of determining which is the acutest of two pains, or the intensest of two pleasurable sensations, except the general suffrage of those who are familiar with both? . . . When, therefore, those feelings and judgment declare the pleasures derived from the higher faculties to be preferable *in kind,* apart from the question of intensity, to those of which the animal nature, disjoined from the higher faculties, is susceptible, they are entitled on this subject to the same regard. . . .

The assailants of utilitarianism seldom have the justice to acknowledge, that the happiness which forms the utilitarian standard of what is right in conduct, is not the agent's own happiness, but that of all concerned. As between his own happiness and that of others, utilitarianism requires him to be as strictly impartial as a disinterested and benevolent spectator. In the golden rule of Jesus of Nazareth, we read the complete spirit of the ethics of utility. To do as one would be done by, and to love one's neighbour as oneself, constitute the ideal perfection of utilitarian morality. As the means of making the nearest approach to this ideal, utility would enjoin, first, that laws and social arrangements should place the happiness, or (as speaking practically it may be called) the interest, of every individual, as nearly as possible in harmony with the interest of the whole; and secondly, that education and opinion, which have so vast a power over human character, should so use that power as to establish in the mind of every individual an indissoluble association between his own happiness and the good of the whole; especially between his own happiness and the practice of such modes of conduct, negative and positive, as regard for the universal happiness prescribes. . . .

The objectors to utilitarianism . . . say it is exacting too much to require that people shall always act from the inducement of promoting the general interests of society. But this is to mistake the very meaning of a standard of morals, and to confound the rule of action with the motive of it. It is the business of ethics to tell us what are our duties, or by what test we may know them; but no system of ethics requires that the sole motive of all we do shall be a feeling of duty; on the contrary, ninety-nine hundredths of all our actions are done from other motives, and rightly so done, if the rule of duty does not condemn them. It is the more unjust to utilitarianism that this particular misapprehension should be made a ground of objection to it, inasmuch as utilitarian moralists have gone beyond almost all others in affirming that the motive has nothing to do with the morality of the action, though much with the worth of the agent. He who saves a fellow creature from drowning does what is morally right, whether his motive be duty, or the hope of being paid for his trouble: he who betrays the friend that trusts him, is guilty of a crime, even if his object be to serve another friend to whom he is under greater obligations. But to speak only of actions done from the motive of duty, and in direct obedience to principle: it is a misapprehension of the utilitarian mode of thought, to conceive it as implying that people should fix their minds upon so wide a generality as the world, or society at large. The great majority of good actions are intended, not for the benefit of the world, but for that of individuals, of which the good of the world is made up; and the thoughts of the most virtuous man need not on these occasions travel beyond the particular persons concerned, except so far as is necessary to assure himself that in benefitting them he is not violating the rights—that is, the legitimate and authorized expectations—of any one else. . . . In the case of abstinences indeed—of things which people forbear to do, from moral considerations, though the consequences in the particular case might be beneficial—it would be unworthy of an intelligent agent not to be consciously aware that the action is of a class which, if practised generally, would be generally injurious, and that this is the ground of the obligation to abstain from it. The amount of regard for the public interest implied in this recog-

nition, is no greater than is demanded by every system of morals; for they all enjoin to abstain from whatever is manifestly pernicious to society. . . .

Defenders of utility often find themselves called upon to reply to such objections as this—that there is not time, previous to action, for calculating and weighing the effects of any line of conduct on the general happiness. . . . The answer to the objection is, that there has been ample time, namely, the whole past duration of the human species. During all that time mankind have been learning by experience the tendencies of actions; on which experience all the prudence, as well as all the morality of life, is dependent. People talk as if the commencement of this course of experience had hitherto been put off, and as if, at the moment when some man feels tempted to meddle with the property or life of another, he had to begin considering for the first time whether murder and theft are injurious to human happiness. . . . It is truly a whimsical supposition that if mankind were agreed in considering utility to be the test of morality, they would remain without any agreement as to what is useful, and would take no measures for having their notions on the subject taught to the young, and enforced by law and opinion. There is no difficulty in proving any ethical standard whatever to work ill, if we suppose universal idiocy to be conjoined with it, but on any hypothesis short of that, mankind must by this time have acquired positive beliefs as to the effects of some actions on their happiness. . . . That the received code of ethics is by no means of divine right; and that mankind have still much to learn as to the effects of actions on the general happiness, I admit, or rather, earnestly maintain. The corollaries from the principle of utility, like the precepts of every practical art, admit of indefinite improvement, and, in a progressive state of the human mind, their improvement is perpetually going on. But to consider the rules of morality as improvable, is one thing; to pass over the intermediate generalizations entirely, and endeavour to test each individual action directly by the first principle, is another. It is a strange notion that the acknowledgment of a first principle is inconsistent with the admission of secondary ones. To inform a traveller respecting the place of his ultimate destination, is not to forbid the use of landmarks and direction-posts on the way. The proposition that happiness is the end and aim of morality, does not mean that no road ought to be laid down to that goal, or that persons going thither should not be advised to take one direction rather than another. Men really ought to leave off talking a kind of nonsense on this subject. . . . Whatever we adopt as the fundamental principle of morality, we require subordinate principles to apply it by. . . .

Chapter IV: Of What Sort of Proof the Principle of Utility Is Susceptible

It has already been remarked, that questions of ultimate ends do not admit of proof, in the ordinary acceptation of the term. To be incapable of proof by reasoning is common to all first principles; to the first premises of our knowledge, as well as to those of our conduct. But the former, being matters of fact, may be the subject of a direct appeal to the faculties which judge of fact—namely, our senses, and our internal consciousness. Can an appeal be made to the same faculties on questions of practical ends? Or by what other faculty is cognizance taken of them?

Questions about ends are, in other words, questions [about] what things are desirable. The utilitarian doctrine is, that happiness is desirable, and the only thing desirable, as an end; all other things being only desirable as means to that end. What ought to be required of this doctrine—what conditions is it requisite that the doctrine should fulfil—to make good its claim to be believed?

The only proof capable of being given that an object is visible, is that people actually see it. The only proof that a sound is audible, is that people hear it: and so of the other sources of our experience. In like manner, I apprehend, the sole evidence it is possible to produce that anything is desirable, is that people do actually desire it. If the end which the utilitarian doctrine proposes to itself were not, in theory, and in practice, acknowledged to be an end, nothing could ever convince any person that it was so. No reason can be given

why the general happiness is desirable, except that each person, so far as he believes it to be attainable, desires his own happiness. This, however, being a fact, we have not only all the proof which the case admits of, but all which it is possible to require, that happiness is a good: that each person's happiness is a good to that person, and the general happiness, therefore, a good to the aggregate of all persons. Happiness has made out its title as *one* of the ends of conduct, and consequently one of the criteria of morality.

But it has not, by this alone, proved itself to be the sole criterion. To do that, it would seem, by the same rule, necessary to show, not only that people desire happiness, but that they never desire anything else. Now it is palpable that they do desire things which, in common language, are decidedly distinguished from happiness. They desire, for example, virtue, and the absence of vice, no less really than pleasure and the absence of pain. The desire of virtue is not as universal, but it is as authentic a fact, as the desire of happiness. . . .

The ingredients of happiness are very various, and each of them is desirable in itself, and not merely when considered as swelling an aggregate. The principle of utility does not mean that any given pleasure, as music, for instance, or any given exemption from pain, as for example health, are to be looked upon as a means to a collective something termed happiness, and to be desired on that account. They are desired and desirable in and for themselves; besides being means, they are a part of the end. Virtue, according to the utilitarian doctrine, is not naturally and originally part of the end, but it is capable of becoming so; and in those who love it disinterestedly it has become so, and is desired and cherished, not as a means to happiness, but as a part of their happiness.

To illustrate this farther, we may remember that virtue is not the only thing, originally a means, and which if it were not a means to anything else, would be and remain indifferent, but which by association with what it is a means to, comes to be desired for itself, and that too with the utmost intensity. What, for example, shall we say of the love of money? There is nothing originally more desirable about money than about any heap of glittering pebbles. Its worth is solely that of the things which it will buy; the desires for other things than itself, which it is a means of gratifying. Yet the love of money is not only one of the strongest moving forces of human life, but money is, in many cases, desired in and for itself; the desire to possess it is often stronger than the desire to use it, and goes on increasing when all the desires which point to ends beyond it, to be encompassed by it, are falling off. It may be then said truly, that money is desired not for the sake of an end, but as part of the end. From being a means to happiness, it has come to be itself a principal ingredient of the individual's conception of happiness. The same may be said of the majority of the great objects of human life—power, for example, or fame; except that to each of these there is a certain amount of immediate pleasure annexed, which has at least the semblance of being naturally inherent in them; a thing which cannot be said of money. Still, however, the strongest natural attraction, both of power and of fame, is the immense aid they give to the attainment of our other wishes; and it is the strong association thus generated between them and all our objects of desire, which gives to the direct desire of them the intensity it often assumes, so as in some characters to surpass in strength all other desires. In these cases the means have become a part of the end, and a more important part of it than any of the things which they are means to. What was once desired as an instrument for the attainment of happiness, has come to be desired for its own sake. In being desired for its own sake it is, however, desired as *part* of happiness. The person is made, or thinks he would be made, happy by its mere possession; and is made unhappy by failure to obtain it. The desire of it is not a different thing from the desire of happiness, any more than the love of music, or the desire of health. They are included in happiness. They are some of the elements of which the desire of happiness is made up. Happiness is not an abstract idea, but a concrete whole; and these are some of its parts. . . .

It results from the preceding considerations, that there is in reality nothing desired except happiness. Whatever is desired otherwise than as a means to some end beyond itself, and ultimately to happiness, is desired as itself a part of happiness, and is not desired for itself until it has become so. . . .

We have now, then, an answer to the question, of what sort of proof the principle of utility is susceptible. If the opinion which I have now stated is psychologically true—if human nature is so constituted as to desire nothing which is not either a part of happiness or a means of happiness, we can have no other proof, and we require no other, that these are the only things desirable. If so, happiness is the sole end of human action, and the promotion of it the test by which to judge of all human conduct; from whence it necessarily follows that it must be the criterion of morality, since a part is included in the whole. . . .

Chapter V: On the Connexion Between Justice and Utility

. . . We do not call anything wrong, unless we mean to imply that a person ought to be punished in some way or other for doing it; if not by law, by the opinion of his fellow creatures; if not by opinion, by the reproaches of his own conscience. This seems the real turning point of the distinction between morality and simple expediency. It is a part of the notion of Duty in every one of its forms, that a person may rightfully be compelled to fulfil it. Duty is a thing which may be *exacted* from a person, as one exacts a debt. Unless we think that it might be exacted from him, we do not call it his duty. Reasons of prudence, or the interest of other people, may militate against actually exacting it; but the person himself, it is clearly understood, would not be entitled to complain. There are other things, on the contrary, which we wish that people should do, which we like or admire them for doing, perhaps dislike or despise them for not doing, but yet admit that they are not bound to do; it is not a case of moral obligation; we do not blame them, that is, we do not think that they are proper objects of punishment. . . . I think there is no doubt that this distinction lies at the bottom of the notions of right and wrong; that we call any conduct wrong, or employ instead, some other term of dislike or dis-paragement, according as we think that the person ought, or ought not, to be punished for it; and we say that it would be right to do so and so, or merely that it would be desirable or laudable, according as we would wish to see the person whom it concerns, compelled or only persuaded and exhorted, to act in that manner. . . .

The term [*justice*] appear[s] generally to involve the idea of a personal right—a claim on the part of one or more individuals, like that which the law gives when it confers a proprietary or other legal right. Whether the injustice consists in depriving a person of a possession, or in breaking faith with him, or in treating him worse than he deserves, or worse than other people who have no greater claims, in each case the supposition implies two things—a wrong done, and some assignable person who is wronged. Injustice may also be done by treating a person better than others; but the wrong in this case is to his competitors, who are also assignable persons. It seems to me that this feature in the case—a right in some person, cor-relative to the moral obligation—constitutes the specific difference between justice, and generosity or beneficence. Justice implies something which it is not only right to do, and wrong not to do, but which some individual person can claim from us as his moral right. No one has a moral right to our generosity or beneficence, because we are not morally bound to practise those virtues towards any given individual. . . .

When we call anything a person's right, we mean that he has a valid claim on society to protect him in the possession of it, either by the force of law, or by that of education and opinion. If he has what we consider a sufficient claim, on whatever account, to have something guaranteed to him by society, we say that he has a right to it. If we desire to prove that anything does not belong to him by right, we think this done as soon as it is admitted that society ought not to take measures for securing it to him, but should leave it to chance, or to his own exertions. . . .

To have a right, then, is, I conceive, to have something which society ought to defend me in the possession of. If the objector goes on to ask why it ought, I can give him no other reason than general utility. . . .

Justice is a name for certain classes of moral rules, which concern the essentials of human well-being more nearly, and are therefore of more absolute obligation, than any other rules for the guidance of life; and the notion which we have found to be of the essence of the idea of justice, that of a right residing in an individual, implies and testifies to this more binding obligation.

The moral rules which forbid mankind to hurt one another (in which we must never forget to include wrongful interference with each other's freedom) are more vital to human well-being than any maxims, however important, which only point out the best mode of managing some department of human affairs.

Review and Discussion Questions

1. Are you persuaded by Mill that some pleasures are higher than others in terms of quality rather than quantity? Do you agree that it is "better to be Socrates dissatisfied than a fool satisfied"? If so, why?

2. How convincing do you find Mill's "proof" of the principle of utility? Are things other than happiness intrinsically desirable? What sort of proof can one expect in ethics?

3. What is significant about Mill's treatment of right and wrong in the final chapter? Do you agree with his theory of justice?

4. Contrast Mill's approach to ethics with those of Kant and Aristotle.

PART II

ISSUES IN APPLIED ETHICS

SUICIDE AND EUTHANASIA

The Morality and Rationality of Suicide

RICHARD B. BRANDT

Richard B. Brandt was professor of philosophy at the University of Michigan for many years and author of *Ethical Theory, A Theory of the Good and the Right,* and *Facts, Values, and Morality.* Elsewhere, he defines suicide "as doing something that results in one's death, from the intention either of ending one's life or to bring about some other state of affairs (such as relief from pain) that one thinks it certain or highly probable can be achieved only by means of death or that will produce death." In this essay, he examines the conditions under which suicide would be morally blameworthy, the moral arguments for and against suicide, the question of when suicide would be rational from the individual's point of view, and the moral obligations of others toward someone contemplating suicide.

Study Questions

1. What is Brandt's definition of "moral blameworthiness," and how does it apply to the case of suicide?

2. What are three types of suicide that can be morally excused even if they are objectively wrong?

3. Explain what Brandt means when he says that there are things we can have some moral obligation to avoid doing even though in particular situations they may be right or even obligatory. How does this principle apply to the analysis of suicide?

4. Restate the theological, the natural law, and the harm-to-others arguments against suicide.

5. What are some of the errors a person must avoid if his or her decision to commit suicide is to be a rational one?

Reprinted by permission from Seymour Perlin, ed., A Handbook for the Study of Suicide *(New York: Oxford University Press, 1975).*

FROM THE POINT OF VIEW of contemporary philosophy, suicide raises the following distinct questions: whether a person who commits suicide (assuming that there is suicide if and only if there is intentional termination of one's own life) is morally blameworthy, reprehensible, sinful in all circumstances; whether suicide is objectively right or wrong, and in what circumstances it is right or wrong, from a moral point of view; and whether, or in which circumstances, suicide is the best or the rational thing to do from the point of view of the agent's personal welfare.

The Moral Blameworthiness of Suicide

In former times the question of whether suicide is sinful was of great interest because the answer to it was considered relevant to how the agent would spend eternity. At present the practical issue is not as great, although a normal funeral service may be denied a person judged to have committed suicide sinfully. The chief practical issue now seems to be that persons may disapprove of a decedent for having committed suicide, and his friends or relatives may wish to defend his memory against moral charges.

The question of whether an act of suicide was sinful or morally blameworthy is not apt to arise unless it is already believed that the agent morally ought not to have done it: for instance, if he really had very poor reason for doing so, and his act foreseeably had catastrophic consequences for his wife and children. But, even if a given suicide is morally wrong, it does not follow that it is morally reprehensible. For, while asserting that a given act of suicide was wrong, we may still think that the act was hardly morally blameworthy or sinful if, say, the agent was in a state of great emotional turmoil at the time. We might then say that, although what he did was wrong, his action is *excusable*, just as in the criminal law it may be decided that, although a person broke the law, he should not be punished because he was *not*

responsible, that is, was temporarily insane, did what he did inadvertently, and so on.

The foregoing remarks assume that to be morally blameworthy (or sinful) on account of an act is one thing, and for the act to be wrong is another. But, if we say this, what after all does it *mean* to say that a person is morally blameworthy on account of an action? We cannot say there is agreement among philosophers on this matter, but I suggest the following account as being safe from serious objection: "*X* is morally blameworthy on account of an action *A*" may be taken to mean "*X* did *A,* and *X* would not have done *A* had not his character been in some respect below standard; and in view of this it is fitting or justified for *X* to have some disapproving attitudes including remorse toward himself, and for some other persons *Y* to have some disapproving attitudes toward *X* and to express them in behavior." . . .

In case the foregoing definition does not seem obviously correct, it is worthwhile pointing out that it is usually thought that an agent is not blameworthy or sinful for an action unless it is a *reflection on him;* the definition brings this fact out and makes clear why.

If someone charges that a suicide was sinful, we may now properly ask, "What defect of character did it show?" Some writers have claimed that suicide is blameworthy because it is *cowardly;* and since being cowardly is generally conceded to be a defect of character, if an act of suicide is admitted to be both objectively wrong and also cowardly, the claim to blameworthiness might be warranted in terms of the above definition. Of course, many people would hesitate to call taking one's own life a cowardly act, and there will certainly be controversy about which acts are cowardly and which are not. But at least we can see part of what has to be done to make a charge of blameworthiness valid.

The most interesting question is the general one: which types of suicide in general are ones that, even if objectively wrong (in a sense to be explained below), are not sinful or blameworthy? Or, in other words, when is a suicide *morally excused* even if it is objectively wrong? We can at least identify some types that are morally excusable.

1. Suppose I *think* I am morally bound to commit suicide because I have a terminal illness and continued medical care will ruin my family financially. Suppose, however, that I am mistaken in this belief, and that suicide in such circumstances is not right. But surely I am not morally blameworthy; for I may be doing, out of a sense of duty to my family, what I would personally prefer not to do and is hard for me to do. What defect of character might my action show? Suicide from a genuine sense of duty is not blameworthy, even when the moral conviction in question is mistaken.

2. Suppose that I commit suicide when I am temporarily of unsound mind, either in the sense of the M'Naghten rule that I do not know that what I am doing is wrong, or of the Durham rule that, owing to a mental defect, I am substantially unable to do what is right. Surely, any suicide in an unsound state of mind is morally excused.

3. Suppose I commit suicide when I could not be said to be temporarily of unsound mind, but simply because I am not myself. For instance, I may be in an extremely depressed mood. Now a person may be in a very depressed mood, and commit suicide on account of being in that mood, when there is nothing the matter with his character—or, in other words, his character is not in any relevant way below standard. What are other examples of being "not myself," of emotional states that might be responsible for a person's committing suicide, and that might render the suicide excusable even if wrong? Being frightened; being distraught; being in almost any highly emotional frame of mind (anger, frustration, disappointment in love); perhaps just being terribly fatigued.

So there are at least three types of suicide which can be morally excused even if they are objectively wrong. The main point is this: Mr. X may commit suicide and it may be conceded that he ought not to have done so, but it is another step to show that he is sinful, or morally blameworthy, for having done so. To make out that further point, it must be shown that his act is attributable to some substandard trait of character. So, Mrs. X after the suicide can concede that her husband ought not to have done what he did, but she can also point out that it is no reflection on his character. . . .

The Moral Reasons For and Against Suicide

Persons who say suicide is morally wrong must be asked which of two positions they are affirming: Are they saying that *every* act of suicide is wrong, *everything considered;* or are they merely saying that there is always *some* moral obligation—doubtless of serious weight—not to commit suicide, so that very often suicide is wrong, although it is possible that there are *countervailing considerations* which in particular situations make it right or even a moral duty? It is quite evident that the first position is absurd; only the second has a chance of being defensible.

In order to make clear what is wrong with the first view, we may begin with an example. Suppose an army pilot's single-seater plane goes out of control over a heavily populated area; he has the choice of staying in the plane and bringing it down where it will do little damage but at the cost of certain death for himself, and of bailing out and letting the plane fall where it will, very possibly killing a good many civilians. Suppose he chooses to do the former, and so, by our definition, commits suicide. Does anyone want to say that his action is morally wrong? Even Immanuel Kant, who opposed suicide in all circumstances, apparently would not wish to say that it is; he would, in fact, judge that this act is not one of suicide, for he says, "It is no suicide to risk one's life against one's enemies, and even to sacrifice it, in order to preserve one's duties towards oneself."[1] . . .

In general . . . there are things [we have] some moral obligation to avoid which, on account of other morally relevant considerations, it is sometimes right or even morally obligatory to do. There may be some obligation to tell the truth on every occasion, but surely in many cases the consequences of telling the truth would be so dire that one is obligated to lie. The same goes for promises. There is some moral obligation to do what one has promised (with a few exceptions); but, if one can keep a trivial promise only at serious cost to another person (i.e., keep an appointment only by failing to give aid to someone injured in an accident), it is surely obligatory to break the promise.

The most that the moral critic of suicide can hold, then, is that there is *some* moral obligation not to do what one knows will cause one's death; but he surely cannot deny that circumstances exist in which there are obligations to do things which, in fact, will result in one's death. If so, then in principle it would be possible to argue, for instance, that in order to meet my obligation to my family, it might be right for me to take my own life as the only way to avoid catastrophic hospital expenses in a terminal illness. Possibly the main point that critics of suicide on moral grounds would wish to make is that it is never right to take one's own life *for reasons of one's own personal welfare,* of any kind whatsoever. Some of the arguments used to support the immorality of suicide, however, are so framed that if they were supportable at all, they would prove that suicide is *never* moral.

One well-known type of argument against suicide may be classified as *theological*. St. Augustine and others urged that the Sixth Commandment ("Thou shalt not kill") prohibits suicide, and that we are bound to obey a divine commandment. To this reasoning one might first reply that it is arbitrary exegesis of the Sixth Commandment to assert that it was intended to prohibit suicide. The second reply is that if there is not some consideration which shows on the merits of the case that suicide is morally wrong, God has no business prohibiting it. It is true that some will object to this point, and I must refer them elsewhere for my detailed comments on the divine-will theory of morality.[2]

Another theological argument with wide support was accepted by John Locke, who wrote: ". . . Men being all the workmanship of one omnipotent and infinitely wise Maker; all the servants of one sovereign Master, sent into the world by His order and about His business; they are His property, whose workmanship they are made to last during His, not one another's pleasure. . . . Every one . . . is bound to preserve himself, and not to quit his station wilfully. . . ."[3] And Kant: "We have been placed in this world under certain conditions and for specific purposes. But a suicide opposes the purpose of his Creator; he arrives in the other world as one who has deserted his post; he must be looked upon as a rebel against God. So long as we remember the truth that it is God's intention to preserve life, we are bound to regulate our activities in conformity with it. This duty is upon us until the time comes when God expressly commands us to leave this life. Human beings are sentinels on earth and may not leave their posts until relieved by another beneficent hand."[4] Unfortunately, however, even if we grant that it is the duty of human beings to do what God commands or intends them to do, more argument is required to show that God does *not* permit human beings to quit this life when their own personal welfare would be maximized by so doing. How does one draw the requisite inference about the intentions of God? The difficulties and contradictions in arguments to reach such a conclusion are discussed at length and perspicaciously by David Hume in his essay "On Suicide," and in view of the unlikelihood that readers will need to be persuaded about these, I shall merely refer those interested to that essay.[5]

A second group of arguments may be classed as arguments *from natural law.* St. Thomas says: "It is altogether unlawful to kill oneself, for three reasons. First, because everything naturally loves itself, the result being that everything naturally keeps itself in being, and resists corruptions as far as it can. Wherefore suicide is contrary to the inclination of nature, and to charity whereby every man should love himself. Hence suicide is always a mortal sin, as being contrary to the natural law and to charity."[6] Here St. Thomas ignores two obvious points. First, it is not obvious why a human being is morally bound to do what he or she has some inclination to do. (St. Thomas did not criticize chastity.) Second, while it is true that most human beings do feel a strong urge to live, the human being who commits suicide obviously feels a stronger inclination to do something else. It is as natural for a human being to dislike, and to take steps to avoid, say, great pain, as it is to cling to life.

A somewhat similar argument by Immanuel Kant may seem better. In a famous passage Kant writes that the maxim of a person who commits suicide is "From self-love I make it my principle to shorten my life if its continuance threatens more evil than it promises pleasure. The only further question to ask is whether this principle of self-love can become a universal law of nature. It is then seen at once that a system of nature by whose law the very same feeling whose function is to stimulate the furtherance of life should actually destroy life would contradict itself and consequently would not subsist as a system of nature. Hence this maxim cannot possibly hold as a universal law of nature and is therefore entirely opposed to the supreme principle of all duty."[7] What Kant finds contradictory is that the motive of self-love (interest in one's own long-range welfare) should sometimes lead one to struggle to preserve one's life, but at other times to end it. But where is the contradiction? One's circumstances change, and, if the argument of the following section in this chapter is correct, one sometimes maximizes one's own long-range welfare by trying to stay alive, but at other times by bringing about one's demise.

A third group of arguments, a form of which goes back at least to Aristotle, has a more modern and convincing ring. These are arguments to show that, in one way or another, a suicide necessarily does harm to other persons, or to society at large. Aristotle says that the suicide treats the *state* unjustly.[8] Partly following Aristotle, St. Thomas says: "Every man is part of the community, and so, as such, he belongs to the community. Hence by killing himself he injures the community."[9] Blackstone held that a suicide is an offense against the king "who hath an interest in the preservation of all his subjects," perhaps following Judge Brown in 1563, who argued that suicide cost the king a subject—"he being the head has lost one of his mystical members."[10] The premise of such arguments is, as Hume pointed out, obviously mistaken in many instances. It is true that Freud would perhaps have injured society had he, instead of finishing his last book, committed suicide to escape the pain of throat cancer. But surely there have been many suicides whose demise was not a noticeable loss to society; an honest man could only say that in some instances society was better off without them.

It need not be denied that suicide is often injurious to other persons, especially the family of a suicide. Clearly it sometimes is. But, we should notice what this fact establishes. Suppose we admit, as generally would be done, that there is some obligation not to perform any action which will probably or certainly be injurious to other people, the strength of the obligation being dependent on various factors, notably the seriousness of the expected injury. Then there is *some* obligation not to commit suicide, when that act would probably or certainly be injurious to other people. But, as we have already seen, many cases of *some* obligation to do something nevertheless are *not* cases of a duty to do that thing, *everything considered*. So it could sometimes be morally justified to commit suicide, even if the act will harm someone. Must a man with a terminal illness undergo excruciating pain because his death will cause his wife sorrow—when she will be caused sorrow a month later anyway, when he is dead of natural causes? Moreover, to repeat, the fact that an individual has some obligation not to commit suicide when that act will probably injure other persons does not imply that, everything considered, it is wrong for him to do it [or] that in all circumstances suicide *as such* is something there is some obligation to avoid.

Is there any sound argument, convincing to the modern mind, to establish that there is (or is not) *some moral obligation* to avoid suicide *as such*, an obligation, of course, which might be overridden by other obligations in some or many cases? . . .

To present all the arguments necessary to answer this question convincingly would take a great deal of space. I shall, therefore, simply state one answer to it which seems plausible to some contemporary philosophers. Suppose it could be shown that it would maximize the long-run welfare of everybody affected if people were taught that there is a moral obligation to avoid suicide—so that people would be motivated to avoid suicide just because they thought it wrong (would have anticipatory guilt feelings at the very idea), and so that other people would be inclined to disapprove of persons who commit suicide unless there were some excuse (such as those mentioned in the first section). One might ask: how could it maximize utility to mold the conceptual and motivational structure of persons in this way? To which the answer might be: feeling in this way might make persons who are impulsively inclined to commit suicide in a bad mood, or a fit of anger or jealousy, take more time to deliberate; hence, some suicides that have bad effects generally might be prevented. In other words, it might be a good thing in its effects for people to feel about suicide in the way they feel about breach of promise or injuring others, just as it might be a good thing for people to feel a moral obligation not to smoke, or to wear seat belts. However, it might be that negative moral feelings about suicide as such would stand in the way of action by those persons whose welfare really is best served by suicide and whose suicide is the best thing for everybody concerned.

When a Decision to Commit Suicide Is Rational from the Person's Point of View

The person who is contemplating suicide is obviously making a choice between future world-courses: the world-course that includes his demise, say, an hour from now, and several possible ones that contain his demise at a later point. One cannot have precise knowledge about many features of the latter group of world-courses, but it is certain that they will all end with death some (possibly short) finite time from now.

Why do I say the choice is between *world*-courses and not just a choice between future life-courses of the prospective suicide, the one shorter than the other? The reason is that one's suicide has some impact on the world (and one's continued life has some impact on the world), and that conditions in the rest of the world will often make a difference in one's evaluation of the possibilities. One *is* interested in things in the world other than just oneself and one's own happiness.

The basic question a person must answer, in order to determine which world-course is best or rational for him to choose, is which he *would* choose under conditions of optimal use of information, when *all* of his desires are taken into account. It is not just a question of what we prefer *now*, with some clarification of all the possibilities being considered. Our preferences change, and the preferences of tomorrow (assuming we can know something about them) are just as legitimately taken into account in deciding what to do now as the preferences of today. Since any reason that can be given today for weighting heavily today's preference can be given tomorrow for weighting heavily tomorrow's preference, the preferences of any time- stretch have a rational claim to an equal vote. Now the importance of that fact is this: we often know quite well that our desires, aversions, and preferences may change after a short while. When a person is in a state of despair—perhaps brought about by a rejection in love or discharge from a long-held position—nothing but the thing he cannot have seems desirable; everything else is turned to ashes. Yet we know quite well that the passage of time is likely to reverse all this; replacements may be found or other types of things that are available to us may begin to look attractive. So, if we were to act on the preferences of today alone, when the emotion of despair seems more than we can stand, we might find death preferable to life; but if we allow for the preferences of the weeks and years ahead, when many goals will be enjoyable and attractive, we might find life much preferable to death. So, if a choice of what is best is to be determined by what we want not only now but later (and later desires on an equal basis with the present ones)—as it should be—then what is the best or preferable world-course will often be quite different from what it would be if the choice, or what is best for one, were fixed by one's desires and preferences now.

Of course, if one commits suicide there are no future desires or aversions that may be compared with present ones and that should be allowed an equal vote in deciding what is best. In that respect the course of action that results in death is different from any other course of action we may undertake. I do not wish to suggest the rosy possibility that it is often or always reasonable to believe that next week "I shall be more interested in living than I am today, if today I take a dim view of continued existence." On the contrary, when a person is seriously ill, for instance, he may have no reason to think that the preference-order will be reversed—it may be that tomorrow he will prefer death to life more strongly.

The argument is often used that one can never be *certain* what is going to happen, and hence one is never rationally justified in doing anything as drastic as committing suicide. But we always have to live by probabilities and make our estimates as best we can. As soon as it is clear beyond reasonable doubt not only that death is now preferable to life, but also that it will be every day from now until the end, the rational thing is to act promptly.

Let us not pursue the question of whether it is rational for a person with a painful terminal illness to commit suicide; it is. However, the issue seldom arises, and few terminally ill patients do commit

suicide. With such patients matters usually get worse slowly so that no particular time seems to call for action. They are often so heavily sedated that it is impossible for the mental processes of decision leading to action to occur; or else they are incapacitated in a hospital and the very physical possibility of ending their lives is not available. Let us leave this grim topic and turn to a practically more important problem: whether it is rational for persons to commit suicide for some reason other than painful terminal physical illness. Most persons who commit suicide do so, apparently, because they face a nonphysical problem that depresses them beyond their ability to bear.

Among the problems that have been regarded as good and sufficient reasons for ending life, we find (in addition to serious illness) the following: some event that has made a person feel ashamed or lose his prestige and status; reduction from affluence to poverty; the loss of a limb or of physical beauty; the loss of sexual capacity; some event that makes it seem impossible to achieve things by which one sets store; loss of a loved one; disappointment in love; the infirmities of increasing age. It is not to be denied that such things can be serious blows to a person's prospects of happiness.

Whatever the nature of an individual's problem, there are various plain errors to be avoided — errors to which a person is especially prone when he is depressed—in deciding whether, everything considered, he prefers a world-course containing his early demise to one in which his life continues to its natural terminus. Let us forget for a moment the relevance to the decision of preferences that he may have tomorrow, and concentrate on some errors that may infect his preference as of today, and for which correction or allowance must be made.

In the first place, depression, like any severe emotional experience, tends to primitivize one's intellectual processes. It restricts the range of one's survey of the possibilities. One thing that a rational person would do is compare the world-course containing his suicide with his *best* alternative. But his best alternative is precisely a possibility he may overlook if, in a depressed mood, he thinks only of how badly off he is and cannot imagine any way of improving his situation. If a person is disappointed in love, it is possible to adopt a vigorous plan of action that carries a good chance of acquainting him with someone he likes at least as well; and if old age prevents a person from continuing the tennis game with his favorite partner, it is possible to learn some other game that provides the joys of competition without the physical demands.

Depression has another insidious influence on one's planning; it seriously affects one's judgment about probabilities. A person disappointed in love is very likely to take a dim view of himself, his prospects, and his attractiveness; he thinks that because he has been rejected by one person he will probably be rejected by anyone who looks desirable to him. In a less gloomy frame of mind he would make different estimates. Part of the reason for such gloomy probability estimates is that depression tends to repress one's memory of evidence that supports a nongloomy prediction. Thus, a rejected lover tends to forget any cases in which he has elicited enthusiastic response from ladies in relation to whom he has been the one who has done the rejecting. Thus his pessimistic self-image is based upon a highly selected, and pessimistically selected, set of data. Even when he is reminded of the data, moreover, he is apt to resist an optimistic inference.

Another kind of distortion of the look of future prospects is not a result of depression, but is quite normal. Events distant in the future feel small, just as objects distant in space look small. Their prospect does not have the effect on motivational processes that it would have if it were of an event in the immediate future. Psychologists call this the "goal-gradient" phenomenon; a rat, for instance, will run faster toward a perceived food box than a distant unseen one. In the case of a person who has suffered some misfortune, and whose situation now is an unpleasant one, this reduction of the motivational influence of events distant in time has the effect that present unpleasant states weigh far more heavily than probable future pleasant ones in any choice of world-courses.

If we are trying to determine whether we now prefer, or shall later prefer, the outcome of one world-course to that of another (and this is leaving aside the questions of the weight of the votes of preferences at a later date), we must take into account these and other infirmities of our "sensing" machinery. Since knowing that the machinery is out of order will not tell us what results it would give if it were working, the best recourse might be to refrain from making any decision in a stressful frame of mind. If decisions have to be made, one must recall past reactions, in a normal frame of mind, to outcomes like those under assessment. But many suicides seem to occur in moments of despair. What should be clear from the above is that a moment of despair, if one is seriously contemplating suicide, ought to be a moment of reassessment of one's goals and values, a reassessment which the individual must realize is very difficult to make objectively, because of the very quality of his depressed frame of mind.

A decision to commit suicide may in certain circumstances be a rational one. But a person who wants to act rationally must take into account the various possible "errors" and make appropriate rectification of his initial evaluations.

The Role of Other Persons

What is the moral obligation of other persons toward those who are contemplating suicide? The question of their moral blameworthiness may be ignored and what is rational for them to do from the point of view of personal welfare may be considered as being of secondary concern. Laws make it dangerous to aid or encourage a suicide. The risk of running afoul of the law may partly determine moral obligation, since moral obligation to do something may be reduced by the fact that it is personally dangerous.

The moral obligation of other persons toward one who is contemplating suicide is an instance of a general obligation to render aid to those in serious distress, at least when this can be done at no great cost to one's self. I do not think this general principle is seriously questioned by anyone, whatever his moral theory; so I feel free to assume it as a premise. Obviously the person contemplating suicide is in great distress of some sort; if he were not, he would not be seriously considering terminating his life.

How great a person's obligation is to one in distress depends on a number of factors. Obviously family and friends have special obligations to devote time to helping the prospective suicide—which others do not have. But anyone in this kind of distress has a moral claim on the time of any person who knows the situation (unless there are others more responsible who are already doing what should be done).

What is the obligation? It depends, of course, on the situation, and how much the second person knows about the situation. If the individual has decided to terminate his life if he can, and it is clear that he is right in this decision, then, if he needs help in executing the decision, there is a moral obligation to give him help. On this matter a patient's physician has a special obligation, from which any talk about the Hippocratic oath does not absolve him. It is true that there are some damages one cannot be expected to absorb, and some risks which one cannot be expected to take, on account of the obligation to render aid.

On the other hand, if it is clear that the individual should not commit suicide, from the point of view of his own welfare, or if there is a presumption that he should not (when the only evidence is that a person is discovered unconscious, with the gas turned on), it would seem to be the individual's obligation to intervene, prevent the successful execution of the decision, and see to the availability of competent psychiatric advice and temporary hospitalization, if necessary. Whether one has a right to take such steps when a clearly sane person, after careful reflection over a period of time, comes to the conclusion that an end to his life is what is best for him and what he wants, is very doubtful, even when one thinks his conclusion a mistaken one; it would seem that a man's own consid-

ered decision about whether he wants to live must command respect, although one must concede that this could be debated.

The more interesting role in which a person may be cast, however, is that of adviser. It is often important to one who is contemplating suicide to go over his thinking with another, and to feel that a conclusion, one way or the other, has the support of a respected mind. One thing one can obviously do, in rendering the service of advice, is to discuss with the person the various types of issues discussed above, made more specific by the concrete circumstances of his case, and help him find whether, in view, say, of the damage his suicide would do to others, he has a moral obligation to refrain, and whether it is rational or best for him, from the point of view of his own welfare, to take this step or adopt some other plan instead.

To get a person to see what is the rational thing to do is no small job. Even to get a person, in a frame of mind when he is seriously contemplating (or perhaps has already unsuccessfully attempted) suicide, to recognize a plain truth of fact may be a major operation. If a man insists, "I am a complete failure," when it is obvious that by any reasonable standard he is far from that, it may be tremendously difficult to get him to see the fact. But there is another job beyond that of getting a person to see what is the rational thing to do; that is to help him *act* rationally, or *be* rational, when he has conceded what would be the rational thing.

How either of these tasks may be accomplished effectively may be discussed more competently by an experienced psychiatrist than by a philosopher. Loneliness and the absence of human affection are states which exacerbate any other problems; disappointment, reduction to poverty, and so forth, seem less impossible to bear in the presence of the affection of another. Hence simply to be a friend, or to find someone a friend, may be the largest contribution one can make either to helping a person be rational or see clearly what is rational for him to do; this service may make one who was contemplating suicide feel that there is a future for him which it is possible to face.

NOTES

1. Immanuel Kant, *Lectures on Ethics* (New York: Harper Torchbook, 1963), p. 150.

2. R. B. Brandt, *Ethical Theory* (Englewood Cliffs, N.J.: Prentice-Hall, 1959), pp. 61–82.

3. John Locke, *Two Treatises of Government*, ch. 2.

4. Kant, *Lectures on Ethics*, p. 154.

5. This essay appears in collections of Hume's works.

6. For an argument similar to Kant's, see also St. Thomas Aquinas, *Summa Theologica*, II, II, Q. 64, Art. 5.

7. Immanuel Kant, *The Fundamental Principles of the Metaphysic of Morals*, trans. H. J. Paton (London: The Hutchinson Group, 1948), ch. 2.

8. Aristotle, *Nicomachean Ethics*, Bk. 5, Ch. 10, p. 1138a.

9. St. Thomas Aquinas, *Summa Theologica*, II, II, Q. 64, Art. 5.

10. Sir William Blackstone, *Commentaries*, 4:189; Brown in *Hales* v. *Petit*, I Plow 253, 75 E.R. 387 (C.B. 1563). Both cited by Norman St. John-Stevas, *Life, Death and the Law* (Bloomington, Ind.: Indiana University Press, 1961), p. 235.

Review and Discussion Questions

1. Assess Brandt's definition of suicide. Does the pilot who stays in the plane commit suicide?

2. Are there suicides that, in your view, show some defect of character and are thus morally blameworthy?

3. Are you persuaded by Brandt's responses to the arguments intended to show that we have some moral obligation to avoid suicide as such? Are there arguments against suicide that Brandt has overlooked?

4. Would it maximize social well-being or the collective good if people were taught that there is a moral obligation to avoid suicide? Explain your answer.

5. Under what circumstances, if any, would it be rational for a person to commit suicide? Given Brandt's discussion of the decisional errors that people contemplating suicide are prone to make, how likely is it that the average suicide attempt reflects a rational decision? What implications does this have for our policy toward suicide?

6. Suppose you learned that a friend, acquaintance, or colleague were contemplating suicide. What would you do? What difference would believing that the person's suicide would be rational or irrational make to your actions? Do we ever have a moral obligation to help someone commit suicide?

Voluntary Active Euthanasia

DAN W. BROCK

Dan W. Brock, professor of philosophy and director of the Center for Biomedical Ethics at Brown University, argues for the moral permissibility of voluntary active euthanasia based on the values of self-determination and individual well-being. Although euthanasia involves the deliberate killing of an innocent person, so does

From the Hastings Center Report, *vol. 22, no. 2 (1992). Reproduced by permission.* © *The Hastings Center. Notes omitted.*

withdrawing life-sustaining treatment at a patient's request and allowing the patient to die. Moreover, euthanasia is not wrongful killing because it does not deprive the victim of a future that he or she values or violate the person's right not to be killed. Turning to public policy, Brock explores the potential good and bad consequences of society's permitting euthanasia. Although he is sensitive to the possible dangers of legalizing euthanasia, he maintains that the benefits of doing so outweigh the risks and that procedural safeguards can substantially reduce the possibility of abuse.

Study Questions

1. What is the difference between physician-assisted suicide and voluntary active euthanasia? Between active and passive euthanasia? Between voluntary, involuntary, and nonvoluntary euthanasia?

2. How do the values of self-determination and individual well-being argue in favor of euthanasia?

3. How does the example of the greedy son support Brock's argument against the common view that withdrawing life-sustaining treatment is not killing but merely "allowing to die"?

4. Brock believes that even if euthanasia is killing and withdrawing life support is not, it doesn't follow that euthanasia is wrongful. Why not?

5. Brock identifies four likely good consequences of permitting euthanasia. What are they?

6. What five potential bad consequences does he identify?

I N THE RECENT BIOETHICS LITERATURE some have endorsed physician-assisted suicide but not euthanasia. Are they sufficiently different that the moral arguments for one often do not apply to the other? A paradigm case of physician-assisted suicide is a patient's ending his or her life with a lethal dose of a medication requested of and provided by a physician for that purpose. A paradigm case of voluntary active euthanasia is a physician's administering the lethal dose, often because the patient is unable to do so. The only difference that need exist between the two is the person who actually administers the lethal dose—the physician or the patient. In each, the physician plays an active and necessary causal role.

In physician-assisted suicide the patient acts last . . . whereas in euthanasia the physician acts last. . . . In both cases, however, the choice rests fully with the patient. In both the patient acts last in the sense of retaining the right to change his or her mind until the point at which the lethal process becomes irreversible. How could there be a substantial moral difference between the two based only on this small difference in the part played by the physician in the causal process resulting in death? Of course, it might be held that the moral difference is clear and important—in euthanasia the physician kills the patient whereas in physician-assisted suicide the patient kills him- or herself. But this is misleading at best. In assisted suicide the physician and patient together kill the patient. . . .

If there is no significant, intrinsic moral difference between the two, it is also difficult to see why public or legal policy should permit one but not the other; worries about abuse or about giving anyone dominion over the lives of others apply equally to either. As a result, I will take the arguments evaluated below to apply to both and will focus on euthanasia.

My concern here will be with *voluntary* euthanasia only—that is, with the case in which a clearly competent patient makes a fully voluntary and persistent request for aid in dying. Involuntary euthanasia, in which a competent patient explicitly refuses or opposes receiving euthanasia, and nonvoluntary euthanasia, in which a patient is incompetent and unable to express his or her wishes about euthanasia, will be considered here only as potential unwanted side effects of permitting voluntary euthanasia. I emphasize as well that I am concerned with *active* euthanasia, not withholding or withdrawing life-sustaining treatment, which some commentators characterize as "passive euthanasia." . . .

The Central Ethical Argument for Voluntary Active Euthanasia

The central ethical argument for euthanasia is familiar. It is that the very same two fundamental ethical values supporting the consensus on patients' rights to decide about life-sustaining treatment also support the ethical permissibility of euthanasia. These values are individual self-determination or autonomy and individual well-being. By self-determination as it bears on euthanasia, I mean people's interest in making important decisions about their lives for themselves according to their own values or conceptions of a good life, and in being left free to act on those decisions. Self-determination is valuable because it permits people to form and live in accordance with their own conception of a good life, at least within the bounds of justice and consistent with others doing so as well. In exercising self-determination people take responsibility for their lives and for the kinds of persons they become. A central aspect of human dignity lies in people's capacity to direct their lives in this way. The value of exercising self-determination presupposes some minimum of decisionmaking

capacities or competence, which thus limits the scope of euthanasia supported by self-determination; it cannot justifiably be administered, for example, in cases of serious dementia or treatable clinical depression.

Does the value of individual self-determination extend to the time and manner of one's death? Most people are very concerned about the nature of the last stage of their lives. This reflects not just a fear of experiencing substantial suffering when dying, but also a desire to retain dignity and control during this last period of life. Death is today increasingly preceded by a long period of significant physical and mental decline, due in part to the technological interventions of modern medicine. Many people adjust to these disabilities and find meaning and value in new activities and ways. Others find the impairments and burdens in the last stage of their lives at some point sufficiently great to make life no longer worth living. For many patients near death, maintaining the quality of one's life, avoiding great suffering, maintaining one's dignity, and insuring that others remember us as we wish them to become of paramount importance and outweigh merely extending one's life. But there is no single, objectively correct answer for everyone as to when, if at all, one's life becomes all things considered a burden and unwanted. If self-determination is a fundamental value, then the great variability among people on this question makes it especially important that individuals control the manner, circumstances, and timing of their dying and death.

The other main value that supports euthanasia is individual well-being. It might seem that individual well-being conflicts with a person's self-determination when the person requests euthanasia. Life itself is commonly taken to be a central good for persons, often valued for its own sake, as well as necessary for pursuit of all other goods within a life. But when a competent patient decides to forgo all further life-sustaining treatment then the patient, either explicitly or implicitly, commonly decides that the best life possible for him or her with treatment is of sufficiently poor quality that it is worse than no further life at all. Life is no longer considered a benefit by the patient, but has now become a burden. The same judgment underlies a request for euthanasia: continued life is seen by the patient as no longer a benefit, but now a burden. Especially in the often severely compromised and debilitated states of many critically ill or dying patients, there is no objective standard, but only the competent patient's judgment of whether continued life is no longer a benefit. . . .

Most opponents do not deny that there are some cases in which the values of patient self-determination and well-being support euthanasia. Instead, they commonly offer two kinds of arguments against it that on their view outweigh or override this support. The first kind of argument is that in any individual case where considerations of the patient's self-determination and well-being do support euthanasia, it is nevertheless always ethically wrong or impermissible. The second kind of argument grants that in some individual cases euthanasia may *not* be ethically wrong, but maintains nonetheless that public and legal policy should never permit it. The first kind of argument focuses on features of any individual case of euthanasia, while the second kind focuses on social or legal policy. In the next section I consider the first kind of argument.

Euthanasia Is the Deliberate Killing of an Innocent Person

The claim that any individual instance of euthanasia is a case of deliberate killing of an innocent person is, with only minor qualifications, correct. Unlike forgoing life-sustaining treatment, commonly understood as allowing to die, euthanasia is clearly killing, defined as depriving of life or causing the death of a living being. [By contrast with] providing morphine for pain relief at doses where the risk of respiratory depression and an earlier death may be a foreseen but unintended side effect of treating the patient's pain, in a case of euthanasia the patient's death is deliberate or intended even if in both the physician's ultimate end may be respecting the patient's wishes. If the deliberate killing of an innocent person is wrong, euthanasia would be nearly always impermissible.

In the context of medicine, the ethical prohibition against deliberately killing the innocent derives some of its plausibility from the belief that nothing in the currently accepted practice of medicine is deliberate killing. . . . The belief that doctors do not in fact kill requires the corollary belief that forgoing life-sustaining treatment, whether by not starting or by stopping treatment, is allowing to die, not killing. Common though this view is, I shall argue that it is confused and mistaken.

Why is the common view mistaken? Consider the case of a patient terminally ill with ALS disease [amyotrophic lateral sclerosis]. She is completely respirator dependent with no hope of ever being weaned. She is unquestionably competent but finds her condition intolerable and persistently requests to be removed from the respirator and allowed to die. Most people and physicians would agree that the patient's physician should respect the patient's wishes and remove her from the respirator, though this will certainly cause the patient's death. The common understanding is that the physician thereby allows the patient to die. But is that correct?

Suppose the patient has a greedy and hostile son who mistakenly believes that his mother will never decide to stop her life-sustaining treatment and that even if she did, her physician would not remove her from the respirator. Afraid that his inheritance will be dissipated by a long and expensive hospitalization, he enters his mother's room while she is sedated, extubates her, and she dies. Shortly thereafter the medical staff discovers what he has done and confronts the son. He replies, "I didn't kill her, I merely allowed her to die. It was her ALS disease that caused her death." I think this would rightly be dismissed as transparent sophistry—the son went into his mother's room and deliberately killed her. But, of course, the son performed just the same physical actions, did just the same thing, that the physician would have done. If that is so, then doesn't the physician also kill the patient when he extubates her?

I underline immediately that there are important ethical differences between what the physician and the greedy son do. First, the physician acts with the patient's consent whereas the son does not. Second, the physician acts with a good motive—to respect the patient's wishes and self-determination—whereas the son acts with a bad motive—to protect his own inheritance. Third, the physician acts in a social role through which he is legally authorized to carry out the patient's wishes regarding treatment whereas the son has no such authorization. These and perhaps other ethically important differences show that what the physician did was morally justified whereas what the son did was morally wrong. What they do *not* show, however, is that the son killed while the physician allowed to die. One can either kill or allow to die with or without consent, with a good or bad motive, within or outside of a social role that authorizes one to do so.

The difference between killing and allowing to die that I have been implicitly appealing to here is roughly that between acts and omissions resulting in death. Both the physician and the greedy son act in a manner intended to cause death, do cause death, and so both kill. One reason this conclusion is resisted is that on a different understanding of the distinction between killing and allowing to die, what the physician does is allow to die. In this account, the mother's ALS is a lethal disease whose normal progression is being held back or blocked by the life-sustaining respirator treatment. Removing this artificial intervention is then viewed as standing aside and allowing the patient to die of her underlying disease. I have argued elsewhere that this alternative account is deeply problematic, in part because it commits us to accepting that what the greedy son does is to allow to die, not kill. . . .

. . . Killing is often understood, especially within medicine, as unjustified causing of death; in medicine it is thought to be done only accidentally or negligently. It is also increasingly widely accepted that a physician is ethically justified in stopping life support in a case like that of the ALS patient. But if these two beliefs are correct, then what the physician does cannot be killing, and so must be allowing to die. Killing patients is not, to put it flippantly, understood to be part of physicians' job description. What is mistaken in this line of reasoning is the assumption that all killings are *unjustified* causings of death. Instead, some killings are ethically justified, including many instances of stopping life support. . . .

Suppose . . . my arguments are mistaken. Suppose that killing is worse than allowing to die and that withdrawing life support is not killing, although euthanasia is. Euthanasia still need not for that reason be morally wrong. To see this, we need to determine the basic principle for the moral evaluation of killing persons. What is it that makes paradigm cases of wrongful killing wrongful? One very plausible answer is that killing denies the victim something that he or she values greatly—continued life or a future. Moreover, since continued life is necessary for pursuing any of a person's plans and purposes, killing brings the frustration of all of these plans and desires as well. In a nutshell, wrongful killing deprives a person of a valued future, and of all the person wanted and planned to do in that future.

A natural expression of this account of the wrongness of killing is that people have a moral right not to be killed. But in this account of the wrongness of killing, the right not to be killed, like other rights, should be waivable when the person makes a competent decision that continued life is no longer wanted or a good, but is instead worse than no further life at all. In this view, euthanasia is properly understood as a case of a person having waived his or her right not to be killed.

This rights view of the wrongness of killing is not, of course, universally shared. Many people's moral views about killing have their origins in religious views that human life comes from God and cannot be justifiably destroyed or taken away, either by the person whose life it is or by another. But in a pluralistic society like our own with a strong commitment to freedom of religion, public policy should not be grounded in religious beliefs which many in that society reject. I turn now to the general evaluation of public policy on euthanasia.

Would the Bad Consequences of Euthanasia Outweigh the Good?

The argument against euthanasia at the policy level is stronger than at the level of individual cases, though even here I believe the case is ultimately unpersuasive, or at best indecisive. The policy level is the place where the main issues lie, however, and where moral considerations that might override arguments in favor of euthanasia will be found, if they are found anywhere. It is important to note two kinds of disagreement about the consequences for public policy of permitting euthanasia. First, there is empirical or factual disagreement about what the consequences would be. This disagreement is greatly exacerbated by the lack of firm data on the issue. Second, since on any reasonable assessment there would be both good and bad consequences, there are moral disagreements about the relative importance of different effects. In addition to these two sources of disagreement, there is also no single, well-specified policy proposal for legalizing euthanasia on which policy assessments can focus. But without such specification, and especially without explicit procedures for protecting against well-intentioned misuse and ill-intentioned abuse, the consequences for policy are largely speculative. Despite these difficulties, a preliminary account of the main likely good and bad consequences is possible. This should help clarify where better data or more moral analysis and argument are needed, as well as where policy safeguards must be developed.

Potential good consequences of permitting euthanasia

What are the likely good consequences? First, if euthanasia were permitted it would be possible to

respect the self-determination of competent patients who want it, but now cannot get it because of its illegality. . . .

One important factor substantially affecting the number of persons who would seek euthanasia is the extent to which an alternative is available. The widespread acceptance in the law, social policy, and medical practice of the right of a competent patient to forgo life-sustaining treatment suggests that the number of competent persons in the United States who would want euthanasia if it were permitted is probably relatively small.

A second good consequence of making euthanasia legally permissible benefits a much larger group. Polls have shown that a majority of the American public believes that people should have a right to obtain euthanasia if they want it. No doubt the vast majority of those who support this right to euthanasia will never in fact come to want euthanasia for themselves. Nevertheless, making it legally permissible would reassure many people that if they ever do want euthanasia they would be able to obtain it. This reassurance would supplement the broader control over the process of dying given by the right to decide about life-sustaining treatment. . . .

A third good consequence of the legalization of euthanasia concerns patients whose dying is filled with severe and unrelievable pain or suffering. When there is a life-sustaining treatment that, if forgone, will lead relatively quickly to death, then doing so can bring an end to these patients' suffering without recourse to euthanasia. For patients receiving no such treatment, however, euthanasia may be the only release from their otherwise prolonged suffering and agony. This argument from mercy has always been the strongest argument for euthanasia in those cases to which it applies. . . .

Specialists in pain control, as for example the pain of terminally ill cancer patients, argue that there are very few patients whose pain could not be adequately controlled, though sometimes at the cost of so sedating them that they are effectively unable to interact with other people or their environment. Thus, the argument from mercy in cases of physical pain can probably be met in a large majority of cases by providing adequate measures of pain relief. . . .

Dying patients often undergo substantial psychological suffering that is not fully or even principally the result of physical pain. The knowledge about how to relieve this suffering is much more limited than in the case of relieving pain, and efforts to do so are probably more often unsuccessful. If the argument from mercy is extended to patients experiencing great and unrelievable psychological suffering, the numbers of patients to which it applies are much greater.

One last good consequence of legalizing euthanasia is that once death has been accepted, it is often more humane to end life quickly and peacefully, when that is what the patient wants. Such a death will often be seen as better than a more prolonged one. People who suffer a sudden and unexpected death, for example by dying quickly or in their sleep from a heart attack or stroke, are often considered lucky to have died in this way. We care about how we die in part because we care about how others remember us, and we hope they will remember us as we were in "good times" with them and not as we might be when disease has robbed us of our dignity as human beings. . . .

Potential bad consequences of permitting euthanasia

Some of the arguments against permitting euthanasia are aimed specifically against physicians, while others are aimed against anyone being permitted to perform it. I shall first consider one argument of the former sort. Permitting physicians to perform euthanasia, it is said, would be incompatible with their fundamental moral and professional commitment as healers to care for patients and to protect life. Moreover, if euthanasia by physicians became common, patients would come to fear that a medication was intended not to treat or care, but instead to kill, and would thus lose trust in their physicians. This position was forcefully stated in a paper by Willard Gaylin and his colleagues:

The very soul of medicine is on trial. This issue touches medicine at its moral center; if this moral center collapses, if physicians become killers or are even licensed to kill, the profession—and, therewith, each physician—will never again be worthy of trust and respect as healer and comforter and protector of life in all its frailty.

. . . If permitting physicians to kill would undermine the very "moral center" of medicine, then almost certainly physicians should not be permitted to perform euthanasia. But how persuasive is this claim? Patients should not fear, as a consequence of permitting *voluntary* active euthanasia, that their physicians will substitute a lethal injection for what patients want and believe is part of their care. If active euthanasia is restricted to cases in which it is truly voluntary, then no patient should fear getting it unless she or he has voluntarily requested it. (The fear that we might in time also come to accept nonvoluntary, or even involuntary, active euthanasia is a slippery slope worry I address below.) Patients' trust of their physicians could be increased, not eroded, by knowledge that physicians will provide aid in dying when patients seek it. . . .

A second bad consequence that some foresee is that permitting euthanasia would weaken society's commitment to provide optimal care for dying patients. We live at a time in which the control of health care costs has become, and is likely to continue to be the dominant focus of health care policy. If euthanasia is seen as a cheaper alternative to adequate care and treatment, then we might become less scrupulous about providing sometimes costly support and other services to dying patients. Particularly if our society comes to embrace deeper and more explicit rationing of health care, frail, elderly, and dying patients will need to be strong and effective advocates for their own health care and other needs, although they are hardly in a position to do this. We should do nothing to weaken their ability to obtain adequate care and services.

This second worry is difficult to assess because there is little firm evidence about the likelihood of the feared erosion in the care of dying patients.

There are at least two reasons, however, for skepticism about this argument. The first is that the same worry could have been directed at recognizing patients' or surrogates' rights to forgo life-sustaining treatment, yet there is no persuasive evidence that recognizing the right to refuse treatment has caused a serious erosion in the quality of care of dying patients. The second reason for skepticism about this worry is that only a very small proportion of deaths would occur from euthanasia if it were permitted. In the Netherlands, where euthanasia under specified circumstances is permitted by the courts, though not authorized by statute, the best estimate of the proportion of overall deaths that result from it is about 2 percent. Thus, the vast majority of critically ill and dying patients will not request it, and so will still have to be cared for by physicians, families, and others. Permitting euthanasia should not diminish people's commitment and concern to maintain and improve the care of these patients. . . .

The [third] potential bad consequence of permitting euthanasia has been developed by David Velleman and turns on the subtle point that making a new option or choice available to people can sometimes make them worse off, even if once they have the choice they go on to choose what is best for them. Ordinarily, people's continued existence is viewed by them as given, a fixed condition with which they must cope. Making euthanasia available to people as an option denies them the alternative of staying alive by default. If people are offered the option of euthanasia, their continued existence is now a choice for which they can be held responsible and which they can be asked by others to justify. We care, and are right to care, about being able to justify ourselves to others. To the extent that our society is unsympathetic to justifying a severely dependent or impaired existence, a heavy psychological burden of proof may be placed on patients who think their terminal illness or chronic infirmity is not a sufficient reason for dying. Even if they otherwise view their life as worth living, the opinion of others around them that it is not can threaten their reason for living and make euthanasia a rational choice. Thus the existence of the option becomes a subtle pressure to request it.

This argument correctly identifies the reason why offering some patients the option of euthanasia would not benefit them. Velleman takes it not as a reason for opposing all euthanasia, but for restricting it to circumstances where there are "unmistakable and overpowering reasons for persons to want the option of euthanasia," and for denying the option in all other cases. But there are at least three reasons why such restriction may not be warranted. First, polls and other evidence support that most Americans believe euthanasia should be permitted. . . . Thus, many more people seem to want the choice than would be made worse off by getting it. Second, if giving people the option of ending their life really makes them worse off, then we should not only prohibit euthanasia, but also take back from people the right they now have to decide about life-sustaining treatment. The feared harmful effect should already have occurred from securing people's right to refuse life-sustaining treatment, yet there is no evidence of any such widespread harm or any broad public desire to rescind that right. Third, since there is a wide range of conditions in which reasonable people can and do disagree about whether they would want continued life, it is not possible to restrict the permissibility of euthanasia as narrowly as Velleman suggests without thereby denying it to most persons who would want it; to permit it only in cases in which virtually everyone would want it would be to deny it to most who would want it.

A [fourth] potential bad consequence of making euthanasia legally permissible is that it might weaken the general legal prohibition of homicide. This prohibition is so fundamental to civilized society, it is argued, that we should do nothing that erodes it. If most cases of stopping life support are killing, as I have already argued, then the court cases permitting such killing have already in effect weakened this prohibition. However, neither the courts nor most people have seen these cases as killing and so as challenging the prohibition of homicide. The courts have usually grounded patients' or their surrogates' rights to refuse life-sustaining treatment in rights to privacy, liberty, self-determination, or bodily integrity, not in exceptions to homicide laws.

Legal permission for physicians or others to perform euthanasia could not be grounded in patients' rights to decide about medical treatment. Permitting euthanasia would require qualifying, at least in effect, the legal prohibition against homicide, a prohibition that in general does not allow the consent of the victim to justify or excuse the act. Nevertheless, the very same fundamental basis of the right to decide about life-sustaining treatment—respecting a person's self-determination—does support euthanasia as well. Individual self-determination has long been a well-entrenched and fundamental value in the law, and so extending it to euthanasia would not require appeal to novel legal values or principles. That suicide or attempted suicide is no longer a criminal offense in virtually all states indicates an acceptance of individual self-determination in the taking of one's own life analogous to that required for voluntary active euthanasia. The legal prohibition (in most states) of assisting in suicide and the refusal in the law to accept the consent of the victim as a possible justification of homicide are both arguably a result of difficulties in the legal process of establishing the consent of the victim after the fact. If procedures can be designed that clearly establish the voluntariness of the person's request for euthanasia, it would under those procedures represent a carefully circumscribed qualification on the legal prohibition of homicide. Nevertheless, some remaining worries about this weakening can be captured in the final potential bad consequence, to which I will now turn.

This final potential bad consequence is the central concern of many opponents of euthanasia and, I believe, is the most serious objection to a legal policy permitting it. According to this "slippery slope" worry, although active euthanasia may be morally permissible in cases in which it is unequivocally voluntary and the patient finds his or her condition unbearable, a legal policy permitting euthanasia would inevitably lead to active euthanasia being performed in many other cases in which it would be morally wrong. To prevent those other wrongful cases of euthanasia we should not permit even morally justified performance of it.

Slippery slope arguments of this form are problematic and difficult to evaluate. From one perspective, they are the last refuge of conservative defenders of the status quo. When all the opponent's objections to the wrongness of euthanasia itself have been met, the opponent then shifts ground and acknowledges both that it is not in itself wrong and that a legal policy which resulted only in its being performed would not be bad. Nevertheless, the opponent maintains, it should still not be permitted because doing so would result in its being performed in other cases in which it is not voluntary and would be wrong. In this argument's most extreme form, permitting euthanasia is the first and fateful step down the slippery slope to Nazism. Once on the slope we will be unable to get off.

Now it cannot be denied that it is *possible* that permitting euthanasia could have these fateful consequences, but that cannot be enough to warrant prohibiting it if it is otherwise justified. A similar *possible* slippery slope worry could have been raised to securing competent patients' rights to decide about life support, but recent history shows such a worry would have been unfounded. It must be relevant how likely it is that we will end with horrendous consequences and an unjustified practice of euthanasia. How *likely* and *widespread* would the abuses and unwarranted extensions of permitting it be? By abuses, I mean the performance of euthanasia that fails to satisfy the conditions required for voluntary active euthanasia, for example, if the patient has been subtly pressured to accept it. By unwarranted extensions of policy, I mean later changes in legal policy to permit not just voluntary euthanasia, but also euthanasia in cases in which, for example, it need not be fully voluntary. Opponents of voluntary euthanasia on slippery slope grounds have not provided the data or evidence necessary to turn their speculative concerns into well-grounded likelihoods.

It is at least clear, however, that both the character and likelihood of abuses of a legal policy permitting euthanasia depend in significant part on the procedures put in place to protect against them. I will not try to detail fully what such procedures might be, but will just give some examples of what they might include:

1. The patient should be provided with all relevant information about his or her medical condition, current prognosis, available alternative treatments, and the prognosis of each.
2. Procedure should ensure that the patient's request for euthanasia is stable or enduring (a brief waiting period could be required) and fully voluntary (an advocate for the patient might be appointed to ensure this).
3. All reasonable alternatives must have been explored for improving the patient's quality of life and relieving any pain or suffering.
4. A psychiatric evaluation should ensure that the patient's request is not the result of a treatable psychological impairment such as depression.

These examples of procedural safeguards are all designed to ensure that the patient's choice is fully informed, voluntary, and competent, and so a true exercise of self-determination. Other proposals for euthanasia would restrict its permissibility further—for example, to the terminally ill—a restriction that cannot be supported by self-determination. Such additional restrictions might, however, be justified by concern for limiting potential harms from abuse. At the same time, it is important not to impose procedural or substantive safeguards so restrictive as to make euthanasia impermissible or practically infeasible in a wide range of justified cases.

These examples of procedural safeguards make clear that it is possible to substantially reduce, though not to eliminate, the potential for abuse of a policy permitting voluntary active euthanasia. Any legalization of the practice should be accompanied by a well-considered set of procedural safeguards together with an ongoing evaluation of its use. Introducing euthanasia into only a few states could be a form of carefully limited and controlled social

experiment that would give us evidence about the benefits and harms of the practice. Even then firm and uncontroversial data may remain elusive, as the continuing controversy over what has taken place in the Netherlands in recent years indicates.

The slip into nonvoluntary active euthanasia

While I believe slippery slope worries can largely be limited by making necessary distinctions both in principle and in practice, one slippery slope concern is legitimate. There is reason to expect that legalization of voluntary active euthanasia might soon be followed by strong pressure to legalize some nonvoluntary euthanasia of incompetent patients unable to express their own wishes. Respecting a person's self-determination and recognizing that continued life is not always of value to a person can support not only voluntary active euthanasia, but some nonvoluntary euthanasia as well. These are the same values that ground competent patients' right to refuse life-sustaining treatment. Recent history here is instructive. In the medical ethics literature, in the courts . . . , and in norms of medical practice, that right has been extended to incompetent patients and exercised by a surrogate who is to decide as the patient would have decided in the circumstances if competent. It has been held unreasonable to continue life-sustaining treatment that the patient would not have wanted just because the patient now lacks the capacity to tell us that. Life-sustaining treatment for incompetent patients is today frequently forgone on the basis of a surrogate's decision, or less frequently on the basis of an advance directive executed by the patient while still competent. The very same logic that has extended the right to refuse life-sustaining treatment from a competent patient to the surrogate of an incompetent patient (acting with or without a formal advance directive from the patient) may well extend the scope of active euthanasia. The argument will be, Why continue to force unwanted life on patients just because they have now lost the capacity to request euthanasia from us? . . .

Even if voluntary active euthanasia should slip into nonvoluntary active euthanasia, with surrogates

acting for incompetent patients, the ethical evaluation is more complex than many opponents of
euthanasia allow. Just as in the case of surrogates'
decisions to forgo life-sustaining treatment for
incompetent patients, so also surrogates' decisions to
request euthanasia for incompetent persons would
often accurately reflect what the incompetent person
would have wanted and would deny the person
nothing that he or she would have considered

worth having. Making nonvoluntary active
euthanasia legally permissible, however, would
greatly enlarge the number of patients on whom
it might be performed and substantially enlarge
the potential for misuse and abuse. As noted above,
frail and debilitated elderly people, often demented
or otherwise incompetent and thereby unable to
defend and assert their own interests, may be especially vulnerable to unwanted euthanasia.

Review and Discussion Questions

1. Do you agree that there is no significant moral difference between physician-assisted
suicide and voluntary active euthanasia?

2. Can premature death ever be said to promote one's well-being? If so, how is this to be
determined?

3. If one withdraws life support from a patient, does one thereby kill the person or merely
allow the person to die? Is the difference between directly killing a person and allowing a
person to die morally significant in and of itself? Explain your answer.

4. Can one waive one's right not to be killed?

5. Examine the five possible bad consequences of permitting euthanasia that Brock discusses. In each case, does he succeed in eliminating or diminishing the worries of the opponent of euthanasia? Has he overlooked any other possible bad consequences? In your view are
the benefits of permitting euthanasia outweighed by the likely costs? Does an answer to this
question settle whether society should or should not permit voluntary active euthanasia?

6. Would Brock's proposed procedural safeguards reduce the possibility of abuse enough
to justify permitting euthanasia, or is any risk of abuse too great? Are there other safeguards
that you would suggest?

7. Would our permitting voluntary euthanasia make it more likely that society will someday permit nonvoluntary euthanasia? If so, is that a good argument against permitting voluntary euthanasia? Is nonvoluntary euthanasia sometimes permissible or is it always wrong?
What about involuntary euthanasia?

When Self-Determination Runs Amok

DANIEL CALLAHAN

Senior fellow at Harvard Medical School and cofounder of the Hastings Center for
the study of bioethics, Daniel Callahan believes that legitimating euthanasia would
push our society in the wrong direction. Rejecting the idea that there are no limits
to an individual's right to self-determination, Callahan contends that this right does

From the Hastings Center Report, *vol. 22, no. 2 (1992). Reproduced by permission.* © *The Hastings Center.*

not justify a doctor's terminating a patient's life, even at the request of the patient, and he maintains that there is an important moral difference between commission and omission and, more specifically, between active euthanasia and withdrawing life-sustaining treatment from a patient. Callahan goes on to argue that permitting euthanasia would have bad consequences, that any law permitting it would inevitably be abused, and that it is not medicine's place to determine when a life is or is not worth living.

Study Questions

1. Callahan believes that permitting euthanasia would push society in the wrong direction with regard to "three important turning points in Western thought." What are they?

2. How does the role of the physician undermine the argument for euthanasia on grounds of self-determination? What is the point of the analogies Callahan draws with slavery and with dueling?

3. What does Callahan have in mind by the difference between "causality and culpability"? According to him, in what three ways is the distinction between the two concepts confused by those who believe there is no morally significant difference between killing a patient and allowing the patient to die?

4. Callahan says that failing to maintain the distinction between killing and allowing to die could have two disturbing results. What are they?

5. Callahan says that the "moral logic of the motives for euthanasia contain within them the ingredients of abuse." Explain what he has in mind.

6. Why does Callahan believe that a doctor who engages in euthanasia abuses the aims of medicine?

THE EUTHANASIA DEBATE is not just another moral debate, one in a long list of arguments in our pluralistic society. It is profoundly emblematic of three important turning points in Western thought. The first is that of the legitimate conditions under which one person can kill another. The acceptance of voluntary active euthanasia would morally sanction what can only be called "consenting adult killing." By the term I mean the killing of one person by another in the name of their mutual right to be killer and killed if they freely agree to play those roles. This turn flies in the face of a long-standing effort to limit the circumstances under which one person can take the life of another, from efforts to control the free flow of guns and arms, to abolish capital punishment, and to more tightly control warfare. Euthanasia would add a whole new category of killing to a society that already has too many excuses to indulge itself in that way.

The second turning point lies in the meaning and limits of self-determination. The acceptance of euthanasia would sanction a view of autonomy holding that individuals may, in the name of their own private, idiosyncratic view of the good life, call upon others, including such institutions as medicine, to help them pursue that life, even at the risk of harm to the common good. This works against the idea that the meaning and scope of our own right to lead our own lives must be conditioned by, and be compatible with, the good of the community, which is more than an aggregate of self-directing individuals.

The third turning point is to be found in the claim being made upon medicine: it should be prepared to make its skills available to individuals to help them achieve their private vision of the good life. This puts medicine in the business of promoting the individualistic pursuit of general human happiness and well-being. It would overturn the traditional belief that medicine should limit its domain to promoting and preserving human health, redirecting it instead to the relief of that suffering which stems from life itself, not merely from a sick body.

I believe that, at each of these three turning points, proponents of euthanasia push us in the wrong direction. Arguments in favor of euthanasia fall into four general categories, which I will take up in turn: (1) the moral claim of individual self-determination and well-being; (2) the moral irrelevance of the difference between killing and allowing to die; (3) the supposed paucity of evidence to show likely harmful consequences of legalized euthanasia; and (4) the compatibility of euthanasia and medical practice.

Self-Determination

Central to most arguments for euthanasia is the principle of self-determination. People are presumed to have an interest in deciding for themselves, according to their own beliefs about what makes life good, how they will conduct their lives. That is an important value, but the question in the euthanasia context is, What does it mean and how far should it extend? If it were a question of suicide, where a person takes their own life without assistance from another, that principle might be pertinent, at least for debate. But euthanasia is not that limited a matter. The self-determination in that case can only be effected by the moral and physical assistance of another. Euthanasia is thus no longer a matter only of self-determina-

tion, but of a mutual, social decision between two people, the one to be killed and the other to do the killing.

How are we to make the moral move from my right of self-determination to some doctor's right to kill me—from *my* right to *his* right? Where does the doctor's moral warrant to kill come from? Ought doctors to be able to kill anyone they want as long as permission is given by competent persons? Is our right to life just like a piece of property, to be given away or alienated if the price (happiness, relief of suffering) is right? And then to be destroyed with our permission once alienated?

In answer to all those questions, I will say this: I have yet to hear a plausible argument why it should be permissible for us to put this kind of power in the hands of another, whether a doctor or anyone else. The idea that we can waive our right to life, and then give to another the power to take that life, requires a justification yet to be provided by anyone.

Slavery was long ago outlawed on the ground that one person should not have the right to own another, even with the other's permission. Why? Because it is a fundamental moral wrong for one person to give over his life and fate to another, whatever the good consequences, and no less a wrong for another person to have that kind of total, final power. Like slavery, dueling was long ago banned on similar grounds: even free, competent individuals should not have the power to kill each other, whatever their motives, whatever the circumstances. Consenting adult killing, like consenting adult slavery or degradation, is a strange route to human dignity.

There is another problem as well. If doctors, once sanctioned to carry out euthanasia, are to be themselves responsible moral agents—not simply hired hands with lethal injections at the ready—then they must have their own *independent* moral grounds to kill those who request such services. What do I mean? As those who favor euthanasia are quick to point out, some people want it because their life has become so burdensome it no longer seems worth living.

The doctor will have a difficulty at this point. The degree and intensity to which people suffer from their diseases and their dying, and whether they find life more of a burden than a benefit, has very little directly to do with the nature or extent of their actual physical condition. Three people can have the same condition, but only one will find the suffering unbearable. People suffer, but suffering is as much a function of the values of individuals as it is of the physical causes of that suffering. Inevitably in that circumstance, the doctor will in effect be treating the patient's values. To be responsible, the doctor would have to share those values. The doctor would have to decide, on her own, whether the patient's life was "no longer worth living."

But how could a doctor possibly know that or make such a judgment? Just because the patient said so? I raise this question because, while in Holland at the euthanasia conference reported by Maurice de Wachter . . ., the doctors present agreed that there is no objective way of measuring or judging the claims of patients that their suffering is unbearable. And if it is difficult to measure suffering, how much more difficult to determine the value of a patient's statement that her life is not worth living?

However one might want to answer such questions, the very need to ask them, to inquire into the physician's responsibility and grounds for medical and moral judgment, points out the social nature of the decision. Euthanasia is not a private matter of self-determination. It is an act that requires two people to make it possible, and a complicit society to make it acceptable.

Killing and Allowing to Die

Against common opinion, the argument is sometimes made that there is no moral difference between stopping life-sustaining treatment and more active forms of killing, such as lethal injection. Instead I would contend that the notion that there is no morally significant dif-ference between omission and commission is just wrong. Consider in its broad implications what the eradication of the distinction implies: that death from disease has been banished, leaving only the actions of physicians in terminating treatment as the cause of death. Biology, which used to bring about death, has apparently been displaced by human agency. Doctors have finally, I suppose, thus genuinely become gods, now doing what nature and the deities once did.

What is the mistake here? It lies in confusing causality and culpability, and in failing to note the way in which human societies have overlaid natural causes with moral rules and interpretations. Causality (by which I mean the direct physical causes of death) and culpability (by which I mean our attribution of moral responsibility to human actions) are confused under three circumstances.

They are confused, first, when the action of a physician in stopping treatment of a patient with an underlying lethal disease is construed as *causing* death. On the contrary, the physician's omission can only bring about death on the condition that the patient's disease will kill him in the absence of treatment. We may hold the physician morally responsible for the death, if we have morally judged such actions wrongful omissions. But it confuses reality and moral judgment to see an omitted action as having the same causal status as one that directly kills. A lethal injection will kill both a healthy person and a sick person. A physician's omitted treatment will have no effect on a healthy person. Turn off the machine on me, a healthy person, and nothing will happen. It will only, in contrast, bring the life of a sick person to an end because of an underlying fatal disease.

Causality and culpability are confused, second, when we fail to note that judgments of moral responsibility and culpability are human constructs. By that I mean that we human beings, after moral reflection, have decided to call some actions right or wrong, and to devise moral rules to deal with them. When physicians could do nothing to stop death, they were not held responsible for it. When, with medical progress, they began to have some power over death—but only its timing and circumstances, not its ultimate inevitability—moral rules were devised to set forth their obligations. Natural causes of death were not thereby banished. They were, instead, overlaid with a medical ethics designed to determine moral culpability in deploying medical power.

To confuse the judgments of this ethics with the physical causes of death—which is the connotation of the word *kill*—is to confuse nature and human action. People will, one way or another, die of some disease; death will have dominion over all of us. To say that a doctor "kills" a patient by allowing this to happen should only be understood as a moral judgment about the licitness of his omission, nothing more. We can, as a fashion of speech only, talk about a doctor *killing* a patient by omitting treatment he should have provided. It is a fashion of speech precisely because it is the underlying disease that brings death when treatment is omitted; that is its cause, not the physician's omission. It is a misuse of the word *killing* to use it when a doctor stops a treatment he believes will no longer benefit the patient—when, that is, he steps aside to allow an eventually inevitable death to occur now rather than later. The only deaths that human beings invented are those that come from direct killing—when, with a lethal injection, we both cause death and are morally responsible for it. In the case of omissions, we do not cause death even if we may be judged morally responsible for it.

This difference between causality and culpability also helps us see why a doctor who has omitted a treatment he should have provided has "killed" that patient while another doctor—performing precisely the same act of omission on another patient in different circumstances—does not kill her, but only allows her to die. The difference is that we have come, by moral convention and conviction, to classify unauthorized or illegitimate omissions as acts of "killing." We call them "killing" in the expanded sense of the term: a culpable action that permits the real cause of death, the underlying disease, to proceed to its lethal conclusion. By contrast, the doctor who, at the patient's request, omits or terminates unwanted treatment does not kill at all. Her underlying disease, not his action, is the physical cause of death; and we have agreed to consider actions of that kind to be morally licit. He thus can truly be said to have "allowed" her to die.

If we fail to maintain the distinction between killing and allowing to die, moreover, there are some disturbing possibilities. The first would be to confirm many physicians in their already too-powerful belief that, when patients die or when physicians stop treatment because of the futility of continuing it, they are somehow both morally and physically responsible for the deaths that follow. That notion needs to be abolished, not strengthened. It needlessly and wrongly burdens the physician, to whom should not be attributed the powers of the gods. The second possibility would be that, in every case where a doctor judges medical treatment no longer effective in prolonging life, a quick and direct killing of the patient would be seen as the next, most reasonable step, on grounds of both humaneness and economics. I do not see how that logic could easily be rejected.

Calculating the Consequences

When concerns about the adverse social consequences of permitting euthanasia are raised, its advocates tend to dismiss them as unfounded and overly speculative. On the contrary, recent data about the Dutch experience suggests that such concerns are right on target. From my own discussions in Holland, and from the articles on that subject. . ., I believe we can now fully see most of the *likely* consequences of legal euthanasia.

Three consequences seem almost certain, in this or any other country: the inevitability of some abuse of the law; the difficulty of precisely writing, and then enforcing, the law; and the inherent slipperiness of the moral reasons for legalizing euthanasia in the first place.

Why is abuse inevitable? One reason is that almost all laws on delicate, controversial matters are to some extent abused. This happens because not everyone will agree with the law as written and will bend it, or ignore it, if they can get away with it. From explicit admissions to me by Dutch proponents of euthanasia, and from the corroborating information provided by the Remmelink Report and the outside studies of Carlos Gomez and John Keown, I am convinced that in the Netherlands there are a substantial number of cases of nonvoluntary euthanasia, that is, euthanasia undertaken without the explicit permission of the person being killed. The other reason abuse is inevitable is that the law is likely to have a low enforcement priority in the criminal justice system. Like other laws of similar status, unless there is an unrelenting and harsh willingness to pursue abuse, violations will ordinarily be tolerated. The worst thing to me about my experience in Holland was the casual, seemingly indifferent attitude toward abuse. I think that would happen everywhere.

Why would it be hard to precisely write, and then enforce, the law? The Dutch speak about the requirement of "unbearable" suffering, but admit that such a term is just about indefinable, a highly subjective matter admitting of no objective standards. A requirement for outside opinion is nice, but it is easy to find complaisant colleagues. A requirement that a medical condition be "terminal" will run aground on the notorious difficulties of knowing when an illness is actually terminal.

Apart from those technical problems there is a more profound worry. I see no way, even in principle, to write or enforce a meaningful law that can guarantee effective procedural safeguards. The reason is obvious yet almost always overlooked. The euthanasia transaction will ordinarily take place within the boundaries of the private and confidential doctor-patient relationship. No one can possibly know what takes place in that context unless the doctor chooses to reveal it. In Holland, less than 10 percent of the physicians report their acts of euthanasia and do so with almost complete legal impunity. There is no reason why the situation should be any better elsewhere. Doctors will have their own reasons for keeping euthanasia secret, and some patients will have no less a motive for wanting it concealed.

I would mention, finally, that the moral logic of the motives for euthanasia contain within them the ingredients of abuse. The two standard motives for euthanasia and assisted suicide are said to be our right of self-determination, and our claim upon the mercy of others, especially doctors, to relieve our suffering. These two motives are typically spliced together and presented as a single justification. Yet if they are considered independently—and there is no inherent reason why they must be linked—they reveal serious problems. It is said that a competent, adult person should have a right to euthanasia for the relief of suffering. But why must the person be suffering? Does not that stipulation already compromise the principle of self-determination? How can self-determination have any limits? Whatever the person's motives may be, why are they not sufficient?

Consider next the person who is suffering but not competent, who is perhaps demented or mentally retarded. The standard argument would deny euthanasia to that person. But why? If a person is suffering but not competent, then it would seem grossly unfair to deny relief solely on the grounds of incompetence. Are the incompetent less entitled to relief from suffering than the competent? Will it only be affluent, middle-class people, mentally fit and savvy about working the medical system, who can qualify? Do the incompetent suffer less because of their incompetence?

Considered from these angles, there are no good moral reasons to limit euthanasia once the principle of taking life for that purpose has been legitimated. If we really believe in self-determination, then any competent person should have a right to be killed by a doctor for any reason that suits him. If we believe in the relief of suffering, then it seems cruel and capricious to deny it to the incompetent. There is, in short, no reasonable or logical stopping point once the turn has been made down the road to euthanasia, which could soon turn into a convenient and commodious expressway.

Euthanasia and Medical Practice

A fourth kind of argument one often hears both in the Netherlands and in this country is that euthanasia and assisted suicide are perfectly compatible with the aims of medicine. I would note at the very outset that a physician who participates in another person's suicide already abuses medicine. Apart from depression (the main statistical cause of suicide), people commit suicide because they find life empty, oppressive, or meaningless. Their judgment is a judgment about the value of continued life, not only about health (even if they are sick). Are doctors now to be given the right to make judgments about the kinds of life worth living and to give their blessing to suicide for those they judge wanting? What conceivable competence, technical or moral, could doctors claim to play such a role? Are we to medicalize suicide, turning judgments about its worth and value into one more clinical issue? Yes, those are rhetorical questions.

Yet they bring us to the core of the problem of euthanasia and medicine. The great temptation of modern medicine, not always resisted, is to move beyond the promotion and preservation of health into the boundless realm of general human happiness and well-being. The root problem of illness and mortality is both medical and philosophical or religious. "Why must I die?" can be asked as a technical, biological question or as a question about the meaning of life.

When medicine tries to respond to the latter, which it is always under pressure to do, it moves beyond its proper role.

It is not medicine's place to lift from us the burden of that suffering which turns on the meaning we assign to the decay of the body and its eventual death. It is not medicine's place to determine when lives are not worth living or when the burden of life is too great to be borne. Doctors have no conceivable way of evaluating such claims on the part of patients, and they should have no right to act in response to them. Medicine should try to relieve human suffering, but only that suffering which is brought on by illness and dying as biological phenomena, not that suffering which comes from anguish or despair at the human condition.

Doctors ought to relieve those forms of suffering that medically accompany serious illness and the threat of death. They should relieve pain, do what they can to allay anxiety and uncertainty, and be a comforting presence. As sensitive human beings, doctors should be prepared to respond to patients who ask why they must die, or die in pain. But here the doctor and the patient are at the same level. The doctor may have no better an answer to those old questions than anyone else; and certainly no special insight from his training as a physician. It would be terrible for physicians to forget this, and to think that in a swift, lethal injection, medicine has found its own answer to the riddle of life. It would be a false answer, given by the wrong people. It would be no less a false answer for patients. They should neither ask medicine to put its own vocation at risk to serve their private interests, nor think that the answer to suffering is to be killed by another. The problem is precisely that, too often in human history, killing has seemed the quick, efficient way to put aside that which burdens us. It rarely helps, and too often simply adds to one evil still another. That is what I believe euthanasia would accomplish. It is self-determination run amok.

Review and Discussion Questions

1. With respect to Callahan's three turning points, do you agree that permitting euthanasia would push our society in the wrong direction?

2. Callahan argues that my right to self-determination does not justify a doctor's killing me. But what about physician-assisted suicide?

3. In the previous essay, Dan W. Brock argued that the value of self-determination supports euthanasia. Callahan argues that it does not. With whom do you agree, and why?

4. Callahan argues that those who say there is no morally significant difference between killing a patient and allowing the patient to die are guilty of confusing causality and culpability. Do you find his reasoning persuasive? Explain why or why not.

5. According to Callahan, some omissions are morally culpable and thus considered "killings." But if some omissions are permissible and others impermissible, must direct killings always be wrongful?

6. Brock appears to believe that the difference between killing and letting die is not morally significant, other things being equal. Callahan would dispute this. With whom do you agree, and why?

7. Callahan believes that a law permitting euthanasia would be difficult to write and to enforce and that abuse is inevitable. In your view, does this constitute an insurmountable objection to legalizing euthanasia?

8. Callahan writes that "if we really believe in self-determination, then any competent person should have a right to be killed by a doctor for any reason that suits him." Do you agree that self-determination implies this? If it does, should we therefore limit individual self-determination or should we simply accept that people have a right to have their lives ended, regardless of their reasons?

9. Is a doctor who participates in euthanasia or assisted suicide guilty of abusing his or her proper role as a physician?

Is There a Duty to Die?

JOHN HARDWIG

Earlier Richard B. Brandt considered situations in which suicide might be rational from the point of view of the person contemplating it, and Dan W. Brock argued that euthanasia can benefit the person killed. In this essay, John Hardwig, professor of philosophy at East Tennessee State University, supports the more radical view that people can have a duty to die—indeed, that they can sometimes have this duty even when they would prefer to go on living. He is particularly concerned with situations in which modern medical technology makes it possible for an elderly person to extend his or her life for a short time but only at a very high cost to his or her loved ones, and he argues that medical ethics is wrong to focus exclusively on the well-being and autonomy of the patient while ignoring the burden that life-prolonging treatment can sometimes place on one's family.

From the Hastings Center Report, *vol. 27, no. 2 (1997). Reproduced by permission.* © *The Hastings Center.*

1. Why does modern medicine raise the question of whether one can have a duty to die?
2. What is the "individualistic fantasy" that Hardwig criticizes?
3. What are the three objections to the idea of a duty to die that he considers?
4. What are the main factors that Hardwig identifies as influencing whether one has a duty to die?
5. Hardwig believes that "we fear death too much." What does he see as the implications of our fear of death?

F OR ME THE QUESTION IS REAL and very important. I feel strongly that I may very well some day have a duty to die. I do not believe that I am idiosyncratic, morbid, mentally ill, or morally perverse in thinking this. I think many of us will eventually face precisely this duty. But I am first of all concerned with my own duty. . . .

Circumstances and a Duty to Die

Do many of us really believe that no one ever has a duty to die? I suspect not. I think most of us probably believe that there is such a duty, but it is very uncommon. Consider Captain Oates, a member of Admiral Scott's expedition to the South Pole. Oates became too ill to continue. If the rest of the team stayed with him, they would all perish. After this had become clear, Oates left his tent one night, walked out into a raging blizzard, and was never seen again. That may have been a heroic thing to do, but we might be able to agree that it was also no more than his duty. It would have been wrong for him to urge—or even to allow—the rest to stay and care for him.

This is a very unusual circumstance—a "lifeboat case"—and lifeboat cases make for bad ethics. But I expect that most of us would also agree that there have been cultures in which what we would call a duty to die has been fairly common. These are relatively poor, technologically simple, and especially nomadic cultures. In such societies, everyone knows that if you manage to live long enough, you will become old and debilitated. Then you will need to take steps to end your life. The old people in these societies regularly did precisely that. Their cultures prepared and supported them in doing so.

Those cultures could be dismissed as irrelevant to contemporary bioethics; their circumstances are so different from ours. But if that is our response, it is instructive. It suggests that we assume a duty to die is irrelevant to us because our wealth and technological sophistication have purchased exemption for us . . . except under very unusual circumstances like Captain Oates's.

But have wealth and technology really exempted us? We like to think of modern medicine as all triumph with no dark side. Our medicine saves many lives and enables us to live longer. That is wonderful, indeed. We are all glad to have access to this medicine. But our medicine also delivers most of us over to chronic illnesses and it enables many of us to survive longer that we can take care of ourselves, longer than we know what to do with ourselves, longer than we even are ourselves.

The costs—and these are not merely monetary—of prolonging our lives when we are no longer able to care for ourselves are often staggering. If further medical advances wipe out many of today's "killer diseases"—cancer, heart attacks, strokes, ALS, AIDS, and the rest—then one day most of us will survive long enough to become demented or debilitated. These developments could generate a fairly widespread duty to die. A fairly common duty to die might turn out to be only the dark side of our life-prolonging medicine and the uses we choose to make of it.

Let me be clear. I certainly believe that there is a duty to refuse life-prolonging medical treatment and also a duty to complete advance directives refusing life-prolonging treatment. But a duty to die can go well beyond that. There can be a duty to die before one's illnesses would cause death, even if treated only with palliative measures. In fact, there may be a fairly common responsibility to end one's life in the absence of any terminal illness at all. Finally, there can be a duty to die when one would prefer to live. Granted, many of the conditions that can generate a duty to die also seriously undermine the quality of life. Some prefer not to live under such conditions. But even those who want to live can face a duty to die. These will clearly be the most controversial and troubling cases; I will, accordingly, focus my reflections on them.

The Individualistic Fantasy

Because a duty to die seems such a real possibility to me, I wonder why contemporary bioethics has dismissed it without serious consideration. I believe that most bioethics still shares in one of our deeply embedded American dreams: the individualistic fantasy. This fantasy leads us to imagine that lives are separate and unconnected, or that they could be so if we chose. If lives were unconnected, things that happened in my life would not or need not affect others. And if others were not (much) affected by my life, I would have no duty to consider the impact of my decisions on others. I would then be free morally to live my life however I please, choosing whatever life or death I prefer for myself. The way I live would be nobody's business but my own. I certainly would have no duty to die if I preferred to live.

Within a health care context, the individualistic fantasy leads us to assume that the patient is the only one affected by decisions about her medical treatment. If only the patient were affected, the relevant questions when making treatment decisions would be precisely those we ask: What will benefit the patient? Who can best decide that? The pivotal issue would always be simply whether the patient wants to live like this and whether she would consider herself better off dead. "Whose life is it, anyway?" we ask rhetorically.

But this is morally obtuse. We are not a race of hermits. Illness and death do not come only to those who are all alone. Nor is it much better to think in terms of the bald dichotomy between "the interests of the patient" and "the interests of society" (or a third-party payer), as if we were isolated individuals connected only to "society" in the abstract or to the other, faceless members of our health maintenance organization.

Most of us are affiliated with particular others and most deeply, with family and loved ones. Families and loved ones are bound together by ties of care and affection, by legal relations and obligations, by inhabiting shared spaces and living units, by interlocking finances and economic prospects, by common projects and also commitments to support the different life projects of other family members, by shared histories, by ties of loyalty. This life together of family and loved ones is what defines and sustains us; it is what gives meaning to most of our lives. We would not have it any other way. We would not want to be all alone, especially when we are seriously ill, as we age, and when we are dying.

But the fact of deeply interwoven lives debars us from making exclusively self-regarding decisions, as the decisions of one member of a family may dramatically affect the lives of all the rest. The impact of my decisions upon my family and loved ones is the source of many of my strongest obligations and also the most plausible and likeliest basis of a duty to die. "Society," after all, is only very marginally affected by how I live, or by whether I live or die.

A Burden to My Loved Ones

Many older people report that their one remaining goal in life is not to be a burden to their loved ones. Young people feel this, too: when I ask my undergraduate students to think about whether their death could come too late, one of their very first responses always is, "Yes, when I become a burden to my family or loved ones." Tragically, there are situations in which my loved ones would be much better off—all things considered, the loss of a loved one notwithstanding—if I were dead.

The lives of our loved ones can be seriously compromised by caring for us. The burdens of providing care or even just supervision twenty-four hours a day, seven days a week are often overwhelming. When this kind of caregiving goes on for years, it leaves the caregiver exhausted, with no time for herself or life of her own. Ultimately, even her health is often destroyed. But it can also be emotionally devastating simply to live with a spouse who is increasingly distant, uncommunicative, unresponsive, foreign, and unreachable. Other family members' needs often go unmet as the caring capacity of the family is exceeded. Social life and friendships evaporate, as there is no opportunity to go out to see friends and the home is no longer a place suitable for having friends in.

We must also acknowledge that the lives of our loved ones can be devastated just by having to pay for health care for us. One part of the recent SUPPORT study documented the financial aspects of caring for a dying member of a family. Only those who had illnesses severe enough to give them less than a 50 percent chance to live six more months were included in this study. When these patients survived their initial hospitalization and were discharged about one-third required considerable caregiving from their families; in 20 percent of the cases a family member had to quit work or make some other major lifestyle change; almost one-third of these families lost all of their savings; and just under 30 percent lost a major source of income.

If talking about money sounds venal or trivial, remember that much more than money is normally at stake here. When someone has to quit work, she may well lose her career. Savings decimated late in life cannot be recouped in the few remaining years of employability, so the loss comprises the quality of the rest of the caregiver's life. For a young person, the chance to go to college

may be lost to the attempt to pay debts due to an illness in the family, and this decisively shapes an entire life. . . .

I am not advocating a crass, quasi-economic conception of burdens and benefits, nor a shallow, hedonistic view of life. Given a suitably rich understanding of benefits, family members sometimes do benefit from suffering through the long illness of a loved one. Caring for the sick or aged can foster growth, even as it makes daily life immeasurably harder and the prospects for the future much bleaker. Chronic illness or drawn-out death can also pull a family together, making the care for each other stronger and more evident. If my loved ones are truly benefiting from coping with my illness or debility, I have no duty to die based on burdens to them.

But it would also be irresponsible to blithely assume that this always happens, that it will happen in my family, or that it will be the fault of my family if they cannot manage to turn my illness into a positive experience. Perhaps the opposite is more common: a hospital chaplain once told me that he could not think of a single case in which a family was strengthened or brought together by what happened at the hospital.

Our families and loved ones also have obligations, of course—they have the responsibility to stand by us and to support us through debilitating illness and death. They must be prepared to make significant sacrifices to respond to an illness in the family. I am far from denying that. Most of us are aware of this responsibility and most families meet it rather well. In fact, families deliver more than 80 percent of the long-term care in this country, almost always at great personal cost. Most of us who are part of a family can expect to be sustained in our time of need by family members and those who love us.

But most discussions of an illness in the family sound as if responsibility were a one-way street. It is not, of course. When we become seriously ill or debilitated, we too may have to make sacrifices. To think that my loved ones must bear whatever burdens my illness, debility, or dying process might impose upon them is to reduce them to means of my well-being. And that would be immoral. Family solidarity, altruism, bearing the burden of a loved one's misfortune, and loyalty are all important virtues of families as well. But they are all also two-way streets.

Objections to a Duty to Die

To my mind, the most serious objections to the idea of a duty to die lie in the effects on my loved ones of ending my life. But to most others, the important objections have little or nothing to do with family and loved ones. Perhaps the most common objections are: (1) there is a higher duty that always takes precedence over a duty to die; (2) a duty to end one's own life would be incompatible with a recognition of human dignity or the intrinsic value of a person; and (3) seriously ill, debilitated, or dying people are already bearing the harshest burdens and so it would be wrong to ask them to bear the burden of ending their own lives. . . .

An example of the first line of argument would be the claim that a duty to God, the giver of life, forbids that anyone take her own life. It could be argued that this duty always supersedes whatever obligations we might have to our families. But what convinces us that we always have such a religious duty in the first place? And what guarantees that it always supersedes our obligations to try to protect our loved ones?

Certainly, the view that death is the ultimate evil cannot be squared with Christian theology. It does not reflect the actions of Jesus or those of his early followers. Nor is it clear that the belief that life is sacred requires that we never take it. . . .

Secondly, religious considerations aside, the claim could be made that an obligation to end one's own life would be incompatible with human dignity or would embody a failure to recognize the intrinsic value of a person. But I do not see that in thinking I had a duty to die I would necessarily be failing to respect myself or appreciate my dignity or worth. Nor would I necessarily be failing to respect you in thinking that you had a similar duty. There is surely also a sense in which

we fail to respect ourselves if in the face of illness or death, we stoop to choosing just what is best for ourselves. Indeed, Kant held that the very best core of human dignity is the ability to act on a self-imposed moral law, regardless of whether it is in our interest to do so. We shall return to the notion of human dignity.

A third objection appeals to the relative weight of burdens and thus, ultimately, to considerations of fairness or justice. The burdens that an illness creates for the family could not possibly be great enough to justify an obligation to end one's life— the sacrifice of life itself would be a far greater burden than any involved in caring for a chronically ill family member.

But is this true? Consider the following case:

> An 87-year-old woman was dying of congestive heart failure. Her APACHE score predicted that she had less than a 50 percent chance to live for another six months. She was lucid, assertive, and terrified of death. She very much wanted to live and kept opting for rehospitalization and the most aggressive life-prolonging treatment possible. That treatment successfully prolonged her life (though with increasing debility) for nearly two years. Her 55-year-old daughter was her only remaining family, her caregiver, and the main source of her financial support. The daughter duly cared for her mother. But before her mother died, her illness had cost the daughter all of her savings, her home, her job, and her career.

This is by no means an uncommon sort of case. Thousands of similar cases occur each year. Now, ask yourself which is the greater burden:

> a) To lose a 50 percent chance of six more months of life at age 87?
>
> b) To lose all your savings, your home, and your career at age 55?

Which burden would you prefer to bear? Do we really believe the former is the greater burden? . . .

I think most of us would agree that (b) is a greater burden. That is the evil we would more hope to avoid in our lives. If we are tempted to say that the mother's disease and impending death are the greater evil, I believe it is because we are taking a "slice of time" perspective rather than a "lifetime perspective." But surely the lifetime perspective is the appropriate perspective when weighing burdens. If (b) is the greater burden, then we must admit that we have been promulgating an ethics that advocates imposing greater burdens on some people in order to provide smaller benefits for others just because they are ill and thus gain our professional attention and advocacy.

A whole range of cases like this one could easily be generated. In some, the answer about which burden is greater will not be clear. But in many it is. Death—or ending your own life—is simply not the greatest evil or the greatest burden.

This point does not depend on a utilitarian calculus. Even if death were the greatest burden (thus disposing of any simple utilitarian argument), serious questions would remain about the moral justifiability of choosing to impose crushing burdens on loved ones in order to avoid having to bear this burden oneself. . . .

I can readily imagine that, through cowardice, rationalization, or failure of resolve, I will fail in this obligation to protect my loved ones. If so, I think I would need to be excused or forgiven for what I did. But I cannot imagine it would be morally permissible to ruin the rest of my partner's life to sustain mine or to cut off my sons' careers, impoverish them, or compromise the quality of their children's lives simply because I wish to live a little longer. This is what leads me to believe in a duty to die.

Who Has a Duty to Die?

Suppose, then, that there can be a duty to die. Who has a duty to die? And when? To my mind, these are the right questions, the questions we should be asking. Many of us may one day badly need answers to just these questions. . . .

I cannot say when someone has a duty to die. Still, I can suggest a few features of one's illness, history, and circumstances that make it more likely that one has duty to die. I present them here without much elaboration or explanation.

1. A duty to die is more likely when continuing to live will impose significant burdens—emotional burdens, extensive caregiving, destruction of life plans, and, yes, financial hardship—on your family and loved ones. This is the fundamental insight underlying a duty to die.

2. A duty to die becomes greater as you grow older. As we age, we will be giving up less by giving up our lives, if only because we will sacrifice fewer remaining years of life and a smaller portion of our life plans. . . .

3. A duty to die is more likely when you have already lived a full and rich life. You have already had a full share of the good things life offers.

4. There is greater duty to die if your loved ones' lives have already been difficult or impoverished, if they have had only a small share of the good things that life has to offer (especially if through no fault of their own).

5. A duty to die is more likely when your loved ones have already made great contributions—perhaps even sacrifices—to make your life a good one. Especially if you have not made similar sacrifices for their well-being or for the well-being of other members of your family.

6. To the extent that you can make a good adjustment to your illness or handicapping condition, there is less likely to be a duty to die. A good adjustment means that smaller sacrifices will be required of loved ones and there is more compensating interaction for them. . . .

7. There is less likely to be a duty to die if you can still make significant contributions to the lives of others, especially your family.

8. A duty to die is more likely when the part of you that is loved will soon be gone or seriously compromised. Or when you soon will no longer be capable of giving love. Part of the horror of dementing disease is that it destroys the capacity to nurture and

sustain relationships, taking away a person's agency and the emotions that bind her to others.

9. There is a greater duty to die to the extent that you have lived a relatively lavish lifestyle instead of saving for illness or old age. Like most upper middle-class Americans, I could easily have saved more. It is a greater wrong to come to your family for assistance if your need is the result of having chosen leisure or a spendthrift lifestyle. . . .

These, then, are some of the considerations that give shape and definition to the duty to die. If we can agree that these considerations are all relevant, we can see that the correct course of action will often be difficult to discern. A decision about when I should end my life will sometimes prove to be every bit as difficult as the decision about whether I want treatment for myself.

Can the Incompentent Have a Duty to Die?

Severe mental deterioration springs readily to mind as one of the situations in which I believe I could have a duty to die. But can incompetent people have duties at all? We can have moral duties we do not recognize or acknowledge, including duties that we never recognized. But can we have duties we are unable to recognize? Duties when we are unable to understand the concept of morality at all? If so, do others have a moral obligation to help us carry out this duty? These are extremely difficult theoretical questions. The reach of moral agency is severely strained by mental incompetence.

I am tempted to simply bypass the entire question by saying that I am talking only about competent persons. But the idea of a duty to die clearly raises the specter of one person claiming that another—one who cannot speak for herself—has such a duty. So I need to say that I can make no sense of the claim that someone has a duty to die if the person has never been able to understand moral obligation at all. To my mind, only those who were formerly capable of making moral decisions could have such a duty.

But the case of formerly competent persons is almost as troubling. Perhaps we should simply stipulate that no incompetent person can have a duty to die, not even if she affirmed belief in such a duty in an advance directive. If we take the view that formerly competent people may have such a duty, we should surely exercise extreme caution when claiming a formerly competent person would have acknowledged a duty to die or that any formerly competent person has an unacknowledged duty to die. Moral dangers loom regardless of which way we decide to resolve such issues.

But for me personally, very urgent practical matters turn on their resolution. If a formerly competent person can no longer have a duty to die (or if other people are not likely to help her carry out this duty), I believe that my obligation may be to die while I am still competent, before I become unable to make and carry out that decision for myself. Surely it would be irresponsible to evade my moral duties by temporizing until I escape into incompetence. And so I must die sooner than I otherwise would have to. On the other hand, if I could count on others to end my life after I become incompetent, I might be able to fulfill my responsibilities while also living out all my competent or semi-competent days. Given our society's reluctance to permit physicians, let alone family members, to perform aid-in-dying, I believe I may well have a duty to end my life when I can see mental incapacity on the horizon.

There is also the very real problem of sudden incompetence—due to a serious stroke or automobile accident, for example. For me, that is the real nightmare. If I suddenly become incompetent, I will fall into the hands of a medical-legal system that will conscientiously disregard my moral beliefs and do what is best for me, regardless of the consequences for my loved ones. And that is not at all what I would have wanted!

Social Policies and a Duty to Die

The claim that there is a duty to die will seem to some a misplaced response to social negligence. If our society were providing for the debilitated, the chronically ill, and the elderly as it should be, there would only be very rare cases of a duty to die. . . .

This much is surely true: there are a number of social policies we could pursue that would dramatically reduce the incidence of such a duty. Most obviously, we could decide to pay for facilities that provide excellent long-term care (not just health care!) for all chronically ill, debilitated, mentally ill, or demented people in this country. We probably could still afford to do this. . . . The duty to die would then be virtually eliminated.

I cannot claim to know whether in some abstract sense a society like ours should provide care for all who are chronically ill or debilitated. But the fact is that we Americans seem to be unwilling to pay for this kind of long-term care, except for ourselves and our own. In fact, we are moving in precisely the opposite direction—we are trying to shift the burdens of caring for the seriously and chronically ill onto families in order to save costs for our health care systems. As we shift the burdens of care onto families, we also dramatically increase the number of Americans who will have a duty to die.

I must not, then, live my life and make my plans on the assumption that social institutions will protect my family from my infirmity and debility. To do so would be irresponsible. More likely, it will be up to me to protect my loved ones.

A Duty to Die and the Meaning of Life

A duty to die seems very harsh, and often it would be. It is one of the tragedies of our lives that someone who wants very much to live can nevertheless have a duty to die. It is both tragic and ironic that it is precisely the very real good of family and loved ones that gives rise to this duty. Indeed, the genuine love, closeness, and supportiveness of family members is a major

source of this duty: we could not be such a burden if they did not care for us. Finally, there is deep irony in the fact that the very successes of our life-prolonging medicine help to create a widespread duty to die.

We fear death too much. Our fear of death has led to a massive assault on it. We still crave after virtually any life-prolonging technology that we might conceivably be able to produce. We still too often feel morally impelled to prolong life—virtually any form of life—as long as possible. As if the best death is the one that can be put off longest.

We do not even ask about meaning in death, so busy are we with trying to postpone it. But we will not conquer death by one day developing a technology so magnificent that no one will have to die. Nor can we conquer death by postponing it ever longer. We can conquer death only by finding meaning in it.

Although the existence of a duty to die does not hinge on this, recognizing such a duty would go some way toward recovering meaning in death. Paradoxically, it would restore dignity to those who are seriously ill or dying. It would also reaffirm the connections required to give life (and death) meaning. I close now with a few words about both of these points.

First, recognizing a duty to die affirms my agency and also my moral agency. I can still do things that make an important difference in the lives of my loved ones. Moreover, the fact that I still have responsibilities keeps me within the community of moral agents. My illness or debility has not reduced me to a mere moral patient (to use the language of the philosophers). Though it may not be the whole story, surely Kant was onto something important when he claimed that human dignity rests on the capacity for moral agency within a community of those who respect the demands of morality. . . .

Second, recovering meaning in death requires an affirmation of connections. If I end my life to spare the futures of my loved ones, I testify in my death that I am connected to them. It is because I love and care for precisely these people (and I know they care for me) that I wish not to be such a burden on them. By contrast, a life in which I am free to choose whatever I want for myself is a life unconnected to others. A bioethics that would treat me as if I had no serious moral responsibilities does what it can to marginalize, weaken, or even destroy my connections with others.

But life without connections is meaningless. The individualistic fantasy, though occasionally liberating, is deeply destructive. When life is good and vitality seems unending, life itself and life lived for yourself may seem quite sufficient. But if not life, certainly death without connection is meaningless. If you are only for yourself, all you have to care about as your life draws to a close is yourself and your life. Everything that you care about will then perish in your death. And that—the end of everything you care about—is precisely the total collapse of meaning. We can, then, find meaning in death only through a sense of connection with something that will survive our death. . . .

If I am correct, death is so difficult for us partly because our sense of community is so weak. Death seems to wipe out everything when we can't fit it into the lives of those who live on. A death motivated by the desire to spare the futures of my loved ones might well be a better death for me than the one I would get as a result of opting to continue my life as long as there is any pleasure in it for me. Pleasure is nice, but meaning is what matters.

I don't know about others, but these reflections have helped me. I am now more at peace about facing a duty to die. Ending my life if my duty required it might still be difficult. But for me, a far greater horror would be dying all alone or stealing the futures of my loved ones in order to buy a little more time for myself. I hope that if the time comes when I have a duty to die, I will recognize it, encourage my loved ones to recognize it too, and carry it out bravely.

Review and Discussion Questions

1. Has Hardwig exaggerated the possible burden that life-prolonging treatment can impose on a patient's loved ones? What about the point that a family can be pulled together and grow by suffering through the drawn-out death of a loved one?

2. Do you agree with Hardwig that one can have a duty to die? If so, why does one have this duty, and under what circumstances does one have it?

3. Does Hardwig successfully answer the three objections to his position that he considers? Are there objections that he overlooks?

4. Does Hardwig's position presuppose a utilitarian approach to ethics? Is he correct to say that he is not advocating a "crass, quasi-economic" approach or a "shallow, hedonistic view of life"?

5. How would you respond to the point that if society were willing to spend the resources necessary for life-prolonging medical care for the elderly, then one would rarely, if ever, have a duty to die?

6. Can a person who is no longer mentally competent have a duty to die? Explain why or why not.

7. Do you agree with Hardwig that we fear death too much? Is it possible to find meaning in death? If so, how? Would recognizing the existence of a duty to die help make death meaningful?

8. Assess the following argument: If society were to acknowledge a duty to die, the consequences would be bad because elderly people would inevitably be pressured (implicitly or explicitly) by family members and others to terminate their lives when they wish to go on living.

ABORTION

An Almost Absolute Value in History

JOHN T. NOONAN, JR.

In this essay, John T. Noonan, Jr., professor of law at the University of California, Berkeley, presents the case against abortion based on the humanity of the fetus. His basic argument is that humanity begins at the moment of conception, when a new being is created with a unique, human genetic code. Noonan argues against attempts to draw a distinction between human and nonhuman life at some later point in fetal development. He specifically rejects arguments that the fetus is not fully human until it is viable, until it has had certain experiences, unless its parents can sense it or would mourn its death, or until it achieves social visibility at birth. All these attempts to distinguish between the human and nonhuman, Noonan argues, fail to mark some morally relevant difference. He argues, furthermore, that a change in biological probabilities supports the position that humanity begins at conception.

Study Questions

1. What does *viability* mean, and why does Noonan reject the idea that it marks the difference between human and nonhuman life (so that abortion would be permissible prior to, but not after, viability)?

2. What are the other attempted distinctions between the human and nonhuman that Noonan criticizes, and what are his criticisms of them?

3. Explain how Noonan appeals to biological probabilities to support his position.

4. Under what circumstances would Noonan permit abortion?

Reprinted by permission from John T. Noonan, Jr., ed., The Morality of Abortion: Legal and Historical Perspectives *(1970). Section titles added.*

I. The Criterion for Humanity

THE MOST FUNDAMENTAL QUESTION involved in the long history of thought on abortion is: How do you determine the humanity of a being? To phrase the question that way is to put in comprehensive humanistic terms what the theologians . . . dealt with as an explicitly theological question under the heading of "ensoulment." . . . But the theological notion of ensoulment could easily be translated into humanistic language by substituting "human" for "rational soul"; the problem of knowing when a man is a man is common to theology and humanism.

If one steps outside the specific categories used by the theologians, the answer they gave can be analyzed as a refusal to discriminate among human beings on the basis of their varying potentialities. Once conceived, the being was recognized as man because he had man's potential. The criterion for humanity, thus, was simple and all-embracing: If you are conceived by human parents, you are human.

II. The Humanity of the Fetus

The strength of this position may be tested by a review of some of the other distinctions offered in the contemporary controversy over legalizing abortion. Perhaps the most popular distinction is in terms of viability. Before an age of so many months, the fetus is not viable, that is, it cannot be removed from the mother's womb and live apart from her. To that extent, the life of the fetus is absolutely dependent on the life of the mother. This dependence is made the basis of denying recognition to its humanity.

There are difficulties with this distinction. One is that the perfection of artificial incubation may make the fetus viable at any time: It may be removed and artificially sustained. Experiments with animals already show that such a procedure is possible. This hypothetical extreme case relates to an actual difficulty: There is considerable elasticity to the idea of viability. Mere length of life is not an exact measure. The via-

bility of the fetus depends on the extent of its anatomical and functional development. The weight and length of the fetus are better guides to the state of its development than age, but weight and length vary. Moreover, different racial groups have different ages at which their fetuses are viable. Some evidence, for example, suggests that Negro fetuses mature more quickly than white fetuses. If viability is the norm, the standard would vary with race and with many individual circumstances.

The most important objection to this approach is that dependence is not ended by viability. The fetus is still absolutely dependent on someone's care in order to continue existence; indeed a child of one or three or even five years of age is absolutely dependent on another's care for existence; uncared for, the older fetus or the younger child will die as surely as the early fetus detached from the mother. The unsubstantial lessening in dependence at viability does not seem to signify any special acquisition of humanity.

A second distinction has been attempted in terms of experience. A being who has had experience, has lived and suffered, who possesses memories, is more human than one who has not. Humanity depends on formation by experience. The fetus is thus "unformed" in the most basic human sense.

This distinction is not serviceable for the embryo, which is already experiencing and reacting. The embryo is responsive to touch after eight weeks and at least at that point is experiencing. At an earlier stage the zygote is certainly alive and responding to its environment. The distinction may also be challenged by the rare case where aphasia has erased adult memory: Has it erased humanity? More fundamentally, this distinction leaves even the older fetus or the younger child to be treated as an unformed inhuman thing. Finally, it is not clear why experience as such confers humanity. It could be argued that certain central experiences such as loving or learning are necessary to make a man human. But then human beings who have failed to love or to learn might be excluded from the class called man.

A third distinction is made by appeal to the sentiments of adults. If a fetus dies, the grief of the parents is not the grief they would have for a living child. The fetus is an unnamed "it" till birth, and is not perceived as personality until at least the fourth month of existence, when movements in the womb manifest a vigorous presence demanding joyful recognition by the parents.

Yet feeling is notoriously an unsure guide to the humanity of others. Many groups of humans have had difficulty in feeling that persons of another tongue, color, religion, sex, are as human as they. Apart from reactions to alien groups, we mourn the loss of a ten-year-old boy more than the loss of his one-day-old brother or his 90-year-old grandfather. The difference felt and the grief expressed vary with the potentialities extinguished, or the experience wiped out; they do not seem to point to any substantial difference in the humanity of baby, boy, or grandfather.

Distinctions are also made in terms of sensation by the parents. The embryo is felt within the womb only after about the fourth month. The embryo is seen only at birth. What can be neither seen nor felt is different from what is tangible. If the fetus cannot be seen or touched at all, it cannot be perceived as man.

Yet experience shows that sight is even more untrustworthy than feeling in determining humanity. By sight, color became an appropriate index for saying who was a man, and the evil of racial discrimination was given foundation. Nor can touch provide the test; a being confined by sickness, "out of touch" with others, does not thereby seem to lose his humanity. . . .

Finally, a distinction is sought in social visibility. The fetus is not socially perceived as human. It cannot communicate with others. Thus, both subjectively and objectively, it is not a member of society. As moral rules are rules for the behavior of members of society to each other, they cannot be made for behavior toward what is not yet a member. Excluded from the society of men, the fetus is excluded from the humanity of men.

By force of the argument from the consequences, this distinction is to be rejected. It is more subtle than that founded on an appeal to physical sensation, but it is equally dangerous in its implications. If humanity depends on social recognition, individuals or whole groups may be dehumanized by being denied any status in their society. Such a fate is fictionally portrayed in *1984* and has actually been the lot of many men in many societies. In the Roman empire, for example, condemnation to slavery meant the practical denial of most human rights; in the Chinese Communist world, landlords have been classified as enemies of the people and so treated as nonpersons by the state. Humanity does not depend on social recognition, though often the failure of society to recognize the prisoner, the alien, the heterodox as human has led to the destruction of human beings. Anyone conceived by a man and a woman is human. Recognition of this condition by society follows a real event in the objective order, however imperfect and halting the recognition. Any attempt to limit humanity to exclude some group runs the risk of furnishing authority and precedent for excluding other groups in the name of the consciousness or perception of the controlling group in the society.

A philosopher may reject the appeal to the humanity of the fetus because he views "humanity" as a secular view of the soul and because he doubts the existence of anything real and objective which can be identified as humanity. One answer to such a philosopher is to ask how he reasons about moral questions without supposing that there is a sense in which he and the others of whom he speaks are human. Whatever group is taken as the society which determines who may be killed is thereby taken as human. A second answer is to ask if he does not believe that there is a right and wrong way of deciding moral questions. If there is such a difference, experience may be appealed to: To decide who is human on the basis of the sentiment of a given society has led to consequences which rational men would characterize as monstrous.

III. Biological Probabilities

The rejection of the attempted distinctions based on viability and visibility, experience and feeling, may be buttressed by the following considerations: Moral judgments often rest on distinctions, but if the distinctions are not to appear arbitrary fiat, they should relate to some real difference in probabilities. There is a kind of continuity in all life, but the earlier stages of the elements of human life possess tiny probabilities of development. Consider, for example, the spermatozoa in any normal ejaculate: There are about 200,000,000 in any single ejaculate, of which one has a chance of developing into a zygote. Consider the oocytes which may become ova: There are 100,000 to 1,000,000 oocytes in a female infant, of which a maximum of 390 are ovulated. But once spermatozoon and ovum meet and the conceptus is formed, such studies as have been made show that roughly in only 20 percent of the cases will spontaneous abortion occur. In other words, the chances are about 4 out of 5 that this new being will develop. At this stage in the life of the being there is a sharp shift in probabilities, an immense jump in potentialities. To make a distinction between the rights of spermatozoa and the rights of the fertilized ovum is to respond to an enormous shift in possibilities. For about twenty days after conception, the egg may split to form twins or combine with another egg to form a chimera, but the probability of either event happening is very small.

It may be asked, What does a change in biological probabilities have to do with establishing humanity? The argument from probabilities is not aimed at establishing humanity but at establishing an objective discontinuity which may be taken into account in moral discourse. As life itself is a matter of probabilities, as most moral reasoning is an estimate of probabilities, so it seems in accord with the structure of reality and the nature of moral thought to found a moral judgment on the change in probabilities at conception. The appeal to probabilities is the most commonsensical of arguments; to a greater or smaller degree all of us base our actions on probabilities, and in morals, as in law, prudence and negligence are often measured by the account one has taken of the probabilities. If the chance is 200,000,000 to 1 that the movement in the bushes into which you shoot is a man's, I doubt if many persons would hold you careless in shooting; but if the chances are 4 out of 5 that the movement is a human being's, few would acquit you of blame. Would the argument be different if only one out of ten children conceived came to term? Of course this argument would be different. This argument is an appeal to probabilities that actually exist, not to any and all states of affairs which may be imagined.

The probabilities as they do exist do not show the humanity of the embryo in the sense of a demonstration in logic any more than the probabilities of the movement in the bush being a man demonstrate beyond all doubt that the being is a man. The appeal is a "buttressing" consideration, showing the plausibility of the standard adopted. The argument focuses on the decisional factor in any moral judgment and assumes that part of the business of a moralist is drawing lines. One evidence of the nonarbitrary character of the line drawn is the difference of probabilities on either side of it. If a spermatozoon is destroyed, one destroys a being which had a chance of far less than 1 in 200,000,000 of developing into a reasonable being, possessed of the genetic code, a heart, and other organs, and capable of pain. If a fetus is destroyed, one destroys a being already possessed of the genetic code, organs, and sensitivity to pain, and one which had an 80 percent chance of developing further into a baby, outside the womb, who, in time, would reason.

The positive argument for conception as the decisive moment of humanization is that at conception the new being receives the genetic code. It is this genetic information which determines his characteristics, which is the biological carrier of the possibility of human wisdom, which makes him a self-evolving being. A being with a human genetic code is man.

IV. Conclusion

This review of current controversy over the humanity of the fetus emphasizes what a fundamental question the theologians resolved in asserting the inviolability of the fetus. To regard the fetus as possessed of equal rights with other humans was not, however, to decide every case where abortion might be employed. It did decide the case where the argument was that the fetus should be aborted for its own good. To say a being was human was to say it had a destiny to decide for itself which could not be taken from it by another man's decision. But human beings with equal rights often come in conflict with each other, and some decision must be made as to whose claims are to prevail. Cases of conflict involving the fetus are different only in two respects: the total inability of the fetus to speak for itself and the fact that the right of the fetus regularly at stake is the right to life itself.

. . . In Catholic moral theology, as it developed, life even of the innocent was not taken as an absolute. Judgments on acts affecting life issued from a process of weighing. In the weighing, the fetus was always given a value greater than zero, always a value separate and independent from its parents. This valuation was crucial and fundamental in all Christian thought on the subject and marked it off from any approach which considered that only the parents' interests needed to be considered.

Even with the fetus weighed as human, one interest could be weighed as equal or superior: that of the mother in her own life. . . .

The perception of the humanity of the fetus and the weighing of fetal rights against other human rights constituted the work of the moral analysts. But what spirit animated their abstract judgments? For the Christian community it was the injunction of Scripture to love your neighbor as yourself. The fetus as human was a neighbor; his life had parity with one's own. The commandment gave life to what otherwise would have been only rational calculation.

The commandment could be put in humanistic as well as theological terms. Do not injure your fellow man without reason. In these terms, once the humanity of the fetus is perceived, abortion is never right except in self-defense. When life must be taken to save life, reason alone cannot say that a mother must prefer a child's life to her own. With this exception, now of great rarity, abortion violates the rational humanist tenet of the equality of human lives.

Review and Discussion Questions

1. Assess Noonan's arguments against each of the five attempts (criticized by him) to distinguish between human and nonhuman at some point in development after conception. How strong are his arguments? Can you think of considerations in favor of any of the "distinctions" that he has ignored? Has Noonan overlooked some other way of distinguishing between human and nonhuman at a later point in development?

2. Are you persuaded that one becomes fully human, with a right to life, at conception? Explain your answer.

3. How relevant and how persuasive do you find Noonan's appeal to biological probabilities?

4. Noonan believes that, even if the fetus is seen as human, its life does not have absolute value—in other words, abortion is not necessarily prohibited in every case. Assuming that the fetus is human, when, if ever, would abortion be permissible?

5. Assume that abortion is immoral except to save the life of the mother. Should it therefore be illegal?

The Moral Status of Abortion

MARY ANNE WARREN

In this essay, Mary Anne Warren, professor of philosophy at San Francisco State University and author of *Moral Status*, defends abortion. She distinguishes between two senses of the term "human being": a genetic sense and a moral sense. An entity is human in the genetic sense if it is a member of our biological species; it is human in the moral sense if it is a person, that is, a member of the moral community with full and equal moral rights. She argues that genetic humanity is neither necessary nor sufficient for personhood and that although fetuses are genetically human, they are not persons in the moral sense because they lack the characteristics that are central to personhood. Although it is possible to extend moral rights to beings that have few or none of these characteristics, Warren argues against doing so in the case of fetuses. She also argues that a fetus's potential to develop into a person does not give it a right to life strong enough to outweigh the moral rights of actual persons.

Study Questions

1. Explain the two senses of "human being" that Noonan and other opponents of abortion confuse. What connection, if any, is there between the senses?

2. According to Warren, what are the six characteristics that are central to the concept of personhood?

3. Why does Warren reject the idea that we should extend moral rights to fetuses even though they lack the morally significant characteristics of persons?

4. In the normal course of events, a fetus will ultimately develop into a person with a right to life; it is thus a potential person. Explain the example that Warren uses to argue that potential persons do not have a significant right to life.

5. A critic of Warren might object that her argument entails that infanticide is morally justifiable. What is her response to this objection?

FOR OUR PURPOSES, abortion may be defined as the act a woman performs in deliberately terminating her pregnancy before it comes to term, or in allowing another person to terminate it. Abortion usully entails the death of a fetus.[1] Nevertheless, I will argue that it is morally permissible, and should be neither legally prohibited nor made needlessly difficult to obtain, e.g., by obstructive legal regulations.

Some philosophers have argued that the moral status of abortion cannot be resolved by rational means.[2] If this is so then liberty should prevail; for it is not a proper function of the law to enforce prohibitions upon personal behavior that cannot clearly be shown to be morally objectionable, and seriously so. But the advocates of prohibition believe that their position is objectively correct, and not merely a result of religious beliefs or personal prejudices. They argue that the humanity of the fetus is a matter of scientific fact, and that abortion is therefore the moral equivalent of murder, and must be prohibited in all or most cases. (Some would make an exception when the woman's life is in danger, or when the pregnancy is due to rape or incest; others would prohibit abortion even in these cases.)

In response, advocates of a right to choose abortion point to the terrible consequences of prohibiting it, especially while contraception is still unreliable, and is financially beyond the reach of much of the world's population. Worldwide, hundreds of thousands of women die each year from illegal abortions, and many more suffer from complications that may leave them injured or infertile. Women who are poor, under-age, disabled, or otherwise vulnerable, suffer most from the absence of safe and legal abortion. Advocates of choice also argue that to deny a woman access to abortion is to deprive her of the right to control her own body—a right so fundamental that without it other rights are often all but meaningless.

These arguments do not convince abortion opponents. The tragic consequences of prohibition leave them unmoved, because they regard the deliberate killing of fetuses as even more tragic. Nor do appeals to the right to control one's own body impress them, since they deny that this right includes the right to destroy a fetus. We cannot hope to persuade those who equate abortion with murder that they are mistaken, unless we can refute the standard anti-abortion argument: that because fetuses are human beings, they have a right to life equal to that of any other human being. Unfortunately, confusion has prevailed with respect to the two important questions which that argument raises: (1) Is a human fetus really a human being at all stages of prenatal development? and (2) If so,

what (if anything) follows about the moral and legal status of abortion?

John Noonan says that "the fundamental question in the long history of abortion is: How do you determine the humanity of a being?"[3] His anti-abortion argument is essentially that of the Roman Catholic Church. In his words,

> . . . it is wrong to kill humans, however poor, weak, defenseless, and lacking in opportunity to develop their potential they may be. It is therefore morally wrong to kill Biafrans. Similarly, it is morally wrong to kill embryos.[4]

Noonan bases his claim that fetuses are human beings from the time of conception upon what he calls the theologians' criterion of humanity: that whoever is conceived of human beings is a human being. . . .

I argue . . . that a fetus is not a member of the moral community—the set of beings with full and equal moral rights. The reason that a fetus is not a member of the moral community is that it is not yet a person, nor is it enough like a person in the morally relevant respects to be regarded the equal of those human beings who are persons. I argue that it is personhood, and not genetic humanity, which is the fundamental basis for membership in the moral community. A fetus, especially in the early stages of its development, satisfies none of the criteria of personhood. Consequently, it makes no sense to grant it moral rights strong enough to override the woman's moral rights to liberty, bodily integrity, and sometimes life itself. Unlike an infant who has already been born, a fetus cannot be granted full and equal moral rights without severely threatening the rights and well-being of women. Nor, as we will see, is a fetus's *potential* personhood a threat to the moral permissibility of abortion, since merely potential persons do not have a moral right to become actual—or none that is strong enough to override the fundamental moral rights of actual persons. . .

The question we must answer in order to determine the moral status of abortion is: How are we to define the moral community, the set of beings with full and equal moral rights? What sort of entity has the inalienable moral rights to life, liberty, and the pursuit of happiness? Thomas Jefferson attributed these rights to all *men,* and he may have intended to attribute them *only* to men. Perhaps he ought to have attributed them to all human beings. If so, then we arrive, first, at Noonan's problem of defining what makes an entity a human being, and second, at the question which Noonan does not consider: What reason is there for identifying the moral community with the set of all human beings, in whatever way we have chosen to define that term?

On the Definition of "Human"

The term "human being" has two distinct, but not often distinguished, senses. This results in a slide of meaning, which serves to conceal the fallacy in the traditional argument that, since (1) it is wrong to kill innocent human beings, and (2) fetuses are innocent human beings, therefore (3) it is wrong to kill fetuses. For if "human being" is used in the same sense in both (1) and (2), then whichever of the two senses is meant, one of these premises is question-begging. And if it is used in different senses then the conclusion does not follow.

Thus, (1) is a generally accepted moral truth, and one that does not beg the question about abortion, only if "human being" is used to mean something like "a full-fledged member of the moral community, who is also a member of the human species." I will call this the *moral* sense of "human being." It is not to be confused with what I will call the *genetic* sense, i.e., the sense in which any individual entity that belongs to the human species is a human being, regardless of whether or not it is rightly considered to be an equal member of the moral community. Premise (1) avoids begging the question only if the moral sense is intended; while premise (2) avoids it only if what is intended is the genetic sense.

Noonan argues for the classification of fetuses with human beings by pointing, first, to the presence of the human genome in the cell nuclei of the human conceptus from conception onwards;

and secondly, to the potential capacity for rational thought.[5] But what he needs to show, in order to support his version of the traditional anti-abortion argument, is that fetuses are human beings in the moral sense—the sense in which all human beings have full and equal moral rights. In the absence of any argument showing that whatever is genetically human is also morally human—and he gives none—nothing more than genetic humanity can be demonstrated by the presence of human chromosomes in the fetus's cell nuclei. And, as we will see, the strictly potential capacity for rational thought can at most show that the fetus may later become human in the moral sense.

Defining the Moral Community

Is genetic humanity sufficient for moral humanity? There are good reasons for not defining the moral community in this way. I would suggest that the moral community consists, in the first instance, of all *persons,* rather than all genetically human entities.[6] It is persons who invent moral rights, and who are (sometimes) capable of respecting them. It does not follow from this that only persons can have moral rights. However, persons are wise not to ascribe to entities that clearly are not persons moral rights that cannot in practice be respected without severely undercutting the fundamental moral rights of those who clearly are.

What characteristics entitle an entity to be considered a person? This is not the place to attempt a complete analysis of the concept of personhood; but we do not need such an analysis to explain why a fetus is not a person. All we need is an approximate list of the most basic criteria of personhood. In searching for these criteria, it is useful to look beyond the set of people with whom we are acquainted, all of whom are human. Imagine, then, a space traveler who lands on a new planet, and encounters organisms unlike any she has ever seen or heard of. If she wants to behave morally toward these organisms, she has somehow to determine whether they are people and thus have full moral rights, or whether they are things that she need not feel guilty about treating, for instance, as a source of food.

How should she go about making this determination? If she has some anthropological background, she might look for signs of religion, art, and the manufacturing of tools, weapons, or shelters, since these cultural traits have frequently been used to distinguish our human ancestors from prehuman beings, in what seems to be closer to the moral than the genetic sense of "human being." She would be right to take the presence of such traits as evidence that the extraterrestrials were persons. It would, however, be anthropocentric of her to take the absence of these traits as proof that they were not, since they could be people who have progressed beyond, or who have never needed, these particular cultural traits.

I suggest that among the characteristics which are central to the concept of personhood are the following:

1. *sentience*—the capacity to have conscious experiences, usually including the capacity to experience pain and pleasure;
2. *emotionality*—the capacity to feel happy, sad, angry, loving, etc.;
3. *reason*—the capacity to solve new and relatively complex problems;
4. *the capacity to communicate,* by whatever means, messages of an indefinite variety of types; that is, not just with an indefinite number of possible contents, but on indefinitely many possible topics;
5. *self-awareness*—having a concept of oneself, as an individual and/or as a member of a social group; and finally
6. *moral agency*—the capacity to regulate one's own actions through moral principles or ideals.

It is difficult to produce precise definitions of these traits, let alone to specify universally valid behavioral indications that these traits are present. But let us assume that our explorer knows approximately what these six characteristics mean, and that she is able to observe whether or not the extraterrestrials possess these mental and behavioral capacities. How should she use her findings to decide whether or not they are persons?

An entity need not have *all* of these attributes to be a person. And perhaps none of them is absolutely necessary. For instance, the absence of emotion would not disqualify a being that was personlike in all other ways. Think, for instance, of two of the *Star Trek* characters, Mr. Spock (who is half human and half alien), and Data (who is an android). Both are depicted as lacking the capacity to feel emotion; yet both are sentient, reasoning, communicative, self-aware moral agents, and unquestionably persons. Some people are unemotional; some cannot communicate well; some lack self-awareness; and some are not moral agents. It should not surprise us that many people do not meet all of the criteria of personhood. Criteria for the applicability of complex concepts are often like this: none may be logically necessary, but the more criteria that are satisfied, the more confident we are that the concept is applicable. Conversely, the fewer criteria are satisfied, the less plausible it is to hold that the concept applies. And if none of the relevant criteria are met, then we may be confident that it does not.

Thus, to demonstrate that a fetus is not a person, all I need to claim is that an entity that has *none* of these six characteristics is not a person. Sentience is the most basic mental capacity, and the one that may have the best claim to being a necessary (though not sufficient) condition for personhood. Sentience can establish a claim to moral considerability, since sentient beings can be harmed in ways that matter to them; for instance, they can be caused to feel pain, or deprived of the continuation of a life that is pleasant to them. It is unlikely that an entirely insentient organism could develop the other mental and behavioral capacities that are characteristic of persons. Consequently, it is odd to claim that an entity that is not sentient, and that has never been sentient, is nevertheless a person. Persons who have permanently and irreparably lost all capacity for sentience, but who remain biologically alive, arguably still have strong moral rights by virtue of what they have been in the past.

But small fetuses, which have not yet begun to have experiences, are not persons yet and do not have the rights that persons do.

The presumption that all persons have full and equal basic moral rights may be part of the very concept of a person. If this is so, then the concept of a person is in part a moral one; once we have admitted that X is a person, we have implicitly committed ourselves to recognizing X's right to be treated as a member of the moral community. The claim that X is a *human being* may also be voiced as an appeal to treat X decently; but this is usually either because "human being" is used in the moral sense, or because of a confusion between genetic and moral humanity.

If (1)–(6) are the primary criteria of personhood, then genetic humanity is neither necessary nor sufficient for personhood. Some genetically human entities are not persons, and there may be persons who belong to other species. A man or woman whose consciousness has been permanently obliterated but who remains biologically alive is a human entity who may no longer be a person; and some unfortunate humans, who have never had any sensory or cognitive capacities at all, may not be people either. Similarly, an early fetus is a human entity which is not yet a person. It is not even minimally sentient, let alone capable of emotion, reason, sophisticated communication, self-awareness, or moral agency.[7] Thus, while it may be greatly valued as a future child, it does not yet have the claim to moral consideration that it may come to have later.

Moral agency matters to moral status, because it is moral agents who invent moral rights, and who can be obliged to respect them. Human beings have become moral agents from social necessity. Most social animals exist well enough, with no evident notion of a moral right. But human beings need moral rights, because we are not only highly social, but also sufficiently clever and self-interested to be capable of undermining our societies through violence and duplicity. For human persons, moral rights are essential for peaceful and mutually beneficial social life. So long as some moral agents are denied basic rights, peaceful existence is difficult, since moral agents justly resent being treated as something less. If animals of some terrestrial species are found to be persons, or if alien persons come from other worlds, or if human beings someday invent machines whose mental and behavioral capacities make them persons, then we will be morally obliged to respect the moral rights of these non-human persons—at least to the extent that they are willing and able to respect ours in turn.

Although only those persons who are moral agents can participate directly in the shaping and enforcement of moral rights, they need not and usually do not ascribe moral rights only to themselves and other moral agents. Human beings are social creatures who naturally care for small children, and other members of the social community who are not currently capable of moral agency. Moreover, we are all vulnerable to the temporary or permanent loss of the mental capacities necessary for moral agency. Thus, we have self-interested as well as altruistic reasons for extending basic moral rights to infants and other sentient human beings who have already been born, but who currently lack some of these other mental capacities. These human beings, despite their current disabilities, are persons and members of the moral community.

But in extending moral rights to beings (human or otherwise) that have few or none of the morally significant characteristics of persons, we need to be careful not to burden human moral agents with obligations that they cannot possibly fulfill, except at unacceptably great cost to their own well-being and that of those they care about. Women often cannot complete unwanted pregnancies, except at intolerable mental, physical, and economic cost to themselves and their families. And heterosexual intercourse is too important a part of the social lives of most men and women to be reserved for times when pregnancy is an acceptable outcome. Furthermore, the world cannot afford the continued rapid population growth which is the inevitable consequence of prohibiting abortion, so long as contraception is neither very reliable nor available to everyone.

If fetuses were persons, then they would have rights that must be respected, even at great social or personal cost. But given that early fetuses, at least, are unlike persons in the morally relevant respects, it is unreasonable to insist that they be accorded exactly the same moral and legal status.

Fetal Development and the Right to Life

Two questions arise regarding the application of these suggestions to the moral status of the fetus. First, if indeed fetuses are not yet persons, then might they nevertheless have strong moral rights based upon the degree to which they *resemble* persons? Secondly, to what extent, if any, does a fetus's potential to *become* a person imply that we ought to accord to it some of the same moral rights? Each of these questions requires comment.

It is reasonable to suggest that the more like a person something is—the more it appears to meet at least some of the criteria of personhood—the stronger is the case for according it a right to life, and perhaps the stronger its right to life is. That being the case, perhaps the fetus gradually gains a stronger right to life as it develops. We should take seriously the suggestion that, just as "the human individual develops biologically in a continuous fashion . . . the rights of a human person . . . develop in the same way."[8]

A seven-month fetus can apparently feel pain, and can respond to such stimuli as light and sound. Thus, it may have a rudimentary form of consciousness. Nevertheless, it is probably not as conscious, or as capable of emotion, as even a very young infant is; and it has as yet little or no capacity for reason, sophisticated intentional communication, or self-awareness. In these respects, even a late-term fetus is arguably less like a person than are many nonhuman animals. Many animals (e.g., large-brained mammals such as elephants, cetaceans, or apes) are not only sentient, but clearly possessed of a degree of reason, and perhaps even of self-awareness. Thus, on the basis of its resemblance to a person, even a late-

term fetus can have no more right to life than do these animals.

Animals may, indeed, plausibly be held to have some moral rights, and perhaps rather strong ones. But it is impossible in practice to accord full and equal moral rights to all animals. When an animal poses a serious threat to the life or well-being of a person, we do not, as a rule, greatly blame the person for killing it; and there are good reasons for this species-based discrimination. Animals, however intelligent in their own domains, are generally not beings with whom we can reason; we cannot persuade mice not to invade our dwellings or consume our food. That is why their rights are necessarily weaker than those of a being who can understand and respect the rights of other beings.

But the probable sentience of late-term fetuses is not the only argument in favor of treating late abortion as a morally more serious matter than early abortion. Many—perhaps most—people are repulsed by the thought of needlessly aborting a late-term fetus. The late-term fetus has features which cause it to arouse in us almost the same powerful protective instinct as does a small infant.

This response needs to be taken seriously. If it were impossible to perform abortions early in pregnancy, then we might have to tolerate the mental and physical trauma that would be occasioned by the routine resort to late abortion. But where early abortion is safe, legal, and readily available to all women, it is not unreasonable to expect most women who wish to end a pregnancy to do so prior to the third trimester. Most women strongly prefer early to late abortion, because it is far less physically painful and emotionally traumatic. Other things being equal, it is better for all concerned that pregnancies that are not to be completed should be ended as early as possible. Few women would consider ending a pregnancy in the seventh month in order to take a trip to Europe. If, however, a woman's own life or health is at stake, or if the fetus has been found to be so severely abnormal as to be unlikely to survive or to have a life worth living, then late abortion may be the morally best choice. For even a late-term fetus is not a person yet, and its rights must yield to those of the woman whenever it is impossible for both to be respected.

Potential Personhood and the Right to Life

We have seen that a presentient fetus does not yet resemble a person in ways which support the claim that it has strong moral rights. But what about its *potential*, the fact that if nurtured and allowed to develop it may eventually become a person? Doesn't that potential give it at least some right to life? The fact that something is a potential person may be a reason for not destroying it; but we need not conclude from this that potential people have a strong right to life. It may be that the feeling that it is better not to destroy a potential person is largely due to the fact that potential people are felt to be an invaluable resource, not to be lightly squandered. If every speck of dust were a potential person, we would be less apt to suppose that all potential persons have a right to become actual.

We do not need to insist that a potential person has no right to life whatever. There may be something immoral, and not just imprudent, about wantonly destroying potential people, when doing so isn't necessary. But even if a potential person does have some right to life, that right could not outweigh the right of a woman to obtain an abortion; for the basic moral rights of an actual person outweigh the rights of a merely potential person, whenever the two conflict. Since this may not be immediately obvious in the case of a human fetus, let us look at another case.

Suppose that our space explorer falls into the hands of an extraterrestrial civilization, whose scientists decide to create a few thousand new human beings by killing her and using some of her cells to create clones. We may imagine that each of these newly created women will have all of the original woman's abilities, skills, knowledge, and so on, and will also have an individual self-concept; in short, that each of them will be a bona fide (though not genetically unique) person. Imagine, further, that our explorer knows all of this, and knows that these people will be treated kindly and

fairly. I maintain that in such a situation she would have the right to escape if she could, thus depriving all of these potential people of their potential lives. For her right to life outweighs all of theirs put together, even though they are all genetically human, and have a high probability of becoming people, if only she refrains from acting.

Indeed, I think that our space traveler would have a right to escape even if it were not her life which the aliens planned to take, but only a year of her freedom, or only a day. She would not be obliged to stay, even if she had been captured because of her own lack of caution—or even if she had done so deliberately, knowing the possible consequences. Regardless of why she was captured, she is not obliged to remain in captivity for *any* period of time in order to permit merely potential people to become actual people. By the same token, a woman's rights to liberty and the control of her own body outweigh whatever right to life a fetus may have merely by virtue of its potential personhood.

The Objection from Infanticide

One objection to my argument is that it appears to justify not only abortion, but also infanticide. A newborn infant is not much more personlike than a nine-month fetus, and thus it might appear that if late-term abortion is sometimes justified, then infanticide must also sometimes be justified. Yet most people believe that infanticide is a form of murder, and virtually never justified.

This objection is less telling than it may seem. There are many reasons why infanticide is more difficult to justify than abortion, even though neither fetuses nor newborn infants are clearly persons. In this period of history, the deliberate killing of newborns is virtually never justified. This is in part because newborns are so close to being persons that to kill them requires a very strong moral justification—as does the killing of dolphins, chimpanzees, and other highly personlike creatures. It is certainly wrong to kill such beings for the sake of convenience, or financial profit, or "sport." Only the most vital human needs, such as the need to defend one's own life and physical integrity, can provide a plausible justification for killing such beings.

In the case of an infant, there is no such vital need, since in the contemporary world there are usually other people who are eager to provide a good home for an infant whose own parents are unable or unwilling to care for it. Many people wait years for the opportunity to adopt a child, and some are unable to do so, even though there is every reason to believe that they would be good parents. The needless destruction of a viable infant not only deprives a sentient human being of life, but also deprives other persons of a source of great satisfaction, perhaps severely impoverishing their lives.

Even if an infant is unadoptable (e.g., because of some severe physical disability), it is still wrong to kill it. For most of us value the lives of infants, and would greatly prefer to pay taxes to support foster care and state institutions for disabled children, rather than to allow them to be killed or abandoned. So long as most people feel this way, and so long as it is possible to provide care for infants who are unwanted, or who have special needs that their parents cannot meet without assistance, it is wrong to let any infant die who has a chance of living a reasonably good life.

If these arguments show that infanticide is wrong, at least in today's world, then why don't they also show that late-term abortion is always wrong? After all, third-trimester fetuses are almost as personlike as infants, and many people value them and would prefer that they be preserved. As a potential source of pleasure to some family, a fetus is just as valuable as an infant. But there is an important difference between these two cases: once the infant is born, its continued life cannot pose any serious threat to the woman's life or health, since she is free to put it up for adoption or to place it in foster care. While she might, in rare cases, prefer that the child die rather than be raised by others, such a preference would not establish a right on her part.

In contrast, a pregnant woman's right to protect her own life and health outweighs other people's desire that the fetus be preserved—just as, when a

person's life or health is threatened by an animal, and when the threat cannot be removed without killing the animal, that person's right to self-defense outweighs the desires of those who would prefer that the animal not be killed. Thus, while the moment of birth may mark no sharp discontinuity in the degree to which an infant resembles a person, it does mark the end of the mother's right to determine its fate. Indeed, if a late abortion can be safely performed without harming the fetus, she has in most cases no right to insist upon its death, for the same reason that she has no right to insist that a viable infant be killed or allowed to die.

It remains true that, on my view, neither abortion nor the killing of newborns is obviously a form of murder. Perhaps our legal system is correct in its classification of infanticide as murder, since no other legal category adequately expresses the force of our disapproval of this action. But some moral distinction remains, and it has important consequences. When a society cannot possibly care for all of the children who are born, without endangering the survival of adults and older children, allowing some infants to die may be the best of a bad set of options. Throughout history, most societies—from those that lived by gathering and hunting to the highly civilized Chinese, Japanese, Greeks, and Romans—have permitted infanticide under such unfortunate circumstances, regarding it as a necessary evil. It shows a lack of understanding to condemn these societies as morally benighted for this reason alone, since in the absence of safe and effective means of contraception and abortion, parents must sometimes have had no morally better options.

Conclusion

I have argued that fetuses are neither persons nor members of the moral community. Furthermore, neither a fetus's resemblance to a person, nor its potential for becoming a person, provides an adequate basis for the claim that it has a full and equal right to life. At the same time, there are medical as well as moral reasons for preferring early to late abortion when the pregnancy is unwanted.

Women, unlike fetuses, are undeniably persons and members of the human moral community. If unwanted or medically dangerous pregnancies never occurred, then it might be possible to respect women's basic moral rights, while at the same time extending the same basic rights to fetuses. But in the real world such pregnancies do occur—often despite the woman's best efforts to prevent them. Even if the perfect contraceptive were universally available, the continued occurrence of rape and incest would make access to abortion a vital human need. Because women are persons, and fetuses are not, women's rights to life, liberty, and physical integrity morally override whatever right to life it may be appropriate to ascribe to a fetus. Consequently, laws that deny women the right to obtain abortions, or that make safe early abortions difficult or impossible for some women to obtain, are an unjustified violation of basic moral and constitutional rights.

NOTES

1. Strictly speaking, a human conceptus does not become a fetus until the primary organ systems have formed, at about six to eight weeks gestational age.

However, for simplicity I shall refer to the conceptus as a fetus at every stage of its prenatal development.

2. For example, Roger Wertheimer argues, in "Understanding the Abortion Argument," *Philosophy and Public Affairs*, 1 (Fall, 1971), that the moral status of abortion is not a question of fact, but only of how one responds to the facts.

3. John Noonan, "Abortion and the Catholic Church: A Summary History," *Natural Law Forum*, 12 (1967), 125.

4. John Noonan, "Deciding Who Is Human," *Natural Law Forum*, 13 (1968), 134.

5. Noonan, "Deciding Who Is Human," 135.

6. From here on, I will use "human" to mean "genetically human," since the moral sense of the term seems closely connected to, and perhaps derived from, the assumption that genetic humanity is both necessary and sufficient for membership in the moral community.

7. Fetal sentience is impossible prior to the development of neurological connections between the sense organs and the brain, and between the various parts of the brain involved in the processing of conscious experience. This stage of neurological development is currently thought to occur at some point in the late second or early third trimester.

8. Thomas L. Hayes, "A Biological View," *Commonweal*, 85 (March 17,1967), 677–678; cited by Daniel Callahan, in *Abortion: Law, Choice, and Morality* (London: Macmillan, 1970).

Review and Discussion Questions

1. Warren rejects the principle, which Noonan appears to accept, that all and only biological human beings are persons. With whom do you agree—Warren or Noonan? Explain why.

2. Does Warren correctly identify the characteristics that are central to the concept of personhood, or should her list be modified in some way? Do you agree that a fetus has none of the characteristics she mentions? Give an example of a being that is genetically human but not a person in the moral sense and an example of a being that is a person but not a human being.

3. Even if a fetus is not a person, we could still choose to extend moral rights to it. Are there sound reasons for doing so, or do you agree with Warren that the consequences of doing so would be unacceptable?

4. Warren concedes that late-term fetuses may be sentient, yet she holds that they are not yet persons. Do you agree, or do all sentient beings have a right to life?

5. Many people have thought that the potential of a fetus to develop full human capacities is of great moral importance, but Warren disagrees. What moral weight, if any, should we place on the fetus's potential for development? How persuasive do you find her argument about the space traveler escaping cloning?

6. Warren argues that even though newborn infants are not persons, infanticide is still wrong. Assess her reasoning. Can infanticide be seriously wrong, as most people believe, if newborn infants lack a right to life?

An Argument That Abortion Is Wrong

DON MARQUIS

Don Marquis, professor of philosophy at the University of Kansas, argues that the debate over whether the fetus has a right to life has reached an impasse and that there are problems with both the standard anti-abortion position (as represented by Noonan) and the standard pro-choice position (as represented by Warren). Turning to the issue of why killing is wrong in the first place, Marquis argues that what makes killing an adult human being wrong is the loss of his or her future. However, because a fetus has a future like ours, killing it would be wrong for the same reason that it would be wrong to kill an adult human being. Accordingly, abortion is seriously wrong (except in rare cases). Marquis goes on to present four arguments in support of his theory and to rebut several objections to it.

Study Questions

1. On what grounds does Marquis criticize the anti-abortion argument that the fetus has a right to life because it is human? Why is he critical of the pro-choice position that the fetus lacks a right to life because it is not a person?

2. What is the Future Like Ours (FLO) account of the wrongness of killing and how does it apply to abortion?

3. Marquis contends that the FLO account yields correct answers to certain life-and-death cases. What examples does he give?

4. Explain the analogy Marquis draws between his anti-abortion argument and the reason it is wrong to cause animals to suffer.

5. How does Marquis respond to the objection that his argument entails that contraception is immoral?

Tнᴇ ᴘᴜʀᴘᴏsᴇ ᴏꜰ ᴛʜɪs ᴇssᴀʏ is to set out an argument for the claim that abortion, except perhaps in rare instances, is seriously wrong.[1] One reason for these exceptions is to eliminate from consideration cases whose ethical analysis should be controversial and detailed for clear-headed opponents of abortion. Such cases include abortion after rape and abortion during the first fourteen days after conception when there is an argument that the fetus is not definitely an individual. Another reason for making these exceptions is to allow for those cases in which the permissibility of abortion is compatible with the argument of this essay. Such cases include abortion when continuation of a pregnancy endangers a woman's life and abortion when the fetus is anencephalic.

When I speak of the wrongness of abortion in this essay, a reader should presume the above qualifications. I mean by an abortion an action intended to bring about the death of a fetus for the sake of the woman who carries it. . . . I mean by a fetus a developing human being from the time of conception to the time of birth. (Thus, as is standard, I call embryos and zygotes, fetuses.)

The argument of this essay will establish that abortion is wrong for the same reason as killing a reader of this essay is wrong. I shall just assume, rather than establish, that killing you is seriously wrong. I shall make no attempt to offer a complete ethics of killing. Finally, I shall make no attempt to resolve some very fundamental and difficult general philosophical issues into which this analysis of the ethics of abortion might lead.

Why the Debate over Abortion Seems Intractable

Symmetries that emerge from the analysis of the major arguments on either side of the abortion debate may explain why the abortion debate seems intractable. Consider the following standard anti-abortion argument: Fetuses are both human and alive. Humans have the right to life. Therefore, fetuses have the right to life. Of course, women have the right to control their own bodies, but the right to life overrides the right of a woman to control her own body. Therefore, abortion is wrong. . . .

Do fetuses have the right to life?

. . . An argument that fetuses either have or lack the right to life must be based upon some general criterion for having or lacking the right to life. Opponents of abortion, on the one hand, look around for the broadest possible plausible criterion, so that fetuses will fall under it. This explains why classic arguments against abortion appeal to the criterion of being human (Noonan, 1970 . . .). This criterion appears plausible: The claim that all humans, whatever their race, gender, religion or age, have the right to life seems evident enough. In addition, because the fetuses we are concerned with do not, after all, belong to another species, they are clearly human. Thus, the syllogism that generates the conclusion that fetuses have the right to life is apparently sound.

On the other hand, those who believe abortion is morally permissible wish to find a narrow, but plausible, criterion for possession of the right to life so that fetuses will fall outside of it. This explains, in part, why the standard pro-choice arguments in the philosophical literature appeal to the criterion of being a person (Warren, 1973 . . .). This criterion appears plausible: The claim that only persons have the right to life seems evident enough. Furthermore, because fetuses neither are rational nor possess the capacity to communicate in complex ways nor possess a concept of self that continues through time, no fetus is a person. Thus, the syllogism needed to generate the conclusion that no fetus possesses the right to life is apparently sound. Given that no fetus possesses the right to life, a woman's right to control her own body easily generates the general right to abortion. The existence of two apparently defensible syllogisms which support contrary conclusions helps to explain why partisans on both sides of the abortion dispute often regard their opponents as either morally depraved or mentally deficient.

Which syllogism should we reject? The anti-abortion syllogism is usually attacked by attacking its major premise: the claim that whatever is biologically human has the right to life. This premise is subject to scope problems because the class of the biologically human includes too much: human cancer-cell cultures are biologically human, but they do not have the right to life. Moreover, this premise also is subject to moral-relevance problems: the connection between the biological and the moral is merely assumed. It is hard to think of a good *argument* for such a connection. If one wishes to consider the category of "human" a moral category, as some people find it plausible to do in other contexts, then one is left with no way of showing that the fetus is fully human without begging the question. Thus, the classic anti-abortion argument appears subject to fatal difficulties.

These difficulties with the classic anti-abortion argument are well known and thought by many to be conclusive. The symmetrical difficulties with the classic pro-choice syllogism are not as well recognized. The pro-choice syllogism can be attacked by attacking its major premise: Only persons have the right to life. This premise is subject to scope problems because the class of persons includes too little: infants, the severely retarded, and some of the mentally ill seem to fall outside the class of persons as the supporter of choice understands the concept. The premise is also subject to moral-relevance problems: Being a person is understood by the pro-choicer as having certain psychological attributes. If the pro-choicer questions the connection between the biological and the moral, the opponent of abortion can question the connection between the psychological and the moral. If one wishes to consider "person" a moral category, as is often done, then one is left with no way of showing that the fetus is not a person without begging the question. . . .

The argument of this section has attempted to establish, albeit briefly, that the classic anti-abortion argument and the pro-choice argument favored by most philosophers both face problems that are mirror images of one another. A stand-off results. The abortion debate requires a different strategy.

The "Future Like Ours" Account of the Wrongness of Killing

Why do the standard arguments in the abortion debate fail to resolve the issue? The general principles to which partisans in the debate appeal are either truisms most persons would affirm in the absence of much reflection, or very general moral theories. All are subject to major problems. A different approach is needed.

Opponents of abortion claim that abortion is wrong because abortion involves killing someone like us, a human being who just happens to be very young. Supporters of choice claim that ending the life of a fetus is not in the same moral category as ending the life of an adult human being. Surely this controversy cannot be resolved in the absence of an account of what it is about killing us that makes killing us wrong. On the one hand, if we know what property we possess that makes killing us wrong, then we can ask whether fetuses have the same property. On the other hand, suppose that we do not know what it is about us that makes killing us wrong. If this is so, we do not understand even easy cases in which killing is wrong. Surely, we will not understand the ethics of killing fetuses, for if we do not understand easy cases, then we will not understand hard cases. Both pro-choicer and anti-abortionist agree that it is obvious that it is wrong to kill us. Thus, a discussion of what it is about us that makes killing us not only wrong, but seriously wrong, seems to be the right place to begin a discussion of the abortion issue.

Who is primarily wronged by a killing? The wrong of killing is not primarily explained in terms of the loss to the family and friends of the victim. Perhaps the victim is a hermit. Perhaps one's friends find it easy to make new friends. The wrong of killing is not primarily explained in terms of the brutalization of the killer. The great wrong to the victim explains the brutalization, not the other way around. The wrongness of killing us is understood in terms of what killing does to us. Killing us imposes on us the misfortune of premature death. That misfortune underlies the wrongness.

Premature death is a misfortune because when one is dead, one has been deprived of life. This misfortune can be more precisely specified. Premature death cannot deprive me of my past life. That part of my life is already gone. If I die tomorrow or if I live thirty more years my past life will be no different. It has occurred on either alternative. Rather than my past, my death deprives me of my future, of the life that I would have lived if I had lived out my natural life span.

The loss of a future biological life does not explain the misfortune of death. Compare two scenarios: In the former I now fall into a coma from which I do not recover until my death in thirty years. In the latter I die now. The latter scenario does not seem to describe a greater misfortune than the former.

The loss of our future conscious life is what underlies the misfortune of premature death. Not any future conscious life qualifies, however. Suppose that I am terminally ill with cancer. Suppose also that pain and suffering would dominate my future conscious life. If so, then death would not be a misfortune for me.

Thus, the misfortune of premature death consists of the loss to us of the future goods of consciousness. What are these goods? Much can be said about this issue, but a simple answer will do for the purposes of this essay. The goods of life are whatever we get out of life. The goods of life are those items toward which we take a "pro" attitude. They are completed projects of which we are proud, the pursuit of our goals, aesthetic enjoyments, friendships, intellectual pursuits, and physical pleasures of various sorts. The goods of life are what makes life worth living. In general, what makes life worth living for one person will not be the same as what makes life worth living for another. Nevertheless, the list of goods in each of our lives will overlap. The lists are usually different in different stages of our lives.

What makes the goods of my future good for me? One possible, but wrong, answer is my desire for those goods now. This answer does not account for those aspects of my future life that I now believe I will later value, but about which I am wrong. Neither does it account for those aspects of my future that I will come to value, but which I don't value now. What is valuable to the young may not be valuable to the middle-aged. What is valuable to the middle-aged may not be valuable to the old. Some of life's values for the elderly are best appreciated by the elderly. Thus it is wrong to say that the value of my future to me is just what I value now. What makes my future valuable to me are those aspects of my future that I will (or would) value when I will (or

would) experience them, whether I value them now or not.

It follows that a person can believe that she will have a valuable future and be wrong. Furthermore, a person can believe that he will not have a valuable future and also be wrong. This is confirmed by our attitude toward many of the suicidal. We attempt to save the lives of the suicidal and to convince them that they have made an error in judgment. This does not mean that the future of an individual obtains value from the value that others confer on it. It means that, in some cases, others can make a clearer judgment of the value of a person's future *to that person* than the person herself. This often happens when one's judgment concerning the value of one's own future is clouded by personal tragedy. . . .

Thus, what is sufficient to make killing us wrong, in general, is that it causes premature death. Premature death is a misfortune. Premature death is a misfortune, in general, because it deprives an individual of a future of value. An individual's future will be valuable to that individual if that individual will come, or would come, to value it. We know that killing us is wrong. What makes killing us wrong, in general, is that it deprives us of a future of value. Thus, killing someone is wrong, in general, when it deprives her of a future like ours. I shall call this "an FLO."

Arguments in Favor of the FLO Theory

At least four arguments support this FLO account of the wrongness of killing.

The considered judgment argument

The FLO account of the wrongness of killing is correct because it fits with our considered judgment concerning the nature of the misfortune of death. The analysis of the previous section is an exposition of the nature of this considered judgment. This judgment can be confirmed. If one were to ask individuals with AIDS or with incurable cancer about the nature of their misfortune, I believe that they would say or imply that their impending loss of an FLO makes their premature death a misfortune. If they would not, then the FLO account would plainly be wrong.

The worst of crimes argument

The FLO account of the wrongness of killing is correct because it explains why we believe that killing is one of the worst of crimes. My being killed deprives me of more than does my being robbed or beaten or harmed in some other way because my being killed deprives me of all of the value of my future, not merely part of it. This explains why we make the penalty for murder greater than the penalty for other crimes.

As a corollary the FLO account of the wrongness of killing also explains why killing an adult human being is justified only in the most extreme circumstances, only in circumstances in which the loss of life to an individual is outweighed by a worse outcome if that life is not taken. Thus, we are willing to justify killing in self-defense, killing in order to save one's own life, because one's loss if one does not kill in that situation is so very great. We justify killing in a just war for similar reasons. We believe that capital punishment would be justified if, by having such an institution, fewer premature deaths would occur. The FLO account of the wrongness of killing does not entail that killing is always wrong. Nevertheless, the FLO account explains both why killing is one of the worst of crimes and, as a corollary, why the exceptions to the wrongness of killing are so very rare. A correct theory of the wrongness of killing should have these features.

The appeal to cases argument

The FLO account of the wrongness of killing is correct because it yields the correct answers in many life-and-death cases that arise in medicine and have interested philosophers.

Consider medicine first. Most people believe that it is not wrong deliberately to end the life of a person who is permanently unconscious. Thus we believe that it is not wrong to remove a feeding tube or a ventilator from a permanently comatose patient, knowing that such a removal will cause death. The FLO account of the wrongness of killing explains why this is so. A patient who is permanently unconscious cannot have a future that she would come to value, whatever her values. Therefore, according to the FLO theory of the wrongness of killing, death could not, *ceteris paribus,* be a misfortune to her. Therefore, removing the feeding tube or ventilator does not wrong her.

By contrast, almost all people believe that it is wrong, *ceteris paribus,* to withdraw medical treatment from patients who are temporarily unconscious. The FLO account of the wrongness of killing also explains why this is so. Furthermore, these two unconsciousness cases explain why the FLO account of the wrongness of killing does not include present consciousness as a necessary condition for the wrongness of killing.

Consider now the issue of the morality of legalizing active euthanasia. Proponents of active euthanasia argue that if a patient faces a future of intractable pain and wants to die, then, *ceteris paribus,* it would not be wrong for a physician to give him medicine that she knows would result in his death. This view is so universally accepted that even the strongest *opponents* of active euthanasia hold it. The official Vatican view . . . is that it is permissible for a physician to administer to a patient morphine sufficient (although no more than sufficient) to control his pain even if she foresees that the morphine will result in his death. Notice how nicely the FLO account of the wrongness of killing explains this unanimity of opinion. A patient known to be in severe intractable pain is presumed to have a future without positive value. Accordingly, death would not be a misfortune for him and an action that would (foreseeably) end his life would not be wrong.

Contrast this with the standard emergency medical treatment of the suicidal. Even though the suicidal have indicated that they want to die, medical personnel will act to save their lives. This supports the view that it is not the mere *desire* to enjoy an FLO which is crucial to our understanding of the wrongness of killing. *Having* an FLO is what is crucial to the account, although one would, of course, want to make an exception in the case of fully autonomous people who refuse life-saving medical treatment. Opponents of abortion can, of course, be willing to make an exception for fully autonomous fetuses who refuse life support.

The FLO theory of the wrongness of killing also deals correctly with issues that have concerned philosophers. It implies that it would be wrong to kill (peaceful) persons from outer space who come to visit our planet even though they are biologically utterly unlike us. Presumably, if they are persons, then they will have futures that are sufficiently like ours so that it would be wrong to kill them. The FLO account of the wrongness of killing shares this feature with the personhood views of the supporters of choice. Classical opponents of abortion who locate the wrongness of abortion somehow in the biological humanity of a fetus cannot explain this.

The FLO account does not entail that there is another species of animals whose members ought not to be killed. Neither does it entail that it is permissible to kill any non-human animal. On the one hand, a supporter of animals' rights might argue that since some nonhuman animals have a future of value, it is wrong to kill them also, or at least it is wrong to kill them without a far better reason than we usually have for killing non-human animals. On the other hand, one might argue that the futures of non-human animals are not sufficiently like ours for the FLO account to entail that it is wrong to kill them. Since the FLO account does not specify which properties a future of another individual must possess so that killing that individual is wrong, the FLO account is indeterminate with respect to this issue. The fact that the FLO account of the wrongness of killing does not give a determinate answer to this question is not a flaw in the theory. A sound ethical account should yield the right answers in the obvious cases; it should not be required to resolve every disputed question.

A major respect in which the FLO account is superior to accounts that appeal to the concept of person is the explanation the FLO account provides of the wrongness of killing infants. There was a class of infants who had futures that included a class of events that were identical to the futures of the readers of this essay. Thus, reader, the FLO account explains why it was as wrong to kill you when you were an infant as it is to kill you now. This account can be generalized to almost all infants. Notice that the wrongness of killing infants can be explained in the absence of an account of what makes the future of an individual sufficiently valuable so that it is wrong to kill that individual. The absence of such an account explains why the FLO account is indeterminate with respect to the wrongness of killing non-human animals.

If the FLO account is the correct theory of the wrongness of killing, then because abortion involves killing fetuses and fetuses have FLOs for exactly the same reasons that infants have FLOs, abortion is presumptively seriously immoral. This inference lays the necessary groundwork for a fourth argument in favor of the FLO account that shows that abortion is wrong.

The analogy with animals argument

Why do we believe it is wrong to cause animals suffering? We believe that, in our own case and in the case of other adults and children, suffering is a misfortune. It would be as morally arbitrary to refuse to acknowledge that animal suffering is wrong as it would be to refuse to acknowledge that the suffering of persons of another race is wrong. It is, on reflection, suffering that is a misfortune, not the suffering of white males or the suffering of humans. Therefore, infliction of suffering is presumptively wrong no matter on whom it is inflicted and whether it is inflicted on persons or nonpersons. Arbitrary restrictions on the wrongness of suffering count as racism or speciesism. Not only is this argument convincing on its own, but it is the only way of justifying the wrongness of animal cruelty. Cruelty toward animals is clearly wrong. (This famous argument is due to Singer, 1979.)

The FLO account of the wrongness of abortion is analogous. We believe that, in our own case and the cases of other adults and children, the loss of a future of value is a misfortune. It would be . . . morally arbitrary to refuse to acknowledge that the loss of a future of value to a fetus is wrong. . . . To deprive someone of a future of value is wrong no matter on whom the deprivation is inflicted and no matter whether the deprivation is inflicted on persons or nonpersons. Arbitrary restrictions on the wrongness of this deprivation count as racism, genocide, or ageism. Therefore, abortion is wrong. This argument that abortion is wrong should be convincing because it has the same form as the argument for the claim that causing pain and suffering to non-human animals is wrong. Since the latter argument is convincing, the former argument should be also. Thus, an analogy with animals supports the thesis that abortion is wrong.

Replies to Objections

The four arguments in the previous section establish that abortion is, except in rare cases, seriously immoral. Not surprisingly, there are objections to this view. There are replies to the [three] most important objections to the FLO argument for the immorality of abortion.

The potentiality objection

The FLO account of the wrongness of abortion is a potentiality argument. To claim that a fetus has an FLO is to claim that a fetus now has the potential to be in a state of a certain kind in the future. It is not to claim that all ordinary fetuses will have FLOs. Fetuses who are aborted, of course, will not. To say that a standard fetus has an FLO is to say that a standard fetus either will have or would have a life it will or would value.

To say that a standard fetus would have a life it would value is to say that it will have a life it will value if it does not die prematurely. The truth of this conditional is based upon the nature of fetuses (including the fact that they naturally age) and this nature concerns their potential.

Some appeals to potentiality in the abortion debate rest on unsound inferences. For example, one may try to generate an argument against abortion by arguing that because persons have the right to life, potential persons also have the right to life. Such an argument is plainly invalid as it stands. The premise one needs to add to make it valid would have to be something like: "If Xs have the right to Y, then potential Xs have the right to Y." This premise is plainly false. Potential presidents don't have the rights of the presidency; potential voters don't have the right to vote.

In the FLO argument potentiality is not used in order to bridge the gap between adults and fetuses as is done in the argument in the above paragraph. The FLO theory of the wrongness of killing adults is based upon the adult's potentiality to have a future of value. Potentiality is in the argument from the very beginning. Thus, the plainly false premise is not required. Accordingly, the use of potentiality in the FLO theory is not a sign of an illegitimate inference.

The argument from interests

A second objection to the FLO account of the immorality of abortion involves arguing that even though fetuses have FLOs, nonsentient fetuses do not meet the minimum conditions for having any moral standing at all because they lack interests. Steinbock (1992, p. 5) has presented this argument clearly:

> Beings that have moral status must be capable of caring about what is done to them. They must be capable of being made, if only in a rudimentary sense, happy or miserable, comfortable or distressed. Whatever reasons we may have for preserving or protecting nonsentient beings, these reasons do not refer to their own interests. For without conscious awareness, beings cannot

have interests. Without interests, they cannot have a welfare of their own. Without a welfare of their own, nothing can be done for their sake. Hence, they lack moral standing or status.

Medical researchers have argued that fetuses do not become sentient until after 22 weeks of gestation (Steinbock, 1992, p. 50). If they are correct, and if Steinbock's argument is sound, then we have both an objection to the FLO account of the wrongness of abortion and a basis for a view on abortion minimally acceptable to most supporters of choice.

Steinbock's conclusion conflicts with our settled moral beliefs. Temporarily unconscious human beings are nonsentient, yet no one believes that they lack either interests or moral standing. Accordingly, neither conscious awareness nor the capacity for conscious awareness is a necessary condition for having interests.

The counter-example of the temporarily unconscious human being shows that there is something internally wrong with Steinbock's argument. The difficulty stems from an ambiguity. One cannot *take* an interest in something without being capable of caring about what is done to it. However, something can be *in* someone's interest without that individual being capable of caring about it, or about anything. Thus, life support can be *in* the interests of a temporarily unconscious patient even though the temporarily unconscious patient is incapable of *taking* an interest in that life support. If this can be so for the temporarily unconscious patient, then it is hard to see why it cannot be so for the temporarily unconscious (that is, nonsentient) fetus who requires placental life support. Thus the objection based on interests fails. . . .

The contraception objection

The strongest objection to the FLO argument for the immorality of abortion is based on the claim that, because contraception results in one less FLO, the FLO argument entails that contraception, indeed, abstention from sex when conception is possible, is immoral. Because neither contraception nor abstention from sex when conception is possible is immoral, the FLO account is flawed.

There is a cogent reply to this objection. If the argument of the early part of this essay is correct, then the central issue concerning the morality of abortion is the problem of whether fetuses are individuals who are members of the class of individuals whom it is seriously presumptively wrong to kill. The properties of being human and alive, of being a person, and of having an FLO are criteria that participants in the abortion debate have offered to mark off the relevant class of individuals. The central claim of this essay is that having an FLO marks off the relevant class of individuals. A defender of the FLO view could, therefore, reply that since, at the time of contraception, there is no individual to have an FLO, the FLO account does not entail that contraception is wrong. The wrong of killing is primarily a wrong to the individual who is killed; at the time of contraception there is no individual to be wronged.

However, someone who presses the contraception objection might have an answer to this reply. She might say that the sperm and egg are the individuals deprived of an FLO at the time of contraception. Thus, there are individuals whom contraception deprives of an FLO and if depriving an individual of an FLO is what makes killing wrong, then the FLO theory entails that contraception is wrong.

There is also a reply to this move. In the case of abortion, an objectively determinate individual is the subject of harm caused by the loss of an FLO. This individual is a fetus. In the case of contraception, there are far more candidates (see Norcross, 1990). Let us consider some possible candidates in order of the increasing number of individuals harmed: (1) The single harmed individual might be the combination of the particular sperm and the particular egg that would have united to form a zygote if contraception had not been used. (2) The two harmed individuals might be the particular sperm itself, and, in addition, the ovum itself that would have physically combined to form the zygote. (This is modeled on the double homicide of two persons who would otherwise in a short time fuse. (1) is modeled on harm to a single entity some of whose parts are not physically contiguous, such as a university.) (3) The many harmed individuals might be the millions of *combinations* of sperm and the released ovum whose (small) chances of having an FLO were reduced by the successful contraception. (4) The even larger class of harmed individuals (larger by one) might be the class consisting of all of the individual sperm in an ejaculate and, in addition, the individual ovum released at the time of the successful contraception. (1) through (4) are all candidates for being the subject(s) of harm in the case of successful contraception or abstinence from sex. Which should be chosen? Should we hold a lottery? There seems to be no non-arbitrarily determinate subject of harm in the case of successful contraception. But if there is no such subject of harm, then no determinate thing was harmed. If no determinate thing was harmed, then (in the case of contraception) no wrong has been done. Thus, the FLO account of the wrongness of abortion does not entail that contraception is wrong.

Conclusion

This essay contains an argument for the view that, except in unusual circumstances, abortion is seriously wrong. Deprivation of an FLO explains why killing adults and children is wrong. Abortion deprives fetuses of FLOs. Therefore, abortion is wrong. This argument is based on an account of the wrongness of killing that is a result of our considered judgment of the nature of the misfortune of premature death. It accounts for why we regard killing as one of the worst of crimes. It is superior to alternative accounts of the wrongness of killing that are intended to provide insight into the ethics of abortion. This account of the wrongness of killing is supported by the way it handles cases in which our moral judgments are settled. This account has an analogue in the most plausible account of the wrongness of causing

animals to suffer. This account makes no appeal to religion. Therefore, the FLO account shows that abortion, except in rare instances, is seriously wrong.

N O T E

1. This essay is an updated version of a view that first appeared in the *Journal of Philosophy* (1989). This essay incorporates attempts to deal with the objections of McInerney (1990), Norcross (1990), Shirley (1995), Steinbock (1992), and Paske (1994) to the original version of the view.

References

Marquis, D. B., "A Future Like Ours and the Concept of Person: A Reply to McInerney and Paske," *The Abortion Controversy: A Reader*, ed. L. P. Pojman and F. J. Beckwith, Boston: Jones and Bartlett, 1994, 354–68.

———, "Fetuses, Futures and Values: A Reply to Shirley," *Southwest Philosophy Review*, 11 (1995): 263–5.

———, "Why Abortion Is Immoral," *Journal of Philosophy*, 86 (1989): 183–202.

McInerney, P., "Does a Fetus Already Have a Future Like Ours?" *Journal of Philosophy*, 97 (1990): 264–8.

Noonan, J., "An Almost Absolute Value in History" [reprinted in this volume].

Norcross, A., "Killing, Abortion, and Contraception: A Reply to Marquis," *Journal of Philosophy*, 87 (1990): 268–77.

Paske, G., "Abortion and the Neo-Natal Right to Life: A Critique of Marquis's Futurist Argument," *The Abortion Controversy: A Reader*, ed. L. P. Pojman and F. J. Beckwith, Boston: Jones and Bartlett, 1994, pp. 343–53.

Shirley, E. S., "Marquis' Argument against Abortion: A Critique," *Southwest Philosophy Review*, 11 (1995): 79–89.

Singer, P., "Not for Humans Only: The Place of Nonhumans in Environmental Issues," *Ethics and Problems of the 21st Century*, ed. K. E. Goodpaster and K. M. Sayre, South Bend: Notre Dame University Press, 1979.

Steinbock, B., *Life Before Birth: The Moral and Legal Status of Embryos and Fetuses*, New York: Oxford University Press, 1992.

Warren, M. A., "On the Moral and Legal Status of Abortion," *Monist*, 57 (1973): 43–61.

Review and Discussion Questions

1. Is the debate over whether the fetus has a right to life deadlocked, as Marquis argues? How persuasive are his arguments against Noonan's anti-abortion position and Warren's pro-choice stance? Is his approach to the abortion issue superior to theirs?

2. Why is it wrong to kill an adult human being? Are there any plausible accounts of why killing is wrong other than Marquis's FLO account?

3. Restate and assess the four arguments that Marquis advances in support of the FLO theory. How persuasive are they? Which argument do you find the most convincing?

4. Assuming that Marquis's account of the wrongness of killing is correct, does it show that abortion is immoral? Assess the following argument: Although fetuses have a FLO, they lack moral standing because, not being sentient, they cannot meaningfully be said to have interests; therefore, abortion is morally permissible.

5. Marquis's position would be implausible if it entailed, as some critics claim it does, that contraception is wrong. Is his defense of his position on this issue successful?

A Defense of Abortion

JUDITH JARVIS THOMSON

The moral debate over abortion has tended to focus on the moral status of the fetus. In this famous article, Judith Jarvis Thomson, professor of philosophy at the Massachusetts Institute of Technology, takes another approach. Conceding for the sake of argument that the fetus is a person with a right to life from the moment of conception, Thomson argues that abortion still is not necessarily wrong. Her essay uses several memorable analogies to make her point that, even if a fetus has a right to life, it may still lack a right to use the mother's body.

Study Questions

1. Explain the example of the kidnapped violinist. How does Thomson use it to challenge the standard anti-abortion argument?

2. What is the extreme anti-abortion view, and what is Thomson's response to it?

3. What is the case of Jones, Smith, and the coat intended to show?

4. What does the Henry Fonda example tell us about the right to life?

5. What argument is Thomson trying to answer with the burglar and people-seeds examples?

6. What is the difference between a Good Samaritan and a Minimally Decent Samaritan? How does this distinction fit into Thomson's defense of abortion?

MOST OPPOSITION TO ABORTION relies on the premise that the fetus is a human being, a person, from the moment of conception. The premise is argued for, but, as I think, not well. Take, for example, the most common argument. We are asked to notice that the development of a human being from conception through birth into childhood is continuous; then it is said that to draw a line, to choose a point in this development and say "before this point the thing is not a person, after this point it is a person" is to make an arbitrary choice, a choice for which in the nature of things no good reason can be given. It is concluded that the fetus is, or anyway that we had better say it is, a person from the moment of conception. But this conclusion does not follow. Similar things might be said about the development of an acorn into an oak tree, and it does not follow that acorns are oak trees, or that we had better say they are. Arguments of this form are sometimes called "slippery slope arguments"—the phrase is perhaps self-explanatory—and it is dismaying that opponents of abortion rely on them so heavily and uncritically.

I am inclined to agree, however, that the prospects for "drawing a line" in the development of the fetus look dim. I am inclined to think also that we shall probably have to agree that the fetus has already become a human person well before birth. Indeed, it comes as a surprise when one first learns how early in its life it begins to acquire human characteristics. By the tenth week, for example, it already has a face, arms and legs, fingers and toes; it has internal organs, and brain activity is detectable. On the other hand, I think that the premise is false, that the fetus is not a person from the moment of conception. A newly fertilized ovum, a newly implanted clump of cells, is no more a person than an acorn is an oak tree. But I shall not discuss any of this. For it seems to me to be of great interest to ask what happens if, for the sake of argument, we allow the premise. How, precisely, are we supposed to get from there to the conclusion that abortion is morally imper-

missible? Opponents of abortion commonly spend most of their time establishing that the fetus is a person, and hardly any time explaining the step from there to the impermissibility of abortion. Perhaps they think the step too simple and obvious to require much comment. . . . Whatever the explanation, I suggest that the step they take is neither easy nor obvious, that it calls for closer examination than is commonly given, and that when we do give it this closer examination we shall feel inclined to reject it.

I propose, then, that we grant that the fetus is a person from the moment of conception. How does the argument go from here? Something like this, I take it. Every person has a right to life. So the fetus has a right to life. No doubt the mother has a right to decide what shall happen in and to her body; everyone would grant that. But surely a person's right to life is stronger and more stringent than the mother's right to decide what happens in and to her body, and so outweighs it. So the fetus may not be killed; an abortion may not be performed.

It sounds plausible. But now let me ask you to imagine this. You wake up in the morning and find yourself back to back in bed with an unconscious violinist. A famous unconscious violinist. He has been found to have a fatal kidney ailment, and the Society of Music Lovers has canvassed all the available medical records and found that you alone have the right blood type to help. They have therefore kidnapped you, and last night the violinist's circulatory system was plugged into yours, so that your kidneys can be used to extract poisons from his blood as well as your own. The director of the hospital now tells you, "Look, we're sorry the Society of Music Lovers did this to you—we would never have permitted it if we had known. But still, they did it, and the violinist now is plugged into you. To unplug you would be to kill him. But never mind, it's only for nine months. By then he will have recovered from his ailment, and can safely be unplugged from you." Is it morally incumbent on you to accede to this situation? No doubt it would be very nice of you if you did, a great kindness. But do you *have* to accede to it? What if it were not nine months, but nine years? Or longer still? What if the director of the hospital says, "Tough luck, I agree, but you've now got to stay in bed, with the violinist plugged into you, for the rest of your life. Because remember this. All persons have a right to life, and violinists are persons. Granted you have a right to decide what happens in and to your body, but a person's right to life outweighs your right to decide what happens in and to your body. So you cannot ever be unplugged from him." I imagine you would regard this as outrageous, which suggests that something really is wrong with that plausible-sounding argument I mentioned a moment ago.

In this case, of course, you were kidnapped; you didn't volunteer for the operation that plugged the violinist into your kidneys. Can those who oppose abortion on the ground I mentioned make an exception for a pregnancy due to rape? Certainly. They can say that persons have a right to life only if they didn't come into existence because of rape; or they can say that all persons have a right to life, but that some have less of a right to life than others, in particular, that those who come into existence because of rape have less. But these statements have a rather unpleasant sound. Surely the question of whether you have a right to life at all, or how much of it you have, shouldn't turn on the question of whether or not you are the product of a rape. And in fact the people who oppose abortion on the ground I mentioned do not make this distinction, and hence do not make an exception in case of rape.

Nor do they make an exception for a case in which the mother has to spend the nine months of her pregnancy in bed. They would agree that would be a great pity, and hard on the mother; but all the same, all persons have a right to life, the fetus is a person, and so on. I suspect, in fact, that they would not make an exception for a case in which, miraculously enough, the pregnancy went on for nine years, or even the rest of the mother's life.

Some won't even make an exception for a case in which continuation of the pregnancy is likely to shorten the mother's life; they regard abortion as impermissible even to save the mother's life. Such cases are nowadays very rare, and many opponents of abortion do not accept this extreme view. All the same, it is a good place to begin: a number of points of interest come out in respect to it.

1. The Extreme Anti-Abortion View

Let us call the view that abortion is impermissible even to save the mother's life "the extreme view." I want to suggest first that it does not issue from the argument I mentioned earlier without the addition of some fairly powerful premises. Suppose a woman has become pregnant, and now learns that she has a cardiac condition such that she will die if she carries the baby to term. What may be done for her? The fetus, being a person, has a right to life, but as the mother is a person too, so has she a right to life. Presumably they have an equal right to life. How is it supposed to come out that an abortion may not be performed? If mother and child have an equal right to life, shouldn't we perhaps flip a coin? Or should we add to the mother's right to life her right to decide what happens in and to her body, which everybody seems to be ready to grant—the sum of her rights now outweighing the fetus' right to life?

The most familiar argument here is the following. We are told that performing the abortion would be directly killing the child, whereas doing nothing would not be killing the mother, but only letting her die. Moreover, in killing the child, one would be killing an innocent person, for the child has committed no crime, and is not aiming at his mother's death. . . . If directly killing an innocent person is murder, and thus is impermissible, then the mother's directly killing the innocent person inside her is murder, and thus is impermissible. But it cannot seriously be thought to be murder if the mother performs an abortion on herself to save her life. It cannot seriously be said that she *must* refrain, that she *must* sit passively by and wait for her death. Let us look again at the case of you and the violinist. There you are, in bed with the violinist, and the director of the hospital says to you, "It's all most distressing, and I deeply sympathize, but you see this is putting an additional strain on your kidneys, and you'll be dead within the month. But you *have* to stay where you are all the same. Because unplugging you would be directly killing an innocent violinist, and that's murder, and that's impermissible." If anything in the world is true, it is that you do not commit murder, you do not do what is impermissible, if you reach around to your back and unplug yourself from that violinist to save your life.

The main focus of attention in writings on abortion has been on what a third party may or may not do in answer to a request from a woman for an abortion. This is in a way understandable. Things being as they are, there isn't much a woman can safely do to abort herself. So the question asked is what a third party may do, and what the mother may do, if it is mentioned at all, is deduced, almost as an afterthought, from what it is concluded that third parties may do. But it seems to me that to treat the matter in this way is to refuse to grant to the mother that very status of person which is so firmly insisted on for the fetus. For we cannot simply read off what a person may do from what a third party may do. Suppose you find yourself trapped in a tiny house with a growing child. I mean a very tiny house, and a rapidly growing child—you are already up against the wall of the house and in a few minutes you'll be crushed to death. The child on the other hand won't be crushed to death; if nothing is done to stop him from growing he'll be hurt, but in the end he'll simply burst open the house and walk out a free man. Now I could well understand it if a bystander were to say, "There's nothing we can do for you. We cannot choose between your life and his, we cannot be the ones to decide who is to live, we cannot intervene." But it cannot be concluded that you too can do nothing, that you cannot attack it to save your life. However innocent the child may be, you do not have to wait passively while it crushes you to death. Perhaps a

pregnant woman is vaguely felt to have the status of [a] house, to which we don't allow the right of self-defense. But if the woman houses the child, it should be remembered that she is a person who houses it.

I should perhaps stop to say explicitly that I am not claiming that people have a right to do anything whatever to save their lives. I think, rather, that there are drastic limits to the right of self-defense. If someone threatens you with death unless you torture someone else to death, I think you have not the right, even to save your life, to do so. But the case under consideration here is very different. In our case there are only two people involved, one whose life is threatened, and one who threatens it. Both are innocent: the one who is threatened is not threatened because of any fault, the one who threatens does not threaten because of any fault. For this reason we may feel that we bystanders cannot intervene. But the person threatened can.

In sum, a woman surely can defend her life against the threat to it posed by the unborn child, even if doing so involves its death. And this shows . . . that the extreme view of abortion is false. . . .

The extreme view could of course be weakened to say that while abortion is permissible to save the mother's life, it may not be performed by a third party, but only by the mother herself. But this cannot be right either. For what we have to keep in mind is that the mother and the unborn child are not like two tenants in a small house which has, by an unfortunate mistake, been rented to both; the mother *owns* the house. The fact that she does adds to the offensiveness of deducing that the mother can do nothing from the supposition that third parties can do nothing. But it does more than this: it casts a bright light on the supposition that third parties can do nothing. Certainly it lets us see that a third party who says "I cannot choose between you" is fooling himself if he thinks this is impartiality. If Jones has found and fastened on a certain coat, which he needs to keep from freezing, but which Smith also needs to keep him from freezing, then it is not impartiality that says "I cannot choose between you" when Smith owns the coat. Women have said again and again, "This body is *my* body!" and they have reason to feel angry, reason to feel that it has been like shouting into the wind. Smith, after all, is hardly likely to bless us if we say to him, "Of course it's your coat, anybody would grant that it is. But no one may choose between you and Jones who is to have it."

We should really ask what it is that says "no one may choose" in the face of the fact that the body that houses the child is the mother's body. It may be simply a failure to appreciate this fact. But it may be something more interesting, namely the sense that one has a right to refuse to lay hands on people, even where it would be just and fair to do so, even where justice seems to require that somebody do so. Thus justice might call for somebody to get Smith's coat back from Jones, and yet you have a right to refuse to be the one to lay hands on Jones, a right to refuse to do physical violence to him. This, I think, must be granted. But then what should be said is not "no one may choose," but only "*I* cannot choose," and indeed not even this, but "*I* will not *act*," leaving it open that somebody else can or should, and in particular that anyone in a position of authority, with the job of securing people's rights, both can and should. So this is no difficulty. I have not been arguing that any given third party must accede to the mother's request that he perform an abortion to save her life, but only that he may. . . .

2. The Right to Life

Where the mother's life is not at stake, the argument I mentioned at the outset seems to have a much stronger pull. "Everyone has a right to life, so the unborn person has a right to life." And isn't the child's right to life weightier than anything other than the mother's own right to life, which she might put forward as ground for an abortion?

This argument treats the right to life as if it were unproblematic. It is not, and this seems to me to be precisely the source of the mistake.

For we should now, at long last, ask what it comes to, to have a right to life. In some views

having a right to life includes having a right to be given at least the bare minimum one needs for continued life. But suppose that what in fact *is* the bare minimum a man needs for continued life is something he has no right at all to be given? If I am sick unto death, and the only thing that will save my life is the touch of Henry Fonda's cool hand on my fevered brow, then all the same, I have no right to be given the touch of Henry Fonda's cool hand on my fevered brow. It would be frightfully nice of him to fly in from the West Coast to provide it. It would be less nice, though no doubt well meaning, if my friends flew out to the West Coast and carried Henry Fonda back with them. But I have no right at all against anybody that he should do this for me. Or again, to return to the story I told earlier, the fact that for continued life that violinist needs the continued use of your kidneys does not establish that he has a right to be given the continued use of your kidneys. He certainly has no right against you that *you* should give him continued use of your kidneys. For nobody has any right to use your kidneys unless you give him such a right; and nobody has the right against you that you shall give him this right—if you do allow him to go on using your kidneys, this is a kindness on your part, and not something he can claim from you as his due. Nor has he any right against anybody else that *they* should give him continued use of your kidneys. Certainly he had no right against the Society of Music Lovers that they should plug him into you in the first place. And if you now start to unplug yourself, having learned that you will otherwise have to spend nine years in bed with him, there is nobody in the world who must try to prevent you, in order to see to it that he is given something he has a right to be given.

Some people are rather stricter about the right to life. In their view, it does not include the right to be given anything, but amounts to, and only to, the right not to be killed by anybody. But here a related difficulty arises. If everybody is to refrain from killing that violinist, then everybody must refrain from doing a great many different sorts of things. Everybody must refrain from slitting his throat, everybody must refrain from shooting him—and everybody must refrain from unplugging you from him. But does he have a right against everybody that they shall refrain from unplugging you from him? To refrain from doing this is to allow him to continue to use your kidneys. It could be argued that he has a right against us that we should allow him to continue to use your kidneys. That is, while he had no right against us that we should give him the use of your kidneys, it might be argued that he anyway has a right against us that we shall not now intervene and deprive him of the use of your kidneys. I shall come back to third-party interventions later. But certainly the violinist has no right against you that *you* shall allow him to continue to use your kidneys. As I said, if you do allow him to use them, it is a kindness on your part, and not something you owe him. . . .

I would stress that I am not arguing that people do not have a right to life—quite to the contrary. . . . I am arguing only that having a right to life does not guarantee having either a right to be given the use of or a right to be allowed continued use of another person's body—even if one needs it for life itself. So the right to life will not serve the opponents of abortion in the very simple and clear way in which they seem to have thought it would.

3. The Right to Use the Mother's Body

There is another way to bring out the difficulty. In the most ordinary sort of case, to deprive someone of what he has a right to is to treat him unjustly. Suppose a boy and his small brother are jointly given a box of chocolates for Christmas. If the older boy takes the box and refuses to give his brother any of the chocolates, he is unjust to him, for the brother has been given a right to half of them. But suppose that, having learned that otherwise it means nine years in bed with that violinist, you unplug yourself from him. You surely are not being unjust to him for you gave

him no right to use your kidneys, and no one else can have given him any such right. But we have to notice that in unplugging yourself, you are killing him; and violinists, like everybody else, have a right to life, and thus in the view we were considering just now, the right not to be killed. So here you do what he supposedly has a right you shall not do, but you do not act unjustly to him in doing it.

The emendation which may be made at this point is this: the right to life consists not in the right not to be killed, but rather in the right not to be killed unjustly. This runs a risk of circularity, but never mind; it would enable us to square the fact that the violinist has a right to life with the fact that you do not act unjustly toward him in unplugging yourself, thereby killing him. For if you do not kill him unjustly, you do not violate his right to life, and so it is no wonder you do him no injustice.

But if this emendation is accepted, the gap in the argument against abortion stares us plainly in the face: it is by no means enough to show that the fetus is a person, and to remind us that all persons have a right to life—we need to be shown also that killing the fetus violates its right to life, i.e., that abortion is unjust killing. And is it?

I suppose we may take it as a datum that in a case of pregnancy due to rape the mother has not given the unborn person a right to the use of her body for food and shelter. Indeed, in what pregnancy could it be supposed that the mother has given the unborn person such a right? It is not as if there were unborn persons drifting about the world, to whom a woman who wants a child says, "I invite you in."

But it might be argued that there are other ways one can have acquired a right to the use of another person's body than by having been invited to use it by that person. Suppose a woman voluntarily indulges in intercourse, knowing of the chance it will issue in pregnancy, and then she does become pregnant; is she not in part responsible for the presence, in fact the very existence, of the unborn person inside her? No doubt she did not invite it in. But doesn't her partial responsibility for its being there itself give it a right to the use of her body? If so, then her aborting it would be more like the boy's taking away the chocolates, and less like your unplugging yourself from the violinist—doing so would be depriving it of what it does have a right to, and thus would be doing it an injustice.

. . . This argument would give the unborn person a right to its mother's body only if her pregnancy resulted from a voluntary act, undertaken in full knowledge of the chance a pregnancy might result from it. It would leave out entirely the unborn person whose existence is due to rape. Pending the availability of some further argument, then, we would be left with the conclusion that unborn persons whose existence is due to rape have no right to the use of their mothers' bodies, and thus that aborting them is not depriving them of anything they have a right to and hence is not unjust killing.

And we should also notice that it is not at all plain that this argument really does go even as far as it purports to. For there are cases and cases, and the details make a difference. If the room is stuffy, and I therefore open a window to air it, and a burglar climbs in, it would be absurd to say, "Ah, now he can stay, she's given him a right to the use of her house—for she is partially responsible for his presence there, having voluntarily done what enabled him to get in, in full knowledge that there are such things as burglars, and that burglars burgle." It would be still more absurd to say this if I had had bars installed outside my windows, precisely to prevent burglars from getting in, and a burglar got in only because of a defect in the bars. It remains equally absurd if we imagine it is not a burglar who climbs in, but an innocent person who blunders or falls in. Again, suppose it were like this: people-seeds drift about in the air like pollen, and if you open your windows, one may drift in and take root in your carpets or upholstery. You don't want children, so you fix up your windows with fine mesh screens, the very best you can buy. As can happen, however, and on very, very rare occasions does happen, one of the screens is defective; and a seed drifts in and takes root. Does the person-plant who now develops have a right to the use of your house? Surely not—despite the fact that you voluntarily opened your windows, you knowingly kept carpets and upholstered furniture, and you knew that screens were sometimes defective. Someone may argue that you are responsible for its rooting, that it does have a right to your house, because after all you *could* have lived out your life with bare floors and furniture, or with sealed windows and doors. But this won't do—for by the same token anyone can avoid a pregnancy due to rape by having a hysterectomy, or anyway by never leaving home without a (reliable!) army.

It seems to me that the argument we are looking at can establish at most that there are *some* cases in which the unborn person has a right to the use of its mother's body, and therefore *some* cases in which abortion is unjust killing. There is room for much discussion and argument as to precisely which, if any. But I think we should sidestep this issue and leave it open, for at any rate the argument certainly does not establish that all abortion is unjust killing.

4. Rights and Sacrifices

There is room for yet another argument here, however. We surely must all grant that there may be cases in which it would be morally indecent to detach a person from your body at the cost of his life. Suppose you learn that what the violinist needs is not nine years of your life, but only one hour: all you need do to save his life is to spend one hour in that bed with him. Suppose also that letting him use your kidneys for that one hour would not affect your health in the slightest. Admittedly you were kidnapped. Admittedly you did not give anyone permission to plug him into you. Nevertheless it seems to me plain you *ought* to allow him to use your kidneys for that hour—it would be indecent to refuse.

Again, suppose pregnancy lasted only an hour, and constituted no threat to life or health. And suppose that a woman becomes pregnant as a result of rape. Admittedly she did not voluntarily do anything to bring about the existence of a child. Admittedly she did nothing at all which would give the unborn person a right to the use of her body. All the same it might well be said, as in the newly emended violinist story, that she *ought* to allow it to remain for that hour—that it would be indecent in her to refuse.

Now some people are inclined to use the term "right" in such a way that it follows from the fact that you ought to allow a person to use your body for the hour he needs, that he has a right to use your body for the hour he needs, even though he has not been given that right by any person or act. They may say that it follows also that if you refuse, you act unjustly toward him. This use of the term is perhaps so common that it cannot be called wrong; nevertheless it seems to me to be an unfortunate loosening of what we would do better to keep a tight rein on. Suppose that that box of chocolates I mentioned earlier had not been given to both boys jointly, but was given only to the older boy. There he sits, stolidly eating his way through the box, his small brother watching enviously. Here we are likely to say "You ought not to be so mean. You ought to give your brother some of those chocolates." My own view is that it just does not follow from the truth of this that the brother has any right to any of the chocolates. If the boy refuses to give his brother any, he is greedy, stingy, callous—but not unjust. I suppose that the people I have in mind will say it does follow that the brother has a right to some of the chocolates, and thus that the boy does act unjustly if he refuses to give his brother any. But the effect of saying this is to obscure what we should keep distinct, namely the difference between the boy's refusal in this case and the boy's refusal in the earlier case, in which the box was given to both boys jointly, and in which the small brother thus had what was from any point of view clear title to half.

A further objection to so using the term "right," that from the fact that A ought to do a thing for B, it follows that B has a right against A that A do it for him, is that it is going to make the question of whether or not a man has a right to a

thing turn on how easy it is to provide him with it; and this seems not merely unfortunate, but morally unacceptable. Take the case of Henry Fonda again. I said earlier that I had no right to the touch of his cool hand on my fevered brow, even though I needed it to save my life. I said it would be frightfully nice of him to fly in from the West Coast to provide me with it, but that I had no right against him that he should do so. But suppose he isn't on the West Coast. Suppose he has only to walk across the room, place a hand briefly on my brow—and lo, my life is saved. Then surely he ought to do it, it would be indecent to refuse. Is it to be said, "Ah, well, it follows that in this case she has a right to the touch of his hand on her brow, and so it would be an unjustice in him to refuse"? So that I have a right to it when it is easy for him to provide it, though no right when it's hard? It's rather a shocking idea that anyone's rights should fade away and disappear as it gets harder and harder to accord them to him.

So my own view is that even though you ought to let the violinist use your kidneys for the one hour he needs, we should not conclude that he has a right to do so—we should say that if you refuse, you are, like the boy who owns all the chocolates and will give none away, self-centered and callous, indecent in fact, but not unjust. And similarly, that even supposing a case in which a woman pregnant due to rape ought to allow the unborn person to use her body for the hour he needs, we should not conclude that he has a right to do so; we should conclude that she is self-centered, callous, indecent, but not unjust, if she refuses. The complaints are no less grave; they are just different. However, there is no need to insist on this point. If anyone does wish to deduce "he has a right" from "you ought," then all the same he must surely grant that there are cases in which it is not morally required of you that you allow that violinist to use your kidneys, and in which he does not have a right to use them, and in which you do not do him an injustice if you refuse. And so also for mother and unborn child. Except in such cases as the unborn person has a right to demand it—and we were leaving open the possibility that there may be such cases—nobody is morally *required* to make large sacrifices, of health, of all other interests and concerns, of all other duties and commitments, for nine years, or even for nine months, in order to keep another person alive.

5. Good Samaritans

We have in fact to distinguish between two kinds of Samaritan: the Good Samaritan and what we might call the Minimally Decent Samaritan. The story of the Good Samaritan, you will remember, goes like this:

> A certain man went down from Jerusalem to Jericho, and fell among thieves, which stripped him of his raiment, and wounded him, and departed, leaving him half dead.
>
> And by chance there came down a certain priest that way; and when he saw him, he passed by on the other side.
>
> And likewise a Levite, when he was at the place, came and looked on him, and passed by on the other side.
>
> But a certain Samaritan, as he journeyed, came where he was; and when he saw him he had compassion on him.
>
> And went to him, and bound up his wounds, pouring in oil and wine, and set him on his own beast, and brought him to an inn, and took care of him.
>
> And on the morrow, when he departed, he took out two pence, and gave them to the host, and said unto him, "Take care of him; and whatsoever thou spendest more, when I come again, I will repay thee."
>
> Luke 10:30–35

The Good Samaritan went out of his way, at some cost to himself, to help one in need of it. We are not told what the options were, that is, whether or not the priest and the Levite could have helped by doing less than the Good Samaritan did, but assuming they could have, then the fact they did nothing at all shows they were not even Minimally Decent Samaritans, not because they were not

Samaritans, but because they were not even minimally decent.

These things are a matter of degree, of course, but there is a difference, and it comes out perhaps most clearly in the story of Kitty Genovese, who, as you will remember, was murdered while thirty-eight people watched or listened, and did nothing at all to help her. A Good Samaritan would have rushed out to give direct assistance against the murderer. Or perhaps we had better allow that it would have been a Splendid Samaritan who did this, on the ground that it would have involved a risk of death for himself. But the thirty-eight not only did not do this, they did not even trouble to pick up a phone to call the police. Minimally Decent Samaritanism would call for doing at least that, and their not having done it was monstrous.

After telling the story of the Good Samaritan, Jesus said, "Go, and do thou likewise." Perhaps he meant that we are morally required to act as the Good Samaritan did. Perhaps he was urging people to do more than is morally required of them. At all events it seems plain that it was not morally required of any of the thirty-eight that he rush out to give direct assistance at the risk of his own life, and that it is not morally required of anyone that he give long stretches of his life—nine years or nine months—to sustaining the life of a person who has no special right (we were leaving open the possibility of this) to demand it.

. . . What we should ask is not whether anybody should be compelled by law to be a Good Samaritan, but whether we must accede to a situation in which somebody is being compelled—by nature, perhaps—to be a Good Samaritan. We have, in other words, to look now at third-party interventions. I have been arguing that no person is morally required to make large sacrifices to sustain the life of another who has no right to demand them, and this even where the sacrifices do not include life itself; we are not morally required to be Good Samaritans or anyway Very Good Samaritans to one another. But what if a man cannot extricate himself from such a situation?

What if he appeals to us to extricate him? It seems to me plain that there are cases in which we can, cases in which a Good Samaritan would extricate him. There you are, you were kidnapped, and nine years in bed with that violinist lie ahead of you. You have your own life to lead. You are sorry, but you simply cannot see giving up so much of your life to the sustaining of his. You cannot extricate yourself, and ask us to do so. I should have thought that—in light of his having no right to the use of your body—it was obvious that we do not have to accede to your being forced to give up so much. We can do what you ask. There is no injustice to the violinist in our doing so.

6. Parental Responsibility

Following the lead of the opponents of abortion, I have throughout been speaking of the fetus merely as a person, and what I have been asking is whether or not the argument we began with, which proceeds only from the fetus' being a person, really does establish its conclusion. I have argued that it does not.

But of course there are arguments and arguments, and it may be said that I have simply fastened on the wrong one. It may be said that what is important is not merely the fact that the fetus is a person, but that it is a person for whom the woman has a special kind of responsibility issuing from the fact that she is its mother. And it might be argued that all my analogies are therefore irrelevant—for you do not have that special kind of responsibility for that violinist. Henry Fonda does not have that special kind of responsibility for me. And our attention might be drawn to the fact that men and women both *are* compelled by law to provide support for their children.

I have in effect dealt (briefly) with this argument . . . above; but a (still briefer) recapitulation now may be in order. Surely we do not have any such "special responsibility" for a person unless we have assumed it, explicitly or implicitly. If a set of parents do not try to prevent pregnancy, do not obtain an abortion, but rather take it home with them, then they have assumed responsibility for it, they have given it rights, and they cannot *now* withdraw support from it at the cost of its life because they now find it difficult to go on providing for it. But if they have taken all reasonable precautions against having a child, they do not simply by virtue of their biological relationship to the child who comes into existence have a special responsibility for it. They may wish to assume responsibility for it, or they may not wish to. And I am suggesting that if assuming responsibility for it would require large sacrifices, then they may refuse. . . .

7. Conclusion

My argument will be found unsatisfactory on two counts by many of those who want to regard abortion as morally permissible. First, while I do argue that abortion is not impermissible, I do not argue that it is always permissible. There may well be cases in which carrying the child to term requires only Minimally Decent Samaritanism of the mother, and this is a standard we must not fall below. I am inclined to think it a merit of my account precisely that it does *not* give a general yes or a general no. It allows for and supports our sense that, for example, a sick and desperately frightened fourteen-year-old schoolgirl, pregnant due to rape, may *of course* choose abortion, and that any law which rules this out is an insane law. And it also allows for and supports our sense that in other cases resort to abortion is even positively indecent. It would be indecent in the woman to request an abortion, and indecent in a doctor to perform it, if she is in her seventh month, and wants the abortion just to avoid the nuisance of postponing a trip abroad. The very fact that the arguments I have been drawing attention to treat all cases of abortion, or even all cases of abortion in which the mother's life is not at stake, as morally on a par ought to have made them suspect at the outset.

Secondly, while I am arguing for the permissibility of abortion in some cases, I am not arguing for the right to secure the death of the unborn child. It is easy to confuse these two things in that up to a certain point in the life of the fetus it is not able to survive outside the mother's body; hence removing it from her body guarantees its death. But they are importantly different. I have argued that you are not morally required to spend nine months in bed, sustaining the life of that violinist; but to say this is by no means to say that if, when you unplug yourself, there is a miracle and he survives, you then have a right to turn around and slit his throat. You may detach yourself even if this costs him his life; you have no right to be guaranteed his death, by some other means, if unplugging yourself does not kill him. There are some people who will feel dissatisfied by this feature of my argument. A woman may be utterly devastated by the thought of a child, a bit of herself, put out for adoption and never seen or heard of again. She may therefore want not merely that the child be detached from her, but more, that it die. Some opponents of abortion are inclined to regard this as beneath contempt—thereby showing insensitivity to what is surely a powerful source of despair. All the same, I agree that the desire for the child's death is not one which anybody may gratify, should it turn out to be possible to detach the child alive.

At this place, however, it should be remembered that we have only been pretending throughout that the fetus is a human being from the moment of conception. A very early abortion is surely not the killing of a person, and so is not dealt with by anything I have said here.

Review and Discussion Questions

1. Some writers have criticized Thomson's vivid analogies for being too bizarre and fanciful. Would you agree, or are her analogies useful and illuminating? Could she have made her case without using analogies?

2. Thomson's criticism of the extreme anti-abortion view assumes that the right to self-defense permits us to kill an innocent person if that person threatens our life. Do you agree? Can you imagine such a case outside of the context of abortion?

3. Thomson writes that "the right to life consists not in the right not to be killed, but rather in the right not to be killed unjustly." Do you agree? Assuming that the fetus has a right to life, under what circumstances would it be unjust to abort it? Under what circumstances just?

4. Assess the following argument: If you as a woman have sex, then you know that, even if you do use birth control, there is a chance you may become pregnant. Therefore, knowing this, if you have sex and do become pregnant, then you must assume responsibility for the fetus and not abort it.

5. Thomson maintains that we are not obligated to make large sacrifices to keep other people alive unless they have a right that we do so. Give examples of when we would and would not be obligated to make such sacrifices. Do you find Thomson's principle morally acceptable? Is Thomson correct in arguing that morality does not require us to be Good Samaritans?

Virtue Theory and Abortion

ROSALIND HURSTHOUSE

The moral debate over abortion typically centers on the moral status of the fetus and the competing rights of the mother. In this essay, Rosalind Hurst-house, professor of philosophy at Auckland University, New Zealand, and author of *On Virtue Ethics*, takes a different approach, examining abortion through the lens of virtue ethics. After succinctly explaining the virtue ethics approach, she shows how it transforms the moral discussion of abortion. Instead of concentrating on the rights of women or on abstract questions about the moral status of the fetus, the virtue ethicist focuses on familiar biological facts about human reproduction and its role in human society. The point is to adopt the right attitude to human life and death, and to pregnancy and family life, and to see whether, in a particular set of circumstances, the decision to terminate a pregnancy would or would not fit with a plausible understanding of what it is for one to live a good human life. This leads Hurst-house to a moderate stance on abortion, one which judges some abortions to be callous, self-indulgent, or irresponsible, but allows that other abortions display no such vices and are compatible with an appropriate appreciation of the value of parenthood and child raising.

Study Questions

1. According to Hurst-house, what is a virtue, and what makes an action right?
2. Why, with regard to abortion, is the issue of women's rights of relatively little importance for virtue ethics?
3. Why would it be mistaken to see abortion as comparable to having a haircut or an appendectomy?
4. How does Hurst-house respond to the point that some societies routinely practice abortion and infanticide?
5. Hurst-house writes that even if abortion is the right decision, it "will be a ground for guilt if getting into those circumstances in the first place itself manifested a flaw in character." Explain what she means.
6. In what way does virtue ethics extend the moral issues surrounding abortion to boys and men?

THE SORT OF ETHICAL THEORY derived from Aristotle, variously described as virtue ethics, virtue-based ethics, or neo-Aristotelianism, is becoming better known, and is now quite widely recognized as at least a possible rival to deontological and utilitarian theories. . . .

Virtue Theory

. . . Let us consider what a skeletal virtue theory looks like. It begins with a specification of right action:

> P.1. An action is right iff it is what a virtuous agent would do in the circumstances.

From Philosophy and Public Affairs, *vol. 20, no. 3 (Summer 1991). Copyright ©1991 Princeton University Press. Reprinted by permission of Princeton University Press. Notes omitted; some section titles added.*

This . . . is a purely formal principle, giving one no guidance as to what to do, that forges the conceptual link between *right action* and *virtuous agent.* . . . It must, of course, go on to specify what the latter is. The first step toward this may appear quite trivial, but is needed to correct a prevailing tendency among many critics to define the virtuous agent as one who is disposed to act in accordance with a deontologist's moral rules.

> P.1a. A virtuous agent is one who acts virtuously, that is, one who has and exercises the virtues.

This subsidiary premise lays bare the fact that virtue theory aims to provide a nontrivial specification of the virtuous agent *via* a nontrivial specification of the virtues, which is given in its second premise:

> P.2. A virtue is a character trait a human being needs to flourish or live well.

This premise forges a conceptual link between *virtue* and *flourishing* (or *living well* or *eudaimonia*). And, just as deontology, in theory, then goes on to argue that each favored rule meets its specification, so virtue ethics, in theory, goes on to argue that each favored character trait meets its.

These are the bare bones of virtue theory . . . .

Abortion

As everyone knows, the morality of abortion is commonly discussed in relation to just two considerations: first, and predominantly, the status of the fetus and whether or not it is the sort of thing that may or may not be innocuously or justifiably killed; and second, and less predominantly (when, that is, the discussion concerns the *morality* of abortion rather than the question of permissible legislation in a just society), women's rights. If one thinks within this familiar framework, one may well be puzzled about what virtue theory, as such, could contribute. . . . But . . . virtue theory quite transforms the discussion of abortion by dismissing the two familiar dominating considerations as, in a way, fundamentally irrelevant. In what way or ways, I hope to make both clear and plausible.

Women's rights

Let us first consider women's rights. Let me emphasize again that we are discussing the *morality* of abortion, not the rights and wrongs of laws prohibiting or permitting it. If we suppose that women do have a moral right to do as they choose with their own bodies, or, more particularly, to terminate their pregnancies, then it may well follow that a *law* forbidding abortion would be unjust. Indeed, even if they have no such right, such a law might be, as things stand at the moment, unjust, or impractical, or inhumane: on this issue I have nothing to say in this article. But, putting all questions about the justice or injustice of laws to one side, and supposing only that women have such a moral right, *nothing* follows from this supposition about the morality of abortion, according to virtue theory, once it is noted (quite generally, not with particular reference to abortion) that in exercising a moral right I can do something cruel, or callous, or selfish, light-minded, self-righteous, stupid, inconsiderate, disloyal, dishonest—that is, act viciously. Love and friendship do not survive their parties' constantly insisting on their rights, nor do people live well when they think that getting what they have a right to is of preeminent importance; they harm others, and they harm themselves. So whether women have a moral right to terminate their pregnancies is irrelevant within virtue theory, for it is irrelevant to the question "In having an abortion in these circumstances, would the agent be acting virtuously or viciously or neither?"

Status of the fetus

What about the consideration of the status of the fetus—what can virtue theory say about that? One might say that this issue is not in the province of *any* moral theory; it is a metaphysical question, and an extremely difficult one at that. Must virtue theory then wait upon metaphysics to come up with the answer?

At first sight it might seem so. For virtue is said to involve knowledge, and part of this knowledge consists in having the *right* attitude to things.

"Right" here does not just mean "morally right" or "proper" or "nice" in the modern sense; it means "accurate, true." One cannot have the right or correct attitude to something if the attitude is based on or involves false beliefs. And this suggests that if the status of the fetus is relevant to the rightness or wrongness of abortion, its status must be known, as a truth, to the fully wise and virtuous person.

But the sort of wisdom that the fully virtuous person has is not supposed to be recondite; it does not call for fancy philosophical sophistication, and it does not depend upon, let alone wait upon, the discoveries of academic philosophers. And this entails the following, rather startling, conclusion: that the status of the fetus—that issue over which so much ink has been spilt—is, according to virtue theory, simply not relevant to the rightness or wrongness of abortion (within, that is, a secular morality).

Or rather, since that is clearly too radical a conclusion, it is in a sense relevant, but only in the sense that the familiar biological facts are relevant. By "the familiar biological facts" I mean the facts that most human societies are and have been familiar with—that, standardly (but not invariably), pregnancy occurs as the result of sexual intercourse, that it lasts about nine months, during which time the fetus grows and develops, that standardly it terminates in the birth of a living baby, and that this is how we all come to be.

It might be thought that this distinction— between the familiar biological facts and the status of the fetus—is a distinction without a difference. But this is not so. To attach relevance to the status of the fetus, in the sense in which virtue theory claims it is not relevant, is to be gripped by the conviction that we must go beyond the familiar biological facts, deriving some sort of conclusion from them, such as that the fetus has rights, or is not a person, or something similar. It is also to believe that this exhausts the relevance of the familiar biological facts, that all they are relevant to is the status of the fetus and whether or not it is the sort of thing that may or may not be killed.

These convictions, I suspect, are rooted in the desire to solve the problem of abortion by getting it to fall under some general rule such as "You ought not to kill anything with the right to life but may kill anything else." But they have resulted in what should surely strike any nonphilosopher as a most bizarre aspect of nearly all the current philosophical literature on abortion, namely, that, far from treating abortion as a unique moral problem, markedly unlike any other, nearly everything written on the status of the fetus and its bearing on the abortion issue would be consistent with the human reproductive facts' (to say nothing of family life) being totally different from what they are. . . .

Right attitudes

Now if we are using virtue theory, our first question is not "What do the familiar biological facts show—what can be derived from them about the status of the fetus?" but "How do these facts figure in the practical reasoning, actions and passions, thoughts and reactions, of the virtuous and the nonvirtuous? What is the mark of having the right attitude to these facts and what manifests having the wrong attitude to them?" This immediately makes essentially relevant not only all the facts about human reproduction I mentioned above, but a whole range of facts about our emotions in relation to them as well. I mean such facts as that human parents, both male and female, tend to care passionately about their offspring, and that family relationships are among the deepest and strongest in our lives—and, significantly, among the longest-lasting.

These facts make it obvious that pregnancy is not just one among many other physical conditions; and hence that anyone who genuinely believes that an abortion is comparable to a haircut or an appendectomy is mistaken. The fact that the premature termination of a pregnancy is, in some sense, the cutting off of a new human life, and thereby, like the procreation of a new human life, connects with all our thoughts about human life and death, parenthood, and family relationships, must make it a serious matter. To disregard this fact about it, to think of abortion as nothing but the killing of something that does not matter, or as nothing but the exercise of some right or rights one has, or as the incidental means to some desirable state of affairs, is to do something callous and light-minded, the sort of thing that no virtuous and wise person would do. It is to have the wrong attitude not only to fetuses, but more generally to human life and death, parenthood, and family relationships.

Although I say that the facts make this obvious, I know that this is one of my tendentious points. In partial support of it I note that even the most dedicated proponents of the view that deliberate abortion is just like an appendectomy or haircut rarely hold the same view of spontaneous abortion, that is, miscarriage. It is not so tendentious of me to claim that to react to people's grief over miscarriage by saying, or even thinking, "What a fuss about nothing!" would be callous and light-minded, whereas to try to laugh someone out of grief over an appendectomy scar or a botched haircut would not be. It is hard to give this point due prominence within act-centered theories, for the inconsistency is an inconsistency in attitude about the seriousness of loss of life, not in beliefs about which acts are right or wrong. Moreover, an act-centered theorist may say, "Well, there is nothing wrong with *thinking* 'What a fuss about nothing!' as long as you do not say it and hurt the person who is grieving. And besides, we cannot be held responsible for our thoughts, only for the intentional actions they give rise to." But the character traits that virtue theory emphasizes are not simply dispositions to intentional actions, but a seamless disposition to certain actions and passions, thoughts and reactions.

To say that the cutting off of a human life is always a matter of some seriousness, at any stage, is not to deny the relevance of gradual fetal development. Notwithstanding the well-worn point that clear boundary lines cannot be drawn, our emotions and attitudes regarding the fetus do change as it develops, and again when it is born, and indeed further as the baby grows. Abortion for shallow reasons in the later stages is much more shocking than abortion for the same reasons in the early stages in a way that matches the fact that deep grief over miscarriage in the later stages

is more appropriate than it is over miscarriage in the earlier stages (when, that is, the grief is solely about the loss of *this* child, not about, as might be the case, the loss of one's only hope of having a child or of having one's husband's child). Imagine (or recall) a woman who already has children; she had not intended to have more, but finds herself unexpectedly pregnant. Though contrary to her plans, the pregnancy, once established as a fact, is welcomed—and then she loses the embryo almost immediately. If this were bemoaned as a tragedy, it would, I think, be a misapplication of the concept of what is tragic. But it may still properly be mourned as a loss. The grief is expressed in such terms as "I shall always wonder how she or he would have turned out" or "When I look at the others, I shall think, "How different their lives would have been if this other one had been part of them.'" It would, I take it, be callous and light-minded to say, or think, "Well, she has already *got* four children; what's the problem?"; it would be neither, nor arrogantly intrusive in the case of a close friend, to try to correct prolonged mourning by saying, "I know it's sad, but it's not a tragedy; rejoice in the ones you have." The application of *tragic* becomes more appropriate as the fetus grows, for the mere fact that one has lived with it for longer, conscious of its existence, makes a difference. To shrug off an early abortion is understandable just because it is very hard to be fully conscious of the fetus's existence in the early stages and hence hard to appreciate that an early abortion is the destruction of life. It is particularly hard for the young and inexperienced to appreciate this, because appreciation of it usually comes only with experience.

I do not mean "with the experience of having an abortion" (though that may be part of it) but, quite generally, "with the experience of life." Many women who have borne children contrast their later pregnancies with their first successful one, saying that in the later ones they were conscious of a new life growing in them from very early on. And, more generally, as one reaches the age at which the next generation is coming up close behind one, the counterfactuals "If I, or she, had had an abortion, Alice, or Bob, would not have been born" acquire a significant application, which casts a new light on the conditionals "If I or Alice have an abortion then some Caroline or Bill will not be born."

The fact that pregnancy is not just one among many physical conditions does not mean that one can never regard it in that light without manifesting a vice. When women are in very poor physical health, or worn out from childbearing, or forced to do very physically demanding jobs, then they cannot be described as self-indulgent, callous, irresponsible, or light-minded if they seek abortions mainly with a view to avoiding pregnancy as the physical condition that it is. To go through with a pregnancy when one is utterly exhausted, or when one's job consists of crawling along tunnels hauling coal, as many women in the nineteenth century were obliged to do, is perhaps heroic, but people who do not achieve heroism are not necessarily vicious. That they can view the pregnancy only as eight months of misery, followed by hours if not days of agony and exhaustion, and abortion only as the blessed escape from this prospect, is entirely understandable and does not manifest any lack of serious respect for human life or a shallow attitude to motherhood. What it does show is that something is terribly amiss in the conditions of their lives, which make it so hard to recognize pregnancy and childbearing as the good that they can be.

. . . Philosophers arguing against anything remotely resembling a belief in the sanctity of life (which the above claims clearly embody) frequently appeal to the existence of other communities in which abortion and infanticide are practiced. We should not automatically assume that it is impossible that some other communities could be morally inferior to our own; maybe some are, or have been, precisely insofar as their members are, typically, callous or light-minded or unjust. But in communities in which life is a great deal tougher for everyone than it is in ours, having the right attitude to human life and death, parenthood, and family relationships might well manifest itself in ways that are unlike ours. When

it is essential to survival that most members of the community fend for themselves at a very young age or work during most of their waking hours, selective abortion or infanticide might be practiced either as a form of genuine euthanasia or for the sake of the community and not, I think, be thought callous or light-minded. But this does not make everything all right; as before, it shows that there is something amiss with the conditions of their lives, which are making it impossible for them to live really well.

The foregoing discussion, insofar as it emphasizes the right attitude to human life and death, parallels to a certain extent those standard discussions of abortion that concentrate on it solely as an issue of killing. But it does not, as those discussions do, gloss over the fact, emphasized by those who discuss the morality of abortion in terms of women's rights, that abortion, wildly unlike any other form of killing, is the termination of a pregnancy, which is a condition of a woman's body and results in *her* having a child if it is not aborted. This fact is given due recognition not by appeal to women's rights but by emphasizing the relevance of the familiar biological and psychological facts and their connection with having the right attitude to parenthood and family relationships. But it may well be thought that failing to bring in women's rights still leaves some important aspects of the problem of abortion untouched.

Good human lives

Speaking in terms of women's rights, people sometimes say things like, "Well, it's her life you're talking about too, you know; she's got a right to her own life, her own happiness." And the discussion stops there. But in the context of virtue theory, given that we are particularly concerned with what constitutes a good human life, with what true happiness or *eudaimonia* is, this is no place to stop. We go on to ask, "And is this life of hers a good one? Is she living well?"

If we are to go on to talk about good human lives, in the context of abortion, we have to bring in our thoughts about the value of love and family life, and our proper emotional development through a natural life cycle. The familiar facts support the view that parenthood in general, and motherhood and childbearing in particular, are intrinsically worthwhile, are among the things that can be correctly thought to be partially constitutive of a flourishing human life. If this is right, then a woman who opts for not being a mother (at all, or again, or now) by opting for abortion may thereby be manifesting a flawed grasp of what her life should be, and be about—a grasp that is childish, or grossly materialistic, or shortsighted, or shallow.

I said "*may* thereby": this *need* not be so. Consider, for instance, a woman who has already had several children and fears that to have another will seriously affect her capacity to be a good mother to the ones she has—she does not show a lack of appreciation of the intrinsic value of being a parent by opting for abortion. Nor does a woman who has been a good mother and is approaching the age at which she may be looking forward to being a good grandmother. Nor does a woman who discovers that her pregnancy may well kill her, and opts for abortion. Nor, necessarily, does a woman who has decided to lead a life centered around some other worthwhile activity or activities with which motherhood would compete.

People who are childless by choice are sometimes described as "irresponsible," or "selfish," or "refusing to grow up," or "not knowing what life is about." But one can hold that having children is intrinsically worthwhile without endorsing this, for we are, after all, in the happy position of there being more worthwhile things to do than can be fitted into one lifetime. Parenthood, and motherhood in particular, even if granted to be intrinsically worthwhile, undoubtedly take up a lot of one's adult life, leaving no room for some other worthwhile pursuits. But some women who choose abortion rather than have their first child, and some men who encourage their partners to choose abortion, are not avoiding parenthood for the sake of other worthwhile

pursuits, but for the worthless one of "having a good time," or for the pursuit of some false vision of the ideals of freedom or self-realization. And some others who say "I am not ready for parenthood yet" are making some sort of mistake about the extent to which one can manipulate the circumstances of one's life so as to make it fulfill some dream that one has. Perhaps one's dream is to have two perfect children, a girl and a boy, within a perfect marriage, in financially secure circumstances, with an interesting job of one's own. But to care too much about that dream, to demand of life that it give it to one and act accordingly, may be both greedy and foolish, and is to run the risk of missing out on happiness entirely. Not only may fate make the dream impossible, or destroy it, but one's own attachment to it may make it impossible. Good marriages, and the most promising children, can be destroyed by just one adult's excessive demand for perfection.

Once again, this is not to deny that girls may quite properly say "I am not ready for motherhood yet," especially in our society, and, far from manifesting irresponsibility or light-mindedness, show an appropriate modesty or humility, or a fearfulness that does not amount to cowardice. However, even when the decision to have an abortion is the right decision—one that does not itself fall under a vice-related term and thereby one that the perfectly virtuous could recommend—it does not follow that there is no sense in which having the abortion is wrong, or guilt inappropriate. For, by virtue of the fact that a human life has been cut short, some evil has probably been brought about, and that circumstances make the decision to bring about some evil the right decision will be a ground for guilt if getting into those circumstances in the first place itself manifested a flaw in character.

What "gets one into those circumstances" in the case of abortion is, except in the case of rape, one's sexual activity and one's choices, or the lack of them, about one's sexual partner and about contraception. The virtuous woman (which here of course does not mean simply "chaste woman" but "woman with the virtues") has such character traits as strength, independence, resoluteness, decisiveness, self-confidence, responsibility, serious-mindedness, and self-determination—and no one, I think, could deny that many women become pregnant in circumstances in which they cannot welcome or cannot face the thought of having *this* child precisely because they lack one or some of these character traits. So even in the cases where the decision to have an abortion is the right one, it can still be the reflection of a moral failing—not because the decision itself is weak or cowardly or irresolute or irresponsible or light-minded, but because lack of the requisite opposite of these failings landed one in the circumstances in the first place. Hence the common universalized claim that guilt and remorse are never appropriate emotions about an abortion is denied. They may be appropriate, and appropriately inculcated, even when the decision was the right one.

Another motivation for bringing women's rights into the discussion may be to attempt to correct the implication, carried by the killing-centered approach, that insofar as abortion is wrong, it is a wrong that only women do, or at least (given the preponderance of male doctors) that only women instigate. I do not myself believe that we can thus escape the fact that nature bears harder on women than it does on men, but virtue theory can certainly correct many of the injustices that the emphasis on women's rights is rightly concerned about. With very little amendment, everything that has been said above applies to boys and men too. Although the abortion decision is, in a natural sense, the woman's decision, proper to her, boys and men are often party to it, for well or ill, and even when they are not, they are bound to have been party to the circumstances that brought it up. No less than girls and women, boys and men can, in their actions, manifest self-centeredness, callousness, and light-mindedness about life and parenthood in relation to abortion. They can be self-centered or courageous about the possibility of disability in their offspring; they need to reflect on their sexual activity and their choices, or the lack of them,

about their sexual partner and contraception; they need to grow up and take responsibility for their own actions and life in relation to fatherhood. If it is true, as I maintain, that insofar as motherhood is intrinsically worthwhile, being a mother is an important purpose in women's lives, being a father (rather than a mere generator) is an important purpose in men's lives as well, and it is adolescent of men to turn a blind eye to this and pretend that they have many more important things to do.

Conclusion

Much more might be said, but I shall end the actual discussion of the problem of abortion here, and conclude by highlighting what I take to be its significant features. . . .

The discussion does not proceed simply by our trying to answer the question "Would a perfectly virtuous agent ever have an abortion and, if so, when?"; virtue theory is not limited to considering "Would Socrates have had an abortion if he were a raped, pregnant fifteen-year-old?" nor automatically stumped when we are considering circumstances into which no virtuous agent would have got herself. Instead, much of the discussion proceeds in the virtue- and vice-related terms whose application, in several cases, yields practical conclusions. . . . These terms are difficult to apply correctly, and anyone might challenge my application of any one of them. So, for example, I have claimed that some abortions, done for certain reasons, would be callous or light-minded; that others might indicate an appropriate modesty or humility; that others would reflect a greedy and foolish attitude to what one could expect out of life. . . .

Proceeding as it does in the virtue-and vice-related terms, the discussion thereby, inevitably, also contains claims about what is worthwhile, serious and important, good and evil, in our lives. So, for example, I claimed that parenthood is intrinsically worthwhile, and that having a good time was a worthless end (in life, not on individual occasions); that losing a fetus is always a serious matter (albeit not a tragedy in itself in the first trimester) whereas acquiring an appendectomy scar is a trivial one; that (human) death is an evil. Once again, these are difficult matters, and anyone might challenge any one of my claims. But what is at issue is, as before, should those difficult claims be there or can one reach practical conclusions about real moral issues that are in no way determined by premises about such matters? . . .

The discussion also thereby, inevitably, contains claims about what life is like (e.g., my claim that love and friendship do not survive their parties' constantly insisting on their rights; or the claim that to demand perfection of life is to run the risk of missing out on happiness entirely). What is at issue is, should those disputable claims be there, or is our knowledge (or are our false opinions) about what life is like irrelevant to our understanding of real moral issues? . . .

Naturally, my own view is that all these concepts should be there in any discussion of real moral issues and that virtue theory, which uses all of them, is the right theory to apply to them.

Review and Discussion Questions

1. Based on Hursthouse's brief sketch of virtue ethics, does it offer, in your opinion, a plausible alternative to deontological or utilitarian theories? What questions of interpretation or application does her sketch raise for you?

2. Hursthouse believes that it is misguided to attempt to solve the abortion issue by focusing on rights or by bringing abortion under some general moral rule about killing. Is she right about this, or is an appeal to rights or to general normative principles inescapable when discussing the rights and wrongs of abortion and related moral issues?

3. Do you agree with her that understanding the morality of abortion does not require any sophisticated philosophical arguments about the status of the fetus?

4. Is terminating a pregnancy always a serious matter? Why? Do you agree with Hursthouse that "abortion for shallow reasons in the later stages is much more shocking than abortion for the same reasons in the early stages"? If so, why? If not, why not?

5. Hursthouse emphasizes the importance of parenthood and childrearing for human flourishing. But how important are they? Is there something deficient about the lives of people who are childless by choice? Do you agree with her that some people who avoid children do so out of a false ideal of freedom or self-realization or in worthless pursuit of "having a good time"? Do you agree that people who say "I am not ready for parenthood yet" are sometimes making a mistake?

6. Hursthouse implies that in most cases women end up facing unwanted pregnancies only because of some moral failing on their part. Explain what she has in mind and whether you agree or disagree.

7. Hursthouse acknowledges that she makes judgments about the virtuousness (or not) of certain types of conduct and about what is worthwhile, serious, and important in a human life. Are her judgments well justified? Do her judgments concern matters about which different people or different societies can usually reach agreement? Sometimes reach agreement? Rarely reach agreement? Suppose two people disagree about whether having an abortion in a particular situation would be compatible with one's being a virtuous person. Is there some way this disagreement can be resolved?

8. Does virtue theory offer an important new perspective on the abortion debate, or does it avoid or beg the difficult questions?

6

ANIMALS AND ENVIRONMENTAL ETHICS

The Place of Nonhumans in Environmental Issues

PETER SINGER

Peter Singer, professor of bioethics at Princeton University, is the author of *Animal Liberation,* a work that has stimulated much of today's interest in and debate over our treatment of animals. In the following essay, Singer argues that the effects of our environmental actions on nonhumans should figure directly in our deliberations about what we ought to do. Because animals can feel pleasure and pain and have the capacity for subjective experience, they can therefore be said to have interests, interests that we must not ignore. Singer contends that we must extend the moral principle of "equal consideration of interests" to include the interests of nonhumans, and he sketches the implications of our doing so—including the necessity of abandoning our present practice of rearing and killing other animals for food.

Study Questions

1. What are the two ways that Singer distinguishes of taking into account the effects of our actions on nonhuman animals?
2. What does Singer mean by "speciesism"?
3. Why does Singer maintain that birds and mammals have interests but plants do not?

4. Why is giving equal consideration to the interests of two different beings not the same as treating them alike or holding their lives to be of equal value?

5. Why does Singer think that the question of animal rights is not so important?

6. Why is Singer against raising and killing animals for food?

I. Humans and Nonhumans

WHEN WE HUMANS change the environment in which we live, we often harm ourselves. If we discharge cadmium into a bay and eat shellfish from that bay, we become ill and may die. When our industries and automobiles pour noxious fumes into the atmosphere, we find a displeasing smell in the air, the long-term results of which may be every bit as deadly as cadmium poisoning. The harm that humans do the environment, however, does not rebound solely, or even chiefly, on humans. It is nonhumans who bear the most direct burden of human interference with nature.

By "nonhumans" I mean to refer to all living things other than human beings, though for reasons to be given later, it is with nonhuman animals, rather than plants, that I am chiefly concerned. It is also important, in the context of environmental issues, to note that living things may be regarded either collectively or as individuals. In debates about the environment the most important way of regarding living things collectively has been to regard them as species. Thus, when environmentalists worry about the future of the blue whale, they usually are thinking of the blue whale as a species, rather than of individual blue whales. But this is not, of course, the only way in which one can think of blue whales, or other animals, and one of the topics I shall discuss is whether we should be concerned about what we are doing to the environment primarily insofar as it threatens entire species of nonhumans, or primarily insofar as it affects individual nonhuman animals.

The general question, then, is how the effects of our actions on the environment of nonhuman beings should figure in our deliberations about what we ought to do. There is an unlimited variety of contexts in which this issue could arise. To take just one: Suppose that it is considered necessary to build a new power station, and there are two sites, A and B, under consideration. In most respects the sites are equally suitable, but building the power station on site A would be more expensive because the greater depth of shifting soil at that site will require deeper foundations; on the other hand to build on site B will destroy a favored breeding ground for thousands of wildfowl. Should the presence of the wildfowl enter into the decision as to where to build? And if so, in what manner should it enter, and how heavily should it weigh?

In a case like this the effects of our actions on nonhuman animals could be taken into account in two quite different ways: directly, giving the lives and welfare of nonhuman animals an intrinsic significance which must count in any moral calculation; or indirectly, so that the effects of our actions on nonhumans are morally significant only if they have consequences for humans. . . .

II. Speciesism

The view that the effects of our actions on other animals have no direct moral significance is not as likely to be openly advocated today as it was in the past; yet it is likely to be accepted implicitly and acted upon. When planners perform cost-benefit studies on new projects, the costs and benefits are costs and benefits for human beings only. This does not mean that the impact of [a] power station or highway on wildlife is ignored altogether, but it is included only indirectly. That a new reservoir would drown a valley teeming with wildlife is taken into account only under some such heading as the value of the facilities for recreation that the valley affords. In calculating this value, the cost-benefit study will be neutral between forms of recreation like hunting and shooting and those like bird watching and bush walking—in fact hunting and shooting are likely to contribute more to the benefit side of the calculations because larger sums of money are spent on them, and they therefore benefit manufacturers and retailers of firearms as well as the hunters and shooters themselves. The suffering experienced by the animals whose habitat is flooded is not reckoned into the costs of the operation; nor is the recreational value obtained by the hunters and shooters offset by the cost to the animals that their recreation involves.

Despite its venerable origin, the view that the effects of our actions on nonhuman animals have no intrinsic moral significance can be shown to be arbitrary and morally indefensible. If a being suffers, the fact that it is not a member of our own species cannot be a moral reason for failing to take its suffering into account. This becomes obvious if we consider the analogous attempt by white slaveowners to deny consideration to the interests of blacks. These white racists limited their moral concern to their own race, so the suffering of a black did not have the same moral significance as the suffering of a white. We now recognize that in doing so they were making an arbitrary distinction, and that the existence of suffering, rather than the race of the sufferer, is what is really morally significant. The point remains true if "species" is substituted for "race." The logic of racism and the logic of the position we have been discussing, which I have elsewhere referred to as "speciesism," are indistinguishable; and if we reject the former then consistency demands that we reject the latter too.[1]

It should be clearly understood that the rejection of speciesism does not imply that the different species are in fact equal in respect of such characteristics as intelligence, physical strength, ability to communicate, capacity to suffer, ability to damage the environment, or anything else. After all, the moral principle of human equality cannot be taken as implying that all humans are equal in these respects either—if it did, we would have to give up the idea of human equality. That

one being is more intelligent than another does not entitle him to enslave, exploit, or disregard the interests of the less intelligent being. The moral basis of equality among humans is not equality in fact, but the principle of equal consideration of interests, and it is this principle that, in consistency, must be extended to any nonhumans who have interests.

III. Nonhumans Have Interests

There may be some doubt about whether any nonhuman beings have interests. This doubt may arise because of uncertainty about what it is to have an interest, or because of uncertainty about the nature of some nonhuman beings. So far as the concept of "interest" is the cause of doubt, I take the view that only a being with subjective experiences, such as the experience of pleasure or the experience of pain, can have interests in the full sense of the term; and that any being with such experiences does have at least one interest, namely, the interest in experiencing pleasure and avoiding pain. Thus consciousness, or the capacity for subjective experience, is both a necessary and a sufficient condition for having an interest. While there may be a loose sense of the term in which we can say that it is in the interests of a tree to be watered, this attenuated sense of the term is not the sense covered by the principle of equal consideration of interests. All we mean when we say that it is in the interests of a tree to be watered is that the tree needs water if it is to continue to live and grow normally; if we regard this as evidence that the tree has interests, we might almost as well say that it is in the interests of a car to be lubricated regularly because the car needs lubrication if it is to run properly. In neither case can we really mean (unless we impute consciousness to trees or cars) that the tree or car has any preference about the matter.

The remaining doubt about whether nonhuman beings have interests is, then, a doubt about whether nonhuman beings have subjective experiences like the experience of pain. I have argued elsewhere that the commonsense view that birds and mammals feel pain is well founded,[2] but more serious doubts arise as we move down the evolutionary scale. Vertebrate animals have nervous systems broadly similar to our own and behave in ways that resemble our own pain behavior when subjected to stimuli that we would find painful; so the inference that vertebrates are capable of feeling pain is a reasonable one, though not as strong as it is if limited to mammals and birds. When we go beyond vertebrates to insects, crustaceans, mollusks and so on, the existence of subjective states becomes more dubious, and with very simple organisms it is difficult to believe that they could be conscious. As for plants, though there have been sensational claims that plants are not only conscious, but even psychic, there is no hard evidence that supports even the more modest claim.

The boundary of beings who may be taken as having interests is therefore not an abrupt boundary, but a broad range in which the assumption that the being has interests shifts from being so strong as to be virtually certain to being so weak as to be highly improbable. The principle of equal consideration of interests must be applied with this in mind, so that where there is a clash between a virtually certain interest and highly doubtful one, it is the virtually certain interest that ought to prevail.

In this manner our moral concern ought to extend to all beings who have interests. . . .

IV. Equal Consideration of Interests

Giving equal consideration to the interests of two different beings does not mean treating them alike or holding their lives to be of equal value. We may recognize that the interests of one being are greater than those of another, and equal consideration will then lead us to sacrifice the being with lesser interests, if one or the other must be sacrificed. For instance, if for some reason a choice has to be made between saving the life of a normal human being and that of a dog, we might well

decide to save the human because he, with his greater awareness of what is going to happen, will suffer more before he dies; we may also take into account the likelihood that it is the family and friends of the human who will suffer more; and finally, it would be the human who had the greater potential for future happiness. This decision would be in accordance with the principle of equal consideration of interests, for the interests of the dog get the same consideration as those of the human, and the loss to the dog is not discounted because the dog is not a member of our species. The outcome is as it is because the balance of interests favors the human. In a different situation—say, if the human were grossly mentally defective and without family or anyone else who would grieve for it—the balance of interests might favor the nonhuman.

The more positive side of the principle of equal consideration is this: Where interests are equal, they must be given equal weight. So where human and nonhuman animals share an interest—as in the case of the interest in avoiding physical pain—we must give as much weight to violations of the interest of the nonhumans as we do to similar violations of the human's interest. This does not mean, of course, that it is as bad to hit a horse with a stick as it is to hit a human being, for the same blow would cause less pain to the animal with the tougher skin. The principle holds between similar amounts of felt pain, and what this is will vary from case to case.

It may be objected that we cannot tell exactly how much pain another animal is suffering, and that therefore the principle is impossible to apply. While I do not deny the difficulty and even, so far as precise measurement is concerned, the impossibility of comparing the subjective experiences of members of different species, I do not think that the problem is different in kind from the problem of comparing the subjective experiences of two members of our own species. Yet this is something we do all the time, for instance when we judge that a wealthy person will suffer less by being taxed at a higher rate than a poor person will gain from the welfare benefits paid for by the tax; or when we decide to take our two children to the beach instead of to a fair, because although the older one would prefer the fair, the younger one has a stronger preference the other way. These comparisons may be very rough, but since there is nothing better, we must use them; it would be irrational to refuse to do so simply because they are rough. Moreover, rough as they are, there are many situations in which we can be reasonably sure which way the balance of interests lies. While a difference of species may make comparisons rougher still, the basic problem is the same, and the comparisons are still often good enough to use, in the absence of anything more precise.

V. Animal Rights

The principle of equal consideration of interests and the indefensibility of limiting this principle to members of our own species means that we cannot deny, as Aquinas and Kant denied, that we have direct duties to members of other species. It may be asked whether this means that members of other species have rights against us. This is an issue on which there has been a certain amount of dispute, but it is, I believe, more a dispute about words than about substantive issues. In one sense of "right," we may say that it follows immediately from the fact that animals come within the scope of the principle of equal consideration of interests that they have at least one right, namely, the right to equal consideration. That is, admittedly, an odd kind of right—it is really a necessary foundation for having rights, rather than a right in itself. But some other rights could be derived from it without difficulty: the right not to have gratuitous pain inflicted would be one such right. There is, however, another sense of "right," according to which rights exist only among those who are part of a community, all members of whom have rights and in turn are capable of respecting the rights of others. On this view, rights are essentially contractual, and hence cannot exist unless both parties are capable of honoring the contract. It would follow that most, if not all, nonhuman animals have no rights. It should be noted, though, that this is a narrower notion of rights than that commonly used in America today; for it follows from this notion of rights that not only nonhuman animals, but also human infants and young children, as well as mentally defective humans, have no rights. Those who put forward this view of rights do not believe that we may do what we like with young or mentally defective humans or nonhuman animals; rather they would say that moral rights are only one kind of constraint on our conduct, and not necessarily the most important. They might, for instance, take account of utilitarian considerations which would apply to all beings capable of pleasure or pain. Thus actions which proponents of the former, broader view of rights may condemn as violations of the rights of animals could also be condemned by those who hold the narrower view, though they would not classify such actions as infringing rights. Seen in this light the question of whether animals have rights becomes less important than it might otherwise appear, for what matters is how we think animals ought to be treated, and not how we employ the concept of a right. Those who deny animal rights will not be likely to refuse to consider their interests, as long as they are reminded that the denial of rights to nonhuman animals does no more than place animals in the same moral category as human infants. Hence I doubt if the claim that animals have rights is worth the effort required in its defense; it is a claim which invites replies which, whatever their philosophical merits, serve as a distraction from the central practical question.

VI. Examples

We can now draw at least one conclusion as to how the existence of nonhuman living things should enter into our deliberations about actions affecting the environment: Where our actions are likely to make animals suffer, that suffering must count in our deliberations, and it should count equally with a like amount of suffering by human beings, insofar as rough comparisons can be made.

The difficulty of making the required comparison will mean that the application of this conclusion is controversial in many cases, but there will be some situations in which it is clear enough. Take, for instance, the wholesale poisoning of animals that is euphemistically known as "pest control." The authorities who conduct these campaigns give no consideration to the suffering they inflict on the "pests," and invariably use the method of slaughter they believe to be cheapest and most effective. The result is that hundreds of millions of rabbits have died agonizing deaths from the artificially introduced disease, myxomatosis, or from poisons like "ten-eighty"; coyotes and other wild dogs have died painfully from cyanide poisoning; and all manner of wild animals have endured days of thirst, hunger, and fear with a mangled limb caught in a leg-hold trap. Granting, for the sake of argument, the necessity for pest control—though this has rightly been questioned—the fact remains that no serious attempts have been made to introduce alternative means of control and thereby reduce the incalculable amount of suffering caused by present methods. It would not, presumably, be beyond modern science to produce a substance which, when eaten by rabbits or coyotes, produced sterility instead of a drawn-out death. Such methods might be more expensive, but can anyone doubt that if a similar amount of human suffering were at stake, the expense would be borne?

Another clear instance in which the principle of equal consideration of interests would indicate methods different from those presently used is in the timber industry. There are two basic methods of obtaining timber from forests. One is to cut only selected mature or dead trees, leaving the forest substantially intact. The other, known as clear-cutting, involves chopping down everything that grows in a given area, and then reseeding. Obviously when a large area is clear-cut, wild animals find their whole living area destroyed in a few days, whereas selected felling makes a relatively minor disturbance. But clear-cutting is

cheaper, and timber companies therefore use this method and will continue to do so unless forced to do otherwise. . . .

VII. The Meat Industry

For the great majority of human beings, especially in urban, industrialized societies, the most direct form of contact with members of other species is at meal-times: We eat them. In doing so we treat them purely as means to our ends. We regard their life and well-being as subordinate to our taste for a particular kind of dish. I say "taste" deliberately—this is purely a matter of pleasing our palate. There can be no defence of eating flesh in terms of satisfying nutritional needs, since it has been established beyond doubt that we could satisfy our need for protein and other essential nutrients far more efficiently with a diet that replaced animal flesh by soy beans, or products derived from soy beans, and other high-protein vegetable products.*

It is not merely the act of killing that indicates what we are ready to do to other species in order to gratify our tastes. The suffering we inflict on the animals while they are alive is perhaps an even clearer indication of our speciesism than the fact that we are prepared to kill them.[†] In order to have

---

* In order to produce 1 lb. of protein in the form of beef or veal, we must feed 21 lbs. of protein to the animal. Other forms of livestock are slightly less inefficient, but the average ratio in the U.S. is still 1:8. It has been estimated that the amount of protein lost to humans in this way is equivalent to 90% of the annual world protein deficit. . . .

[†]Although one might think that killing a being is obviously the ultimate wrong one can do to it, I think that the infliction of suffering is a clearer indication of speciesism because it might be argued that at least part of what is wrong with killing a human is that most humans are conscious of their existence over time and have desires and purposes that extend into the future—see, for instance, M. Tooley, "Abortion and Infanticide," *Philosophy and Public Affairs*, vol. 2, no. 1 (1972). Of course, if one took this view one would have to hold—as Tooley does—that killing a human infant or mental defective is not in itself wrong, and is less serious than killing certain higher mammals that probably do have a sense of their own existence over time.

meat on the table at a price that people can afford, our society tolerates methods of meat production that confine sentient animals in cramped, unsuitable conditions for the entire durations of their lives. Animals are treated like machines that convert fodder into flesh, and any innovation that results in a higher "conversion ratio" is liable to be adopted. As one authority on the subject has said, "cruelty is acknowledged only when profitability ceases."[3] So hens are crowded four or five to a cage with a floor area of twenty inches by eighteen inches, or around the size of a single page of the *New York Times*. The cages have wire floors, since this reduces cleaning costs, though wire is unsuitable for the hens' feet; the floors slope, since this makes the eggs roll down for easy collection, although this makes it difficult for the hens to rest comfortably. In these conditions all the birds' natural instincts are thwarted: They cannot stretch their wings fully, walk freely, dust-bathe, scratch the ground, or build a nest. Although they have never known other conditions, observers have noticed that the birds vainly try to perform these actions. Frustrated at their inability to do so, they often develop what farmers call "vices," and peck each other to death. To prevent this, the beaks of young birds are often cut off.

This kind of treatment is not limited to poultry. Pigs are now also being reared in cages inside sheds. These animals are comparable to dogs in intelligence, and need a varied, stimulating environment if they are not to suffer from stress and boredom. Anyone who kept a dog in the way in which pigs are frequently kept would be liable to prosecution, in England at least, but because our interest in exploiting pigs is greater than our interest in exploiting dogs, we object to cruelty to dogs while consuming the produce of cruelty to pigs. Of the other animals, the condition of veal calves is perhaps worst of all, since these animals are so closely confined that they cannot even turn around or get up and lie down freely. In this way they do not develop unpalatable muscle. They are also made anaemic and kept short of roughage, to keep their flesh pale, since white veal fetches a higher price; as a result they develop a craving for iron and roughage, and have been observed to gnaw wood off the sides of their stalls, and lick greedily at any rusty hinge that is within reach.

Since, as I have said, none of these practices cater to anything more than our pleasures of taste, our practice of rearing and killing other animals in order to eat them is a clear instance of the sacrifice of the most important interests of other beings in order to satisfy trivial interests of our own. To avoid speciesism we must stop this practice, and each of us has a moral obligation to cease supporting the practice. Our custom is all the support that the meat industry needs. The decision to cease giving it that support may be difficult, but it is no more difficult than it would have been for a white Southerner to go against the traditions of his society and free his slaves; if we do not change our dietary habits, how can we censure those slaveholders who would not change their own way of living?

NOTES

1. For a fuller statement of this argument, see my *Animal Liberation* (New York: A New York Review Book, 1975), especially ch. 1.
2. *Ibid.*
3. Ruth Harrison, *Animal Machines* (London: Stuart, 1964). This book provides an eye-opening account of intensive farming methods for those unfamiliar with the subject.

Review and Discussion Questions

1. Describe the human practices that most clearly demonstrate speciesism.
2. What does the principle of "equal consideration of interests" imply for our treatment of animals? What does it not imply?
3. Do you agree that animals can have interests that human beings must take into account? If so, which animals and what interests? What about plants?

4. Give examples of how adherence to the principle of equal consideration would change the conduct of human beings.

5. Do you believe that animals have rights? If so, which animals have rights, and what rights do they have? Explain.

6. Most people take for granted that there is nothing immoral about eating meat. What are Singer's reasons for challenging this assumption? How compelling is his reasoning? Do you think that meat eating can be morally justified?

Do Animals Have Rights?

TIBOR R. MACHAN

In the previous essay, Peter Singer argued that the moral principle of equal consideration of interests should be extended to animals—that is, that animal interests should be weighed equally with human interests in our moral deliberations. Other moral philosophers have put the point in terms of rights, arguing that animals have certain basic moral rights that humans must respect. In this essay Tibor R. Machan, professor of philosophy at Auburn University, rejects these arguments, contending that animals have no rights and that their interests do not count equally with those of human beings.

Study Questions

1. What is it to have a right, according to Machan? What is the argument for extending rights to animals?

2. Explain why, according to Machan, human beings may use animals for their own purposes.

3. Why are human rights important? How does the answer to this question imply that there is no room for animal rights?

4. Does Machan believe that we are morally permitted to do whatever we want to animals?

Iℕ RECENT YEARS the doctrine of animals' rights has found champions in important circles where the general doctrine of rights is itself well respected. For example, Professor Tom Regan, in his important book *The Case For Animal Rights* . . ., finds the idea of natural rights intellectually congenial but then extends this idea to cover animals near humans on the evolutionary scale. The tradition from within which Regan works is clearly Lockean, only he does not agree that human nature is distinctive enough, in relevant respects, to restrict the scope of natural rights to human beings alone.

Following a different tradition, namely, utilitarianism, the idea of animal liberation has emerged. And this idea comes to roughly the same thing, practically speaking. Only the argument is different because for utilitarians what is important is not that someone or something must have a specific sphere of dominion but that they be well off in their lives. So long as the bulk of the relevant creatures enjoy a reasonably high living standard, the moral and political objectives for us will have been met. But if this goal is neglected, moral and political steps are required to improve on the situation. Animal liberation is such a step.

This essay will maintain that animals have no rights and need no liberation. I will argue that to think they do is a category mistake—it is, to be blunt, to unjustifiably anthropomorphize animals, to treat them as if they were what they are not, namely, human beings. Rights and liberty are political concepts applicable to human beings because human beings are moral agents, in need of what Harvard philosopher Robert Nozick calls "moral space," that is, a definite sphere of moral jurisdiction where their authority to act is respected and protected so it is they, not intruders, who govern themselves and either succeed or fail in their moral tasks.

Oddly, it is clearly admitted by most animal rights or liberation theorists that only human beings are moral agents—for example, they never urge animals to behave morally (by, e.g., standing up for their rights, by leading a political revolution). No animal rights theorist proposes that animals be tried for crimes and blamed for moral wrongs.

If it is true that the moral nature of human beings gives rise to the conception of basic rights and liberties, then by this alone animal rights and liberation theorists have made an admission fatal to their case.

Before getting under way I want to note that rights and liberty are certainly not the whole of moral concern to us. There are innumerable other moral issues one can raise, including about the way human beings relate to animals. In particular, there is the question how should people treat animals. Should they be hunted even when this does not serve any vital human purpose? Should they be utilized in hurtful—indeed, evidently agonizing—fashion even for trivial human purposes? Should their pain and suffering be ignored in the process of being made use of for admittedly vital human purposes?

It is clear that once one has answered the question of whether animals have rights (or ought to be liberated from human beings) in the negative, one has by no means disposed of these other issues. In this essay I will be dealing mostly with the issue of animal rights and liberation. Yet I will also touch briefly on the other moral issues just raised. I will indicate why they may all be answered in the negative without it being the case that animals have rights or should be liberated—i.e., without raising any serious political issues.

Why Might Animals Have Rights?

To have a right amounts to having those around one who have the choice to abstain from intruding on one within a given sphere of jurisdiction. If I have the right to the use of our community swimming pool, no one may prevent me from making the decision as to whether I do or do not use the pool. Someone's having a right is a kind of freedom from the unavoidable interference of moral agents, beings who are capable of choosing whether they will interfere or not interfere with the rights holder.

When a right is considered natural, the freedom involved in having this right is supposed to be justified by reference to the kind of being one is, one's nature as a certain kind of entity. The idea of natural rights was formulated in connection with the issue of the proper relationship between human beings, especially citizens and governments. The idea goes back many centuries. . . .

The major political thinker with an influential doctrine of natural rights was John Locke. In his *Second Treatise on Government* he argued that each human being is responsible to follow the Law of Nature, the source of morality. But to do so, each also requires a sphere of personal authority, which is identified by the principle of the natural right to property—including one's person and estate. In other words, to be a morally responsible being in the company of other persons one needs what Robert Nozick has called "moral space," i.e., a sphere of sovereignty or personal jurisdiction so that one can engage in self-government—for better or for worse. . . .

In our time numerous philosophers and social commentators have made the attempt to demonstrate that if we are able to ascribe basic rights to life, liberty and property to human beings, we can do the same for many of the higher animals. In essentials their arguments can be broken down into two parts. First, they subscribe to Darwin's thesis that no difference of kind, only a difference of degree, can be found between other animals and human beings.[1] Second, even if there were a difference in kind between other animals—especially mammals—and human beings, since they both can be shown to have interests (e.g., the avoidance of pain or suffering), for certain moral and legal purposes the difference does not matter, only the similarity does. In connection with both of these arguments the central conclusion is that if human beings can be said to have certain basic rights—e.g., to life, liberty or consideration for their capacity to suffer—then so do (higher) animals.*

Now I do not wish to give the impression that no diversity exists among those who defend animal rights. Some do so from the viewpoint of natural rights, treating animals' rights as basic limiting principles which may not be ignored except when it would also make sense to disregard the rights of human beings. Even on this matter there are serious differences among defenders of animals'

rights—some do not allow any special regard for human beings,[†] some hold that when it comes to a choice between a person and a dog, it is ordinarily the person who should be given protection.[‡] But others choose to defend animal rights on utilitarian grounds—to the extent that it amounts to furthering overall pleasure or happiness in the world, animals must be given equal consideration to what human beings receive. Thus only if there really is demonstrable contribution to the overall pleasure or happiness on earth may an animal capable of experiencing pleasure or happiness be sacrificed for the sake of some human purpose. Barring such demonstrable contribution, animals and humans enjoy equal rights.[§]

At times the argument for animal rights begins with the rather mild point that "reason requires that other animals are as much within the scope of moral concern as are men" but then moves on to the more radical claim that therefore "we must view our entire history as well as all aspects of our daily lives from a new perspective."[2]

Of course, people have generally invoked some moral considerations as they treated animals—I can recall living on a farm in Hungary when I was 11 and getting all kinds of lectures about how I ought to treat the animals, receiving severe rebuke when I mistreated a cat and lots of praise when I took the favorite cow grazing every day and established a close bond with it over time. Hardly anyone can have escaped one or another moral lecture from parents or neighbors concerning the

*On these points both the deontologically oriented Tom Regan and the utilitarian Peter Singer tend to agree, although they differ considerably in their arguments.

[†]Peter Singer holds that "we would be on shaky grounds if we were to demand equality for blacks, women, and other groups of oppressed humans while denying equal consideration to nonhumans." "All Animals Are Equal," *op. cit.*, Regan & Singer, *Animal Rights,* p. 150.
[‡]Tom Regan contends that "[it] is not to say that practices that involve taking the lives of animals cannot possibly be justified . . . in order to seriously consider approving such a practice [it] would [have to] prevent, reduce, or eliminate a much greater amount of evil . . . there is no other way to bring about these consequences . . . and . . . we have very good reason to believe that these consequences will obtain." "Do Animals Have a Right to Life?" *op. cit.*, Regan & Singer, *Animal Rights,* pp. 204–5.
[§]This is the gist of Singer's thesis.

treatment of pets, household animals, or birds. When a young boy once tried out an air gun by shooting a pigeon sitting on a telephone wire before the apartment house in which he lived, I recall that there was no end of rebuke in response to his wanton callousness. Yet none of those who engaged in the moralizing ever entertained the need to "view our entire history as well as all aspects of our daily lives from a new perspective." Rather they seemed to have understood that reckless disregard for the life or well being of animals shows a defect of character, lack of sensitivity, callousness—realizing, at the same time, that numerous human purposes justify our killing and using animals in the various ways most of us do use them.

And this really is the crux of the matter. But why? Why is it more reasonable to think of animals as available for our sensible use rather than owed the kind of respect and consideration we ought to extend to other human beings? It is one thing to have this as a common sense conviction, it is another to know it as a sound viewpoint, in terms of which we may confidently conduct ourselves.

Why We May Use Animals

While I will return to the arguments for animal rights, let me first place on record the case for the use of animals for human purposes. Without this case reasonably well established, it will not be possible to critically assess the case for animal rights. After all, this is a comparative matter—which viewpoint makes better sense, which is, in other words, more likely to be true?

One reason for the propriety of our use of animals is that we are more important or valuable than other animals and some of our projects may require animals for them to be successful. Notice that this is different from saying that human beings are "uniquely important," a position avidly ridiculed by Stephen R. L. Clark, who claims that "there seems no decent ground in reason or revelation to suppose that man is uniquely important or significant."[3] If man were uniquely important, that would mean that one could not assign any

value to plants or non-human animals apart from their relationship to human beings. That is not the position I am defending. I argue that there is a scale of importance in nature, and among all the various kinds of being, human beings are the most important—even while it is true that some members of the human species may indeed prove themselves to be the most vile and worthless, as well.

How do we establish that we are more important or valuable? By considering whether the idea of lesser or greater importance or value in the nature of things makes clear sense and applying it to an understanding of whether human beings or other animals are more important. If it turns out that ranking things in nature as more or less important makes sense, and if we qualify as more important than other animals, there is at least the beginning of a reason why we may make use of other animals for our purposes.

That there are things of different degree of value in nature is admitted by animal rights advocates, so there is no great need here to argue about that. When they insist that we treat animals differently from the way we treat, say, rocks or iron ore—so that while we may not use the former as we choose, we may use the latter—they testify, at least by implication, that animals are more important than, say, iron ore. Certainly they invoke some measure of importance or value and place animals higher in line with this measure than they place other aspects of nature. They happen, also, to deny that human beings rank higher than animals, or at least they do not admit that human beings' higher ranking warrants their using animals for their purposes. But that is a distinct issue which we can consider later.

Quite independently of the implicit acknowledgment by animal rights advocates of the hierarchy of nature, there simply is evidence through the natural world of the existence of beings of greater complexity and of higher value. For example, while it makes no sense to evaluate as good or bad such things as planets or rocks or pebbles—except as they may relate to human purposes—when it comes to plants and animals the process of evaluation commences very naturally indeed. We can speak of better or worse trees, oaks, redwoods, or zebras, foxes or chimps. While at this point we confine our evaluation to the condition or behavior of such beings without any intimation of their responsibility for being better or worse, when we start discussing human beings our evaluation takes on a moral component. Indeed, none are more ready to testify to this than animal rights advocates who, after all, do not demand any change of behavior on the part of non-human animals and yet insist that human beings conform to certain moral edicts as a matter of their own choice. This means that even animal rights advocates admit outright that to the best of our knowledge it is with human beings that the idea of moral goodness and moral responsibility enters the universe.

Clearly this shows a hierarchical structure in nature: some things do not invite evaluations at all—it is a matter of no significance or of indifference whether they are or are not or what they are or how they behave. Some things invite evaluation but without implying any moral standing with reference to whether they do well or badly. And some things—namely, human beings—invite moral evaluation. The level of importance or value may be noted to move from the inanimate to the animate world, culminating, as far as we now know, with human life. Normal human life involves moral tasks, and that is why we are more important than other beings in nature—we are subject to moral appraisal, it is a matter of our doing whether we succeed or fail in our lives.

Now when it comes to our moral task, namely, to succeed as human beings, we are dependent upon reaching sensible conclusions about what we should do. We can fail to do this and too often do so. But we can also succeed. The process that leads to our success involves learning, among other things, what it is that nature avails us with to achieve our highly varied tasks in life. Clearly among these highly varied tasks could be some that make judicious use of animals—for example, to find out whether some medicine is safe for human use, we might wish to use animals. To do this is the rational thing for us to do, so as to make the best use of nature for our success in living our lives. That does not mean there need be no guidelines involved in how we might make use of animals—any more than there need be no guidelines involved in how we use anything else.

Why Individual Human Rights?

Where do individual *human* rights come into this picture? The rights being talked of in connection with human beings have as their source, as we have noted earlier, the human capacity to make moral choices. We have the right to life, liberty and property—as well as more specialized rights connected with politics, the press, religion—because we have as our central task in life to act morally. And in order to be able to do this throughout the scope of our lives, we require a reasonably clear sphere of personal jurisdiction—a dominion where we are sovereign and can either succeed or fail to live well, to do right, to act properly.

If we did not have rights, we would not have such a sphere of personal jurisdiction and there would be no clear idea as to whether we are acting in our own behalf or those of other persons. No one could be blamed or praised for we would not know clearly enough whether what the person is doing is in his or her authority to do or in someone else's. This is precisely the problem that arises in communal living and, especially, in totalitarian countries where everything is under forced collective governance. The reason moral distinctions are still possible to make under such circumstances is that in fact—as distinct from law—there is always some sphere of personal jurisdiction wherein people may exhibit courage, prudence, justice, honesty and other virtues. But where collectivism has been successfully enforced, there is no individual responsibility at play and people's morality and immorality is submerged within the group.

Indeed the main reason for governments has for some time been recognized to be nothing other than that our individual human rights should be protected. . . .

Where Is There Room for Animal Rights?

We have seen that the most sensible and influential doctrine of human rights rests on the fact that human beings are indeed members of a discernibly different species—the members of which have a moral life to aspire to and must have principles upheld for them in communities that make their aspiration possible. Now there is plainly no valid intellectual place for rights in the nonhuman world, the world in which moral responsibility is for all practical purposes absent. Some would want to argue that some measure of morality can be found within the world of at least higher animals—e.g., dogs. For example, Rollin holds that "In actual fact, some animals even seem to exhibit behavior that bespeaks something like moral agency or moral agreement."[4] His argument for this is rather anecdotal but it is worth considering:

Canids, including the domesticated dog, do not attack another when the vanquished bares its throat, showing a sign of submission. Animals typically do not prey upon members of their own species. Elephants and porpoises will and do feed injured members of their species. Porpoises will help humans, even at risk to themselves. Some animals will adopt orphaned young of other species. (Such cross-species "morality" would certainly not be explainable by simple appeal to mechanical evolution, since there is no advantage whatever to one's own species.) Dogs will act "guilty" when they break a rule such as one against stealing food from a table and will, for the most part, learn not to take it.[5]

Animal rights advocates such as Rollin maintain that it is impossible to clearly distinguish between human and non-human animals, including on the grounds of the former's characteristic as a moral agent. Yet what they do to defend this point is to invoke borderline cases, imaginary hypothesis, and anecdotes.

In contrast, in his book *The Difference of Man and the Difference It Makes,* Mortimer Adler undertakes the painstaking task of showing that even with the full acknowledgment of the merits of Darwinian and, especially, post-Darwinian evolutionary theory, there is ample reason to uphold the doctrine of species-distinction—a distinction, incidentally, that is actually presupposed within Darwin's own work.[6] Adler shows that although the theistic doctrine of radical species differences is incompatible with current evolutionary theory, the more naturalistic view that species are superficially (but non-negligibly) different is indeed necessary to it. The fact of occasional borderline cases is simply irrelevant—what is crucial is that the generalization is true that human beings are basically different from other animals—by virtue of "a crucial threshold in a continuum of degrees." As Adler explains:

. . . distinct species are genetically isolated populations between which interbreeding is impossible, arising (except in the case of polyploidy) from varieties between which interbreeding was not impossible, but between which it was prevented. Modern theorists, with more assurance than Darwin could manage, treat distinct species as natural kinds, not as man-made class distinctions.[7]

Adler adds that "Without the critical insight provided by the distinction between superficial and radical differences in kind, biologists [as well as animal rights advocates, one should add] might be tempted to follow Darwin in thinking that all differences in kind must be apparent, not real."[8]

Since Locke's admittedly incomplete—sometimes even confusing—theory had gained respect and, especially, practical import (e.g., in British and American political history), it became clear enough that the only justification for the exercise of state power—namely the force of the law—is that the rights of individuals are being or have been violated. But as with all successful doctrines, Locke's idea became corrupted by innumerable efforts to concoct rights that government must protect, rights that were actually disguised special interest objectives—values that some people, perhaps quite legitimately, wanted very badly to have secured for them.

While it is no doubt true that many animal rights advocates sincerely believe that they have found a justification for the actual existence of animal rights, it is equally likely that if the Lockean doctrine of rights had not become so influential, they would now be putting their point differently—in a way, namely, that would secure for them what they, as a special interest group, want: the protection of animals they have such love and sympathy for.

Closing Reflections

As with most issues on the minds of many intelligent people as well as innumerable crackpots, a discussion of whether there are animal rights and how we ought to treat animals cannot be concluded with dogmatic certainty one way or the other. Even though those who defend animal rights are certain almost beyond a shadow of doubt, all I can claim is to being certain beyond a reasonable doubt. Animals are not the sort of beings with basic rights to life, liberty and property, whereas human beings, in the main, are just such beings. Yet we know that animals can feel pain and can enjoy themselves and this must give us pause when we consider using them for our legitimate purposes. We ought to be humane, we ought to kill them and rear them and train them and hunt them in a fashion consistent with such care about them as sentient beings.

NOTES

1. Charles Darwin, *The Descent of Man*, Chpts. 3 and 4. Reprinted in Tom Regan and Peter Singer, eds., *Animal Rights and Human Obligations* (Englewood Cliffs, NJ: Prentice-Hall, 1976), pp. 72–81.

2. Bernard E. Rollin, *Animal Rights and Human Morality* (Buffalo, NY: Prometheus Books, 1981), p. 4.

3. Stephen R. L. Clark, *The Moral Status of Animals* (Oxford, England: Clarendon Press, 1977), p. 13.

4. Rollin, *Animal Rights*, p. 14.

5. *Ibid.*

6. See a discussion of this in Mortimer Adler, *The Difference of Man and the Difference It Makes* (New York: World Publishing Co., 1968), pp. 73ff.

7. *Ibid.*

8. *Ibid.*, p. 75.

Review and Discussion Questions

1. Contrast the practical implications of Machan's essay and those of Singer's essay for our treatment of animals, in particular for meat eating and animal experimentation.

2. Do you agree with Machan that human beings are more important or valuable than animals? How could this conclusion be established? Would our being more valuable show that we are morally permitted to use animals for our own purposes?

3. Most people would agree that animals cannot make moral decisions and therefore are not moral agents. If not, does it follow that animals cannot have rights or that their interests count less than human interests?

4. Machan believes that moral considerations still govern our treatment of animals, even if they lack rights and even if we are not obligated to give equal consideration to their interests. Assuming Machan is correct, what are the moral limits on our treatment of animals, and why?

5. How would you respond to Machan's argument if you were Singer? Is Machan guilty of "speciesism"?

Should Trees Have Standing?
Toward Legal Rights for Natural Objects

CHRISTOPHER D. STONE

Professor of law Christopher D. Stone argues that we should extend legal rights to forests, oceans, rivers, and other natural objects. Although the proposal may sound absurd, so did earlier proposals to extend rights, for example, to blacks and women. Stone discusses what it means to be a holder of legal rights and how extending rights to natural objects would dramatically change our approach to environmental protection. Stone's proposal is in part pragmatic: a legal move to enable environmentalists to better protect the environment. But it also reflects the view that nature deserves to be protected for its own sake.

Study Questions

1. Why does the extension of rights to some new entity always sound absurd?
2. What three criteria must something satisfy to be a "holder of legal rights"?
3. How does the example of the pollution of a stream illustrate the fact that natural objects lack legal rights?
4. How does Stone address the problem that natural objects like forests cannot speak for themselves or claim their rights?
5. What is the new conception advocated by Stone of the relationship of human beings to the rest of nature?

T HROUGHOUT LEGAL HISTORY, each successive extension of rights to some new entity has been, theretofore, a bit unthinkable. We are inclined to suppose the rightlessness of rightless "things" to be a decree of Nature, not a legal convention acting in support of some status quo. It is thus that we defer considering the choices involved in all their moral, social, and economic dimensions. And so the United States Supreme Court could straightfacedly tell us in *Dred Scott* that Blacks had been denied the rights of citizenship "as a subordinate and inferior class of beings, who had been subjugated by the dominant race. . . ."[1] In the nineteenth century, the highest court in California explained that Chinese had not the right to testify against white men in criminal matters because they were "a race of people whom nature has marked as inferior, and who are incapable of progress or intellectual development beyond a certain point . . . between whom and ourselves nature has placed an impassable difference."[2] The popular conception of the

Excerpted from Christopher D. Stone, "Should Trees Have Standing? Toward Legal Rights for Natural Objects," 45 Southern California Law Review 450–501 (1972). Reprinted with the permission of the Southern California Law Review.

Jew in the thirteenth century contributed to a law which treated them as "men *ferae naturae,* protected by a quasi-forest law. Like the roe and the deer, they form an order apart."[3] Recall, too, that it was not so long ago that the foetus was "like the roe and the deer." In an early suit attempting to establish a wrongful death action on behalf of a negligently killed foetus (now widely accepted practice), Holmes, then on the Massachusetts Supreme Court, seems to have thought it simply inconceivable "that a man might owe a civil duty and incur a conditional prospective liability in tort to one not yet in being."[4] The first woman in Wisconsin who thought she might have a right to practice law was told that she did not, in the following terms:

> The law of nature destines and qualifies the female sex for the bearing and nurture of the children of our race and for the custody of the homes of the world. . . . [A]ll life-long callings of women, inconsistent with these radical and sacred duties of their sex, as is the profession of the law, are departures from the order of nature; and when voluntary, treason against it. . . . The peculiar qualities of womanhood, its gentle graces, its quick sensibility, its tender suscepti- bility, its purity, its delicacy, its emotional impulses, its subordination of hard reason to sympathetic feeling, are surely not qualifications for forensic strife. Nature has tempered woman as little for the juridical conflicts of the court room, as for the physical conflicts of the battle field. . . .[5]

The fact is, that each time there is a move- ment to confer rights onto some new "entity," the proposal is bound to sound odd or fright- ening or laughable. This is partly because until the rightless thing receives its rights, we cannot see it as anything but a *thing* for the use of "us"—those who are holding rights at the time. In this vein, what is striking about the Wisconsin case above is that the court, for all its talk about women, so clearly was never able to see women as they are (and might become). All it could see was the popular "idealized" version of *an object it needed.* Such is the way the slave South looked upon the Black. There is something of a seamless web involved; there will be resist- ance to giving the thing "rights" until it can be seen and valued for itself; yet, it is hard to see it and value it for itself until we can bring our- selves to give it "rights"—which is almost inevitably going to sound inconceivable to a large group of people.

The reason for this little discourse on the unthinkable, the reader must know by now, if only from the title of the paper. I am quite seri- ously proposing that we give legal rights to forests, oceans, rivers, and other so-called "natu- ral objects" in the environment—indeed, to the natural environment as a whole. . . .

Toward Rights for the Environment

Now, to say that the natural environment should have rights is not to say anything as silly as that no one should be allowed to cut down a tree. We say human beings have rights, but—at least as of the time of this writing—they can be executed. Corpo- rations have rights, but they cannot plead the fifth amendment; *In re Gault* gave fifteen-year-olds certain rights in juvenile proceedings, but it did not give them the right to vote. Thus, to say that the environment should have rights is not to say that it should have every right we can imagine, or even the same body of rights as human beings have. Nor is it to say that everything in the envi- ronment should have the same rights as every other thing in the environment. . . .

For a thing to be *a holder of legal rights* some- thing more is needed than that some authorita- tive body will review the actions and processes of those who threaten it. As I shall use the term, "holder of legal rights," each of three additional criteria must be satisfied. All three, one will observe, go towards making a thing *count* jurally—to have a legally recognized worth and dignity in its own right, and not merely to serve as a means to benefit "us" (whoever the con- temporary group of rights-holders may be). They are, first, that the thing can institute legal actions *at its behest;* second, that in determining the granting of legal relief, the court must take *injury to it* into account; and, third, that relief must run to the *benefit of it*. . . .

The Rightlessness of Natural Objects at Common Law

Consider, for example, the common law's posture toward the pollution of a stream. True, courts have always been able, in some circumstances, to issue orders that will stop the pollution. . . . But the stream itself is fundamentally rightless, with implications that deserve careful reconsideration.

The first sense in which the stream is not a rights-holder has to do with standing. The stream itself has none. So far as the common law is concerned, there is in general no way to challenge the polluter's actions save at the behest of a lower riparian—another human being—able to show an invasion of *his* rights. . . .

The second sense in which the common law denies "rights" to natural objects has to do with the way in which the merits are decided in those cases in which someone is competent and willing to establish standing. At its more primitive levels, the system protected the "rights" of the property owning human with minimal weighing of any values. . . . Today we have come more and more to make balances—but only such as will adjust the economic best interests of identifiable humans. . . .

Thus, we find the highest court of Pennsylvania refusing to stop a coal company from discharging polluted mine water into a tributary of the Lackawana River because a plaintiff's "grievance is for a mere personal inconvenience; and . . . mere private personal inconveniences . . . must yield to the necessities of a great public industry, which although in the hands of a private corporation, subserves a great public interest."[6] The stream itself is lost sight of in "a quantitative compromise between *two* conflicting interests."[7]

The third way in which the common law makes natural objects rightless has to do with who is regarded as the beneficiary of a favorable judgment. Here, too, it makes a considerable difference that it is not the natural object that counts in its own right. To illustrate this point let me begin by observing that it makes perfectly good sense to speak of, and ascertain, the legal damage to a natural object, if only in the sense of "making it whole" with respect to the most obvious factors. The costs of making a forest whole, for example, would include the costs of reseeding, repairing watersheds, restocking wildlife—the sorts of costs the Forest Service undergoes after a fire. Making a polluted stream whole would include the costs of restocking with fish, water-fowl, and other animal and vegetable life, dredging, washing out impurities, establishing natural and/or artificial aerating agents, and so forth. Now, what is important to note is that, under our present system, even if a plaintiff riparian wins a water pollution suit for damages, no money goes to the benefit of the stream itself to repair *its* damages. . . .

None of the natural objects, whether held in common or situated on private land, has any of the three criteria of a rights-holder. They have no standing in their own right; their unique damages do not count in determining outcome; and they are not the beneficiaries of awards. In such a fashion, these objects have traditionally been regarded by the common law, and even by all but the most recent legislation, as objects for man to conquer and master and use—in such a way as the law once looked upon "man's" relationships to African Negroes. Even where special measures have been taken to conserve them, as by seasons on game and limits on timber cutting, the dominant motive has been to conserve them *for us*—for the greatest good of the greatest number of human beings. Conservationists, so far as I am aware, are generally reluctant to maintain otherwise. As the name implies, they want to conserve and guarantee *our* consumption and *our* enjoyment of these other living things. In their own right, natural objects have counted for little, in law as in popular movements.

As I mentioned at the outset, however, the rightlessness of the natural environment can and should change; it already shows some signs of doing so.

Toward Having Standing in Its Own Right

It is not inevitable, nor is it wise, that natural objects should have no rights to seek redress in their own behalf. It is no answer to say that streams and forests cannot have standing because streams and forests cannot speak. Corporations cannot speak either; nor can states, estates, infants, incompetents, municipalities, or universities. Lawyers speak for them, as they customarily do for the ordinary citizen with legal problems. One ought, I think, to handle the legal problems of natural objects as one does the problems of legal incompetents—human beings who have become vegetable. If a human being shows signs of becoming senile and has affairs that he is de jure incompetent to manage, those concerned with his well being make such a showing to the court, and someone is designated by the court with the authority to manage the incompetent's affairs. . . .

On a parity of reasoning we should have a system in which, when a friend of a natural object perceives it to be endangered, he can apply to a court for the creation of a guardianship. . . .

The potential "friends" that such a statutory scheme would require will hardly be lacking. The Sierra Club, Environmental Defense Fund, Friends of the Earth, Natural Resources Defense Counsel, and the Izaak Walton League are just some of the many groups which have manifested unflagging dedication to the environment and which are becoming increasingly capable of marshalling the requisite technical experts and lawyers. If, for example, the Environmental Defense Fund should have reason to believe that some company's strip mining operations might be irreparably destroying the ecological balance of large tracts of land, it could, under this procedure,

apply to the court in which the lands were situated to be appointed guardian. As guardian, it might be given rights of inspection (or visitation) to determine and bring to the court's attention a fuller finding on the land's condition. If there were indications that under the substantive law some redress might be available on the land's behalf, then the guardian would be entitled to raise the land's rights in the land's name, *i.e.*, without having to make the roundabout and often unavailing demonstration . . . that the "rights" of the club's members were being invaded. . . .

One reason for making the environment itself the beneficiary of a judgment is to prevent it from being "sold out" in a negotiation among private litigants who agree not to enforce rights that have been established among themselves. Protection from this will be advanced by making the natural object a party to an injunctive settlement. Even more importantly, we should make it a beneficiary of money awards. . . .

The idea of assessing damages as best we can and placing them in a trust fund is far more realistic than a hope that a total "freeze" can be put on the environmental status quo. Nature is a continuous theatre in which things and species (eventually man) are destined to enter and exit. In the meantime, co-existence of man and his environment means that *each* is going to have to compromise for the better of both. Some pollution of streams, for example, will probably be inevitable for some time. Instead of setting an unrealizable goal of enjoining absolutely the discharge of all such pollutants, the trust fund concept would (a) help assure that pollution would occur only in those instances where the social need for the pollutant's product (via his present method of production) was so high as to enable the polluter to cover *all* homocentric costs, plus some estimated costs to the environment *per se,* and (b) would be a corpus for preserving monies, if necessary, while the technology developed to a point where repairing the damaged portion of the environment was feasible. Such a fund might even finance the requisite research and development. . . .

A radical new conception of man's relationship to the rest of nature would not only be a step towards solving the material planetary problems; there are strong reasons for such a changed consciousness from the point of making us far better humans. If we only stop for a moment and look at the underlying human qualities that our present attitudes toward property and nature draw upon and reinforce, we have to be struck by how stultifying of our own personal growth and satisfaction they can become when they take rein of us. Hegel, in "justifying" private property, unwittingly reflects the tone and quality of some of the needs that are played upon:

> A person has as his substantive end the right of putting his will into any and every thing and thereby making it his, because it has no such end in itself and derives its destiny and soul from his will. This is the absolute right of appropriation which man has over all "things."[8]

What is it within us that gives us this need not just to satisfy basic biological wants, but to extend our wills over things, to object-ify them, to make them ours, to manipulate them, to keep them at a psychic distance? Can it all be explained on "rational" bases? Should we not be suspect of such needs within us, cautious as to why we wish to gratify them? When I first read that passage of Hegel, I immediately thought not only of the emotional contrast with Spinoza, but of the passage in Carson McCullers' "A Tree, a Rock, a Cloud," in which an old derelict has collared a twelve-year-old boy in a streetcar cafe. The old man asks whether the boy knows "how love should be begun."

> The old man leaned closer and whispered:
> "A tree. A rock. A cloud."
> "The weather was like this in Portland," he said. "At the time my science was begun. I meditated and I started very cautious. I would pick up something from the street and take it home with me. I bought a goldfish and I concentrated on the goldfish and I loved it. I graduated from one thing to another. Day by day I was getting this technique.

> . . . "For six years now I have gone around by myself and built up my science. And now I am a master. Son, I can love anything. No longer do I have to think about it even. I see a street full of people and a beautiful light comes in me. I watch a bird in the sky. Or I meet a traveler on the road. Everything, Son. And anybody. All stranger and all loved! Do you realize what a science like mine can mean?"[9]

To be able to get away from the view that Nature is a collection of useful senseless objects is, as McCullers' "madman" suggests, deeply involved in the development of our abilities to love—or, if that is putting it too strongly, to be able to reach a heightened awareness of our own, and others' capacities in their mutual interplay. To do so, we have to give up some psychic investment in our sense of separateness and specialness in the universe. And this, in turn, is hard giving indeed, because it involves us in a fight backwards, into earlier stages of civilization and childhood in which we had to trust (and perhaps fear) our environment, for we had not then the power to master it. Yet, in doing so, we—as persons—gradually free ourselves of needs for supportive illusions. Is not this one of the triumphs for "us" of our giving legal rights to (or acknowledging the legal rights of) the Blacks and women? . . .

The time may be on hand when these sentiments, and the early stirrings of the law, can be coalesced into a radical new theory or myth—felt as well as intellectualized—of man's relationships to the rest of nature. I do not mean "myth" in a demeaning sense of the term, but in the sense in which, at different times in history, our social "facts" and relationships have been comprehended and integrated by reference to the "myths" that we are co-signers of a social contract, that the Pope is God's agent, and that all men are created equal. Pantheism, Shinto, and Tao all have myths to offer. But they are all, each in its own fashion, quaint, primitive, and archaic. What is needed is a myth that can fit our growing body of knowledge of geophysics, biology, and the cosmos. In this vein, I do not think it too remote that we may come to regard the Earth, as some have suggested, as one organism, of which Mankind is a functional part—the mind, perhaps: different from the rest of nature, but different as a man's brain is from his lungs.

NOTES

1. *Dred Scott v. Sanford,* 60 U.S. (19 How.) 396, 404–05 (1856).
2. *People v. Hall,* 4 Cal. 399, 405 (1854).

3. Schechter, "The Rightlessness of Medieval English Jewry," 45 *Jewish Q. Rev.* 121, 135 (1954) quoting from M. Bateson, *Medieval England* 139 (1904).
4. *Dietrich v. Inhabitants of Northampton,* 138 Mass. 14, 16 (1884).
5. *In re Goddell,* 39 Wisc. 232, 245 (1875).
6. *Pennsylvania Coal Co. v. Sanderson,* 113 Pa. 126, 149, 6 A. 453, 459 (1886).
7. Hand, J., in *Smith v. Staso Milling Co.,* 18 F.2d 736, 738 (2d Cir. 1927) (emphasis added).
8. G. Hegel, *Hegel's Philosophy of Right,* 41 (T. Knox transl. 1945).
9. C. McCullers, *The Ballad of the Sad Cafe and Other Stories,* 150–51 (1958).

Review and Discussion Questions

1. Do you think the idea of granting legal rights to natural objects is workable? What would be the practical results of doing so? Would it significantly strengthen efforts to preserve the natural environment?

2. Assess Stone's argument in light of the previous essay by Tibor Machan. How do their positions contrast, and whose viewpoint seems more persuasive? Can natural objects have either legal, political, or moral rights? If so, which natural objects and what rights?

3. Peter Singer states that "consciousness, or the capacity for subjective experience, is both a necessary and a sufficient condition for having an interest." This suggests that he would disagree with Stone's talk of protecting the "interests" of nature. Whose point of view is more plausible?

4. Would embracing Stone's proposal lead to a change in our conception of our relationship to nature? Does our conception need to be radically changed, as Stone suggests?

People or Penguins

WILLIAM F. BAXTER

In contrast to Christopher D. Stone, William F. Baxter defends a more traditional, human-centered, cost-benefit approach to environmental issues. According to him, the impact of our actions on, for example, penguins, sugar pines, or geological marvels is irrelevant except insofar as it affects human interests. Baxter argues that this is the only realistic approach to take and that, in any case, what is good for humans is in many respects good for plant and animal life as well. He also rejects the claim that we have an obligation to respect the "balance of nature" or to "preserve the environment."

Reprinted by permission from William F. Baxter, People or Penguins: The Case for Optimal Pollution. *Copyright © 1974 Columbia University Press.*

No natural or morally correct state of nature exists, and even pollution is only defined by reference to the needs of human beings. For Baxter, the goal is not pure air and water but the "optimal state of pollution"—that is, the level of pollution that yields the greatest amount of human satisfaction.

Study Questions

1. How does the example of DDT and penguins illustrate Baxter's position?

2. For what reasons does Baxter believe that his position is the only tenable starting place for analysis?

3. Why does Baxter reject the notion that there is a "right" or "morally correct" state of nature to which we should return?

4. What does Baxter mean when he writes that our objective is "not pure air or water but rather some optimal state of pollution"? How are we to determine that optimal state?

I START WITH THE MODEST PROPOSITION that, in dealing with pollution, or indeed with any problem, it is helpful to know what one is attempting to accomplish. Agreement on how and whether to pursue a particular objective, such as pollution control, is not possible unless some more general objective has been identified and stated with reasonable precision. We talk loosely of having clean air and clean water, of preserving our wilderness areas, and so forth. But none of these is a sufficiently general objective: each is more accurately viewed as a means rather than as an end.

With regard to clean air, for example, one may ask, "how clean?" and "what does clean mean?" It is even reasonable to ask, "why have clean air?" Each of these questions is an implicit demand that a more general community goal be stated—a goal sufficiently general in its scope and enjoying sufficiently general assent among the community of actors that such "why" questions no longer seem admissible with respect to that goal.

If, for example, one states as a goal the proposition that "every person should be free to do whatever he wishes in contexts where his actions do not interfere with the interests of other human beings," the speaker is unlikely to be met with a response of "why." The goal may be criticized as uncertain in its implications or difficult to implement, but it

is so basic a tenet of our civilization—it reflects a cultural value so broadly shared, at least in the abstract—that the question of "why" is seen as impertinent or imponderable or both. . . .

Without any expectation of obtaining unanimous consent to them, let me set forth four goals that I generally use as ultimate testing criteria in attempting to frame solutions to problems of human organization. My position regarding pollution stems from these four criteria. . . .

My criteria are as follows:

1. The spheres of freedom criterion stated above.

2. Waste is a bad thing. The dominant feature of human existence is scarcity—our available resources, our aggregate labors, and our skill in employing both have always been, and will continue for some time to be, inadequate to yield to every man all the tangible and intangible satisfactions he would like to have. Hence, none of those resources, or labors, or skills, should be wasted—that is, employed so as to yield less than they might yield in human satisfactions.

3. Every human being should be regarded as an end rather than as a means to be used for the betterment of another. Each should be afforded dignity and regarded as having an absolute claim to an evenhanded application of such rules as the community may adopt for its governance.

4. Both the incentive and the opportunity to improve his share of satisfactions should be preserved to every individual. Preservation of incentive is dictated by the "no-waste" criterion and enjoins against the continuous, totally egalitarian redistribution of satisfactions, or wealth; but subject to that constraint, everyone should receive, by continuous redistribution if necessary, some minimal share of aggregate wealth so as to avoid a level of privation from which the opportunity to improve his situation becomes illusory.

The relationship of these highly general goals to the more specific environmental issues at hand may not be readily apparent, and I am not yet ready to demonstrate their pervasive implications. Recently scientists have informed us that use of DDT in food production is causing damage to the penguin population. For the present purposes let us accept that assertion as an indisputable scientific fact. The scientific fact is often asserted as if the correct implication—that we must stop agricultural use of DDT—followed from the mere statement of the fact of penguin damage. But plainly it does not follow if my criteria are employed.

My criteria are oriented to people, not penguins. Damage to penguins, or sugar pines, or geological marvels is, without more, simply irrelevant. One must go further, by my criteria, and say: Penguins are important because people enjoy seeing them walk about rocks; and furthermore, the well-being of people would be less impaired by halting use of DDT than by giving up penguins. In short, my observations about environmental problems will be people-oriented, as are my criteria. I have no interest in preserving penguins for their own sake.

It may be said by way of objection to this position that it is very selfish of people to act as if each person represented one unit of importance and

nothing else was of any importance. It is undeniably selfish. Nevertheless I think it is the only tenable starting place for analysis for several reasons. First, no other position corresponds to the way most people really think and act—i.e., corresponds to reality.

Second, this attitude does not portend any massive destruction of nonhuman flora and fauna, for people depend on them in many obvious ways, and they will be preserved because and to the degree that humans do depend on them.

Third, what is good for humans is, in many respects, good for penguins and pine trees—clean air for example. So that humans are, in these respects, surrogates for plant and animal life.

Fourth, I do not know how we could administer any other system. Our decisions are either private or collective. Insofar as Mr. Jones is free to act privately, he may give such preferences as he wishes to other forms of life: he may feed birds in winter and do with less himself, and he may even decline to resist an advancing polar bear on the ground that the bear's appetite is more important than those portions of himself that the bear may choose to eat. In short my basic premise does not rule out private altruism to competing life-forms. It does rule out, however, Mr. Jones' inclination to feed Mr. Smith to the bear, however hungry the bear, however despicable Mr. Smith.

Insofar as we act collectively, on the other hand, only humans can be afforded an opportunity to participate in the collective decisions. Penguins cannot vote now and are unlikely subjects for the franchise—pine trees more unlikely still. Again each individual is free to cast his vote so as to benefit sugar pines if that is his inclination. But many of the more extreme assertions that one hears from some conservationists amount to tacit assertions that they are specially appointed representatives of sugar pines, and hence that their preferences should be weighted more heavily than the preferences of other humans who do not enjoy equal rapport with "nature." The simplistic assertion that agricultural use of DDT must stop at once because it is harmful to penguins is of that type.

Fifth, if polar bears or pine trees or penguins, like men, are to be regarded as ends rather than means, if they are to count in our calculus of social organization, someone must tell me how much each one counts, and someone must tell me how these life-forms are to be permitted to express their preferences, for I do not know either answer. If the answer is that certain people are to hold their proxies, then I want to know how those proxy-holders are to be selected: self-appointment does not seem workable to me.

Sixth, and by way of summary of all the foregoing, let me point out that the set of environmental issues under discussion—although they raise very complex technical questions of how to achieve any objective—ultimately raise a normative question: what *ought* we to do? Questions of *ought* are unique to the human mind and world—they are meaningless as applied to a nonhuman situation.

I reject the proposition that we *ought* to respect the "balance of nature" or to "preserve the environment" unless the reason for doing so, express or implied, is the benefit of man.

I reject the idea that there is a "right" or "morally correct" state of nature to which we should return. The word "nature" has no normative connotation. Was it "right" or "wrong" for the earth's crust to heave in contortion and create mountains and seas? Was it "right" for the first amphibian to crawl up out of the primordial ooze? Was it "wrong" for plants to reproduce themselves and alter the atmospheric composition in favor of oxygen? For animals to alter the atmosphere in favor of carbon dioxide both by breathing oxygen and eating plants? No answers can be given to these questions because they are meaningless questions.

All this may seem obvious to the point of being tedious, but much of the present controversy over environment and pollution rests on tacit normative assumptions about just such nonnormative phenomena: that it is "wrong" to impair penguins with DDT, but not to slaughter cattle for prime rib roasts. That it is wrong to kill stands of sugar pines with industrial fumes, but not to cut sugar pines and build housing for the poor. Every man is entitled to his own preferred definition of Walden Pond, but there is no definition that has any moral superiority over another, except by reference to the selfish needs of the human race.

From the fact that there is no normative definition of the natural state, it follows that there is no normative definition of clean air or pure water—hence no definition of polluted air—or of pollution—except by reference to the needs of man. The "right" composition of the atmosphere is one which has some dust in it and some lead in it and some hydrogen sulfide in it—just those amounts that attend a sensibly organized society thoughtfully and knowledgeably pursuing the greatest possible satisfaction for its human members.

The first and most fundamental step toward solution of our environmental problems is a clear recognition that our objective is not pure air or water but rather some optimal state of pollution. That step immediately suggests the question: How do we define and attain the level of pollution that will yield the maximum possible amount of human satisfaction?

Low levels of pollution contribute to human satisfaction but so do food and shelter and education and music. To attain ever lower levels of pollution, we must pay the cost of having less of these other things. I contrast that view of the cost of pollution control with the more popular statement that pollution control will "cost" very large numbers of dollars. The popular statement is true in some senses, false in others; sorting out the true and false senses is of some importance. The first step in that sorting process is to achieve a clear understanding of the difference between dollars and resources. Resources are the wealth of our nation; dollars are merely claim checks upon those resources. Resources are of vital importance; dollars are comparatively trivial.

Four categories of resources are sufficient for our purposes: at any given time a nation, or a planet if you prefer, has a stock of labor, of technological skill, of capital goods, and of natural resources (such as mineral deposits, timber, water, land, etc.). These resources can be used in various combinations to yield goods and services of all kinds—in some limited quantity. The quantity will be larger if they are combined efficiently, smaller if combined inefficiently. But in either event the resource stock is limited, the goods and services that they can be made to yield are limited; even the most efficient use of them will yield less than our population, in the aggregate, would like to have.

If one considers building a new dam, it is appropriate to say that it will be costly in the sense that it will require x hours of labor, y tons of steel and concrete, and z amount of capital goods. If these resources are devoted to the dam, then they cannot be used to build hospitals, fishing rods, schools, or electric can openers. That is the meaningful sense in which the dam is costly.

Quite apart from the very important question of how wisely we can combine our resources to produce goods and services is the very different question of how they get distributed—who gets how many goods? Dollars constitute the claim checks which are distributed among people and which control their share of national output. Dollars are nearly valueless pieces of paper except to the extent that they do represent claim checks to some fraction of the output of goods and services. Viewed as claim checks, all the dollars outstanding during any period of time are worth, in the aggregate, the goods and services that are available to be claimed with them during that period—neither more nor less.

It is far easier to increase the supply of dollars than to increase the production of goods and services—printing dollars is easy. But printing more dollars doesn't help because each dollar then simply becomes a claim to fewer goods, i.e., becomes worth less.

The point is this: many people fall into error upon hearing the statement that the decision to build a dam, or to clean up a river, will cost $X million. It is regrettably easy to say: "It's only money. This is a wealthy country, and we have lots of money." But you cannot build a dam or clean a river with $X million—unless you also have a match, you can't even make a fire. One builds a dam or cleans a river by diverting labor and steel and trucks and factories from making one kind of goods to making another. The cost in dollars is merely a shorthand way of describing the extent of the diversion necessary. If we build a dam for $X million, then we must recognize that we will have $X million less housing and food and medical care and electric can openers as a result.

Similarly, the costs of controlling pollution are best expressed in terms of the other goods we will have to give up to do the job. This is not to say the job should not be done. Badly as we need more housing, more medical care, and more can openers, and more symphony orchestras, we could do with somewhat less of them, in my judgment at least, in exchange for somewhat cleaner air and rivers. But that is the nature of the trade-off, and analysis of the problem is advanced if that unpleasant reality is kept in mind. Once the trade-off relationship is clearly perceived, it is possible to state in a very general way what the optimal level of pollution is. I would state it as follows:

People enjoy watching penguins. They enjoy relatively clean air and smog-free vistas. Their health is improved by relatively clean water and air. Each of these benefits is a type of good or service. As a society we would be well advised to give up one washing machine if the resources that would have gone into that washing machine can yield greater human satisfaction when diverted into pollution control. We should give up one hospital if the resources thereby freed would yield more human satisfaction when devoted to elimination of noise in our cities. And so on, trade-off by trade-off, we should divert our productive capacities from the production of existing goods and services to the production of a cleaner, quieter, more pastoral nation up to—and no further than—the point at which we value more highly the next washing machine or hospital that we would have to do without than we value the next unit of environmental improvement that the diverted resources would create.

Now this proposition seems to me unassailable but so general and abstract as to be unhelpful—at least unadministerable in the form stated. It assumes we can measure in some way the incremental units of human satisfaction yielded by very different types of goods. The proposition must remain a pious abstraction until I can explain how this measurement process can occur. . . . But I insist that the proposition stated describes the result for which we should be striving—and again, that it is always useful to know what your target is even if your weapons are too crude to score a bull's eye.

Review and Discussion Questions

1. What are the practical implications of Baxter's human-centered, cost-benefit approach to environmental issues? How sympathetic are you to his approach? What do you see as its strong points? Its weak points?

2. Assess each of Baxter's six reasons for claiming that his is the best starting point for examining environmental issues.

3. What exactly does Baxter mean by saying that "questions of *ought* are unique to the human mind and world—they are meaningless as applied to a nonhuman situation"? Does the fact that only human beings are moral agents imply that human beings can have moral responsibilities only to other human beings?

4. Is Baxter right in arguing that there is no right or wrong level of pollution independent of human needs?

5. How would Peter Singer reply to Baxter's arguments? How does Stone's perspective contrast with Baxter's?

6. Does the idea of an optimal level of pollution make sense? If so, how do we determine that level? Is it possible to calculate it or to reach agreement on trade-offs between environmental goods and other goods?

The Search for an Environmental Ethic

J. BAIRD CALLICOTT

J. Baird Callicott, professor of philosophy at the University of Wisconsin, Stevens Point, and author of *In Defense of the Land Ethic,* rejects traditional human-centered approaches to environmental ethics like William F. Baxter's and is also critical of attempts like Peter Singer's to extend traditional morality to include nonhuman sentient beings. Instead, Callicott advocates a holistic or ecocentric environmental ethic based on the "land ethic" of environmentalist Aldo Leopold. Central to an ecosystemic or holistic environmental ethic is the concept of the global ecosystem or biotic community, of which all forms of life on our planet are fellow members. Human beings are members of this community, not the conquerors of nature. Such a perspective, Callicott insists, implies respect for fellow members of the community and for the biotic community as a whole. Callicott defends an ecocentric environmental ethic against the charge that it is anti-human and concludes by discussing what living in accord with such an ethic would mean for our lives.

Study Questions

1. What is the traditional humanistic approach to environmental ethics? On what basis does Callicott criticize it?

2. What is "extensionism"? What are Callicott's reasons for rejecting it as an adequate environmental ethic?

3. What does Callicott mean by describing his ethic as "holistic," "ecocentric," and "ecosystemic"?

4. How do some traditional American Indian cultures illustrate the ethical perspective Callicott advocates?

5. What are the implications of Callicott's ethic for our treatment of animals?

Three Secular Approaches to Environmental Ethics

Since the emergence of a broad awareness of the environmental crisis and an evolutionary-ecological world view, professional philosophers have attempted to construct a logically coherent, adequate, and practicable *theory* of environmental ethics without reference to God or to his "creation." Three main secular theoretical approaches have, in this interval, clearly emerged. They are as follows:

1. *Traditional and protracted humanism:* business-as-usual Western human-centered ethics, in which moral standing is sometimes accorded to human beings of future generations.

2. *Extensionism:* the extension of moral standing and/or moral rights from human beings inclusively to wider and wider classes of *individual* nonhuman natural entities.

3. *Ecocentrism:* moral consideration for the ecosystem *as a whole* and for its various subsystems as well as for human and non-human natural entities severally.

I shall argue that the third approach, ecocentrism, is the best approach to environmental ethics. It is, I think, by far the most coherent in both senses, viz., that it is (1) self-consistent and, just as important, (2) consistent with the larger pattern of ideas that gave rise to environmental awareness and concern in the first place. It is, I also think, the most adequate: it *directly* and *effectively* addresses the moral problems that it is supposed to help us resolve. And finally, of the three secular approaches to environmental ethics so far developed, I think it is the most practicable—in the sense that the limitations it would impose on human behavior vis-à-vis the environment are limitations that will help the environment to prosper *and* human beings to live and live well.

Traditional and Protracted Humanism

The traditional humanistic approach to environmental ethics treats the environment merely as a "pool" of "resources" and as an "arena" of human interaction and potential conflict that the science of ecology has recently revealed to be much more complex than previously supposed. The adverse effects human beings may have upon other human beings *indirectly* through things they may do *directly* to the environment—like "developing" and consuming it and treating it as a sink for wastes—have recently become amplified, moreover, by ballooning human numbers and more powerful and/or more toxic technologies. According to philosopher Kristin Shrader-Frechette, a leading advocate of this approach,

> it is difficult to think of an action which would do irreparable damage to the environment or ecosystem, but which would not also threaten human well-being. . . . if a polluter dumps toxic wastes in a river, this action could be said to be wrong . . . because the "interests" of the river are violated, but also . . . because there are human interests in having clean water (e.g. for recreation and for drinking).[1]

Therefore, we don't need a *new* environmental ethic to set out what human beings may and may not do to nonhuman natural entities and nature as a whole. Our old ethics of equal moral consideration and/or justice for all human beings are quite adequate—especially if by "all" we intend future as well as presently existing human beings, as in protracted humanism.

A Critique of the Traditional and Protracted Humanism Approach

. . . I . . . doubt that a human-centered ethic for the use of the environment would in fact prohibit human harms to the environment as strictly as any other ethic. To take Shrader-Frechette's own example, a polluting industry might generously compensate the affected *people* for the loss of the recreational amenity afforded by a clean river and provide them an alternative source of drinking water. Upon this approach to environmental ethics, the industry could then ethically go on using the river as a dump for its toxic wastes. Although fish, birds, and the river itself would continue to suffer disease, death, and degradation, the "interests" of the affected human parties would be fairly balanced.

However, *even if Shrader-Frechette is right* that "existing utilitarian and egalitarian ethical theories [are adequate] to safeguard the environment," an inconsistency . . . lies at the core of this approach to environmental ethics. Its advocates seem at once ecologically well informed and ecologically unenlightened. According to both the traditional and protracted humanistic approaches to environmental ethics, ecology only complicates human-to-human intercourse, both in the present and across generations; it does not transform our vision of what it means to be human.

Norwegian philosopher Arne Naess and his American exponents Bill Devall and George Sessions call these approaches to environmental ethics "shallow" as opposed to "deep" ecology. Ecology is acknowledged or intellectually affirmed in one area or at one level of thought—relations of cause and effect in the nonhuman natural environment—but it is ignored or denied at another level or area of thought—the general structure of nature and the embeddedness of people within that structure. From an evolutionary-ecological point of view, we are "kin" to the fellow members of the biotic community. Our actions in respect to these fellow members should somehow be *directly* morally accountable, and the integrity of this community per se, the health of the planetary organism, should somehow be of *direct* moral concern. . . .

Extensionism

A second approach to environmental ethics attempts conceptually to articulate and theoretically to ground moral concern *directly* for the environment by extending or stretching traditional Western humanistic moral theory so that it recognizes the moral standing of some nonhuman natural entities. It was first developed, most notably by Peter Singer, as a theory which would extend moral considerability to fellow *sentient* beings (beings capable of experiencing pleasure and pain) without reference to the environment at large or environmental problems per se.[2] . . .

Peter Singer's criterion of sentiency for equal consideration or equal moral standing is not an adequate basis for an ethical theory to address the major moral issues of animal welfare, let alone an adequate basis for a theory of environmental ethics. Singer himself considers meat eating immoral and, throughout his book *Animal Liberation*, insists that people ought, *morally* ought, to become vegetarians. Bentham, the original advocate of sentiency as a criterion for moral considerability, however, recognized that it is perfectly possible to raise animals in comfort and to slaughter them painlessly; thus he would support the view that human carnivorousness is perfectly consistent with a sentiency-based animal welfare ethic. If everyone were a vegetarian, many fewer cows, pigs, chickens, and other domestic livestock would be raised and thus many fewer animals would have the opportunity, for an allotted time, to pursue happiness. One might therefore argue, on Singer's own grounds, that people have a positive moral obligation to eat meat *provided that the animals raised for human consumption were raised in comfort and given the opportunity to live happily.* Even sport hunting—long regarded by some concerned about animal welfare to be the most odious because the most gratuitous abuse of animals—would be permissible on Singer's grounds *provided that hunters deliver a clean kill and by so doing preserve animals from greater suffering from the vicissitudes of life in the wild,* while as a bonus benefit also giving themselves pleasure.

Recognizing these (and other) inadequacies of Singer's moral theory in relation to the moral problems of the treatment of animals, Tom Regan has advocated a "rights" approach to address them.[3] Regan postulates that some individual animals have "inherent worth" because they are, like ourselves, not only sentient but *subjects of a life* that from their point of view can be better or worse. Inherent worth, in turn, may be the grounds of basic moral rights. I am persuaded that Regan's representation of animal rights in his book *The Case for Animal Rights* adequately supports the basic moral agenda of those concerned primarily for individual animal welfare: an end to (1) meat eating, (2) the use of animals in "scientific" experimentation, and (3) hunting and trapping.

A Critique of Extensionism in Relation to Environmental Problems

Clearly, however, neither Singer's theory of animal liberation nor Regan's theory of animal rights will do double duty as an environmental ethic. For one thing, most obviously neither animal liberation nor animal rights provides for direct moral consideration of plants and all the many animals that may not be either sentient or, more restrictively still, "subjects of a life." But the brunt of environmental destruction is borne by plants helplessly in the path of chain saws and bulldozers, and the bulk of rare and endangered species are neither sentient nor subjects of a life as Regan defines this concept. . . .

A *sentiency centered* and/or *subject-of-a-life centered* environmental ethic would result, no less than traditional and protracted humanism, in a mere management ethic, an ethic for using the environment by sentient or subject-of-a-life animals (including humans, of course) for their own sake. While not an anthropocentric ethic, it would nonetheless be a management ethic. Animal liberation/rights broaden the base class of morally considerable beings (the former more widely than the latter), but not by very much relative to the millions of plant and invertebrate forms of life making up earth's biotic community. So plants and invertebrate animals, the vast majority of earth's living denizens, remain mere means to be managed for the good of the morally privileged class of sentient or subject-of-a-life animals. . . .

Animal liberation/animal rights seems very well informed by one of modern biology's two great theoretical cornerstones, the theory of evolution, while not at all by the other, ecology.

Animal liberation/rights rests in part on the basic notion that there is no essential *morally relevant* difference between mankind and mankind's closest kin in the phylogenetic scale. But the *ecological* order of nature is premised on one fundamental principle—all life (even plant life, for plant nutrients must be recycled) depends upon death. Death and often pain are at the heart of nature's economy. To the extent that the animal liberation/animal rights ethics condemn the taking of life (as a violation of the rights of a subject of life) or the infliction of pain on a sentient being, they are irreconcilably at odds with the ecological "facts of life."

To develop this point more particularly, a ruthlessly consistent deduction of the consequences of both the Singerian and Reganic ethics *might* imply a program of humane predator extermination. For sound ecological reasons, the conservation and reintroduction of predators are among the highest priorities on the agenda of current environmental goals. Predatory fishes, reptiles, birds, and mammals, however, cause a great deal of suffering to other innocent animals. If carnivorous animals could be rounded up, housed comfortably in zoos, fed soyburgers, sterilized, and allowed to die natural deaths, then only herbivorous animals would remain in nature and the total amount of pain and suffering might be vastly reduced. . . .

Both Singer and Regan . . . admit that rare and endangered species are provided no special, preemptory status by their respective theories. And yet species extirpation and extinction is today widely recognized as the single most pressing problem among the spectrum of problems collectively called the environmental crisis. The specimens of most endangered species, moreover, are neither sentient nor subjects of a life. They are, rather, plants and invertebrates. Hence, if there were a mortal conflict between, say, an endangered plant *species* and *individual* sentient or subject-of-a-life animals, there could be no *moral* reason to choose to save the plant species at the expense of the lives of plentiful individual animals, according to animal liberation/rights.

Environmental philosopher Holmes Rolston III reports with approval an action of the National Park Service in which hundreds of rabbits on Santa Barbara Island were killed "to protect a few plants . . . once thought extinct and curiously called the Santa Barbara Live Forever."[4] Since in this and similar cases, the animal liberation/rights ethics would give preference to the sentient/subject-of-a-life animals, the environmental problem of species extinction would be not merely ignored; it would be aggravated, at least for the vast majority of threatened species.

Animal liberation/rights, finally, does not discriminate between the value of domestic and wild animals, since both are equally sentient and/or subjects of a life. However, most environmentalists regard the intrusion of domestic animals into natural ecosystems as very destructive and therefore prima facie contrary to an environmental ethic. . . . Since domestic livestock and wild animals are equally sentient and/or equally subjects of a life and a pasture can support more cows than deer in a woods of the same size, the animal liberation/animal rights ethic cannot, as an environmentalist would prefer, condemn the former and commend the latter.

An ecologically well-informed environmental ethic would draw a moral distinction among animals along another axis than that drawn by animal liberation/rights. Rather than providing moral standing or rights to animals that are sentient or subjects of a life and withholding standing or rights from those that are not, an ecologically oriented environmental ethic would provide preferred moral consideration (and possibly rights) to wild animals, whether or not sentient or subjects of a life, and regard domestic animals as, for all practical purposes, a kind of human technology to be evaluated, like all other technologies, in terms of environmental impact. The environmental impact of domestic animals might be benign—as, for example, that of domestic bees—but from the ecological point of view, environmental impact should be the *primary* consideration governing the treatment of man-made animals originally designed for human utility. . . .

A Plea for a Holistic Approach to Environmental Ethics

. . . A holistic or ecocentric environmental ethic was outlined in *A Sand County Almanac,* the widely read and admired "gospel" of environmental philosophy by Aldo Leopold. For the most part, contemporary moral philosophers searching for a coherent, adequate, and practicable environmental ethic have failed to explore and develop Leopold's "land ethic" to the extent that they have, for example, Bentham's even briefer remarks about the moral considerability of sentient animals. This is, in large measure, because a holistic approach to ethics is so unfamiliar and represents such a radical departure from long-established modern traditions of Western moral philosophy. . . .

Transition from Humanistic to Environmental Ethics

According to Aldo Leopold, "All ethics so far evolved rest upon a single premise: that the individual is a member of a community of interdependent parts. . . . The land ethic simply enlarges the boundaries of the community to include soils, waters, plants, and animals, or collectively: the land."[5] . . .

Now, the general world view of the modern life sciences *represents* all forms of life on the planet Earth both as *kin* and as fellow members of a social unit—*the biotic community.* The Earth may now be *perceived* not, as once it was, the unique physical center of the universe but rather a mere planet orbiting around an ordinary star at the edge of a galaxy containing billions of similar stars in a universe containing billions of such galaxies. In the context of this universal spatial-temporal frame of reference, the planet Earth is very small and very local indeed, an island paradise in a vast desert of largely empty space containing physically hostile foreign bodies separated from Earth by immense distances. All the denizens of this cosmic island paradise evolved into their myriad contemporary forms from a simple, single-cell common ancestor. All contemporary forms of life thus are represented to be *kin, relatives, members of one extended family.* And all are equally members in good standing of one *society* or *community,* the biotic community or global ecosystem.

This cosmic/evolutionary/ecological picture of the Earth and its biota can actuate the moral sentiments of affection, respect, love, and sympathy with which we human mammals are genetically endowed. It also actuates the special sentiment or feeling (call it "patriotism"), noticed by both Hume and Darwin, that we have for the *group as a whole* to which we belong, the *family* per se, the *tribe,* and the *country* or *nation.* From the point of view of modern biology, the earth with its living mantle is our tribe and each of its myriad species is, as it were, a separate clan.

Thus the land ethic—in sharp contrast to traditional Western humanism and its protracted and extended variations—provides moral standing for both environmental *individuals* and for the environment *as a whole.* In Leopold's words, "a land ethic changes the role of *Homo sapiens* from conqueror of the land community to plain member and citizen of it. It implies respect for fellow-members *and also* respect for the community as such."[6]

Holism

Respect for wholes, for the community as such and its various subsystems, is a theoretical possibility for the land ethic because it is conceptually and historically related to the Humean-Darwinian theoretical complex. Both individual members of society and the community as such, the social whole (together with its component divisions), are the objects of certain special, naturally selected moral sentiments. Beauty may be in the eye of the beholder, but it does not follow from this that only the eye of the beholder is beautiful. Similarly, there may be no value without valuers, but it does not follow from this that only valuers are valuable. Both beauty and intrinsic value are bivalent concepts; that is, both involve subjective and objective factors. *Intrinsic value* is, as it were, "projected" onto appropriate objects by virtue of certain naturally selected and inherited *intentional* feelings, some of which (patriotism, or love of country, is perhaps the most familiar example) simply have social wholes as their natural objects. We may value our community per se, for the sake of itself, just as we may value our children for the sake of themselves. Wholes may thus have intrinsic value no less problematically than individuals. . . .

The stress upon the value of the biotic community is the distinguishing characteristic of the land ethic and its cardinal strength as an *adequate* environmental ethic. The land ethic directs us to take the welfare of nature—the diversity, stability, and integrity of the biotic community or, to mix metaphors, the health of the land organism—to be the standard of the moral quality, the rightness or wrongness, of our actions. Practically, this means that we should assess the "environmental impact" of any proposed project, whether it be a personal, corporate, or public undertaking, and choose that course of action which will enhance the diversity, integrity, beauty, and stability of the biotic community, the health and well-being of the land organism. . . .

The Dangers of an Untempered Holistic Environmental Ethic

But, as with so many things, the cardinal strength of the land ethic is also its cardinal weakness. What are the moral (to say nothing of the economic) costs of the land ethic? Most seriously, it would seem to imply a draconian policy toward the human population, since almost all ecologists and environmentalists agree that, from the perspective of the integrity, diversity, and stability of the biotic community, there are simply too many people and too few redwoods, white pines, wolves, bears, tigers, elephants, whales, and so on. Philosopher William Aiken has recoiled in horror from the land ethic, since in his view it would imply that "massive human diebacks would be good. It is our species' duty to eliminate 90 percent of our numbers."[7] It would also seem to imply a merciless attitude toward nonhuman individual members of

the biotic community. Sentient members of overabundant species, like rabbits and deer, may be (as actually presently they are) routinely culled, for the sake of the ecosystems of which they are a part, by hunting or other methods of liquidation. . . . From the perspective of both humanism and its humane extension, the land ethic appears nightmarish in its own peculiar way. It seems more properly the "ethic" of a termitarium or beehive than of anything analogous to a human community. It appears richly to deserve Tom Regan's epithet "environmental fascism."

The Relation of the Land Ethic to Prior Accretions

Despite Leopold's narrative drift away from attention to *members* of the biotic community to the *community per se* and despite some of Leopold's more radical exponents who have confrontationally stressed the holistic dimension of the land ethic, its theoretical foundations yield a subtler, richer, far more complex system of morals than simple environmental holism. The land ethic is the latest step in an evolutionary sequence, according to its own theoretical foundations. Each succeeding step in social-moral evolution—from the savage clan to the family of man—does not cancel or invalidate the earlier stages. Rather, each succeeding stage is layered over the earlier ones, which remain operative. . . . That I am now a member of the global human community, and hence have correlative moral obligations to all mankind, does not mean that I am no longer a member of my own family and citizen of my local community and of my country or that I am relieved of the peculiar and special limitations on freedom of action attendant upon these relationships.

The Place of Human Beings in the Land Ethic

Therefore, just as the existence of a global human community with its humanitarian ethic does not submerge and override smaller, more primitive human communities and their moral codes, neither does the newly discovered existence of a global biotic community and its land ethic submerge and override the global human community and its humanitarian ethic. To seriously propose, then, that to preserve the integrity, beauty, and stability of the biotic community we ought summarily to eliminate 90 percent of the current human population is . . . morally skewed. . . .

To agree that the human population should not, in gross and wanton violation of our humanitarian moral code, be immediately reduced by deliberate acts of war or by equally barbaric means does not imply that the human population should not be scaled down, as time goes on, by means and methods that are conscionable from a humanitarian point of view. How obligations across the outermost rings of our nested sociomoral matrix may be weighed and compared is admittedly uncertain—just as uncertain as how one should weigh and compare one's duty, say, to one's family against one's duty to one's country. . . .

The Place of Individual Nonhumans in the Land Ethic

Richard Sylvan and Val Plumwood have developed the view that Leopold briefly suggests, namely, that an ecosystemic ethic primarily provides not rights but *respect* for individual nonhuman members of the biotic community. Although the concept of respect is singular and simple, its practical implications are varied and complex. These thinkers further suggest that American Indian environmental attitudes and values provide a well-developed, rich exemplar of *respectful* participation in the economy of nature, a participation that permits human beings morally to eat and otherwise consumptively to utilize their fellow citizens of the organic society:

> The view that the land, animals, and the natural world should be treated with *respect* was a common one in many hunting-gathering societies. . . . Respect adds a moral dimension to

relations with the natural world. . . . The conventional wisdom of Western society tends to offer a false dichotomy of use versus respectful non-use . . . of using animals, for example, in the ways characteristic of large-scale mass-production farming . . . *or* on the other hand of not making use of animals at all. . . . What is left out of this choice is the alternative the Indians . . . recognized . . . of limited and respectful use. . . .[8]

A great deal of controversy has surrounded the hypothesis of an American Indian land ethic. Recent studies, empirically based upon actual cultural materials, have shown beyond reasonable doubt that at least some American Indian cultures did in fact have an ecosystemic or environmental ethic *and* that such an ethic maps conceptually upon the Leopold land ethic.[9] In other words, some American Indian cultures—among them, for example, the Ojibwa of the western Great Lakes—represented the plants and animals of their environment as engaged in *social* and *economic* intercourse with one another and with human beings. And such a social picture of human-environment interaction gave rise to correlative moral attitudes and behavioral restraints. The Ojibwa cultural narratives (myths, stories, and tales), which served as the primary vehicles of enculturation or education, repeatedly stress that animals, plants, and even rocks and rivers (natural entities that Western culture regards as inanimate) are *persons* engaged in reciprocal, mutually beneficial exchange with human beings. A cardinal precept embellished again and again in these narratives is that nonhuman natural entities, both individually and as species, must be treated with respect and restraint. The Ojibwa were primarily a hunting-gathering people, which perforce involved them in killing animals as well as plants for food, clothing, and shelter. But they nevertheless represented the animals and plants of their biotic community as *voluntarily* participating in a mannerized economic exchange with people who, for their part, gave tokens of gratitude and reimbursement and offered guest friendship. . . .

Modern Life in Accordance with an Ecosystemic Environmental Ethic

Of course, most people today do not live by hunting and gathering. Nevertheless, the general ideal provided by American Indian cultures of respectful, restrained, mutually beneficial human use of the environment is certainly applicable in today's context. An ecosystemic environmental ethic does not prohibit human use of the environment; it requires, rather, that that use be subject to two ethical limitations. The first is holistic, the second individualistic.

The first requires that human use of the environment, as nearly as possible, should enhance the diversity, integrity, stability, and beauty of the biotic community. Biologist René Dubos has argued that Western Europe was, prior to the industrial revolution, biologically richer *as a result* of human settlement and cultivation. The creation and cultivation of small fields, hedgerows, and forest edges measurably (objectively and quantitatively) enhanced the diversity and integrity and certainly the beauty of the preindustrial European landscape. . . . Human occupation and use of the environment from the perspective of the quality of the environment as a whole does not *have* to be destructive. On the contrary, it can be. . . . mutually beneficial.

The second, individualistic ethical limitation on human use of the environment requires that trees cut for shelter or to make fields, animals slain for food or for fur, and so on should be thoughtfully selected, skillfully and humanely dispatched, and carefully used so as to neither waste nor degrade them. The *individual* plant, animal, or even rock or river consumed or transformed by human use deserves to be used respectfully.

Surely we can envision an eminently livable, modern, systemic, *civilized* technological society well adapted to and at peace and in harmony with its organic environment. Human technological civilization can live not merely in peaceful coexistence but in benevolent symbiosis with nature.

Is our current *mechanical* technological civilization the only one imaginable? Aren't there alternative technologies? Isn't it possible to envision, for example, a human civilization based upon non-polluting solar energy for domestic use, manufacturing, and transportation and small-scale, soil-conserving organic agriculture? There would be fewer material *things* and more *services, information,* and opportunity for aesthetic and recreational *activities;* fewer people and more bears; fewer parking lots and more wilderness. I think it is possible. . . .

In the meantime, while such an adaptive organic civilization gradually evolves out of our present grotesque mechanical civilization, the most important injunction of ecosystemic ethics remains the one stressed by Leopold—subject, of course, to the humanitarian, humane, and life-respecting qualifications that, as I have just argued, are theoretically consistent with it. We should strive to preserve the diversity, stability, and integrity of the biotic community.

Before ending, it is appropriate to ask what the implications of an ecocentric ethic would be for our daily lives. After all, one value of this ethic, no less than any other, is that it gives meaning to choices that otherwise remain unconscious or arbitrary. If, as I have claimed, an ecocentric ethic is the most practicable environmental ethic, how does it actually inform our real-life choices?

Integrating an ecocentric ethic into our lives would provide new criteria for choices we make everyday in virtually every arena of our lives. Some of these choices are obvious; others, less so.

Most obviously, because a vegetarian diet, more directly and efficiently than a meat-centered diet, conducts solar energy into human bodies, the practice of vegetarianism could not only help reduce human hunger and animal suffering, it would free more land and solar energy for the restoration of natural communities. (Note that eating wild game, respectfully, lawfully, and humanely harvested, would be an exception to the vegetarian implications of ecocentric ethics. Only grain-fed, domestic live-stock should in general be avoided.)

Above all, one should try to avoid fast-food beef (McDonald's, Hardee's, and the like) made mostly from the imported carcasses of cattle, not only because consuming such food contributes to the political and economic causes of hunger in the countries from which it is exported, but also because it is produced on lands once covered by rain-forests. Hence, the consumption of such foods not only implicates one (in all probability) in the destructive politics of world hunger and the disrespectful use of animals, it implicates one (almost certainly) in the extinction of endemic species (those specifically adapted to particular rain-forest habitats).

But what we eat is only the most obvious link between our daily choices and the integrity of the biotic community of which we are part. In a multitude of other roles, our choices either contribute to its regeneration or its continued ruin. As *consumers,* do we weigh our purchases according to the environmental consequences of their production? As *students,* do we utilize our learning time to hone our knowledge and sensibilities so as to more effectively live an eco-centric ethic? As *citizens,* of both a nation and a community, do we elect leaders whose policies ignore the need for environmental protection and reparation? As *workers,* do we choose to be employed by corporations whose activities degrade the environment? As *parents and indi-viduals whose opinions necessarily influence others,* do we work to impart to others an understand-ing of the importance of an ecocentric ethic? As *decisionmakers over resources*—from real estate to other large or small assets—do we assume responsibility for their use? Or do we simply turn a blind eye, allowing others to use them for envi-ronmentally destructive ends?

Asking ourselves such questions, we discover that the implications of an ecocentric ethic cannot be reduced to one or even several major life choices. Rather, the contribution of an ecocentric ethic is to be found in the myriad of mundane, even banal decisions we make everyday. A

grounding in an ecocentric ethic would thus shape the entire unfolding of one's life.

The second most serious moral issue of our times—second only to our individual and collec-tive responsibility to prevent thermonuclear holocaust—is our responsibility to preserve the biological diversity of the earth. Later, when an appropriately humble, sane, ecocentric civiliza-tion comes into being, as I believe it will, its gov-ernment and citizens will set about rehabilitating this bruised and tattered planet. For their work, they must have as great a library of genetic mate-rial as it is possible for us to save. Hence, it must be our immediate goal to prevent further destruc-tion of the biosphere, to save what species we can, and to preserve the biotic diversity and beauty that remain.

NOTES

1. K. S. Shrader-Frechette, *Environmental Ethics.* Pacific Grove, Calif.: Boxwood, 1981, p. 17.
2. Peter Singer, *Animal Liberation: A New Ethics for Our Treatment of Animals.* New York: Avon, 1975.
3. Tom Regan, *The Case for Animal Rights.* Berkeley, Calif.: The University of California Press, 1983.
4. Holmes Rolston III, "Duties to Endangered Species," p. 8. Unpublished paper presented to the Environmental Ethics—New Directions Conference, Oct. 4–6, 1984, at the University of Georgia.
5. Aldo Leopold, *A Sand County Almanac.* New York: Ballantine, 1966, p. 239.
6. *Ibid.,* p. 240.
7. William Aiken, "Ethical Issues in Agriculture," in Tom Regan, ed., *Earthbound: New Introductory Essays in Environmental Ethics.* New York: Random House, 1984, p. 269.
8. Richard Sylvan and Val Plumwood, "Human Chauvinism and Environmental Ethics," in D. Mannison, M. McRobbie, and R. Routley, eds., *Environmental Philosophy.* Canberra, Australia: Australian National University, 1980, pp. 178–179.
9. Cf. Thomas W. Overholt and J. Baird Callicott, *Clothed-in-Fur and Other Tales: An Introduction to an Ojibwa World View.* Washington, D.C.: University Press of America, 1982; and J. Baird Callicott, "American Indian and Western European Attitudes Toward Nature: An Overview," *Environmental Ethics* 4 (1982): 293–318.

Review and Discussion Questions

1. What are the practical implications for our day-to-day lives of Callicott's holistic environmental ethic? Do you find these implications acceptable?

2. How would Baxter respond to Callicott's rejection of a humanistic approach? With whom do you agree, and why?

3. Callicott is critical of Singer's position, which he finds less adequate than a "rights" approach. How persuasive do you find his criticism?

4. Assess Callicott's reasons for arguing that extensionism does not provide a satisfactory environmental ethic. How do you think extensionists like Singer and Regan (cited in this essay) would respond?

5. How does Callicott's approach differ from the extensionists' with regard to our treatment of animals? Whose perspective do you find the soundest and most plausible?

6. At the beginning of the essay, Callicott claims that his ethic is more coherent, addresses the moral problems more directly and effectively, and is more practicable than rival environmental ethics. Assess these claims.

Why You Are Committed to the Immorality of Eating Meat

MYLAN ENGEL, JR.

This essay by Mylan Engel, Jr., professor of philosophy at Northern Illinois University, returns to an issue raised by Peter Singer and touched upon by J. Baird Callicott, namely, the morality or immorality of eating meat. Engel's essay appears at the end of this section because he endeavors to develop the ethical case against eating meat and for vegetarianism in a way that is independent of the various philosophical issues disputed by Singer, Machan, Stone, Baxter, and Callicott, for example, whether speciesism is warranted, whether only human beings have rights, whether human beings and animals have comparable value, and whether we should transcend traditional human-centered ethics toward a more bio-centered moral perspective. Engel argues that, given the reality of factory farming and given the fact that eating meat is not nutritionally necessary, various commonplace moral beliefs—beliefs that readers of this book almost certainly hold—imply that eating meat is immoral. In other words, the things you already believe commit you, on pain of inconsistency, to becoming a vegetarian.

Study Questions

1. What is Engel's basic argumentative strategy and how does it differ from that of Peter Singer?

2. What are the main reasons given by Engel for believing that factory farming is cruel?

3. What are the main ethical beliefs that, according to Engel, imply that we should stop purchasing and consuming meat?

4. What impact does the meat industry have on the environment?

5. What is the main evidence that meat consumption is not necessary for human survival?

MOST ARGUMENTS FOR THE MORAL OBLIGATORINESS of vegetarianism take one of two forms. Either they follow Singer's lead and demand equal consideration for animals on utilitarian grounds, or they follow Regan's deontological rights-based approach and insist that most of the animals we routinely consume possess the very same rights-conferring properties that confer rights on humans. While many people have been persuaded to alter their dietary habits on the basis of one of these arguments, most philosophers have not. . . . My aim is to . . . provid[e] an argument for the immorality of eating meat that does not rest on any particular ethical theory. Rather, it rests on beliefs that you already hold.[1]

Before turning to your beliefs, two prefatory observations are in order. First, unlike other ethical arguments for vegetarianism, my argument is *not* predicated on the wrongness of speciesism,[2] *nor* does it depend on your believing that all animals are equal or that all animals have a right to life. . . . My argument is . . . compatible with both an anthropocentric and a biocentric worldview. In short, my argument is designed to show that even those of you who are steadfastly committed to valuing humans over nonhumans are nevertheless committed to the immorality of eating meat, given your other beliefs.

Second, ethical arguments are often context-dependent in that they presuppose a specific audience in a certain set of circumstances. Recognizing what that intended audience and context is, and what it is not, can prevent confusions about the scope of the ethical claim being made. My argument is context-dependent in precisely this way. It is not aimed at those relatively few indigenous peoples who, because of the paucity of edible vegetable matter available, must eat meat to survive. Rather, it is directed at people, like you, who live in agriculturally bountiful societies in which a wealth of nutritionally adequate alternatives to meat are readily available. Thus, I intend to show that your beliefs commit you to the view that eating meat is morally wrong for anyone who is in the circumstances in which you typically find yourself and *a fortiori* that it is morally wrong for you to eat meat in these circumstances. Enough by way of preamble, on to your beliefs.

1. The Things You Believe

The beliefs attributed to you herein would normally be considered noncontentious. In most contexts, we would take someone who didn't hold these beliefs to be either morally defective or irrational. Of course, in most contexts, these beliefs are not a threat to enjoying hamburgers, hot dogs, steaks, and ribs; but even with burgers in the balance, you will, I think, readily admit believing the following propositions: (p_1) Other things being equal, a world with less pain and suffering is better than a world with more pain and suffering; and (p_2) A world with less unnecessary suffering is better than a world with more unnecessary suffering.[3] . . . Since you think that unnecessary suffering is an intrinsically bad state of affairs, you no doubt also believe: (p_3) Unnecessary cruelty is wrong and *prima facie* should not be supported or encouraged. You probably believe: (p_4) We ought to take steps to make the world a better place. But even if you reject (p_4) on the grounds that we have no positive duties to benefit, you still think there are negative duties to do no harm, and so you believe: (p_4) We ought to do what we reasonably can to avoid making the world a worse place. You also believe: (p_5) A morally good person will take steps to make the world a better place and even stronger steps to avoid making the world a worse place; and (p_6) Even a "minimally decent person"[4] would take steps to help reduce the amount of unnecessary pain and suffering in the world, *if s/he could do so with little effort on her/his part.*

You also have beliefs about yourself. You believe one of the following propositions . . . : (p_7) I am a morally good person; or (p_8) I am at least a minimally decent person. You also believe of yourself: (p_9) I am the sort of person who certainly would take steps to help reduce the amount of pain and suffering in the world, *if I could do so with little effort on my part.* Enough about you. On to your beliefs about nonhuman animals and our obligations toward them.

You believe: (p_{10}) Many nonhuman animals (certainly all vertebrates) are capable of feeling pain. I do not have to prove (p_{10}). You already believe it, as evidenced by your other beliefs: (p_{11}) Other things being equal, it is morally wrong to cause an animal pain or suffering; and (p_{12}) It is morally wrong and despicable to treat animals inhumanely *for no good reason.* . . . In addition to your beliefs about the wrongness of causing animals unnecessary pain, you also have beliefs about the appropriateness of killing animals, for example, you believe: (p_{13}) We ought to euthanize untreatably injured, suffering animals to put them out of their misery whenever feasible; and (p_{14}) Other things being equal, it is worse to kill a conscious sentient animal than it is to kill a plant. Finally, you believe: (p_{15}) We have a duty to help preserve the environment for future generations (at least for future *human* generations); and consequently, you believe: (p_{16}) One ought to minimize one's contribution toward environmental degradation, *especially in those ways requiring minimal effort on one's part.*

2. Factory Farming and Modern Slaughter: The Cruelty Behind the Cellophane

Before they become someone's dinner, most farm animals raised in the United States are forced to endure intense pain and suffering in "factory farms." Factory farms are intensive confinement facilities where animals are made to live in inhospitable unnatural conditions for the duration of their lives. The first step in intensive farming is early separation of mother and offspring. Chickens are separated from their mothers *before* birth, as they are hatched in incubators and never get to see their mothers; veal calves are removed from their mothers within a few days; and piglets are separated from their mothers two to three weeks after birth. The offspring are then housed in overcrowded confinement facilities. Broiler chickens and turkeys are warehoused in sheds containing anywhere from 10,000–100,000 birds (the poultry industry recommends—but does not require—that each chicken be allotted seven-tenths of a square foot of floor space); veal calves are kept in crates 22″ × 54″ and are chained at the neck, rendering them unable to move or turn around; pigs are confined in metal crates (which provide 6 square feet of living space) situated on concrete slatted floors with no straw or bedding; and beef cattle are housed in feedlots containing up to 100,000 animals. The inappropriate, unforgiving surfaces on which the animals must stand produce chronic foot and leg injuries. Since they cannot move about, they must stand in their own waste. In these cramped, unsanitary conditions, virtually all of the animals' basic instinctual urges (e.g., to nurse, stretch, move around, root, groom, build nests, rut, establish social orders, select mates, copulate, procreate, and rear offspring) are frustrated, causing boredom and stress in the animals. . . .

The animals react to these inhumane, stressful conditions by developing "stereotypies" (i.e., stress- and boredom-induced, neurotic repetitive behaviors) and other unnatural behaviors including cannibalism. For example, chickens unable to develop a pecking order often try to peck each other to death, and pigs, bored due to forced immobility, routinely bite the tail of the pig caged in front of them. To prevent losses due to cannibalism and aggression, the animals receive preemptive mutilations. To prevent chickens and turkeys from pecking each other to death, the birds are "debeaked" using a scalding hot blade that slices through the highly sensitive horn of the beak leaving blisters in the mouth; and to prevent these birds from scratching each other to death (which the industry refers to as "back ripping"), their toes are amputated using the same hot knife machine. Other routine mutilations include dubbing (surgical removal of the combs and wattles of male chickens and turkeys), tail docking, branding, dehorning, ear tagging, ear clipping, teeth pulling, castration, and ovariectomy. In the interest of cost efficiency, *all* of these excruciating procedures are performed *without* anaesthesia. *Unanaesthetized* branding, dehorning, ear tagging, ear clipping, and castration are standard procedures on nonintensive family farms, as well.

Lives of frustration and torment finally culminate as the animals are inhumanely loaded onto trucks and shipped long distance to slaughterhouses without food or water and without adequate protection from the elements. Each year millions of animals die or are severely injured as a result of such handling and transportation. For example, in 1998, USDA inspectors condemned 28,500 ducks, 768,300 turkeys, and 37.6 million chickens before they entered the slaughter plant, because they were either dead or severely injured upon arrival. Once inside the slaughterhouse, the animals are hung upside down (pigs, cattle, and sheep are suspended by one hind leg, which often breaks) and are brought via conveyor to the slaughterer who slits their throats and severs their carotid arteries and jugular veins. In *theory,* animals covered by the Federal Humane Slaughter Act are to be rendered unconscious by electric current or by captive bolt pistol (a pneumatic gun that, when aimed properly, renders the animal unconscious by firing an eight-inch pin

into the animal's skull). Chickens, turkeys, ducks, and geese are not considered animals under the act and receive no protection at all. In *practice,* the act is not enforced, and as a result, many slaughterhouses elect not to use the captive bolt pistol in the interest of cost efficiency. As for electric shock, it is unlikely that being shocked into unconsciousness is a painless process, based on reports of people who have experienced electroconvulsive therapy. A consequence of the lax enforcement of the Federal Humane Slaughter Act is that in many cases (and all kosher cases), the animals are fully conscious throughout the entire throat-slitting ordeal. For some, the agony does not even end here. According to Gail Eisnitz, chief investigator for the Humane Farming Association, the killing line speeds are so fast in modern slaughterhouses that animals frequently do not have time to bleed out before reaching the skinners and leggers. As a result, those animals that were unstunned or improperly stunned often have their legs cut off and their skin removed while they are still alive.

These animal rearing and slaughtering techniques are by no means rare: 97% of all poultry are produced in 100,000+ bird operations, 98% of pigs are raised in confinement systems, 59% of the nation's dairy cows are raised in confinement systems, all veal calves are crate-raised by definition, and 74% of beef cattle experience feedlot confinement before slaughter. To see just how many animals suffer the institutionalized cruelties of factory farming, consider the number slaughtered in the United States each year. According to the National Agricultural Statistics Service (NASS), 35.6 million cattle, 1.5 million veal calves, 101.2 million pigs, 3.9 million sheep and lambs, 23.5 million ducks, 273.0 million turkeys, and 7,995.4 million chickens were slaughtered in the United States in 1998. In sum, 8.43 *billion* animals are raised and slaughtered in the United States annually (not counting horses, goats, rabbits, emu, other poultry, or fish). . . . Suffice it to say that no other human activity results in more pain, suffering, frustration, and death than factory farming and animal agribusiness.

3. The Implications of Your Beliefs: Why You Are Committed to the Immorality of Eating Meat

I will now offer an argument for the immorality of eating meat predicated on *your* beliefs (p_1)–(p_{16}). Actually I will offer a family of related arguments, all predicated on different subsets of the set $\{(p_1), (p_2), \ldots, (p_{16})\}$. While you do not have to believe all of (p_1)–(p_{16}) for my argument to succeed, the more of these propositions you believe, the greater *your* commitment to the immorality of eating meat. For convenience, (p_1)–(p_{16}) have been compiled in an appendix at the end of the article.

Your beliefs (p_{10})–(p_{13}) show that you already believe that animals are capable of experiencing intense pain and suffering. I don't have to prove to you that *unanaesthetized* branding, castration, debeaking, tail docking, tooth extraction, and so forth cause animals severe pain. You already believe these procedures to be excruciatingly painful. Consequently, given the husbandry techniques and slaughtering practices documented above, you must admit the fact that: (f_1) Virtually all commercial animal agriculture, *especially* factory farming, causes animals intense pain and suffering and, thus, *greatly increases* the amount of pain and suffering in the world. (f_1) and your belief (p_1) together entail that, other things being equal, the world would be better without animal agriculture and factory farms. It is also a fact that: (f_2) In modern societies the consumption of meat is *in no way necessary* for human survival, and so, the pain and suffering that results from meat production is entirely *unnecessary*, as are all the cruel practices inherent in animal agriculture. Since no one *needs* to eat flesh, all of the inhumane treatment to which farm animals are routinely subjected is done *for no good reason*, and so, your belief that it is morally wrong and despicable to treat animals inhumanely *for no good reason* $[(p_{12})]$ forces you to admit that factory farming and animal agribusiness are morally wrong and despicable. Furthermore, your belief that a world with less unnecessary suffering is better than a world with more unnecessary suffering $[(p_2)]$,

together with (f_2), entails that the world would be better if there were less animal agriculture and fewer factory farms, and better still if there were no animal agriculture and no factory farms. Moreover, your belief in (p_3) commits you to the view that factory farming is wrong and *prima facie* ought not be supported or encouraged. When one buys factory farm-raised meat, one *is* supporting factory farms monetarily and thereby encouraging their *unnecessary* cruel practices. The only way to avoid actively supporting factory farms is to stop purchasing their products. . . .

Since, per (p_3), you have a *prima facie* obligation to stop supporting factory farming and animal agriculture, you have a *prima facie* obligation to become a vegetarian. Of course, *prima facie* obligations are overridable. Perhaps they can even be overridden simply by the fact that fulfilling them would be excessively burdensome or require enormous effort and sacrifice on one's part. Perhaps, but this much is clear: When one can fulfill *prima facie* obligation O *with little effort on one's part and without thereby failing to perform any other obligation*, then obligation O becomes very stringent indeed.

As for your *prima facie* obligation to stop supporting factory farming, you can easily satisfy it without thereby failing to perform any of your other obligations simply by refraining from eating meat and eating something else instead. For example, you can eat Boca burgers rather than hamburgers, pasta with marinara sauce rather than meat sauce, bean burritos or bean tostadas rather than beef tacos, red beans and rice rather than Cajun fried chicken, barbecued tofu rather than barbecued ribs, moo shoo vegetables rather than moo shoo pork, minestrone rather than chicken soup, hummus-filled whole wheat pitas rather than BLTs, five-bean vegetarian chili rather than chili with ground beef, chick pea salad rather than chicken salad, fruit and whole wheat toast rather than bacon and eggs, scrambled tofu vegetable frittatas rather than ham and cheese omelets, and so forth.[5] These examples underscore the *ease* with which one can avoid consuming flesh, a fact which often seems to elude meat eaters.

From your beliefs (p_1), (p_2), and $(p_{4'})$, it follows that we ought to do what we reasonably can to avoid contributing to the amount of unnecessary suffering in the world. Since one thing we reasonably can do is stop contributing to factory farming with our purchases, it follows that we ought to stop purchasing and consuming meat.

Your other beliefs support the same conclusion. You believe: (p_5) A morally good person will take steps to make the world a better place and even stronger steps to avoid making the world a worse place; and (p_6) Even a "minimally decent person" would take steps to help reduce the amount of unnecessary pain and suffering in the world, *if s/he could do so with little effort on her/his part*. You also believe that you are a morally good person $[(p_7)]$ or at least a minimally decent one $[(p_8)]$. Moreover, you believe that you are the kind of person who would take steps to help reduce the amount of pain and suffering in the world, *if you could do so with little effort on your part* $[(p_9)]$. As shown above, *with minimal effort* you could take steps to help reduce the amount of unnecessary suffering in the world just by eating something other than meat. Accordingly, given (p_6), you ought to refrain from eating flesh. Given (p_9), if you really are the kind of person you think you are, you will quit eating meat, opting for cruelty-free vegetarian fare instead.

Finally, animal agriculture is an extremely wasteful, inefficient, environmentally devastating means of food production. A full discussion of the inefficiencies and environmental degradations associated with animal agriculture is beyond the scope of the present paper, but consider five examples:

(1) Animal agriculture is an extremely energy-intensive method of food production. It takes an average of 28 kcal of fossil energy to produce 1 kcal of animal protein, compared with an average of 3.3 kcal of fossil energy per kcal of grain protein, making animal production on average more than eight times less energy efficient than grain production.

(2) Animal production is extremely inefficient in its water usage, compared to vegetable and grain production. Producing 1 kg of animal protein requires around 100 times more water than producing 1 kg of plant protein, for example, it takes 500 liters of water to grow 1 kg of potatoes and 900 liters of water to grow 1 kg of wheat, but it requires 100,000 liters of water to produce 1 kg of beef. Hence, agricultural water usage, which currently accounts for 87% of the world's freshwater consumption, could be drastically reduced by a shift toward an entirely plant-based agriculture.

(3) Animal agriculture is also extremely nutrient inefficient. By cycling grains through livestock to produce animal protein, we lose 90% of that grain's protein, 96% of its calories, 100% of its carbohydrates, and 100% of its fiber.

(4) Another negative by-product of the livestock industry is soil erosion. Much of arable land in the United States is devoted to feed crop production. Eighty percent of the corn and 95% of the oats grown in the United States are fed to livestock, and the excessive cultivation of our farmlands needed to produce these crops is responsible for the loss of 7 billion tons of topsoil each year. . . . The United States is losing soil at a rate thirteen times faster than the rate of soil formation.

And (5) animal agriculture creates enormous amounts of hazardous waste in the form of excrement. U.S. livestock produce 250,000 pounds of excrement *per second*, resulting in *1 billion tons* of unrecycled waste per year. According to the U.S. General Accounting Office's Report to the U.S. Senate Committee on Agriculture, Nutrition, and Forestry, animal waste run-off from feedlots and rangeland is a significant factor in water quality, affecting about 72% of impaired rivers and streams, 56% of impaired lake acres, and 43% of impaired estuary miles. . . .

The upshot is this: Animal agriculture is, by far and away, the most resource intensive, inefficient, environmentally harmful and ecologically unsound means of human food production, and consequently, one of the easiest direct actions one can take to help protect the environment and preserve resources for future generations, *one requiring minimal effort*, is to stop eating meat. And so, since you believe that we have a duty to preserve the environment for future generations [(p_{15})], and you believe that one ought to minimize one's contribution toward environmental degradation [(p_{16})], your beliefs commit you to the obligatoriness of becoming vegetarian, since doing so is a simple way to help preserve the environment. . . .

4. Is Meat Consumption Really Unnecessary?

A crucial premise in my argument is: (CP1) The pain and suffering that inevitably results from meat production is entirely *unnecessary*. I defended (CP1) on the grounds that in modern societies meat consumption is *in no way necessary* for human survival [(f_2)]. But (CP1) does not follow from (f_2), since eating meat might be necessary for some reason other than survival. Hence, one might object: "While eating meat is not necessary for survival, it *might* still be necessary for humans to thrive and flourish, in which case (CP1) would be false since the pain and suffering experienced by farm animals would be *necessary* for a significant human benefit."

If meat consumption were *necessary* for humans to flourish, my argument would be seriously compromised, so let us examine the evidence. First, consider the counterexamples. Since world-class athletic competition is one of the most grueling and physically strenuous activities in which humans can engage, one would not expect there to be any highly successful vegetarian athletes or vegetarian world record holders, *if* meat consumption were necessary for humans to thrive and flourish. However, the list of world-class vegetarian athletes is quite long and includes Dave Scott (six-time winner of Hawaii's Ironman Triathlon), Sixto Linares (world-record holder for the 24-hour triathlon), Edwin Moses (400-meter hurdler undefeated in international competition for eight straight years), Paavo Nurmi (20 world records, 9 Olympic medals), Andreas Cahling (1980 Mr. International title in body

building), and Ridgely Abele (U.S. Karate Association World Champion), to name a few, which strongly suggests that eating meat is *not* necessary for humans to flourish.

Second, consider the diseases associated with the consumption of meat and animal products—heart disease, cancer, stroke, osteoporosis, diabetes, hypertension, arthritis, and obesity—as documented in numerous, highly regarded studies. Four examples must suffice: (1) The Loma Linda study, involving over 24,000 people, found that lacto-ovo-vegetarian men (who consume eggs and dairy products, but no meat) had a 61% lower coronary heart disease (CHD) mortality rate than California's general population. Pure vegetarian men (who consume no animal products) fared even better: The CHD mortality rate for these males was 86% lower than that of the California general population. (2) The ongoing Framingham heart study has been tracking the daily living and eating habits of thousands of residents of Framingham, Massachusetts, since 1948. Dr. William Castelli, director of the study for the last fifteen years, maintains that based on his research the most heart healthy diet is a *pure* vegetarian diet. . . . [A]ccording to Dr. Castelli . . . "Vegetarians not only outlive the rest of us, they also aren't prey to other degenerative diseases, such as diabetes, strokes, etc., that slow us down and make us chronically ill." (3) The Cornell-Oxford-China Health Project systematically monitored the diet, lifestyle, and disease patterns of 6,500 families from 65 different counties in Mainland China and Taiwan. The data collected in this study has led its director, Dr. T. Colin Campbell, to conclude that 80–90% of all cancers can be controlled or prevented by a lowfat (10–15% fat) pure vegetarian diet. And (4), the Dean Ornish study demonstrated that *advanced* coronary artery disease could be *reversed* through a combination of stress reduction and an extremely lowfat vegetarian diet (10% fat). . . .

These and countless other studies have led the American Dietetic Association, the leading nutritional organization in the country, to assert:

Scientific data suggest positive relationships between a vegetarian diet and reduced risk for several chronic degenerative diseases and conditions, including obesity, coronary artery disease, hypertension, diabetes mellitus, and some types of cancer. . . . *It is the position of The American Dietetic Association (ADA) that appropriately planned vegetarian diets are healthful, are nutritionally adequate, and provide health benefits in the prevention and treatment of certain diseases.*

An article in *The Journal of the American Medical Association* concurs, claiming: "A vegetarian diet can prevent 90% of our thrombo-embolic disease and 97% of our coronary occlusions." . . . The evidence is unequivocal: A vegetarian diet is nutritionally superior to a meat-based diet. One cannot reject my crucial premise—(CP1) The pain and suffering that inevitably results from meat production is entirely *unnecessary*—on the grounds that eating meat is necessary for human flourishing, because it isn't. Rather, eating meat is *detrimental* to human health and well-being. Simply put, eating meat serves no human need that cannot be better met with plant-based foods.

Since all of our nutritional needs can be met and can be met better with plant-based foods than they can with meat and animal-based foods, all of the pain and suffering farm animals are forced to endure to wind up on our dinner plates really is unnecessary. Since purchasing and eating meat does contribute to unnecessary suffering, and since you believe it is wrong to contribute to unnecessary suffering [(p₂)], your beliefs entail that eating meat is wrong.

5. Conclusion

The implications of your beliefs are clear. Given your beliefs, it follows that eating meat is morally wrong. This conclusion was not derived from some highly contentious ethical theory that you can easily reject, but from your own firmly held beliefs. Furthermore, this conclusion follows, regardless of your views on speciesism, animal equality, and animal rights. Even those of you who are staunch speciesists are committed to the immorality of eating meat, given your other beliefs. Consequently, consistency (your own beliefs) demands that you embrace the immorality of eating meat and modify your behavior accordingly.

Appendix

(p₁) Other things being equal, a world with less pain and suffering is better than a world with more pain and suffering.

(p₂) A world with less unnecessary suffering is better than a world with more unnecessary suffering.

(p₃) Unnecessary cruelty is wrong and *prima facie* should not be supported or encouraged.

(p₄) We ought to take steps to make the world a better place.

(p₄') We ought to do what we reasonably can to avoid making the world a worse place.

(p₅) A morally good person will take steps to make the world a better place and even stronger steps to avoid making the world a worse place.

(p₆) Even a minimally decent person would take steps to reduce the amount of unnecessary pain and suffering in the world, *if s/he could do so with little effort on her/his part.*

(p₇) I am a morally good person.

(p₈) I am at least a minimally decent person.

(p₉) I am the sort of person who certainly would take steps to help reduce the amount of pain and suffering in the world, *if I could do so with little effort on my part.*

(p₁₀) Many nonhuman animals (certainly all vertebrates) are capable of feeling pain.

(p₁₁) Other things being equal, it is morally wrong to cause an animal pain or suffering.

(p₁₂) It is morally wrong and despicable to treat animals inhumanely for *no good reason*.

(p₁₃) We ought to euthanize untreatably injured, suffering animals to put them out of their misery whenever feasible.

(p₁₄) Other things being equal, it is worse to kill a conscious sentient animal than it is to kill a plant.

(p₁₅) We have a duty to help preserve the environment for future generations (at least for future human generations).

(p₁₆) One ought to minimize one's contribution toward environmental degradation, *especially in those ways requiring minimal effort on one's part*.

NOTES

1. Obviously, if you do not hold these beliefs (or enough of them), my argument will have no force for you, nor is it intended to. It is only aimed at those of you who do hold these widespread commonsense beliefs.

2. *Speciesism* is the widespread view that one's own species is superior to and more valuable than the other species and that, therefore, members of one's own species have the right to dominate members of these other species. While "speciesism" and its cognates are often used pejoratively in the animal rights literature, I use them only descriptively and imply no negative or condescending appraisal of the individual so described.

3. By "*unnecessary* suffering" I mean suffering that serves no greater, outweighing justifying good. If some instance of suffering is required to bring about a greater good (e.g., a painful root canal may be the only way to save a person's tooth), then that suffering is *not* unnecessary. Thus, in the case of (p₂), no *ceteris paribus* clause is needed, since if other things are *not* equal such that the suffering in question is justified by an overriding, justifying good that can only be achieved by allowing that suffering, then that suffering is *not* necessary.

4. By a "minimally decent person" I mean a person who does the very minimum required by morality and no more. I borrow this terminology from Judith Jarvis Thomson who distinguishes a *good* Samaritan from an *minimally decent* Samaritan. See her "A Defense of Abortion" [reprinted in this volume].

5. It is worth noting that in every case just mentioned the vegetarian option is significantly more nutritious, more healthful, and much lower in fat, saturated fat, and cholesterol than its meat-based counterpart. In fact, none of the vegetarian options listed contain any cholesterol whatsoever.

Review and Discussion Questions

1. Is Engel correct to say that his case for vegetarianism avoids reliance on any controversial ethical theory?

2. Is factory farming cruel and immoral? Is it bad for the environment?

3. Examine carefully each of the seventeen propositions listed in the Appendix. Which are the most important for Engel's argument? Which are the most controversial or debatable? For each of the propositions, state whether you believe it. If you do, how firmly are you committed to it? If you do not believe it, why not?

4. Is the consumption of meat by human beings nutritionally (a) necessary, (b) not necessary but beneficial, (c) neither beneficial nor harmful, or (d) harmful?

5. Are you persuaded by Engel's argument for vegetarianism? If not, why not? Are there arguments against his position that he has overlooked or failed to answer adequately?

6. Assess the following argument: "I agree that factory farming is cruel and inhumane. However, my not eating meat won't make any difference. Therefore, it is not wrong for me to continue eating meat."

7. Assess Engel's argument from the point of view of Tibor Machan and William Baxter. Are they committed to the morality of eating meat?

7

PORNOGRAPHY AND SEXUAL MORALITY

Pornography, Oppression, and Freedom

HELEN E. LONGINO

After presenting the traditional conception of pornography, Helen E. Longino, professor of philosophy and women's studies at Rice University, offers her own definition. In her view, sexually explicit or erotic material constitutes pornography only if it endorses the degrading or demeaning treatment of women. This is what makes pornography wrong. She argues further that pornography distorts our view of women, reinforces their oppression and exploitation, and encourages violence against them.

Study Questions

1. What does Longino mean by distinguishing "between questions of sexual mores and questions of morality"?

2. What is Longino's definition of pornography? According to her, sexually explicit material is not necessarily pornographic; indeed, not all explicit representations of sexually abusive treatment of women constitute pornography. Explain.

3. In what ways does pornography communicate its endorsement of sexual behavior that demeans women?

4. What does Longino mean when she writes that pornography lies about women and denies their equality to men?

5. Why does she believe that pornography is connected to crimes of violence against women?

Reprinted by permission of the author from "Pornography, Oppression, and Freedom: A Closer Look" in Laura Lederer, ed., Take Back the Night: Women on Pornography *(1980). Some notes omitted.*

I. Introduction

. . . TRADITIONALLY, PORNOGRAPHY WAS condemned as immoral because it presented sexually explicit material in a manner designed to appeal to "prurient interests" or a "morbid" interest in nudity and sexuality, material which furthermore lacked any redeeming social value and which exceeded "customary limits of candor." While these phrases, taken from a definition of "obscenity" proposed in the 1954 American Law Institute's *Model Penal Code,* require some criteria of application to eliminate vagueness, it seems that what is objectionable is the explicit description or representation of bodily parts or sexual behavior for the purpose of inducing sexual stimulation or pleasure on the part of the reader or viewer. This kind of objection is part of a sexual ethic that subordinates sex to procreation and condemns all sexual interactions outside of legitimated marriage. It is this code which was the primary target of the sexual revolutionaries in the 1960's, and which has given way in many areas to more open standards of sexual behavior.

One of the beneficial results of the sexual revolution has been a growing acceptance of the distinction between questions of sexual mores and questions of morality. This distinction underlies the old slogan, "Make love, not war," and takes harm to others as the defining characteristic of immorality. What is immoral is behavior which causes injury to or violation of another person or people. Such injury may be physical or it may be psychological. To cause pain to another, to lie to another, to hinder another in the exercise of her or his rights, to exploit another, to degrade another, to misrepresent and slander another are instances of immoral behavior. Masturbation or engaging voluntarily in sexual intercourse with another consenting adult of the same or the other sex, as long as neither injury nor violation of either individual or another is involved, is not immoral. Some sexual behavior is morally objectionable, but not because of its sexual character. Thus, adultery is immoral not because it involves sexual intercourse with someone to whom one is not legally married, but because it involves breaking a promise (of sexual and emotional fidelity to one's spouse). Sadistic, abusive, or forced sex is immoral because it injures and violates another.

The detachment of sexual chastity from moral virtue implies that we cannot condemn forms of sexual behavior merely because they strike us as distasteful or subversive of the Protestant work ethic, or because they depart from standards of behavior we have individually adopted. It has thus seemed to imply that no matter how offensive we might find pornography, we must tolerate it in the name of freedom from illegitimate repression. I wish to argue that this is not so, that pornography is immoral because it is harmful to people.

II. What Is Pornography?

I define pornography as *verbal or pictorial explicit representations of sexual behavior that,* in the words of the Commission on Obscenity and Pornography, *have as a distinguishing characteristic "the degrading and demeaning portrayal of the role and status of the human female . . . as a mere sexual object to be exploited and manipulated sexually."*[1] In pornographic books, magazines, and films, women are represented as passive and as slavishly dependent upon men. The role of female characters is limited to the provision of sexual services to men. To the extent that women's sexual pleasure is represented at all, it is subordinated to that of men and is never an end in itself as is the sexual pleasure of men. What pleases women is the use of their bodies to satisfy male desires. While the sexual objectification of women is common to all pornography, women are the recipients of even worse treatment in violent pornography, in which women characters are killed, tortured, gang-raped, mutilated, bound, and otherwise abused, as a means of providing sexual stimulation or pleasure to the male characters. It is this development which has attracted the attention of feminists and been the stimulus to an analysis of pornography in general.

Not all sexually explicit material is pornography, nor is all material which contains representations of sexual abuse and degradation pornography.

A representation of a sexual encounter between adult persons which is characterized by mutual respect is, once we have disentangled sexuality and morality, not morally objectionable. Such a representation would be one in which the desires and experiences of each participant were regarded by the other participants as having a validity and a subjective importance equal to those of the individual's own desire and experiences. In such an encounter, each participant acknowledges the other participant's basic human dignity and personhood. Similarly, a representation of a nude human body (in whole or in part) in such a manner that the person shown maintains self-respect—e.g., is not portrayed in a degrading position—would not be morally objectionable. The educational films of the National Sex Forum, as well as a certain amount of erotic literature and art, fall into this category. While some erotic materials are beyond the standards of modesty held by some individuals, they are not for this reason immoral.

A representation of a sexual encounter which is not characterized by mutual respect, in which at least one of the parties is treated in a manner beneath her or his dignity as a human being, is no longer simple erotica. That a representation is of degrading behavior does not in itself, however, make it pornographic. Whether or not it is pornographic is a function of contextual features. Books and films may contain descriptions or representations of a rape in order to explore the consequences of such an assault upon its victim. What is being shown is abusive or degrading behavior which attempts to deny the humanity and dignity of the person assaulted, yet the context surrounding the representation, through its exploration of the consequences of the act, acknowledges and reaffirms her dignity. Such books and films, far from being pornographic, are (or can be) highly moral, and fall into the category of moral realism.

What makes a work a work of pornography, then, is not simply its representation of degrading and abusive sexual encounters, but its implicit, if not explicit, approval and recommendation of sexual behavior that is immoral, i.e., that physically or psychologically violates the personhood of one of the participants. Pornography, then, is verbal or pictorial material which represents or describes sexual behavior that is degrading or abusive to one or more of the participants in *such a way as to endorse the degradation*. The participants so treated in virtually all heterosexual pornography are women or children, so heterosexual pornography is, as a matter of fact, material which endorses sexual behavior that is degrading and/or abusive to women and children. As I use the term "sexual behavior," this includes sexual encounters between persons, behavior which produces sexual stimulation or pleasure for one of the participants, and behavior which is preparatory to or invites sexual activity. Behavior that is degrading or abusive includes physical harm or abuse, and physical or psychological coercion. In addition, behavior which ignores or devalues the real interests, desires, and experiences of one or more participants in any way is degrading. Finally, that a person has chosen or consented to be harmed, abused, or subjected to coercion does not alter the degrading character of such behavior.

Pornography communicates its endorsement of the behavior it represents by various features of the pornographic context: the degradation of the female characters is represented as providing pleasure to the participant males and, even worse, to the participant females, and there is no suggestion that this sort of treatment of others is inappropriate to their status as human beings. These two features are together sufficient to constitute endorsement of the represented behavior. The contextual features which make material pornographic are intrinsic to the material. In addition to these, extrinsic features, such as the purpose for which the material is presented—i.e., the sexual arousal/pleasure/satisfaction of its (mostly) male consumers—or an accompanying text, may reinforce or make explicit the endorsement. Representations which in and of themselves do not show or endorse degrading behavior may be put into a pornographic context by juxtaposition with others that are degrading, or by a text which invites or recommends degrading behavior toward the subject represented. In such a case the whole complex—the series of representations or representations with text—is pornographic.

The distinction I have sketched is one that applies most clearly to sequential material—a verbal or pictorial (filmed) story—which represents an action and provides a temporal context for it. In showing the before and after, a narrator or film-maker has plenty of opportunity to acknowledge the dignity of the person violated or clearly to refuse to do so. It is somewhat more difficult to apply the distinction to single still representations. The contextual features cited above, however, are clearly present in still photographs or pictures that glamorize degradation and sexual violence. Phonograph album covers and advertisements offer some prime examples of such glamorization. Their representations of women in chains (the Ohio Players), or bound by ropes and black and blue (the Rolling Stones) are considered high-quality commercial "art" and glossily prettify the violence they represent. Since the standard function of prettification and glamorization is the communication of desirability, these albums and ads are communicating the desirability of violence against women. Representations of women bound or chained, particularly those of women bound in such a way as to make their breasts, or genital or anal areas vulnerable to any passerby, endorse the scene they represent by the absence of any indication that this treatment of women is in any way inappropriate.

To summarize: Pornography is not just the explicit representation or description of sexual behavior, nor even the explicit representation or description of sexual behavior which is degrading and/or abusive to women. Rather, it is material that explicitly represents or describes degrading and abusive sexual behavior so as to endorse and/or recommend the behavior as described. The contextual features, moreover, which communicate such endorsement are intrinsic to the material; that is, they are features whose removal or alteration would change the representation or description.

This account of pornography is underlined by the etymology and original meaning of the word "pornography." *The Oxford English Dictionary* defines pornography as "Description of the life, manners, etc. of prostitutes and their patrons [from πορνη (*porne*) meaning "harlot" and γραφειν (*graphein*) meaning "to write"]; hence the expression or suggestion of obscene or unchaste subjects in literature or art."

Let us consider the first part of the definition for a moment. In the transactions between prostitutes and their clients, prostitutes are paid, directly or indirectly, for the use of their bodies by the client for sexual pleasure. Traditionally males have obtained from female prostitutes what they could not or did not wish to get from their wives or women friends, who, because of the character of their relation to the male, must be accorded some measure of human respect. While there are limits to what treatment is seen as appropriate toward women as wives or women friends, the prostitute as prostitute exists to provide sexual pleasure to males. The female characters of contemporary pornography also exist to provide pleasure to males, but in the pornographic context no pretense is made to regard them as parties to a contractual arrangement. Rather, the anonymity of these characters makes each one Everywoman, thus suggesting not only that all women are appropriate subjects for the enactment of the most bizarre and demeaning male sexual fantasies, but also that this is their primary purpose. The recent escalation of violence in pornography—the presentation of scenes of bondage, rape, and torture of women for the sexual stimulation of the male characters or male viewers—while shocking in itself, is from this point of view merely a more vicious extension of a genre whose success depends on treating women in a manner beneath their dignity as human beings.

III. Pornography: Lies and Violence Against Women

What is wrong with pornography, then, is its degrading and dehumanizing portrayal of women (and *not* its sexual content). Pornography, by its very nature, requires that women be subordinate to men and mere instruments for the fulfillment of male fantasies. To accomplish this, pornography must lie. Pornography lies when it says that our sexual life is or ought to be subordinate to the service of men, that our pleasure consists in pleasing men and not ourselves, that we are depraved, that we are fit subjects for rape, bondage, torture, and murder. Pornography lies explicitly about women's sexuality, and through such lies fosters more lies about our humanity, our dignity, and our personhood.

Moreover, since nothing is alleged to justify the treatment of the female characters of pornography save their womanhood, pornography depicts all women as fit objects of violence by virtue of their sex alone. Because it is simply being female that, in the pornographic vision, justifies being violated, the lies of pornography are lies about all women. Each work of pornography is on its own libelous and defamatory, yet gains power through being reinforced by every other pornographic work. The sheer number of pornographic productions expands the moral issue to include not only assessing the morality or immorality of individual works, but also the meaning and force of the mass production of pornography.

The pornographic view of women is thoroughly entrenched in a booming portion of the publishing, film, and recording industries, reaching and affecting not only all who look to such sources for sexual stimulation, but also those of us who are forced into an awareness of it as we peruse magazines at newsstands and record albums in record stores, as we check the entertainment sections of city newspapers, or even as we approach a counter to pay for groceries. It is not necessary to spend a great deal of time reading or viewing pornographic material to absorb its male-centered definition of women. No longer confined within plain brown wrappers, it jumps out from billboards that proclaim "Live X-rated Girls!" or "Angels in Pain" or "Hot and Wild," and from magazine covers displaying a woman's genital area being spread open to the viewer by her own fingers.[2] Thus, even men who do not frequent pornographic shops and movie houses are supported in the sexist objectification of women by their environment. Women, too, are crippled by internalizing as self-images those that are presented to us by pornographers. Isolated from one another and with no source of support for an alternative view of female sexuality, we may not always find the strength to resist a message that dominates the common cultural media.

The entrenchment of pornography in our culture also gives it a significance quite beyond its explicit sexual messages. To suggest, as pornography does, that the primary purpose of women is to provide sexual pleasure to men is to deny that women are independently human or have a status equal to that of men. It is, moreover, to deny our equality at one of the most intimate levels of human experience. This denial is especially powerful in a hierarchical, class society such as ours, in which individuals feel good about themselves by feeling superior to others. Men in our society have a vested interest in maintaining their belief in the inferiority of the female sex, so that no matter how oppressed and exploited by the society in which they live and work, they can feel that they are at least superior to someone or some category of individuals—a woman or women. Pornography, by presenting women as wanton, depraved, and made for the sexual use of men, caters directly to that interest. The very intimate nature of sexuality which makes pornography so corrosive also protects it from explicit public discussion. The consequent lack of any explicit social disavowal of the pornographic image of women enables this image to continue fostering sexist attitudes even as the society publicly proclaims its (as yet timid) commitment to sexual equality.

In addition to finding a connection between the pornographic view of women and the denial to us of our full human rights, women are beginning to connect the consumption of pornography with committing rape and other acts of sexual violence against women. Contrary to the findings of the Commission on Obscenity and Pornography a growing body of research is documenting (1) a correlation between exposure to representations of violence and the committing of violent acts generally, and (2) a correlation between exposure to pornographic materials and the committing of sexually abusive or violent acts against women.[3] While more study is needed to establish precisely what the causal relations are, clearly so-called hard-core pornography is not innocent.

From "snuff" films and miserable magazines in pornographic stores to *Hustler*, to phonograph album covers and advertisements, to *Vogue*, pornography has come to occupy its own niche in the communications and entertainment media and to acquire a quasi-institutional character (signaled by the use of diminutives such as "porn" or "porno" to refer to pornographic material, as though such familiar naming could take the hurt out). Its acceptance by the mass media, whatever the motivation, means a cultural endorsement of its message. As much as the materials themselves, the social tolerance of these degrading and distorted images of women in such quantities is harmful to us, since it indicates a general willingness to see women in ways incompatible with our fundamental human dignity and thus to justify treating us in those ways. The tolerance of pornographic representations of the rape, bondage, and torture of women helps to create and maintain a climate more tolerant of the actual physical abuse of women. The tendency on the part of the legal system to view the victim of a rape as responsible for the crime against her is but one manifestation of this.

In sum, pornography is injurious to women in at least three distinct ways:

1. Pornography, especially violent pornography, is implicated in the committing of crimes of violence against women.
2. Pornography is the vehicle for the dissemination of a deep and vicious lie about women. It is defamatory and libelous.

3. The diffusion of such a distorted view of women's nature in our society as it exists today supports sexist (i.e., male-centered) attitudes, and thus reinforces the oppression and exploitation of women.

Society's tolerance of pornography, especially pornography on the contemporary massive scale, reinforces each of these modes of injury: By not disavowing the lie, it supports the male-centered myth that women are inferior and subordinate creatures. Thus, it contributes to the maintenance of a climate tolerant of both psychological and physical violence against women. . . .

IV. Conclusion

I have defined pornography in such a way as to distinguish it from erotica and from moral realism, and have argued that it is defamatory and libelous toward women, that it condones crimes against women, and that it invites tolerance of the social, economic, and cultural oppression of women. The production and distribution of pornographic material is thus a social and moral wrong. Contrasting both the current volume of pornographic production and its growing infiltration of the communications media with the status of women in this culture makes clear the necessity for its control. . . .

Appeals for action against pornography are sometimes brushed aside with the claim that such action is a diversion from the primary task of feminists—the elimination of sexism and of sexual inequality. This approach focuses on the enjoyment rather than the manufacture of pornography, and sees it as merely a product of sexism which will disappear when the latter has been overcome and the sexes are socially and economically equal. Pornography cannot be separated from sexism in this way: Sexism is not just a set of attitudes regarding the inferiority of women but the behaviors and social and economic rules that manifest such attitudes. Both the manufacture and distribution of pornography and the enjoyment of it are instances of sexist behavior. The enjoyment of pornography on the part of individuals will presumably decline as such individuals begin to accord women their status as fully human. A cultural climate which tolerates the degrading representation of women is not a climate which facilitates the development of respect for women. Furthermore, the demand for pornography is stimulated not just by the sexism of individuals but by the pornography industry itself. Thus, both as a social phenomenon and in its effect on individuals, pornography, far from being a mere product, nourishes sexism. The campaign against it is an essential component of women's struggle for legal, economic, and social equality, one which requires the support of all feminists.

NOTES

1. *Report of the Commission on Obscenity and Pornography* (New York: Bantam Books, 1979), p. 239. The Commission, of course, concluded that the demeaning content of pornography did not adversely affect male attitudes toward women.

2. This was a full-color magazine cover seen in a rack at the check-out counter of a corner delicatessen.

3. Urie Bronfenbrenner, *Two Worlds of Childhood* (New York: Russell Sage Foundation, 1970); H. J. Eysenck and D. K. B. Nias, *Sex, Violence and the Media* (New York: St. Martin's Press, 1978); and Michael Goldstein, Harold Kant, and John Hartman, *Pornography and Sexual Deviance* (Berkeley: University of California Press, 1973).

Review and Discussion Questions

1. Do you agree with Longino's definition of pornography? Can something be erotic, explicit, and sexually stimulating without being pornographic?

2. When is sexual behavior degrading or demeaning toward women, and how is this to be judged? What does it mean for a book or film to endorse such behavior? Could something be pornographic because it endorses sexual conduct that is demeaning toward men?

3. What, if anything, makes pornography (as Longino defines it) worse than degrading or dehumanizing nonsexual portrayals of women?

4. Explain and assess Longino's contention that pornography is "defamatory and libelous" to women.

5. Longino believes that pornography is connected to violence against women. Do you agree? What reason or evidence supports this belief? If true, what are its implications?

6. Do you agree with Longino that it is necessary to control pornography? If so, how should it be regulated? Should pornography be banned altogether?

Feminism, Moralism, and Pornography

ELLEN WILLIS

In the previous essay, Helen E. Longino attacked pornography from a feminist perspective. In this essay, Ellen Willis, professor of journalism at New York University, challenges the idea that opposition to pornography is a feminist cause. She is critical of attempts to distinguish erotica from pornography, arguing that they rest on an unre-

Ellen Willis, *"Feminism, Moralism, and Pornography" from* Beginning to See the Light. *© 1992 Wesleyan University Press. Reprinted by permission.*

alistic view of sexuality. She sees the antipornography movement as problematic from a feminist point of view because it is hostile to lust, refuses to acknowledge that women can enjoy pornography, and has a "goody-goody concept of eroticism."

Study Questions

1. How, in Willis's view, have antipornography feminists attempted to redefine pornography? Why is she critical of attempts to distinguish it from erotica?

2. Why is Willis skeptical of the claim that pornography causes violence against women?

3. Why is Willis critical of the view of sex that has emerged from the antipornography movement? Explain why she believes that the feminist campaign against pornography will not improve the position of women.

4. Why is Willis worried about attempts to ban or censor pornography?

FEMINIST CRITICISM of sexist and misogynist pornography is nothing new; porn is an obvious target insofar as it contributes to larger patterns of oppression—the reduction of the female body to a commodity (the paradigm being prostitution), the sexual intimidation that makes women regard the public streets as enemy territory (the paradigm being rape), sexist images and propaganda in general. But what is happening now is different. By playing games with the English language, antiporn activists are managing to rationalize as feminism a single-issue movement divorced from any larger political context and rooted in conservative moral assumptions that are all the more dangerous for being unacknowledged.

When I first heard there was a group called Women Against Pornography (WAP), I twitched. Could I define myself as Against Pornography? Not really. In itself, pornography—which, my dictionary and I agree, means any image or description intended or used to arouse sexual desire—does not strike me as the proper object of a political crusade. As the most cursory observation suggests, there are many varieties of porn, some pernicious, some more or less benign. About the only generalization one can make is that pornography is the return of the repressed, of feelings and fantasies driven underground by a culture that atomizes sexuality, defining love as

a noble affair of the heart and mind, lust as a base animal urge centered in unmentionable organs. Prurience—the state of mind I associate with pornography—implies a sense of sex as forbidden, secretive pleasure, isolated from any emotional or social context. I imagine that in utopia, porn would wither away along with the state, heroin, and Coca-Cola. At present, however, the sexual impulses that pornography appeals to are part of virtually everyone's psychology. For obvious political and cultural reasons nearly all porn is sexist in that it is the product of a male imagination and aimed at a male market; women are less likely to be consciously interested in pornography, or to indulge that interest, or to find porn that turns them on. But anyone who thinks women are simply indifferent to pornography has never watched a bunch of adolescent girls pass around a trashy novel. Over the years I've enjoyed various pieces of pornography—some of them of the sleazy Forty-Second Street paperback sort—and so have most women I know. Fantasy, after all, is more flexible than reality, and women have learned, as a matter of survival, to be adept at shaping male fantasies to their own purposes. If feminists define pornography, per se, as the enemy, the result will be to make a lot of women ashamed of their sexual feelings and afraid to be honest about them. And the last thing women need is more sexual shame, guilt, and hypocrisy—this time served up as feminism.

So why ignore qualitative distinctions and in effect condemn all pornography as equally bad? WAP organizers answer—or finesse—this question by redefining pornography. They maintain that pornography is not really about sex but about violence against women. Or, in a more colorful formulation, "Pornography is the theory, rape is the practice." Part of the argument is that pornography causes violence; much is made of the fact that Charles Manson and David Berkowitz had porn collections. This is the sort of inverted logic that presumes marijuana to be dangerous because most heroin addicts started with it. It is men's hostility toward women—combined with their power to express that hostility and for the most part get away with it—that causes sexual violence. Pornography that gives sadistic fantasies concrete shape—and, in today's atmosphere, social legitimacy—may well encourage suggestible men to act them out. But if *Hustler* were to vanish from the shelves tomorrow, I doubt that rape or wife-beating statistics would decline.

Even more problematic is the idea that pornography depicts violence rather than sex. Since porn is by definition overtly sexual, while most of it is not overtly violent, this equation requires some fancy explaining. . . . Robin Morgan and Gloria Steinem . . . distinguish pornography from erotica. According to this argument, erotica (whose etymological root is "eros," or sexual love) expresses an integrated sexuality based on mutual affection and desire between equals; pornography (which comes from another Greek root—"porne," meaning prostitute) reflects a dehumanized sexuality based on male domination and exploitation of women. The distinction sounds promising, but it doesn't hold up. The accepted meaning of erotica is literature or pictures with sexual themes; it may or may not serve the essentially utilitarian function of pornography. Because it is less specific, less suggestive of actual sexual activity, "erotica" is regularly used

as a euphemism for "classy porn." Pornography expressed in literary language or expensive photography and consumed by the upper middle class is "erotica"; the cheap stuff, which can't pretend to any purpose but getting people off, is smut. The erotica-versus-porn approach evades the (embarrassing?) question of how porn is *used*. It endorses the portrayal of sex as we might like it to be and condemns the portrayal of sex as it too often is, whether in action or only in fantasy. But if pornography is to arouse, it must appeal to the feelings we have, not those that by some utopian standard we ought to have. Sex in this culture has been so deeply politicized that it is impossible to make clear-cut distinctions between "authentic" sexual impulses and those conditioned by patriarchy. Between, say, *Ulysses* at one end and *Snuff* at the other, erotica/pornography conveys all sorts of mixed messages that elicit complicated and private responses. In practice, attempts to sort out good erotica from bad porn inevitably come down to "What turns me on is erotic; what turns you on is pornographic."

It would be clearer and more logical simply to acknowledge that some sexual images are offensive and some are not. But logic and clarity are irrelevant—or rather, inimical—to the underlying aim of the antiporners, which is to vent the emotions traditionally associated with the word "pornography." . . . There is a social and psychic link between pornography and rape. In terms of patriarchal morality both are expressions of male lust, which is presumed to be innately vicious, and offenses to the putative sexual innocence of "good" women. But feminists supposedly begin with different assumptions—that men's confusion of sexual desire with predatory aggression reflects a sexist system, not male biology; that there are no good (chaste) or bad (lustful) women, just women who are, like men, sexual beings. From this standpoint, to lump pornography with rape is dangerously simplistic. Rape is a violent physical assault. Pornography can be a psychic assault, both in its content and in its public intrusions on our attention, but for women as for men it can also be a source of erotic pleasure. A woman who is raped is a victim; a woman who enjoys pornography (even if that means enjoying a rape fantasy) is in a sense a rebel, insisting on an aspect of her sexuality that has been defined as a male preserve. Insofar as pornography glorifies male supremacy and sexual alienation, it is deeply reactionary. But in rejecting sexual repression and hypocrisy—which have inflicted even more damage on women than on men—it expresses a radical impulse.

That this impulse still needs defending, even among feminists, is evident from the sexual attitudes that have surfaced in the antiporn movement. In the movement's rhetoric pornography is a code word for vicious male lust. To the objection that some women get off on porn, the standard reply is that this only shows how thoroughly women have been brainwashed by male values—though a WAP leaflet goes so far as to suggest that women who claim to like pornography are lying to avoid male opprobrium. (Note the good-girl-versus-bad-girl theme, reappearing as healthy-versus-sick, or honest-versus-devious; for "brainwashed" read "seduced.") And the view of sex that most often emerges from talk about "erotica" is as sentimental and euphemistic as the word itself: lovemaking should be beautiful, romantic, soft, nice, and devoid of messiness, vulgarity, impulses to power, or indeed aggression of any sort. Above all, the emphasis should be on *relationships,* not (yuck) *organs.* This goody-goody concept of eroticism is not feminist but feminine. It is precisely sex as an aggressive, unladylike activity, an expression of violent and unpretty emotion, an exercise of erotic power, and a specifically genital experience that has been taboo for women. Nor are we supposed to admit that we, too, have sadistic impulses, that our sexual fantasies may reflect forbidden urges to turn the tables and get revenge on men. (When a woman is aroused by a rape fantasy, is she perhaps identifying with the rapist as well as the victim?)

. . . Lesbian separatists argue that pornography reflects patriarchal sexual relations; patriarchal sexual relations are based on male power backed by force; ergo, pornography is violent.

This dubious syllogism, which could as easily be applied to romantic novels, reduces the whole issue to hopeless mush. If all manifestations of patriarchal sexuality are violent, then opposition to violence cannot explain why pornography (rather than romantic novels) should be singled out as a target. Besides, such reductionism allows women no basis for distinguishing between consensual heterosexuality and rape. . . . To attack pornography, and at the same time equate it with heterosexual sex, is implicitly to condemn not only women who like pornography, but women who sleep with men. This is familiar ground. The argument that straight women collaborate with the enemy has often been, among other things, a relatively polite way of saying that they consort with the beast. . . . Proponents of the separatist line . . . [are] like the modern equivalents of women who, in an era when straightforward prudery was socially acceptable, joined convents to escape men's rude sexual demands. . . . Their revulsion against heterosexuality . . . [serves] as the thinnest of covers for disgust with sex itself. In any case, sanitized feminine sexuality, whether straight or gay, is as limited as the predatory masculine kind and as central to women's oppression; a major function of misogynist pornography is to scare us into embracing it. . . .

Self-righteousness has always been a feminine weapon, a permissible way to make men feel bad. Ironically, it is socially acceptable for women to display fierce aggression in their crusades against male vice, which serve as an outlet for female anger without threatening male power. The temperance movement, which made alcohol the symbol of male violence, did not improve the position of women; substituting porn for demon rum won't work either. One reason it won't is that it bolsters the good girl–bad girl split. Overtly or by implication it isolates women who like porn or "pornographic" sex or who work in the sex industry. WAP has refused to take a position on prostitution, yet its activities—particularly its support for cleaning up Times Square—will affect prostitutes' lives. Prostitution raises its own set of complicated questions. But it is clearly not in women's interest to pit "good" feminists against "bad" whores (or topless dancers, or models for skin magazines).

So far, the issue that has dominated public debate on the antiporn campaign is its potential threat to free speech. Here too the movement's arguments have been full of contradictions. Susan Brownmiller and other WAP organizers claim not to advocate censorship and dismiss the civil liberties issue as a red herring dragged in by men who don't want to face the fact that pornography oppresses women. Yet at the same time, WAP endorses the Supreme Court's contention that obscenity is not protected speech, a doctrine I—and most civil libertarians—regard as a clear infringement of First Amendment rights. Brownmiller insists that the First Amendment was designed to protect political dissent, not expressions of woman-hating violence. But to make such a distinction is to defeat the amendment's purpose, since it implicitly cedes to the government the right to define "political." (Has there ever been a government willing to admit that its opponents are anything more than antisocial troublemakers?) Anyway, it makes no sense to oppose pornography on the grounds that it's sexist propaganda, then turn around and argue that it's not political. Nor will libertarians be reassured by WAP's statement that "we want to change the definition of obscenity so that it focuses on violence, not sex." Whatever their focus, obscenity laws deny the right of free expression to those who transgress official standards of propriety. . . . The basic purpose of obscenity laws is and always has been to reinforce cultural taboos on sexuality and suppress feminism, homosexuality, and other forms of sexual dissidence. No pornographer has ever been punished for being a woman hater, but not too long ago information about female sexuality, contraception, and abortion was assumed to be obscene. In a male supremacist society the only obscenity law that will not be used against women is no law at all.

As an alternative to an outright ban on pornography, Brownmiller and others have advocated restricting its display. There is a plausible case to be made for the idea that antiwoman images displayed so prominently that they are impossible to avoid are coercive, a form of active harassment that oversteps the bounds of free speech. But aside from the evasion involved in simply equating pornography with misogyny or sexual sadism, there are no legal or logical grounds for treating sexist material any differently from (for example) racist or anti-Semitic propaganda; an equitable law would have to prohibit any kind of public defamation. And the very thought of such a sweeping law has to make anyone with an imagination nervous. Could Catholics claim they were being harassed by nasty depictions of the pope? Could Russian refugees argue that the display of Communist literature was a form of psychological torture? Would proabortion material be taken off the shelves on the grounds that it defamed the unborn? I'd rather not find out.

At the moment the First Amendment issue remains hypothetical; the movement has concentrated on raising the issue of pornography through demonstrations and other public actions. This is certainly a legitimate strategy. Still, I find myself more and more disturbed by the tenor of antipornography actions and the sort of consciousness they promote; increasingly their focus has shifted from rational feminist criticism of specific targets to generalized, demagogic moral outrage. Picketing an antiwoman movie, defacing an exploitative billboard, or boycotting a record company to protest its misogynist album covers conveys one kind of message, mass marches Against Pornography quite another. Similarly, there is a difference between telling the neighborhood news dealer why it pisses us off to have *Penthouse* shoved in our faces and choosing as a prime target every right-thinking politician's symbol of big-city sin, Times Square.

In contrast to the abortion rights movement, which is struggling against a tidal wave of energy from the other direction, the antiporn campaign is respectable. It gets approving press and . . . has begun to attract women whose perspective on other matters is in no way feminist ("I'm anti-abortion," a participant in WAP's march on Times Square told a reporter, "but this is something I can get into"). Despite the insistence of WAP organizers that they support sexual freedom, their line appeals to the antisexual emotions that feed the backlash.

Review and Discussion Questions

1. Longino believes, and Willis denies, that there is a difference between erotica and pornography. With whom do you agree, and why?

2. Do you agree with Willis that women can enjoy pornography? How is this contention relevant to her argument? How might a critic of pornography, like Longino, respond to it?

3. Explain and assess Willis's claim that pornography is "deeply reactionary" and yet "expresses a radical impulse."

4. Is opposition to pornography really hostility toward lust and an attempt to repress people's unruly sexual feelings and fantasies, as Willis suggests, or is it a legitimate effort to free sexuality from sexism and misogyny, as Longino would claim?

5. Would banning pornography violate free speech? What about regulating its display?

6. Longino argues that "the campaign against [pornography] is an essential component of women's struggle for legal, economic, and social equality, one which requires the support of all feminists." Why would Willis reject this proposition? With whom do you agree, and why? Should feminists oppose pornography?

Alcohol and Rape

NICHOLAS DIXON

A man who has sex with a woman who has passed out after consuming large quantities of alcohol is guilty of rape while a man who has sex with a woman who is slightly tipsy but who later regrets their lovemaking is innocent of rape. In this essay, Nicholas Dixon, professor of philosophy at Alma College in Michigan, explores the problematic intermediate cases of what he calls "impaired sex," in which a woman responds to a man's sexual advances when she is very drunk but later wishes she had not. Is this rape? Dixon critically assesses two rival approaches to this question: the communicative sexuality model of Lois Pineau and the "women's responsibility for sex" view, associated with Katie Roiphe and Camille Paglia. Although he concurs with Pineau that men have a moral obligation to ensure that their partners consent to sex, Dixon raises some difficulties for the idea of criminalizing impaired sex.

Reprinted by permission from Public Affairs Quarterly, *vol. 15, no. 4 (October 2001). Copyright © 2001* Public Affairs Quarterly.

Study Questions

1. In the crime of rape, what do *actus reus* and *mens rea* refer to?
2. What does Dixon mean by impaired sex? How does it differ from his two limiting cases?
3. What approach to impaired sex do Katie Roiphe and Camille Paglia take?
4. What is the central tenet of Pineau's model of communicative sexuality? From her perspective, why might a man's explicitly asking a woman for consent sometimes be insufficient?
5. What exceptions are there to the demand that men always refrain from impaired sex?
6. What two reasons does Dixon give for believing that making impaired sex a felony would be unfair to men?

M ANY DATE OR ACQUAINTANCE RAPES, especially those that occur in a college setting, involve the use of alcohol by both rapist and victim. To what extent, if any, should the fact that a woman has been drinking alcohol before she has sexual relations affect our determination of whether or not she has been raped? I will consider the impact of the woman's intake of alcohol on both the *actus reus* ("guilty act") and *mens rea* ("guilty mind") elements of rape. A man is guilty of rape only if he not only commits the *actus reus* of rape—sex without his partner's consent—but does so with the requisite guilty mind, that is, intentionally, knowingly, recklessly, or negligently. I will take for granted that, regardless of a woman's alcoholic intake, she has been raped whenever a man forces himself on her after she says "no" or otherwise resists. I will focus instead on situations when women who have been drinking provide varying levels of acquiescence to sex. Let us begin by considering two relatively straightforward examples, which we can use as limiting cases, of sexual encounters involving alcohol.

I. Two Limiting Cases

A. Fraternity gang rape

In 1988 four Florida State University fraternity members allegedly had sex with an 18-year-old female student after she had passed out with an almost lethal blood alcohol level of .349 percent.

Afterwards, she was allegedly "dumped" in a different fraternity house.

If these events, which led to a five-year ban on the fraternity chapter, really happened, the woman was certainly raped. Since a woman who is unconscious after heavy drinking is unable to consent, the fraternity members committed the *actus reus* of rape. Moreover, any claim that they were unaware of her lack of consent, thus potentially negating the *mens rea* requirement, would ring hollow. We may extrapolate beyond this extreme case to situations where a person is so drunk that, while she is conscious, she is barely aware of where she is and who her partner is, and she has no recollection of what has happened the following day. She may acquiesce and give the physiological responses that indicate consent, and she may even say "yes" when asked whether she wants to have sex, but her mental state is so impaired by alcohol that she cannot give a sufficiently meaningful level of consent to rebut rape charges against the man with whom she has sexual relations.

B. A regretted sexual encounter

A male and female college student go on a dinner date, and both drink a relatively small amount of alcohol, say a glass of wine or beer. The conversation flows freely, and she agrees to go back to his place to continue the evening. They have one more drink there, start kissing and making out, and he asks her to spend the night. She is not drunk and, impressed by his gentle and communicative manner, accepts his offer. However, she is not used to drinking, and, although she is not significantly cognitively impaired—her speech is not slurred and her conversation is lucid—her inhibitions have been markedly lowered by the alcohol. When she wakes up alongside him the following morning, she bitterly regrets their lovemaking.

No rape has occurred. While she now regrets having spent the night with her date, and would quite likely not have agreed to do so had she not drunk any alcohol, her consent at the time was sufficiently voluntary to rule out any question of rape. While their sexual encounter violated her more lasting values, this no more entails that she did not "really" consent than the fact that my overeating at dinner violates my long-term plan to diet entails that my indulgence was not an autonomous action. Moreover, even if we granted for the sake of argument the far fetched claim that the *actus reus* of rape occurred, his belief that she did consent was perfectly reasonable, so he would still fail to exhibit the requisite *mens rea*. We do not have to agree with Katie Roiphe's controversial views on date rape to accept her point that a distinction exists between rape and bad sex.[1] Unwisely having sex after unwisely drinking alcohol is not necessarily rape. We do a lot of unwise things when drinking, like *continuing* to drink too long and getting a bad hangover, and staying up too late when we have to work the next day. In neither case would we question our consent to our act of continuing to drink or staying up late. Why should a person's consent to sex after moderate amounts of drinking be any more suspect?

II. Problematic Intermediate Cases: Impaired Sex

Real sexual encounters involving alcohol tend to fall in between these two limiting cases. Imagine, for instance, a college student who gets very drunk at a party. Her blood alcohol level is well above the legal limit for driving. She is slurring her words and is unsteady on her feet, but she knows where she is and with whom she is speaking or dancing. She ends up spending the night with a guy at the party—perhaps someone she has just met, perhaps an acquaintance, but no one with whom she is in an ongoing relationship. She willingly responds to his sexual advances, but, like the woman in case I.B, horribly regrets her sexual encounter the next day. Although she remembers going home with the guy from the party, she cannot recall much else from the evening and night. Let us call this intermediate case, in which the woman's judgment is significantly impaired by alcohol, "impaired sex." Has she been raped?

In the next two subsections I will examine two competing analyses of impaired sex, each one suggested by one of the limiting cases in section I. First, though, I pause to consider how relevant the degree to which the man has helped to bring about the woman's impaired state is to the question of whether rape has occurred. Suppose that he has deliberately got her drunk, cajoling her to down drink after drink, with the intention of lowering her resistance to his planned sexual advances? The very fact that he uses such a strategy implies that he doubts that she would agree to have sex with him if she were sober. Should she bring rape charges, on the ground that her acquiescence to sex when she was drunk was invalid, his claim that he believed that she voluntarily consented would appear disingenuous. His recklessness in disregarding doubts about the voluntariness of her consent arguably meets the *mens rea* requirement. (Remember that in this section we are discussing women who are very drunk to the point of slurring their words and being unsteady on their feet, not those who are less inhibited after drinking a moderate amount of alcohol.)

For the remainder of this paper, I will focus instead on the more difficult variant of impaired sex in which the man does not use alcohol as a tool for seduction. Instead, he meets the woman when she is already drunk, or else he drinks with her with no designs on getting her drunk. In either case, he spontaneously takes advantage of the situation in which he finds himself. Is he guilty of rape?

A. *Women's responsibility for their own actions*

Few would deny that the woman in section I.B is responsible for her own unwise decision to engage in a sexual encounter that she now regrets. Katie Roiphe and Camille Paglia would extend this approach to impaired sex, involving a woman who is very drunk but not incoherent. Roiphe insists that women are autonomous adults who are responsible for the consequences of their use of alcohol and other drugs.[2] And Paglia argues that sex is an inherently risky business, in which rape is an ever-present danger. Rather than complain about sexual assault, women who desire to be sexually active should take steps to minimize its danger, by being alert to warning signs, learning self-defense, and avoiding getting drunk when doing so would put them at risk for rape.[3]

Both Roiphe and Paglia are vulnerable to powerful criticisms. For instance, Roiphe's blanket dismissal of the extensive date rape literature is based on her own flimsy anecdotal evidence and a superficial reading of the studies. And, among multiple outrageous, offensive comments about uncontrollable male sexuality and women's desire to be with abusive he-men, Paglia is especially guilty of blatant victim-blaming. Even if it does result from a woman's recklessness, rape is still rape and the rapist is primarily to blame. We would not dream of exonerating a Central Park mugger because the victim was foolish to go there at 4 a.m. Indeed, the whole point of "Take Back the Night" marches is precisely that the burden is on *aggressors* to stop their violence, not on women to change their behavior to accommodate aggressors.

However, we can isolate from their more dubious views a relatively uncontroversial underlying principle, which is surely congenial to liberal and most other types of feminists: namely, that we should respect women's status as agents, and we should not degrade them by treating them as incapable of making autonomous decisions

about alcohol and sexuality. We should, instead, hold women at least partly responsible for the consequences of their voluntary decision to drink large amounts of alcohol, made in full knowledge that it may result in choices that they will later regret. This principle would count against regarding impaired sex as rape. A plausible corollary of this principle is that women, as autonomous beings, have a duty to make their wishes about sex clear to their partners. When a woman drinks heavily and ends up having a sexual encounter that she later regrets she has failed to exercise this positive duty of autonomous people. Her actions have sent the wrong message to her partner, and to blame him for the sex in which she willingly engages but that she later regrets seems unfair. Even if we allow that her consent is so impaired that the *actus reus* of rape has occurred, on this view he does not fulfill the *mens rea* element of the crime of rape. The onus is on the woman to communicate her lack of consent and, in the absence of such communication, his belief in her consent is quite reasonable. In sum, proponents of this approach hesitate to regard impaired sex as rape, because doing so suggests that women are unable to make autonomous decisions about alcohol and sexuality, and because it ignores women's positive duty to exercise their autonomy by clearly communicating their considered preferences (and not just their momentary passion) about sex.

B. *Communicative sexuality: Men's duty to ensure that women consent*

The "women's responsibility for sex" approach is very plausible in case I.B, where a woman later regrets sex in which she willingly engaged after moderate drinking. However, men's accountability for unwanted sex becomes unavoidable in the gang rape described in subsection I.A. Granted, the female student may have voluntarily and very unwisely chosen to drink massive amounts of alcohol, but once she had passed out, the four fraternity members who allegedly had intercourse with her had absolutely no reason to believe that she consented to sex. Regardless of whether they deliberately got her drunk or, on the other hand, took advantage of her after finding her in this condition, they are guilty of recklessly ignoring the evident risk that she did not consent, and hence fulfill the *mens rea* requirement for rape.

In cases such as this, Lois Pineau's model of "communicative sexuality" becomes enormously plausible.[4] While Pineau's view does not preclude regarding women as having a duty to clearly communicate their wishes regarding sexual intimacy—indeed, such a duty may be an integral part of communicative sexuality—its central tenet is that men too are responsible for ensuring that effective communication occurs. In particular, the burden is on men to ensure that their female partners really do consent to sexual intimacy, and they should refrain from sexual activity if they are not sure of this consent. A reasonable belief that a woman consented to sex will still count as a defense against rape, but the reasonableness of this belief will itself be judged on whether it would have been reasonable, from the woman's point of view, to consent to sex. Since virtually no woman would want four men to have sex with her after she has passed into an alcoholic coma, in the absence of some miraculous evidence that the female student actually wanted sex in such unpleasant circumstances, the four fraternity members blatantly violated their duty to be sure of the woman's consent, and are indeed guilty of rape.

More generally, Pineau argues that it is never reasonable to assume that a woman consents to "aggressive noncommunicative sex." Not only does her approach regard the extreme case of sex with an unconscious person as rape, but it would put any man who fails to take reasonable precautions to ensure that a woman consents to sex at risk for a rape conviction should she later declare that she did not consent. When doubt exists about consent, the burden is on the man to *ask*. The much-discussed Antioch University "Sexual Offense Policy," which requires explicit consent to each new level of sexual intimacy every time it

occurs, is a quasi-legal enactment of Pineau's model of communicative sexuality.

Pineau's approach entails a very different analysis of our central case of impaired sex than the "women's responsibility for sex" model discussed in the previous section. At first blush, one might think that all that Pineau would require of a man would be to ask the woman whether she is really sure that she wants to continue with sexual intimacy. If he boldly forges ahead without even asking the woman this question, and if the woman later claims that she was too drunk for her acquiescence to sex to constitute genuine consent, he risks being found guilty of Pineau's proposed category of "nonaggravated sexual assault," which would carry a lighter penalty than "standard" rape when a woman communicates her lack of consent by saying "no" or otherwise resisting.

But even explicitly asking the woman for consent may be insufficient to protect him from blame and liability under the communicative sexuality model. The issue is precisely whether the word "yes," when spoken by a woman who is very drunk, is sufficient evidence of her consent. Being very drunk means that her judgment is impaired, as is evident from her horror and regret the following morning when she realizes what she has done. Given that we are only too aware of our propensity to do things that we later regret when we are very drunk, the man in this situation has good reason to doubt whether the woman's acquiescence to his advances and her "yes" to his explicit question is a fully autonomous reflection of lasting values and desires. Since he cannot be reasonably sure that the woman consents, he should refrain from sexual intercourse. Even if he is unaware of the danger that she does not consent, he *should* be aware and is, therefore, guilty of negligence. His belief that she consents may be sincere, but it is unreasonable and does not provide a defense to charges of nonaggravated sexual assault. On Pineau's "communicative sexuality" model, then, the man who proceeds with impaired sex meets both the *actus reus* and *mens rea* requirements of nonaggravated sexual assault.

III. Should We Punish Men for Impaired Sex?

Pineau's claim that men have a *moral obligation* to ensure that their partners consent to sex is very plausible. Given alcohol's tendency to cloud people's judgment, men should be especially careful to ensure that a woman consents to sex when she is very drunk. In most circumstances, this requires simply refraining from sexual activity. Imposing this relatively minor restriction on men's sexual freedom seems amply justified by the goal of preventing the enormous harm of rape. However, whether we should find men who fail to meet this duty and proceed to have sex with very drunk women guilty of rape—or even of nonaggravated sexual assault or a similar felony carrying a lighter penalty than "standard" rape— is much more controversial.

A. The importance of context

Alan Soble criticizes the Antioch University policy on the ground that it fails to distinguish between different types of sexual encounters. Its demand that people obtain explicit verbal consent to each new level of sexual activity during each sexual encounter may be appropriate for one night stands with strangers. However, it seems unduly intrusive in the context of an ongoing, committed relationship, when the partners may well be sufficiently well attuned to one another's body language to be reasonably sure that both people consent to sex. Under Antioch's policy, "[t]he history of the relationship, let alone the history of the evening, counts for nothing."[5]

A similar criticism applies to the demand that men always refrain from impaired sex. While the existence of a long-term, committed relationship does not provide a man with immunity from charges of sexual misconduct—marital rape, after all, can occur—men may reasonably proceed with sexual intimacy with long-term partners who are very drunk when doing so with a stranger would be wrong. In the case of a stranger, the only clue to her wishes that he has is her current, drunken acquiescence, whereas his history of consenting lovemaking with his partner, presumably often when both are sober, gives him every reason to believe that her current consent is fully voluntary and reflective of her ongoing desires. Another exception that could apply even in the case of one-night stands would be when a woman, while sober, gives her advance consent to consuming large amounts of alcohol followed by sexual activity. So if we do criminalize sex with women whose judgment is impaired by large amounts of alcohol, we need to build in exceptions for ongoing relationships and advance consent.

B. Social conventions on consent to sex

Pineau herself recognizes that a just rape law must "ensur[e] that men are not convicted of felonies they could not reasonably have known they were committing."[6] Thus it is precisely because the man in case I.B had no reason to suspect that his partner did not consent that he is innocent of rape. Husak and Thomas fear that "narrowing the 'mistake of fact' defense" to rape—and such would certainly be the effect of criminalizing impaired sex—will result in the unjust conviction of men who reasonably believed that their partner consented to sex. The problem is that social conventions concerning how women demonstrate consent and nonconsent to sex are likely to lag behind any reformist rape laws, and "the punishment of persons whose behavior is reasonable according to existing conventions is manifestly unjust."[7] Similarly, while Catharine Wells supports the goal of better protecting women against nonconsensual sex, she is "concerned that individual criminals are not scapegoated for societal sexism. Criminal liability is a serious matter—it is hardly the place to experiment with rearrangements of social relations."[8]

While such concerns are reasonable, they do not provide a fatal objection to the proposed change to the rape law concerning alcohol. As Pineau points out in defense of her proposal to reform rape law in accordance with the need for communicative sexuality,

Provided that a law is duly promulgated, we expect citizens to adjust their behavior to conform with the law. This expectation is indeed one of the most fundamental tenets of the legal system. It is formulated as the maxim "Ignorance of the law is no excuse." Without this principle and the principle of fair notice (that the law be promulgated), it would indeed be impossible to make legal changes fairly.[9]

If we were indeed to make impaired sex a category of rape, the massive publicity that such a controversial reform would likely bring would guarantee all men fair warning of the new restriction.

C. Imprecise distinctions and fairness to men

Because of the risk of the substantial harm of sex without a woman's fully voluntary consent, men should normally not have impaired sex. And, provided that we widely publicize the change in rape law and allow exceptions for established relationships and advance consent, criminalizing impaired sex would not be inherently unfair to men. The strongest reason against doing so is that implementing such a law would be a logistical nightmare that would indeed create the risk of unjustly convicting men.

Distinctions that are morally significant are difficult to translate into law. For instance, whether a man deliberately encourages a woman to drink large amounts of alcohol in order to make her more responsive to his sexual advances or, on the other hand, encounters her when she is already drunk or else innocently drinks with her with no intention of taking advantage of her, is relevant to our judgment of his actions. However, proving such subtle differences in intention would be extremely difficult, especially when the prosecution's star witness, the woman who was allegedly assaulted, was drunk at the crucial time.

The biggest logistical problem of all concerns drawing boundaries. The only clear cases are of the type discussed in section I: sex with a woman who is unconscious or incoherent due to alcohol (rape), and communicative sex with a lucid,

slightly tipsy woman who later regrets it (no rape). In between these limiting cases is a vast array of situations, whose diversity is concealed by my use of the blanket category of impaired sex. Just how impaired does a woman's judgment have to be to fall into this category? At what point does a woman progress from being merely tipsy, and responsible for any poor judgments that she makes as a result of her condition, to being so impaired that a man who proceeds to have sex with her recklessly or negligently runs the risk of sex without her fully voluntary consent? We saw in the last subsection that criminalizing a behavior that was previously considered acceptable is not inherently unfair. But the vagueness of the meaning of "significantly impaired" does indeed create doubts about whether men would have fair warning about how to conform their behavior to this new law. Saying that when in doubt, men should err on the side of caution is fair enough, but the only way to be completely sure of avoiding conviction for this felony would be to completely abstain from sex with women who have drunk any alcohol, and this would be an unreasonable restriction on sexual freedom. A law that gives fair warning requires a certain amount of precision about the forbidden behavior, and this is hard to come by in matters of impairment due to alcohol. Setting a certain blood alcohol level as the cutoff point seems arbitrary, and requiring a man to be aware of his partner's reading on this scale seems unreasonable and even absurd.

In defense of criminalizing impaired sex, one might argue that making judgment calls about how a legal rule applies to a particular case is precisely what courts are supposed to do. This approach works well when courts are asked to determine how a clear-cut rule applies to the often messy details of a case. The problem here, though, is that the distinction on which impaired sex is based is itself fuzzy, making judgments about whether rape has occurred doubly difficult.

Those who would make impaired sex a felony might point out the analogy with drunk driving laws, in which we set a more or less arbitrary blood alcohol level as the legally acceptable limit, in full knowledge that this limit corresponds only approximately with drivers' level of impairment. The overwhelmingly good overall consequences of a law that deters drunk driving help us to accept the occasional minor injustice of convicting a person whose driving ability was, despite his or her illegal blood alcohol level, not significantly affected. In this light, my dismissal of a blood alcohol level as a cutoff point for impaired sex may have been premature. Such a law would give men a strong incentive to refrain from sex when they have any doubts that their potential partner may be too impaired to give fully voluntary consent.

However, criminalizing impaired sex when the woman's blood alcohol level is above a certain limit is unacceptable for several reasons. First, it places an onerous burden on the man to know his partner's blood alcohol level, in contrast to drunk driving laws, which require us to monitor our *own* intake of intoxicants. Even a man who accompanies his partner throughout her drinking may be unaware of her tolerance level, which may be unusually low. Men who meet women who have already been drinking would have even less reason to be sure that their blood alcohol level is within the legal limit. To be sure of escaping conviction for rape, men in these circumstances would have to either administer portable breathalyzer tests to their partners or else simply abstain from sex. Now showing such restraint may be precisely the kind of caring, thoughtful behavior that we, following Pineau's communicative sexuality model, want to encourage. But to require men to do so, on pain of criminal sanctions (typically imprisonment), seems to be an unduly heavy-handed intrusion into the sex lives of two adults.

Second, measuring a woman's blood alcohol level in order to secure convictions for rape will very likely not be feasible in most cases. Courts need to know her level of impairment at the time of the alleged rape, but in very few cases will a woman be available for a blood test immediately after the sexual encounter. Even an hour after-

wards may be too late, in that her blood alcohol level may have dropped below the legal limit for her partner to be at risk for impaired sex. Due to the emotional trauma or the effects of alcohol, many women will not report the incident until several hours afterwards or even the next day, by which time most or all of the alcohol will have worked its way through her system.

In sum, making impaired sex a felony would be unfair to men, in that the concept "significantly impaired" is too vague for (1) courts to be able to make non-arbitrary judgments to distinguish the guilty from the innocent or (2) men to have fair warning to enable them to conform their behavior to the law. If, on the other hand, we make the law more precise and objective by specifying a blood alcohol content above which a woman's sexual partner would be liable for prosecution for impaired sex, we are placing an undue burden on men whose potential sexual partners have been drinking. Moreover, few women who believe that they have been raped will submit to blood alcohol tests early enough to secure convictions for impaired sex.

One way we might soften the blow of concerns with fair warning would be to make impaired sex a misdemeanor rather than a felony. Such a law would protect women, while the occasional injustice done to men who are convicted though they reasonably believe that their partners consent would result only in such minimal penalties as suspended sentences, fines, or community service. Granted, these minimal penalties might provide little deterrence to men, but they would at least send the desired message that men should exercise care in sexual intimacy when alcohol is involved. And the fact that the penalties are light would minimize whatever danger might exist of frivolous or vindictive complaints against men. However, even if we reduce it to a misdemeanor, we would be hard pressed to rid impaired sex of the connotations of moral turpitude that currently attach to rape and other sexual offenses, so the issue of fair warning would remain significant. Moreover, even though the penalties for a misdemeanor would be slight, we should hesitate to involve courts in prosecuting cases that are very difficult to prove and that people may well sometimes justly perceive as unfair to defendants.

IV. Conclusion

Existing rape laws probably suffice to convict men for clear cases of sexual misconduct involving alcohol, such as sex with unconscious women or with women who are drunk to the point of incoherence. In jurisdictions where such laws do not exist, we should create a category of rape—on the lines of "sex with a partner who is incapable of consent"—that would criminalize such cases. Granted, complications would arise. We would probably have to allow for exceptions for advance consent and for ongoing relationships. And, as in all rape cases, proving guilt may often be difficult, often reducing to "her word against his." But the harm done by men who take advantage of women in such circumstances is great enough to justify taking on these problems.

However, we would do better to deal with impaired sex by means of moral disapproval and educational measures rather than legal sanctions. The dangers of unjustly convicting men on the basis of unworkable distinctions, and of simultaneously degrading women (however inadvertently) and being unfair to men by underestimating women's ability to take responsibility for their alcohol intake and sexuality, are too great. Instead, we should regard impaired sex as a moral wrong on the lines of obtaining sexual gratification by means of trickery, such as concealing the fact that one has a spouse or significant other, or declaring one's undying love when all one wants is a brief fling. In the case of both impaired sex and trickery, one's partner is prevented from making a fully autonomous decision about her sexual activity: either because her judgment is clouded by alcohol, or because she has been denied vital information. Both are wrong, and both are better dealt with by informal sanctions than by inevitably heavy-handed and sometimes unfair legal interventions.

NOTES

1. The relevant passage from Roiphe's book *The Morning After* is reprinted in Robert Trevas, Arthur Zucker, and Donald Borchert (eds.), *Philosophy of Sex and Love: A Reader* (Upper Saddle River, N.J.: Prentice Hall, 1997), p. 366.
2. *Ibid.*, p. 365.
3. Camille Paglia, "Date Rape: Another Perspective," William H. Shaw (ed.), *Social and Personal Ethics*, 2nd edition (Belmont, Calif.: Wadsworth Publishing Co., 1996).
4. Lois Pineau, "Date Rape: A Feminist Analysis," *Law and Philosophy* 8 (1989).
5. See Alan Soble, "Antioch's 'Sexual Offense Policy': A Philosophical Exploration," *Journal of Social Philosophy*, vol. 28, no. 1 (Spring 1997) for an excellent analysis and critique of Antioch's policy, p. 30.
6. Pineau, "Date Rape," p. 146.
7. Douglas N. Husak and George C. Thomas III, "Date Rape, Social Convention, and Reasonable Mistakes," Lori Gruen and George E. Panichas (eds.), *Sex, Morality and the Law* (London: Routledge, 1997), p. 453.
8. Catharine Pierce Wells, "Date Rape and the Law: Another Feminist View," p. 43.
9. Lois Pineau, "A Response to My Critics," Leslie Francis (ed.), *Date Rape*, p. 85.

Review and Discussion Questions

1. Is impaired sex a kind of rape? Contrast the view of Katie Roiphe and Camille Paglia with that of Lois Pineau. Whose view is the most plausible?

2. Is it morally wrong for a man to have sex with a willing woman if he suspects that if she were sober, she would not consent? Explain why or why not. Suppose he believes that she would probably consent even if sober, but he's not sure. What should he do?

3. Suppose that a woman would not have had sex with a man if she hadn't been drunk. But she doesn't regret it the next day. Does this constitute impaired sex?

4. Suppose a women becomes intoxicated, knowing that this will make it more likely that she will have a sexual encounter that she will regret. Does this diminish her partner's responsibility to avoid impaired sex? Do women have a moral obligation to avoid impaired sex, or do only men have this obligation? If women do have it, is this an obligation that women have to men?

5. Dixon believes that impaired sex is wrong because it is harmful to women. But what about men—can impaired sex be harmful to them? How detrimental is it to have sex that you agree to at the time but later regret?

6. Dixon believes that men have a moral obligation to avoid impaired sex. But suppose that both the man and woman are drunk when they have impaired sex. Does Dixon's position imply that the man is morally responsible for his drunken conduct, but the woman is not?

7. Critically assess Antioch University's "Sexual Offense Policy." Is it a good idea? Is it viable? Does it rest on a plausible understanding of sexuality? Should universities have official policies governing alcohol and sexual intimacy between students?

8. Would making impaired sex a misdemeanor have good social consequences?

9. Dixon compares impaired sex to obtaining sexual gratification by trickery, but what if the man is not responsible for the woman's drunken condition?

Why Shouldn't Tommy and Jim Have Sex?

JOHN CORVINO

In this essay, John Corvino, a philosophy professor at Wayne State University, argues for the morality of homosexuality. Many people believe that homosexuality is wrong because it is unnatural. Corvino examines several possible meanings of "unnatural" and argues that none of them support moral criticism of homosexual activity. He goes on to disarm religious objections to it and to defend it against the charge that it harms those who engage in it, endangers children, or threatens society. Because there are no reasonable moral objections to homosexual conduct, and because it promotes the happiness and well-being of homosexually inclined people, we should abandon society's traditional rejection of it.

Study Questions

1. Why does one need a strong reason to deny a sexual relationship to Tommy and Jim?

2. What are the five possible meanings of "unnatural" that Corvino discusses?

3. Corvino criticizes both those who say that homosexuals are born that way and therefore it is natural and right for them to form homosexual relationships and those who say that homosexuality is a lifestyle choice and therefore unnatural and wrong. Explain.

From John Corvino, ed., Same Sex: Debating the Ethics, Science, and Culture of Homosexuality *(Lanham, Md.: Rowman & Littlefield Publishers, 1997). Reprinted by permission of the publisher.*

4. Why does Corvino reject the idea that homosexuality is unnatural because it cannot lead to procreation?

5. Corvino contends that even if there were reliable statistical evidence linking homosexual activity to promiscuity, suicide, depression, or other harms, this would still not establish what the critic of gay rights purports to prove. Explain.

6. How does he respond to the argument that homosexuality threatens children?

7. Explain how interpreting the Bible in historical context shows that its strictures against usury or homosexuality are not relevant to contemporary banking or contemporary homosexuality.

T OMMY AND JIM ARE A HOMOSEXUAL couple I know. Tommy is an accountant; Jim is a botany professor. They are in their forties and have been together fourteen years, the last five of which they've lived in a Victorian house that they've lovingly restored. Although their relationship has had its challenges, each has made sacrifices for the sake of the other's happiness and the relationship's long-term success.

I assume that Tommy and Jim have sex with each other (although I've never bothered to ask). Furthermore, I contend that they probably *should* have sex with each other. For one thing, sex is pleasurable. But it is also much more than that: a sexual relationship can unite two people in a way that virtually nothing else can. It can be an avenue of growth, of communication, and of lasting interpersonal fulfillment. These are reasons why most heterosexual couples have sex even if they don't want children, don't want children yet, or don't want additional children. And if these reasons are good enough for most heterosexual couples, then they should be good enough for Tommy and Jim.

Of course, having a reason to do something does not preclude there being an even better reason for not doing it. Tommy might have a good reason for drinking orange juice (it's tasty and nutritious) but an even better reason for not doing so (he's allergic). The point is that one would need a pretty good reason for denying a sexual relationship to Tommy and Jim, given the intense benefits widely associated with such relationships. The question I shall consider in this paper is thus quite simple: Why shouldn't Tommy and Jim have sex?

Homosexual Sex Is "Unnatural"

Many contend that homosexual sex is "unnatural." But what does that mean? Many things that people value—clothing, houses, medicine, and government, for example—are unnatural in some sense. On the other hand, many things that people detest—disease, suffering, and death, for example—are "natural" in the sense that they occur "in nature." If the unnaturalness charge is to be more than empty rhetorical flourish, those who levy it must specify what they mean. Borrowing from Burton Leiser, I will examine several possible meanings of "unnatural."[1]

What is unusual or abnormal is unnatural

One meaning of "unnatural" refers to that which deviates from the norm, that is, from what most people do. Obviously, most people engage in heterosexual relationships. But does it follow that it is wrong to engage in homosexual relationships? Relatively few people read Sanskrit, pilot ships, play the mandolin, breed goats, or write with both hands, yet none of these activities is immoral simply because it is unusual. As the Ramsey Colloquium, a group of Jewish and Christian scholars who oppose homosexuality, writes, "The statistical frequency of an act does not determine its moral status."[2] So while homosexuality might be unnatural in the sense of being unusual, that fact is morally irrelevant.

What is not practiced by other animals is unnatural

Some people argue, "Even animals know better than to behave homosexually; homosexuality must be wrong." This argument is doubly flawed. First, it rests on a false premise. Numerous studies—including Anne Perkins's study of "gay" sheep and George and Molly Hunt's study of "lesbian" seagulls—have shown that some animals do form homosexual pair-bonds. Second, even if animals did not behave homosexually, that fact would not prove that homosexuality is immoral. After all, animals don't cook their food, brush their teeth, participate in religious worship, or attend college; human beings do all of these without moral censure. Indeed, the idea that animals could provide us with our standards—especially our sexual standards—is simply amusing.

What does not proceed from innate desires is unnatural

Recent studies suggesting a biological basis for homosexuality have resulted in two popular positions. One side proposes that homosexual people are "born that way" and that it is therefore natural (and thus good) for them to form homosexual relationships. The other side maintains that homosexuality is a lifestyle choice, which is therefore unnatural (and thus wrong). Both sides assume a connection between the origin of homosexual orientation, on the one hand, and the moral value of homosexual activity, on the other. And insofar as they share that assumption, both sides are wrong.

Consider first the pro-homosexual side: "They are born that way; therefore it's natural and good." This inference assumes that all innate desires are good ones (i.e., that they should be acted upon). But that assumption is clearly false. Research suggests that some people are born with a predisposition toward violence, but such people have no more right to strangle their neighbors than anyone else. So while people like Tommy and Jim may be born with homosexual tendencies, it doesn't follow that they ought to act on them. Nor does it follow that they ought *not* to act on them, even if the tendencies are not innate. I probably do not have any innate tendency to write with my left hand (since I, like everyone else in my family, have always been right-handed), but it doesn't follow that it would be immoral for me to do so. So simply asserting that homosexuality is a lifestyle choice will not show that it is an immoral lifestyle choice.

Do people "choose" to be homosexual? People certainly don't seem to choose their sexual *feelings*, at least not in any direct or obvious way. (Do you? Think about it.) Rather, they find certain people attractive and certain activities arousing, whether they "decide" to or not. Indeed, most people at some point in their lives wish that they could control their feelings more—for example, in situations of unrequited love—and find it frustrating that they cannot. What they *can* control to a considerable degree is how and when they act upon those feelings. In that sense, both homosexuality and heterosexuality involve lifestyle choices. But in either case, determining the origin of the feelings will not determine whether it is moral to act on them.

What violates an organ's principal purpose is unnatural

Perhaps when people claim that homosexual sex is unnatural they mean that it cannot result in procreation. The idea behind the argument is that human organs have various natural purposes: eyes are for seeing, ears are for hearing, genitals are for procreating. According to this argument, it is immoral to use an organ in a way that violates its particular purpose.

Many of our organs, however, have multiple purposes. Tommy can use his mouth for talking, eating, breathing, licking stamps, chewing gum, kissing women, or kissing Jim; and it seems rather arbitrary to claim that all but the last use are "natural." (And if we say that some of the other uses are "unnatural, but not immoral," we have failed to specify a morally relevant sense of the term "natural.")

Just because people can and do use their sexual organs to procreate, it does not follow that they should not use them for other purposes. Sexual organs seem very well suited for expressing love, for giving and receiving pleasure, and for celebrating, replenishing, and enhancing a relationship—even when procreation is not a factor. Unless opponents of homosexuality are prepared to condemn heterosexual couples who use contraception or individuals who masturbate, they must abandon this version of the unnaturalness argument. Indeed, even the Roman Catholic Church, which forbids contraception and masturbation, approves of sex for sterile couples and of sex during pregnancy, neither of which can lead to procreation. The Church concedes here that intimacy and pleasure are morally legitimate purposes for sex, even in cases where procreation is impossible. But since homosexual sex can achieve these purposes as well, it is inconsistent for the Church to condemn it on the grounds that it is not procreative.

One might object that sterile heterosexual couples do not *intentionally* turn away from procreation, whereas homosexual couples do. But this distinction doesn't hold. It is no more possible for Tommy to procreate with a woman whose uterus has been removed than it is for him to procreate with Jim. By having sex with either one, he is intentionally engaging in a nonprocreative sexual act.

Yet one might press the objection further and insist that Tommy and the woman *could* produce children if the woman were fertile: whereas homosexual relationships are essentially infertile, heterosexual relationships are only incidentally so. But what does that prove? Granted, it might require less of a miracle for a woman without a uterus to become pregnant than for Jim to become pregnant, but it would require a miracle nonetheless. Thus it seems that the real difference here is not that one couple is fertile and the other not, nor that one couple "could" be fertile (with the help of a miracle) and the other not, but rather that one couple is male-female and the other male-male. In other words, sex between Tommy and Jim is wrong because it's male-male—i.e., because it's homosexual. But that, of course, is no argument at all.

What is disgusting or offensive is unnatural

If often seems that when people call homosexuality "unnatural" they really just mean that it's disgusting. But plenty of morally neutral activities—handling snakes, eating snails, performing autopsies, cleaning toilets, and so on—disgust people. Indeed, for centuries, most people found interracial relationships disgusting, yet that feeling—which has by no means disappeared—hardly proves that such relationships are wrong. In sum, the charge that homosexuality is unnatural, at least in its most common forms, is longer on rhetorical flourish than on philosophical cogency. At best it expresses an aesthetic judgment, not a moral judgment.

Homosexual Sex Is Harmful

One might instead argue that homosexuality is harmful. The Ramsey Colloquium, for instance, argues that homosexuality leads to the breakdown of the family and, ultimately, of human society, and it points to the "alarming rates of sexual promiscuity, depression, and suicide and the ominous presence of AIDS within the homosexual subculture."[3] Thomas Schmidt marshals copious statistics to show that homosexual activity undermines physical and psychological health.[4] Such charges, if correct, would seem to provide strong evidence against homosexuality. But are the charges correct? And do they prove what they purport to prove?

One obvious (and obviously problematic) way to answer the first question is to ask people like

Tommy and Jim. It would appear that no one is in a better position to judge the homosexual lifestyle than those who know it firsthand. Yet it is unlikely that critics would trust their testimony. Indeed, the more homosexual people try to explain their lives, the more critics accuse them of deceitfully promoting an agenda. . . .

One might instead turn to statistics. An obvious problem with this tack is that both sides of the debate bring forth extensive statistics and "expert" testimony, leaving the average observer confused. There is a more subtle problem as well. Because of widespread antigay sentiment, many homosexual people won't acknowledge their romantic feelings to themselves, much less to researchers. I have known a number of gay men who did not "come out" until their forties and fifties, and no amount of professional competence on the part of interviewers would have been likely to open their closets sooner. Such problems compound the usual difficulties of finding representative population samples for statistical study.

Yet even if the statistical claims of gay rights opponents were true, they would not prove what they purport to prove, for several reasons. First, as any good statistician realizes, correlation does not equal cause. Even if homosexual people were more likely to commit suicide, be promiscuous, or contract AIDS than the general population, it would not follow that their homosexuality causes them to do these things. An alternative—and very plausible—explanation is that these phenomena, like the disproportionately high crime rates among African Americans, are at least partly a function of society's treatment of the group in question. Suppose you were told from a very early age that the romantic feelings that you experienced were sick, unnatural, and disgusting. Suppose further that expressing these feelings put you at risk of social ostracism or, worse yet, physical violence. Is it not plausible that you would, for instance, be more inclined to depression than you would be without such obstacles? And that such depression could, in its extreme forms, lead to suicide or other self-destructive behaviors? (It is indeed remarkable

that couples like Tommy and Jim continue to flourish in the face of such obstacles.)

A similar explanation can be given for the alleged promiscuity of homosexuals. The denial of legal marriage, the pressure to remain in the closet, and the overt hostility toward homosexual relationships are all more conducive to transient, clandestine encounters than they are to long-term unions. As a result, that which is challenging enough for heterosexual couples—settling down and building a life together—becomes far more challenging for homosexual couples. . . .

But what about AIDS? Opponents of homosexuality sometimes claim that even if homosexual sex is not, strictly speaking, immoral, it is still a bad idea, since it puts people at risk for AIDS and other sexually transmitted diseases. But that claim is misleading: it is infinitely more risky for Tommy to have sex with a woman who is HIV-positive than with Jim, who is HIV-negative. Obviously, it's not homosexuality that's harmful, it's the virus; and the virus may be carried by both heterosexual and homosexual people.

Now it may be true (in the United States, at least) that homosexual males are statistically more likely to carry the virus than heterosexual females and thus that homosexual sex is *statistically* more risky than heterosexual sex (in cases where the partner's HIV status is unknown). But opponents of homosexuality need something stronger than this statistical claim. For if it is wrong for men to have sex with men because their doing so puts them at a higher AIDS risk than heterosexual sex, then it is also wrong for women to have sex with men because their doing so puts them at a higher AIDS risk than homosexual sex (lesbians as a group have the lowest incidence of AIDS). Purely from the standpoint of AIDS risk, women ought to prefer lesbian sex.

If this response seems silly, it is because there is obviously more to choosing a romantic or sexual partner than determining AIDS risk. And a major part of the decision, one that opponents of homosexuality consistently overlook, is considering whether one can have a mutually fulfilling relationship with the partner. For many people like Tommy and Jim, such fulfillment—which most heterosexuals recognize to be an important component of human flourishing—is only possible with members of the same sex. . . .

In sum, there is nothing *inherently* risky about sex between persons of the same gender. It is only risky under certain conditions: for instance, if they exchange diseased bodily fluids or if they engage in certain "rough" forms of sex that could cause tearing of delicate tissue. Heterosexual sex is equally risky under such conditions. Thus, even if statistical claims like those of Schmidt and the Ramsey Colloquium were true, they would not prove that homosexuality is immoral. At best, they would prove that homosexual people—like everyone else—ought to take great care when deciding to become sexually active.

Of course, there's more to a flourishing life than avoiding harm. One might argue that even if Tommy and Jim are not harming each other by their relationship, they are still failing to achieve the higher level of fulfillment possible in a heterosexual relationship, which is rooted in the complementarity of male and female. But this argument just ignores the facts: Tommy and Jim are homosexual *precisely because* they find relationships with men (and, in particular, with each other) more fulfilling than relationships with women. Even evangelicals (who have long advocated "faith healing" for homosexuals) are beginning to acknowledge that the choice for most homosexual people is not between homosexual relationships and heterosexual relationships, but rather between homosexual relationships and celibacy. What the critics need to show, therefore, is that no matter how loving, committed, mutual, generous, and fulfilling the relationship may be, Tommy and Jim would flourish more if they were celibate. Given the evidence of their lives (and of others like them), this is a formidable task indeed.

Thus far I have focused on the allegation that homosexuality harms those who engage in it. But what about the allegation that homosexuality harms other, nonconsenting parties? Here I will

briefly consider two claims: that homosexuality threatens children and that it threatens society.

Those who argue that homosexuality threatens children may mean one of two things. First, they may mean that homosexual people are child molesters. Statistically, the vast majority of reported cases of child sexual abuse involve young girls and their fathers, stepfathers, or other familiar (and presumably heterosexual) adult males. But opponents of homosexuality argue that when one adjusts for relative percentage in the population, homosexual males appear more likely than heterosexual males to be child molesters. As I argued above, the problems with obtaining reliable statistics on homosexuality render such calculations difficult. Fortunately, they are also unnecessary.

Child abuse is a terrible thing. But when a heterosexual male molests a child (or rapes a woman or commits assault), the act does not reflect upon all heterosexuals. Similarly, when a homosexual male molests a child, there is no reason why that act should reflect upon all homosexuals. Sex with adults of the same sex is one thing; sex with *children* of the same sex is quite another. Conflating the two not only slanders innocent people, it also misdirects resources intended to protect children. Furthermore, many men convicted of molesting young boys are sexually attracted to adult women and report no attraction to adult men. To call such men "homosexual," or even "bisexual," is probably to stretch such terms too far.[5]

Alternatively, those who charge that homosexuality threatens children might mean that the increasing visibility of homosexual relationships makes children more likely to become homosexual. The argument for this view is patently circular. One cannot prove that doing X is bad by arguing that it causes other people to do X, which is bad. One must first establish independently that X is bad. That said, there is not a shred of evidence to demonstrate that exposure to homosexuality leads children to become homosexual.

But doesn't homosexuality threaten society? A Roman Catholic priest once put the argument to me as follows: "Of course homosexuality is bad for society. If everyone were homosexual, there would be no society." Perhaps it is true that if everyone were homosexual, there would be no society. But if everyone were a celibate priest, society would collapse just as surely, and my friend the priest didn't seem to think that he was doing anything wrong simply by failing to procreate. . . .

From the fact that the continuation of society requires procreation, it does not follow that *everyone* must procreate. Moreover, even if such an obligation existed, it would not preclude homosexuality. At best, it would preclude *exclusive* homosexuality: homosexual people who occasionally have heterosexual sex can procreate just fine. And given artificial insemination, even those who are exclusively homosexual can procreate. In short, the priest's claim—if everyone were homosexual, there would be no society—is false; and even if it were true, it would not establish that homosexuality is immoral. . . .

I have argued that Tommy and Jim's sexual relationship harms neither them nor society. On the contrary, it benefits both. It benefits them because it makes them happier—not merely in a short-term, hedonistic sense, but in a long-term, "big picture" sort of way. And, in turn, it benefits society, since it makes Tommy and Jim more stable, more productive, and more generous than they would otherwise be. In short, their relationship—including its sexual component—provides the same kinds of benefits that infertile heterosexual relationships provide (and perhaps other benefits as well). Nor should we fear that accepting their relationship and others like it will cause people to flee in droves from the institution of heterosexual marriage. After all, . . . the usual response to a gay person is not "How come *he* gets to be gay and I don't?"

Homosexuality Violates Biblical Teaching

At this point in the discussion, many people turn to religion. "If the secular arguments fail to prove that homosexuality is wrong," they say, "so much

the worse for secular ethics. This failure only proves that we need God for morality." Since people often justify their moral beliefs by appeal to religion, I will briefly consider the biblical position.

At first glance, the Bible's condemnation of homosexual activity seems unequivocal. Consider, for example, the following two passages, one from the "Old" Testament and one from the "New":

> You shall not lie with a male as with a woman; it is an abomination. (Lev. 18:22)

> For this reason God gave them up to degrading passions. Their women exchanged natural intercourse for unnatural, and in the same way also the men, giving up natural intercourse with women, were consumed with passion for one another. Men committed shameless acts with men and received in their own persons the due penalty for their error. (Rom. 1:26–27)

Note, however, that these passages are surrounded by other passages that relatively few people consider binding. For example, Leviticus also declares,

> The pig . . . is unclean for you. Of their flesh you shall not eat, and their carcasses you shall not touch; they are unclean for you. (11:7–8)

Taken literally, this passage not only prohibits eating pork, but also playing football, since footballs are made of pigskin. . . .

Similarly, St. Paul, author of the Romans passage, also writes, "Slaves, obey your earthly masters with fear and trembling, in singleness of heart, as you obey Christ" (Eph. 6:5)—morally problematic advice if there ever were any. Should we interpret this passage (as Southern plantation owners once did) as implying that it is immoral for slaves to escape? After all, God himself says in Leviticus,

> [Y]ou may acquire male and female slaves . . . from among the aliens residing with you, and from their families that are with you, who have been born in your land; and they may be your property. You may keep them as a possession for your children after you, for them to inherit as property. (25:44–46)

How can people maintain the inerrancy of the Bible in light of such passages? The answer, I think, is that they learn to interpret the passages *in their historical context.*

Consider the Bible's position on usury, the lending of money for interest (for *any* interest, not just excessive interest). The Bible condemns this practice in no uncertain terms. . . . Should believers therefore close their savings accounts? Not necessarily. According to orthodox Christian teaching, the biblical prohibition against usury no longer applies. The reason is that economic conditions have changed substantially since biblical times, such that usury no longer has the same negative consequences it had when the prohibitions were issued. Thus, the practice that was condemned by the Bible differs from contemporary interest banking in morally relevant ways.[6]

Yet are we not in a similar position regarding homosexuality? Virtually all scholars agree that homosexual relations during biblical times were vastly different from relationships like Tommy and Jim's. Often such relations were integral to pagan practices. In Greek society, they typically involved older men and younger boys. If those are the kinds of features that the biblical authors had in mind when they issued their condemnations, and such features are no longer typical, then the biblical condemnations no longer apply. As with usury, substantial changes in cultural context have altered the meaning and consequences—and thus the moral value—of the practice in question. Put another way, using the Bible's condemnations of homosexuality against contemporary homosexuality is like using its condemnations of usury against contemporary banking.

Let me be clear about what I am *not* claiming here. First, I am not claiming that the Bible has been wrong before and therefore may be wrong this time. The Bible may indeed be wrong on some matters, but for the purpose of this argument I am assuming its infallibility. Nor am I claiming that the Bible's age renders it entirely inapplicable to today's issues. Rather, I am claiming that when we do apply it, *we must pay attention to morally relevant cultural differences between biblical times and today.* Such attention will help us distinguish between specific time-bound prohibitions (for example, laws against usury or homosexual relations) and the enduring moral values they represent (for example, generosity or respect for persons). And as the above argument shows, my claim is not very controversial. Indeed, to deny it is to commit oneself to some rather strange views on slavery, usury, women's roles, astronomy, evolution, and the like.

Here, one might also make an appeal to religious pluralism. Given the wide variety of religious beliefs (e.g., the Muslim belief that women should cover their faces, the Orthodox Jewish belief against working on Saturday, and Hindu belief that cows are sacred and should not be eaten), each of us inevitably violates the religious beliefs of others. But we normally don't view such violations as occasions for moral censure, since we distinguish between beliefs that depend on particular revelations and beliefs that can be justified independently (e.g., that stealing is wrong). Without an independent justification for condemning homosexuality, the best one can say is, "My religion says so." But in a society that cherishes religious freedom, that reason alone does not normally provide grounds for moral or legal sanctions. That people still fall back on that reason in discussions of homosexuality suggests that they may not have much of a case otherwise.

Conclusion

As a last resort, opponents of homosexuality typically change the subject: "But what about incest, polygamy, and bestiality? If we accept Tommy and Jim's sexual relationship, why shouldn't we accept those as well?" Opponents of interracial marriage used a similar slippery-slope argument in the 1960s when the Supreme Court struck down antimiscegenation laws. It was a bad argument then, and it is a bad argument now.

Just because there are no good reasons to oppose interracial or homosexual relationships, it does not follow that there are no good reasons to oppose incestuous, polygamous, or bestial relationships. . . .

Why, then, do critics continue to push this objection? Perhaps it's because accepting homosexuality requires them to give up one of their favorite arguments: "It's wrong because we've always been taught that it's wrong." This argument—call it the argument from tradition—has an obvious appeal: people reasonably favor tried-and-true ideas over unfamiliar ones, and they recognize the foolishness of trying to invent morality from scratch. But the argument from tradition is also a dangerous argument, as any honest look at history will reveal.

I conclude that Tommy and Jim's relationship, far from being a moral abomination, is exactly what it appears to be to those who know them: a morally positive influence on their lives and on others. Accepting this conclusion takes courage, since it entails that our moral traditions are fallible. But when these traditions interfere with people's happiness for no sound reason, they defeat what is arguably the very point of morality: promoting individual and communal well-being. To put the argument simply, Tommy and Jim's relationship makes them better people. And that's not just good for Tommy and Jim: that's good for everyone.

NOTES

1. Burton M. Leiser, *Liberty, Justice, and Morals: Contemporary Value Conflicts* (New York: Macmillan, 1986), 51–57.

2. The Ramsey Colloquium, "The Homosexual Movement," *First Things* (March 1994), 15–20.

3. The Ramsey Colloquium, "Homosexual Movement," 19.

4. Thomas Schmidt, "The Price of Love" in *Straight and Narrow? Compassion and Clarity in the Homosexuality Debate* (Downers Grove, IL: InterVarsity Press, 1995), chap. 6.

5. Part of the problem here arises from the grossly simplistic categorization of people into two (or, at best, three) sexual orientations: heterosexual, homosexual, and bisexual. Clearly, there is great variety within (and beyond) these categories. See Frederick Suppe, "Explaining Homosexuality: Philosophical Issues, and Who Cares Anyhow?" in Timothy F. Murphy, ed., *Gay Ethics: Controversies in Outing, Civil Rights, and Sexual Science* (New York: Harrington Park Press, 1994), esp. 223–268, published simultaneously in the *Journal of Homosexuality* 27, nos. 3–4: 223–268.

6. See Richard P. McBrien, *Catholicism*, study ed. (San Francisco: Harper & Row, 1981), 1020.

Review and Discussion Questions

1. Critically assess Corvino's responses to each of the five different ways in which homosexuality might be thought to be unnatural. Do you find his reasoning convincing? Has he overlooked some other way in which homosexuality might be considered unnatural?

2. If homosexuality is not unnatural, is it therefore natural? What do you mean when you use the words *natural* and *unnatural*? Is something's naturalness or unnaturalness ever relevant to its rightness or wrongness?

3. Why are some people oriented toward partners of the same sex? Does it result from free choice, genetic makeup, one's early psychological formation, or something else? What explains society's traditional disapproval of homosexuality? Why do so many people believe it to be wrong or disgusting?

4. Is homosexual behavior risky? Is there some way in which it is a threat to society? Does exposure to homosexuals have any negative effects on children?

5. Assess Corvino's claim that because of cultural changes, Biblical condemnations of homosexuality no longer apply.

6. In defending homosexual activity against Biblical strictures, Corvino claims that he is not challenging the infallibility of the Bible. Is he correct about this, or does his argument presuppose that the Bible is mistaken on some matters?

7. Is discrimination against homosexuals always wrong? Should they be permitted to marry?

Homosexuality and the Common Good

MICHAEL PAKALUK

In the previous essay, John Corvino dismissed the idea that homosexuality poses a threat to society. In this essay, Michael Pakaluk, professor of philosophy at Clark University and a translator of Aristotle's *Nicomachean Ethics,* maintains to the contrary that laws prohibiting discrimination against gays or permitting same-sex marriages would undermine the family and society at large. After arguing that anti-sodomy laws serve a valuable function even if they are unenforceable, Pakaluk contends that the legal changes sought by advocates of gay rights would radically alter our society, that they would involve wrongly bringing the power of the state against those who believe homosexuality is immoral, and that they would undermine the traditional and correct social understanding of marriage and family.

Study Questions

1. What valuable functions do anti-sodomy laws have? What is the "modern European consensus" on homosexuality?
2. How would anti-discrimination laws make life more difficult for those who believe that homosexuality is immoral?
3. Pakaluk writes that shared beliefs can be part of "the common good." What does he mean by this, and how does it apply to society's understanding of marriage and the family?
4. What point is Pakaluk making when he refers to a famous statement of Martin Luther King, Jr.?
5. Why does Pakaluk believe that same-sex marriages are absurd and impossible?

IT IS SOMETIMES CLAIMED that, if laws were uniformly changed to prohibit discrimination based upon sexual orientation or preference, or if same-sex partners were allowed by law to enter into contracts regarded as the equivalent of marriage and having similar privileges and rights, these changes would undermine the family and society at large. My purpose in this paper is to spell out some of the reasons why that claim is true, and what exactly the claim means, that is,

what the "undermining" of the family and society would amount to in this case.

We should acknowledge that the claim strikes many people, and not only "gay activists," as absurd. Fr. John F. Tuohey . . . provided a good example of this response in an article in *America* magazine.[1] Fr. Tuohey is criticizing a letter sent by the Vatican to American bishops. . . . That letter, echoing a 1986 Vatican document,[2] stated that "the view that homosexual activity is equivalent to,

Reprinted by permission of the American Public Philosophy Institute from Christopher Wolfe, ed., Homosexuality and American Public Life *(Dallas, TX: Spence Publishing, 1999).*

or as acceptable as, the sexual expression of conjugal love has a direct impact on society's understanding of the nature and rights of the family and puts them in jeopardy." Fr. Tuohey complains that "Nowhere does the statement attempt to show that recognizing the civil rights of gay and lesbian persons would harm the 'genuine' family or the common good." Indeed, "The absence of any evidence . . . that gay and lesbian persons pose a threat to society is easy to explain. No credible evidence exists. On the contrary, there is evidence to suggest exactly the opposite." He then describes the many contributions that homosexuals have made to their communities, implying that what they may do in private has no bearing on how they act as citizens and that, if so, they can hardly constitute any "threat" to anyone else.

Or, again, on a gay-activist web page, I encountered the following argument: "Giving gay couples the right to marry would not take away any of the rights heterosexual couples currently enjoy; it would only extend those rights and responsibilities to everyone in our society"—as if the proposed changes would only increase freedom, not limit it, and only add to the benefits people enjoy, not in any way diminish them. But, if so, the changes would leave everything else intact: heterosexual couples and families could continue thriving and flourishing as much, or as little, as they were before. This is the way some people look at the matter, then, and any claims to the contrary strike them as exaggerated, even hysterical, and absurd.

Before proceeding, we should make clear the various sorts of legislative change that are at stake:

1. the extension of anti-discrimination laws, making it illegal to discriminate, especially in matters of housing or hiring, on the basis of sexual orientation or activity;
2. the legal recognition of same-sex couples as equivalent to marriage;
3. permitting same-sex couples to adopt or to serve as foster parents;
4. the repeal of anti-sodomy laws.

I want to say something about the last of these points in order to put the subject aside, since,

although important, it is not my primary concern. In fact, the claim is *not* often made that repealing anti-sodomy laws would undermine the family or society. Although two dozen states presently retain anti-sodomy laws, it is not uncommon even for social conservatives to regard these laws as unwise and dispensable on the grounds that they are in general unenforceable.

But I think that view is a mistake. It is better to retain such laws where they exist, unless it were clear that they would be repealed as part of what was a larger, *de facto* societal compromise, for anti-sodomy laws have a valuable function, even if they are unenforceable. First, they constitute a kind of link with the past, a link to society as it was *before* the sexual revolution, when our insight into matters sexual was clearer. We should retain such laws, then, as a kind of deference to the wisdom of the past. We accept them "on authority," so to speak, even if we do not directly grasp their point and force. And then, also, unenforceable laws may have the function of expressing a view and instructing: Anti-sodomy laws are an expression, in law, of the view that homosexual activity is inherently wrong—and that is the key truth that we have to preserve in the debates over each of the points I mentioned. Unenforceable or unenforced laws can also play an indirect role in deciding matters that *are* "enforceable." For example, in child custody decisions, it may become relevant that one parent rather than the other regularly engages in activity that is contrary to some unenforced law—the child then goes to the one who does *not* fornicate, or commit adultery, or engage in sodomy.

It is important not to acquiesce in *bad* reasons for repealing anti-sodomy laws, for instance, because they are argued to be excluded by an alleged constitutional right to privacy, or because they are claimed to be exceptions to Mill's harm principle. In fact, it is only if we hold that the state *could*, licitly and in principle, retain anti-sodomy laws, that we can then regard the repeal of such laws as an element in a stable compromise. John Finnis has referred, approvingly, to what he calls the "modern European consensus" on homosexuality, that is, the legal arrangement whereby, roughly, *private* homosexual acts are not proscribed, but public acts, and the public promotion of homosexuality, are proscribed. That arrangement, like indeed most stable social arrangements in which there are competing interests or desires, involves reciprocity: Society relinquishes legislation over homosexual acts in private, but those who engage in such acts relinquish any claim of right to them, which their public performance or advocacy would imply. Yet such an arrangement is not possible, once it is conceded, as it should not be, that society has no competence to legislate against homosexual acts in the first place.

Plus Ça Change?

How can we make out the claim that the *other* sorts of legal changes *would* tend to undermine society or the family? A first step is to argue that the proposed changes would not be slight changes in degree—say, the extension of benefits or rights to a larger class—but rather changes in *kind*, of a very radical nature. This makes it more plausible, at least, that the changes might undermine society or the family: Presumably, a change that was not radical could not be the sort of thing that would pose such a threat. This, I take it, is the force of the argument that Hadley Arkes and others have advanced,[3] that if same-sex "marriages" were recognized, then there would be no reason, in principle, why a marriage should be between only two persons. There is a certain ambiguity in the current legal category of marriage. The old view remains vestigially that a marriage is the founding of a family; but alongside this is another competing view, that a marriage can be simply a long-term erotic friendship. The older view retains a kind of natural pride of place and in some sense overmasters the other. But once same-sex marriages are recognized, we resolve the ambiguity decisively in one direction, severing "marriage" from procreation—in which case there is no reason why only two should marry, any more than why only two should be friends. So the change,

clearly, is a radical one—of the sort, we might suspect, which would be mischievous in unpredictable ways, even if its immediate effects do not appear so damaging. The change does not extend marriage but alters its nature.

That is the force, too, of the argument that, if anti-discrimination laws are extended to include sexual orientation, then we shall soon afterwards be met with affirmative action for professed homosexuals. Of course this will follow: If it is wrong, *now*, to take homosexuality into account in any decisions about hiring or housing, then it was wrong throughout past decades and centuries as well. But that is to say that homosexuals may claim a long history of unjust oppression, just as African-Americans and other minorities. And the recognized remedy for that sort of thing is affirmative action. It is clear, then, that we have, not a mere incremental change, which *allows* some additional citizens to do what they wish to do, but a radical change, namely, the mobilization of the entire apparatus of social justice, which originated in the civil rights movement, to *promote* and *advance* a certain way of life.

That is the first step, to argue that the proposed changes are radical, not slight. The second step is similar. We saw that proponents of gay rights legislation argue that the changes they favor would leave everything else in place, as before, while simply increasing the freedoms and benefits enjoyed by homosexuals. Therefore, one advances the argument to the contrary that the proposed changes would imply the use of the coercive power of the state, brought to bear against citizens who are not homosexual, precisely insofar as they act in support of marriage and the family as these are traditionally conceived. So, for instance, a Christian who lets a room in a small apartment building will no longer be allowed to refuse to provide, as he sees it, an "occasion for sin" (to use the traditional terminology) by renting to a same-sex couple: he finds his Christian sentiments blocked and checked by the force of law—by a law, one should recall, which was supposed merely to let others do what *they* wanted.[4] Or, again, parents who teach their children one thing about sexuality and the family will find that state funds are used, and regulations are established, directly in opposition to them in government schools, since, *of course*, if discrimination on the basis of sexual orientation is strictly analogous to that based on race, it will need to be similarly warned against in the schools, and this from the earliest ages.

The second step, then, is to argue that things are not at all left in place by the proposed changes; it is not simply a matter of allowing an additional view. And then it begins to appear even more plausible that the proposed changes could undermine society and the family—if, that is, they are radical and imply the use of coercive state power against dispositions and actions that we regard as *good*, that is, those of honest citizens acting in accordance with their religious convictions, or simply aiming to teach their children well.

The Common Good

But this leads to the third step of the argument, which is the most fundamental and, in a sense, the most obvious, but also the most subtle. At this point we need to go back and point out that Fr. Tuohey was not correct when he made his complaint. The Vatican letter he criticized *did* give an argument, albeit a very compressed one, for how the proposed legislative changes would harm society and the family. It gave the argument, in fact, in the very passage I quoted earlier: "the *view* that homosexual activity is equivalent to, or as acceptable as, the sexual expression of conjugal love has a direct impact on society's *understanding* of the nature and rights of the family and puts them in jeopardy" (my emphasis). What is at stake, most fundamentally, is a *view*—how it is that society looks upon something—and the view that we have is a part of the common good, and it involves immediate and manifold consequences.

Let me explain what I mean by saying something about the notion of a "common good" and what it is for society to have a *view* or belief about something. (This is in fact to explore the ancient idea of

concordia: agreement on practical matters which is constitutive of social unity and civic friendship.)

I shall assume that people form associations, any association whatsoever, to procure or achieve something which they could not get at all, or could not get easily, if they acted each on his own. In that case, what they get through their association, and the instruments they use together in getting this, are, we can say, "common goods." For instance, in a large town or city, it would be either impossible or very difficult for each person to get water on his own—the water source is too small, or too far away, and hauling buckets takes too much time. So the town builds a system of reservoirs and pipes to supply water. The reserved water would then be a common good, and so too the reservoirs and supply system, the common instruments for procuring that good.

It should be noted that rarely is a common good simply a "thing" or material object. Even a water supply system, of any but the crudest sort, needs engineers to oversee it and skilled workers to maintain it. Their knowledge and habits of work—their virtues—have to be counted as part of that common good. But then, also, very often a *belief* is a common good. To give a simple example: Some commandos synchronize their watches and agree to rendezvous at a certain time. They must all believe that doing so essential to their accomplishing their task; if an enemy could somehow befuddle some of them about that, he would foil their mission. Or, less trivially, it is a common good for both husband and wife to regard their marriage as indissoluble and for them to tailor their actions accordingly. If one member of the couple changes his mind about that, they both fail to achieve what they associated together for in the first place. Or, to take a political example, and one closer to our purposes, Lincoln held that the shared belief, among citizens in a republic, in the principles expressed in the Declaration of Independence, was essential to the practice of democracy. Their common belief in those "axioms of democracy," as Lincoln called them, is, we might say, an important common good. The shared belief in them is essential if citizens are to work together and assist one another, in a coordinated fashion, in maintaining and building up a free society.

A belief is held in common, we should note, not simply when each member of a group happens to hold it, but rather when each is furthermore *aware* that the others hold it, and is aware that the others are aware that *he* holds it. Typically, the way in which this sort of agreement is achieved in political society is through a law, a public resolution having the force of law, or some practice itself regulated by law. For instance, it is only after a declaration of war is passed by the legislature that everyone in a society becomes aware that a particular nation is regarded as a hostile power in the minds of all other fellow citizens as well. The declaration of war at once expresses and brings about this consensus. There are in fact many things which we thus believe in common, and which we must so believe, if our type of government is to work and endure. For example, we all believe that a life of productive work is better than one of listless unemployment, that literacy is a great good, and so on. It is an important mark of beliefs that are held in common, that they are transmitted effortlessly, with hardly any need of explicit teaching (which, by the way, is precisely why it is easy to neglect them). In a modern liberal state, in fact, it is typically left to religion to refresh and reinvigorate the shared beliefs most necessary to the state's existence, and rightly so; the government for its part has aimed, generally, not to place itself at odds with the promotion or encouragement of these beliefs.

We can say that a law implies a certain belief if the law could not be regarded as desirable or appropriate, except on that belief; also, that a law implies the *falsity* of a belief if it could be regarded as desirable or appropriate, *only* given the falsity of that belief. It was Lincoln's point against Douglas, for instance, that Douglas's idea of self-government implied a rejection of the principles of the Declaration of Independence: to accept a law which left it up to individual states, as something indifferent, whether they would be free or slave, was to abandon a shared belief in the basic equality of human beings, in virtue of their

humanity. Douglas's conception of self-government could be regarded as desirable only given the falsity of the principles of the Declaration; thus it implied the rejection of those principles.

Finally, we can distinguish between beliefs which it is in some sense *natural* to hold in common, because they are regarded, correctly, as fulfillments or completions of other things believed, and those which it is not natural to hold in common, and which can be sustained, then, only artificially and through devices of coercion. For instance, the doctrine of communism, that all property should be held in common, proved itself to be unnatural, something which could not really be believed, and which therefore had to be upheld, if it was to be maintained at all, through extreme or illegitimate coercion. In this sense, the belief that the unborn child has a right to life is natural: It is the easy extension, to the unborn, of a belief we are prepared to hold as regards any human being. But the belief that a woman's so-called right to choose is more fundamental is like Douglas's view of self-government: It is unnatural and can only be maintained by the corruption of the institutions of medicine, the law, and the media.

Now, to apply these considerations to the case at hand. Consider first laws that would prohibit discrimination on the basis of sexual orientation. Such laws are, of course, modeled on civil rights legislation of the 1960s. Now it is necessary, if one is to *rule out* discrimination of some kinds as being inappropriate, to have in mind reasons on the basis of which discrimination, or the drawing of distinctions, or the assignment of rank, *would* be appropriate. You cannot rule out some types of features, as a basis of judgment, except to clear the way for others. The correct view in this matter was articulated by Martin Luther King, when he said famously that his ideal was a society in which people judged each other, not by the color of their skin, but by the content of their character. And of course matters that have a bearing on morality are precisely those that, potentially, should enter into decisions about how we are to associate with others and on what conditions. If we grant this, then to say that a certain characteristic is *not* one that should be used for drawing distinctions is to say that it is *not* related to questions of morality or character. Anyone, then, who believed that homosexual acts were morally wrong, and who accepted this sound understanding of the point of anti-discrimination laws, could *not* regard it as appropriate or desirable to proscribe by law all discrimination on that basis; thus, laws which proscribe such behavior imply the view—and indeed propose it as a shared belief—that homosexual acts are not morally wrong. (Actually, one is left with an alternative: *either* homosexual acts are not morally wrong, *or* the apparatus of social justice originating in the civil rights movement works to no coherent purpose.)

What follows from this? If homosexual acts are not morally wrong, then, obviously, it is not the case that sexual activity *ought* to be confined to marriage. But that it ought to be is the correct view of the matter, and one that is most consistent with other deeply held common beliefs. Thus, for a society to accept such non-discrimination laws is for it to reject the true view of sexuality and marriage. We might say, then, that under the guise of a slight change in the law, motivated, apparently, by a concern for fairness, such laws embody or express the basic belief of the sexual revolution. They, so to speak, enshrine the sexual revolution in law.

The Culture War

Of course it might be objected at this point that, if there is any threat to the family or society in this regard, it comes, rather, from the sexual revolution itself, and the evident change in society's mores then, not from some consequent change in law which assumes, as a *fait accompli,* the changes already introduced by the sexual revolution. But this objection underestimates the importance of law and fails to take into account the dividedness of society, that is, that there is indeed a culture war over sexual morality, which has continued to this point, and which will not be brought to a conclusion until the sexual revolution attains full legitimacy. Law is to society as principle and conscience are to an individual. A man may be a repeat adulterer, but so long as he recognizes that his marriage vow is binding upon him, he can reform. There are actually few, if any, legal changes since the 1960s which so directly imply the falsity of the view that sexual activity should be confined to marriage, as do gay rights laws. To accept such laws is to reject the principle, the claim of "conscience," by which, perhaps, the mores of the sexual revolution *could* be reversed.

Furthermore, although it is difficult to live in a society such as ours presently is, in which the true view of marriage and sexuality is hardly ever affirmed, it is much more difficult to live in one in which it is explicitly denied, and this with the power of the state. Currently, parents who wish to teach chastity and marital fidelity to their children are like the townspeople who needed water in our example, but where the water supply system has been disabled by a social upheaval, so that those who want water have to find a bucket and a water source and haul it in on their own. But once the negation of what such parents believe gets embodied into law—and law, too, which has the appearance of being righteous and progressive—it is as if the town then poisons its water supply, so that one has to be concerned, not only with getting fresh water, but also with not drinking the fouled water.

Consider next laws that would recognize same-sex couples as marriages. I consider it a telling fact that one never hears anyone saying, simply, that the proposed change is outright *impossible,* that two persons of the same sex *cannot* be married, whatever the state may say about it. Really, the only healthy reaction to the idea of same-sex "marriage" would be a kind of chuckle at the absurdity of it, and an internal resolve to ignore, as though nothing at all, both this fiction and anything any government might say in support of it. It is as though the government were to declare monkeys to be men, or men not to be men. Well, we have not done so well in resisting this last idea—the government *has* declared some men not to be men, and we go along with it—so I suppose it is not surprising that there are no signs of the appropriate response to the idea of men marrying men.

What these reflections suggest is the following. No one who thought that marriage had an objective character, prior to the state, could regard it as appropriate or desirable that there be a law by which the state defined and indeed altered, as by fiat, the character of marriage. Thus, laws recognizing gay marriage imply the falsity of the view that marriage is an objective reality prior to the state. Note too that parental authority must stand or fall with marriage. If the bond of husband and wife is not by nature, then neither is the government of those who share in that bond over any children that might result. Thus, laws recognizing gay marriage imply, similarly, that parents have no objective and natural authority over their children, prior to that of the state.

We are familiar with the idea, and, as I have said, we have acquiesced in it, that belief in the inherent dignity of all human beings is a subjective preference, a whim or fancy, which some fringe members of society—the right-to-life extremists—may perhaps regard as decisive in their *own* lives, because they hold to particular religious beliefs which involve this belief as a consequence. To accept gay "marriage," similarly, is to endorse the position that the belief in the family as having its own nature prior to the state is a mere whim or preference, springing from a religious viewpoint, perhaps, which the state is not bound to honor—in fact, which it cannot honor, without violating the separation of church and state.

If, indeed, gay "marriage" were to be recognised in law—a state of affairs which would itself be regrettable, since the required beliefs underlying it would be "unnatural" beliefs, in the sense I have explained, and which therefore could only be sustained by illegitimate force and coercion—then I do not doubt that it would not be long before it became regarded as unjust, that *some* couples, the heterosexual ones, can have children, but others cannot—just as, presently, women who accept the "pro-choice" ideology regard it as unjust that *they* can bear children, but men cannot. As much as possible, then, in a society in which the proposed

changes have been fully implemented, children will be raised directly by the state. That biological parents have some special claim over their children will be seen as some kind of mysterious superstition, perhaps even a disguised animus against others, which can in any case be easily trumped by the state's concern for what it would regard as the well-being and proper education of citizens.

These are some of the developments that may be in store for us—at least we cannot say that we would be tending to avoid them—if we endorse gay rights and gay marriage. Of course, it might be objected that this is all fantastical and preposterous. But I am certain that gay marriage and partial birth abortion would have seemed much more fantastical and preposterous in 1965. And in any case the burden has been discharged, the challenge overthrown. Why is it not absurd to hold that gay rights laws undermine society and the family? Because they imply beliefs which are incompatible with the common pursuit of goods which one wishes to obtain in marriage and family life. They remove a common good, a correct shared belief about the nature and good of marriage, which enables us to assist one another in realizing marriage and attaining its good, and they substitute—again, in the guise of something praiseworthy and just—a view which can only be sustained with coercion, and which will lead to suffering and unhappiness to the extent to which it is acted upon.

NOTES

1. "The C.D.F. and Homosexuals: Rewriting the Moral Tradition," in *America*, 167, no. 6, September 12, 1992.

2. Congregation for the Doctrine of the Faith, "Letter to the Bishops of the Catholic Church on the Pastoral Care of Homosexual Persons," Rome, October 1, 1986, no. 9.

3. See for instance Hadley Arkes, "The Implications of Gay Marriage," presented at a July 2, 1996 Capitol Hill briefing regarding the Defense of Marriage Act (DOMA).

4. See Richard Duncan, "Who Wants to Stop the Church: Homosexual Rights Legislation, Public Policy, and Religious Freedom," *Notre Dame Law Review* 69:3.

Review and Discussion Questions

1. Does a social compromise on homosexuality—what Pakaluk refers to as the "modern European consensus"—presuppose, as he says it does, that the state is within its rights to outlaw sodomy?

2. Assess Pakaluk's claim that ending discrimination on the basis of sexual orientation would lead to affirmative action for homosexuals and that it would wrongly involve bringing the coercive power of the state against those who believe that homosexuality is immoral.

3. Does society have a shared or common understanding of sexuality, family, and marriage, and would ending discrimination against gays or permitting same-sex marriage undermine this understanding? If so, would this be a bad thing?

4. Does marriage have an objective reality prior to the state, or is it a creation of the law?

5. Does Pakaluk provide any reasons for believing that homosexuality is immoral, or do his arguments merely presuppose that it is? Is there, in fact, anything immoral about homosexual conduct? Who is right about this—Pakaluk or John Corvino?

6. People disagree about the morality of homosexuality. Given this, would the government wrongly be taking one side of this moral debate by prohibiting discrimination against homosexuals or permitting same-sex marriages?

Adultery and Fidelity

MIKE W. MARTIN

The previous essay raised the question of the meaning of marriage and sexuality in our society. In this essay, Mike W. Martin, professor of philosophy at Chapman University, takes up the morality of adultery. Trying to steer a course between "conventional absolute prohibitions" and "trendy permissiveness," he maintains that a rule-oriented approach is unsatisfactory. Instead, he focuses on the moral ideals traditionally associated with marriage, in particular, love, commitment, and trust. Although traditional marriage arrangements are morally optional and couples are free to develop their own particular commitments and understandings, for those who do opt for traditional marriage, a commitment to love implies sexual exclusivity, and sexual fidelity is a virtue because it supports love. However, commitments can change, relationships can deteriorate, and spouses can sometimes fall in love with others, thus complicating the ethics of adultery. Although adultery within traditional marriage is generally immoral, in some circumstances, Martin believes, it may be justified or at least excusable.

From the Journal of Social Philosophy, vol. 25, no. 3 (Winter 1994). Reprinted by permission of the Journal of Social Philosophy.

Study Questions

1. How does Martin define "adultery"? Do you agree with his definition? What does he mean by "marriage"?

2. How does his approach to the ethics of adultery differ from a "rule-oriented approach"?

3. What are the descriptive and normative senses of "love"?

4. According to Martin, how does sexual exclusivity express and protect love? Why does he want to avoid saying that it is "intrinsically valuable or a feature of all genuine love"?

5. People can renegotiate their understandings and commitments. But what two difficulties can changing commitments give rise to?

6. Is love-inspired adultery always wrong?

ADULTERY IS MORALLY COMPLEX. . . . Whether as moral judges assessing the character of adulterers or as moral agents confronted with making our own decisions about adultery, we often find ourselves immersed in confusions and ambiguities that are both personally and philosophically troublesome.

I will seek a middle ground between conventional absolute prohibitions and trendy permissiveness. A humanistic perspective should embrace a pluralistic moral outlook that affirms a variety of forms of sexual relationships, including many traditional marriages. It can justify a strong presumption against adultery for individuals who embrace traditional marital ideals.

The ethics of adultery divides into two parts: making commitments and keeping them. The ethics of making commitments centers primarily on commitments to love, where love is a value-guided relationship, and secondarily on the promise of sexual exclusivity (the promise to have sex only with one's spouse) which some couples make in order to support the commitment to love. The ethics of keeping commitments has to do with balancing initial marital commitments against other moral considerations.

Making Commitments

What is adultery? Inspired by the New Testament, some people employ a wide definition that applies to any significant sexual interest in someone besides one's spouse: "You have heard that it was said, 'Do not commit adultery.' But I tell you that anyone who looks at a woman lustfully has already committed adultery with her in his heart."[1] Other people define adultery narrowly to match their particular scruples: for them extramarital genital intercourse may count as adultery, but not oral sex; or falling in love with someone besides one's spouse may count as adultery but not "merely" having sex. Whatever definition we might adopt there will always be borderline cases, if only those created by "brinkmanship"—going as far as possible without having intercourse (e.g., lying naked together in bed).

In this paper, "adultery" refers to married persons having sexual intercourse (of any kind) with someone other than their spouses. I am aware that the word "adultery" is not purely descriptive and evokes a range of emotive connotations. Nevertheless, I use the word without implying that adultery is immoral; that is a topic left open for investigation in specific cases. Like "deception," the world "adultery" raises moral questions about possible misconduct but it does not answer them. By contrast, I will use a wider sense of "marriage" that refers to all monogamous (two-spouse) relationships formally established by legal or religious ceremonies *and* closely analogous moral relationships such as committed relationships between homosexual or heterosexual couples who are not legally married.

A moral understanding of adultery turns on an understanding of morality. If we conceive morality as a set of rules, we will object to adultery insofar as it violates those rules. "Do not commit adultery" is not an irreducible moral principle, but many instances of adultery violate other familiar roles. As Richard Wasserstrom insightfully explained, much adultery violates one or more of these rules: Do not break promises (*viz.*, the wedding vows to abjure outside sex, vows which give one's partner "reasonable expectations" of sexual fidelity); do not deceive (whether by lying, withholding information, or pretending about the affair); do not be unfair (by enjoying outside sex forbidden to one's spouse); and do not cause undeserved harm (to one's spouse who suspects or hears of the affair).[2] Wasserstrom points out that all these rules are *prima facie*: In some situations they are overridden by other moral considerations, thereby justifying some instances of adultery.

Moreover, adultery is not even *prima facie* wrong when spouses have an "open marriage" in which they give each other permission to have extramarital affairs. In this connection Wasserstrom raises questions about the reasonableness of traditional marital promises of sexual exclusivity. Wouldn't it be wiser to break the conventional ties between sex and love, so that the pleasures of adultery can be enjoyed along with those of marriage? Alternatively, should we maintain the connection between sex and love but break the exclusive tie between sexual love and one's spouse, thus tolerating multiple simultaneous loves for one's spouse and for additional partners? No doubt the linking of love, sex, and exclusivity has an *instrumental* role in promoting marriages, but so would the patently unreasonable practices of allowing people to eat decent meals (beyond bread and water) only with their spouses.

In my view, a rule-oriented approach to morality lacks the resources needed to answer the important questions Wasserstrom raises. We need an expanded conception of morality as encompassing ideals and virtues, in particular the moral ideals of love which provide the point of marital commitments and the virtues manifested in pursuing those ideals. The ethics of adultery centers on the moral ideals of and commitments to love—which include ideals of constancy (or faithfulness), honesty, trust, and fairness—that make possible special ways of caring for persons. The ideals are morally optional in that no one is obligated to embrace them. Nevertheless, strong obligations to avoid adultery arise for those couples who embrace the ideals as a basis for making traditional marital commitments. The primary commitment is to love each other, while the commitment of sexual exclusivity is secondary and supportive. This can be seen by focusing on three ideas that Wasserstrom devotes little attention to: love, commitments to love, and trust.

1. What is *love*? Let us set aside the purely descriptive (value-neutral) senses in which "love" refers to (a) a strong positive attraction or emotion or (b) a complex attitude involving many emotions—not only strong affection, but also excitement, joy, pride, hope, fear, jealousy, anger, and so on. Let us focus instead on the normative (value-laden) sense in which we speak of "true love" or "the real thing." Cogent disputes arise concerning the values defining true love, though ultimately individuals have a wide area of personal discretion in the ideals they pursue in relationships of erotic love.

In its value-laden senses, "love" refers to special ways of valuing persons. As an attitude, love is valuing the beloved, cherishing her or him as unique. Erotic love includes sexual valuing, but the valuing is focused on the person as a unity, not just a body. As a relationship, love is defined by reciprocal attitudes of mutual valuing. The precise nature of this valuing turns on the ideals one accepts, and hence those ideals are part of the very meaning of "love."

2. According to the traditional ideal (or set of ideals) of interest here, marriage is based on a *commitment to love*: "to have and to hold from this day forward, for better for worse, for richer for poorer, in sickness and in health, to love and to cherish, till death us do part." This is not just a commitment to have continuous feelings of strong affection—feelings which are beyond our immediate voluntary control. Instead, it is a commitment to create and sustain a relationship conducive to those feelings, as well as conducive to the happiness and fulfillment of both partners. Spouses assume responsibility for maintaining conditions for mutual caring which in turn foster recurring emotions of deep affection, delight, shared enthusiasm, and joy. The commitment to love is not a promise uttered once during a wedding ceremony; it is an ongoing willingness to assume responsibility for a value-guided relationship.

The commitment to love implies a web of values and virtues. It is a commitment to create a lifelong relationship of deep caring that promises happiness through shared activities (including sexual ones) and through joining interests in mutually supportive ways involving shared decision-making, honesty, trust, emotional intimacy, reciprocity, and (at least in modern versions) fair and equal opportunities for self-expression and personal growth. This traditional ideal shapes how spouses value each other, both symbolically and substantively. Commitments to love throughout a lifetime show that partners value each other as having paramount importance and also value them as a unity, as persons-living-throughout-a-lifetime. Time-limited commitments, such as to remain together only while in college, express at most a limited affirmation of the importance of the other person in one's life.

Valuing each other is manifested in a willingness to make accommodations and sacrifices to support the marriage. For most couples, some of those sacrifices are sexual. The promise of sexual exclusivity is a distinct wedding vow whose supportive status is symbolized by being mentioned in a subordinate clause, "and, forsaking all others, keep thee only unto her/him." Hopefully couples who make the vow of sexual exclusivity are not under romantic illusions that their present sexual preoccupation with each

other will magically abolish sexual interests in other people and temptations to have extramarital affairs. They commit themselves to sexual exclusivity as an expression of their love and with the aim of protecting that love.

How does sexual exclusivity express and protect love? In two ways. First, many spouses place adultery at the top of the list of actions which threaten their marriage. They are concerned, often with full justification, that adultery might lead to another love that would damage or destroy their relationship. They fear that the affection, time, attention, and energy (not to mention money) given to an extramarital partner would lessen the resources they devote to sustaining their marriage. They also fear the potential for jealousy to disrupt the relationship. As long as it does not become excessive, jealousy is a healthy reaction of anger, fear, and hurt in response to a perceived loss of an important good. Indeed, if a spouse feels no jealousy whatsoever, the question is raised (though not answered) about the depth of love.

Second, sexual exclusivity is one way to establish the symbolism that "making love" is a singular affirmation of the partner. The love expressed is not just strong affection, but a deep valuing of each other in the ways defined by the ideals embedded in the marriage. Sex is especially well-suited (far more than eating) to express that love because of its extraordinary physical and emotional intimacy, tenderness, and pleasure. The symbolic meaning involved is not sentimental fluff; it makes possible forms of expression that enter into the substance of love.

In our culture sex has no uniform meaning, but couples are free to give it personal meanings. Janet Z. Giele notes two extremes: "On the one hand, the body may be viewed as the most important thing the person has to give, and sexual intercourse therefore becomes the symbol of the deepest and most far-reaching commitment, which is to be strictly limited to one pair-bond. On the other hand, participants may define sexual activity as merely a physical expression that, since it does not importantly envelop the whole personality nor commit the pair beyond the pleasures of the moment, may be regulated more permissively."[3] Between the two extremes lie many variations in the personal symbolism that couples give to sex, and here we are exploring only those variations found in traditional marital vows.

3. *Trust* is present at the time when couples undertake commitments to love, and in turn those commitments provide a framework for sustaining trust. Trust implies but is not reducible to Wasserstrom's "reasonable expectations" about a partner's conduct. Expectations are epistemic attitudes, whereas trust is a moral attitude of relying on others to act responsibly, with goodwill, and (in marriage) with love and support. We have a reasonable expectation that the earth will continue to orbit the sun throughout our lifetime, but no moral relationship of trust is involved. As a way of giving support to others, underwriting their endeavors, and showing the importance of their lives to us, trust and trustworthiness is a key ingredient in caring.

To be sure, trust is not always good. It is valuable when it contributes to valuable relationships, in particular to worthwhile marriages. Marital trust is confidence in and dependence upon a spouse's morally responsible love. As such, it provides a basis for ongoing intimacy and mutual support. It helps spouses undergo the vulnerabilities and risks (emotional, financial, physical) inherent in intimate relationships.

The trust of marital partners is broad-scoped. Spouses trust each other to actively support the marriage and to avoid doing things that might pull them away from it. They trust each other to maintain the conditions for preserving intimacy and mutual happiness. Violating marital trust does more than upset expectations and cause pain. It violates trust, honesty, fairness, caring, and the other moral ideals defining the relationship. It betrays one's spouse. And it betrays one's integrity as someone committed to their ideals.

To sum up, I have avoided Wasserman's narrow preoccupation with the promise of sexual exclusivity. Commitments of sexual exclusivity find their rationale in wider commitments to love each other *if* a couple decides that exclusivity will support their commitments to love *and* where love is understood as a special way to value persons within lasting relationships based on mutual caring, honesty, and trust. Accordingly, marital faithfulness (or constancy) in loving is the primary virtue; sexual fidelity is a supporting virtue. And sexual fidelity must be understood in terms of the particular commitments and understandings that couples establish.

I have also avoided saying that sexual exclusivity is intrinsically valuable or a feature of all genuine love. . . . In my view, the intrinsic good lies in fulfilling love relationships, rather than sexual exclusivity *per se,* thereby recognizing that some couples sustain genuine love without sexual exclusivity. For some couples sexual exclusivity does contribute to the goods found in traditional relationships, but other couples achieve comparable goods through nontraditional relationships, for example open marriages that tolerate outside sex without love. We can recognize the value of traditional relationships while also recognizing the value of alternative relationships, as chosen autonomously by couples.

Keeping Commitments

A complete ethics of keeping commitments of exclusivity would focus on the virtues of responsibility, faithfulness, and self-control. Here, however, I wish to defend Wasserstrom's view that even in traditional relationships the prohibition against adultery is *prima facie.* However strong the presumption against adultery in traditional relationships, it does not yield an exceptionless, all-things-considered judgment about wrong doing and blameworthiness in specific cases. I will discuss four of the many complicating factors. What if partners wish to change their commitments? What happens when love comes to an end? What if one spouse falls in love with an additional partner? And what about the sometimes extraordinary self-affirmation extramarital affairs may bring?

(i) *Changing Commitments.* Some spouses who begin with traditional commitments later revise them. Buoyed by the exuberance of romance, most couples feel confident they will not engage in adultery (much less be among the fifty percent of couples who divorce). Later they may decide to renegotiate the guidelines for their marriage in light of changing attitudes and circumstances, though still within the framework of their commitments to love each other. One study suggests that 90% of couples believe sexual exclusivity to be essential when they marry, but only 60% maintain this belief after several years of marriage (with the changes occurring primarily among those who had at least one affair).

Vita Sackville-West and Harold Nicolson provide an illuminating if unusual example. They married with the usual sexual attraction to each other and for several years were sexually compatible. As that changed, they gave each other permission to pursue extramarital affairs, primarily homosexual ones. Yet their original commitment to love each other remained intact. Indeed, for forty-nine years, until Vita died in 1962, their happy marriage was a model of mutual caring, deep affection, and trust. . . .

Just as we respect the mutual autonomy of couples in forming their initial understanding about their relationship, we should also respect their autonomy in renegotiating that understanding. The account I have offered allows us to distinguish between the primary commitment to love and the secondary commitment of sexual exclusivity. The secondary commitment is made in order to support the primary one, and if a couple agrees that it no longer is needed they are free to revoke it. Renegotiations can also proceed in the reverse directions: Spouses who initially agree on an open marriage may find that allowing extramarital affairs creates unbearable strains on their relationship, leading them to make commitments of exclusivity.

Changing commitments raise two major difficulties. First, couples are sometimes less than explicit about the sexual rules for their relationship. One or both partners may sense that their understandings have changed over the years but fail to engage in discussions that establish explicit new understandings. As a result, one spouse may believe something is acceptable to the other spouse when in fact it is not. . . . Lack of shared understanding generates moral vagueness and ambiguity concerning adultery, whereas periodic forthright communication helps establish clear moral boundaries.

Second, what happens when only one partner wants to renegotiate an original understanding? The mere desire to renegotiate does not constitute a betrayal, nor does it by itself justify adultery if one's spouse refuses to rescind the initial vow of sexual exclusivity. In such cases the original presumption against adultery continues but with an increased risk that the partner wishing to change it may feel adultery is more excusable. Such conflicts may or may not be resolved in a spirit of caring and compromise that enables good relationships to continue. Lacking such resolution, the moral status of adultery may become less clear-cut.

(ii) *Lost Love.* Couples who make traditional commitments sometimes fall out of love, singly or together, or for other reasons find themselves unwilling to continue in a marriage. Sometimes the cause is adultery, and sometimes adultery is a symptom of irresponsibility and poor judgment that erodes the relationship in additional ways. But other times there is little or no fault involved. Lasting love is a creation of responsible conduct *and* luck. No amount of conscientiousness can replace the good fortune of emotional compatibility and conducive circumstances.

In saying that traditional commitments to love are intended to be lifelong, we need not view them as unconditional. Typically they are based on tacit conditions. One condition is embedded in the wedding ceremony in which *mutual* vows are exchanged, namely, that one's spouse will take the marital vows seriously. Others are presupposed as background conditions, for example, that the spouse will not turn into a murderer, rapist, spouse-beater, child-abuser, or psychopathic monster. Usually there are more specific tacit assumptions that evolve before the marriage, for example, that the spouses will support each other's careers. Above all, there is the background hope that with sincere effort the relationship will contribute to the overall happiness of both partners. All these conditions remain largely tacit, as a matter of faith. When that faith proves ill-founded or just unlucky, the ethics of adultery becomes complicated.

As relationships deteriorate, adultery may serve as a transition to new and perhaps better relationships. In an ideal world, marriages would be ended cleanly before new relationships begin. But then, in an ideal world people would be sufficiently prescient not to make traditional commitments that are unlikely to succeed. Contemplating adultery is an occasion for much self-deception, but at least sometimes there may be good reasons for pursuing alternative relationships before officially ending a bad marriage.

(iii) *New Loves.* Some persons claim to (erotically) love both their spouse and an additional lover. They may be mistaken, as they later confess to themselves, but is it impossible to love two (or more) people simultaneously? "Impossible" in what sense?

Perhaps for some people it is a psychological impossibility, but, again, other individuals report a capacity to love more than one person at a time. For many persons it is a practical impossibility, given the demands of time, attention, and affection required in genuine loving. But that would seem to allow that resourceful individuals can finesse (psychologically, logistically, financially, and so forth) multiple simultaneous relationships. I believe that the impossibility is moral and conceptual—*if* one embraces traditional ideals that define marital love as a singular affirmation of one's spouse and *if* a couple establishes sex as a symbolic and substantive way to convey that

exclusive love. Obviously people can experience additional romantic attractions after they make traditional vows, but it is morally impossible for them to actively engage in loving relationships with additional partners without violating the love defined by their initial commitments.

Richard Taylor disagrees in *Having Love Affairs,* a book-length defense of adultery. No doubt this book is helpful for couples planning open marriages, but Taylor concentrates on situations where traditional vows have been made and then searches for ways to minimize the harm to spouses that results from extramarital love affairs.[4] In that regard his book is morally subversive in that it systematically presents only one side of the story. . . .

Bonnie Steinbock affirms an opposite view. She suggests that to fall in love with someone other than one's spouse is already a betrayal: "Sexual infidelity has significance as a sign of a deeper betrayal—falling in love with someone else. It may be objected that we cannot control the way we feel, only the way we behave; that we should not be blamed for falling in love, but only for acting on the feeling. While we may not have direct control over our feelings, however, we are responsible for getting ourselves into situations in which certain feelings naturally arise."[5] I agree that spouses who make traditional vows are responsible for avoiding situations that they know (or should know) foster extramarital love. Nevertheless, deeply committed people occasionally do fall in love with third parties without being blameworthy for getting into situations that spark that love. Experiencing a strong romantic attraction is not by itself an infidelity, and questions of betrayal may arise only when a person moves in the direction of acting on the love in ways that violate commitments to one's spouse.

Having said all this, I know of no argument that absolutely condemns all love-inspired adultery as immoral, all things considered and in all respects, even within traditional relationships. Nonetheless, as I have been concerned to emphasize, there is a serious betrayal of one's spouse. But to say that ends the matter would make the commitment to love one's spouse a moral absolute, with no exceptions whatsoever. Tragic dilemmas overthrow such absolutes, and we need to set aside both sweeping condemnations and wholesale defenses of love-inspired adultery.

To mention just one type of case, when marriages are profoundly unfulfilling, and when constricting circumstances prevent other ways of meeting important needs, there is a serious question whether love-inspired adultery is sometimes justifiable or at least excusable—witness *The Scarlet Letter, Anna Karenina, Madame Bovary, Lady Chatterly's Lover,* and *The Awakening.* Moreover, our deep ambivalence about some cases of love-inspired adultery reflect how there is some good and some bad involved in conduct that we cannot fully justify nor fully condemn.

(iv) *Sex and Self-Esteem.* Extramarital affairs are often grounded in attractions less grand than love. Affection, friendship, or simple respect may be mixed with a desire for exciting sex and the enhanced self-esteem from being found sexually desirable. The sense of risk may add to the pleasure that one is so desirable that a lover will take added risks. Are sex and self-esteem enough to justify violating marital vows? It would seem not. The obligations created through marital commitments are moral requirements, whereas sex and self-esteem pertain to one's self-interest. Doesn't morality trump self-interest?

But things are not so simple. Morality includes rights and responsibilities to ourselves to pursue our happiness and self-fulfillment. Some marriages are sexually frustrating or damaging in other ways to self-respect. Even when marriages are basically fulfilling, more than a few individuals report their extramarital affairs were liberating and transforming, whether or not grounded in love. For example, many women make the following report about their extramarital affair: "It's given me a whole new way of looking at myself . . . I felt attractive again. I

hadn't felt that way in years, really. It made me very, very confident."

In addition, the sense of personal enhancement may have secondary benefits. Occasionally it strengthens marriages, especially after the extramarital affair ends, and some artists report an increase in creative activity. These considerations do not automatically outweigh the dishonesty and betrayal that may be involved in adultery, and full honesty may never be restored when spouses decide against confessing an affair to their partners. But nor are considerations of enhanced self-esteem and its secondary benefits irrelevant.

I have mentioned some possible justifications or excuses for specific instances of adultery after traditional commitments are made. I conclude with a caveat. Specific instances are one thing; general attitudes about adultery are another. Individuals who make traditional commitments and who are fortunate enough to establish fulfilling relationships based on those commitments ought to maintain a general attitude that for them to engage in adultery would be immoral (as well as stupid). The "ought" is stringent, as stringent as the commitment to sexual exclusivity. Rationalizing envisioned adultery with anecdotes about the joys of extramarital sex or statistics about the sometimes beneficial effects of adultery is a form of moral duplicity. It is also inconsistent with the virtues of both sexual fidelity and faithfulness in sustaining commitments to love.

NOTES

1. Matthew 5:27–28, *New International Version.*
2. Richard Wasserstrom, "Is Adultery Immoral?" *Philosophical Forum* 5 (1974): 513–528.
3. Janet Z. Giele, as quoted by Philip E. Lampe, "The Many Dimensions of Adultery," in Philip E. Lampe, ed., *Adultery in the United States* (Amherst, N.Y.: Prometheus Books, 1987), p. 56.
4. Richard Taylor, *Having Love Affairs* (Amherst, N.Y.: Prometheus Books, 1982), pp. 67–68.
5. Bonnie Steinbock, "Adultery," in Alan Soble, ed., *The Philosophy of Sex* (Savage, Md.: Rowman & Littlefield, 1991), p. 192.

Review and Discussion Questions

1. What does Wasserstrom say about adultery? Would you agree that his approach is limited and that Martin's is better?

2. According to Martin, the traditional ideal of marriage is that it is based on a commitment to love. Do you agree? If not, why not? If so, then what, in your view, does a "commitment to love" involve?

3. What is the relation of sexual exclusivity to love? What is the relation of trust to love?

4. What ethical problems are posed by the fact that people's commitments can change over time?

5. Martin believes that adultery inspired by love cannot be absolutely condemned. Why not? Do you agree or disagree?

6. Because marital commitments are moral requirements, they would seem to trump the self-interested reasons for which people usually have affairs (like the pleasure of exciting sex or enhancing one's self-esteem). Yet Martin believes that "things are not so simple." Why not?

7. Assume that a couple has undertaken a traditional commitment to sexual exclusivity. In your view, under what circumstances, if any, would adultery be justified? Under what circumstances, if any, might adultery be excused even if not justified?

8

LIBERTY, PATERNALISM, AND FREEDOM OF EXPRESSION

On Liberty

JOHN STUART MILL

The freedom of the individual to choose and to act as he or she sees fit is a fundamental value, cherished by almost everyone, and clearly the upholding of personal liberty shows respect for persons as moral agents and contributes to human happiness. Yet any society must place limits on individual conduct. In the following excerpt from his classic essay *On Liberty,* John Stuart Mill examines one of the most fundamental questions of moral and social philosophy: What are the proper limits to society's power over the individual? Mill's answer is that society may interfere with an individual's actions only to prevent the individual from harming others. In line with this idea, Mill turns first to freedom of thought and expression, vigorously upholding freedom of opinion regardless of whether the viewpoint that the majority wishes to stifle is true or false. Mill then elaborates on his general principle, arguing that society may not compel the individual to do (or not do) something solely because society judges that it would be in the individual's own interest to do it.

Study Questions

1. What is Mill's basic principle, and on what ultimate ethical basis does he say that it rests?
2. Assume that the belief society wishes to suppress is false. Why would suppressing it be wrong, in Mill's view?
3. How does Mill answer the objection that his doctrine is "one of selfish indifference"?

From John Stuart Mill, On Liberty *(1859).*

4. What does Mill mean when he writes that "the inconveniences which are strictly inseparable from the unfavorable judgment of others" are the only ones a person should suffer for conduct that affects only himself or herself?

5. From Mill's perspective, why is there an important difference between punishing a person for being drunk and punishing a police officer for being drunk on duty?

6. How does Mill answer the argument that society needs the power to coerce people to take proper care of themselves, in order to bring its weaker members up to ordinary standards of rational conduct?

7. What does Mill see as the strongest argument against public interference in purely personal conduct?

Introductory

THE OBJECT OF THIS ESSAY is to assert one very simple principle, as entitled to govern absolutely the dealings of society with the individual in the way of compulsion and control, whether the means used be physical force in the form of legal penalties or the moral coercion of public opinion. That principle is, that the sole end for which mankind are warranted, individually or collectively, in interfering with the liberty of action of any of their number, is self-protection. That the only purpose for which power can be rightfully exercised over any member of a civilized community, against his will, is to prevent harm to others. His own good, either physical or moral, is not a sufficient warrant. He cannot rightfully be compelled to do or forbear because it will be better for him to do so, because it will make him happier, because, in the opinions of others, to do so would be wise or even right. These are good reasons for remonstrating with him, or reasoning with him, or persuading him, or entreating him, but not for compelling him or visiting him with any evil in case he do otherwise. To justify that, the conduct from which it is desired to deter him must be calculated to produce evil to someone else. The only part of the conduct of anyone, for which he is amenable to society, is that which concerns others. In the part which merely concerns himself, his independence is, of right, absolute. Over himself, over his own body and mind, the individual is sovereign.

It is, perhaps, hardly necessary to say that this doctrine is meant to apply only to human beings in the maturity of their faculties. We are not speaking of children, or of young persons below the age which the law may fix as that of manhood or womanhood. Those who are still in a state to require being taken care of by others, must be protected against their own actions as well as against external injury. For the same reason, we may leave out of consideration those backward states of society in which the race itself may be considered as in its nonage. . . .

It is proper to state that I forego any advantage which could be derived to my argument from the idea of abstract right, as a thing independent of utility. I regard utility as the ultimate appeal on all ethical questions; but it must be utility in the largest sense, grounded on the permanent interests of a man as a progressive being. These interests, I contend, authorize the subjection of individual spontaneity to external control, only in respect to those actions of each which concern the interest of other people. If anyone does an act hurtful to others, there is a *prima facie* case for punishing him, by law, or, where legal penalties are not safely applicable, by general disapprobation. There are also many positive acts for the benefit of others, which he may rightfully be compelled to perform: such as to give evidence in a court of justice; to bear his fair share in the common defense, or in any other joint work necessary to the interest of the society of which he enjoys the protection; and to perform certain acts of individual beneficence, such as saving a fellow-creature's life, or interposing to protect the defenseless against ill-usage, things which whenever it is obviously a man's duty to do, he may rightfully be made responsible to society for not doing. A person may cause evil to others not only by his actions but by his inaction, and in either case he is justly accountable to them for the injury. . . .

But there is a sphere of action in which society, as distinguished from the individual, has, if any, only an indirect interest; comprehending all that portion of a person's life and conduct which affects only himself, or if it also affects others, only with their free, voluntary, and undeceived consent and participation. When I say only himself, I mean directly, and in the first instance; for whatever affects himself, may affect others through himself; and the objection which may be grounded on this contingency, will receive consideration in the sequel. This, then is the appropriate region of human liberty. It comprises, *first,* the inward domain of consciousness; demanding liberty of conscience in the most comprehensive sense; liberty of thought and feeling; absolute freedom of opinion and sentiment on all subjects, practical or speculative, scientific, moral or theological. The liberty of expressing and publishing opinions may seem to fall under a different principle, since it belongs to that part of the conduct of an individual which concerns other people; but, being almost of as much importance as the liberty of thought itself, and resting in great part on the same reasons, is practically inseparable from it. *Secondly,* the principle requires liberty of tastes and pursuits; of framing the plan of our life to suit our own character; of doing as we like, subject to such consequences as may follow: without impediment from our fellow-creatures, so long as what we do does not harm them, even though they should think our conduct foolish, perverse, or wrong. *Thirdly,* from this liberty of each individual, follows the liberty, within the same limits, of combinations among individuals; freedom to unite, for any purpose not involving harm to others: the persons combining being supposed to be of full age, and not forced or deceived.

No society in which these liberties are not, on the whole, respected, is free, whatever may be its form of government; and none is completely free in which they do not exist absolute and unqualified. The only freedom which deserves the name, is that of pursuing our own good in our own way, as long as we do not attempt to deprive others of theirs, or impede their efforts to obtain it. Each is the proper guardian of his own health, whether bodily, or mental and spiritual. Mankind are greater gainers by suffering each other to live as seems good to themselves, than by compelling each to live as seems good to the rest. . . .

Of the Liberty of Thought and Discussion

The time, it is to be hoped, is gone by, when any defense would be necessary of the "liberty of the press" as one of the securities against corrupt or tyrannical government. No argument, we may suppose, can now be needed against permitting a legislature or an executive, not identified in interest with the people, to prescribe opinions to them, and determine what doctrines or what arguments they shall be allowed to hear. . . . Let us suppose . . . that the government is entirely at one with the people, and never thinks of exerting any power of coercion unless in agreement with what it conceives to be their voice. But I deny the right of the people to exercise such coercion, either by themselves or by their government. The power itself is illegitimate. The best government has no more title to it than the worst. It is as noxious, or more noxious, when exerted in accordance with public opinion than when in opposition to it. If all mankind minus one were of one opinion, mankind would be no more justified in silencing that one person than he, if he had the power, would be justified in silencing mankind. Were an opinion a personal possession of no value except to the owner, if to be obstructed in the enjoyment of it were simply a private injury, it would make some difference whether the injury was inflicted only on a few persons or on many. But the peculiar evil of silencing the expression of an opinion is that it is robbing the human race, posterity as well as the existing generation—those who dissent from the opinion, still more than those who hold it. If the opinion is right, they are deprived of the opportunity of exchanging error for truth; if wrong, they lose, what is almost as great a benefit, the clearer perception and livelier impression of truth produced by its collision with error.

It is necessary to consider separately these two hypotheses, each of which has a distinct branch of the argument corresponding to it. We can never be sure that the opinion we are endeavoring to stifle is a false opinion; and if we were sure, stifling it would be an evil still.

First, the opinion which it is attempted to suppress by authority may possibly be true. Those who desire to suppress it, of course, deny its truth; but they are not infallible. They have no authority to decide the question for all mankind and exclude every other person from the means of judging. To refuse a hearing to an opinion because they are sure that it is false is to assume that *their* certainty is the same thing as *absolute* certainty. All silencing of discussion is an assumption of infallibility. Its condemnation may be allowed to rest on this common argument, not the worse for being common.

Unfortunately for the good sense of mankind, the fact of their fallibility is far from carrying the weight in their practical judgment which is always allowed to it in theory; for while everyone well knows himself to be fallible, few think it necessary to take any precautions against their own fallibility, or admit the supposition that any opinion of which they feel very certain may be one of the examples of the error to which they acknowledge themselves to be liable. . . .

The objection likely to be made to this argument would probably take some such form as the following. There is no greater assumption of infallibility in forbidding the propagation of error than in any other thing which is done by public authority on its own judgment and responsibility. . . . It is the duty of governments, and of individuals, to

form the truest opinions they can; to form them carefully, and never impose them upon others unless they are quite sure of being right. But when they are sure (such reasoners may say), it is not conscientiousness but cowardice to shrink from acting on their opinions and allow doctrines which they honestly think dangerous to the welfare of mankind, either in this life or in another, to be scattered abroad without restraint, because other people, in less enlightened times, have persecuted opinions now believed to be true. . . . There is no such thing as absolute certainty, but there is assurance sufficient for the purposes of human life. We may, and must, assume our opinion to be true for the guidance of our own conduct; and it is assuming no more when we forbid bad men to pervert society by the propagation of opinions which we regard as false and pernicious.

I answer, that it is assuming very much more. There is the greatest difference between presuming an opinion to be true because, with every opportunity for contesting it, it has not been refuted, and assuming its truth for the purpose of not permitting its refutation. Complete liberty of contradicting and disproving our opinion is the very condition which justifies us in assuming its truth for purposes of action; and on no other terms can a being with human faculties have any rational assurance of being right. . . .

Let us now pass to the second division of the argument, and dismissing the supposition that any of the received opinions may be false, let us assume them to be true and examine into the worth of the manner in which they are likely to be held when their truth is not freely and openly canvassed. However unwillingly a person who has a strong opinion may admit the possibility that his opinion may be false, he ought to be moved by the consideration that, however true it may be, if it is not fully, frequently, and fearlessly discussed, it will be held as a dead dogma, not a living truth. . . .

If the cultivation of the understanding consists in one thing more than in another, it is surely in learning the grounds of one's own opinions. Whatever people believe, on subjects on which it is of the first importance to believe rightly, they ought to be able to defend against at least the common objections. . . . He who knows only his own side of the case knows little of that. His reasons may be good, and no one may have been able to refute them. But if he is equally unable to refute the reasons on the opposite side, if he does not so much as know what they are, he has no ground for preferring either opinion. The rational position for him would be suspension of judgment, and unless he contents himself with that, he is either led by authority or adopts, like the generality of the world, the side to which he feels most inclination. Nor is it enough that he should hear the arguments of adversaries from his own teachers, presented as they state them, and accompanied by what they offer as refutations. That is not the way to do justice to the arguments or bring them into real contact with his own mind. He must be able to hear them from persons who actually believe them, who defend them in earnest and do their very utmost for them. He must know them in their most plausible and persuasive form; he must feel the whole force of the difficulty which the true view of the subject has to encounter and dispose of, else he will never really possess himself of the portion of truth which meets and removes that difficulty. . . .

The fact . . . is that not only the grounds of the opinion are forgotten in the absence of discussion, but too often the meaning of the opinion itself. The words which convey it cease to suggest ideas, or suggest only a small portion of those they were originally employed to communicate. Instead of a vivid conception and a living belief, there remain only a few phrases retained by rote; or, if any part, the shell and husk only of the meanings is retained, the finer essence being lost. The great chapter in human history which this fact occupies and fills cannot be too earnestly studied and meditated on. . . .

We have hitherto considered only two possibilities: that the received opinion may be false, and some other opinion, consequently, true; or that, the received opinion being true, a conflict with the opposite error is essential to a clear apprehension and deep feeling of its truth. But there is a commoner case than either of these:

when the conflicting doctrines, instead of being one true and the other false, share the truth between them, and the nonconforming opinion is needed to supply the remainder of the truth of which the received doctrine embodies only a part. Popular opinions, on subjects not palpable to sense, are often true, but seldom or never the whole truth. They are a part of the truth, sometimes a greater, sometimes a smaller part, but exaggerated, distorted, and disjointed from the truths by which they ought to be accompanied and limited. Heretical opinions, on the other hand, are generally some of these suppressed and neglected truths, bursting the bonds which kept them down, and either seeking reconciliation with the truth contained in the common opinion, or fronting it as enemies, and setting themselves up, with similar exclusiveness, as the whole truth. The latter case is hitherto the most frequent, as, in the human mind, one-sidedness has always been the rule, and many-sidedness the exception. . . . Such being the partial character of prevailing opinions, even when resting on a true foundation, every opinion which embodies somewhat of the portion of truth which the common opinion omits ought to be considered precious, with whatever amount of error and confusion that truth may be blended. . . .

We have now recognized the necessity to the mental well-being of mankind (on which all their other well-being depends) of freedom of opinion, and freedom of the expression of opinion, on four distinct grounds, which we will now briefly recapitulate:

First, if any opinion is compelled to silence, that opinion may, for aught we can certainly know, be true. To deny this is to assume our own infallibility.

Secondly, though the silenced opinion be an error, it may, and very commonly does, contain a portion of truth; and since the general or prevailing opinion on any subject is rarely or never the whole truth, it is only by the collision of adverse opinions that the remainder of the truth has any chance of being supplied.

Thirdly, even if the received opinion be not only true, but the whole truth; unless it is suffered to be, and actually is, vigorously and earnestly contested, it will, by most of those who receive it, be held in the manner of a prejudice, with little comprehension or feeling of its rational grounds. And not only this, but, fourthly, the meaning of the doctrine itself will be in danger of being lost or enfeebled, and deprived of its vital effect on the character and conduct: the dogma becoming a mere formal profession, inefficacious for good, but cumbering the ground and preventing the growth of any real and heartfelt conviction from reason or personal experience. . . .

Of the Limits to the Authority of Society over the Individual

. . . As soon as any part of a person's conduct affects prejudicially the interests of others, society has jurisdiction over it, and the question whether the general welfare will or will not be promoted by interfering with it, becomes open to discussion. But there is no room for entertaining any such question when a person's conduct affects the interests of no persons besides himself, or need not affect them unless they like (all the persons concerned being of full age, and the ordinary amount of understanding). In all such cases, there should be perfect freedom, legal and social, to do the action and stand the consequences.

It would be a great misunderstanding of this doctrine to suppose that it is one of selfish indifference, which pretends that human beings have no business with each other's conduct in life, and that they should not concern themselves about the well-doing or well-being of one another, unless their own interest is involved. . . . Human beings owe to each other help to distinguish the better from the worse, and encouragement to choose the former and avoid the latter. They should be forever stimulating each other to increased exercise of their higher faculties, and increased direction of their feelings and aims towards wise instead of foolish, elevating instead

of degrading, objects and contemplations. But neither one person, nor any number of persons, is warranted in saying to another human creature of ripe years, that he shall not do with his life for his own benefit what he chooses to do with it. He is the person most interested in his own well-being: the interest which any other person, except in cases of strong personal attachment, can have in it, is trifling, compared with that which he himself has; the interest which society has in him individually (except as to his conduct to others) is fractional, and altogether indirect; while with respect to his own feelings and circumstances, the most ordinary man or woman has means of knowledge immeasurably surpassing those that can be possessed by anyone else. The interference of society to overrule his judgment and purposes in what only regards himself must be grounded on general presumptions; which may be altogether wrong, and even if right, are as likely as not to be misapplied to individual cases, by persons no better acquainted with the circumstances of such cases than those are who look at them merely from without. In this department, therefore, of human affairs, individuality has its proper field of action. In the conduct of human beings towards one another it is necessary that general rules should for the most part be observed, in order that people may know what they have to expect; but in each person's own concerns his individual spontaneity is entitled to free exercise. Considerations to aid his judgment, exhortations to strengthen his will, may be offered to him, even obtruded on him, by others: but he himself is the final judge. All errors which he is likely to commit against advice and warning are far outweighed by the evil of allowing others to constrain him to what they deem his good. . . .

Though doing no wrong to anyone, a person may so act as to compel us to judge him, and feel to him, as a fool, or as a being of an inferior order; and since this judgment and feeling are a fact which he would prefer to avoid, it is doing him a service to warn him of it beforehand, as of any other disagreeable consequence to which he exposes himself. . . . We have a right, also, in various ways, to act upon our unfavorable opinion of anyone, not to the oppression of his individuality, but in the exercise of ours. We are not bound, for example, to seek his society; we have a right to avoid it (though not to parade the avoidance), for we have right to choose the society most acceptable to us. We have a right, and it may be our duty, to caution others against him, if we think his example or conversation likely to have a pernicious effect on those with whom he associates. We may give others a preference over him in optional good offices, except those which tend to his improvement. In these various modes a person may suffer very severe penalties at the hands of others for faults which directly concern only himself; but he suffers these penalties only in so far as they are the natural and, as it were, the spontaneous consequences of the faults themselves, not because they are purposely inflicted on him for the sake of punishment. . . .

What I contend for is, that the inconveniences which are strictly inseparable from the unfavorable judgment of others, are the only ones to which a person should ever be subjected for that portion of his conduct and character which concerns his own good, but which does not affect the interest of others in their relations with him. Acts injurious to others require a totally different treatment. Encroachment on their rights; infliction on them of any loss or damage not justified by his own rights; falsehood or duplicity in dealing with them; unfair or ungenerous use of advantages over them; even selfish abstinence from defending them against injury—these are fit objects of moral reprobation, and, in grave cases, of moral retribution and punishment. And not only these acts, but the dispositions which lead to them, are properly immoral, and fit subjects of disapprobation which may rise to abhorrence. . . .

The distinction here pointed out between the part of a person's life which concerns only himself, and that which concerns others, many persons will refuse to admit. How (it may be asked) can any part of the conduct of a member of society be a matter of indifference to the other members? No person is an entirely isolated being; it is impos-

sible for a person to do anything seriously or permanently hurtful to himself, without mischief reaching at least to his near connections, and often far beyond them. If he injures his property, he does harm to those who directly or indirectly derived support from it, and usually diminishes, by a greater or less amount, the general resources of the community. If he deteriorates his bodily or mental faculties, he not only brings evil upon all who depended on him for any portion of their happiness, but disqualifies himself for rendering the services which he owes to his fellow-creatures generally; perhaps becomes a burden on their affection or benevolence; and if such conduct were very frequent, hardly an offense that is committed would detract more from the general sum of good. Finally, if by his vices or follies a person does no direct harm to others, he is nevertheless (it may be said) injurious by his example; and ought to be compelled to control himself, for the sake of those whom the sight or knowledge of his conduct might corrupt or mislead.

And even (it will be added) if the consequences of misconduct could be confined to the vicious or thoughtless individual, ought society to abandon to their own guidance those who are manifestly unfit for it? If protection against themselves is confessedly due to children and persons under age, is not society equally bound to afford it to persons of mature years who are equally incapable of self-government? If gambling, or drunkenness, or incontinence, or idleness, or uncleanliness, are as injurious to happiness, and as great a hindrance to improvement, as many or most of the acts prohibited by law, why (it may be asked) should not law, so far as is consistent with practicability and social convenience, endeavor to repress these also? And as a supplement to the unavoidable imperfections of law, ought not opinion at least to organize a powerful police against these vices, and visit rigidly with social penalties those who are known to practice them? There is no question here (it may be said) about restricting individuality, or impeding the trial of new and original experiments in living. The only things it is sought to prevent are things which have been tried and condemned from the beginning of the world until now; things which experience has shown not to be useful or suitable to any person's individuality. There must be some length of time and amount of experience after which a moral or prudential truth may be regarded as established: and it is merely desired to prevent generation after generation from falling over the same precipice which has been fatal to their predecessors.

I fully admit that the mischief which a person does to himself may seriously affect, both through their sympathies and their interests, those nearly connected with him and, in a minor degree, society at large. When, by conduct of this sort, a person is led to violate a distinct and assignable obligation to any other person or persons, the case is taken out of the self-regarding class and becomes amenable to moral disapprobation in the proper sense of the term. If, for example, a man, through intemperance or extravagance, becomes unable to pay his debts, or, having undertaken the moral responsibility of a family, becomes from the same cause incapable of supporting or educating them, he is deservedly reprobated, and might be justly punished; but it is for the breach of duty to his family or creditors, not for the extravagance. If the resources which ought to have been devoted to them, had been diverted from them for the most prudent investment, the moral culpability would have been the same. George Barnwell murdered his uncle to get money for his mistress, but if he had done it to set himself up in business he would equally have been hanged. Again, in the frequent case of a man who causes grief to his family by addiction to bad habits, he deserves reproach for his unkindness or ingratitude; but so he may for cultivating habits not in themselves vicious, if they are painful to those with whom he passes his life, or who from personal ties are dependent on him for their comfort. Whoever fails in the consideration generally due to the interests and feelings of others, not being compelled by some more imperative duty, or justified by allowable self-preference, is a subject of moral disapprobation for that failure, but not for the cause of it, nor for the errors, merely personal

to himself, which may have remotely led to it. In like manner, when a person disables himself, by conduct purely self-regarding, from the performance of some definite duty incumbent on him to the public, he is guilty of a social offense. No person ought to be punished simply for being drunk; but a soldier or policeman should be punished for being drunk on duty. Whenever, in short, there is a definite damage, or a definite risk of damage, either to an individual or to the public, the case is taken out of the province of liberty and placed in that of morality or law.

But with regard to the merely contingent or, as it may be called, constructive injury which a person causes to society by conduct which neither violates any specific duty to the public, nor occasions perceptible hurt to any assignable individual except himself, the inconvenience is one which society can afford to bear, for the sake of the greater good of human freedom. If grown persons are to be punished for not taking proper care of themselves, I would rather it were for their own sake than under pretense of preventing them from impairing their capacity or rendering to society benefits which society does not pretend it has a right to exact. But I cannot consent to argue the point as if society had no means of bringing its weaker members up to its ordinary standard of rational conduct, except waiting till they do something irrational, and then punishing them, legally or morally, for it. Society has had absolute power over them during all the early portion of their existence; it has had the whole period of childhood and nonage in which to try whether it could make them capable of rational conduct in life. The existing generation is master both of the training and the entire circumstances of the generation to come; it cannot indeed make them perfectly wise and good, because it is itself so lamentably deficient in goodness and wisdom; and its best efforts are not always, in individual cases, its most successful ones; but it is perfectly well able to make the rising generation, as a whole, as good as, and a little better than, itself. If society lets any considerable number of its members grow up mere children, incapable of being acted on by rational consideration of distant motives, society has itself to blame for the consequences. Armed not only with all the powers of education, but with the ascendency which the authority of a received opinion always exercises over the minds who are least fitted to judge for themselves, and aided by the *natural* penalties which cannot be prevented from falling on those who incur the distaste or the contempt of those who know them—let not society pretend that it needs, besides all this, the power to issue commands and enforce obedience in the personal concerns of individuals in which, on all principles of justice and policy, the decision ought to rest with those who are to abide the consequences. . . . With respect to what is said of the necessity of protecting society from the bad example set to others by the vicious or the self-indulgent, it is true that bad example may have a pernicious effect, especially the example of doing wrong to others with impunity to the wrongdoer. But we are now speaking of conduct which, while it does no wrong to others, is supposed to do great harm to the agent himself; and I do not see how those who believe this can think otherwise than that the example, on the whole, must be more salutary than hurtful, since, if it displays the misconduct, it displays also the painful or degrading consequences which, if the conduct is justly censured, must be supposed to be in all or most cases attendant on it.

But the strongest of all the arguments against the interference of the public with purely personal conduct is that, when it does interfere, the odds are that it interferes wrongly and in the wrong place. On questions of social morality, of duty to others, the opinion of the public, that is, of an overruling majority, though often wrong, is likely to be still oftener right, because on such questions they are only required to judge of their own interests, of the manner in which some mode of conduct, if allowed to be practiced, would affect themselves. But the opinion of a similar majority, imposed as a law on the minority, on questions of self-regarding conduct is quite as likely to be wrong as right, for in these cases public opinion means, at the best, some people's opinion of what is good or bad for other people, while very often it does not even mean that—the public, with the most perfect indifference, passing over the pleasure or convenience of those whose conduct they censure and considering only their own preference. There are many who consider as an injury to themselves any conduct which they have a distaste for, and resent it as an outrage to their feelings; as a religious bigot, when charged with disregarding the religious feelings of others, has been known to retort that they disregard his feelings by persisting in their abominable worship or creed. But there is no parity between the feeling of a person for his own opinion and the feeling of another who is offended at his holding it, no more than between the desire of a thief to take a purse and the desire of the right owner to keep it. And a person's taste is as much his own peculiar concern as his opinion or his purse. It is easy for anyone to imagine an ideal public which leaves the freedom and choice of individuals in all uncertain matters undisturbed and only requires them to abstain from modes of conduct which universal experience has condemned. But where has there been seen a public which set any such limit to its censorship? Or when does the public trouble itself about universal experience? In its interferences with personal conduct it is seldom thinking of anything but the enormity of acting or feeling differently from itself.

Review and Discussion Questions

1. Is no doctrine or opinion so pernicious that it may justifiably be outlawed? Must society tolerate the expression of any opinion? What about those who advocate Nazism, racial oppression, satanism, or the overthrow of the government?

2. Would violent pornography be protected by Mill?

3. In light of Mill's basic principle, assess the legitimacy of laws (a) requiring motorists to wear seat belts and motorcyclists to wear helmets, (b) preventing people from walking naked in public parks, (c) forbidding people to take drugs like cocaine or heroin, or (d) outlawing skateboarding in certain areas.

4. Does Mill satisfactorily answer the criticism that distinguishing between actions that concern only ourselves and actions that affect others is impossible?

5. Has Mill gone too far in restricting the power of society over individual conduct?

6. Some critics of Mill have doubted that he can square his commitment to individual liberty with his underlying utilitarianism. Do you think utilitarianism might sometimes require us to limit individual freedom in ways that *On Liberty* opposes in order to enhance total social welfare?

Paternalism

GERALD DWORKIN

Gerald Dworkin, professor of philosophy at the University of California-Davis, examines John Stuart Mill's objections to interfering with a person's liberty on paternalistic grounds—that is, in order to promote the person's own good or happiness. Dworkin lists various examples of paternalistic legislation and distinguishes between "pure" and "impure" forms of paternalism. Dworkin argues that Mill implicitly used two types of argument—one utilitarian, the other based on the absolute value of free choice. Utilitarian argument, however, can establish only a presumption but not an absolute prohibition against interference with personal choice. And even the second type of argument allows for certain sorts of paternalism.

Study Questions

1. What is the difference between "pure" and "impure" paternalism?

2. Why is legislation preventing employees from working more than forty hours per week not necessarily paternalistic?

3. Why, according to Dworkin, does utilitarianism provide a presumption—but not an absolute prohibition—against interference with personal conduct?

4. What justifies parental paternalism, and what limits the exercise of such parental power?

5. What are the two distinct ways in which one can behave in a nonrational fashion?

6. Dworkin argues that rational people would agree to society's imposing restrictions on self-regarding conduct in certain situations. What are three examples?

7. What two principles does he propose in order to limit such paternalistic restrictions?

From Richard A. Wasserstrom, ed., Morality and the Law. *Copyright © 1971 Wadsworth Publishing Company. Reprinted by permission of the author and the publisher.*

I TAKE AS MY STARTING POINT the "one very simple principle" proclaimed by Mill in *On Liberty* . . .

> That principle is, that the sole end for which mankind are warranted, individually or collectively, in interfering with the liberty of action of any of their number, is self-protection. That the only purpose for which power can be rightfully exercised over any member of a civilized community, against his will, is to prevent harm to others. He cannot rightfully be compelled to do or forbear because it will be better for him to do so, because it will make him happier, because, in the opinion of others, to do so would be wise, or even right.

This principle is neither "one" nor "very simple." It is at least two principles: one asserting that self-protection or the prevention of harm to others is sometimes a sufficient warrant and the other claiming that the individual's own good is *never* a sufficient warrant for the exercise of compulsion either by the society as a whole or by its individual members. I assume that no one, with the possible exception of extreme pacifists or anarchists, questions the correctness of the first half of the principle. This essay is an examination of the negative claim embodied in Mill's principle—the objection to paternalistic interferences with a man's liberty.

I

By paternalism I shall understand roughly the interference with a person's liberty of action justified by reasons referring exclusively to the welfare, good, happiness, needs, interests or values of the person being coerced. One is always well-advised to illustrate one's definitions by examples but it is not easy to find "pure" examples of paternalistic interferences. For almost any piece of legislation is justified by several different kinds of reasons and even if historically a piece of legislation can be shown to have been introduced for purely paternalistic motives, it may be that advocates of the legislation with an antipaternalistic outlook can find sufficient reasons justifying the legislation without appealing to the reasons which were originally adduced to support it. Thus, for example, it may be that the original legislation requiring motorcyclists to wear safety helmets was introduced for purely paternalistic reasons. But the Rhode Island Supreme Court recently upheld such legislation on the grounds that it was "not persuaded that the legislature is powerless to prohibit individuals from pursuing a course of conduct which could conceivably result in their becoming public charges," thus clearly introducing reasons of a quite different kind. Now I regard this decision as being based on reasoning of a very dubious nature but it illustrates the kind of problem one has in finding examples. The following is a list of the kinds of interferences I have in mind as being paternalistic.

II

1. Laws requiring motorcyclists to wear safety helmets when operating their machines.
2. Laws forbidding persons from swimming at a public beach when lifeguards are not on duty.
3. Laws making suicide a criminal offense.
4. Laws making it illegal for women and children to work at certain types of jobs.
5. Laws regulating certain kinds of sexual conduct, for example, homosexuality among consenting adults in private.
6. Laws regulating the use of certain drugs which may have harmful consequences to the user but do not lead to antisocial conduct.
7. Laws requiring a license to engage in certain professions with those not receiving a license subject to fine or jail sentence if they do engage in the practice.
8. Laws compelling people to spend a specified fraction of their income on the

purchase of retirement annuities (Social Security).

9. Laws forbidding various forms of gambling (often justified on the grounds that the poor are more likely to throw away their money on such activities than the rich who can afford to).

10. Laws regulating the maximum rates of interest for loans.

11. Laws against duelling.

In addition to laws which attach criminal or civil penalties to certain kinds of action there are laws, rules, regulations, decrees which make it rather difficult or impossible for people to carry out their plans and which are also justified on paternalistic grounds. Examples of this are:

1. Laws regulating the types of contracts which will be upheld as valid by the courts, for example (an example of Mill's to which I shall return), no man may make a valid contract for perpetual involuntary servitude.

2. Not allowing assumption of risk as a defense to an action based on the violation of a safety statute.

3. Not allowing as a defense to a charge of murder or assault the consent of the victim.

4. Requiring members of certain religious sects to have compulsory blood transfusions. This is made possible by not allowing the patient to have recourse to civil suits for assault and battery and by means of injunctions.

5. Civil commitment procedures when these are specifically justified on the basis of preventing the person being committed from harming himself. The D.C. Hospitalization of the Mentally Ill Act provides for involuntary hospitalization of a person who "is mentally ill, and because of that illness, is likely to injure himself or others if allowed to remain at liberty." The term injure in this context applies to unintentional as well as intentional injuries.

All of my examples are of existing restrictions on the liberty of individuals. Obviously one can think of interferences which have not yet been imposed. Thus one might ban the sale of cigarettes, or require that people wear safety belts in automobiles (as opposed to merely having them installed), enforcing this by not allowing motorists to sue for injuries even when caused by other drivers if the motorist was not wearing a seat belt at the time of the accident. . . .

III

Bearing these examples in mind, let me return to a characterization of paternalism. I said earlier that I meant by the term, roughly, interference with a person's liberty for his own good. But, as some of the examples show, the class of persons whose good is involved is not always identical with the class of persons whose freedom is restricted. Thus, in the case of professional licensing it is the practitioner who is directly interfered with but it is the would-be patient whose interests are presumably being served. Not allowing the consent of the victim to be a defense to certain types of crime primarily affects the would-be aggressor but it is the interests of the willing victim that we are trying to protect. Sometimes a person may fall into both classes as would be the case if we banned the manufacture and sale of cigarettes and a given manufacturer happened to be a smoker as well.

Thus we may first divide paternalistic interferences into "pure" and "impure" cases. In "pure" paternalism the class of persons whose freedom is restricted is identical with the class of persons whose benefit is intended to be promoted by such restrictions. Examples: the making of suicide a crime, requiring passengers in automobiles to wear seat belts, requiring a Christian Scientist to receive a blood transfusion. In the case of "impure" paternalism in trying to protect the welfare of a class of persons we find that the only way to do so will involve restricting the freedom of other persons besides those who are benefitted. Now it might be thought that there are not cases of "impure" paternalism since any such case could always be justified on nonpaternalistic grounds, that is, in terms of preventing harm to others. Thus we might ban cigarette manufacturers from continuing to manufacture their product on the grounds that we are preventing them from causing illness to others in the same way that we prevent other manufacturers from releasing pollutants into the atmosphere, thereby causing danger to the members of the community. The difference is, however, that in the former but not the latter case the harm is of such a nature that it could be avoided by those individuals affected if they so chose. The incurring of the harm requires, so to speak, the active cooperation of the victim. It would be mistaken theoretically and hypocritical in practice to assert that our interference in such cases is just like our interference in standard cases of protecting others from harm. At the very least someone interfered with in this way can reply that no one is complaining about his activities. It may be that impure paternalism requires arguments or reasons of a stronger kind in order to be justified, since there are persons who are losing a portion of their liberty and they do not even have the solace of having it be done "in their own interest." Of course in some sense, if paternalistic justifications are ever correct, then we are protecting others, we are preventing some from injuring others, but it is important to see the differences between this and the standard case.

Paternalism then will always involve limitations on the liberty of some individuals in their own interest but it may also extend to interferences with the liberty of parties whose interests are not in question.

IV

Finally, by way of some more preliminary analysis, I want to distinguish paternalistic interference with liberty from a related type with which it is often confused. Consider, for example, legislation which forbids employees to work more than, say, forty hours per week. It is sometimes argued that such legislation is paternalistic for if employees desired such a restriction on their hours of work they could agree among themselves to impose it voluntarily. But because they do not the society imposes its own conception of their best interests upon them by the use of coercion. Hence this is paternalism. . . .

There are restrictions which are in the interests of a class of persons taken collectively but are such that the immediate interest of each individual is furthered by his violating the rule when others adhere to it. In such cases the individuals involved may need the use of compulsion to give effect to their collective judgment of their own interest by guaranteeing each individual compliance by the others. In these cases compulsion is not used to achieve some benefit which is not recognized to be a benefit by those concerned, but rather because it is the only feasible means of achieving some benefit which *is* recognized as such by all concerned. This way of viewing matters provides us with another characterization of paternalism in general. Paternalism might be thought of as the use of coercion to achieve a good which is not recognized as such by those persons for whom the good is intended. Again while this formulation captures the heart of the matter—it is surely what Mill is objecting to in *On Liberty*—the matter is not always quite like that. For example, when we force motorcyclists to wear helmets we are trying to promote a good—the protection of the person from injury—which is surely recognized by most of the individuals concerned. It is not that a cyclist doesn't value his bodily integrity; rather, as a supporter of such legislation would put it, he either places, perhaps irrationally, another value or good (freedom from wearing a helmet) above that of physical well-being or, perhaps, while recognizing the danger in the abstract, he either does not fully appreciate it or he underestimates the likelihood of its occurring. But now we are approaching the question of possible justifications of paternalistic measures and the rest of this essay will be devoted to that question.

V

I shall begin for dialectical purposes by discussing Mill's objections to paternalism and then go on to discuss more positive proposals.

An initial feature that strikes one is the absolute nature of Mill's prohibitions against paternalism. It is so unlike the carefully qualified admonitions of Mill and his fellow utilitarians on other moral issues. He speaks of self-protection as the *sole* end warranting coercion, of the individual's own goals as *never* being a sufficient warrant. . . .

Clearly the operative premise here is . . . bolstered by claims about the status of the individual as judge and appraiser of his welfare, interests, needs, etc.:

> With respect to his own feelings and circumstances, the most ordinary man or woman has means of knowledge immeasurably surpassing those that can be possessed by any one else.
>
> He is the person most interested in his own well-being: the interest which any other person, except in cases of strong personal attachment, can have in it is trifling, compared to that which he himself has.

These claims are used to support the following generalizations concerning the utility of compulsion for paternalistic purposes:

> The interference of society to overrule his judgment and purposes in what only regards himself must be grounded on general presumptions; which may be altogether wrong, and even if right, are as likely as not to be misapplied to individual cases.
>
> But the strongest of all the arguments against the interference of the public with purely personal conduct is that when it does interfere, the odds are that it interferes wrongly and in the wrong place.
>
> All errors which [the individual] is likely to commit against advice and warning are far outweighed by the evil of allowing others to constrain him to what they deem his good.

Performing the utilitarian calculation by balancing the advantages and disadvantages, we find that: "Mankind are greater gainers by suffering each other to live as seems good to themselves, than by compelling each other to live as seems good to the rest.". . .

This is clearly the main channel of Mill's thought and it is one which has been subjected to vigorous attack from the moment it appeared— most often by fellow utilitarians. The link that they have usually seized on is, as Fitzjames Stephen put it in *Liberty, Equality, Fraternity,* the absence of proof that the "mass of adults are so well acquainted with their own interests and so much disposed to pursue them that no compulsion or restraint put upon them by any others for the purpose of promoting their interest can really promote them.". . .

Now it is interesting to note that Mill himself was aware of some of the limitations on the doctrine that the individual is the best judge of his own interests. In his discussion of government intervention in general (even where the intervention does not interfere with liberty but provides alternative institutions to those of the market) after making claims which are parallel to those just discussed, for example, "People understand their own business and their own interests better, and care for them more, than the government does, or can be expected to do," he goes on to an intelligent discussion of the "very large and conspicuous exceptions" to the maxim. . . .

In short, we get a presumption, not an absolute prohibition. The question is why doesn't the argument against paternalism go the same way?

I suggest that the answer lies in seeing that in addition to a purely utilitarian argument Mill uses another as well. . . . When Mill states that "there is a part of the life of every person who has come to years of discretion, within which the individuality of that person ought to reign uncontrolled either by any other person or by the public collectively," he is saying something about what it means to be a person, an autonomous agent. It is because coercing a person for his own good denies this status as an independent entity that Mill objects to it so strongly and in such absolute terms. To be able to choose is a good that is independent of the wisdom of what is chosen. A man's "mode of laying out his existence is the best, not because it is the best in itself, but because it is his own mode." It is the privilege and proper condition of a human being, arrived at the maturity of his faculties, to use and interpret experience in his own way. . . .

What I have tried to show so far is that there are two strains of argument in Mill—one a straight-forward utilitarian mode of reasoning and one which relies not on the goods which free choice leads to but on the absolute value of the choice itself. The first cannot establish any absolute prohibition but at most a presumption and indeed a fairly weak one given some fairly plausible assumptions about human psychology; the second, while a stronger line of argument, seems to me to allow on its own grounds a wider range of paternalism than might be suspected. I turn now to a consideration of these matters.

VI

We might begin looking for principles governing the acceptable use of paternalistic power in cases where it is generally agreed that it is legitimate. Even Mill intends his principles to be applicable only to mature individuals, not those in what he calls "nonage." What is it that justifies us in interfering with children? The fact that they lack some of the emotional and cognitive capacities required in order to make fully rational decisions. It is an empirical question to just what extent children have an adequate conception of their own present and future interests but there is not much doubt that there are many deficiencies. For example, it is very difficult for a child to defer gratification for any considerable period of time. Given these deficiencies and given the very real and permanent dangers that may befall the child, it becomes not only permissible but even a duty of the parent to restrict the child's freedom in various ways. There is however an important moral limitation on the exercise of such parental power which is provided by the notion of the child eventually coming to see the correctness of his parent's interventions. Parental paternalism may be thought of as a wager by the parent on the child's subsequent recognition of the wisdom of the restrictions. There is an emphasis on what could be called future-oriented consent—on what the child will come to welcome, rather than on what he does welcome. . . .

Let me start by considering a case where the consent is not hypothetical in nature. Under certain conditions it is rational for an individual to agree that others should force him to act in ways which, at the time of action, the individual may not see as desirable. If, for example, a man knows that he is subject to breaking his resolves when temptation is present, he may ask a friend to refuse to entertain his requests at some later stage.

A classical example is given in the Odyssey when Odysseus commands his men to tie him to the mast and refuse all future orders to be set free, because he knows the power of the Sirens to enchant men with their songs. Here we are on relatively sound ground in later refusing Odysseus' request to be set free. He may even claim to have changed his mind but, since it is *just* such changes that he wished to guard against, we are entitled to ignore them.

A process analogous to this may take place on a social rather than individual basis. An electorate may mandate its representatives to pass legislation which when it comes time to "pay the price" may be unpalatable. I may believe that a tax increase is necessary to halt inflation though I may resent the lower pay check each month. However in both this case and that of Odysseus, the measure to be enforced is specifically requested by the party involved and at some point in time there is genuine consent and agreement on the part of those persons whose liberty is infringed. Such is not the case for the paternalistic measures we have been speaking about. What must be involved here is not consent to specific measures but rather consent to a system of government, run by elected representatives, with an understanding that they may act to safeguard our interests in certain limited ways.

I suggest that since we are all aware of our irrational propensities, deficiencies in cognitive and emotional capacities, and avoidable and unavoidable ignorance, it is rational and prudent for us to in effect take out "social insurance policies." We may argue for and against proposed paternalistic measures in terms of what fully rational individuals would accept as forms of protection. Now clearly, since the initial agreement is not about specific measures we are dealing with a more-or-less blank check and therefore there have to be carefully defined limits. What I am looking for are certain kinds of conditions which make it plausible to suppose that rational men could reach agreement to limit their liberty even when other men's interests are not affected. . . .

Let me suggest types of situations in which it seems plausible to suppose that fully rational individuals would agree to having paternalistic restrictions imposed upon them. It is reasonable to suppose that there are "goods" such as health which any person would want to have in order to pursue his own good—no matter how that good is conceived. This is an argument used in connection with compulsory education for children but it seems to me that it can be extended to other goods which have this character. Then one could agree that the attainment of such goods should be promoted even when not recognized to be such, at the moment, by the individuals concerned.

An immediate difficulty arises from the fact that men are always faced with competing goods and that there may be reasons why even a value such as health—or indeed life—may be overridden by competing values. Thus the problem with the Christian Scientist and blood transfusions. It may be more important for him to reject "impure substances" than to go on living. The difficult problem that must be faced is whether one can give sense to the notion of a person irrationally attaching weights to competing values.

Consider a person who knows the statistical data on the probability of being injured when not wearing seat belts in an automobile and knows the types and gravity of the various injuries. He also insists that the inconvenience attached to fastening the belt every time he gets in and out

of the car outweighs for him the possible risks to himself. I am inclined in this case to think that such a weighing is irrational. Given his life plans, which we are assuming are those of the average person, his interests and commitments already undertaken, I think it is safe to predict that we can find inconsistencies in his calculations at some point. I am assuming that this is not a man who for some conscious or unconscious reasons is trying to injure himself nor is he a man who just likes to "live dangerously." I am assuming that he is like us in all the relevant respects but just puts an enormously high negative value on inconvenience—one which does not seem comprehensible or reasonable.

It is always possible, of course, to assimilate this person to creatures like myself. I, also, neglect to fasten my seat belt and I concede such behavior is not rational but not because I weigh the inconvenience differently from those who fasten the belts. It is just that having made (roughly) the same calculation as everybody else, I ignore it in my actions. A plausible explanation for this deplorable habit is that although I know in some intellectual sense what the probabilities and risks are I do not fully appreciate them in an emotionally genuine manner.

We have two distinct types of situation in which a man acts in a nonrational fashion. In one case he attaches incorrect weights to some of his values; in the other he neglects to act in accordance with his actual preferences and desires. Clearly there is a stronger and more persuasive argument for paternalism in the latter situation. Here we are really not—by assumption—imposing a good on another person. But why may we not extend our interference to what we might call evaluative delusions? After all, in the case of cognitive delusions we are prepared, often, to act against the expressed will of the person involved. If a man believes that when he jumps out the window he will float upwards—Robert Nozick's example—would not we detain him, forcibly if necessary? The reply will be that this man doesn't wish to be injured and if we could convince him that he is mistaken as to the consequences of his action, he would not wish to perform the action. But part of what is involved in claiming that the man who doesn't fasten his seat belts is attaching an incorrect weight to the inconvenience of fastening them is that if he were to be involved in an accident and severely injured he would look back and admit that the inconvenience wasn't as bad as all that. So there is a sense in which, if I could convince him of the consequences of his action, he also would not wish to continue his present course of action. . . . Let me now consider another factor which comes into play in some of these situations which may make an important difference in our willingness to consent to paternalistic restrictions.

Some of the decisions we make are of such a character that they produce changes which are in one or another way irreversible. Situations are created in which it is difficult or impossible to return to anything like the initial stage at which the decision was made. In particular, some of these changes will make it impossible to continue to make reasoned choices in the future. I am thinking specifically of decisions which involve taking drugs that are physically or psychologically addictive and those which are destructive of one's mental and physical capacities.

I suggest we think of the imposition of paternalistic interferences in situations of this kind as being a kind of insurance policy which we take out against making decisions which are far-reaching, potentially dangerous and irreversible. Each of these factors is important. . . .

A second class of cases concerns decisions which are made under extreme psychological and sociological pressures. I am not thinking here of the making of the decision as being something one is pressured into—for example, a good reason for making duelling illegal is that unless this is done many people might have to manifest their courage and integrity in ways in which they would rather not do so—but rather of decisions, such as that to commit suicide, which are usually made at a point where the individual is not thinking clearly and calmly about the nature of his decision. In addition, of course, this comes under the previous

heading of all-too-irrevocable decisions. Now there are practical steps which a society could take if it wanted to decrease the possibility of suicide— for example not paying social security benefits to the survivors or, as religious institutions do, not allowing persons to be buried with the same status as natural deaths. I think we may count these as interferences with the liberty of persons to attempt suicide and the question is whether they are justifiable.

Using my argument schema the question is whether rational individuals would consent to such limitations. I see no reason for them to consent to an absolute prohibition but I do think it is reasonable for them to agree to some kind of enforced waiting period. Since we are all aware of the possibility of temporary states, such as great fear or depression, that are inimical to the making of well-informed and rational decisions, it would be prudent for all of us if there were some kind of institutional arrangement whereby we were restrained from making a decision which is so irreversible. What this would be like in practice is difficult to envisage and it may be that if no practical arrangements were feasible we would have to conclude that there should be no restriction at all on this kind of action. But we might have a "cooling off" period, in much the same way that we now require couples who file for divorce to go through a waiting period. Or, more far-fetched, we might imagine a Suicide Board composed of a psychologist and another member picked by the applicant. The Board would be required to meet and talk with the person proposing to take his life, though its approval would not be required.

A third class of decisions—these classes are not supposed to be disjoint—involves dangers which are either not sufficiently understood or appreciated correctly by the persons involved. Let me illustrate, using the example of cigarette smoking, a number of possible cases.

1. A man may not know the facts—e.g., smoking between 1 and 2 packs a day shortens life expectancy 6.2 years, the

costs and pain of the illness caused by smoking, etc.

2. A man may know the facts, wish to stop smoking, but not have the requisite will-power.

3. A man may know the facts but not have them play the correct role in his calculation because, say, he discounts the danger psychologically since it is remote in time and/or inflates the attractiveness of other consequences of his decision which he regards as beneficial.

In case 1 what is called for is education, the posting of warnings, et cetera. In case 2 there is no theoretical problem. We are not imposing a good on someone who rejects it. We are simply using coercion to enable people to carry out their own goals. (Note: There obviously is a difficulty in that only a subclass of the individuals affected wish to be prevented from doing what they are doing.) In case 3 there is a sense in which we are imposing a good on someone in that given his current appraisal of the facts he doesn't wish to be restricted. But in another sense we are not imposing a good since what is being claimed— and what must be shown or at least argued for— is that an accurate accounting on his part would lead him to reject his current course of action. Now we all know that such cases exist, that we are prone to disregarding dangers that are only possibilities, that immediate pleasures are often magnified and distorted.

If in addition the dangers are severe and far-reaching, we could agree to allow the state a certain degree of power to intervene in such situations. The difficulty is in specifying in advance, even vaguely, the class of cases in which intervention will be legitimate.

A related difficulty is that of drawing a line so that it is not the case that all ultra-hazardous activities are ruled out, for example, mountain-climbing, bull-fighting, sports-car racing, et cetera. There are some risks—even very great ones—which a person is entitled to take with his life.

A good deal depends on the nature of the deprivation—for example, does it prevent the person from engaging in the activity completely or merely limit his participation—and how important to the nature of the activity is the absence of restriction when this is weighed against the role that the activity plays in the life of the person. In the case of automobile seat belts, for example, the restriction is trivial in nature, interferes not at all with the use or enjoyment of the activity, and does, I am assuming, considerably reduce a high risk of serious injury. Whereas, for example, making mountain-climbing illegal completely prevents a person from engaging in an activity which may play an important role in his life and his conception of the person he is.

In general, the easiest cases to handle are those which can be argued about in the terms which Mill thought to be so important—a concern not just for the happiness or welfare, in some broad sense, of the individual but rather a concern for the autonomy and freedom of the person. I suggest that we would be most likely to consent to paternalism in those instances in which it preserves and enhances for the individual his ability to rationally consider and carry out his own decisions.

I have suggested in this essay a number of types of situations in which it seems plausible that rational men would agree to granting the legislative powers of a society the right to impose restrictions on what Mill calls "self-regarding" conduct. However, rational men knowing something about the resources of ignorance, ill-will and stupidity available to the lawmakers of a society—a good case in point is the history of drug legislation in the United States—will be concerned to limit such intervention to a minimum. I suggest in closing two principles designed to achieve this end.

In all cases of paternalistic legislation there must be a heavy and clear burden of proof placed on the authorities to demonstrate the exact nature of the harmful effects (or beneficial consequences) to be avoided (or achieved) and the probability of their occurrence. The burden of proof here is twofold—what lawyers distinguish as the burden of going forward and the burden of persuasion. That the authorities have the burden of going forward means that it is up to them to raise the question and bring forward evidence of the evils to be avoided. Unlike the case of new drugs, where the manufacturer must produce some evidence that the drug has been tested and found not harmful, no citizen has to show with respect to self-regarding conduct that it is not harmful or promotes his best interest. In addition the nature and cogency of the evidence for the harmfulness of the course of action must be set at a high level. To paraphrase a formulation of the burden of proof for criminal proceedings—better ten men ruin themselves than one man be unjustly deprived of liberty.

Finally, I suggest a principle of the least restrictive alternative. If there is an alternative way of accomplishing the desired end without restricting liberty although it may involve great expense, inconvenience, etc., the society must adopt it.

Review and Discussion Questions

1. Do you agree with Dworkin that Mill's argument in *On Liberty* relies on nonutilitarian moral considerations?

2. What are the arguments, paternalistic and nonpaternalistic, for requiring motorcyclists to wear helmets? What is the argument against helmet laws? With which side do you agree?

3. Assess Dworkin's reason for maintaining that paternalistic interference might be justified in the case of certain drugs.

4. Do you think Mill would accept Dworkin's argument that paternalism can be justified in certain cases in order to enhance the individual's ability rationally to weight and carry out his or her own decisions?

5. Consider the examples Dworkin gives in section II. Which of these laws and regulations, if any, are justified? In each case, explain why or why not.

Permissible Paternalism: Saving Smokers from Themselves

ROBERT E. GOODIN

Robert E. Goodin, professorial fellow in philosophy at the Australian National University and the author of *No Smoking,* argues that public policy directed toward discouraging smoking is an instance of permissible paternalism. In the eyes of many moral theorists, paternalism conflicts with individual rights because the point of rights is to protect an individual's choices. However, Goodin argues that the conflict between rights and paternalism is not so sharp if the paternalistic intervention is grounded on the person's own interests or values. After examining whether the desire of smokers to continue smoking reflects a preference that is their own and that is also relevant, settled, and "preferred," Goodin argues that there is a strong case for government policies intended to stop people from smoking.

Study Questions

1. What two different accounts of rights does Goodin distinguish? On which account is there a conflict between rights and paternalism? Explain. How does Goodin's approach to smoking attempt to lessen this conflict?

2. Goodin believes that paternalism can only be justified for "big decisions." What does he mean by this?

3. Goodin argues that often the preferences of smokers are neither "relevant" nor "settled." What does he mean by this?

4. How does the concept of "preferred preferences" apply to the case of smoking?

5. Why does Goodin reject the idea that, in framing public policy, we should ignore people's preferences when they have been induced by advertising?

PATERNALISM IS DESPERATELY out of fashion. Nowadays notions of "children's rights" severely limit what even parents may do to their own offspring, in their children's interests but against their will. What public officials may properly do to adult citizens, in their interests but against their will, is presumably even more tightly circumscribed. So the project I have set for myself—carving out a substantial sphere of morally permissible paternalism—might seem simply preposterous in present political and philosophical circumstances.

Here I shall say no more about the paternalism of parents toward their own children. My focus will instead be upon ways in which certain public policies designed to promote people's interests might be morally justifiable even if those people were themselves opposed to such policies.

Neither shall I say much more about notions of rights. But in focusing upon people's interests rather than their rights, I shall arguably be sticking closely to the sorts of concerns that motivate rights theorists. Of course, what it is to have a right is itself philosophically disputed; and on at least one account (the so-called "interest theory") to have a right is nothing more than to have a legally protected interest. But on the rival account

(the so-called "choice theory") the whole point of rights is to have a legally protected choice. There, the point of having a right is that your choice in the matter will be respected, even if that choice actually runs contrary to your own best interests.

It is that understanding of rights which leads us to suppose that paternalism and rights are necessarily at odds, and there are strict limits in the extent to which we might reconcile the two positions. Still, there is some substantial scope for compromise between the two positions.

Those theorists who see rights as protecting people's choices rather than promoting their interests would be most at odds with paternalists who were proposing to impose upon people what is judged to be *objectively* good for them. That is to say, they would be most at odds if paternalists were proposing to impose upon people outcomes which are judged to be good for those people, whether or not there were any grounds for that conclusion in those people's own subjective judgments of their own good.

Rights theorists and paternalists would still be at odds, but less at odds, if paternalists refrained from talking about interests in so starkly objective a way. Then, just as rights command respect for people's choices, so too would paternalists be insisting that we respect choices that people themselves have or would have made. The two are not quite the same, to be sure, but they are much more nearly the same than the ordinary contrast between paternalists and rights theorists would seem to suggest.

That is precisely the sort of conciliatory gesture that I shall here be proposing. In paternalistically justifying some course of action on the grounds that it is in someone's interests, I shall always be searching for some warrant in that person's own value judgments for saying that it is in that person's interests.

"Some warrant" is a loose constraint, to be sure. Occasionally will we find genuine cases of what philosophers call "weakness of will": people being possessed of a powerful, conscious present desire to do something that they nonetheless just cannot bring themselves to do. Then public policy forcing them to realize their own desire, though arguably paternalistic, is transparently justifiable even in terms of people's own subjective values. More often, though, the subjective value to which we are appealing is one which is present only in an inchoate form, or will only arise later, or can be appreciated only in retrospect.

Paternalism is clearly paternalistic in imposing those more weakly-held subjective values upon people in preference to their more strongly held ones. But, equally clearly, it is less offensively paternalistic thanks to this crucial fact: at least it deals strictly in terms of values that are or will be subjectively present, at some point or another and to some extent or another, in the person concerned.

I. The Scope of Paternalism

When we are talking about public policies (and maybe even when we are talking of private, familial relations), paternalism surely can only be justified for the "big decisions" in people's lives. No one, except possibly parents and perhaps not even they, would propose to stop you from buying candy bars on a whim, under the influence of

seductive advertising and at some marginal cost to your dental health.

So far as public policy is concerned, certainly, to be a fitting subject for public paternalism a decision must first of all involve high stakes. Life-and-death issues most conspicuously qualify. But so do those that substantially shape your subsequent life prospects. Decisions to drop out of school or to begin taking drugs involve high stakes of roughly that sort. If the decision is also substantially irreversible—returning to school is unlikely, the drug is addictive—then that further bolsters the case for paternalistic intervention.

The point in both cases is that people would not have a chance to benefit by learning from their mistakes. If the stakes are so high that losing the gamble once will kill you, then there is no opportunity for subsequent learning. Similarly, if the decision is irreversible, you might know better next time but be unable to benefit from your new wisdom.

II. Evaluating Preferences

The case for paternalism, as I have cast it, is that the public officials might better respect your own preferences than you would have done through your own actions. That is to say that public officials are engaged in evaluating your (surface) preferences, judging them according to some standard of your own (deeper) preferences. Public officials should refrain from paternalistic interference, and allow you to act without state interference, only if they are convinced that you are acting on:

- *relevant* preferences;
- *settled* preferences;
- *preferred* preferences; and, perhaps,
- *your own* preferences.

In what follows, I shall consider each of those requirements in turn. My running example will be the problem of smoking and policies to control it. Nothing turns on the peculiarities of that example, though. There are many others like it in relevant respects.

It often helps, in arguments like this, to apply generalities to particular cases. So, in what follows, I shall further focus in on the case of one particular smoker, Rose Cipollone. Her situation is nowise unique—in all the respects that matter here, she might be considered the prototypical smoker. All that makes her case special is that she (or more precisely her heir) was the first to win a court case against the tobacco companies whose products killed her.

In summarizing the evidence presented at that trial, the judge described the facts of the case as follows.

> Rose . . . Cipollone . . . began to smoke at age 16 . . . while she was still in high school. She testified that she began to smoke because she saw people smoking in the movies, in advertisements, and looked upon it as something "cool, glamorous and grown-up" to do. She began smoking Chesterfields . . . primarily because of advertising of "pretty girls and movie stars," and because Chesterfields were described . . . as "mild.". . .
>
> Mrs. Cipollone attempted to quit smoking while pregnant with her first child . . . , but even then she would sneak cigarettes. While she was in labor she smoked an entire pack of cigarettes, provided to her at her request by her doctor, and after the birth . . . she resumed smoking. She smoked a minimum of a pack a day and as much as two packs a day.
>
> In 1955, she switched . . . to L&M cigarettes . . . because . . . she believed that the filter would trap whatever was "bad" for her in cigarette smoking. She relied upon advertisements which supported that contention. She . . . switched to Virgina Slims . . . because the cigarettes were glamorous and long, and were associated with beautiful women—and the liberated woman. . . .
>
> Because she developed a smoker's cough and heard reports that smoking caused cancer, she tried to cut down her smoking. These attempts were unsuccessful. . . .
>
> Mrs. Cipollone switched to lower tar and nicotine cigarettes based upon advertising from which she concluded that those cigarettes were safe or safer . . . [and] upon the recommendation of her family physician. In 1981 her cancer

was diagnosed, and even though her doctors advised her to stop she was unable to do so. She even told her doctors and her husband that she had quit when she had not, and she continued to smoke until June of 1982 when her lung was removed. Even thereafter she smoked occasionally—in hiding. She stopped smoking in 1983 when her cancer had metastasized and she was diagnosed as fatally ill.

This sad history containing many of the features that I shall be arguing make paternalism most permissible.

Relevant preferences

The case against paternalism consists in the simple proposition that, morally, we ought to respect people's own choices in matters that affect themselves and by-and-large only themselves. But there are many questions we first might legitimately ask about those preferences, without in any way questioning this fundamental principle of respecting people's autonomy.

One is simply whether the preferences in play are genuinely *relevant* to the decision at hand. Often they are not. Laymen often make purely factual mistakes in their means–ends reasoning. They think—or indeed, as in the case of Rose Cipollone, are led by false advertising to suppose—that an activity is safe when it is not. They think that an activity like smoking is glamorous, when the true facts of the matter are that smoking may well cause circulatory problems requiring the distinctly unglamorous amputation of an arm or leg.

When people make purely factual mistakes like that, we might legitimately override their surface preferences (the preference to smoke) in the name of their own deeper preferences (to stay alive and bodily intact). Public policies designed to prevent youngsters from taking up smoking when they want to, or to make it harder (more expensive or inconvenient) for existing smokers to continue smoking when they want to, may be paternalistic in the sense of running contrary to people's own manifest choices in the matter. But this overriding of their choices is grounded in their own deeper preferences, so such paternalism would be minimally offensive from a moral point of view.

Settled preferences

We might ask, further, whether the preferences being manifested are "settled" preferences or whether they are merely transitory phases people are going through. It may be morally permissible to let people commit euthanasia voluntarily, if we are sure they really want to die. But if we think that they may subsequently change their minds, then we have good grounds for supposing that we should stop them.

The same may well be true with smoking policy. While Rose Cipollone herself thought smoking was both glamorous and safe, youngsters beginning to smoke today typically know better. But many of them still say that they would prefer a shorter but more glamorous life, and that they are therefore more than happy to accept the risks that smoking entails. Say what they may at age sixteen, though, we cannot help supposing that they will think differently when pigeons eventually come home to roost. The risk-courting preferences of youth are a characteristic product of a peculiarly dare-devil phase that virtually all of them will, like their predecessors, certainly grow out of.

Insofar as people's preferences are not settled—insofar as they choose one option now, yet at some later time may wish that they had chosen another—we have another ground for permissible paternalism. Policy-makers dedicated to respecting people's own choices have, in effect, two of the person's own choices to choose between. How such conflicts should be settled is hard to say. We might weigh the strength or duration of the preferences, how well they fit with the person's other preferences, and so on.

Whatever else we do, though, we clearly ought not privilege one preference over another just because it got there first. Morally, it is permissible for policy-makers to ignore one of a person's present preferences (to smoke, for example) in deference to another that is virtually certain later to emerge (as was Rose Cipollone's wish to live, once she had cancer).

Preferred preferences

A third case for permissible paternalism turns on the observation that people have not only multiple and conflicting preferences but also preferences for preferences. Rose Cipollone wanted to smoke. But, judging from her frequent (albeit failed) attempts to quit, she also wanted *not to want* to smoke.

In this respect, it might be said, Rose Cipollone's history is representative of smokers more generally. The US Surgeon General reports that some 90 percent of regular smokers have tried and failed to quit. That recidivism rate has led the World Health Organization to rank nicotine as an addictive substance on a par with heroin itself.

That classification is richly confirmed by the stories that smokers themselves tell about their failed attempts to quit. Rose Cipollone tried to quit while pregnant, only to end up smoking an entire pack in the delivery room. She tried to quit once her cancer was diagnosed, and once again after her lung was taken out, even then only to end up sneaking an occasional smoke.

In cases like this—where people want to stop some activity, try to stop it but find that they cannot stop—public policy that helps them do so can hardly be said to be paternalistic in any morally offensive respect. It overrides people's preferences, to be sure. But the preferences which it overrides are ones which people themselves wish they did not have.

The preferences which it respects—the preferences to stop smoking (like preferences of reformed alcoholics to stay off drink, or of the obese to lose weight)—are, in contrast, preferences that the people concerned themselves prefer. They would themselves rank those preferences above their own occasional inclinations to backslide. In helping them to implement their own preferred preferences, we are only respecting people's own priorities.

Your own preferences

Finally, before automatically respecting people's choices, we ought to make sure that they are really their *own* choices. We respect people's choices because in that way we manifest respect for them as persons. But if the choices in question were literally someone else's—the results of a post-hypnotic suggestion, for example—then clearly there that logic would provide no reason for our respecting those preferences.

Some people say that the effects of advertising are rather like that. No doubt there is a certain informational content to advertising. But that is not all there is in it. When Rose Cipollone read the tar and nicotine content in advertisements, what she was getting was information. What she was getting when looking at the accompanying pictures of movie stars and glamorous, liberated women was something else altogether.

Using the power of subliminal suggestion, advertising implants preferences in people in a way that largely or wholly by-passes their judgment. Insofar as it does so, the resulting preferences are not authentically that person's own. And those implanted preferences are not entitled to the respect that is rightly reserved for a person's authentic preferences, in consequence.

Such thoughts might lead some to say that we should therefore ignore altogether advertising-induced preferences in framing our public policy. I demur. There is just too much force in the rejoinder that, "Wherever those preferences came from in the first instance, they are mine now." If we want our policies to respect people by (among other things) respecting their preferences, then we will have to respect all of those preferences with which people now associate themselves.

Even admitting the force of that rejoinder, though, there is much that still might be done to curb the preference-shaping activities of, for example, the tobacco industry. Even those who say "they're my preferences now" would presumably have preferred, ahead of time, to make up their own minds in the matter. So there we have a case, couched in terms of people's own (past) preferences, for severely restricting the advertising and promotion of products—especially ones which people will later regret having grown to like, but which they will later be unable to resist.

III. Conclusions

What, in practical policy terms, follows from all that? Well, in the case of smoking, which has served as my running example, we might ban the sale of tobacco altogether or turn it into a drug available only on prescription to registered users. Or, less dramatically, we might make cigarettes difficult and expensive to obtain—especially for youngsters, whose purchases are particularly price-sensitive. We might ban all promotional advertising of tobacco products, designed as it is to attract new users. We might prohibit smoking in all offices, restaurants, and other public places, thus making it harder for smokers to find a place to partake and providing a further inducement for them to quit.

All of those policies would be good for smokers themselves. They would enjoy a longer life expectancy and a higher quality of life if they stopped smoking. But that is to talk the language of interests rather than of rights and choices. In those latter terms, all those policies clearly go against smokers' manifest preferences, in one sense or another. Smokers want to keep smoking. They do not want to pay more or drive further to get their cigarettes. They want to be able to take comfort in advertisements constantly telling them how glamorous their smoking is.

In other more important senses, though, such policies can be justified even in terms of the preferences of smokers themselves. They do not want to die, as a quarter of them eventually will (and ten to fifteen years before their time) of smoking-related diseases; it is only false beliefs or wishful thinking that make smokers think that continued smoking is consistent with that desire not to avoid a premature death. At the moment they may think that the benefits of smoking outweigh the costs, but they will almost certainly revise that view once those costs are eventually sheeted home. The vast majority of smokers would like to stop smoking but, being addicted, find it very hard now to do so.

Like Rose Cipollone, certainly in her dying days and intermittently even from her early adulthood, most smokers themselves would say that they would have been better off never starting. Many even agree that they would welcome anything (like a workplace ban on smoking) that might now make them stop. Given the internally conflicting preferences here in play, smokers also harbor at one and the same time preferences pointing in the opposite direction; that is what might make helping them to stop seem unacceptably paternalistic. But in terms of other of their preferences—and ones that deserve clear precedence, at that—doing so is perfectly well warranted.

Smoking is unusual, perhaps, in presenting a case for permissible paternalism on all four of the fronts here canvassed. Most activities might qualify under only one or two of the headings.

However, that may well be enough. My point here is not that paternalism is always permissible but merely that it may always be.

In the discourse of liberal democracies, the charge of paternalism is typically taken to be a knock-down objection to any policy. If I am right, that knee-jerk response is wrong. When confronted with the charge of paternalism, it should always be open to us to say, "Sure, this proposal is paternalistic—but is the paternalism in view permissible or impermissible, good or bad?" More often than not, I think we will find, paternalism might prove perfectly defensible along the lines sketched here.

Further Reading

Goodin, Robert E., "The Ethics of Smoking." *Ethics,* 99 (April 1989), 575–624.
Goodin, Robert E., *No Smoking: The Ethical Issues,* Chicago and London: University of Chicago Press, 1989.

Review and Discussion Questions

1. Goodin believes that public officials should refrain from paternalistic interference with you only if they are convinced that you are acting on relevant preferences, settled preferences, preferred preferences, and preferences that are your own. Do you agree with this principle? Explain why or why not.

2. Goodin argues that smoking presents a case for permissible paternalism on all four of the above points. Assess smoking in terms of each category of preferences.

3. Do cigarette smokers fully understand the risks of smoking? Do they voluntarily assume those risks? How important is cigarette advertising in encouraging people to smoke? Is such advertising manipulative or unfair?

4. Is cigarette smoking (always, sometimes, never) irrational? Explain your answer. Is the answer to this question relevant to the determination of a justifiable smoking policy?

5. How difficult is it to quit smoking? Are most cigarette smokers addicts? How, if at all, is the answer to these questions relevant to the permissibility of paternalistic anti-smoking policies?

6. How would you assess the overall costs and benefits of smoking, both to the individual and to society? Does Goodin overlook the pleasure smokers get from smoking?

7. Would the suppression of cigarette advertising be compatible with our society's commitment to freedom of expression?

8. Is it compatible with Mill's liberty principle for society to undertake to reduce or eliminate smoking? Should society pursue more aggressive policies to discourage or eliminate smoking? If so, what policies? Should over-the-counter cigarette sales be outlawed?

A Drug-Free America—or a Free America?

DAVID BOAZ

David Boaz, executive vice president of the Cato Institute, advocates the legalization of drugs. The "War on Drugs" has failed, he argues, because efforts to restrict the drug trade simply increase the financial incentives for drug dealers. But while drug prohibition has failed to curtail drug use, it has severely limited some fundamental American liberties and violated our fundamental right to live our lives in the way we choose. Unlike many advocates of drug liberalization, however, Boaz rejects the view that addiction is a disease, over which the individual has no control. Instead, he argues that we need to restore traditional notions of individual responsibility.

Study Questions

1. How does prohibition create financial incentives for drug dealers?
2. What are the prohibitionists' arguments against the presumption in favor of individual liberty?
3. What is the "disease concept of addiction"?
4. What evidence does Boaz advance to support the claim that there has been "a flight from individual responsibility" in recent decades?

Introduction: The Drug Problem

HUMAN BEINGS HAVE USED mind-altering substances throughout recorded history. Why? Perhaps because, as one acquaintance put it in a recent conversation, there is a God-shaped void in most people's lives. Perhaps because we fail to love one another as we should. Perhaps because of the social pressure for success. Perhaps because—and this is what really irks the prohibitionists—we enjoy drugs' mind-altering effects.

Though the reasons for drug use are numerous, the governmental response has been singular: almost as long as humans have used drugs, governments have tried to stop them. In the sixteenth century the Egyptian government banned coffee. In the seventeenth century the Czar of Russia and the Sultan of the Ottoman Empire executed tobacco smokers. In the eighteenth century England tried to halt gin consumption and China penalized opium sellers with strangulation.

The drug prohibition experiment most familiar to Americans is the prohibition of alcohol in the 1920s. The period has become notorious for the widespread illegal consumption of alcohol and the resultant crime. Movies such as *Some Like It Hot* typify the popular legend of the era. The failure of Prohibition, however, is not just legendary. Consumption of alcohol probably fell slightly at the beginning of Prohibition but then rose steadily throughout the period. Alcohol became more potent, and there were reportedly more illegal speakeasies than there had been legal saloons. More serious for nondrinkers, the per capita murder rate and the assault-by-firearm rate both rose throughout Prohibition.

Most of the same phenomena are occurring with today's prohibition of marijuana, cocaine, and heroin. Use of these drugs has risen and fallen during the seventy-seven years since Congress passed the Harrison Narcotics Act, with little relationship to the level of enforcement. In the past decade, the decade of the "War on Drugs," use of these drugs seems to have declined, but no faster than the decline in the use of the legal drugs alcohol and tobacco. Over the past twenty years Americans became more health- and fitness-conscious, and use of all drugs seems to have correspondingly decreased. Drug prohibition, however, has not stopped twenty-three million people from trying cocaine and seventy-two million people from trying marijuana. Prohibition also has not stopped the number of heroin users from increasing by one hundred fifty percent and the number of cocaine users from increasing by ten thousand percent. Moreover, prohibition has not kept drugs out of the hands of children: in 1999 fifty-five percent of high school seniors admitted to having tried illicit drugs; eighty-nine percent said it was fairly easy or very easy to obtain marijuana; and forty-four percent said the same about cocaine.

Although drug prohibition has not curtailed drug use, it has severely limited some fundamental American liberties. Programs such as "Zero Tolerance," which advocates seizing a car or boat on the mere allegation of a law enforcement official that the vehicle contains drugs, ignore the constitutional principle that a person is innocent until proven guilty.

In attempting to fashion a solution to "the drug problem," one first needs to define the problem society is trying to solve. If the problem is the age-old human instinct to use mind-altering substances, then the solution might be God, or evolution, or stronger families, or Alcoholics Anonymous. History suggests, however, that the

solution is unlikely to be found in the halls of Congress. If, on the other hand, the problem is the soaring murder rate, the destruction of inner-city communities, the creation of a criminal subculture, and the fear millions of Americans experience on their own streets, then a solution may well be found in Congress—not in the creation of laws but in their repeal.

This article proposes that the repeal of certain laws will force individuals to take responsibility for their actions; the repeal of other laws will provide individuals the right to make important decisions in their lives free from outside interference. Together these changes will create the society in which drugs can, and must, be legalized. Legalization of drugs, in turn, will end the need for the government to make the intrusions into our fundamental rights as it does so often in its War on Drugs.

I. The Futility of Prohibition

A. The War on Drugs

Prohibition of drugs is not the solution to the drug problem. For the past twenty years the United States has waged a "War on Drugs." The goals of this War were simple: prohibit the cultivation or manufacture of drugs, prohibit the import of drugs, and prohibit the use of drugs. As the aforementioned statistics demonstrate, the War has not achieved its goals.

Prohibitionists, however, sometimes claim that the United States has not yet "really fought a drug war." The prohibitionists argue that a "true drug war" would sharply lower drug use. They feel that the government has not fully committed itself to winning this battle. One need only look at the War on Drugs' record, however, to see the commitment:

- Congress passed stricter anti-drug laws in 1984, 1986, 1988, 1994, and 1998. Congress and state legislators steadily increased penalties for drug law violations, mandating jail time even for first offenders, imposing large civil fines, seizing property,

denying federal benefits to drug law violators, and evicting tenants from public
housing.

- Federal drug war outlays increased by
  more than 1150% between 1981 and
  1999, and the federal government spent
  more than $75 billion on anti-drug activi-
  ties during the last five years. Adjusted for
  inflation, the federal government spends
  twenty-five times as much on drug law
  enforcement every year as it spent on
  Prohibition enforcement throughout the
  Roaring Twenties.
- Police officers made more than 1.5 million
  drug law arrests in 1999, about eighty percent of them for drug possession.
- The number of drug busts tripled during
  the 1980s, and the number of convictions
  doubled. Arrests continued to rise throughout the 1990s, and the average sentence
  for drug offenses nearly doubled.
- America's prison population quadrupled
  between 1981 and 1999, from 344,283 to
  1,366,721. More than six million people
  were on probation, in jail or prison, or on
  parole at year end 1999—3.1 percent of all
  U.S. adult residents. On December 31,
  1999, state prisons were operating at
  between one percent and seventeen percent
  above capacity, while federal prisons were
  operating at thirty-two percent above
  capacity. More prisoners are in jail for nonviolent drug law violations than ever before.
- The armed services, Coast Guard, and
  Civil Air Patrol became more active in the
  drug fight, providing search and pursuit
  planes, helicopters, ocean interdiction, and
  radar. Defense Department spending on
  the War on Drugs rose from $200 million
  in 1988 to $800 million in 1990.
- The Central Intelligence Agency (CIA)
  and National Security Agency began using
  spy satellites and communications listening
  technology as part of the drug war. The
  CIA also designed a special Counter
  Narcotics Center.

- The federal government forced drug testing upon public employees and required
  contractors to establish "drug-free" work-
  places. Drug testing has also expanded
  among private companies.
- Seizures of cocaine rose from 2,000 kilograms in 1981 to 120,034 kilograms in
  1998.

Despite this enormous effort, drugs are more
readily available than ever before. The War on
Drugs has failed to achieve its primary goal of
diminishing the availability and use of drugs.

B. Prohibition creates financial incentives

One reason for the failure of the War on Drugs
is that it ignores the fact that prohibition sets up
tremendous financial incentives for drug dealers
to supply the demand. Prohibition, at least initially, reduces the supply of the prohibited substance and thus raises the price. In addition, a
large risk premium is added onto the price. One
has to pay a painter more to paint the Golden
Gate Bridge than to paint a house because of the
added danger. Similarly, drug dealers demand
more money to sell cocaine than to sell alcohol.
Those who are willing to accept the risk of arrest
or murder will be handsomely—sometimes unbe-
lievably—rewarded.

Drug dealers, therefore, whatever one may
think of them morally, are actually profit-seeking
entrepreneurs. Drug researcher James Ostrowski
points out that "[t]he public has the false impression that drug enforcers are highly innovative,
continually devising new schemes to catch drug
dealers. Actually, the reverse is true. The dealers,
like successful businessmen, are usually one step
ahead of the 'competition.'"[1]

New examples of the drug dealers' entrepreneurial skills appear every day. For example, partly
because the Supreme Court upheld surveillance
flights over private property to look for marijuana
fields, marijuana growers have been moving
indoors and underground. The Drug Enforcement
Administration seized about 130 indoor marijuana

gardens in California in 1989. In 1999 they seized 1,048 gardens, or 87,019 plants.

Overseas exporters have also been showing off their entrepreneurial skills. Some have been sending drugs into the United States in the luggage of children traveling alone, on the assumption that authorities will not suspect children and will go easy on them if they are caught. Others have concealed drugs in anchovy cans, bean sprouts, washing machines, fuel tanks, and T-shirts. At least one man surgically implanted a pound of cocaine in his thighs. Some smugglers swallow drugs before getting on international flights. Professor Ethan Nadelmann has explained the spread of overseas exporters as the "push-down/pop-up factor": push down drug production in one country, and it will pop up in another.[2] For example, Nadelmann notes that "Colombian marijuana growers rapidly expanded production following successful eradication efforts in Mexico during the mid-1970s. Today, Mexican growers are rapidly taking advantage of recent Colombian government successes in eradicating marijuana."

Prohibition of drugs creates tremendous profit incentives. In turn, the profit incentives induce drug manufacturers and dealers to creatively stay one step ahead of the drug enforcement officials. The profit incentives show the futility of eradication, interdiction, and enforcement and make one question whether prohibition will ever be successful. . . .

II. Individual Rights

Many of the drug enforcement ideas the prohibitionists suggest trample upon numerous constitutional and natural rights. In any discussion of government policies, it is necessary to examine the effect on natural rights for one simple reason: individuals have rights that governments may not violate. In the Declaration of Independence, Thomas Jefferson defined these rights as life, liberty, and the pursuit of happiness. I argue that these inviolable rights can actually be classified as one fundamental right: individuals have the right to live their lives in any way they choose so long

as they do not violate the equal rights of others. To put this idea in the drug context, what right could be more basic, more inherent in human nature, than the right to choose what substances to put in one's own body? Whether it is alcohol, tobacco, laetrile, AZT, saturated fat, or cocaine, this is a decision that the individual should make, not the government. This point seems so obvious to me that it is, to borrow Jefferson's words, self-evident.

The prohibitionists, however, fail to recognize this fundamental freedom. They advance several arguments in an effort to rebut the presumption in favor of liberty. First, they argue, drug users are responsible for the violence of the drug trade and the resulting damage to innocent people. The erstwhile Drug Czar, William Bennett, when asked how his nicotine addiction differed from a drug addiction, responded, "I didn't do any drive-by shootings."[3] Similarly, former First Lady Nancy Reagan said, "The casual user may think when he takes a line of cocaine or smokes a joint in the privacy of his nice condo, listening to his expensive stereo, that he's somehow not bothering anyone. But there is a trail of death and destruction that leads directly to his door. I'm saying that if you're a casual drug user, you are an accomplice to murder."[4]

The comments of both Mr. Bennett and Mrs. Reagan, however, display a remarkable ignorance about the illegal-drug business. Drug use does not cause violence. Alcohol did not cause the violence of the 1920s, Prohibition did. Similarly, drugs do not cause today's soaring murder rates, drug prohibition does. The chain of events is obvious: drug laws reduce the supply and raise the price of drugs. The high price causes addicts to commit crimes to pay for a habit that would be easily affordable if obtaining drugs was legal. The illegality of the business means that business disputes—between customers and suppliers or between rival suppliers—can be settled only through violence, not through the courts. The violence of the business then draws in those who have a propensity—or what economists call a comparative advantage—for violence. When

Congress repealed Prohibition, the violence went out of the liquor business. Similarly, when Congress repeals drug prohibition, the heroin and cocaine trade will cease to be violent. As columnist Stephen Chapman put it, "the real accomplices to murder" are those responsible for the laws that make the drug business violent.[5]

Another prohibitionist argument against the right to take drugs is that drug use affects others, such as automobile accident victims and crack babies. With regard to the former, certainly good reasons exist to strictly penalize driving (as well as flying or operating machinery) while under the influence of drugs. It hardly seems appropriate, however, to penalize those who use drugs safely in an attempt to stop the unsafe usage. As for harm to babies, this is a heart-rending problem (though perhaps not as large a problem as is sometimes believed). Again, however, it seems unnecessary and unfair to ban a recreational drug just because it should not be used during pregnancy. Moreover, drug-affected babies have one point in common with driving under the influence: misuse of legal drugs (alcohol, tobacco, codeine, caffeine), as well as illegal drugs, contributes to both problems. Thus, if society wants to ban cocaine and marijuana because of these drugs' potential for misuse, society should logically also ban alcohol, tobacco, and similar legal drugs.

The question of an individual right to use drugs comes down to this: if the government can tell us what we can put into our own bodies, what can it not tell us? What limits on government action are there? We would do well to remember Jefferson's advice: "Was the government to prescribe to us our medicine and diet, our bodies would be in such keeping as our souls are now."[6]

III. The Solution: Re-establish Individual Responsibility

For the past several decades a flight from individual responsibility has taken place in the United States. Intellectuals, often government funded, have concocted a whole array of explanations as to why nothing that happens to us is our own fault. These intellectuals tell us that the poor are not responsible for their poverty, the fat are not responsible for their overeating, the alcoholic are not responsible for their drinking. Any attempt to suggest that people are sometimes responsible for their own failures is denounced as "blaming the victim."

These nonresponsibility attitudes are particularly common in discussions of alcohol, tobacco, and other drugs. Development of these attitudes probably began in the 1930s with the formulation of the classic disease theory of alcoholism. The disease theory holds that alcoholism is a disease that the alcoholic cannot control. People have found it easy to apply the theory of addiction to tobacco, cocaine, heroin, even marijuana. In each case, according to the theory, people get "hooked" and simply cannot control their use. Author Herbert Fingarette, however, stated that "*no* leading research authorities accept the classic disease concept [for alcoholism]."[7] Many scientists, though, believe it is appropriate to mislead the public about the nature of alcoholism in order to induce what they see as the right behavior with regard to alcohol.

In the popular press the addiction theory has spread rapidly. Popular magazines declare everything from sex to shopping to video games an addiction that the addicted person has no power to control. As William Wilbanks said, the phrase "I can't help myself" has become the all-purpose excuse of our time.[8]

The addiction theory has also gained prominence in discussions of illegal drugs. Both prohibitionists and legalizers tend to be enamored of the classic notion of addiction. Prohibitionists say that because people cannot help themselves with respect to addictive drugs, society must threaten them with criminal sanctions to protect them from their own failings. Legalizers offer instead a "medical model": treat drug use as a disease, not a crime. The legalizers urge that the billions of dollars currently spent on drug enforcement be transferred to treatment programs so that government can supply "treatment on demand" for drug addicts.

Despite the popular affection for the addiction theory, numerous commentators denounce the theory. For example, addiction researcher Stanton Peele deplores the effects of telling people that addictive behavior is uncontrollable:

> [O]ne of the best antidotes to addiction is to teach children responsibility and respect for others and to insist on ethical standards for everyone—children, adults, addicts. Cross-cultural data indicate, for instance, that when an experience is defined as uncontrollable, many people experience such loss of control and use it to justify their transgressions against society. For example, studies find that the "uncontrollable" consequences of alcohol consumption vary from one society to another, depending upon cultural expectations.[9]

Spreading the disease concept of addiction is not the only way society has undermined the idea of individual responsibility. Some of the other ways have had their greatest impact on America's poorest citizens. For example, author Charles Murray points out that in the 1960s policymakers and opinion molders were seized with the grand idea that poverty could and should be eliminated in the United States.[10] One of the policymakers' first steps was to tell the poor that their poverty was not their own fault. Seeking to eliminate the "stigma" attached to poverty, the policymakers made welfare easier to get. They made it more difficult to throw disruptive or uncooperative students out of school, and they made it more difficult to put criminals in jail. As a result, America ended up with more people on welfare, fewer students learning in the schools, and more crime.

By reducing society's disapproval of people who do not study, do not work, and do not meet their obligations to family and community, the policymakers took away the respectability formerly accorded to those who do study, do work, and do meet their obligations. As Murray wrote, the intelligentsia and the policymakers began treating the poor "in ways that they would never consider treating people they respected."[11]

Recently, Murray has extended his analysis in a penetrating discussion of the drug problem.[12] He cites numerous examples in which the government has taken from people the power to do something about drugs in their own lives. First, in an attempt to prevent school principals from using their power in an arbitrary or racially discriminatory manner, the government has made it very difficult for principals to expel students for disruptive behavior or drug use. Second, legislatures and courts are making it increasingly difficult for employers to dismiss employees: wrongful-discharge suits and federal investigations have replaced the old doctrine of employment at will. Finally, the government has made it more burdensome for landlords to maintain standards in their buildings by taking away the landlords' power to decide—albeit sometimes arbitrarily—to whom to rent and whom to turn away.

Murray proposes solutions designed to give individuals more control over their own lives: school vouchers to allow parents to choose the schools their children will attend, with the schools free to set their own relaxed or zero-tolerance policies toward drugs; freedom for workers and employers to decide on the conditions of employment with regard to drug use without interference from courts and governments; wide discretion for landlords (and tenant committees in public housing) to screen applicants. Murray's basic argument is that "legalization [of drugs will] work in a society where people are held responsible for the consequences of their actions."[13]

. . . Americans might take other steps to restore traditional notions of individual responsibility. Laws regarding drugs should only punish persons who violate the rights of others; private actions should go unpunished. Thus, laws should strictly punish those who drive while under the influence of alcohol or other drugs. Intoxication, moreover, should not be a legal defense against charges of theft, violence, or other rights violations, nor should a claim of "shopping addiction" excuse people from having to pay their debts. Physicians, intellectuals, and religious leaders should recognize that the denial of responsibility has gone too far, and they should begin to stress the moral value of individual responsibility, the self-respect such responsibility brings, and the utilitarian benefits of living in a society in which all persons are held responsible for the consequences of their actions.

Conclusion

Society cannot really make war on drugs, which are just chemical substances. Society can only wage wars against people, in this case people who use and sell drugs. Before America continues a war that has cost many billions of dollars and many thousands of lives—more than eight thousand lives per year even before the skyrocketing murder rates of the late 1980s—Americans should be sure that the benefits exceed the costs. Remarkably, all of the high-ranking officers in the Reagan administration's drug war reported in 1988 that they knew of no studies showing that the benefits of prohibition exceeded the costs.

There is a good reason for the lack of such a study. Prohibition is futile. We cannot win the War on Drugs. We cannot even keep drugs out of our prisons. Thus, we could turn the United States into a police state, and we still would not win the War on Drugs. The costs of prohibition, however, are very real: tens of billions of dollars a year, corruption of law enforcement officials, civil liberties abuses, the destruction of inner-city communities, black-market murders, murders incident to street crime by addicts seeking to pay

for their habit, and the growing sense that our major cities are places of uncontrollable violence.

Hundreds, perhaps thousands, of years of history teach us that we will never make our society drug-free. In the futile attempt to do so, however, we may well make our society unfree.

NOTES

1. Ostrowski, "Thinking About Drug Legalization," 121 *Policy Analysis,* May 25, 1989, at 34. . . .
2. Nadelmann, "The Case for Legalization," 92 *Public Interest* 3, 9 (1988). . . .
3. Isikoff, "Bennett Rebuts Drug Legalization Ideas," *Washington Post,* Dec. 12, 1989, at A10, col. 1.
4. Chapman, "Nancy Reagan and the Real Villains in the Drug War," *Chicago Tribune,* March 6, 1988, sec. 4, at 3, col. 1. . . .
5. Chapman, *supra* note 4.
6. T. Jefferson, "Notes on Virginia," in *The Life and Selected Writings of Thomas Jefferson* 187, 275 (1944).
7. H. Fingarette, *Heavy Drinking* at 3 (1988). . . .
8. Wilbanks, "The New Obscenity," 54 *Vital Speeches of the Day* 658, 658–59 (1988).
9. S. Peele, "Control Yourself," *Reason,* Feb. 1990, at 25.
10. C. Murray, *Losing Ground: American Social Policy, 1950–1980* 26–29, 42 (1984). . . .
11. *Id.* at 222.
12. Murray, "How to Win the War on Drugs," *New Republic,* May 21, 1990, at 19, 19–25.
13. *Id.* at 19.

Review and Discussion Questions

1. Is Boaz correct in saying that the war on drugs is futile? How persuasive is the analogy with alcohol prohibition in the 1920s?
2. Do you agree with Boaz that people have a fundamental right to ingest whatever substances they choose?
3. Opponents of drug legalization point to the undeniable social costs of drug abuse and to the enormous harm it causes individuals. Has Boaz effectively addressed these concerns about the dangers of drug abuse?
4. In what ways does Boaz's essay appeal to both utilitarian and nonutilitarian (or Kantian) considerations? Which of Boaz's points do you find the strongest? Which is the weakest?

5. In a previous essay, Gerald Dworkin presented a rationale for paternalistic drug laws that seems to square with the central concerns of John Stuart Mill's *On Liberty*. What is Boaz's view of addiction, and how would he respond to Dworkin's argument?

6. Boaz's point about the financial incentives created by prohibition seems to assume that drug use is price inelastic—that is, that drug users will keep on paying ever higher prices. Presumably, they will pay more because they are addicted to the drugs. But if, in fact, the demand for drugs depends on addiction, is Boaz's focus on individual responsibility undercut?

7. In the previous essay, Robert E. Goodin defended paternalism in the case of smoking by critically examining the character of smokers' preferences. Apply his arguments to the drugs that Boaz wants to legalize. How strong are those arguments, and how might Boaz respond to them?

If He Hollers Let Him Go: Regulating Racist Speech on Campus

CHARLES R. LAWRENCE III

John Stuart Mill's *On Liberty* makes a compelling case for unabridged freedom of expression, and the First Amendment to the U.S. Constitution enshrines free speech as a cardinal value of our political system. In recent years, however, incidents of racially abusive speech on college campuses have instigated a debate over the exact limits of freedom of expression. Some colleges and universities have adopted regulations forbidding racist speech; others have resisted these sorts of regulations, regarding them as a violation of the principle of free expression. Charles R. Lawrence, professor of law at Stanford University, is sensitive to the conflicting values at stake in this debate, but he argues that racist insults—like so-called "fighting words"—are not constitutionally protected. In addition, racist speech reduces the total amount of speech entering the marketplace of ideas. Emphasizing the importance of listening to the victims of racist speech, Lawrence describes the genuine harms that it causes African Americans and other subordinated groups—harms that are too readily overlooked when we decide to tolerate racist speech.

Study Questions

1. What are the "very strong reasons for protecting even racist speech"?
2. What two reasons does Lawrence give to support the view that face-to-face racial insults are undeserving of First Amendment protection?

From Duke Law Journal, vol. 1990, no. 2. Copyright © 1990 Charles R. Lawrence III. Reprinted by permission of the author and Duke Law Journal. *Most footnotes omitted. The full text of this essay appears in Matsuda, Lawrence, et al.,* "Fighting Words": Critical Race Perspectives on Hate Speech and the First Amendment *(Boulder, Colo.: Westview Press, 1992).*

3. What point does the experience of the gay student, Michael, illuminate?

4. What point is illustrated by the reactions of whites to the racist incident in Wilmington?

5. Why does Lawrence find it misleading to cast the debate in terms of "offensive" speech?

6. How does racist speech distort the marketplace of ideas?

Introduction

IN RECENT YEARS, American campuses have seen a resurgence of racial violence and a corresponding rise in the incidence of verbal and symbolic assault and harassment to which blacks and other traditionally subjugated groups are subjected. There is a heated debate in the civil liberties community concerning the proper response to incidents of racist speech on campus. Strong disagreements have arisen between those individuals who believe that racist speech . . . should be regulated by the university or some public body and those individuals who believe that racist expression should be protected from all public regulation. At the center of the controversy is a tension between the constitutional values of free speech and equality. Like the debate over affirmative action in university admissions, this issue has divided old allies and revealed unrecognized or unacknowledged differences in the experience, perceptions, and values of members of long-standing alliances. It also has caused considerable soul-searching by individuals with long-time commitments to both the cause of political expression and the cause of racial equality.

I write this article from within the cauldron of this controversy. I make no pretense of dispassion or objectivity, but I do claim a deep commitment to the values that motivate both sides of the debate. As I struggle with the tension between these constitutional values, I particularly appreciate the experience of both belonging and not belonging that gives to African Americans and other outsider groups a sense of duality. W. E. B. Du Bois—scholar and founder of the National Association for the Advancement of Colored People—called the gift and burden inherent to the dual, conflicting heritage of all African Americans their "second-sight."[1]

The "double consciousness" of groups outside the ethnic mainstream is particularly apparent in the context of this controversy. Blacks know and value the protection the first amendment affords those of us who must rely upon our voices to petition both government and our neighbors for redress of grievances. Our political tradition has looked to "the word," to the moral power of ideas, to change a system when neither the power of the vote nor that of the gun are available. This part of us has known the experience of belonging and recognizes our common and inseparable interest in preserving the right of free speech for all. But we also know the experience of the outsider. The Framers excluded us from the protection of the first amendment.* The same Constitution that established rights for others endorsed a story that proclaimed our inferiority. It is a story that remains deeply ingrained in the American psyche.

We see a different world than that which is seen by Americans who do not share this historical experience. We often hear racist speech when our white neighbors are not aware of its presence.[†]

It is not my purpose to belittle or trivialize the importance of defending unpopular speech against the tyranny of the majority. There are very strong reasons for protecting even racist

---

*In *Dred Scott v. Sanford,* 60 U.S. (19 How.) 393 (1857), the Court declared that at the time of the Declaration of Independence, and when the Constitution of the United States was framed and adopted, "[blacks] had no rights which the white man was bound to respect." . . .

[†]*See* Matsuda, "Public Response to Racist Speech: Considering the Victim's Story," 87 *Mich. L. Rev.* 2320 (1989). Matsuda points out that the "mainstream press often ignores these stories [of racist speech and violence], giving rise to the view of racist and anti-Semitic incidents as random and isolated, and the corollary that isolated incidents are inconsequential." *Id.* at 2331.

speech. Perhaps the most important reasons are that it reinforces our society's commitment to the value of tolerance, and that, by shielding racist speech from government regulation, we will be forced to combat it as a community. These reasons for protecting racist speech should not be set aside hastily, and I will not argue that we should be less vigilant in protecting the speech and associational rights of speakers with whom most of us would disagree.

But I am deeply concerned about the role that many civil libertarians have played, or the roles we have failed to play, in the continuing, real-life struggle through which we define the community in which we live. I fear that by framing the debate as we have—as one in which the liberty of free speech is in conflict with the elimination of racism—we have advanced the cause of racial oppression and have placed the bigot on the moral high ground, fanning the rising flames of racism. Above all, I am troubled that we have not listened to the real victims, that we have shown so little empathy or understanding for their injury, and that we have abandoned those individuals whose race, gender, or sexual orientation provokes others to regard them as second class citizens. These individuals' civil liberties are most directly at stake in the debate. . . .

Racist Speech as the Functional Equivalent of Fighting Words

Much recent debate over the efficacy of regulating racist speech has focused on the efforts by colleges and universities to respond to the burgeoning incidents of racial harassment on their campuses. At Stanford, where I teach, there has been considerable controversy over the questions whether racist and other discriminatory verbal harassment should be regulated and what form that regulation should take. Proponents of regulation have been sensitive to the danger of inhibiting expression, and the current regulation (which was drafted by my colleague Tom Grey) manifests that sensitivity. . . .

This regulation and others like it have been characterized in the press as the work of "thought police," but it does nothing more than prohibit intentional face-to-face insults, a form of speech that is unprotected by the first amendment. When racist speech takes the form of face-to-face insults, catcalls, or other assaultive speech aimed at an individual or small group of persons, then it falls within the "fighting words" exception to first amendment protection.* The Supreme Court has held that words that "by their very utterance inflict injury or tend to incite an immediate breach of the peace"[2] are not constitutionally protected.

Face-to-face racial insults, like fighting words, are undeserving of first amendment protection for two reasons. The first reason is the immediacy of the injurious impact of racial insults. The experience of being called "nigger," "spic," "Jap," or "kike" is like receiving a slap in the face. The injury is instantaneous. There is neither an opportunity for intermediary reflection on the idea conveyed nor an opportunity for responsive speech. The harm to be avoided is both clear and present. The second reason that racial insults should not fall under protected speech relates to the purpose underlying the first amendment. If the purpose of the first amendment is to foster the greatest amount of speech, then racial insults disserve that purpose. Assaultive racist speech functions as a preemptive strike. The racial invective is experienced as a blow, not a proffered idea, and once the blow is struck, it is unlikely that dialogue will follow. Racial insults are undeserving of first amendment protection because the perpetrator's

---

*The fighting words doctrine requires that the words be "directed to the person of the hearer." *Cohen v. California*, 403 U.S. 15, 20 (1971). This requirement strikes a balance between our concern for protecting the individual from unavoidable personalized attack (one is not given an opportunity to avoid the speech by averting the eyes or leaving the room) and our concern for allowing space for even the most offensive speech in a public forum ("one man's vulgarity is another's lyric," *id*. at 25). I would argue that the face-to-face requirement be expanded in the case of racist verbal assaults to include those words that are intentionally spoken in the presence of members of the denigrated group. . . .

intention is not to discover truth or initiate dialogue but to injure the victim.

The fighting words doctrine anticipates that the verbal "slap in the face" of insulting words will provoke a violent response with a resulting breach of the peace. When racial insults are hurled at minorities, the response may be silence or flight rather than a fight, but the preemptive effect on further speech is just as complete as with fighting words. Women and minorities often report that they find themselves speechless in the face of discriminatory verbal attacks. This inability to respond is not the result of oversensitivity among these groups, as some individuals who oppose protective regulation have argued. Rather, it is the product of several factors, all of which reveal the non-speech character of the initial preemptive verbal assault. The first factor is that the visceral emotional response to personal attack precludes speech. Attack produces an instinctive, defensive psychological reaction. Fear, rage, shock, and flight all interfere with any reasoned response. Words like "nigger," "kike," and "faggot" produce physical symptoms that temporarily disable the victim, and the perpetrators often use these words with the intention of producing this effect. Many victims do not find words of response until well after the assault when the cowardly assaulter has departed.

A second factor that distinguishes racial insults from protected speech is the preemptive nature of such insults—the words by which to respond to such verbal attacks may never be forthcoming because speech is usually an inadequate response. When one is personally attacked with words that denote one's subhuman status and untouchability, there is little (if anything) that can be said to redress either the emotional or reputational injury. This is particularly true when the message and meaning of the epithet resonates with beliefs widely held in society. This preservation of widespread beliefs is what makes the face-to-face racial attack more likely to preempt speech than are other fighting words. The racist name-caller is accompanied by a cultural chorus of equally demeaning speech and symbols.

The subordinated victim of fighting words also is silenced by her relatively powerless position in

society. Because of the significance of power and position, the categorization of racial epithets as "fighting words" provides an inadequate paradigm; instead one must speak of their "functional equivalent." The fighting words doctrine presupposes an encounter between two persons of relatively equal power who have been acculturated to respond to face-to-face insults with violence. The fighting words doctrine is a paradigm based on a white male point of view. In most situations, minorities correctly perceive that a violent response to fighting words will result in a risk to their own life and limb. Since minorities are likely to lose the fight, they are forced to remain silent and submissive. This response is most obvious when women submit to sexually assaultive speech or when the racist name-caller is in a more powerful position—the boss on the job or the mob. . . .

One of my students, a white, gay male, related an experience that is quite instructive in understanding the inadequacy and potential of the fighting words doctrine. In response to my request that students describe how they experienced the injury of racist speech, Michael told a story of being called "faggot" by a man on a subway. His description included all of the speech inhibiting elements I have noted previously. He found himself in a state of semi-shock, nauseous, dizzy, unable to muster the witty, sarcastic, articulate rejoinder he was accustomed to making. He suddenly was aware of the recent spate of gay-bashing in San Francisco, and how many of these had escalated from verbal encounters. Even hours later when the shock receded and his facility with words returned, he realized that any response was inadequate to counter the hundreds of years of societal defamation that one word—"faggot"—carried with it. Like the word "nigger" and unlike the word "liar," it is not sufficient to deny the truth of the word's application, to say, "I am not a faggot." One must deny the truth of the word's meaning, a meaning shouted from the rooftops by the rest of the world a million times a day. Although there are many of us who constantly and in myriad ways seek to counter the lie spoken in the meaning of hateful words like "nigger" and "faggot," it is a nearly impossible burden to bear when one encounters hateful speech face-to-face.

But there was another part of my discussion with Michael that is equally instructive. I asked if he could remember a situation when he had been verbally attacked with reference to his membership in a superordinate group. Had he ever been called a "honkie," a "chauvinist pig," or "mick"? (Michael is from a working class Irish family in Boston.) He said that he had been called some version of all three and that although he found the last one more offensive than the first two, he had not experienced—even in that subordinated role—the same disorienting powerlessness he had experienced when attacked for his membership in the gay community. The question of power, of the context of the power relationships within which speech takes place, must be considered as we decide how best to foster the freest and fullest dialogue within our communities. It is apparent that regulation of face-to-face verbal assault in the manner contemplated by the Stanford provision will make room for more speech than it chills. The provision is clearly within the spirit, if not the letter, of existing first amendment doctrine. . . .

Knowing the Injury and Striking the Balance: Understanding What Is at Stake in Racist Speech Cases

. . . The argument most commonly advanced against the regulation of racist speech goes something like this: We recognize that minority groups suffer pain and injury as the result of racist speech, but we must allow this hatemongering for the benefit of society as a whole. Freedom of speech is the lifeblood of our democratic system. It is a freedom that enables us to persuade others to our point of view. Free speech is especially important for minorities because often it is their only vehicle for rallying support for redress of their grievances. We cannot allow the public regulation of racist invective and vilification because any prohibition precise enough to prevent racist speech

would catch in the same net forms of speech that are central to a democratic society. . . .

*Understanding the injury
inflicted by racist speech*

There can be no meaningful discussion about how to reconcile our commitment to equality and our commitment to free speech until we acknowledge that racist speech inflicts real harm and that this harm is far from trivial. I should state that more strongly: To engage in a debate about the first amendment and racist speech without a full understanding of the nature and extent of the harm of racist speech risks making the first amendment an instrument of domination rather than a vehicle of liberation. Not everyone has known the experience of being victimized by racist, misogynist, and homophobic speech, and we do not share equally the burden of the societal harm it inflicts. Often we are too quick to say we have heard the victims' cries when we have not; we are too eager to assure ourselves we have experienced the same injury, and therefore we can make the constitutional balance without danger of mismeasurement. For many of us who have fought for the rights of oppressed minorities, it is difficult to accept that—by underestimating the injury from racist speech—we too might be implicated in the vicious words we would never utter. Until we have eradicated racism and sexism and no longer share in the fruits of those forms of domination, we cannot justly strike the balance over the protest of those who are dominated. My plea is simply that we listen to the victims.

Members of my own family were involved in a recent incident at a private school in Wilmington, Delaware that taught me much about both the nature of the injury racist speech inflicts and the lack of understanding many whites have of that injury.

As a good Quaker school dedicated to a deep commitment to and loving concern for all the members of its community, Wilmington Friends School also had been a haven for white families fleeing the court ordered desegregation of the

Wilmington public schools. In recent years, the school strove to meet its commitment to human equality by enrolling a small (but significant) group of minority students and hiring an even smaller number of black faculty and staff. My sister Paula, a gifted, passionate, and dedicated teacher, was the principal of the lower school. Her sons attend the high school. My brother-in-law, John, teaches geology at the University of Delaware. He is a strong, quiet, loving man, and he is white. My sister's family had moved to Wilmington shouldering the extra burdens and anxieties borne by an interracial family moving to a town where, not long ago, the defamatory message of segregation graced the doors of bathrooms and restaurants. Within a year they had made their place as well-loved and respected members of the community, particularly the school community, where Paula was viewed as a godsend and my nephews had made many good friends.

In May of their second year in Wilmington, an incident occurred that shook the entire school community but was particularly painful to my sister's family and others who found themselves the objects of hateful speech. In a letter to the school community explaining a decision to expel four students, the school's headmaster described the incident as follows:

> On Sunday evening, May 1, four students in the senior class met by prearrangement to paint the soccer kickboard, a flat rectangular structure, approximately 8 ft. by 25 ft., standing in the midst of the Wilmington Friends School playing fields. They worked for approximately one hour under bright moonlight and then went home.
>
> What confronted students and staff the following morning, depicted on the kickboard, were racist and anti-Semitic slogans and, most disturbing of all, threats of violent assault against one clearly identified member of the senior class. The slogans written on the kickboard included "Save the land, join the Klan," and "Down with Jews"; among the drawings were at least twelve hooded Ku Klux Klansmen, Nazi swastikas, and a burning cross. The most frightening and disturbing depictions, however, were those that threatened violence against one of our senior

black students. He was drawn, in cartoon figure, identified by his name, and his initials, and by the name of his mother. Directly to the right of his head was a bullet, and farther to the right was a gun with its barrel directed toward the head. Under the drawing of the student, three Ku Klux Klansmen were depicted, one of whom was saying that the student "dies." Next to the gun was a drawing of a burning cross under which was written "Kill the Tarbaby."

When I visited my sister's family a few days after this incident, the injury they had suffered was evident. The wounds were fresh. My sister, a care-giver by nature and vocation, was clearly in need of care. My nephews were quiet. Their faces betrayed the aftershock of a recently inflicted blow and a newly discovered vulnerability. I knew the pain and scars were no less enduring because the injury had not been physical. And when I talked to my sister, I realized the greatest part of her pain came not from the incident itself but rather from the reaction of white parents who had come to the school in unprecedented numbers to protest the offending students' expulsion. "It was only a prank." "No one was physically attacked." "How can you punish these kids for mere words, mere drawings." Paula's pain was compounded by the failure of these people, with whom she had lived and worked, to recognize that she had been hurt, to understand in even the most limited way the reality of her pain and that of her family.

Many people called the incident "isolated." But black folks know that no racial incident is "isolated" in America. That is what makes the incidents so horrible, so scary. It is the knowledge that they are not the isolated unpopular speech of a dissident few that makes them so frightening. These incidents are manifestations of an ubiquitous and deeply ingrained cultural belief system, an American way of life. Too often in recent months, as I have debated this issue with friends and colleagues, I have heard people speak of the need to protect "offensive" speech. The word offensive is used as if we were speaking of a difference in taste, as if I should learn to be less sensitive to words that "offend" me. I cannot help but believe that those people who speak of offense—those who argue that this speech must go unchecked—do not understand the great difference between offense and injury: They have not known the injury my sister experienced, have not known the fear, vulnerability, and shame. . . . There is a great difference between the offensiveness of words that you would rather not hear—because they are labeled dirty, impolite, or personally demeaning—and the *injury* inflicted by words that remind the world that you are fair game for physical attack, evoke in you all of the millions of cultural lessons regarding your inferiority that you have so painstakingly repressed, and imprint upon you a badge of servitude and subservience for all the world to see. . . .

The other side of the balance: does the suppression of racial epithets weigh for or against speech?

. . . Blacks and other people of color are . . . skeptical about the absolutist argument that even the most injurious speech must remain unregulated because in an unregulated marketplace of ideas the best ideas will rise to the top and gain acceptance. Our experience tells us the opposite. We have seen too many demagogues elected by appealing to America's racism. We have seen too many good, liberal politicians shy away from the issues that might brand them as too closely allied with us. The American marketplace of ideas was founded with the idea of the racial inferiority of non-whites as one of its chief commodities, and ever since the market opened, racism has remained its most active item in trade.*

But it is not just the prevalence and strength of the idea of racism that makes the unregulated marketplace of ideas an untenable paradigm for those individuals who seek full and equal personhood for all. The real problem is that the idea of the racial

inferiority of non-whites infects, skews, and disables the operation of the market (like a computer virus, sick cattle, or diseased wheat). Racism is irrational and often unconscious. Our belief in the inferiority of non-whites trumps good ideas that contend with it in the market, often without our even knowing it. In addition, racism makes the words and ideas of blacks and other despised minorities less saleable, regardless of their intrinsic value, in the marketplace of ideas. It also decreases the total amount of speech that enters the market by coercively silencing members of those groups who are its targets.

Racism is an epidemic infecting the marketplace of ideas and rendering it dysfunctional. Racism is ubiquitous. We are all racists.[†] Racism is also irrational. Individuals do not embrace or reject racist beliefs as the result of reasoned deliberation. For the most part, we do not recognize the myriad ways in which the racism pervading our history and culture influences our beliefs. In other words, most of our racism is unconscious. . . .

Prejudice that is unconscious or unacknowledged causes even more distortions in the market. When racism operates at a conscious level, opposing ideas may prevail in open competition for the rational or moral sensibilities of the market participant. But when an individual is unaware of his prejudice, neither reason nor moral persuasion will likely succeed.

Racist speech also distorts the marketplace of ideas by muting or devaluing the speech of blacks and other non-whites. An idea that would be embraced by large numbers of individuals if it were offered by a white individual will be rejected or given less credence because its author

---

*See Lawrence, [39 *Stan. L. Rev.* (1987)], at 330 ("[Racism] is a part of our common historical experience and, therefore, a part of our culture. . . . We attach significance to race even when we are not aware that we are doing so. . . . Racism's universality renders it normal").

[†]*See* Lawrence, previous note, where he describes America's racist heritage: "Americans share a common historical and cultural heritage in which racism has played and still plays a dominant role. Because of this shared experience, we also inevitably share many ideas, attitudes, and beliefs that attach significance to an individual's race and induce negative feelings and opinions about non-whites. To the extent that this cultural belief system has influenced all of us, we are all racists" (*Id.* at 322).

belongs to a group demeaned and stigmatized by racist beliefs.

An obvious example of this type of devaluation would be the black political candidate whose ideas go unheard or are rejected by white voters, although voters would embrace the same ideas if they were championed by a white candidate. Racial minorities have the same experiences on a daily basis when they endure the microaggression of having their words doubted, or misinterpreted, or assumed to be without evidentiary support, or when their insights are ignored and then appropriated by whites who are assumed to have been the original authority.

Finally, racist speech decreases the total amount of speech that reaches the market. I noted earlier in this article the ways in which racist speech is inextricably linked with racist conduct. The primary purpose and effect of the speech/conduct that constitutes white supremacy is the exclusion of non-whites from full participation in the body politic. Sometimes the speech/conduct of racism is direct and obvious. When the Klan burns a cross on the lawn of a black person who joined the NAACP or exercised his right to move to a formerly all-white neighborhood, the effect of this speech does not result from the persuasive power of an idea operating freely in the market. It is a threat, a threat made in the context of a history of lynchings, beatings, and economic reprisals that made good on earlier threats, a threat that silences a potential speaker. The black student who is subjected to racial epithets is likewise threatened and silenced. Certainly she, like the victim of a cross-burning, may be uncommonly brave or foolhardy and ignore the system of violence in which this abusive speech is only a bit player. But it is more likely that we, as a community, will be denied the benefit of many of her thoughts and ideas. . . .

Asking victim groups to pay the price

Whenever we decide that racist hate speech must be tolerated because of the importance of toler-ating unpopular speech we ask blacks and other subordinated groups to bear a burden for the good of society—to pay the price for the societal benefit of creating more room for speech. And we assign this burden to them without seeking their advice, or consent. This amounts to white domination, pure and simple. It is taxation without representation. We must be careful that the ease with which we strike the balance against the regulation of racist speech is in no way influenced by the fact the cost will be borne by others. We must be certain that the individuals who pay the price are fairly represented in our deliberation, and that they are heard. . . .

Epilogue

"Enie, menie, minie, mo."

It is recess time at the South Main Street School. It is 1952, and I am nine. Eddie Becker, Muck Makowski, John Thomas, Terry Flynn, Howie Martin, and I are standing in a circle. Right feet thrust forward, the toes of our black, high-top Keds sneakers touching, forming a tight hub of white rubber at the center, our skinny blue-jeaned legs extend like spokes from the hub. Heads bowed, we are intently watching Muck, who is hunkered down on one knee so that he can touch our toes as he calls out the rhyme. We are enthralled and entranced by the drama of this boyhood ritual, this customary pre-game incantation. It is no less important than the game itself.

But my mind is not on the ritual. I have lost track of the count that will determine whose foot must be removed from the hub, who will no longer have a chance to be a captain in this game. I hardly feel Muck's index finger as it presses through the rubber to my toes. My mind is on the rhyme. I am the only black boy in this circle of towheaded prepubescent males. Time stands still for me. My palms are sweaty and I feel a prickly heat at the back of my neck. I know that Muck will not say the word.

"Catch a tiger by the toe."

The heads stay down. No one looks at me. But I know that none of them is picturing the capture of a large striped animal. They are thinking of me, imagining my toe beneath the white rubber of my Keds sneaker—my toe attached to a large, dark, thick lipped, burr-headed American fantasy/nightmare.

"If he hollers let him go."

Tigers don't holler. I wish I could right now.

My parents have told me to ignore this word that is ringing unuttered in my ears. "You must not allow those who speak it to make you feel small or ugly," they say. They are proud, Mississippi-bred black professionals and long- time political activists. Oft-wounded veterans of the war against the racist speech/conduct of Jim Crow and his many relations, they have, on countless occasions, answered the bad speech/conduct of racism with the good speech/conduct of their lives—representing the race, being smarter, cleaner and more morally upright than white folk to prove that black folk are equal, are fully human—refuting the lies of the cultural myth that is American racism. "You must know that it is their smallness, their ugliness of which this word speaks," they say.

I am struggling to heed their words, to follow their example, but I feel powerless before this word and its minions. In a moment's time it has made me an other. In an instant it has rebuilt the wall between my friends' humanity and my own, the wall that I have so painstakingly disassembled.

I was good at games, not just a good athlete, but a strategist, a leader. I knew how to make my teammates feel good about themselves so that they played better. It just came naturally to me. I could choose up a team and make them feel like family. When other folks felt good, I felt good too. Being good at games was the main tool I used to knock down the wall I'd found when I came to this white school in this white town. I looked forward to recess because that was when I could do the most damage to the wall. But now this rhyme, this word, had undone all my labors.

"Enie menie minie mo."

I have no memory of who got to be captain or what game we played. I just wished Muck had used "one potato, two potato . . ." We always used that at home.

NOTES

1. W. E. B. Du Bois, *The Souls of Black Folk* 16–17 (1953). . . .

2. *Chaplinsky* v. *New Hampshire*, 315 U.S. 568, 572 (1942).

Review and Discussion Questions

1. Do you believe that universities should have policies that discourage or restrict racist speech? If so, what exactly should the policies be? How far should the university go to prevent speech that may be hurtful? What is the best way to deal with racist speech?

2. Should ethnic jokes be prohibited?

3. To what extent does racist speech fall into the "fighting words" category? Are regulations against face-to-face insults sufficient to prevent the harms that concern Lawrence?

4. Has Lawrence overlooked or failed to address adequately any arguments against the restriction of racist speech on campus?

5. Is Lawrence right in saying that those who advocate tolerance for racist speech do not understand or fail to consider the real injuries it causes? Has Lawrence exaggerated the pain caused by racist speech?

6. Do you think John Stuart Mill would be persuaded by Lawrence's argument?

7. Will restrictions on racist speech encourage or discourage the exchange of ideas on campus?

9

THE RESPONSIBILITIES OF CITIZENS

Crito

PLATO

Plato was born into an aristocratic family in Athens around 427 B.C.E. Socrates (470–399 B.C.E.) was a friend of Plato's family from the time Plato was a schoolboy. Although a young Athenian of Plato's class would normally have pursued a political career, Plato fell under the influence of Socrates and chose philosophy instead, going on to become one of the world's greatest and most influential philosophers. In 387 B.C.E. Plato founded the Academy, a school of higher education and research. Aristotle spent twenty years there, first as a student, then as a colleague of Plato. Plato continued as the head of the Academy until his death at the age of 80, after which the school continued for 900 years.

Plato wrote around twenty-five dialogues, including *Crito*. Based on historical events, *Crito* is a reconstruction of a conversation between Socrates and his friend Crito. It takes place in the prison where Socrates has been sent to await execution—which in ancient Athens was carried out by the prisoner's drinking hemlock—after having been condemned to death for corrupting the youth of the city through his teaching. Crito tries to convince Socrates to allow his friends to save his life by assisting him to escape, but Socrates will agree only if he can be persuaded that it would not be unjust of him to violate the law. After presenting the arguments that he imagines "the laws and government" of Athens would make to him, Socrates remains convinced that it would be wrong for him to escape, and soon after the scene portrayed, he was executed. *Crito* thus sets the stage for centuries of debate over the nature and extent of a citizen's obligation to obey the law.

Translated by Benjamin Jowett.

Study Questions

1. Why does Socrates reject the idea that we should let the "opinion of the many" determine our conduct? What about the fact that the many can kill us?

2. According to Socrates, is it ever permissible to do wrong? What basic moral principle does he affirm?

3. At one point "the laws" of Athens say that "he who disobeys us is . . . thrice wrong." What are the three reasons a citizen would be wrong to disobey?

4. According to "the laws," Socrates has agreed to obey their commands. What is the proof of this agreement?

5. According to the argument of "the laws," what would be the consequences if Socrates were to escape?

SOCRATES: Why have you come at this hour, Crito? it must be quite early?

CRITO: Yes, certainly.

SOCRATES: What is the exact time?

CRITO: The dawn is breaking.

SOCRATES: I wonder that the keeper of the prison would let you in.

CRITO: He knows me, because I often come, Socrates; moreover, I have done him a kindness.

SOCRATES: And are you only just come?

CRITO: No, I came some time ago.

SOCRATES: Then why did you sit and say nothing, instead of awakening me at once?

CRITO: Why, indeed, Socrates, I myself would rather not have all this sleeplessness and sorrow. But I have been wondering at your peaceful slumbers, and that was the reason why I did not awaken you, because I wanted you to be out of pain. I have always thought you happy in the calmness of your temperament; but never did I see the like of the easy, cheerful way in which you bear this calamity.

SOCRATES: Why, Crito, when a man has reached my age he ought not to be repining at the prospect of death.

CRITO: And yet other old men find themselves in similar misfortunes and age does not prevent them from repining.

SOCRATES: That may be. But you have not told me why you come at this early hour.

CRITO: I come to bring you a message which is sad and painful; not, as I believe, to yourself, but to all of us who are your friends, and saddest of all to me.

SOCRATES: What! I suppose that the ship has come from Delos, on the arrival of which I am to die?

CRITO: No, the ship has not actually arrived, but she will probably be here today, as persons who have come from Sunium tell me that they left her there; and therefore tomorrow, Socrates, will be the last day of your life.

SOCRATES: Very well, Crito; if such is the will of God, I am willing. . . .

CRITO: . . . Oh! my beloved Socrates, let me entreat you once more to take my advice and escape. For if you die I shall not only lose a friend who can never be replaced, but there is another evil: people who do not know you and me will believe that I might have saved you if I had been willing to give money, but that I did not care. Now, can there be a worse disgrace than this—that I should be thought to value money more than the life of a friend? For the many will not be persuaded that I wanted you to escape, and that you refused.

SOCRATES: But why, my dear Crito, should we care about the opinion of the many? Good men, and they are the only persons who are worth considering, will think of these things truly as they happened.

CRITO: But do you see, Socrates, that the opinion of the many must be regarded, as is evident in your own case, because they can do the very greatest evil to any one who has lost their good opinion.

SOCRATES: I only wish, Crito, that they could; for then they could also do the greatest good, and that would be well. But the truth is, that they can do neither good nor evil: they can not make a man wise or make him foolish; and whatever they do is the result of chance.

CRITO: Well, I will not dispute about that; but please tell me, Socrates, whether you are not acting out of regard to me and your other friends: are you not afraid that if you escape hence we may get into trouble with the informers for having stolen you away, and lose either the whole or a great part of our property; or that even a worse evil may happen to us? Now, if this is your fear, be at ease; for in order to save you, we ought surely to run this, or even a greater risk; be persuaded, then, and do as I say.

SOCRATES: Yes, Crito, that is one fear which you mention, but by no means the only one.

CRITO: Fear not. There are persons who at no great cost are willing to save you and bring you out of prison; and as for the informers, you may observe that they are far from being exorbitant in their demands; a little money will satisfy them. My means, which, as I am sure, are ample, are at your service, and if you have a scruple about spending all mine, here are strangers who will give you the use of theirs; and one of them, Simmias the Theban, has brought a sum of money for this very purpose; and Cebes and many others are willing to spend their money too. I say therefore, do not on that account hesitate about making your escape, and do not say, as you did in the court, that you will have a difficulty in knowing what to do with yourself if you escape. For men will love you in other places to which you may go, and not in Athens only; there are friends of mine in Thessaly, if you like to go to them, who will value and protect you, and no Thessalian will give you any trouble. Nor can I think that you are justified, Socrates, in betraying your own life when you might be saved; this is playing into the hands of your enemies and destroyers; and moreover I should say that you were betraying your children; for you might bring them up and educate them; instead of which you go away and leave them, and they will have to take their chance; and if they do not meet with the usual fate of orphans, there will be small thanks to you. No man should bring children into the world who is unwilling to persevere to the end in their nurture and education. But you are choosing the easier part, as I think, not the better and manlier, which would rather have become one who professes virtue in all his actions, like yourself. And indeed, I am ashamed not only of you, but of us who are your friends, when I reflect that this entire business of yours will be attributed to our want of courage. The trial need never have come on, or might have been brought to another issue; and the end of all, which is the crowning absurdity, will seem to have been permitted by us, through cowardice and baseness, who might have saved you, as you might have saved yourself, if we had been good for anything (for there was no difficulty in escaping); and we did not see how disgraceful, Socrates, and also miserable all this will be to us as well as to you. Make your mind up then, or rather have your mind already made up, for the time of deliberation is over, and there is only one thing to be done, which must be done, if at all, this very night, and which any delay will render all but impossible; I beseech you therefore, Socrates, to be persuaded by me, and to do as I say.

SOCRATES: Dear Crito, your zeal is invaluable, if a right one; but if wrong, the greater the zeal the greater the evil; and therefore we ought to consider whether these things shall be done or not. For I am and always have been one of those natures who must be guided by reason, whatever the reason may be which upon reflection appears to me to be the best; and now that this fortune has come upon me, I can not put away the reasons which I have before given: the principles which I have hitherto honored and revered I still honor, and unless we can find other and better principles on the instant, I am certain not to agree with you; no, not even if the power of the multitude could inflict many more imprisonments, confiscations, deaths, frightening us like children with hobgoblin terrors. But what will be the fairest way of considering the question? Shall I return to your old argument about the opinions of men some of which are to be regarded, and others, as we were saying, are not to be regarded? Now were we right in maintaining this before I was condemned? And has the argument which was once good now proved to be talk for the sake of talking;—in fact an amusement only, and altogether vanity? That is what I want to consider with your help, Crito:—whether, under my present circumstances, the argument appears to be in any way different or not; and is to be allowed by me or disallowed. That argument, which, as I believe, is maintained by many who assume to be authorities, was to the effect, as I was saying, that the opinions of some men are to be regarded, and of other men not to be regarded. Now you, Crito, are a disinterested person who are not going to die tomorrow—at least, there is no human probability of this, and you are therefore not liable to be deceived by the circumstances in which you are placed. Tell me then, whether I am right in saying that some opinions, and the opinions of some men only, are to be valued, and other opinions and the opinions of other men, are not to be valued. I ask you whether I was right in maintaining this?

CRITO: Certainly. . . .

SOCRATES: Very good; and is not this true, Crito, of other things which we need not separately enumerate? In the matter of just and unjust, fair and foul, good and evil, which are the subjects of our present consultation, ought we to follow the opinion of the many and to fear them; or the opinion of the one man who has understanding, and whom we ought to fear and reverence more than all the rest of the world: and whom deserting we shall destroy and injure that principle in us which may be assumed to be improved by justice and deteriorated by injustice;—is there not such a principle?

CRITO: Certainly there is, Socrates.

SOCRATES: Take a parallel instance: if, acting under the advice of men who have no understanding, we destroy that which is improvable by health and deteriorated by disease—when that

has been destroyed, I say, would life be worth having? And that is—the body?

CRITO: Yes.

SOCRATES: Could we live, having an evil and corrupted body?

CRITO: Certainly not.

SOCRATES: And will life be worth having, if that higher part of man be depraved, which is improved by justice and deteriorated by injustice? Do we suppose that principle, whatever it may be in man, which has to do with justice and injustice, to be inferior to the body?

CRITO: Certainly not.

SOCRATES: More honored, then?

CRITO: Far more honored.

SOCRATES: Then, my friend, we must not regard what the many say of us; but what he, the one man who has understanding of just and unjust, will say, and what the truth will say. And therefore you begin in error when you suggest that we should regard the opinion of the many about just and unjust, good and evil, honorable and dishonorable.—Well, some one will say, "but the many can kill us."

CRITO: Yes, Socrates; that will clearly be the answer.

SOCRATES: That is true, but still I find with surprise that the old argument is, as I conceive, unshaken as ever. And I should like to know whether I may say the same of another proposition—that not life, but a good life, is to be chiefly valued?

CRITO: Yes, that also remains.

SOCRATES: And a good life is equivalent to a just and honorable one—that hold also?

CRITO: Yes, that holds.

SOCRATES: From these premises I proceed to argue the question whether I ought not to try and escape without the consent of the Athenians: and if I am clearly right in escaping, then I will make the attempt; but if not, I will abstain. The other considerations which you mention, of money and loss of character and the duty of educating children, are, as I fear, only the doctrines of the multitude, who would be as ready to call people to life, if they were able, as they are to put them to death—and with as little reason. But now, since the argument has thus far prevailed, the only question which remains to be considered is, whether we shall do rightly either in escaping or in suffering others to aid in our escape and paying them in money and thanks, or whether we shall not do rightly; and if the latter, then death or any other calamity which may ensure on my remaining here must not be allowed to enter into the calculation.

CRITO: I think that you are right, Socrates; how then shall we proceed?

SOCRATES: Let us consider the matter together, and do you either refute me if you can, and I will be convinced; or else cease, my dear friend, from repeating to me that I ought to escape against the wishes of the Athenians: for I am extremely desirous to be persuaded by you, but not against my own better judgment. And now please consider my first position, and do your best to answer me.

CRITO: I will do my best.

SOCRATES: Are we to say that we are never intentionally to do wrong, or that in one way we ought and in another way we ought not to do wrong, or is doing wrong always evil and dishonorable, as I was just now saying, and as has been already acknowledged by us? Are all our former admissions which were made within a few days to be thrown away? And have we, at our age, been earnestly discoursing with one another all our life long only to discover that we are no better than children? Or are we to rest assured, in spite of the opinion of the many, and in spite of consequences whether better or worse, of the truth of what was then said, that injustice is always an evil and dishonor to him who acts unjustly? Shall we affirm that?

CRITO: Yes.

SOCRATES: Then we must do no wrong?

CRITO: Certainly not.

SOCRATES: Nor when injured injure in return, as the many imagine; for we must injure no one at all?

CRITO: Clearly not.

SOCRATES: Again, Crito, may we do evil?

CRITO: Surely not, Socrates.

SOCRATES: And what of doing evil in return for evil, which is the morality of the many—is that just or not?

CRITO: Not just.

SOCRATES: For doing evil to another is the same as injuring him?

CRITO: Very true.

SOCRATES: Then we ought not to retaliate or render evil for evil to any one, whatever evil we may have suffered from him. But I would have you consider, Crito, whether you really mean what you are saying. For this opinion has never been held, and never will be held, by any considerable number of persons; and those who are agreed and those who are not agreed upon this point have no common ground, and can only despise one another when they see how widely they differ. Tell me, then, whether you agree with and assent to my first principle, that neither injury nor retaliation nor warding off evil by evil is ever right. And shall that be the premise of our argument? Or do you decline and dissent from this? For this has been of old and is still my opinion; but, if you are of another opinion, let me hear what you have to say. If, however, you remain of the same mind as formerly, I will proceed to the next step.

CRITO: You may proceed, for I have not changed my mind.

SOCRATES: Then I will proceed to the next step, which may be put in the form of a question: Ought a man to do what he admits to be right, or ought he to betray the right?

CRITO: He ought to do what he thinks right.

SOCRATES: But if this is true, what is the application? In leaving the prison against the will of the Athenians, do I wrong any? or rather do I not wrong those whom I ought least to wrong? Do I not desert the principles which were acknowledged by us to be just? What do you say?

CRITO: I can not tell, Socrates, for I do not know.

SOCRATES: Then consider the matter in this way: Imagine that I am about to play truant (you may call the proceeding by any name which you like), and the laws and the government come and interrogate me: "Tell us, Socrates," they say; "what are you about? are you going by an act of yours to overturn us—the laws and the whole state, as far as in you lies? Do you imagine that a state can subsist and not be overthrown, in which the decisions of law have no power, but are set aside and overthrown by individuals?" What will be our answer, Crito, to these and the like words? Any one, and especially a clever rhetorician, will have a good deal to urge about the evil of setting aside the law which requires a sentence to be carried out; and we might reply, "Yes; but the state has injured us and given an unjust sentence." Suppose I say that?

CRITO: Very good, Socrates.

SOCRATES: "And was that our agreement with you?" the law would say; "or were you to abide by the sentence of the state?" And if I were to express astonishment at their saying this, the law would probably add: "Answer, Socrates, instead of opening your eyes: you are in the habit of asking and answering questions. Tell us what complaint you have to make against us which justifies you in attempting to destroy us and the state? In the first place did we not bring you into existence? Your father married your mother by our aid and begat you. Say whether you have any objection to urge against those of us who regulate marriage?" None, I should reply. "Or against those of us who regulate the system of nurture and education of children in which you were trained? Were not the laws, who have the charge of this, right in commanding your father to train you in music and gymnastic?" Right, I should reply, "Well then, since you were brought into the world and nurtured and educated by us, can you deny in the first place that you are our child and slave, as your fathers were before you? And if this is true you are not on equal terms with us; nor can you think that you have a right to do to us what we are doing to you. Would you have any right to strike or revile or do any other evil to a father or to your master, if you had one, when you have been struck or reviled by him, or received some other evil at his hands?—you

would not say this? And because we think right to destroy you, do you think that you have any right to destroy us in return, and your country as far as in you lies? And will you, O professor of true virtue, say that you are justified in this? Has a philosopher like you failed to discover that our country is more to be valued and higher and holier far than mother or father or any ancestor, and more to be regarded in the eyes of the gods and of men of understanding? Also to be soothed, and gently and reverently entreated when angry, even more than a father, and if not persuaded, obeyed? And when we are punished by her, whether with imprisonment or stripes, the punishment is to be endured in silence; and if she lead us to wounds or death in battle, thither we follow as is right; neither may any one yield or retreat or leave his rank, but whether in battle or in a court of law, or in any other place, he must do what his city and his country order him; or he must change their view of what is just: and if he may do no violence to his father or mother, much less may he do violence to his country." What answer shall we make to his, Crito? Do the laws speak truly, or do they not?

CRITO: I think that they do.

SOCRATES: Then the laws will say: "Consider, Socrates, if this is true, that in your present attempt you are going to do us wrong. For, after having brought you into the world, and nurtured and educated you, and given you and every other citizen a share in every good that we had to give, we further proclaim and give the right to every Athenian, that if he does not like us when he has come of age and has seen the ways of the city, and made our acquaintance, he may go where he pleases and take his goods with him; and none of us laws will forbid him or interfere with him. Any of you who does not like us and the city, and who wants to go to a colony or to any other city, may go where he likes, and take his goods with him. But he who has experience of the manner in which we order justice and administer the state, and still remains, has entered into an implied contract that he will do as we command him. And he who disobeys us is, as we maintain, thrice wrong; first, because in disobeying us he is disobeying his parents; secondly, because we are the authors of his education; thirdly, because he has made an agreement with us that he will duly obey our commands; and he neither obeys them nor convinces us that our commands are wrong; and we do not rudely impose them, but give them the alternative of obeying or convincing us;—that is what we offer, and he does neither. These are the sort of accusations to which, as we were saying, you, Socrates, will be exposed if you accomplish your intentions; you, above all other Athenians." Suppose I ask, why is this? They will justly retort upon me that I above all other men have acknowledged the agreement. "There is clear proof," they will say, "Socrates, that we and the city were not displeasing to you. Of all Athenians you have been the most constant resident in the city, which, as you never leave, you may be supposed to love. For you never went out of the city either to see the games, except once when you went to the Isthmus, or to any other place unless you were on military service; nor did you travel as other men do. Nor had you any curiosity to know other states or their laws: your affections did not go beyond us and our state; we were your special favorites, and you acquiesced in our government of you; and this is the state in which you begat your children, which is a proof of your satisfaction. Moreover, you might, if you had liked, have fixed the penalty at banishment in the course of the trial—the state which refuses to let you go now would have let you go then. But you pretended that you preferred death to exile, and that you were not grieved at death. And now you have forgotten these fine sentiments, and pay no respect to us the laws, of whom you are the destroyer; and are doing what only a miserable slave would do, running away and turning your back upon the compacts and agreements which you made as a citizen. And first of all answer this very question: Are we right in saying that you agreed to be governed according to us in deed, and not in word only?

Is that true or not?" How shall we answer that, Crito? Must we not agree?

CRITO: There is no help, Socrates.

SOCRATES: Then will they not say: "You, Socrates, are breaking the covenants and agreements which you made with us at your leisure, not in any haste or under any compulsion or deception, but having had seventy years to think of them, during which time you were at liberty to leave the city, if we were not to your mind, or if our covenants appeared to you to be unfair. You had your choice, and might have gone either to Lacedaemon or Crete, which you often praise for their good government, or to some other Hellenic or foreign state. Whereas you, above all other Athenians, seemed to be so fond of the state, or, in other words, of us her laws (for who would like a state that has no laws), that you never stirred out of her; the halt, the blind, the maimed were not more stationary in her than you were. And now you run away and forsake your agreements. Not so, Socrates, if you will take our advice; do not make yourself ridiculous by escaping out of the city."

"For just consider, if you transgress and err in this sort of way, what good will you do either to yourself or to your friends? That your friends will be driven into exile and deprived of citizenship, or will lose their property, is tolerably certain; and you yourself, if you fly to one of the neighboring cities, as, for example, Thebes or Megara, both of which are well-governed cities, will come to them as an enemy, Socrates, and their government will be against you, and all patriotic citizens will cast an evil eye upon you as a subverter of the laws, and you will confirm in the minds of the judges the justice of their own condemnation of you. For he who is a corruptor of the laws is more than likely to be corruptor of the young and foolish portion of mankind. Will you then flee from well-ordered cities and virtuous men? and is existence worth having on these terms? Or will you go to them without shame, and talk to them, Socrates? And what will you say to them? What you say here about virtue and justice and institutions and laws being the best things among men. Would that be decent of you?

Surely not. But if you go away from well-governed states to Crito's friends in Thessaly, where there is a great disorder and license, they will be charmed to have the tale of your escape from prison, set off with ludicrous particulars of the manner in which you were wrapped in a goatskin or some other disguise, and metamorphosed as the fashion of runaways is—that is very likely; but will there be no one to remind you that in your old age you violated the most sacred laws from a miserable desire of a little more life. Perhaps not, if you keep them in a good temper; but if they are out of temper you will hear many degrading things; you will live, but how?—as the flatterer of all men, and the servant of all men; and doing what?—eating and drinking in Thessaly, having gone abroad in order that you may get a dinner. And where will be your fine sentiments about justice and virtue then? Say that you wish to live for the sake of your children, that you may bring them up and educate them—will you take them into Thessaly and deprive them of Athenian citizenship? Is that the benefit which you would confer upon them? Or are you under the impression that they will be better cared for and educated here if you are still alive, although absent from them; for that your friends will take care of them? Do you fancy that if you are an inhabitant of Thessaly they will take care of them, and if you are an inhabitant of the other world they will not take care of them? Nay; but if they who call themselves friends are truly friends, they surely will.

"Listen, then, Socrates, to us who have brought you up. Think not of life and children first, and of justice afterwards, but of justice first, that you may be justified before the princes of the world below. For neither will you nor any that belong to you be happier or holier or juster in this life, or happier in another, if you do as Crito bids. Now you depart in innocence, a sufferer and not a doer of evil; a victim, not of the laws, but of men. But if you go forth, returning evil for evil, and injury for injury, breaking the covenants and agreements which you have made with us, and wronging those whom you ought least to wrong, that is to say, yourself, your friends, your country, and us, we shall be angry with you while you live, and our brethren, the laws in the world below, will receive you as an enemy; for they will know that you have done your best to destroy us. Listen, then, to us and not to Crito."

This is the voice which I seem to hear murmuring in my ears, like the sound of the flute in the ears of the mystic; that voice, I say, is humming in my ears, and prevents me from hearing any other. And I know that anything more which you may say will be vain. Yet speak, if you have anything to say.

CRITO: I have nothing to say, Socrates.

SOCRATES: Then let me follow the intimations of the will of God.

Review and Discussion Questions

1. Socrates maintains that it is wrong to retaliate, that is, to do an injury or evil to someone in return for an injury or evil done to you. Explain why you agree or disagree with this principle. Does this principle rule out self-defense or the possibility of justified punishment?

2. Assess the argument of "the laws" that it is impossible for a state to subsist and not be overthrown if individuals set aside the decisions of the law. When, if ever, is it permissible for citizens to disobey the law?

3. Do we owe our government or society gratitude for our upbringing and for making it possible for us to live the lives we do? If so, does this give us some obligation to obey society's laws and rules?

4. Is there anything to the idea, suggested by the laws, that one's country or government is more important than any one person and deserves the same respect we would show our parents?

5. Is Socrates bound to obey the laws of Athens because he has agreed to do so, either explicitly or implicitly? By living here and benefiting from our society, are you tacitly agreeing to obey its laws? If one has in fact made such an agreement, would it be wrong to break it under any circumstances?

6. The laws say that Socrates has the alternative of obeying or convincing them that their commands are mistaken. Is this point relevant to a citizen's obligation to obey in a democracy?

7. In escaping from prison against the will of the Athenians, would Socrates have done wrong? What would you have done in his place?

Moral Judgment, Historical Reality, and Civil Disobedience

DAVID LYONS

Although he believed the verdict of the Athenian court sentencing him to death was wrong, Socrates accepted it because he also believed, as he explains in *Crito,* that he had an obligation to respect the city's laws and to obey its rulings. Many have seen in Socrates a precursor of modern civil disobedience, in which a citizen violates the law to protest injustice but accepts punishment for doing so out of respect for the law and a sense of political obligation. In this essay, David Lyons, professor of law and philosophy at Boston University, challenges this view of civil disobedience—in particular, the idea that there is a moral presumption in favor of obedience to the law that a person engaging in civil disobedience has to overcome in order to justify his or her actions. Rather, he denies that those who are civilly disobedient have a duty to obey the law in the first place. Moreover, he argues, such a view of civil disobedience does not reflect the thought and actions of Thoreau, Gandhi, and Martin Luther King, Jr. These three important protestors did not believe that they had an obligation to obey the laws of the systems they were fighting.

Study Questions

1. What is the difference between the narrow and the broad definitions of civil disobedience?

2. Lyons says that there is an important limit on political obligation. What is it?

3. Why might one have strong reason to abide by the law even in the absence of a political obligation to do so?

4. Explain the nature of the injustices that Thoreau, Gandhi, and King opposed. According to Lyons, what was their assessment of the systems they were protesting?

5. What were the two dilemmas that King faced in the Birmingham campaign of 1963?

6. According to Lyons, what explains the fact that theorists of civil disobedience assume that disobeying laws supporting slavery, colonialism, or Jim Crow requires moral justification?

From Philosophy & Public Affairs, *vol. 27, no. 1 (Winter 1998). Copyright © 1998 Princeton University Press. Reprinted by permission of Princeton University Press. Most notes omitted.*

THIS ARTICLE CONCERNS TWO STRANDS of civil disobedience theory. One involves the moral judgment of theorists. The other concerns moral judgments that theorists ascribe to those who engage in civil disobedience.

Our philosophical literature on civil disobedience is largely a product of the late 1960s and early 1970s. Responding to critics of the civil rights and anti-Vietnam War movements, philosophers argued that unlawful protest can sometimes be justified. For a number of these writers, justifying civil disobedience means overcoming a serious moral objection. They assume we have a moral obligation to obey the law—in other words, political obligation. Regarding this first strand of civil disobedience theory, I argue that the assumption of political obligation is morally untenable.

. . . I propose a moral condition for political obligation, and I argue that this condition is clearly violated in paradigmatic cases of civil disobedience. As a consequence, we cannot assume civil disobedience requires moral justification, because we cannot assume there is a moral obligation to obey the law.

Regarding the second strand of civil disobedience theory, some theorists assume that civil disobedients consider the prevailing system as "reasonably just" and accordingly seek limited reform, not radical change. This interpretation might seem to explain why civil disobedients accept arrest and punishment: their submission signifies acceptance of the prevailing system and acknowledges a moral obligation to obey the law. I argue that this view of civil disobedients is historically untenable.

The issue might seem to turn uninterestingly on how civil disobedience is delimited by theorists. In everyday speech, any principled disobedience to law may be counted as civil disobedience. But theorists often define it narrowly, distinguishing civil disobedience from other forms of principled noncompliance with law, and they may have perfectly good reason to do so.

But when theorists regard as civil disobedience only acts of individuals who accept the prevailing system (and presumably recognize an obligation to comply with its laws), they impute such an outlook to paradigm practitioners of civil disobedience, such as Henry David Thoreau, Mohandas K. Gandhi, and Martin Luther King, Jr. The result is a false picture of historically significant resistance.

Thus my criticisms of civil disobedience theory center on three paradigm resisters and the targets of their resistance: chattel slavery, British colonial rule, and Jim Crow. I argue that none of these three regarded the prevailing system as "reasonably just" or accepted a moral presumption favoring obedience to law, and that their views were sound.

I am not concerned here with the definition of civil disobedience. I am concerned with the fact that some theorists embrace untenable judgments of American society and a false picture of political resistance.

Section I discusses the idea of political obligation that is implicit in civil disobedience theory. Section II argues that political obligation could not plausibly be imagined to have existed in the relevant settings. Section III argues that none of the paradigm resisters had a favorable appraisal of the prevailing system and that none endorsed political obligation. Section IV notes some arbitrary lines drawn by civil disobedience theory and seeks to explain the untenable judgments found within it.

I

Theorists . . . assume that civil disobedience is morally problematic and requires moral justification. . . . Civil disobedience may be understood broadly, as principled nonviolent disobedience to law. But theorists commonly understand it narrowly, as, say, public protest aimed as persuading others that a law or governmental policy is morally indefensible and must be changed, performed by someone who respects the prevailing system and willingly suffers the legal consequences of disobedience. On either a broad or narrow definition, the . . . only plausible explanation for this set of views—that nonviolent civil disobedience requires justification but obedience to law does not—is a moral presumption favoring obedience to law (political obligation).

I say "moral presumption" because political obligation is reasonably understood by theorists to be defeasible, not absolute. If it exists, moral justification is required for disobedience to law. Theorists commonly assume that adequate justification may be available, in which case political obligation is outweighed.

It seems reasonable to suppose that just laws merit respect. But the same cannot be said of unjust laws. Because political obligation argues for obedience to both just and unjust laws and unjust laws do not automatically merit respect, theorists understand that political obligation itself requires justification.

There may be sound arguments for political obligation, but they would be limited by the principles they invoke. Consent principles, for example, apply when, but only when, there is genuine consent.

My concern here is with *moral* limits to such arguments. I assume that one cannot acquire a moral obligation to do certain things, such as participate in genocide or force someone into slavery, simply by consenting to do so. Like limits presumably apply to open-ended commitments, such as consenting to abide by the decisions to be made by some group of persons, which might include decisions to engage in genocide or to enslave others. Thus consent arguments for political obligation are morally limited.

Champions of the fairness argument believe that one is obligated to comply with social rules whose benefits one has sought and enjoyed. They apply the fairness principle to social systems as a whole. But fairness does not require one to acquiesce in an unjustly small share of benefits or an unjustly large share of burdens. Fairness arguments for political obligation assume a just distribution of benefits and burdens.

Such limits have their limits. If the point is to argue for obedience to unjust laws, we must assume that political obligation is possible in systems that are not perfectly just. To allow for the possibility that an obligation based on fairness might call for compliance with unjust laws, a fairness argument for political obligation cannot require a perfectly just distribution of benefits and burdens.

Thus theorists assume that political obligation can obtain when a system is not perfect, but is (as may be said) "nearly just," "reasonably just," or "fundamentally just." Such terms suggest the truism on which I shall now focus: there are limits to the injustice that is compatible with political obligation. . . .

My argument requires one limit on political obligation . . .: political obligation cannot coexist with significant, systematic injustice that is deeply entrenched. Although there can be reasonable disagreement about the application of these terms to some cases, that will not affect the present argument. The three examples I shall later discuss provide clear illustrations of deeply entrenched, significant, systematic injustice.

Before turning to the main argument, I should emphasize that I am not calling for disobedience to law. Political obligation is not the only moral factor favoring compliance. Other considerations can provide strong reason to abide by law, even when there is significant, deeply entrenched, systematic injustice.

Here are some examples. Some moral principles argue, in effect, for compliance with those laws that prohibit immoral behavior. One does not normally have the moral right to assault, cheat, coerce, harass, imprison, or kill another human being. . . .

Even those who are treated unjustly can have moral reason to comply with the culpable laws—when, for example, disobedience would expose innocent persons to risks they have not agreed to assume. And we can have moral reason to support a regime that is profoundly unjust—when it is endangered for example, by forces that threaten to impose much worse injustice. . . .

II

I turn now to the three examples and begin with what is presumably the easiest case.

Chattel slavery

Thoreau's chief concern was slavery in the United States. Its atrocities began with the commercial trade in slaves, in which vast numbers of Africans lost freedom, family, and homeland, and very many their lives, under horrible conditions. Survivors of the Middle Passage and their descendants were then treated as property to be used at their owners' pleasure or as outlets for their owners' cruelty. Slaves' economic value was the principal check on slavery's brutality. When the international slave trade was outlawed and reduced, it was supplemented by an internal trade built upon the systematic "breeding" of slaves. . . .

I assume there could be no moral presumption favoring obedience by slaves to laws that support their enslavement. That precludes political obligation. Some federal and state laws under slavery were no doubt worthy of respect, and the circumstances of specific actions could create good reasons to comply with laws supporting slavery, but all that is compatible with the present point.

Colonial rule

Gandhi resisted British colonial rule first in South Africa and then in South Asia. Consider Gandhi's view of the latter case: The British made India bear the cost of unnecessary wars, "maintained a ruinously costly civil and military administration, destroyed indigenous industries and de-industrialised India, ignored its agricultural development, caused massive unemployment and famine, and in general mercilessly exploited it." The British, Gandhi argued, "sapped the foundations of Indian civilization, de-nationalised the Indians, ridiculed their society and religion, and foisted their values on them." British rule was moreover racist, degrading, violent, and brutal.

Now consider the following contrast. In the U.S. it is widely assumed that by 1776 Britain had forfeited any right to rule its American colonies. This judgment is based largely on Britain's efforts to tax them. Britain's relations with its own colonists were benevolent by comparison with its subjugation of indigenous peoples in Africa and Asia.

British colonial rule there involved significant, deeply entrenched, systematic injustice. Neither Africans nor Asians could plausibly be regarded as morally obligated to accept British rule and obey laws that supported their subjugation. Some British colonial laws were no doubt worthy of respect, and the circumstances of specific actions could generate reason to comply with laws supporting British rule, but that is compatible with the present point.

Jim Crow

King's resistance activities were primarily directed against the system known as Jim Crow. This was not primarily an arrangement of racial separation but a system of White supremacy—degrading, exploitative, and secured by terror.

After slavery was abolished, the federal Constitution was amended to secure basic rights for African Americans. In 1877, however, the federal government aborted efforts to enforce those rights. Violence and fraud were permitted to eliminate the remnants of Reconstruction and White supremacy was soon reestablished. State laws and constitutions were modified to exclude African Americans from the political process. Protections against rape, kidnapping, harassment, and murder were denied African Americans. All that was possible because of unlawful behavior by officials, the acquiescence of some, and the indifference of others.

The United States was publicly committed to due process, equal protection, and the rule of law, but for many decades government sanctioned their brutal, systematic denial to African Americans. Local officials would rarely interfere with, no less prosecute, violence against Blacks; they were frequently involved. And the federal government would not interfere. For African Americans, the rule of law was a false promise.

The Jim Crow system involved significant, deeply entrenched, systematic injustice. It is implausible to hold that a sound moral presumption favored obedience to all the laws of the land, including those that supported Jim Crow. Some federal and state laws were worthy of respect, and the circumstances of specific actions could generate reasons to comply with Jim Crow laws, but that is compatible with the present point.

Jim Crow provides a third refutation of the notion that civil disobedience can be assumed to require moral justification. Insofar as civil disobedience theory assumes that political resistance requires moral justification even in settings that are morally comparable to Jim Crow, it is premised on serious moral error.

III

I turn now to the notion that those who engage in civil disobedience assume that their unlawful conduct requires moral justification. True civil disobedients are supposed by theorists to regard the systems under which they live as morally flawed but basically just and requiring modest reform rather than fundamental change. Evidence of this outlook is seen in the disobedients' nonviolent methods and use of moral suasion rather than violent rebellion. Their submitting to arrest and punishment is taken as further evidence of respect for legal authority and recognition of a moral obligation to obey. Theorists who mention specific resisters generally assume this is true of King; many include Gandhi; some add Thoreau.

Thoreau and Gandhi are of course very closely associated with the idea and practice of civil disobedience, as the term is used in everyday speech. Theorists do not deny that obvious point; and I do not object to their restricting the term "civil disobedience" to just one species of principled resistance. My concern is the resulting suggestion that the most respected resisters favorably appraised their systems and embraced a moral presumption favoring obedience to their most unjust laws.

Given the settings of their resistance, reviewed in Section II, it would not have been reasonable for Thoreau, Gandhi, or King to have regarded the prevailing system as sufficiently just to support political obligation. As these were not unreasonable men, the second part of my argument might end here. But to strengthen the argument, I shall consider their views more fully.

Thoreau, Gandhi, and King believed, with good reason, that their systems required fundamental change. They did not regard themselves as morally bound to obey unjust laws. No such notion framed the dilemmas they confronted when contemplating unlawful resistance. Their acceptance of legal sanctions signified a strategic, not a moral, judgment.

Gandhi's and King's rejection of violence reflected both moral scruples and prudent judgment, not an outlook favoring modest reform. Violence was not a promising means of effecting the sort of social changes they sought, which included the support of those who were bound to lose their privileged status in a more equitable society.

Thoreau

In his lecture on civil disobedience,[1] Thoreau linked his refusal to pay the Massachusetts poll tax to his state's support of the federal government's favorable policies towards chattel slavery.

That essay also reveals his view that government possesses no moral authority. "Government is at best an expedient; but most governments are usually, and all governments are sometimes inexpedient." Now conducting an aggressive, expansionist war against Mexico, which promised more scope for slavery, the U.S. government, he said, was "each instant losing some of its integrity." One "cannot without disgrace be associated" with "this American government today. . . . I cannot for an instant recognize that political organization as *my* government which is the *slave's* government also."

Thoreau regarded law no more favorably: "Law never made men a whit more just; and, by means of their respect for it, even the well-disposed are daily made the agents of injustice." Undue respect for law leads the "mass of men [to] serve the state . . . not as men mainly, but as machines, with their bodies. . . . Others . . . serve the state chiefly with their heads; and, as they rarely make any moral distinctions, they are as likely to serve the devil, without intending it, as God."

Thoreau believed we should sometimes comply with unjust law. "If the injustice is part of the necessary friction of government, let it go, let it go: perchance it will wear smooth." But "when the friction comes to have its machine, and oppression and robbery are organized, I say, let us not have such a machine any longer."

. . . When asked by the tax collector for payment, Thoreau invited arrest, which he seems to have sought in order to dramatize his protest. As he expected, all of Concord soon learned of his jailing. His subsequent lecture implored others to act on their own anti-slavery convictions. If we regard his lecture as part of his continuing tax resistance, then the latter qualifies as civil disobedience, even under a narrow definition, and Thoreau provides a counter-example to the notion that civil disobedients have a favorable judgment of the prevailing system and accordingly acknowledge a moral presumption favoring obedience to law.

Gandhi

Gandhi championed public, nonviolent protest, conduct that was calculated to cause opponents to consider grievances from the petitioners' point of view, and acceptance of punishment for unlawful resistance. These facts may suggest that Gandhi accepted the legitimacy of British rule and acknowledged a moral obligation to obey the law. But that would be a mistake.

Gandhi went to South Africa in 1893 to do some legal work. Soon becoming an outspoken critic of racist practices under British rule, he remained for two decades, mobilizing Asians and developing his theory of *satyagraha*. He first sought reforms by appealing to the doctrine of equal rights for all British subjects. But experience destroyed his respect for British rule and Britain's notion of civilization.

For the last three decades of his life, Gandhi labored for Indian independence. He led major

campaigns in the 1920s and 1930s and developed the "Quit India" program of the 1940s, which called on the British to leave despite the Japanese invasion.

Ghandi held that, by its broken promises as well as its degrading and brutal treatment of Indians following World War I, Britain had "forfeited all claim to his allegiance." The colonial government showed "utter contempt" for the rights and dignity of its subjects. The colonial administration was corrupt and relied on terror. Indians "had a *right* to disobey it . . . and a duty to do so because as moral beings they had a duty to fight for the self-respect and dignity of their fellow-citizens." Although Gandhi believed a good state "deserved the benefit of the doubt," he held that one had no duty to comply with unjust laws.[2]

Thus Gandhi rejected both the prevailing system and a moral presumption favoring obedience to all of its laws.

King[3]

If any civil disobedient might be imagined to accept the moral legitimacy of the prevailing system and recognize an obligation to obey its laws, it would be Martin Luther King, Jr. King called on the federal government to enforce the law. He agonized over disobeying patently unlawful court orders. He said that his campaigns expressed "the highest respect for law."

But we must look more closely. First, we should not be misled by the limited aims of King's resistance activities. Campaigns for social justice usually advance goals that are more modest than the participants' ultimate objectives. The Montgomery bus boycott made very limited demands, which did not even include an end to segregation, but the boycotters' ultimate aim was clear. As King said at the time, "What the Negro wants—and will not stop until he gets—is absolute and unqualified freedom and equality."

Modest goals were important because Jim Crow was firmly entrenched. Blacks lacked power in the system, and many doubted their ability to effect even modest goals. King stressed that rights could not be realized without persistent mass action. To mobilize participants, campaigns must have realizable goals. To maintain participation, campaigns must sometimes succeed. . . .

Second, King's commitment to nonviolence did not reflect favorably on the system. He emphasized that violent protest was not only immoral but impractical. Although violence was justifiably used in self-defense, it had no place in organized resistance, where it would divert attention from the issues and defeat the long-term goal of improving relations with Whites. And it would be futile, as Blacks were outnumbered and outgunned.

Third, acceptance of punishment was strategic. "If you confront a man who has been cruelly misusing you, and say 'Punish me, if you will; I do not deserve it, but I will accept it, so that the world will know I am right and you are wrong,' then you wield a powerful and just weapon."

Fourth, King called the system not only "unjust" but "evil." "The thing to do is get rid of the system." It might be thought that King condemned only a local aberration. But legally enforced discrimination was pervasive. White domination was maintained by violent and degrading criminal activities that were officially sanctioned rather than prosecuted. Only the federal courts had taken dramatic steps in the direction of reform, but these were still quite limited, and the results were uncertain.

Fifth, King's references to "the highest respect for law" accompanied his distinction between just and unjust law. King, like Gandhi, held that unjust laws merit no respect, and went on to refute a presumption favoring obedience.

In his "Letter from Birmingham City Jail," for example, his review of the distinction between just and unjust law introduces a condemnation of Jim Crow. He first explains how it wrongs the individual. Then he stresses that Jim Crow law is imposed by a majority on a minority that is excluded from the political process. This clearly anticipates and rebuts an argument for political obligation that invokes the notion of democracy. Jim Crow laws *cannot* merit respect as products of a democratic process because the process that generates Jim Crow law excludes African Americans and is inherently *un*democratic.

Finally, King never suggested that when he contemplated civil disobedience he faced a moral dilemma which included an obligation to obey the law. His first decision to violate a court order illustrates the point.

The Birmingham campaign of 1963 included a boycott of downtown stores to pressure the owners into ending racist practices. It was important because it followed an unsuccessful campaign in Albany, Georgia. Birmingham was, moreover, a stronghold of segregation.

Two moral dilemmas developed. Demonstrations had been postponed to avoid involvement in a municipal election. But as the Easter shopping season was ending, demonstrations were needed to strengthen the boycott. A march planned for Good Friday was then banned by an illicit court order. King had obeyed such an order in Albany, which he now regretted. But the Birmingham organizers feared that defiance of a court order might appear unprincipled to financial supporters—inconsistent with King's reliance on law. And financial help would be needed to bail out arrested demonstrators. That was the first dilemma. When King and his colleagues were satisfied that they could persuade their supporters of the importance of the march, they decided to defy the order, and the first dilemma was resolved.

A second dilemma arose the evening prior to the march. The city told a local bondsman who supplied bail for the demonstrators that he could not continue because his financial assets were inadequate. King later recalled:

> It was a serious blow. We had used up all the money we had on hand for cash bonds. There were our people in jail, for whom we had a moral responsibility. Fifty more were to go with Ralph [Abernathy] and me. . . . Without bail facilities, how could we guarantee their eventual release?

The organizers met the next morning to decide what to do. One said:

Martin . . . this means you can't go to jail. We need money. We need a lot of money. We need it now. You are the only one who has the contacts to get it. If you go to jail, we are lost. The battle of Birmingham is lost.

King resolved this dilemma as follows:

I walked to another room. . . . I thought of the three hundred, waiting in prison. I thought of the Birmingham Negro community, waiting. Then . . . . I thought of the twenty million black people who dreamed that someday they might be able to cross the Red Sea of injustice and find their way to the promised land of integration and freedom. There was no more room for doubt.

King and his associates marched and were arrested.

Both dilemmas involved moral considerations and practical uncertainties. Neither involved a moral presumption favoring obedience to law.

King did appeal to the central values that we associate with the Declaration of Independence and the Constitution. But he stressed that America's commitments had not been translated into practice. He did not confuse promise with achievement. He praised our ideals but condemned our practice.

King did not regard racism as a peripheral problem of American society, and he was right. He too refutes the notion that civil disobedients accept an obligation of obedience to law.

IV

I want now to suggest some lessons to be drawn from my argument.

Lawful and unlawful conduct

Much of civil disobedience theory assumes there is a morally significant difference between lawful and unlawful resistance. The first part of my argument shows that assumption to be mistaken in leading cases. In the absence of a blanket moral obligation to comply with law, we cannot assume that the distinction has moral significance. If the condition I employed in that argument is sound, then I think the assumption can rarely, if ever, be made. Few, if any, human societies have been free of significant, deeply entrenched, systematic injustice.

The second part of my argument reveals that the distinction between lawful and unlawful resistance had practical but not moral importance to Thoreau, Gandhi, and King. I would suggest that the same is true of principled resisters generally. Those with grievances serious enough to lead them into perilous conflict with dominant groups do not typically embrace a favorable appraisal of the prevailing system; nor do they think of themselves as morally bound to obey laws that seem to them outrageously unjust. . . .

Insofar as civil disobedience theory assumes political obligation, it distorts the outlook of principled resisters. The literature also tends to ignore the governments' repression of lawful protest and dissent.

Moral misjudgment

Given the first part of my argument, one cannot help wondering why theorists of civil disobedience should have imagined a moral presumption favoring compliance with laws supporting brutally oppressive institutions. For the injustices addressed have been significant, systematic, and deeply entrenched, and the theorists have usually been sympathetic to the resisters' grievances.

. . . How could philosophers of good will have assumed that moral justification was required to disobey laws supporting chattel slavery, racist colonialism, or Jim Crow? If I am right in regarding that assumption as morally indefensible, then we must entertain the possibility of a systematic defect in the moral framework that obtained. The judgment of those of us who took political obligation for granted—despite the obvious existence of intolerable, deeply entrenched, systematic injustice against clearly identified groups within our society—was distorted by inadequate sensitivity to the palpable impact of the oppression, especially on those of color.

Many Americans of European ancestry disapproved of White supremacy but did little about it. Their moral judgment affected their choice of political party and of candidates for public office, but not much else. White supremacy was not perceived as a pressing moral problem that called for concerted action.

That was a moral failing. The discounting and resultant toleration of outrageous, deeply entrenched, systematic injustice amounted to culpable indifference.

Racism often involves naked hostility, inhuman cruelty, and brutal violence toward persons who are identified in racial terms. It often involves harsh measures to secure status in a racial hierarchy. It often involves such overtly racist behavior—but not always. I suggest it can also involve, for example, tolerance of racist conduct or of racist social arrangements because of a failure to attach proper importance to known facts which primarily concern people with whom one does not identify in racial terms.[4]

My suggestion, then, is that theorists' endorsement of political obligation, while possessing sufficient knowledge of settings like Jim Crow, can reasonably be characterized as a derivative but socially important form of racism.

Two qualifications are required. First, most of the relevant literature is now twenty-five years old or more. Political philosophy has since changed. Many of us have become skeptics about political obligation.

Our moral sensibilities have also changed. It is more difficult than ever before for one to discount the interests of groups that are identified in racial terms. The related difficulty that we now face is the idea that the legacy of racial injustice can be rectified by "color blind" political policies. But that is a subject for another occasion.

Second, although White supremacy remains a major feature of American society, it would be a mistake to depict the moral failing to which I have referred in purely racial terms. Analogous attitudes have affected judgment and conduct concerning women as well as various ethnic groups. In these connections, too, moral sensibilities have improved. It remains to be seen by how much and whether we shall develop collective action that is calculated to overcome the significant, deeply entrenched, systematic injustice that remains.

NOTES

1. Thoreau's lecture is reprinted in Henry D. Thoreau, *Reform Papers*, ed. W. Glick (Princeton: Princeton University Press, 1973), pp. 63–90, under its original title, "Resistance to Civil Government." . . . For more on Thoreau's essay, see my "Political Responsibility and Resistance to Civil Government," *Philosophic Exchange* (1995–96): 5–25.

2. Bhikhy Parekh, *Gandhi's Political Philosophy*, (London: Macmillan, 1991), pp. 125–29.

3. Quotations in this section are from *Testament of Hope: The Essential Writings and Speeches of Martin Luther King, Jr.*, ed. J. M. Washington (San Francisco: HarperCollins, 1991).

4. Racism can take other forms, e.g., neglecting to learn about such phenomena when one is vaguely aware of their existence.

Review and Discussion Questions

1. Lyons briefly discusses consent and fairness as bases of political obligation. Assess those arguments. Do citizens today have an obligation to obey the law either because we have consented to our system of government or because it would be unfair of us to violate the rules of the system whose benefits we have enjoyed?

2. Critically assess Lyons's principle that political obligation cannot coexist with significant, systematic, and entrenched injustices. Is the U.S. free of such injustices? Is any society? Does Lyons's principle imply that, in reality, there is no such thing as political obligation? If a society is marred by injustice, does this imply that one has no obligation to obey any of its laws?

3. Lyons believes that those who are unjustly oppressed have no obligation to obey the law. Do you agree? What about those who are not oppressed by the system?

4. Assess the following argument: "I agree that it is sometimes right to violate unjust laws, but it is wrong to protest by breaking laws that are not unjust (for example, laws against trespass, disturbing the peace, blocking traffic, or not paying one's taxes). One still has an obligation to obey those laws."

5. Lyons correctly states that Thoreau, Gandhi, and King did not regard themselves as morally bound to obey unjust laws. But did they regard themselves as having an obligation to obey other laws, or did they see themselves, as Lyons suggests, as having no political obligation at all?

6. Do you agree with Lyons that racism underlies the traditional theory of civil disobedience?

Is There a Duty to Vote?

LOREN E. LOMASKY AND GEOFFREY BRENNAN

Citizens have a duty to vote. That's what we are frequently told, and that's what most people seem to believe. In this essay, Loren E. Lomasky, professor of philosophy at Bowling Green State University, and Geoffrey Brennan, professor of economics at Australian National University, challenge this piece of conventional wisdom. After closely examining several arguments for such a duty—based on prudence, act consequentialism, generalization, and expressive ethics—they conclude that citizens of modern democracies have no obligation to vote. Their essay ends by speculating about why the belief that there is such a duty is so widespread.

Study Questions

1. Why doesn't prudence (or self-interest) give us a reason to vote?

2. What point do Parfit and Barry make? How do the authors respond to it?

3. The authors suggest that, in calculating the utilitarian benefit of voting for one candidate over another, a person must "discount for" (or take account of) five possibilities. What are they?

4. Why in an election in a stable modern democracy is it unlikely that matters of huge moment will be at stake?

5. Why does the "What if everybody did that?" argument work in the case of Throckmorton's cutting across the newly seeded lawn, but not in the case of Dalrymple's giving up farming?

6. Explain the expressive argument for a duty to vote. What is the main problem the authors raise for it?

7. According to the authors, three factors help to explain why a belief in a duty to vote is so widespread. What are they?

Reprinted by permission of Cambridge University Press from Social Philosophy & Policy, *vol. 17, no. 1 (Winter 2000). Copyright © 2000 Social Philosophy and Policy Foundation.*

I. Introduction

. . . GOOD CITIZENSHIP IN THE FINAL DECADE of the twentieth century does not seem to require much of the individual beyond simple law-abidingness. . . . However, there exists a remarkable degree of consensus that voting is requisite, that one who fails to exercise the franchise is thereby derelict. Candidates for the nation's highest office publicly proclaim that duty; so do one's neighbors and associates. . . . We call that consensus remarkable because, as will become evident, it is exceedingly difficult to develop a persuasive rationale for the existence of a duty to vote. Often that duty is simply taken for granted. Where arguments are given, they typically invoke either fallacious reasoning or dubious empirical premises. . . . But we wish to advance a bolder conclusion: There is no satisfactory rationale for a duty to vote. Contra the popular wisdom, an individual who chooses not to exercise the franchise does not thereby fall short with regard to any responsibility entailed by citizenship.

. . . We argue that, under standard circumstances, voting is not morally superior to abstention. One does not do morally better to vote than, say, to spend the time playing golf instead. That is not to maintain that individuals have no reason to vote. Some do, some don't. The same is true for golfing: if voting/golfing affords one enjoyment or otherwise contributes to leading one's preferred mode of life, then one has reason to vote/play golf; otherwise one does not. . . .

II. The Argument Delimited

Sometimes one does wrong not to vote. An impaneled juror who declines to cast a ballot concerning the guilt or innocence of the defendant fails to fulfill one of the duties attached to that office. Similarly, a university faculty member who absents herself from a departmental decision concerning a junior colleague's tenure and promotion case is, exceptional considerations aside, derelict. In both instances the duty to vote is consequent on the

individual's occupying a special office or role, the satisfactory performance of which requires, but is not confined to, casting a vote. . . .

One may, in virtue of special circumstances, be morally obligated to vote in a general election. If, for example, Jones has promised her spouse that she will cast a ballot in the upcoming presidential election, then she stands under an obligation to do so as an entailment of the duty to keep promises one has made. If Smith is an active member of a political party who has aligned himself with others in the task of securing its victory at the polls, then he may be guilty of bad faith, of letting the side down, if he chooses to spend election day sharpening his short iron play. The former explicitly, and the latter implicitly, voluntarily took on a commitment that created an obligation to vote which, in the absence of that undertaking, would not have obtained. . . .

The subsequent discussion of the duty to vote is not meant to apply to cases like these. We explicitly restrict our discussion to voting in general elections by people who are under no special obligation to exercise the franchise and who are not required by law to do so. We further confine our attention to the kinds of elections that characteristically occur in modern nation-states and their substantial political subunits in which populations number in the hundreds of thousands or millions and in which, for most individuals, political activity is only an occasional, part-time pursuit. When there is reference in what follows to a *citizen's duty to vote*, that is the context we have in mind.

III. The Argument from Prudence

How things go with a person can be substantially affected by collective determinations. "Your vote makes a difference," the pre-election propaganda intones. If that is so, then prudent individuals will vote in order to augment the probability that electoral outcomes will favor their interests. If prudence is a duty (or, if not a duty in the strict sense, then a virtue), then one ought to vote.

Whether individuals owe duties to themselves, including a duty of prudence, is debatable. That question can, though, be set to one side here, because the key premise of the prudential argument is defective. In any election with a large number of voters, the chance that my vote will make a difference to the outcome is small. On most electoral occasions it will be infinitesimal. Therefore, one aiming to maximize her own utility may have many alternative paths for doing so, but almost surely one of the least efficacious will be to bestir herself to cast a ballot in order to influence electoral outcomes. That will be so even if much hangs on the results of the election. . . .

Voting is costly in the opportunity sense. The time and effort and perhaps other resources that go into casting a ballot have alternative employments. These costs will vary from individual to individual, but for virtually everyone these will be orders of magnitude greater than the expected return to a vote. . . . Therefore, a rationally self-interested individual will vote neither for A nor for B, but will instead refrain from voting. At least that will be so if voting is exclusively an investment in electoral outcomes. . . . Casting a ballot, then, is similar to bowling or tending petunias or listening to a "Metallica's Greatest Hits" tape: if one appreciates that sort of activity, then one has reason to engage in it; otherwise one does not. From the perspective of prudence there is nothing intrinsically commendable or inadvisable about any of these activities.

IV. The Argument from Act-Consequentialism

The result of the preceding section is not likely to prove upsetting to many exponents of a citizen's duty to vote. Few will have conceived it to be primarily a self-regarding duty. To the contrary: even if the act of voting involves some measure

of personal sacrifice it is meritorious because of the benefits thereby conferred on the population at large. That is precisely the point of speaking of it as a *citizen's* duty.

Nonetheless, a shift of perspective from prudence to the well-being of the entire community does not remove the sting of the preceding section's analysis. If the inconsequentiality of voting renders it unimportant with regard to one's own self-interest whether one bothers to cast a ballot, then that inconsequentiality also infects the claim that one is producing some public good through exercising the franchise. It seems on first blush, then, that only a slightly modified version of the argument from prudence is needed to dispose of the argument from act-consequentialism. Why should minute probabilities draw one to the polls in the latter case if they do not in the former?

The answer the consequentialist will give is: because the stakes are disproportionate. When appraising voting prudentially, only *one's own* utility enters into the picture, but when thinking about how a vote can bear on the political community's well-being, *everyone's* utility counts. Moving from the micro to the macro dimension effects a change in degree which, because it is so great, becomes a difference in kind as well. Derek Parfit offers an analogy:

> It may be objected that it is *irrational* to consider very tiny chances. When our acts cannot affect more than a few people, this may be so. But this is because the stakes are here comparatively low. Consider the risks of causing accidental death. It may be irrational to give any thought to a one-in-a million chance of killing one person. But if I was a nuclear engineer, would I be irrational to give any thought to the same chance of killing a million people? This is what most of us believe. . . . When the stakes are very high, no chance, however, small, should be ignored.[1]

Some hyperbole in the concluding sentence aside, Parfit's point seems undeniable: even very small probabilities that bear heavily on the well-being of a multitude ought to be incorporated in the deliberations preceding one's decision on how to act. Brian Barry interprets this as a generally applicable utilitarian rationale for voting:

> If an act-utilitarian really gives full weight to the consequences for *everyone* that he expects will be affected, this will normally provide an adequate reason for voting. If I think that one party will increase the GNP by 1/4 percent over five years more than the other party, that for a utilitarian is a big aggregate difference. Are there *really* so many more beneficial things one could do with fifteen minutes?[2]

Do these observations indicate, then, that if we extend the scope of our concern from one solitary individual to many, there is a directly consequentialist rationale for a duty to vote despite the minuscule likelihood of altering the outcome? In a word, no. We have no quarrel with the other sides of the respective analogies: it is, indeed, for almost all people almost all of the time, a worthwhile moral bargain to expend fifteen minutes to avert a one-in-a-million chance of a nuclear power plant meltdown or to bring about a one-quarter percent increase in GNP over five years. What we deny is the relevance of these analogies to voting. . . .

By way of contrast to the Parfit/Barry analogies, a more recognizable (although still greatly simplified) rendering of the voter's scenario might go something like this. Party A proposes a set of economic policies that have some hard-to-quantify but non-negligible likelihood of generating a higher national product over the next five years than those of Party B: a best rough estimate is something on the order of one-quarter percent per year. Party B's economic program, however, seems likely to yield somewhat less inflation over the course of those five years. Complicating matters further are conflicting estimates concerning the economic policies' respective merits with regard to effects on capital investment, unemployment, the trade balance, and measures of economic equality. All that one can be reasonably confident of is that A's policies will do better with

regard to some of these, and B's policies will do better with regard to others. And beyond the parties' economic programs there are another two dozen or so major areas of dispute—over defense, civil rights, education, housing, environmental policy, etc. With regard to each, a greater or lesser degree of murkiness obtains; different trade-offs are on offer; both sides swear fealty to the common good. What is the conscientious act-utilitarian now to do? Does it still seem so apparent that spending fifteen minutes to cast a ballot is one of the most socially beneficial things one can do with one's time—especially if one has not previously invested for each of those minutes several dozen hours devoted to securing and assessing relevant political information?

. . . First, . . . one has to discount for mistakes in assigning comparative weights to the various competing goods (or, more rarely, for having identified as a good something that is a bad, or vice versa). Second, one has to discount for the fallibility inherent in empirical assessments concerning matters of fact and causal judgments concerning the instrumental effects of alternative policy options.

Third, one must then discount by the likelihood that the platform on which the party is running is indicative of the actions that it will indeed undertake should it gain office. That is, even if one knew with certainty that giving effect to the A platform would be superior to realizing the B platform, the return to a vote for A has to be discounted by the probability that A will defect from its own standard. It is not only inordinate cynicism about politicians and their campaign promises that might induce one to attach substantial weight to this factor; political history is full of spectacular and momentous turnarounds. To take just twentieth-century United States presidential elections as examples, in 1916 Woodrow Wilson ran for reelection on the slogan "He kept us out of war!" He was duly reelected and then didn't. In 1964, Lyndon Johnson alleged that if the wrong candidate was elected the U.S. would find itself mired in an unwinnable land war in Asia. So it proved. And of course there is the whimsically delightful insouciance of George Bush's "Read my lips; no new taxes!"

Fourth, one must discount for historical accidents and inadvertencies. Unpredictable wars, assassinations, stock market crashes, famine, or incapacity of the officeholder might turn what had *ex ante* seemed to be a good bet into an *ex post* loser. Fifth and finally, one must discount all of the above by a measure of one's own judiciousness or lack of same as a political evaluator, asking: How well-attested is the data on which I rely? How adequate are my technical capabilities in economics, international affairs, defense studies, social policy, etc. for supporting the instrumental analyses I bring to competing policy proposals? Is my judgment liable to be affected by any hidden biases or blind spots? How successfully have I managed to detach myself from evanescent enthusiasms so as to preserve a cool objectivity? And the like.

If, after all the discounts are appropriately assigned, it still seems manifest that A is the better party/candidate, then one may have some utilitarian reason to cast a ballot for A. But even then, perhaps not. If knowledge of the superiority of A is not confined to some esoteric coterie but rather is possessed by me because it is readily available to the citizenry at large, and if members of that citizenry for the most part will vote against a palpably inferior candidate should they bother to vote at all, then employing one's fifteen minutes to vote may, on utilitarian grounds, be inadvisable. . . . If, say, for any representative voter in an electorate in which one million individuals cast ballots, it is .6 likely that she will recognize B to be inferior and thus vote in opposition, then the likelihood of one's own vote being decisive is so indescribably small as to be entirely negligible. (If the question is, "Should we bestir ourselves to avert nuclear meltdowns?", how likely is it that my vote will be needed to tip the balance?) To oversimplify a bit, on those occasions when one's vote is most likely to make the sort of difference that stirs the hearts of act-consequentialists, there will rarely be any firm indication concerning for whom it ought to be cast; and when there is

unmistakable evidence concerning which is the better candidate or policy, it is almost inconceivable that one's vote will be needed.

Suppose, for the sake of argument, that all the preceding cautions could be met by an exceptional public-spirited citizen confident of her ability to evaluate the issues, judge the fitness of the candidates, and cast a well-directed ballot. That would still not support a general duty to vote. Rather, it would at most show that there are consequentialist reasons for *someone who is good at voting* to do so—and consequentialist reasons for someone who is bad at voting to abstain. If, for example, despite my best efforts I am more likely than not to be a sucker for an inferior candidate (this is my track record; past attempts to mend my ways have met with no success; etc.), then I confer on the citizenry a benefit by staying at home on election day. It follows that there cannot be a completely general citizen's duty to vote, because *I* am a citizen and it does not include me. . . .

There is a further reason why the consequentialist case for a duty to vote is strained. The argument hinges on there being matters of huge moment at stake so as to offset the tiny likelihood of one's own vote tipping the balance. However, there are good reasons in general to think that this will not often be the case—at least if democracy is working tolerably well. It is a well-established proposition in the formal literature on electoral competition that parties/candidates will be constrained to offer policy platforms that lie not too far from that which the median voter prefers. In two-party electoral races of the familiar kind, political equilibrium, if it exists, will be characterized by the parties/candidates locating themselves in near-proximity to each other. . . . Competition tends to restrict the policies that parties will offer, to the extent that those parties are interested in maximizing their chances of being elected. . . . In the limit, when rival candidates offer virtually identical policies, it seems inordinately precious to insist that we should all turn out because of some putative democratic duty. At least that is so within an act-consequentialist scheme.

We conclude that on every front the argument from act-consequentialism fails. It cannot support a duty to vote except when the stakes are very high, a circumstance which we have given reason to believe is rarer than is commonly made out. Even then, act-consequentialism does not support a duty to vote but rather a duty to vote *right*. Thus, it is not a duty of the citizenry at large, but only of the political cognoscenti. Even for political junkies, a healthy does of confidence that one is in fact voting right is rarely justified; and the more likely it is that such confidence is justified, the less likely it is that one's vote will be needed to tip the balance. Conclusion: On any list of the top thousand or so ways an ordinary citizen can usefully augment social well-being, casting a ballot on election day will either rank low or not be present at all.

V. The Argument from Generalization

> But what if everyone were to stay home and not vote? The results would be disastrous! Therefore, I (you/she) should vote.

Some version of the preceding is, by our casual tally, the most commonly adduced justification for a duty to vote. It can be presented as a reflection on the utility ramifications of a general practice of nonvoting, or it can take on a more Kantian wrapping in which willing the universalized form of the maxim "Vote only if it involves no sacrifice of one's own interests" is shown to embody an inconsistency. . . .

To begin, we note in passing that the claim that it would be disastrous if no one voted is far from evident. That is because the scenario under which abstention becomes universal has not been specified. . . . Suppose that people abstain from voting because political determinations are largely irrelevant to their interests: Collective action beyond that in which people voluntarily engage is almost never required to secure any appreciable good, and when it is required, one candidate for office is as likely as any other to do a creditable job

in orchestrating it. So no one bothers to vote. Is this a woeful world in which to find oneself? To our eyes it has more the aspects of a paradise! . . .

Such qualms duly noted, let it be granted for the sake of argument that generalized nonvoting would indeed be undesirable. Still, the indicated conclusion ("Therefore I/you/she ought to vote") does not automatically follow. It is notoriously easy to produce arguments that display the same surface form as the generalized-failure-to-vote argument, yet yield preposterous conclusions. For example, suppose that Dalrymple is considering leaving the farm to pursue a career as a dentist. The question is put to her, "What if no one grew fruits and vegetables?" The result, Dalrymple admits, would be disastrous. Therefore, it is urged, she would do wrong to abandon farming for dentistry. Against this suffices the retort, "But *not everyone will* give up farming!"

By way of contrast, Throckmorton is about to take a shortcut across the newly seeded lawn and is brought up by the reproof, "Well, what if everyone were to walk across the lawn? All the grass would be killed!" The reply, "But not everyone will cut across the lawn; most people take more heed of signs than I do," carries distinctly less conviction. The two cases display the same surface form, yet one intuitively is weak and the other strong. What accounts for the difference? . . .

Sometimes by doing or refraining from some action one thereby perpetrates an *unfairness*. This will be so when one benefits from or otherwise assigns positive value to the opposite type of performance on the part of others. By not doing as others do, one takes a free ride on their compliance. When Throckmorton ignores the "Keep Off the Grass!" sign and cuts across the newly seeded lawn, he thereby secures a quicker route to his destination; when others comply with the directive, they get to enjoy a flourishing green lawn—but so too does Throckmorton. The individual who picks an apple from the orchard saying, "One won't be missed," may be entirely correct, but he is thereby presuming that the disappearance of this particular apple will not be followed by the like disappearance of bushels more;

that is, he is presuming that others are more firmly bound than he is himself by norms of property ownership. And similarly for the causal litterer, the tax evader, the illicit occupier of "Handicapped Only" parking spots, and their numerous kin.

In many though not all cases of such free-riding behavior, initial defection by one or a small number of persons tends to promote further defections. In the extreme case the equilibrium outcome is universal defection. Suppose that one individual backs out of paying her share of the cost required to produce some public good. That single act of defection increases the per-person cost of the good to the remainder of the group, which may, in turn, induce others to back out, and so on, until production is no longer sustainable and the free-riding behavior becomes self-annihilating. This is one (not very Kantian) way of reconstructing Kant's demonstration in the *Grundlegung* of the inconsistency generated by application of the Categorical Imperative to a practice of borrowing money in the expectation that one will not be able to pay back the loan when it comes due.

In cases such as these, generalization is useful, if only as a heuristic device. It simultaneously levels the playing field and puts the tendency of an individual's action under a moral microscope through which the wrongness of the conduct is rendered evident. Free-riding, when generalized, is shown to be no more viable than the village in which everyone made a living by taking in others' washing. Strictly speaking, what makes an ungeneralizable action wrong is not that it fails the generalization test. Rather, it fails the generalization test because of underlying unfairness, and it is the unfairness that accounts for the action's wrongness. Passing a generalization test is secondary; fairness or the lack of some is what is primary.

That is why some arguments that exhibit disastrous results of a certain generalized practice fail to persuade. They are examples in which the universal practice of S would indeed be unfortunate, but not because of any unfairness embedded in an individual instance of S. Such is the case with the decision to abandon farming in order to take up

dentistry. When Dalrymple ceases to farm she does not thereby perpetrate any unfairness on those who remain in farming. Rather, each remaining farmer is, all else equal, rendered better off at the margin in virtue of the lower level of competition. In a large economy the effect may be so small as to be entirely unnoticeable, but the key point is its direction, not the magnitude. Moreover, as one person or several people leave farming, there is no tendency to set up a spiral of further departures; just the reverse. The process is self-stabilizing, with inducements to remain (or, once having left, to return) growing progressively greater the more who withdraw. The equilibrium that emerges is morally satisfactory; there will be both dentists and farmers, and neither reaps unfair advantage at the expense of the other.

Abstaining from voting is more like choosing a profession of dentistry than it is like cutting across a newly seeded lawn or failing to pay one's share of taxes. . . . When an eligible voter abstains, thereby lowering the total size of the electorate, the probability of one's own vote proving decisive increases. That is, each remaining voter is rendered better off by the lower level of electoral competition. In a large electorate, as with a large economy, the effect of one person's withdrawal may be so small as to be entirely unnoticeable, but the key point is its direction, not the magnitude. Therefore, as in the preceding example, the process tends to be self-stabilizing. An equilibrium emerges that does not have any evident morally unsatisfactory properties.

Some will respond by objecting that this equilibrium may be substantially less than full citizen participation, perhaps well under 50 percent of the eligible population, and therefore is objectionable for being less democratic than full participation. We are unmoved by this response because we are unsure what it means to be "more/less democratic" and why in this context being more democratic should be deemed better than being less democratic. If "more democratic" simply *means* displaying greater levels of citizen participation, then of course it is true that high rates of voting are more democratic than lower ones, but it would be begging the question to take that definitional circumstance as a reason for preferring greater participation. . . . We do not find it obvious that election outcomes would be "better" or political institutions more "legitimate" (in whatever nontrivial senses of these words might be supplied) if voting were to take place at 90 percent rather than 50 percent or even 5 percent participation levels. And even if more did mean better, it would still require further argument to show that this establishes a duty to vote. Wishing not to prejudge such complex questions, we conclude this section by observing that no such duty emerges straightforwardly from a generalization argument.

VI. Expressive Ethics and Voting

. . . Commonly during classroom discussions of the ethics of democratic participation . . . some student [will] rouse himself to a greater than customary pitch of moral seriousness and exclaim, "If you don't bother to vote, then you don't have any right to complain afterward about what the government does!" Often this rebuke elicits a buzz of approval from the other students.

It is not difficult to find any number of reasons to dismiss this declaration as more passionate than cogent. In no actually legislated bill of rights or credible theory of free expression is a right to complain about the activities of government contingent on one's prior electoral participation. And if there were such a theory, what would it look like? Would someone who has voted for A over B have no right to complain about anything the government subsequently does should A in fact defeat B? . . .

The dismissal is too quick . . . The student's response is, to be sure, naïve, but it conceals a promising insight that has largely been banished from more sophisticated ethical theories. Interpreted charitably, the response maintains that alongside, and to a considerable extent independent of, direct or indirect consequential considerations there exist *norms of expression*. Through one's spoken utterances and other expressive activ-

ity, one aligns oneself with certain values and opposes others. To the extent that it is inherently and not simply instrumentally good to identify— and to identify oneself with—that which is good (and evil to align oneself with that which is evil), an ethics of expression is not reducible to even a sophisticated consequentialism. . . .

It is in the nature of democratic politics that matters presented and widely acknowledged as items of momentous concern to all members of the polity are held up to examination, debated, and eventually put to popular determination through elections. Even in the age of the professionally packaged candidate and the ten-second sound bite, a certain measure of pomp and ceremony still attaches to the electoral process, thereby emphasizing that it is indeed serious business. The individual in her capacity as *citizen* has an assigned role in this process. Outsiders may be affected by the polity's electoral determinations, but the citizen is, additionally, an *agent* of those determinations. Through appearing at the polls and casting a ballot, she expresses her engagement with the concerns and undertakings of her compatriots and displays her assent to the legitimacy of the public enterprise through which she and they are bound together as partners within civil society.

Conversely, it can be argued, someone who chooses to be absent from the polls thereby expresses detachment from the enterprise, if not indeed active disdain. The doings of the polity are not his affair, he proclaims through his absence. It can go on without him—and he very well without it. That which is a matter of profound significance to his neighbors does not merit the allocation of even a few minutes of token symbolic support. It is for this reason that one who fails to vote imperils any right subsequently to complain about the government—not in the technical sense of being legally barred from doing so, but as an implication of common decency. One ought not bother others by raising matters that are none of one's business, and insofar as one who is eligible to vote declines to do so, one is expressing a disinclination to acknowledge the business of the *res publica* as one's own. To complain after the fact may be within the law, but it is base. It is like fulsomely bemoaning at the end of the season the also-ran finish of the Yankees after making no prior effort to take in a game, to apprise oneself of the team's fortunes, or even to cheer from a distance. It is anomalous in the same way as gnashing one's teeth and weeping bitter tears at the passing of someone of whom, in life, one was oblivious. It is, we might say, an exercise of bad faith and is to be condemned as such. That is the fleshed-out rendering of the student's exclamation.

Abstention by itself is not bad faith. It is, though, arguably discreditable. The office of citizen is no mean one, and to fail to display adequate regard for the station can be categorized as inherently condemnable. Not voting, so construed, is akin to declining to stand at the playing of the national anthem or trampling on the flag. Each is an expressively laden action that aligns one with certain political values and against others. Therefore, they are properly subject to praise or blame in virtue of what they *mean,* not simply because of what they *bring about.* The expressive argument for a duty to vote maintains that one evinces a minimally decent level of regard for the political weal by periodic appearances at the polls; to do less is to do too little.

Of all the rationales for a duty to vote, we find the expressive account strongest, if only by default. At one time we pronounced ourselves half-persuaded that the case it makes is sound,[3] but that now seems to be an overestimation. The chief inadequacies of the expressive case for a duty to vote are internal: the mere act of showing up at the polls every several years and grabbing some levers is palpably inadequate to qualify as a significant act of political expression.

Is exercise of the franchise to be construed as the expression of fidelity to the country's democratic institutions? Day-by-day residence within its borders and adherence to its laws and customs attests more explicitly and continuously to one's allegiance. Should the act of voting instead be construed as expressing some appreciation of the significance to the polity of the particular issues

and debates that are spotlighted by the current election campaign? That is to read rather a lot into the act of voting. As exponents of a duty to vote often remark, for most people voting is a low-cost activity. No political literacy test must be passed before one is allowed to matriculate at the polls. Because the ballot is secret, the direction of one's vote is not subject to scrutiny and thus lacks the expressive dimensions of a genuinely public performance. A vote cast from habitual allegiance to one party or TV-ad-induced prejudice or whimsy counts as much as one that is the product of diligent pre-election scrutiny of the candidates and issues. . . . There is, however, no sense in attaching to a perfunctory political performance more expressive weight than it can bear.

Finally, there is the simple point that refraining from voting can be no less expressive than voting. One may wish to record one's total contempt for all the candidates, or one's conscientious objection to some policy that is a feature of all the major candidates' platforms, or one's belief that the entire enterprise is a fraud and a delusion. Turning one's back on the entire business, refusing to be implicated—these may not be the most extreme forms of civic rebellion, but they are ones that the democratic form characteristically admits. And compared to rushing to the barricades or joining the Michigan Militia, they have the added merit of civic gentleness. We might disagree in particular cases concerning the moral advisability of expressive abstention, but it is certainly not an incoherent practice.

VII. Belief in a Duty to Vote

One question raised by the foregoing is why, if grounding for a duty to vote is so distinctly shaky, belief in its existence should be widespread and insistent. . . . Three factors suggest themselves.

First, in some political environments ancestral to that of contemporary representative liberal democracy, the persona of the activist citizen was central in a way it need not and cannot be today. In republics where free adult males possessing affluence sufficient to allow attention to affairs of state were a small minority of a small population, the demand that all who were entitled to participate should do so enjoyed considerable cogency. We are heirs to the political tradition of Aristotle's *Politics*, Renaissance humanism, the *Federalist Papers*. It is not surprising that we remain partially in thrall to ideals that were informed by very different conditions. Civic republicanism is an ideology crafted by and for political elites. Its classical formulations have nothing to say about vast mega-states, universal enfranchisement, widely shared economic affluence, far-advanced division of political labor with concomitant specialization of function, neutral public bureaucracies, moderated party competition, and a host of other shifts in circumstance that separate us from our republican forebears. It is no longer possible, let alone desirable, that all free citizens devote themselves intensively to public concerns. Insofar, though, as traces of that superannuated republicanism linger, they support an ethos of universal participation, the lowest common denominator of which is periodic appearance at the polls.

Second, belief in a duty to vote promotes the self-esteem of voters. The public rhetoric of democracies is redolent with invocations of the dignity of active citizenship. . . . Yet most individuals find themselves, in their daily affairs, distant from the precincts in which governance is exercised. The gulf of separation . . . will be eased if one can establish for oneself solid lines of association with "the people" who are supposed to be sovereign within a democracy. The act of voting constitutes such a connection. One who votes can say, "Well, I did *something*." If that something can, additionally, be characterized as the discharge of a solemn civic trust, there is comfort to be taken in its fulfillment, no matter how meager the demands thereby placed on one's wit and energies, the irrelevance of one's vote to the emergence of political outcomes, and the paucity of expressive potential in casting a ballot. Cheap grace is, after all, still grace.

Third, we ask, *Cui bono?* Who are the major beneficiaries of the myth of a duty to vote? . . . Unlike the general run of citizens for whom political activity is an occasional thing, for a minority it is the primary business. Its rewards include position, prominence, power, and financial prosperity, and the fact that there is never a shortage of aspirants willing to enter the fray is some evidence that the magnitude of those rewards is substantial.

For the circle that thrives on the practice of politics it is, therefore, a matter of no small significance that those who foot the bill remain, if not eager to do so, then at least complaisant. If citizens come to believe that their abbreviated appearances at the polls suffice to render them crucial contributors to democratic affairs, respected and heeded by those who bid for their votes, then they are more likely to feel satisfied with the rules of the game as it is actually played rather than grump about the shortness of their end of the stick. From the perspective of political elites, widespread belief in a duty to vote passes the Goldilocks test: it is not too small, it is not too big; it is just right. If citizens were to believe that political activity had no moral claim on them at all, then they might feel alienated from its practice, especially as the costs they must bear to sustain democratic forms are not negligible. If, on the other hand, citizens believed that they were morally obligated to understand the issues, scrutinize carefully the performances of officeholders, investigate gaps between promised benefits and realized outcomes, and organize independent campaigns whenever they determined that the current political establishment was lax in its attention to the public weal, they would make terrible pests of themselves. The mean between these defective states is just enough participation to make ordinary citizens feel importantly implicated in the process and no more. Belief that voting is necessary and sufficient to enjoy the status *good citizen* is the perfect moral underpinning for that mean. No wonder, then, that it receives such enthusiastic support from political elites. Belief in a duty to vote is the opiate of democratic masses.

VIII. Conclusion

We have argued that a duty to vote cannot be sustained on prudential grounds, nor can it be justified through act-consequentialistic, generalization, or expressive reasoning. There are, though, several plausible explanations of why such a belief, though groundless, can be expected to enjoy wide currency among citizens of contemporary democracies.

That is not, of course, to argue that voting by citizens is morally wrong. Nor is it to call into question the supreme importance of the right to vote enjoyed by citizens of a democracy; on that matter we chant in unison with the civics textbooks and profess ourselves well-pleased to live in jurisdictions in which suffrage is universal and elections vigorously contested rather than, say, Burma or Cuba. It is not even to argue against legally compulsory voting. This much should be clear. But we know based on responses to prior versions of this essay that some people will take us to be saying that voting is irrational, "a waste of time." Not so. There are numerous good and sufficient reasons why someone might decide to vote. The point is merely that the belief that there is a general citizen's duty to do so is not among them. Through voting I can "get it off my chest"; I can evince solidarity with some cause or candidate; I can occupy a walk-on role within the ongoing kaleidoscopic civil drama; or I can simply take comfort from being in step with my neighbors. In short, voting is like playing golf or being a member of a choral group or piecing together patchwork quilts: if it is the sort of thing in which one enjoys participating then there is a reason to do so, but morality does not nudge, one way or the other, except in special cases. And special cases do not make for a general duty.

NOTES

1. Derek Parfit, *Reasons and Persons* (Oxford: Oxford University Press, 1984), 74–75 (emphasis in the original).

2. Brian Barry, "Comment," in *Political Participation*, ed. Stanley Benn (Canberra: Australian National University Press, 1978), 39 (emphases in the original).

3. See Brennan and Lomasky, *Democracy and Decision* (New York: Cambridge University Press, 1993), 186–89.

Review and Discussion Questions

1. Have you been taught that citizens have a responsibility to vote? Do you in fact vote? Explain why or why not.

2. Do you agree with the authors that, from the perspective of self-interest, voting doesn't pay off? If so, why do so many people vote?

3. Suppose that you are a utilitarian and seek always to maximize the general good. Does your moral theory require you to vote?

4. Would there be disastrous results if no one voted? Assume there would be. Does this give one a moral obligation to vote? Explain why or why not. Does one's not voting hurt other people in any way? Or are the authors correct to suggest that one's not voting, in fact, benefits other people by increasing the value of their votes?

5. If more people voted, would this make our system more democratic, election outcomes better, or our institutions more legitimate?

6. The authors believe that little expressive weight can be attached to voting. Yet they also believe that not voting can have expressive value. Can these two beliefs be squared?

7. Assess the authors' contention that it is in the interest of politicians that ordinary people believe that voting is necessary and sufficient for good citizenship.

8. Are you persuaded by the authors that we have no duty to vote? Or is there some argument they have overlooked or failed to give due consideration to?

Some Arguments for Conscription

WILLIAM A. GALSTON

After the war in Vietnam, the United States abolished the military draft and instituted an All-Volunteer Force (AVF). By relying on quality volunteers with extensive training and top-notch equipment, the U.S. has developed a very formidable military force, which enjoys high public confidence. However, Professor William A. Galston, director of the Institute for Philosophy and Public Policy at the University of Maryland, believes that reliance on the AVF has also entailed significant costs for the country. In particular, it has contributed to an impoverished understanding of the meaning and responsibilities of citizenship and has widened the gap between the orientation and experience of military personnel and that of ordinary citizens. Rejecting the idea that conscription is an abuse of state power, Galston recommends moving toward some form of universal (military or civilian) service for all high school graduates.

Study Questions

1. What does Galston mean by "optional citizenship"? What is "spectatorial citizenship"? What is the Principle of Personal Integrity, proposed by Ryan?

2. On what basis does Galston contend that Posner has misinterpreted John Stuart Mill's position?

3. Why does Galston reject Posner's contention that conscription is a form of slavery?

4. What point is Galston trying to make with his four thought experiments?

5. What was the point of Stephen Hess's letter to his sons?

6. What two interim steps does Galston propose, if moving toward a system of universal service is not politically feasible?

IN THE RUN UP to the war against Iraq, an op-ed by congressional representative Charles Rangel (D-NY) rekindled a debate about the military draft; unexpectedly, because most scholars and an overwhelming majority of senior military leaders regarded this matter as settled. The Vietnam-era draft was regarded as arbitrary and unfair, and it was held responsible for dissension within the military as well as the wider society.

In the immediate wake of its disaster in Vietnam, the United States made an historic decision to end the draft and institute an All-Volunteer Force (AVF). On one level, it is hard to argue with success. The formula of high quality volunteers, combined with intensive training and investment in state of the art equipment has produced by far the most formidable military in history. Evidence suggests that the military's performance, especially since 1990, has bolstered public trust and confidence. For example, a recent Gallup Poll of public opinion trends since the end of the Vietnam war in 1975

Reprinted by permission from Philosophy & Public Policy Quarterly *23 (Summer 2003).*

indicates that while the percentage of Americans expressing confidence in religious leaders fell from 68 to 45, and from 40 to 29 for Congress, the percentage expressing confidence in the military rose from under 30 to 78. Among 18 to 29 year olds, the confidence level rose from 20 to 64 percent. (Remarkably, these figures reflect sentiment in late 2002, *before* the impressive victory in Iraq.)

These gains in institutional performance and public confidence are impressive and significant, but they hardly end the discussion. As every reader of Machiavelli (or the Second Amendment) knows, the organization of the military is embedded in larger issues of citizenship and civic life. It is along these dimensions that the decision in favor of the AVF has entailed significant costs. First, the AVF reflects, and has contributed to the development of, what I call *optional citizenship*, the belief that being a citizen involves rights without responsibilities and that we need do for our country only what we choose to do. Numerous studies have documented the rise of individual choice as the dominant norm of contemporary American culture, and many young people today believe being a good person— decent, kind, caring, and tolerant—is all it takes to be a good citizen. This duty-free understanding of citizenship is comfortable and undemanding; it is also profoundly mistaken.

Second, the AVF contributes to what I call *spectatorial citizenship*—the premise that good citizens need not be active but can watch others doing the public's work on their behalf. This spectatorial outlook makes it possible to decouple the question of whether *we* as a nation should do X from the question of whether *I* would do or participate in X. In a discussion with his students during the Gulf War, philosophy professor Cheyney Ryan was struck by "how many of them saw no connection between whether the country should go to war and whether they would . . . be willing to fight in it." A similar disconnect exists today. Young adults have been more supportive of the war against Iraq than any other age group (with more than 70 percent in favor), but recent surveys have found an equal percentage would refuse to participate themselves.

As a counterweight to this decoupling, Ryan proposes what he calls the Principle of Personal Integrity: You should only endorse those military actions of your country in which you yourself would be wiling to give your life. The difficulty is that integrity does not seem to require this kind of personal involvement in other public issues. For example, a citizen of integrity can favor a costly reform of the welfare system without being required to serve as a welfare caseworker. Presumably it is enough if citizens are willing to contribute their fair share of the program's expenses. So one might ask: why is it not enough for citizens to contribute their fair share to maintain our expensive military establishment? Why should integrity require direct participation in the case of the military but not in other situations? This raises the question, to which I shall return, of when monetary contributions are morally acceptable substitutes for direct participation, and why.

Finally, the AVF has contributed to a widening gap between the orientation and experience of military personnel and that of the citizenry as a whole. To be sure, this is an empirically contested area, but some facts are not in dispute. First, since the inauguration of the AVF, the share of officers identifying themselves as Republican has nearly doubled, from 33 to 64 percent. (To be sure, officers were always technically volunteers, but as I can attest from personal experience, the threat of the draft significantly affected the willingness of young men to volunteer for officer candidacy.) Second, and more significantly, the share of elected officials with military experience has declined sharply. From 1900 through 1975, the percentage of members of Congress who were veterans was always higher than in the comparable age cohort of the general population. Since the mid-1990s, the congressional percentage has been lower, and it continues to fall.

Lack of military experience does not necessarily imply hostility to the military. Rather, it means ignorance of the nature of military service, as well as diminished capacity and confidence to assess critically the claims that military leaders make.

(It is no accident that of all the post-war presidents, Dwight Eisenhower was clearly the most capable of saying no to the military's strategic assessments and requests for additional resources.)

For these reasons, among others, I believe that as part of a reconsideration of the relation between mandatory service and citizenship, we should review and revise the decision we made thirty years ago to institute an all-volunteer armed force. I hasten to add that I do not favor reinstituting anything like the Vietnam-era draft. It is hard to see how a reasonable person could prefer that fatally flawed system to today's arrangements. The question, rather, is whether feasible reforms could preserve the gains of the past thirty years while enlisting the military more effectively in the cause of civic renewal.

An Abuse of State Power?

My suggestion faces a threshold objection, however, to the effect that any significant shift back toward a mandatory system of military manpower would represent an abuse of state power. In a recent article, Judge Richard Posner drafts nineteenth-century political theorist John Stuart Mill as an ally in the cause of classical liberalism—a theory of limited government that provides an "unobtrusive framework for private activities." Limited government so conceived, Posner asserts, "has no ideology, no 'projects,' but is really just an association for mutual protection." Posner celebrates the recent emergence of what he calls the "Millian center"—a form of politics that (unlike the left) embraces economic liberty and (unlike the right) endorses personal liberty, and he deplores modern communitarianism's critique of untrammeled personal liberty in the name of the common good. High on Posner's bill of particulars is the recommendation of some (not all) communitarians to reinstitute a draft.

Mill misapplied

Before engaging Posner's own argument, I should note that his attempt to appropriate Mill's

On Liberty to support an anti-conscription stance is deeply misguided. To clinch this point, I need only cite a few of the opening sentences from Chapter Four, entitled "Of the Limits to the Authority of Society Over the Individual":

> [E]veryone who receives the protection of society owes a return for the benefit, and the fact of living in society renders it indispensable that each should be bound to observe a certain line of conduct toward the rest. This conduct consists, first, in not injuring the interests of one another, or rather certain interests which, either by express legal provision or by tacit understanding, ought to be considered as rights; *and secondly, in each person's bearing his share (to be fixed on some equitable principle) of the labors and sacrifices incurred for defending the society or its members from injury and molestation. These conditions society is justified in enforcing at all costs to those who endeavor to withhold fulfillment.*

Posner's view of Mill would make sense only if Mill had never written the words I have italicized.

The fair share argument

It is not difficult to recast Mill's position in the vocabulary of contemporary liberal political thought. Begin with a conception of society as a system of cooperation for mutual advantage. Society is legitimate when the criterion of mutual advantage is broadly satisfied (versus, say, a situation in which the government or some group systematically coerces some for the sake of others). When society meets the standard of broad legitimacy, each citizen has a duty to do his or her fair share to sustain the social arrangements from which all benefit, and society is justified in using its coercive power when necessary to ensure the performance of this duty. That legitimate society coercion may include mandatory military service in the nation's defense.

A counterargument urged by the late political philosopher Robert Nozick is that we typically do not consent to the social benefits we receive and that the involuntary receipt of benefits does not trigger a duty to contribute. Mill anticipated, and rejected, that thesis, insisting that the duty to contribute does not rest on a social contract or voluntarist account of social membership. Besides, the argument Socrates imputes to the Laws in the *Crito* is a compelling one: if a society is not a prison, if as an adult you remain when you have the choice to leave, then you have in fact accepted the benefits, along with whatever burdens the principle of social reciprocity may impose.

Economist Robert Litan has recently suggested that citizens should be "required to give something to their country in exchange for the full range of rights to which citizenship entitles them." Responding in a quasi-libertarian vein, public policy expert Bruce Chapman charges that this proposal has "no moral justification." Linking rights to concrete responsibilities is "contrary to the purposes for which [the United States] was founded and has endured." This simply is not true. For example, the right to receive GI Bill benefits is linked to the fulfillment of military duties. Even the right to vote (and what could be more central to citizenship than that?) rests on law-abidingness; many states disenfranchise convicted felons for extended periods. As Litan points out, this linkage is hardly tyrannical moralism. Rather, it reflects the bedrock reality that "the rights we enjoy are not free" and that it takes real work—contributions from citizens—to sustain constitutional institutions.

Conscription as slavery

Now on to the main event. Posner contends that "Conscription could be described as a form of slavery, in the sense that a conscript is a person deprived of the ownership of his own labor." If slavery is immoral, so is the draft. In a similar vein, Nozick once contended that "taxation of earnings from labor is on a par with forced labor." (If Nozick were right, then the AVF that Posner supports, funded as it is with tax dollars, could also be described as on a par with forced labor.)

Both Posner's and Nozick's arguments prove too much. If each individual's ownership of his or her own labor is seen as absolute, then society as such becomes impossible, because no political community can operate without resources, which must ultimately come from *someone*. Public choice theory predicts, and all of human history proves, that no polity of any size can subsist through voluntary contributions alone; the inevitable free riders must be compelled by law, backed by force, to ante up.

Posner might object, reasonably enough, that this argument illustrates the difference between taxation and conscription: while political community is inconceivable without taxation, it is demonstrably sustainable without conscription. It is one thing to restrict self-ownership of labor out of necessity, but a very different matter to restrict it out of choice. The problem is that this argument proves too little. Posner concedes that "there are circumstances in which military service is an obligation of citizenship." But there are no circumstances in which slavery is an obligation of citizenship. Moreover, it is not morally impermissible to volunteer for military service. But it is impermissible, and rightly forbidden, to voluntarily place oneself in slavery. Therefore, slavery and military service differ in kind, not degree. And if there are circumstances in which military service is an obligation of citizenship, then the state is justified in enforcing that obligation through conscription, which is not impermissible forced labor, let alone a form of slavery. QED. For the purposes of this article, then, I will suppose that a legitimate government would not be exceeding its rightful authority if it chose to move toward a more mandatory system of military recruitment.

Celebrating the cash nexus: four thought experiments

But this is not the end of the argument, because Posner has another arrow in his quiver. He rejects the claim, advanced by Michael Sandel and other communitarians, that substituting market for non-market services represents a degrading "commodification" of social and civic life. Indeed,

Posner celebrates what communitarians deplore. "Commodification promotes prosperity," he informs us, "and prosperity alleviates social ills." Moreover, commodification enables individuals to transform burdensome obligations into bearable cash payments: middle-aged couples can purchase both care for their children and assisted living for their parents, and so forth.

Posner charges that communitarian theory is incapable of drawing a line between matters that rightly belong within the scope of the market and those that do not. Posner's celebration of the cash nexus is exposed to precisely the same objection. Rather than scoring rhetorical points, I will offer a series of examples designed to help delimit the proper sphere of non-market relations.

Paying people to obey the law. Suppose we offered individuals a "compliance bonus"—a cash payment at the end of each year completed without being convicted of a felony or significant misdemeanor. It is not hard to imagine situations in which the benefits of this policy (measured in reduced enforcement costs) would outweigh the outlays for bonuses. What (if anything) is wrong with this?

My answer: at least two things. First, it alters for the worse the expressive meaning of law. In a legitimate order, criminal law represents an authoritative declaration of the behavior the members of society expect of one another. The authoritativeness of the law is supposed to be a sufficient condition for obeying it and internalizing the sense of law as authoritative is supposed to be a sufficient motive for obedience. To offer compliance payments is to contradict the moral and motivation sufficiency of the law.

Second, payment for compliance constitutes a moral version of Gresham's law: lower motives will tend to drive out higher, and the more comfortable to drive out the more demanding. When those who are inclined to obey the law for its own sake see others receiving compensation, they are likely to question the reasonableness of their conduct and to begin thinking of themselves as suckers. Most would end up accepting payment

and coming to resemble more closely those who began by doing so.

Paying citizens for jury duty. Consider the analogy (or disanalogy) between national defense and domestic law enforcement. The latter is divided into two subcategories: voluntary service (there is no draft for police officers) and mandatory service (e.g., jury duty). Our current system of military manpower is all "police" and no "jury." If we conducted domestic law enforcement on our current military model we'd have what might be called "The All-Volunteer Jury," in which we'd pay enough to ensure a steady flow of the jurors the law enforcement system requires to function.

There are two compelling reasons not to move in this direction. First, citizens who self-select for jury duty are unlikely to be representative of the population as a whole. Individuals who incur high opportunity costs (those who are gainfully employed, for example) would tend not to show up. The same considerations that militate against forced exclusion of racial and ethnic groups from jury pools should weigh equally against voluntary self-exclusion based upon income or employment status. (We should ask ourselves why these considerations do not apply to the composition of the military.)

Second, it is important for all citizens to understand that citizenship is an *office*, not just a *status*. As an office, citizenship comprises matters of both rights and duties—indeed, some matters that are both. Service on juries is simultaneously a right, in the sense that that there is a strong presumption against exclusion, and a duty, in the sense that there is a strong presumption against evasion. To move jury duty into the category of voluntary, compensated acts would be to remove one of the last reminders that citizenship is more than a legal status.

Paying foreigners to do our fighting for us. Consider: we might do as well or better to hire foreigners (the All-Mercenary Armed Forces) as kings and princes did regularly during the eighteenth century. The cost might well be lower, and the military performance just as high. Besides, if we hire foreigners to pick our grapes, why not hire them to do our fighting?

There is of course a practical problem, discussed by Machiavelli among others: a pure cash nexus suggests the mercenaries' openness to opportunistic side-switching in response to a better offer, as happened in Afghanistan. In addition, what Abraham Lincoln called the "last full measure of devotion" would be less likely to be forthcoming in the handful of extreme situations in which it is required.

Beyond these practical considerations lies a moral intuition: even if a mercenary army were reliable and effective, it would be wrong, even shameful, to use our wealth to get non-citizens to do our fighting for us. This is something we ought to do for ourselves, as a self-respecting people. I want to suggest that a similar moral principle does some real work in the purely domestic sphere, among citizens.

Paying other citizens to do our fighting for us. Consider military recruitment during the Civil War. In April 1861 President Lincoln called for, and quickly received, 75,000 volunteers. But the expectation of a quick and easy Union victory was soon dashed, and the first conscription act was passed in March, 1863. The act contained two opt-out provisions: an individual facing conscription could pay a fee of $300 to avoid a specific draft notice; and an individual could avoid service for the entire war by paying a substitute to volunteer for three years.

This law created a complex pattern of individual incentives and unanticipated social outcomes, such as anti-conscription riots among urban workers. Setting these aside, was there anything wrong in principle with these opt-out provisions? I think so. In the first place, there was an obvious distributional unfairness: the well off could afford to avoid military service, while the poor and working class could not. Second, even if income and wealth had been more nearly equal, there would have been something wrong in principle with the idea that dollars could purchase exemption from an important civic duty.

The Legacy of the AVF: Economic and Social Stratification

We can now ask: What is the difference between the use of personal resources to opt *out* of military service and the impact of personal resources on the decision to opt *in*? My answer: as both a practical and a moral matter, less than the defenders of the current system would like to believe. To begin with, the decision to implement an AVF has had a profound effect on the educational and class composition of the U.S. military. During World War Two and the Korean War—indeed, through the early 1960s—roughly equal percentages of high school and college graduates saw military service, and about one third of college graduates were in the enlisted (that is, non-officer) ranks. Today, enlisted men and women are rarely college graduates, and elite colleges other than the service academies are far less likely to produce military personnel of any rank, officer or enlisted. As a lengthy *New York Times* feature story recently put it, today's military "mirrors a working-class America." Of the first twenty-eight soldiers to die in Iraq, only one came from a family that could be described as well off.

Many have argued that this income skew is a virtue, not a vice, because the military extends good career opportunities to young men and women whose prospects are otherwise limited. There is something to this argument, of course. But the current system purchases social mobility at the expense of social integration. Today's privileged young people tend to grow up hermetically sealed from the rest of society. Episodic volunteering in soup kitchens does not really break the seal. Military service is one of the few experiences that can.

In an evocative letter to his sons, Brookings Institution scholar Stephen Hess reflects on his experiences as a draftee and defends military service as a vital socializing experience for children from fortunate families. His argument is instructive: "Being forced to be the lowest rank . . ., serving for long enough that you can't clearly see 'the light at the end of the tunnel,' is as close as you will ever come to being a member of society's underclass. To put it bluntly, you will feel in your gut what it means to be at the bottom of the heap. . . . Why should you want to be deprived of your individuality? You shouldn't, of course. But many people are, and you should want to know how this feels, especially if you someday have some responsibility over the lives of other people." It is a matter, not just of compassion, but of respect: "The middle class draftee learns to appreciate a lot of talents (and the people who have them) that are not part of the lives you have known, and, after military duty, will know again for the rest of your lives. This will come from being thrown together with—and having to depend on—people who are very different from you and your friends."

A modern democracy, in short, combines a high level of legal equality with an equally high level of economic and social stratification. It is far from inevitable, or even natural, that democratic leaders who are drawn disproportionately from the upper ranks of society will adequately understand the experiences or respect the contributions of those from the lower. Integrative experiences are needed to bring this about. In a society in which economic class largely determines residence and education and in which the fortunate will not willingly associate with the rest, only non-voluntary institutions cutting across class lines can hope to provide such experiences. If some kind of sustained mandatory service does not fill this bill, it is hard to see what will.

The Importance of Universal Service

The inference I draw from this analysis is far from original: to the extent that circumstances permit, we should move toward a system of universal eighteen-month service for all high school graduates (and in the case of dropouts, all eighteen year olds) who are capable of performing it. Within the limits imposed by whatever ceiling is imposed on military manpower, those subject to this system would be able to choose between military and full-time civilian service. (If all military slots are filled, then some form of civilian service would be the only option.) The cost of fully implementing this proposal (a minimum of $60 billion per year) would certainly slow the pace of implementation and might well impose a permanent ceiling on the extent of implementation. The best response to these constraints would be a lottery to which all are exposed and from which none except those unfit to serve can escape.

It might be argued that a program of this sort would have little if any effect on the armed forces, which would continue to draw their manpower from the current stream of volunteers. That may be the case if the military does not expand during the next decade.

But there are reasons to believe that it will. It is fast becoming evident that the post-war occupation of Iraq will take more troops and last longer than administration officials had predicted. As an interim response, the military has already moved away from the all-volunteer principle. The U.S. Marine Corps has frozen enlistments for all of the 175,000 personnel currently on active duty. Marines whose period of voluntary enlistment has expired are required to remain in the service, on active duty, until the freeze expires. Other services have imposed similar if more limited freezes. It is likely, moreover, that the prospect of being sent to Iraq as part of a vulnerable long-term occupation force will depress voluntary enlistments, especially in the Army and Marines.

There is evidence suggesting that movement toward a less purely voluntary system of military and civilian service could pass the test of democratic legitimacy. For example, a 2002 survey sponsored by the Center for Information and Research on Civic Learning and Engagement (CIRCLE) found 60 percent-plus support for such a move across lines of gender, race and ethnicity, partisan affiliation, and ideology. Still, it is plausible that intense opposition on the part of young adults and their parents could stymie such a change. Assuming that this is the case, there are some feasible interim steps that could yield civic rewards. Let me mention just two.

First, we could follow the advice of former secretary of the navy John Lehman and eliminate the current bias of military recruiters in favor of career personnel and against those willing to serve for shorter periods. As Lehman puts it, we should "actively seek to attract the most talented from all backgrounds with service options that allow them to serve their country . . . without having to commit to six to ten years' active duty." He makes a strong case that this change would markedly increase the number of young men and women from elite colleges and universities who would be willing to undergo military service.

Second, the Congress could pass legislation sponsored by senators John McCain (R-AZ) and Evan Bayh (D-IN) that would dramatically expand AmeriCorps (the Clinton-era national and community service program) from its current level of 50,000 to 250,000 full-time volunteers each year. Survey evidence shows overwhelming (80 percent-plus) support for the basic tenet of this program, that young people should have the opportunity to serve full-time for a year or two and earn significant post-service benefits that can be used for higher education and advanced technical training. As Sen. McCain rightly puts it, "one of the curious truths of our era is that while opportunities to serve ourselves have exploded . . . opportunities to spend some time serving our country have dwindled." In this context, the ongoing resistance to AmeriCorps in some quarters of Congress verges on incomprehensible.

It would be wrong to oversell the civic benefits that might accrue from the revisions to the AVF that I propose, let alone the more modest steps I have just sketched. Still, some of our nation's best social scientists see a link between World War Two-era military service and that generation's subsequent dedication to our nation's civic life. If reconsidering a decision about military manpower made three decades ago could yield even a fraction of this civic improvement, it would be well worth the effort.

Review and Discussion Questions

1. Do you agree that Americans increasingly view citizenship as optional or spectatorial? If so, does this have bad consequences for our society? Critically assess the Principle of Personal Integrity.

2. Restate the conflicting views of Robert Litan and Bruce Chapman on the linkage between the rights and responsibilities of citizens. With whom do you agree, and why?

3. Is conscription a kind of slavery, as Richard Posner alleges? Is conscription an unjust violation of individual liberty, or is it simply one of the responsibilities of citizenship?

4. Examine each of Galston's four thought experiments. Do you agree with him that they would they be bad policies for us to adopt? Explain why or why not. Do his thought experiments support the case for conscription?

5. Do you agree with Galston that the Civil War system of conscription that allowed men who were drafted to pay a fee instead of serving or to hire someone to take their place was unfair? If so, is there a moral difference between that system and the AVF?

6. With the AVF, fewer college graduates and fewer young people from middle-class homes serve as enlisted personnel than in the past. Does this enhance class stratification or have other bad consequences for our society? Is it a problem we should do something about?

7. Do you favor Galston's universal service plan? Explain why or why not. Would either it or Galston's two interim steps be feasible? Political practicality aside, is conscription a good idea in principle? Would it make for a better society?

10

GUN CONTROL

The False Promise of Gun Control

DANIEL D. POLSBY

From the Second Amendment to images of violence in popular culture, guns have long been a noteworthy feature of American society and a significant aspect of its political and cultural history. Today, however, Americans are more worried about crime and gun-related violence than ever before, and many people advocate stricter regulation or even the outright prohibition of guns, especially handguns. But gun control is a controversial issue, which raises difficult sociological questions about the causes and control of crime as well as philosophical questions about the liberties, rights, and responsibilities of citizens.

Rejecting the proposition that firearms cause violence, Daniel D. Polsby, professor of law at Northwestern University, argues that gun-control laws do not work, that their effects are counterproductive, and that they divert attention from the roots of our crime problem. For certain people, criminal conduct is a rational occupational choice, and gun-control laws are unlikely to keep guns out of their hands. Given this and given the limits on what we can expect the police to do, citizens need firearms to protect themselves.

Study Questions

1. Unlike some other opponents of gun control, Polsby does not appeal to the Second Amendment. Explain why not.
2. What is the point of Polsby's discussion of the "demand curve" for guns? What evidence does he provide that firearms do not increase violence and crime?
3. What is the "futility theorem"? What practical problems would a prohibition on handguns face?
4. What does Polsby see as the "most important reason for criminal behavior"? Will more prisons and more police diminish the crime rate?

DURING THE 1960s and 1970s the robbery rate in the United States increased sixfold, and the murder rate doubled; the rate of handgun ownership nearly doubled in that period as well. Handguns and criminal violence grew together apace, and national opinion leaders did not fail to remark on the coincidence.

It has become a bipartisan article of faith that more handguns cause more violence. . . .

Alas, however well accepted, the conventional wisdom about guns and violence is mistaken. Guns don't increase national rates of crime and violence—but the continued proliferation of gun-control laws almost certainly does. Current rates of crime and violence are a bit below the peaks of the late 1970s, but because of a slight oncoming bulge in the at-risk population of males aged fifteen to thirty-four, the crime rate will soon worsen. The rising generation of criminals will have no more difficulty than their elders did in obtaining the tools of their trade. Growing violence will lead to calls for laws still more severe. Each fresh round of legislation will be followed by renewed frustration.

Gun-control laws don't work. What is worse, they act perversely. While legitimate users of firearms encounter intense regulation, scrutiny, and bureaucratic control, illicit markets easily adapt to whatever difficulties a free society throws in their way. Also, efforts to curtail the supply of firearms inflict collateral damage on freedom and privacy interests that have long been considered central to American public life. Thanks to the seemingly never-ending war on drugs and long experience attempting to suppress prostitution and pornography, we know a great deal about how illicit markets function and how costly the public attempts to control them can be. It is essential that we make use of this experience in coming to grips with gun control.

The thousands of gun-control laws in the United States are of two general types. The

older kind sought to regulate how, where, and by whom firearms could be carried. More recent laws have sought to make it more costly to buy, sell, or use firearms (or certain classes of firearms, such as assault rifles, Saturday-night specials, and so on) by imposing fees, special taxes, or surtaxes on them. The Brady bill is of both types: it has a background-check provision, and its five-day waiting period amounts to a "time tax" on acquiring handguns. All such laws can be called scarcity-inducing, because they seek to raise the cost of buying firearms, as figured in terms of money, time, nuisance, or stigmatization. . . .

Opponents of gun control have traditionally wrapped their arguments in the Second Amendment to the Constitution. Indeed, most modern scholarship affirms that so far as the drafters of the Bill of Rights were concerned, the right to bear arms was to be enjoyed by everyone, not just a militia, and that one of the principal justifications for an armed populace was to secure the tranquillity and good order of the community. But most people are not dedicated antiquarians, and would not be impressed by the argument "I admit that my behavior is very dangerous to public safety, but the Second Amendment says I have a right to do it anyway." That would be a case for repealing the Second Amendment, not respecting it.

Fighting the Demand Curve

Everyone knows that possessing a handgun makes it easier to intimidate, wound, or kill someone. But the implication of this point for social policy has not been so well understood. It is easy to count the bodies of those who have been killed or wounded with guns, but not easy to count the people who have avoided harm because they had access to weapons. Think about uniformed police officers, who carry handguns in plain view not in order to kill people but simply to daunt potential attackers. And it works. Criminals generally do not single out police officers for opportunistic attack. Though officers can expect to draw their guns from time to time, few even in big-city departments will actually fire a shot (except in target practice) in the course of a year. This observation points to an important truth: people who are armed make comparatively unattractive victims. A criminal might not know if any one civilian is armed, but if it becomes known that a large number of civilians do carry weapons, criminals will become warier. . . .

In order to predict who will comply with gun-control laws, we should remember that guns are economic goods that are traded in markets. Consumers' interest in them varies. For religious, moral, aesthetic, or practical reasons, some people would refuse to buy firearms at any price. Other people willingly pay very high prices for them.

Handguns, so often the subject of gun-control laws, are desirable for one purpose—to allow a person tactically to dominate a hostile transaction with another person. The value of a weapon to a given person is a function of two factors: how much he or she wants to dominate a confrontation if one occurs, and how likely it is that he or she will actually be in a situation calling for a gun.

Dominating a transaction simply means getting what one wants without being hurt. Where people differ is in how likely it is that they will be involved in a situation in which a gun will be valuable. Someone who *intends* to engage in a transaction involving a gun—a criminal, for example— is obviously in the best possible position to predict that likelihood. Criminals should therefore be willing to pay more for a weapon than most other people would. Professors, politicians, and newspaper editors are, as a group, at very low risk of being involved in such transactions, and they thus systematically underrate the value of defensive handguns. (Correlative, perhaps, is their uncritical readiness to accept studies that debunk the utility of firearms for self-defense.) The class of people we wish to deprive of guns, then, is the very class with the most inelastic demand for them—criminals—whereas the people most likely to comply

with gun-control laws don't value guns in the first place.

Do Guns Drive Up Crime Rates?

Which premise is true—that guns increase crime or that the fear of crime causes people to obtain guns? . . .

If firearms increased violence and crime, then rates of spousal homicide would have skyrocketed, because the stock of privately owned handguns has increased rapidly since the mid-1960s. But according to an authoritative study of spousal homicide in the *American Journal of Public Health,* by James Mercy and Linda Saltzman, rates of spousal homicide in the years 1976 to 1985 fell. If firearms increased violence and crime, the crime rate should have increased throughout the 1980s, while the national stock of privately owned handguns increased by more than a million units in every year of the decade. It did not. Nor should the rates of violence and crime in Switzerland, New Zealand, and Israel be as low as they are, since the number of firearms per civilian household is comparable to that in the United States. Conversely, gun-controlled Mexico and South Africa should be islands of peace instead of having murder rates more than twice as high as those here. The determinants of crime and law-abidingness are, of course, complex matters, which are not fully understood and certainly not explicable in terms of a country's laws. But gun-control enthusiasts, who have made capital out of the low murder rate in England, which is largely disarmed, simply ignore the counterexamples that don't fit their theory.

If firearms increased violence and crime, Florida's murder rate should not have been falling since the introduction, seven years ago, of a law that makes it easier for ordinary citizens to get permits to carry concealed handguns. Yet the murder rate has remained the same or fallen every year since the law was enacted, and it is now lower than the national murder rate (which has been rising). As of last November 183,561 permits had been issued, and only seventeen of the permits had been revoked because the holder was involved in a firearms offense. It would be precipitate to claim that the new law has "caused" the murder rate to subside. Yet here is a situation that doesn't fit the hypothesis that weapons increase violence.

If firearms increased violence and crime, programs of induced scarcity would suppress violence and crime. But—another anomaly—they don't. Why not? A theorem, which we could call the futility theorem, explains why gun-control laws must either be ineffectual or in the long term actually provoke more violence and crime. Any theorem depends on both observable fact and assumption. An assumption that can be made with confidence is that the higher the number of victims a criminal assumes to be armed, the higher will be the risk—the price—of assaulting them. By definition, gun-control laws should make weapons scarcer and thus more expensive. By our prior reasoning about demand among various types of consumers, after the laws are enacted criminals should be better armed, compared with noncriminals, than they were before. Of course, plenty of noncriminals will remain armed. But even if many noncriminals will pay as high a price as criminals will to obtain firearms, a larger number will not.

Criminals will thus still take the same gamble they already take in assaulting a victim who might or might not be armed. But they may appreciate that the laws have given them a freer field, and that crime still pays—pays even better, in fact, than before. What will happen to the rate of violence? Only a relatively few gun-mediated transactions—currently, five percent of armed robberies committed with firearms—result in someone's actually being shot (the statistics are not broken down into encounters between armed assailants and unarmed victims, and encounters in which both parties are armed). It seems reasonable to fear that if the number of such transactions were to increase because criminals thought they faced fewer deterrents, there would be a corresponding increase in shootings. Conversely, if

gun-mediated transactions declined—if criminals initiated fewer of them because they feared encountering an armed victim or an armed good Samaritan—the number of shootings would go down. The magnitude of these effects is, admittedly, uncertain. Yet it is hard to doubt the general tendency of a change in the law that imposes legal burdens on buying guns. The futility theorem suggests that gun-control laws, if effective at all, would unfavorably affect the rate of violent crime. . . .

Are there empirical studies that can serve to help us choose between the futility theorem and the hypothesis that guns increase violence? Unfortunately, no: the best studies of the effects of gun-control laws are quite inconclusive. Our statistical tools are too weak to allow us to identify an effect clearly enough to persuade an open-minded skeptic. But it is precisely when we are dealing with undetectable statistical effects that we have to be certain we are using the best models available of human behavior.

Sealing the Border

Handguns are not legally for sale in the city of Chicago, and have not been since April of 1982. Rifles, shotguns, and ammunition are available, but only to people who possess an Illinois Firearm Owner's Identification card. It takes up to a month to get this card, which involves a background check. Even if one has a FOID card there is a waiting period for the delivery of a gun. In few places in America is it as difficult to get a firearm legally as in the city of Chicago.

Yet there are hundreds of thousands of unregistered guns in the city, and new ones arriving all the time. It is not difficult to get handguns—even legally. Chicago residents with FOID cards merely go to gun shops in the suburbs. Trying to establish a city as an island of prohibition in a sea of legal firearms seems an impossible project.

Is a state large enough to be an effective island, then? Suppose Illinois adopted Chicago's handgun ban. Same problem again. Some people could just get guns elsewhere: Indiana actually borders the city, and Wisconsin is only forty miles away. . . .

Even if many states outlawed sales of handguns, then, they would continue to be available, albeit at a somewhat higher price, reflecting the increased legal risk of selling them. Mindful of the way markets work to undermine their efforts, gun-control proponents press for federal regulation of firearms, because they believe that only Congress wields the authority to frustrate the interstate movement of firearms.

Why, though, would one think that federal policing of illegal firearms would be better than local policing? The logic of that argument is far from clear. Cities, after all, are comparatively small places. Washington, D.C., for example, has an area of less than 45,000 acres. Yet local officers have had little luck repressing the illegal firearms trade there. Why should federal officers do any better watching the United States' 12,000 miles of coastline and millions of square miles of interior? Criminals should be able to frustrate federal police forces just as well as they can local ones. Ten years of increasingly stringent federal efforts to abate cocaine trafficking, for example, have not succeeded in raising the street price of the drug. . . .

In firearms regulation, translating theory into practice will continue to be difficult, at least if the objective is to lessen the practical availability of firearms to people who might abuse them. On the demand side, for defending oneself against predation there is no substitute for a firearm. Criminals, at least, can switch to varieties of law-breaking in which a gun confers little or no advantage (burglary, smash-and-grab), but people who are afraid of confrontations with criminals, whether rationally or (as an accountant might reckon it) irrationally, will be very highly motivated to acquire firearms. Long after the marijuana and cocaine wars of this century have been forgotten, people's demand for personal security and for the tools they believe provide it will remain strong.

On the supply side, firearms transactions can be consummated behind closed doors. Firearms buyers, unlike those who use drugs, pornography, or prostitution, need not recurrently expose themselves to legal jeopardy. One trip to the marketplace is enough to arm oneself for life. This could justify a consumer's taking even greater precautions to avoid apprehension, which would translate into even steeper enforcement costs for the police. . . .

Seeing that local firearms restrictions are easily defeated, gun-control proponents have latched onto national controls as a way of finally making gun control something more than a gesture. But the same forces that have defeated local regulation will defeat further national regulation. Imposing higher costs on weapons ownership will, of course, slow down the weapons trade to some extent. But planning to slow it down in such a way as to drive down crime and violence, or to prevent motivated purchasers from finding ample supplies of guns and ammunition, is an escape from reality. And like many another such, it entails a morning after.

Administering Prohibition

. . . Unless people are prepared to surrender their guns voluntarily, how can the U.S. government confiscate an appreciable fraction of our country's nearly 200 million privately owned firearms? We know that it is possible to set up weapons-free zones in certain locations—commercial airports and many courthouses and, lately, some troubled big-city high schools and housing projects. The sacrifices of privacy and convenience, and the costs of paying guards, have been thought worth the (perceived) gain in security. No doubt it would be possible, though it would probably not be easy, to make weapons-free zones of shopping centers, department stores, movie theaters, ball parks. But it is not obvious how one would cordon off the whole of an open society.

Voluntary programs have been ineffectual. From time to time community-action groups or police departments have sponsored "turn in your gun" days, which are nearly always disappointing.

Sometimes the government offers to buy guns at some price. . . . If the price offered exceeds that at which a gun can be bought on the street, one can expect to see plans of this kind yield some sort of harvest—as indeed they have. But it is implausible that these schemes will actually result in a less-dangerous population. Government programs to buy up surplus cheese cause more cheese to be produced without affecting the availability of cheese to people who want to buy it. So it is with guns.

One could extend the concept of intermittent roadblocks of the sort approved by the Supreme Court for discouraging drunk driving. Metal detectors could be positioned on every street corner, or ambulatory metal-detector squads could check people randomly, or hidden magnetometers could be installed around towns, to detect concealed weapons. As for firearms kept in homes (about half of American households), warrantless searches might be rationalized on the well-established theory that probable cause is not required when authorities are trying to correct dangers to public safety rather than searching for evidence of a crime. . . .

Ignoring the Ultimate Sources of Crime and Violence

The American experience with prohibition has been that black marketeers—often professional criminals—move in to profit when legal markets are closed down or disturbed. In order to combat them, new laws and law-enforcement techniques are developed, which are circumvented almost as soon as they are put in place. New and yet more stringent laws are enacted, and greater sacrifices of civil liberties and privacy demanded and submitted to. But in this case the problem, crime and violence, will not go away, because guns and ammunition (which, of course, won't go away either) do not cause it. One cannot expect people to quit seeking new weapons as long as the tactical advantages of

weapons are seen to outweigh the costs imposed by prohibition. Nor can one expect large numbers of people to surrender firearms they already own. The only way to make people give up their guns is to create a world in which guns are perceived as having little value. This world will come into being when criminals choose not to use guns because the penalties for being caught with them are too great, and when ordinary citizens don't think they need firearms because they aren't afraid of criminals anymore.

Neither of these eventualities seems very likely without substantial departures in law-enforcement policy. Politicians' nostrums—increasing the punishment for crime, slapping a few more death-penalty provisions into the code—are taken seriously by few students of the crime problem. The existing penalties for predatory crimes are quite severe enough. The problem is that they are rarely meted out in the real world. The penalties formally published by the code are in practice steeply discounted, and criminals recognize that the judicial and penal systems cannot function without bargaining in the vast majority of cases. . . .

The problem is not simply that criminals pay little attention to the punishments in the books. Nor is it even that they also know that for the majority of crimes, their chances of being arrested are small. The most important reason for criminal behavior is this: the income that offenders can earn in the world of crime, as compared with the world of work, all too often makes crime appear to be the better choice.

. . . More prisons means that fewer violent offenders will have to be released early in order to make space for new arrivals; perhaps fewer plea bargains will have to be struck—all to the good. Yet a moment's reflection should make clear that one more criminal locked up does not necessarily mean one less criminal on the street. The situation is very like one that conservationists and hunters have always understood. Populations of game animals readily recover from hunting seasons but not from loss of habitat. Mean streets, when there are few legitimate entry-level opportunities for young men, are a criminal habitat, so to speak, in the social ecology of modern American cities. Cull however much one will, the habitat will be reoccupied promptly after its previous occupant is sent away. So social science has found.

Similarly, whereas increasing the number of police officers cannot hurt, and may well increase people's subjective feelings of security, there is little evidence to suggest that doing so will diminish the rate of crime. . . .

Communities must, in short, organize more effectively to protect themselves against predators. No doubt this means encouraging properly qualified private citizens to possess and carry firearms legally. It is not morally tenable—nor, for that matter, is it even practical—to insist that police officers, few of whom are at a risk remotely as great as are the residents of many city neighborhoods, retain a monopoly on legal firearms. It is needless to fear giving honest men and women the training and equipment to make it possible for them to take back their own streets.

Over the long run, however, there is no substitute for addressing the root causes of crime—bad education and lack of job opportunities and the disintegration of families. Root causes are much out of fashion nowadays as explanations of criminal behavior, but fashionable or not, they are fundamental. *The root cause of crime is that for certain people, predation is a rational occupational choice.* Conventional crime-control measures, which by stiffening punishments or raising the probability of arrest aim to make crime pay less, cannot consistently affect the behavior of people who believe that their alternatives to crime will pay virtually nothing.

Young men who did not learn basic literacy and numeracy skills before dropping out of their wretched public schools may not [be] . . . worth hiring at the minimum wage. . . . Their legitimate opportunities, always precarious in a society where race and class still matter, often diminish to the point of being for all intents and purposes absent. . . .

The solution to the problem of crime lies in improving the chances of young men. Easier said than done, to be sure. No one has yet proposed a convincing program for checking all the dislocating forces that government assistance can set in motion. One relatively straightforward change would be reform of the educational system. Nothing guarantees prudent behavior like a sense of the future, and with average skills in reading, writing, and math, young people can realistically look forward to constructive employment and the straight life that steady work makes possible.

But firearms are nowhere near the root of the problem of violence. As long as people come in unlike sizes, shapes, ages, and temperaments, as long as they diverge in their taste for risk and their willingness and capacity to prey on other people or to defend themselves from predation, and above all as long as some people have little or nothing to lose by spending their lives in crime, dispositions to violence will persist.

This is what makes the case for the right to bear arms, not the Second Amendment. It is foolish to let anything ride on hopes for effective gun control. As long as crime pays as well as it does, we will have plenty of it, and honest folk must choose between being victims and defending themselves.

Review and Discussion Questions

1. Have you known anyone who has been threatened with a gun or affected in some way by gun-related violence?

2. Polsby argues that firearms do not increase violence and crime. Are you persuaded by his reasoning? Explain why or why not. Would restricting the ownership of handguns or even banning them altogether make us safer?

3. Assess Polsby's demand curve argument and the futility theorem. Would banning handguns be counterproductive, causing even more violent crime? What about other possible restrictions on handgun ownership?

4. Polsby's argument implies that we should encourage private citizens to arm themselves. Would this be a sensible idea?

5. Polsby believes that legal efforts to ban or restrict firearms are unrealistic and unworkable. Are you persuaded that such efforts can have no benefits? Is it impossible for gun-control laws to stem the flow of guns or do any good at all?

6. Polsby asserts that firearms are not the root cause of crime and violence. What is? Polsby suggests that an armed citizenry is the best prevention against crime and that "honest folk must choose between being victims and defending themselves [with guns]." Do you agree? Is he right that police and prisons can do little to control crime? Would crime be reduced if more citizens went armed?

Handguns and Violent Crime

NICHOLAS DIXON

In the previous essay, Daniel Polsby argued that gun-control laws are ineffective and that trying to ban or restrict handguns would be counterproductive. Nicholas Dixon disagrees. In this essay, he makes a utilitarian case for banning handguns. Basing his argument on international comparisons and on the correlation over recent decades between the number of handguns and the number of homicides in the United States, Dixon contends that a high rate of handgun ownership is one of the causes of our high rate of homicide and that banning handguns is likely to reduce the overall rate of violent crime. He criticizes the Brady Bill as inadequate and responds to both utilitarian and rights-based objections to a ban on handguns.

Study Questions

1. How does our rate of handgun ownership and handgun homicide compare with that of other countries? What do the statistics about handgun ownership in the U.S. over the years and the overall rate of homicide reveal?

2. How does Dixon respond to the objection that other factors besides the ownership of handguns affect the homicide rate? Why does he believe that a reduction in handgun ownership is likely to lower the overall rate of violent crime?

3. What does the Brady Bill require, and on what grounds does Dixon criticize it?

Reprinted from Nicholas Dixon, "Handguns, Violent Crime, and Self-Defense," The International Journal of Applied Philosophy, *Vol. 13:2 (Fall 1999), pp. 239–260 by permission of the Editor. Some notes omitted.*

4. What is "substitution theory" and what is Dixon's criticism of it? How does he respond to the argument that a ban on handguns would actually increase violent crime by denying peaceful citizens the use of handguns in self-defense?

5. How does Dixon respond to the argument that banning handguns would violate people's rights by restricting their freedom?

O VER THE LAST TWENTY YEARS, philosophers have written extensively on such public policy issues as abortion, euthanasia, and the death penalty. I believe that the debate over handgun control in the United States should be added to this list. My goal in this paper is twofold. First, I want to persuade applied ethicists that handgun control is worthy of their attention. Second, drawing in part on data and arguments that I have published elsewhere,[1] I will argue that an outright handgun ban is the best policy.

A. The Initial Case for Restricting Handguns

The following table compares handgun ownership and handgun homicide rates per 100,000 people in selected countries. The left-hand column is an estimate of handgun ownership rates in 1991, roughly the midpoint of the time span under investigation, based on FBI projections and on independent inquiries to the police departments in each country. The handgun homicide rates are calculated from data provided by Handgun Control, Inc., which obtained the information from each country's police department.[2]

The first stage of my argument is to contend that these data are most plausibly explained by a causal relationship between handgun ownership and handgun homicide rates. First, the method of concomitant variation supports this causal assertion, based on the perfect coincidence between the rank orderings in terms of handgun ownership and average handgun homicide rates.[3] Second, and more important, in view of the vast disparity between the United States and all of the other countries in terms of both handgun ownership and handgun homicide, the method of difference supports the claim that the United States' extremely high handgun ownership rate is a cause of its extremely high handgun homicide rate.[4] To complete this stage of my causal argument, and

	Handgun Ownership Per 100,000	Handgun Homicide Rate Per 100,000							
		1980	1983	1985	1988	1990	1992	1996	Average
U.S.A.	22,696	4.60	3.60	3.23	3.56	4.22	5.28	3.75	4.03
Israel	3,716	0.50	N/A	0.39	0.54	N/A	N/A	N/A	0.48
Sweden	3,700	0.22	0.08	N/A	0.23	0.16	0.43	N/A	0.22
Canada	2,301	0.03	0.02	0.02	0.03	0.26	0.50	0.41	0.18
Australia	1,596	0.02	0.06	0.03	0.07	0.06	0.08	0.08	0.06
U.K.	837	0.01	0.01	0.01	0.01	0.04	0.06	0.05	0.03

to minimize the likelihood that the correlations I cite are purely coincidental, I need a causal theory to explain how the causation that I assert works. My theory is based on common sense: Handguns are necessary for handgun homicides, so a higher ownership rate is likely to lead to a higher homicide rate. Simplistic though my causal theory is, I suggest that the correlations I have produced are so striking that the burden of proof is on those who would deny my causal argument.

I do not claim that the handgun ownership rate is the only determinant of homicide and other violent crimes committed with handguns. Two societies may have identical handgun ownership rates yet very different rates of violent crime, both with and without handguns. Economic and racial inequities, unemployment, and countless historical and cultural factors are doubtless also important causal factors. I claim only that the handgun ownership rate is one important determinant of handgun violence rates.

Opponents of handgun prohibition could concede that handgun ownership is causally connected with handgun homicide, while denying that it has any relationship with overall homicide rates. The vital second step in my causal argument, then, is showing that a reduction in handgun homicide and violence in the United States would reduce its overall rate of homicide and other violent crime. Note that I do not assert that a reduction in the handgun violence rate in other countries will substantially reduce their overall rate of violent crime. Handgun ownership and crime in most other countries is so low as to have a negligible impact on their overall crime rate.

I offer two arguments as to why a reduction in handgun violence in the United States will substantially decrease its overall level of violent crime. First, a huge number and a substantial percentage of its homicides and other violent crimes are committed with handguns. Since 1970, over 50% of homicides in this country have been committed with handguns, standing at 53% in 1997.[5] In

the United States in 1997, 39.7% of its 497,950 robberies and 20% of its 1,022,492 aggravated assaults involved firearms.[6] Handguns are used in over 80% of firearms-related robberies[7] and 86% of firearms-related aggravated assaults.[8] Second, because of their lethality, cheapness, ease of use, and small size (and hence ease of concealability), handguns are uniquely suited to homicide and other violent crimes. The importance of concealability of weapons for use in crime was reinforced by a study of crime weapons seized by the police done by the Bureau of Alcohol, Tobacco, and Firearms: "Seventy-one percent, or 7,538 of the handguns submitted for tracing, had a barrel length of 3 inches or less. Sixty-one percent, or 6,476, had a caliber of .32 or less. Since both of these factors relate to the size of the weapon, these figures indicate that concealability is an overriding factor in selecting a handgun for use in crime."[9]

The connection between handgun ownership and the overall homicide rate is further confirmed by a comparison of the number of handguns and the overall homicide rate in the United States in the last four decades.

	Number of Handguns	Handguns Per 100,000	Homicides Per 100,000
1950	12 million	7,931	4.6
1960	16 million	8,924	5.1
1970	27 million	13,281	7.8
1980	48 million	21,192	10.2
1990	66 million	26,358	9.4[10]

From 1950 until 1970, the increase in the handgun ownership rate was matched by a steady increase in the overall homicide rate. Since the early 1970s, the annual homicide rate has become relatively stable, deviating very little from the 8 to 10 per 100,000 range. The likely reason why the homicide rate has not risen appreciably since the early 1970s, even though the handgun ownership rate has continued to rise, is that the United States has become "saturated" with sufficient handguns to supply potential murderers.

I now summarize my main argument. First, the extremely high handgun ownership rate in the United States is a major cause of its high rate of homicides and other violent crimes committed with handguns. A reduction in its handgun ownership rate is therefore likely to reduce its rate of handgun violence. Second, because of the high percentage of violent crimes currently committed in the United States with handguns, and because of the special effectiveness of handguns in committing violent crimes, a reduction in the rate of handgun violence is likely to reduce its overall rate of violent crime. In the next section I argue that an outright ban on handguns is the only realistic way to effect such a reduction.[11]

B. Why the Brady Bill Doesn't Go Far Enough

Arguments such as the foregoing may have played a role in the final passage by Congress of a version of the Brady Bill at the end of 1993. The bill imposes a waiting period of a few days, during which a "background check" is conducted, before a handgun can be purchased. Those found to have criminal records or a history of mental illness will be denied legal access to handguns. It is a "targeted" ban, designed to keep handguns out of the hands of those who are allegedly most likely to abuse them. It is hailed as a compromise that will reduce handgun violence, while respecting law-abiding citizens' right to bear arms. In reality, the one benefit of the Brady Bill is that it may have moved this country slightly closer to considering meaningful handgun control. In itself, the Brady Bill is likely to have little effect in reducing handgun crime.

The only people whose legal access to handguns will be ended will be those who have been convicted of felonies and those with documented mental illness. While opponents of handgun prohibition point out that a high percentage of murders are committed by people with prior arrest records, they estimate that only 25% of murderers have felony convictions. Seventy-five percent of murderers, then, will be unaffected by the Brady Bill. Moreover, lawbreakers who have thus far eluded conviction will be untouched by the Bill, as will those who will buy handguns in order to begin a career of violent crime. This is to say nothing of previously law-abiding handgun owners who lose their temper and use the weapon to kill or maim after arguments.

The situation is even worse for supporters of the Brady Bill when we turn to illegal access to handguns. Its supporters are vulnerable to an objection often raised against a general handgun prohibition. The objection is that only law-abiding citizens are likely to obey a general handgun ban, while felons are likely to keep the handguns they already own, and have continued access to handguns by theft and illegal transfers. The result of a general handgun ban, then, is alleged to be the disarmament of peaceful citizens, while violent types will maintain or even increase their possession of handguns. However, this argument is more damaging as an objection to a targeted ban, such as the Brady Bill, than it is to my proposal for a general handgun ban.

This is because the bill will do nothing to restrict wrongdoers' access to handguns through the illegal channels that already exist: theft and illegal transfers. Felons will be able to get friends with "clean" records to "buy" for them, with no more difficulty than is currently experienced by teenagers in search of alcohol. Handgun "brokers" have already begun to legally purchase large amounts of handguns, which they then illegally sell on the streets to customers with criminal records. The Brady Bill will allow unlimited access (except a few days' wait) to unlimited numbers of handguns for the vast majority of people. Since on average well over two million new handguns have been made available for sale in the United States every year since 1980,[12] there is every reason to believe that the U.S. arsenal of privately owned handguns, which will remain subject to theft and illegal transfer, will continue to grow rapidly.

In contrast, the outright ban that I propose will immediately stem this influx of handguns, which is especially important in view of the fact that a disproportionate number of handgun crimes are committed with new handguns.[13] The pool of sixty-six million handguns already in private hands or available for sale can be gradually reduced by voluntary return by their owners, with the aid of amnesty and buyback schemes, and by police seizure of weapons from felons. Of course, a handgun ban will never be completely effective in removing all sixty-six million handguns from circulation, but "a handgun ban does not need to be perfectly effective to lead to a major decrease in handgun violence."[14]

The Brady Bill is inadequate, then, because it will allow continued legal access to handguns to the majority of future violent criminals, and because it will allow the pool of handguns available for theft and illegal transfer to grow ever larger.

C. Utilitarian Objections to Handgun Prohibition

I present my argument that a handgun ban will reduce violent crime in the United States as an empirical hypothesis supported by striking correlations between handgun ownership and handgun homicide rates, and by a simple, intuitively plausible causal theory. Replies thus far given to my argument for handgun prohibition make the elementary error of treating it and other arguments for prohibition as if they were advanced as deductively valid. These replies consist of thought experiments or conjectures showing how handgun prohibition may conceivably fail to reduce violent crime. While this is indeed sufficient to show that my argument is not deductively valid (a point that I readily concede), it does nothing to undermine my actual claim: Handgun

prohibition will probably reduce violent crime. To refute my actual claim, opponents need to show that it is probably false, not just that it may be false.

Both steps of my argument have been contested. I begin with the second step, in which I claim that a reduction in handgun violence in this country will reduce overall violent crime. The most common response is what I call "substitution theory": If handguns are banned, criminals will simply turn to even more lethal long guns and other weapons, with no net reduction in the amount of violent crime. Kates and Benenson argue that if only 30% of potential murderers were to "upgrade" to long guns (rifles and shotguns) in the event of a handgun ban, while the other 70% "downgraded" to knives, there would still be a "substantial increase" in homicide.[15] Based on the results of prisoner surveys, Gary Kleck asserts that an even higher rate of substitution of more lethal guns is likely to occur.[16]

The problem with these arguments for substitution theory is the flimsy nature of their empirical support. First, the responses of prisoners to surveys scarcely establish Kleck's intuitively implausible prediction of widespread use of bulky, long guns in crime. Second, Kates and Benenson calculated their 30% "threshold" (which is widely cited in the anti–gun control literature) by comparing the relative lethality of long gun and handgun wounds, without considering the fact that it is far easier to inflict wounds in the first place with small, concealable handguns. Given the fact that substitution theory is advanced by opponents of handgun prohibition in order to deny the intuitively plausible view that a reduction in handgun violence will result in a reduction in overall violence, the burden of proof is on its proponents to provide much better support for it. The weakness of substitution theory is especially damaging for those opponents of handgun prohibition who concede that a ban would reduce the level of handgun violence.

Further presumptive evidence against substitution theory is provided by the fact that the

U.S. overall homicide rate is substantially higher than that of the comparison countries. In fact, it is higher, in most cases by several hundred percent, than that of all the other seventeen countries in a recent study. If substitution of other, more lethal weapons were likely to occur in the United States, then we would expect these other countries with low handgun ownership rates to have high non-handgun homicide rates to "compensate" for their low handgun homicide rates; but they do not.

I turn next to the first stage of my argument, in which I claim that a handgun ban would reduce the amount of handgun violence in the United States. The usual strategy of opponents is to argue that the extremely high rate of handgun violence in the United States is attributable to factors unrelated to its high handgun ownership rate. The weakness of most such arguments is that they give little or no analysis of these alleged factors. The unsupported assertion that there may be causes of handgun violence unrelated to handgun ownership rates fails for two reasons to undercut my argument. First, as explained above, showing the bare logical possibility that my causal hypothesis is false does nothing to undercut it. Second, since I claim only that the high handgun ownership rate is one of the causes of our rampant handgun violence rate, the existence of other causes in no way weakens my argument. If anything, the existence of multiple causes of handgun violence makes the striking international correlation between ownership and homicide rates even harder to dismiss as a coincidence. . . .

The strongest objection to handgun prohibition is the claim that it would cause an increase in violent crime by denying peaceful citizens the use of handguns in defense of self and property. Any benefits of a handgun ban have to be weighed against a possible reduction in the defensive use of handguns.

The first weakness of this objection is once again the flimsy nature of the empirical evidence adduced in its support. The sole evidence for the effectiveness and the frequency of the defensive

uses of handguns is provided by highly suspect surveys of prisoners and gun owners, and a conjecture that the number of justified self-defensive homicides is underreported by the FBI. Second, the argument that the use of handguns in self-defense causes a net decrease in violent crime is further weakened by the fact that a substantial percentage of the very violent crimes that handgun ownership is supposed to prevent are themselves committed with handguns. Rather than acquiescing in an endless spiral of increasingly heavily armed aggressors and victims, we would do better to strive for a society in which neither aggressors nor victims have handguns. Third, underlying the self-defense argument against handgun prohibition may be the fear that it would leave ordinary law-abiding citizens helpless against gun-wielding predators. In reality, however, this distinction between peaceful handgun owners and predators is suspect. Even a handgun purchased for purely defensive purposes may be used offensively, since we are all capable of heated arguments that can easily turn lethal when a handgun is available. In about one half of all murders, the victim is a relative or acquaintance of the murderer, and about one third of murders result from arguments, which are hardly circumstances that apply only to predators. A recent study directly supports my claim that the risk of offensive abuses of handguns outweighs their defensive utility: "Despite the widely held belief that guns are effective for protection, our results suggest that they actually pose a substantial threat to members of the household."[17]

The comparative international data cited above also counts against the hypothesis that handgun ownership reduces violence because of the defensive use of handguns. The more handguns that are owned in a given country, we may assume, the more times they will be used defensively and, according to the hypothesis we are considering, the less violent crimes will occur. But the data indicates the direct opposite: the higher the handgun ownership rate, the higher the handgun homicide rate. In particular, the United States,

which far outstrips its rivals in handgun ownership, is also the clear leader in terms of both the
handgun and overall homicide rate. . . .

D. Utilitarianism, Handgun Prohibition, and Individual Rights

The objections discussed in the previous section
did not challenge the utilitarian framework in
which my argument is expressed, and I need to
pause to consider rights-based objections to
handgun prohibition. The U.S. legal system does
not regard the prevention of violence as an
absolute value. We provide defendants with an
extensive array of rights, with the result that some
people are acquitted even though they committed the violent act of which they are accused. This
indicates that we regard protecting individual
rights as an important constraint on the utilitarian goal of reducing violent crime. How do these
objections affect my utilitarian argument for banning handguns?

A general defense of utilitarianism is both
beyond the scope of a paper in applied ethics and
unnecessary in order to defend my proposal. My
strategy in responding to these objections will be
to show that handgun prohibition does not violate individual moral rights, so that the overwhelming utilitarian arguments for prohibition
prevail.

Handgun prohibition undeniably restricts
people's freedom. They are prevented from
owning handguns, which they may desire for
target shooting, collectors' items, or self-defense.
However, the right to life and bodily integrity of
innocent victims of handgun violence—which, if
my main thesis is sound, are constantly endangered by the prevalence of handguns—is arguably
far stronger than any rights that are allegedly violated by banning handguns. Gun collectors would
remain free to own other types of firearms, and
handguns would still be available for enthusiasts
at government-run shooting ranges. The most
substantial freedom that would be curtailed by my

proposal, and the one to which I devote the rest
of this section, is the use of handguns in self-
defense; but my arguments in the last section
showed that defensive uses of handguns are heavily outweighed by offensive abuses. Of what
moral force is an alleged right to defend ourselves
with handguns if (1) exercising this "right"
endangers rather than protects gun owners, and
(2) the widespread handgun ownership necessary
for the exercise of this freedom causes the death
or wounding of thousands of innocent people,
violating their unquestioned right to life and
bodily integrity?

Now opponents of prohibition could adopt
an "absolutist" stance, and insist that central to
the very meaning of the concept of a right is that
it cannot be "trumped" by rival moral considerations. According to this view, my right to defend
myself with a handgun is inviolable, regardless of
the pernicious consequences that my exercise of
this right may have for the rest of society (and,
indeed, for myself). However, the implausibility
of such an absolutist approach is glaring.

First, we cannot sidestep conflicts of rights by
simply declaring one of the rival rights to be
absolute. For instance, we cannot solve the abortion debate by a fiat that the fetus's (or the pregnant woman's) rights are inviolable. Instead,
arguments are needed to explain why one right
takes precedence over another. Thus opponents
of handgun prohibition need to explain exactly
why my right to defend myself with a handgun
outweighs the rights of innocent victims of the
violent crimes that occur as a result of widespread
ownership of handguns.

Second, while my right to defend myself
against harm arguably is absolute, in the sense
that I may always respond to aggression, it is not
unconditional. . . . The right to use violence in
self-defense is qualified by such requirements as
necessity and proportionality. The general right
to self-defense does not entail the right to use
any particular method that I happen to desire.
Thus arguments, and not just a bare assertion, are
needed to support the claim that we have a right

to use handguns in self-defense. The view that enshrines the use of handguns in self-defense as a right simply because some people desire to do so—i.e., that the right to self-defense is unlimited—is easily reduced to absurdity. Paranoid anti-government survivalist militias doubtless believe that possessing huge arsenals of automatic weapons and explosives (and quite likely, if they could get their hands on them, nuclear weapons) is necessary to protect themselves against the constant threat of governmental tyranny. Unless we are willing to accept the consequence that militia members would indeed have the right to own such weaponry, we need a more substantial argument for the right to own handguns for defensive purposes than the mere fact that some people desire to do so. . . .

Handgun prohibition is based on the least controversial ground for restricting freedom: preventing harm to others. Even the most innocuous laws—for instance, those prohibiting people from driving at speeds over 100 mph, privately owning anti-tank weapons or nuclear warheads, or making child pornography—restrict people's freedom, on the ground that these activities pose an unacceptable risk or certainty of harm to others. These familiar examples show that, just as we do not regard preventing harm to others as an absolute value, and are prepared to tolerate some such harm in order to preserve individual rights, neither do we regard protecting individual freedom as sacrosanct. We restrict freedom without violating rights when doing so will prevent substantial harm to others, while imposing minimal restraints on people's behavior. Handgun prohibition falls well within this familiar rationale. . . .

E. Conclusion: Is Handgun Prohibition Realistic?

The most common response that I have encountered to my proposal to ban handguns is that it is too "idealistic." Those who give this response may grant my contention that eradicating hand-

guns would reduce violent crime without violating individual rights, but they insist that handgun prohibition is not a practical goal in the United States. Underlying this skepticism is the belief that we cannot realistically expect the U.S. Congress to pass legislation to ban handguns, and that, even if such a ban were passed, it would be unenforceable.

I have already addressed the issue of enforceability above in section B. While no legislation will ever completely rid the country of handguns, a federal ban would immediately halt the current legal sale of over two million new handguns per year, while voluntary buyback programs and the seizure of weapons used in crime will gradually reduce the arsenal of handguns in private hands. And this reduction will, in turn, reduce the level of violent crime.

As for whether handgun prohibition legislation could be enacted in the first place, the recent passage of precisely such a measure in the United Kingdom, in response to the Dunblaine massacre, shows that it can actually be done. The only way to maintain the view that handgun prohibition is impossible to enact in the United States is to insist that the socio-political realities unique to this country make it so. These realities include the powerful influence of the gun lobby in Congress, the long tradition of gun ownership, and the fervent belief held by a significant minority that owning a handgun is necessary for self-protection.

Little doubt exists that such factors do indeed make the passage of a handgun ban in the United States currently unattainable. However, to count this as a refutation of my position is to adopt a truly disturbing view about the role of applied ethics. We surely need to distinguish between prescribing what we should do—this is the appropriate role for applied ethicists—and, on the other hand, predicting what Congress actually will do, which falls instead into the province of political science. The question of what we should do is prior to the question of what is currently attainable. Compromise and accommodation to practical realities should only be discussed after we have first determined what would be the fair and just thing to do.

NOTES

1. Nicholas Dixon, "Why We Should Ban Handguns in the United States," *Saint Louis University Public Law Review* 12:2 (1993), pp. 243–283; and "Perilous Protection: A Reply to Kopel," *Ibid,* pp. 361–391.

2. For more detail on the derivation of many of these statistics, see Nicholas Dixon, "Why We Should Ban Handguns in the United States," pp. 248–250, and "Perilous Protection: A Reply to Kopel," pp. 372–373.

3. When the amount or rate of the effect E (in this case, handgun homicide) varies according to the amount or rate of antecedent factor X (handgun ownership), the method of concomitant variation indicates that X is probably a cause of E.

4. When the effect E (in this case, an extremely high handgun homicide rate) occurs in the presence of antecedent factor X (an extremely high handgun ownership rate) but not in its absence, the method of difference indicates that X is probably a cause of E.

5. *Uniform Crime Reports for the United States 1970–97* (Washington, D.C.: Federal Bureau of Investigations, U.S. Department of Justice, 1971–98).

6. *Uniform Crime Reports* 1997, pp. 31, 34.

7. Franklin E. Zimring, "Firearms, Violence and Public Policy," *Scientific American,* November 1991, p. 50.

8. This statistic, which comes from 1967, is cited by Franklin E. Zimring and Gordon Hawkins, *The Citizen's Guide to Gun Control* (New York: Macmillan, 1987), p. 38.

9. "Project Identification: A Study of Handguns Used in Crime" (Department of Treasury, May 1976), p. 2.

10. Handgun ownership numbers are based on the Bureau of Alcohol, Tobacco, and Firearms data on the number of handguns available for sale in the United States since 1899. See "Civilian Firearms—Domestic Production, Importation, Exportation, and Availability for Sale," BATF document, 1991. Overall United States homicide rates are taken from *Uniform Crime Reports,* 1950, 1960, 1970, 1980, and 1990.

11. For detail on the exceptions I propose to handgun prohibition, see "Why We Should Ban Handguns," pp. 244–247.

12. "Civilian Firearms—Domestic Production, Importation, Exportation, and Availability for Sale," BATF document.

13. Studies have shown that over half the handguns used in crime were first purchased from retailers within five years of the crime. See Zimring and Hawkins, *The Citizen's Guide to Gun Control,* pp. 39–41. See also Robert J. Spitzer, *The Politics of Gun Control* (Chatham, NJ: Chatham House Publishers, Inc., 1995), p. 80.

14. Nicholas Dixon, "Perilous Protection: A Reply to Kopel," p. 379.

15. See, e.g., Don B. Kates, Jr. and Mark K. Benenson, "Handgun Prohibition and Homicide: A Plausible Theory Meets the Intractable Facts," in Kates (ed.), *Restricting Handguns: The Liberal Skeptics Speak Out* (North River Press, 1979), p. 111.

16. Kleck, "Policy Lessons from Recent Gun Control Research," *Law and Contemporary Problems* 49.

17. Arthur Kellermann et al, "Gun Ownership as a Risk Factor for Homicide in the Home," *New England Journal of Medicine* 329:15 (1993), p. 1090.

Review and Discussion Questions

1. How persuasive do you find the statistics that Dixon presents? Do they establish a strong case for restricting handguns? How important a cause of our high rate of violent crime is handgun ownership?

2. Dixon believes that handguns increase homicide and violent crime. Daniel Polsby argues the opposite. Compare and assess their reasoning. Who is right? What evidence would it take to settle this issue?

3. Would reducing the number of handguns or restricting their availability reduce the amount of violent crime and make us safer? Which would be best—a complete ban on handguns, tighter restrictions without a general ban, or no restrictions at all?

4. Assess the argument that handguns reduce crime by enabling citizens to defend themselves. What about the argument that, if handguns are banned, then criminals will simply use other weapons, with results that are just as bad?

5. The Second Amendment states: "A well regulated Militia, being necessary to the security of a free State, the right of the people to keep and bear Arms, shall not be infringed." Do individuals have either a moral or political right to own handguns?

6. Dixon believes that a handgun ban is a defensible restriction of people's liberty. Do you agree? Assess the banning of handguns from the perspective of Mill's *On Liberty*.

7. Do proponents of gun control like Dixon and opponents like Polsby disagree only about certain factual matters or are there philosophical or ethical differences between them?

Is There a Right to Own a Gun?

MICHAEL HUEMER

In the previous essay, Nicholas Dixon rejected the idea that prohibiting handguns would wrongly infringe the rights of citizens. Michael Huemer, professor of philosophy at the University of Colorado, Boulder, challenges this. He contends that individuals have a right to own firearms, that this is a weighty right, which protects important interests, and that it is not overridden by utilitarian considerations of the sort advanced by Dixon. After some preliminary remarks about the nature of rights, Huemer argues not only that individuals have a right to own guns but also that the recreational value of guns and the importance of the right of self-defense make this right an important one. Violations of it are serious, and very strong reasons would be needed to override it. In particular, the advantages of banning guns would have to be much greater than the costs of doing so in order to outweigh this right. In fact, Huemer maintains, the evidence runs the other way: The benefits of private gun ownership overshadow the harms.

Study Questions

1. We normally have a right to do as we wish unless there is a reason why we should not be allowed to do so. Huemer gives three examples of such reasons. What are they?

2. What's the difference between a fundamental and a derivative right? Between an absolute and a prima facie right? What three factors affect the weight of a right?

3. Huemer believes there is a prima facie right to own a gun. For what two reasons is this right a significant right?

4. How does Huemer respond to the argument, based on international comparisons, that the high homicide rate in the United States is due to its high rate of gun ownership?

5. What does Huemer see as the major benefits of gun ownership?

Reprinted by permission from Social Theory and Practice, *vol. 29, no. 4 (April 2003). Copyright © 2003 by Social Theory and Practice. Most notes omitted.*

1. Introduction

Gun control supporters often assume that the acceptability of gun control laws turns on whether they increase or decrease crime rates. The notion that such laws might violate rights, independently of whether they decrease crime rates, is rarely entertained. Nor are the interests of gun owners in keeping and using guns typically given great weight. Thus, a colleague who teaches about the issue once remarked to me that from the standpoint of rights, as opposed to utilitarian considerations, there wasn't much to say. The only right that might be at stake, he said, was "a trivial right—'the right to own a gun'." Similarly, Nicholas Dixon has characterized his own proposed ban on all handguns as "a minor restriction," and the interests of gun owners in retaining their weapons as "trivial" compared to the dangers of guns.[1]

I believe these attitudes are misguided. I contend that individuals have a prima facie right to own firearms, that this right is weighty and protects important interests, and that it is not overridden by utilitarian considerations. In support of the last point, I shall argue that the harms of private gun ownership are probably less than the benefits, and that in any case, these harms would have to be many times greater than the benefits in order for the right to own a gun to be overridden.

2. Preliminary Remarks about Rights

2.1. Assumptions about the nature of rights

I begin with some general remarks about the moral framework that I presuppose. I assume that individuals have at least some moral rights that are logically prior to the laws enacted by the state, and that these rights place restrictions on what sort of laws ought to be made. I assume that we may appeal to intuitions to identify some of these rights. An example is the right to be free from physical violence: intuitively, it is, ceteris paribus, wrong for people to do violence to one another, and this limits what sort of laws may, morally, be made. . . .

I further assume that we normally have a right to do as we wish unless there is a reason why we should not be allowed to do so—and hence that someone who denies our right to act in a particular way has the dialectical burden to provide reasons against the existence of the right in question. In contrast, one who asserts a right need only respond to these alleged reasons.

What sort of reasons would show that we have no right to engage in a particular activity? Consider three relevant possibilities:

(i) Plausibly, we lack even a prima facie right to engage in activities that harm others, treat others as mere means, or use others without their consent. Thus, I have no claim at all (as opposed to having a claim that is outweighed by competing claims) to be allowed to beat up or rob other people.

(ii) Perhaps we lack a prima facie right to engage in activities that, even unintentionally, impose high *risks* on others, even if those risks do not eventuate. If my favorite form of recreation involves shooting my gun off in random directions in the neighborhood, even if I am not trying to hit anyone, my would-be right to entertain myself is at least overridden, but perhaps wholly erased, because of the danger to others.

(iii) Perhaps we lack a prima facie right to engage in activities that *reasonably appear* to evince an intention to harm or impose unacceptable risks on others. For example, I may not run towards you brandishing a sword, even if I do not in fact intend to hurt you. The principle also explains why we punish people for merely *attempting* or *conspiring* to commit crimes.

There may be other sorts of reasons for excepting an activity from the presumption in favor of liberty. The above list, however, seems to exhaust the reasons that might be relevant to the existence of a right to own a gun. I assume, in particular, that the following sort of consideration would *not* suffice to reject a prima facie right to do *A*: that a modest statistical correlation exists between doing *A* and engaging in other, wrongful activities.[2] Thus, suppose that people who read the *Communist Manifesto* are slightly more likely than the average person to attempt the violent overthrow of the government. . . . I take it that this would not show that there is no prima facie right to read the *Communist Manifesto*. . . .

2.2. What sort of right is the right to own a gun?

First, I distinguish between *fundamental* and *derivative* rights. A right is derivative when it derives at least some of its weight from its relationship to another, independent right. A right is fundamental when it has some force that is independent of other rights. On these definitions, it is possible for a right to be both fundamental and derivative. Derivative rights are usually related to fundamental rights as means to the protection or enforcement of the latter, though this need not be the only way in which a right may be derivative. I claim that the right to own a gun is both fundamental and derivative; however, it is in its *derivative* aspect—as derived from the right of self-defense—that it is most important.

Second, I distinguish between *absolute* and *prima facie* rights. An absolute right is one with overriding importance, such that no considerations can justify violating it. A prima facie right is one that must be given some weight in moral deliberation but that can be overridden by sufficiently important countervailing considerations. Thus, if it would be permissible to steal for sufficiently important reasons—say, to save someone's life—then property rights are not absolute but at most prima facie. It is doubtful whether any rights are absolute. At any rate, I do not propose any absolute rights; I argue only that there is a strong prima facie right to own a gun. . . .

2.3. Weighing rights

The more *weight* a right has, the more serious its violation is and the more difficult it is to override

the right. I assume three broad principles about the weighing of rights.

First: Ceteris paribus, the weight of a fundamental right increases with the importance of the right to an individual's plans for his own life or other purposes. This is not to say that every action that interferes with an individual's aims is a rights violation, but only that *if* an action violates rights, it does so more seriously as it interferes more with the victim's aims. . . .

Second: In the case of a derivative right, the seriousness of its violation is proportional to the importance of the other right that it subserves. Thus, a derivative right that functions to protect the right to life is more important, other things being equal, than one that protects the right to property.

Third: The seriousness of a violation of a derivative right also depends upon how important the derivative right is to the other right that it subserves. For example, censorship of books criticizing the government would be a more serious violation of free speech than censorship of pornographic material, because the ability to publish political criticism is more important to protecting other rights than the ability to publish pornography. . . .

3. Is There a Prima Facie Right to Own a Gun?

Given the presumption in favor of liberty, there is at least a prima facie right to own a gun, unless there are positive grounds of the sort discussed in §2.1 for denying such a right. . . .

It is difficult to deny the existence of at least a *prima facie* right to own a gun. But this says nothing about the *strength* of this right, nor about the grounds there may be for overriding it. Most gun control advocates would claim, not that there is not even a prima facie right to own a gun, but that the right is a minor one, and that the harms of private gun ownership, in comparison, are very large.

4. Is the Right to Own a Gun Significant?

I shall confine my consideration of gun control to the proposal to ban all private firearms ownership. This would violate the prima facie right to own a gun. I contend that the rights violation would be very serious, owing both to the importance of gun ownership in the lives of firearms enthusiasts, and to the relationship between the right to own a gun and the right of self-defense.

4.1. The recreational value of guns

The recreational uses of guns include target shooting, various sorts of shooting competitions, and hunting. In debates over gun control, participants almost never attach any weight to this recreational value—perhaps because that value initially appears minor compared with the deaths caused or prevented by guns. The insistence that individuals have a right to engage in their chosen forms of recreation may seem frivolous in this context. But it is not. . . .

4.2. The right of self-defense

The main argument on the gun rights side goes like this:

1. The right of self-defense is an important right.
2. A firearms prohibition would be a significant violation of the right of self-defense.
3. Therefore, a firearms prohibition would be a serious rights violation.

The strength of the conclusion depends upon the strength of the premises: the more important the right of self-defense is, and the more serious gun control is as a violation of that right, the more serious a rights violation gun control is.

I begin by arguing that the right of self-defense is extremely weighty. Consider this scenario:

Example 1: A killer breaks into a house, where two people—"the victim" and "the accom-

plice"—are staying. (The "accomplice" need have no prior interaction with the killer.) As the killer enters the bedroom where the victim is hiding, the accomplice enters through another door and proceeds, for some reason, to hold the victim down while the killer stabs him to death.

In this scenario, the killer commits what may be the most serious kind of rights violation possible. What about the accomplice who holds the victim down? Most would agree that his crime is, if not equivalent to murder, something close to murder in degree of wrongness, even though he neither kills nor injures the victim. Considered merely as the act of holding someone down for a few moments, the accomplice's action seems a minor rights violation. What makes it so wrong is that it prevents the victim from either defending himself or fleeing from the killer—that is, it violates the right of self-defense. (To intentionally and forcibly prevent a person from exercising a right is to violate that right.) We may also say that the accomplice's crime was that of assisting in the commission of a murder—this is not, in my view, a competing explanation of the wrongness of his action, but rather an elaboration on the first explanation. Since the right of self-defense is a derivative right, serving to protect the right to life among other rights, violations of the right of self-defense will often cause or enable violations of the right to life. . . .

We turn to premise 2, that gun prohibition is serious as a violation of the right of self-defense. Consider:

Example 2: As in example 1, except that the victim has a gun by the bed, which he would, if able, use to defend himself from the killer. As the killer enters the bedroom, the victim reaches for the gun. The accomplice grabs the gun and runs away, with the result that the killer then stabs his victim to death.

The accomplice's action in this case seems morally comparable to his action in example 1. Again, he has intentionally prevented the victim from defending himself, thereby in effect assisting in the murder. The arguments from the criteria for the seriousness of rights violations are the same.

The analogy between the accomplice's action in this case and a general firearms prohibition should be clear. A firearms ban would require confiscating the weapons that many individuals keep for self-defense purposes, with the result that some of those individuals would be murdered, robbed, raped, or seriously injured. If the accomplice's action in example 2 is a major violation of the right of self-defense, then gun prohibition seems to be about equally serious as a violation of the right of self-defense. . . .

5. Are Gun Rights Overridden?

I have argued that there is a strong prima facie right to own a gun. Nevertheless, firearms prohibition might be justified, if the reasons for prohibition were strong enough to override that right. To determine whether this is the case, we consider three questions: First, how great are the harms of private gun ownership? Second, how great are the benefits? Third, what must be cost/benefit ratio be like, for the right to own a gun to be overridden? I shall argue, first, that the harms of private gun ownership have been greatly exaggerated; second, that the benefits of private gun ownership are large and in fact greater than the harms; and third, that the harms would have to be many times greater than the benefits in order to override the right to own a gun.

There is a vast empirical literature concerning the effects of gun ownership and gun control. Here we can only overview a few of the most prominent arguments deriving from that literature.

5.1. The case against guns

. . . [One] type of argument often used by gun-control proponents relies on comparisons of homicide rates between the United States and other industrialized democracies, such as Canada, Great Britain, Sweden, and Australia. The United States is found to have vastly higher homicide rates, and it is argued that this is due largely to the high gun-ownership rates in the U.S.

Skeptics suggest that the United States has a number of unique cultural factors that influence the murder rate and that invalidate such cross-country comparisons. Some find this claim more plausible than do others. Fortunately, we need not rely on intuitions. Instead, we can test the claim empirically, by examining data within the United States, across jurisdictions with varying gun laws and gun ownership rates and over time periods with changing gun laws and gun ownership rates—this would effectively control for the cultural factors allegedly affecting the murder rate. When we do this, we find that (i) jurisdictions with stricter gun laws tend to have higher crime rates, (ii) shifts to more permissive gun laws tend to be followed by drops in crime rates, (iii) areas with higher gun ownership rates have lower crime rates, and (iv) historically, crime rates have fluctuated with no discernible pattern as the civilian gun stock has increased drastically.

I do not claim to have *proved* that gun laws cause increased crime or that civilian gun ownership fails to do so. Nor do I deny that there is any evidence on the gun control advocates' side. What I am claiming at this point is that the evidence presented by gun control advocates fails to make a very convincing case for the net harmfulness of private gun ownership. The casual comparisons between countries discussed here typically use only a handful of data points, exclude many countries from consideration, and make no attempt to control statistically for any other factors that might affect crime rates. In contrast, far more rigorous studies are available to the other side, as we shall see presently. Thus, at a minimum, one cannot claim justified belief that gun prohibition would be beneficial overall.

5.2. The benefits of guns

Frequency of Defensive Gun Uses. Guns are used surprisingly often by private citizens in the United States for self-defense purposes. Fifteen surveys, excluding the one discussed in the following paragraph, have been conducted since 1976, yielding estimates of between 760,000 and 3.6 million defensive gun uses per year, the average estimate being 1.8 million. Probably among the more reliable is Kleck and Gertz's 1993 national survey, which obtained an estimate of 2.5 million annual defensive gun uses, excluding military and police uses and excluding uses against animals. Gun users in 400,000 of these cases believe that the gun certainly or almost certainly saved a life. While survey respondents almost certainly overestimated their danger, if even one tenth of them were correct, the number of lives saved by guns each year would exceed the number of gun homicides and suicides. For the purposes of Kleck and Gertz's study, a "defensive gun use" requires respondents to have actually seen a person (as opposed, for example, to merely hearing a suspicious noise in the yard) whom they believed was committing or attempting to commit a crime against them, and to have at a minimum threatened the person with a gun, but not necessarily to have fired the gun. Kleck's statistics imply that defensive gun uses outnumber crimes committed with guns by a ratio of about 3:1.[3] . . .

The Benefits of Concealed Weapons. In the United States, some states prohibit the carrying of concealed weapons. Others have "discretionary" permit laws, meaning that local officials may, at their discretion, issue permits to carry concealed weapons to citizens who apply for such permits (in such states, officials commonly restrict permits to citizens with special circumstances, such as jobs that require them to carry large sums of money). Others have "nondiscretionary" or "shall-issue" laws, which require officials to issue permits to all applicants who meet specified, objective conditions (these conditions may include absence of a criminal record, payment of a fee, some minimum age, and/or completion of a firearms safety course). Shall-issue laws result in many more permits being issued. Finally, the state of Vermont allows the carrying of concealed weapons with no need for a permit. Several discretionary states converted to nondiscretionary laws during the 1980s and 1990s.

John Lott and David Mustard conducted a study, probably the most rigorous and comprehensive study in the gun control literature, on the effects of nondiscretionary laws on crime rates.[4] Lott's study uses time-series and cross-sectional data for all 3,054 counties in the United States from 1977 to 1992. Overall, states with shall-issue laws have a violent crime rate just over half (55%) of the rate in other states. This alone does not establish that the more restrictive gun laws are a *cause* of the dramatically higher violent crime rates in the states that have them, since the correlation could be explained by the hypothesis that states that already have higher crime rates are more likely to pass restrictive gun laws. The latter hypothesis, however, would not explain why violent crime rates fell after states adopted shall-issue concealed carry laws. After performing a multiple-regression analysis to control for numerous other variables—such as arrest and conviction rates, prison sentence lengths, population density, income levels, and racial and gender makeup of counties—Lott found that upon the adoption of shall-issue laws, murder rates declined immediately by about 8%, rapes by 5%, and aggravated assaults by 7%, with declines continuing in subsequent years (Lott explains the latter fact by the gradually increasing numbers of individuals obtaining permits).

Gun control proponents may find these statistics theoretically surprising: Increasing the availability of one important means of committing violent crimes, they believe, should increase the violent crime rate. But an alternative theory gives the opposite prediction: Increased availability of guns to citizens, including the ability to carry concealed weapons, increases the risks to would-be criminals of experiencing undesired consequences as a result of attempting a violent crime. These consequences include being shot, being detained by the would-be victim until the police arrive, and simply being unable to complete the crime. Thus, other things being equal, increased availability of guns to the general public should result in decreased violent crime. . . .

5.3. Why a gun ban must have much greater benefits than harms to be justified

In order to be justified as a case of the overriding of prima facie rights, gun prohibition would have to save many times as many lives as it cost, for:

1. It is wrong to murder a person, even to prevent several other killings. (premise)
2. A violation of a person or group's right of self-defense, predictably resulting in the death of one of the victims, is morally comparable to murder. (premise)
3. If it is wrong to commit a murder to prevent several killings, then it is wrong to commit a rights violation comparable to murder to prevent several killings. (premise)
4. Therefore, it is wrong to violate a person or group's right of self-defense, predictably resulting in the death of one of the victims, even to prevent several killings. (from 1, 2, 3)
5. Therefore, it is wrong to violate a group of people's right of self-defense, predictably resulting in the deaths of many of the victims, even to prevent several times as many killings. (from 4)
6. Gun prohibition would violate a group of people's right of self-defense, predictably resulting in the deaths of many of the victims. (premise)
7. Therefore, gun prohibition is wrong, even if it would prevent several times as many killings as it contributed to. (from 5, 6)

Similar arguments can be made concerning other rights—including, for example, the right to engage in one's chosen form of recreation—the general point of which would be that the overriding of a right for consequentialist reasons requires a benefit not merely greater, but *very much* greater than the harm to the rights-bearer. . . .

While my premises may support some prima facie right to own all manner of weapons, from machine guns to nuclear missiles, the arguments of §4 do not imply that all such prima facie rights are equally weighty, nor do those of §5 imply that the reasons for overriding all such prima facie rights are of equal strength. Based on empirical evidence discussed above, firearms, particularly handguns, are the most effective means of self-defense against violent criminals, while both handguns and rifles are commonly used for recreational purposes. It would be, to say the least, difficult to make a case for the importance of nuclear missiles for either recreational or self-defense purposes, while it would be easy to make a case for the overriding of any prima facie right to own a nuclear missile. The reader may make his own assessment of the case for various other weapons.

6. Extensions of the Argument

Thus far, we have considered gun control only in the extreme form of a ban on all guns. What of more limited measures? Here I mention just two of the more common measures proposed or enacted. First, many support a ban on all *handguns*. Second, many states either prohibit or place severe restrictions on the carrying of concealed weapons in public places. What do our arguments based on the right to own a gun imply about these measures?

I think that these measures are also serious rights violations, though not as serious as a complete gun ban. The reason is that they (would) create severe impediments to individuals defending themselves. The features of handguns that make them useful to criminals are also the features that make them the most suitable weapons for self-defense purposes—the fact that they are small and light, require little strength or skill to wield effectively, and are widely feared. Furthermore, for various reasons, almost no one in our society would carry a gun for self-protection unless she was able to carry it concealed. Almost no one would carry any kind of gun other than a handgun for self-protection. So laws that prevent law-abiding citizens from carrying concealed weapons, or from owning handguns at all, effectively eliminate self-defense uses of guns outside the home, to the extent that the laws are obeyed. We have seen that the best available evidence indicates that such laws increase rather than decrease crime; thus, there is no case for overriding victims' self-defense rights. All mentally competent, non-criminal adults should therefore be allowed to own and carry concealed handguns. The fewer impediments or costs that are placed in the way of their doing so, the better, since any such impediments can be expected to decrease the rate at which victims defend themselves much more than they can be expected to decrease the rate at which criminals carry guns.

NOTES

1. Nicholas Dixon, "Why We Should Ban Handguns in the United States," *St. Louis University Public Law Review* 12 (1993): 243–83, pp. 283, 244.

2. It may, however, provide grounds for overriding the prima facie right to do *A*. . . .

3. Gary Kleck and Marc Gertz, "Armed Resistance to Crime: The Prevalence and Nature of Self-Defense with a Gun," *Journal of Criminal Law and Criminology* 86 (1995): 150–87; discussed at greater length in Kleck, *Targeting Guns.* . . .

4. John Lott and David Mustard, "Crime, Deterrence, and Right-to-Carry Concealed Handguns," *Journal of Legal Studies* 26 (1997): 1–68; discussed at greater length in Lott, *More Guns.*

Review and Discussion Questions

1. Huemer believes that there is a prima facie right to own a gun because of the presumption in favor of liberty. Do you agree, or are there considerations like those discussed in section 2.1 for denying the existence of such a right?

2. Assuming there is a prima facie right to own a gun, is this right a significant one, the violation of which would be a serious offense? Explain why or why not. How important are guns as a means of recreation? Would banning guns violate our right to self-defense?

3. Huemer believes that the high homicide rate in the U.S. is not a result of its high rate of gun ownership. Nicholas Dixon believes the opposite. Who is right about this?

4. In your judgment, how strong is the evidence that guns are a valuable means of defense? How strong is the evidence that permitting citizens to carry concealed weapons reduces crime? Is Huemer correct in maintaining that the benefits of private gun ownership outweigh the case for gun control?

5. Huemer believes that, to be justified, a ban on handguns "would have to save many times as many lives as it cost." Assess his argument for this proposition. Do you agree with it, or would it be sufficient that the lives saved outnumber the lives lost?

6. Does Huemer's argument imply that one has a right to own bazookas, machine guns, or hand grenades? If it does, is this an objection to Huemer's argument, or does one in fact have a right to own weapons like these?

7. What outstanding factual issues separate Huemer and Polsby, on the one hand, from Dixon, on the other? How might these issues be resolved? What moral or philosophical differences separate these writers?

11

PUNISHMENT AND THE DEATH PENALTY

Punishment and the Criminal Justice System

WILLIAM H. SHAW

When we punish people, we do to them something that it is normally wrong to do to other people: We restrict their liberty, take away their property, harm them physically, or even deprive them of their lives. On what basis then, if any, can punishment be morally justified? In this excerpt from his book *Contemporary Ethics: Taking Account of Utilitarianism*, William H. Shaw presents the utilitarian approach to punishment and to criminal justice. He explains how deterrence works and argues against retributivist theories of punishment. He concludes by addressing the criticism that a utilitarian approach to punishment might require us to punish an innocent person if doing so maximized overall social benefit.

Study Questions

1. According to Shaw, what is the point of criminal law? By contrast, what do "minimalists" believe? What do "maximalists" believe?

2. According to the utilitarian theory, under what circumstances is punishment justified?

3. In what three ways can punishment affect the future conduct of the criminal? How does it affect the conduct of others?

4. What is Mill's point about the death penalty?

5. What does a utilitarian approach to punishment imply about the severity of punishment?

6. What is the retributivist view of punishment, and how does it differ from the utilitarian approach?

7. Explain the "hanging the innocent man" objection to utilitarianism.

Reprinted from Contemporary Ethics: Taking Account of Utilitarianism *(Oxford and Malden, Mass.: Blackwell, 1999). Reprinted by permission of Blackwell Publishers.*

A WORLD OF PERFECTLY MORAL AGENTS could do without a criminal justice system with its police, judges, and prisons, for there would be no wrongdoers to catch and punish. Laws, or at least public rules and regulations of some kind, would probably be needed to coordinate people's actions and direct them in mutually beneficial ways. However, any violations of those laws or rules would be inadvertent or unintentional, the result of accident, error, miscalculation, or minor negligence, rather than malicious intent, gross recklessness, or criminal design. Unfortunately, we live in a different world. Society needs criminal laws not only to steer the conduct of morally motivated people in socially useful directions, but also, among other things, to restrain those with weaker internal moral inhibitions from injuring others. Society also needs an apparatus to enforce those laws.

Although the details of a welfare-maximizing criminal code do not concern us here, it seems beyond debate that utilitarianism firmly underwrites the core provisions of traditional criminal law. For people's lives to go well, they must be protected from extortion, battery, and rape, their homes secured from trespass, burglary, and vandalism, and their possessions preserved from theft, embezzlement, and malicious destruction. Not only do such crimes directly harm people, but the fear and insecurity they provoke diminish people's well-being and the quality of their lives. An efficient and effective system of criminal justice is not valuable for its own sake, nor generally speaking does it directly enhance individual well-being. Rather, by making possible a civilized and secure social existence, it facilitates our obtaining various social and material goods that are central to our lives going well.

That the point of criminal law is to promote our collective welfare may seem obvious, but there are those who would deny it. On the one hand, minimalists believe that the purpose of criminal laws is more modest: not to enhance general welfare, but only to secure respect for people's rights. On the other hand, maximalists believe that the function of criminal law is broader: to root out and punish immoral conduct. [Elsewhere this book] argues that utilitarianism takes rights seriously (and, in fact, provides the soundest theoretical account of them), but nevertheless the theory approaches criminal justice with broader goals than just the protection of rights. Not all crimes violate people's rights. Indeed, utilitarianism can justify criminalizing conduct that is not otherwise wrongful (parking one's car on the sidewalk) or that in a particular instance risks little harm to others (the carrying of a loaded firearm by an experienced but nonviolent marksman) if the gains from doing so outweigh the costs. However, contrary to the maximalists, even when conduct is clearly wrong—for example, callously inducing an emotionally distressed person to commit suicide—utilitarian considerations may argue against criminalizing it. The criminal justice apparatus is a blunt instrument, and bringing it to bear on some types of wrongful conduct will prove too costly and intrusive. Whether a certain kind of conduct is right or wrong is one issue. Whether the state should outlaw the conduct and punish those guilty of it is an entirely separate matter.

Utilitarianism makes sense of the core content of criminal law and certain basic and familiar legal doctrines. Among these are the following principles: that laws be public; that they not be applied retroactively; that necessity or self-defense can sometimes justify conduct that would otherwise be criminal; that certain considerations are exculpatory, such as a mistake of fact or the insanity of the defendant; and that various mitigating factors may reduce the seriousness of the crime, as when one person kills another, not with premeditation, but impulsively or in the heat of passion. Putting the legal details aside, the point is that utilitarianism provides solid grounds for these and a number of other well-established principles of criminal law.

The Utilitarian Approach to Punishment

Punishment is the flip side of the criminal law: "If you can't do the time," the saying goes, "don't do the crime." Because of this, we tend to take its moral legitimacy for granted. Yet our practice of punishment is disquieting, and not just because one can question the effectiveness of existing penal institutions. Even under the best of circumstances, whenever we punish people, we are doing to them something that it is normally wrong to do to people. We restrict their liberty, take away their property, harm them physically, or even deprive them of their lives. On what basis, if any, can punishment be justified?

The utilitarian answer is straightforward. Punishment is justified if and only if (1) the pain and suffering (or, more broadly, the loss of welfare) to those who are punished is outweighed by the benefits of punishment and (2) those benefits cannot be achieved with less suffering or at a lower cost to those punished. On the basis of this formula, utilitarians have something to say not only about the considerations that support the practice of punishment in general, but also about what sort of conduct should be criminalized and about the appropriateness of particular punishments for specific types of crimes. However, before we pursue these matters further, bear in mind that punishment is an after the fact response to antisocial behavior. Utilitarians, like other social theorists and reformers, will be concerned not only with society's response to criminals, but also with understanding and confronting the social and psychological circumstances that conduce to crime.

As an institutional practice, the punishment of lawbreakers benefits society as a whole by reducing the amount of criminal activity. It does this in several ways. To begin with, punishment can affect the future conduct of the criminal who has been caught, along three different avenues. First, if it involves incarceration, exile, or execution, punishment removes the delinquent from society and physically prevents him from committing any

other crimes for the duration of his sentence. Second, punishing the miscreant can teach him a lesson and discourage him from violating the law in the future. Having been punished once, the ex-convict will be reluctant to risk being punished again and will therefore be more likely than he was before to abstain from illicit conduct. Third, punishment can sometimes reform or rehabilitate the criminal, making him a better person—someone who is motivated less by the threat of punishment than by the desire to be a law-abiding and productive citizen.

It is important to be clear about two things. First, the issue for utilitarians is not whether we can identify the specific benefits of punishing a given individual for a particular crime. That is usually impossible. Rather, the issue is the benefits that come from the general practice of punishing those who violate the law. Second, utilitarianism does not claim that our system of punishment, as it actually functions in the United States, succeeds in rehabilitating very many convicted criminals or in discouraging them from future wrongdoing. The evidence that it does so is slight, and many suspect that prisons, as they exist today, only harden inmates and reinforce a criminal orientation toward life.[1] To the extent that our system of punishment fails to rehabilitate the criminal or deter him from future misconduct, the less likely it is to be justified on utilitarian grounds.

Punishing a lawbreaker not only discourages him from future crimes, it can also deter other potential wrongdoers from committing the same crime. This deterrent effect is an extremely important part of the rationale for punishment and is often singled out as if it were the one and only utilitarian reason for punishment. Deterrence reflects the sad fact that sanctions are necessary to give some people an incentive to obey the law. For example, car theft causes inconvenience, distress, and financial loss to its victims, and the specter of it spreads insecurity and worry. Although the thief profits from his larceny, there is an overall loss of welfare. Other things being equal, the less car theft there is, the better off society as a whole will be. For this reason we have laws against taking a motor vehicle without its owner's permission. Nevertheless, there are those who will be tempted to do just that, for fun or profit. Unless we make it a practice to attempt to catch and then punish car thieves, no potential thief has an incentive to refrain from stealing cars. Thus, punishment not only dissuades the criminal who is caught from breaking the law again, but it also deters those people who would otherwise be tempted to do the crime if doing so brought no risk of punishment.

To be sure, the threat of criminal punishment is not what deters most people from criminal activity. They refrain from stealing, not because they fear punishment, but because they believe that theft is wrong and are strongly disposed not to do it. Abolishing the laws against car theft would be unlikely to cause most people to try their hand at stealing cars. Although the risk of punishment is not what prevents moral people from doing wrong, punishment may nevertheless be one factor in their moral education. It may be a component of a socialization process that has shaped their moral character so that they are strongly averse to robbing, injuring, or killing other people. Punishing a wrongdoer teaches a moral lesson to others. When society punishes someone for a crime, it sends a vivid, forceful, and public message that it rejects certain conduct, and that message can profoundly influence the norms that people absorb. The revulsion that law-abiding people feel toward serious crime and their aversion to engaging in it themselves may derive in part from the vivid association of crime with punishment.

Discussions of punishment often overlook this important utilitarian consideration, but John Stuart Mill saw it clearly. Writing about the death penalty, he refers to the "efficacy of a punishment which acts principally through the imagination . . . by the impression it makes on those who are still innocent." It does this "by the horror with which it surrounds the first promptings of guilt [and] the restraining influence it exercises over the beginning of the thought, which, if indulged,

would become a temptation"[2] Mill's argument illuminates an important feature of punishment in general, but it is far from conclusive with respect to whether execution or life imprisonment (or some other punishment) is the most effective response to murder. Some writers believe that capital punishment teaches the enormity of murder more effectively than any other punishment.[3] Others believe that execution should go the way of torture: progress in civilization is characterized by our refusing to inflict horrible punishments even on wicked people.[4] In this view, killing criminals sends the wrong moral message. This dispute turns on controversial matters of social psychology and moral development. Although these elude simple answer, they are of crucial importance for anyone approaching capital punishment from a utilitarian perspective.

Understanding Deterrence

Most people are moral, and except in situations of unusual temptation, the prospect of punishment does not deter them from crime because their consciences already restrain them. On the other hand, some people are hotheaded or imprudent, lack the self-control of normal adults, or are prone to irrational or self-destructive behavior. The prospect of punishment may deter such people only weakly or not at all. For any given type of crime, however, there will be some people who will be deterred by the risk of punishment. Their number will vary with the likelihood and severity of the punishment in question.

Thus, as we have seen, a policy of punishing car thieves is justified because it discourages people from stealing cars who would otherwise be tempted to do so. The cost to the convicted thieves is outweighed by the greater benefit to society of a lower level of car theft. For utilitarians, however, not only must the benefits of reducing car theft be greater than the cost of enforcement and punishment, but we must be unable to achieve those benefits at a lower cost. Because utilitarians want to increase *net* welfare as much as possible, they consider both the costs and the benefits of any policy or practice. For instance, if speeding were a capital crime, far fewer drivers would violate the speed limit, and we would all be a little safer on the road. But clearly the benefit to society of increased compliance with this traffic law would be outweighed by the harm done to the executed drivers and their loved ones and by the worry and insecurity that knowledge of such draconian punishment would cause drivers in general.

If the deterrent effect of two punishments is the same, then, all other things being equal, utilitarianism requires us to choose the less severe punishment. If imprisoning burglars for two years deters potential burglars as effectively as a policy of imprisoning them for three years, then one can justify the harsher sentencing policy only if it provides some non-deterrent benefit. This issue is central to the debate over capital punishment. Does execution prevent homicide more effectively than life imprisonment? In other words, can we reasonably expect the threat of capital punishment to lower the rate of murder? If it does, then executing murderers will save innocent lives, and that fact would provide a compelling utilitarian argument for capital punishment. On the other hand, if executing murderers deters potential killers no more effectively than life imprisonment does, then capital punishment would be difficult to justify on utilitarian grounds (assuming, as most people do, that it is worse to be executed than to spend one's life in prison). From a utilitarian perspective, it cannot be right to increase the harm done to wrongdoers if this brings no offsetting benefit to them or to the rest of society.

If no crime ever went unresolved and unpunished, then relatively mild penalties would suffice to deter wrongdoers. For instance, if every burglary were solved and every burglar captured, even a clement punishment would eliminate any gains to the burglar and make committing the crime pointless. Not all crimes are solved, however, and a calculating criminal might reasonably believe, let's suppose, that there is only a one out of twenty chance that he will be caught and convicted for stealing a car. If so, the punishment for car theft

must be at least twenty times more costly to the thief than his gain from stealing the car. This is because the rational car thief will discount the disutility of being punished by the likelihood of capture and conviction. If few car thieves are ever caught, very severe punishments may be needed to deter car theft. Of course, real life is complicated, and thieves do not always rationally calculate the costs and benefits of the crimes they contemplate. Nevertheless, the simple but often neglected point holds that deterrence is a function of both the severity of the punishment and the likelihood of its being inflicted.

In fact, we know surprisingly little about the comparative deterrent effect of different punishments, and some commentators doubt that putting criminals in prison achieves anything that could not be accomplished by less harsh means, such as monetary fines, community service, house arrest with electronic monitoring, intermittent incarceration (on weekends, for instance), or halfway houses with close supervision.[5] Utilitarians will consider and perhaps experiment with these and other alternatives to conventional punishment. They are not wedded to the status quo but, rather, favor whatever system of criminal justice and whatever forms and mechanisms of punishment produce the greatest expected net benefit for society as a whole. Determining this is no easy matter, and utilitarian reformers will doubtless proceed in an incremental fashion, basing their recommendations on the best available empirical data and on whatever insights psychology, social theory, and scientific criminology can provide.

Against Retributivism

Retributivists advance the non-utilitarian thesis that punishment is justified because it is the morally appropriate response to wrongdoing. It is right and fitting that wrongdoers be punished. Having done evil, they should be paid back for what they have done; they deserve to suffer. Retributivists urge that whereas utilitarianism concerns itself with the future effects of punishment,

punishment is properly backward looking. It looks to the past, to what people deserve because of what they have done. Just as someone can merit praise or reward for doing something well, so a person can deserve blame or punishment for doing wrong. No further justification, in terms of social benefit or anything else, is called for. Staunch retributivists believe that it is right to punish wrongdoers even if doing so has no positive social benefits whatsoever.

Retributivism enjoys some commonsense appeal, but it is debatable whether desert is the independent moral variable retributivists take it to be. Given an established practice, or within the context of certain rules, people can appropriately be said to deserve the reward or penalties they incur. A prizefighter can deserve to be judged the winner of a heavyweight bout; a basketball player can deserve to be thrown out of the game for an egregious foul. Likewise, assuming that the laws are reasonable and people are aware of them, we can say that, having broken the "rules of the game" by assaulting someone, stealing a purse, or embezzling money, a person can deserve to be punished. Utilitarians have no problem with this way of talking. However, they will insist that desert is always relative to some institutional framework or to some system of rules, norms, or established expectations, which system is itself subject to consequentialist assessment. In their view, desert is not an antecedent or free-standing moral factor capable of showing what laws we should have in the first place, which transgressions we should punish, or what penalties we should mete out.

Likewise, utilitarians can accommodate the point (urged by a number of philosophers) that punishment is justified on grounds of fair play. Criminals take advantage of law-abiding citizens by breaking rules that those citizens have adhered to. In this way, they attempt to benefit themselves unfairly at the expense of others. Society therefore has a right to punish criminals, these philosophers argue, to restore an equitable distribution of benefits and burdens. Although utilitarians do not center their analysis of punishment on the idea of fair play, the underlying point is

perfectly compatible with a utilitarian approach. Those who adhere to rules that others get away with breaking may come to feel resentful or aggrieved, especially if obeying the rules requires an effort on their part or if the rule breakers injure their interests. A failure to punish lawbreakers can jeopardize the allegiance of the law abiding. From a utilitarian perspective, this point highlights another positive social effect of punishment. Like desert, however, the idea of fair play is parasitic on existing institutional arrangements; it does not tell us what conduct should be criminalized, what type of punishment is the appropriate response, or how severe that punishment should be.

Retributivists would dispute this. They affirm, not just that criminals deserve to be punished, but also that they deserve to be punished in proportion to the evil they have done; the worse the crime, the harsher the punishment should be. This is a sensible precept, to be sure, and it is one that utilitarians can easily endorse. Unfortunately, the principle that the severity of the punishment should correspond to the gravity of the deed provides little practical guidance. Some retributivists embrace the ancient tenet of "an eye for an eye," at least in the case of murder. The thought that those who kill deserve to die has to be modified, of course, if it is to accommodate different degrees of murder (first degree, second degree, manslaughter, etc.) or to determine the appropriate punishment for attempted murder. Some people who think that they agree with "an eye for an eye" implicitly assume that execution has a greater deterrent effect than life imprisonment. If they came to believe otherwise, then they might cease to believe that the death penalty is a moral imperative. They would almost certainly cease to believe this if they thought that capital punishment actually increased the murder rate (because, say, state-sponsored executions cause some impressionable citizens to become less averse to killing people in other circumstances).

Some retributivists fear that a utilitarian approach to punishment will lead us to let criminals off too easily, not punishing them as fully as they deserve. Kant, for instance, firmly believed in capital punishment and was vexed by the thought that utilitarian reasoning might induce us to refrain from executing murderers.[6] There is, however, no more substantial ground for this belief than for its opposite, that utilitarians will punish criminals too harshly. For instance, one might contend that if a certain kind of crime is very difficult to detect, then a utilitarian society might have to punish the few violators it catches more severely than they deserve. Or suppose that someone who commits a crime has himself been wronged or abused or received less than a fair share of society's resources; one might argue that the criminal is more sinned against than sinning and thus does not deserve the punishment that utilitarianism might authorize. The fact that some retributivists allege that a utilitarian approach to punishment is too harsh whereas others allege that it is too lenient highlights a weakness of retributivism. It provides no agreed upon framework from which questions of punishment can be systematically addressed. In practice, retributivists fall back on their sometimes conflicting intuitions about what criminals deserve or don't deserve under different circumstances.

The criminal justice system of any advanced society comprises several complex institutions and practices. Utilitarians seek to shape these institutions and practices so as to direct and modify people's behavior in welfare-enhancing directions. By contrast, for retributivists the prime or perhaps only point of these institutions is to see that people get what they morally deserve. But assessing people's desert is problematic.[7] Moreover, retributivists have relatively little interest in the impact that these institutions have on social well-being (for instance, their effect on the overall level of crime and anti-social behavior). This stance seems, at best, misguided.

Hanging the Innocent Man

Retributivists contend that utilitarianism ignores considerations of desert and argue that, as a result, the theory could conceivably require us to punish an innocent person if doing so maximized overall social benefit. To illustrate their point, they ask us to imagine a sheriff in a small town where a heinous, racially inflammatory crime has been committed.[8] The local community is restless and upset, demanding that the culprit be caught and punished. Unless this happens soon, there will be (the sheriff knows) violent rioting resulting in several deaths and much future bitterness. The sheriff has a suspect in custody but learns that he is innocent. Nevertheless, the sheriff could plausibly frame the suspect for the crime. If he does, then the potential riot will be averted, public faith in law enforcement renewed, and widespread fear and anxiety replaced by a sense of safety and security. The retributivist contends, then, that if the sheriff is a utilitarian, he should frame the innocent man and see him hanged because it is better that one man dies than that a riot occurs with multiple deaths. (To make his argument tighter, the critic might stipulate further imaginary details. The true criminal confesses his crime to the sheriff immediately before dying. Unfortunately, there is no other evidence of his guilt, and he is so well regarded and the circumstances so strange that nobody would be likely to believe the sheriff's report.)

To this line of argument, utilitarians respond that the imagined case is too fanciful to take seriously and that the same is true of any other story that one might concoct in an effort to show the utility of executing an innocent person. The example assumes as certainties what are only extremely risky possibilities. For one thing, the sheriff cannot know with confidence what he is supposed to know. He cannot be sure that proceeding honestly and setting the innocent man free really would have dire consequences, nor can he safely assume that no one will ever figure out what he has done. And if the truth ever leaked out, the results would be extremely bad.

Furthermore, the example rests on a naive view of human psychology and institutional life. It clearly promotes long-run utility for the rule of law to prevail and for people working in the criminal justice system to follow established professional standards. Yet we are to suppose that somehow the sheriff (and perhaps others) could decide to break the law this one time and yet on all other occasions be firmly committed to acting legally and professionally. Yet if the sheriff believes that he is right to fabricate evidence when he knows an accused person is innocent, he will surely be tempted to invent evidence against people he firmly believes to be guilty. This is something it would be madness to encourage.

There is another and deeper point here as well. Judicial punishment is part of a larger criminal justice system, and it is the rules and practices of that system that utilitarianism seeks to assess and possibly reform. As a number of writers have stressed, one must distinguish between justifying a practice or institution and justifying conduct within that practice or institution.[9] With regard to the former, there are conclusive utilitarian objections to a legal (or quasi-legal) system that instructs or permits its officials to frame innocent people whenever those officials deem it necessary for the benefit of society. The potential for abuse is so great that the contention that utilitarians would favor and attempt to design such a system is preposterous.

Assume that we have a democratic society with a morally defensible criminal justice system in place. Once the legislature has decided what the punishment is for a particular crime, then it follows that although judges may have some discretion in the sentencing of individual lawbreakers (taking into account, for instance, age or prior convictions), their role is essentially to determine legal guilt or innocence and to assign a reasonable and appropriate penalty (within a predetermined range). It is not to calculate what precise social benefit, if any, will come from sentencing this particular person to jail. By analogy, in baseball the umpire's job is to call balls and strikes, rather than to determine on utilitarian grounds whether a particular batter should be allowed extra swings.

Retributivists contend that utilitarianism fails to give moral weight to the fact that criminals deserve to be punished. Utilitarianism is forward looking, they say, whereas punishment properly looks back to what the criminal has done. But we can now see that this contention is simplistic. In assessing different systems of punishment, util-

itarians do, to be sure, approach the whole issue in terms of benefits and costs. If they approve of a particular system, it will be on forward-looking grounds. However, a judge within that system looks backward and attempts to determine what the accused person did and whether it fits the legally established criteria of the crime in question. Likewise, other officials will have specific institutional roles to play. For them to ignore both the rules of the system and their own institutional duties whenever they think that doing so is best would have very poor long-term results. Rather, utilitarians will want officials to stick to established institutional procedures and perform their assigned roles as well as possible.

NOTES

1. C. L. Ten, *Crime, Guilt, and Punishment* (Oxford: Oxford University Press, 1987), pp. 8–13.

2. "Capital Punishment," in John Stuart Mill, *Public and Parliamentary Speeches* (*Collected Works of John Stuart Mill*, vol. XXVIII). J. M. Robson and B. L. Kinzer, eds. (Toronto: University of Toronto Press, 1988), p. 269.

3. Steve Goldberg, "On Capital Punishment," *Ethics*, vol. 85, no. 1 (October 1974), pp. 67–79.

4. Jeffrey H. Reiman, "Justice, Civilization, and the Death Penalty" [reproduced later in this volume].

5. Richard B. Brandt, *Facts, Values, and Morality* (Cambridge: Cambridge University Press, 1996), p. 258.

6. Immanuel Kant, *Practical Philosophy* (Cambridge Edition of the Works of Immanuel Kant), ed. M. J. Gregor (Cambridge: Cambridge University Press, 1996), p. 473.

7. If incompatabilists or hard determinists are correct that our actions are determined and therefore we are not responsible for them, then retributivists will have a problem making sense of talk of moral desert. Their position assumes either that we have free will or that our normal ideas about responsibility are compatible with the truth of determinism. Utilitarianism, by contrast, is neutral with respect to the debate over free will, determinism, and responsibility.

8. This much-discussed example originated in H. J. McCloskey, "An Examination of Restricted Utilitarianism," *Philosophical Review*, vol. 66, no. 4 (October 1957), pp. 466–485.

9. John Rawls, "Two Concepts of Rules," *Philosophical Review*, vol. 64, no. 1 (January 1955), pp. 3–32. Mill, Austin, and others anticipated this distinction.

Review and Discussion Questions

1. What factors are relevant to the issue of whether a particular punishment is an effective deterrent? Besides deterrence, what other considerations might a utilitarian take into account in determining whether a particular punishment, or a particular system of criminal justice, is justified?

2. Do you think our system of criminal punishment as it actually exists today is justifiable on utilitarian grounds? Is it justifiable on retributivist grounds? Should our system of punishment be reformed in some way?

3. Explain and contrast the retributivist and utilitarian approaches to punishment. Which approach do you find the most attractive?

4. Explain Shaw's response to the "hanging the innocent man" objection. Do you find it convincing? Explain why or why not. Are there objections to the utilitarian approach to punishment that Shaw has ignored or failed to do justice to?

5. Assess capital punishment from a utilitarian point of view. Assess it from a retributivist point of view.

The Ultimate Punishment: A Defense

ERNEST VAN DEN HAAG

A long-time defender of capital punishment, Ernest van den Haag, formerly John M. Olin Professor of Jurisprudence and Public Policy at Fordham University, states the case for the death penalty in this essay and answers various criticisms of it. Van den Haag believes in the deterrent effect of the death penalty, and he also maintains that retribution supplies an independent moral justification of it. Critics of capital punishment contend that it is administered in a discriminatory or capricious way. Van den Haag replies that such discrimination is not inherent in capital punishment and that neither its maldistribution nor the fact that innocent people have been executed would justify abolishing it. He concludes by responding to the argument that the death penalty is excessive and degrading.

Study Questions

1. Van den Haag writes that "justice is independent of distributional inequalities." How is this point relevant to his defense of capital punishment?

2. Why does van den Haag believe that the death penalty has a greater deterrent effect than imprisonment?

3. Why does van den Haag believe that "the death penalty cannot be unjust to the guilty criminal"?

4. How does van den Haag respond to the charge that the death penalty is excessive and degrading?

Reprinted by permission from Harvard Law Review *99 (1986). Copyright © 1986 by Harvard Law Review Association. Some notes omitted.*

I n an average year about 20,000 homicides occur in the United States. Fewer than 300 convicted murderers are sentenced to death. But because no more than thirty murderers have been executed in any recent year, most convicts sentenced to death are likely to die of old age. Nonetheless, the death penalty looms large in discussions: it raises important moral questions independent of the number of executions.

The death penalty is our harshest punishment.* It is irrevocable: it ends the existence of those punished, instead of temporarily imprisoning them. Further, although not intended to cause physical pain, execution is the only corporal punishment still applied to adults.[1] These singular characteristics contribute to the perennial, impassioned controversy about capital punishment.

I. Distribution

Consideration of the justice, morality, or usefulness of capital punishment is often conflated with objections to its alleged discriminatory or capricious distribution among the guilty. Wrongly so. If capital punishment is immoral *in se*, no distribution among the guilty could make it moral. If capital punishment is moral, no distribution would make it immoral. Improper distribution cannot affect the quality of what is distributed, be it punishments or rewards. Discriminatory or capricious distribution thus could not justify abolition of the death penalty. Further, maldistribution inheres no more in capital punishment than in any other punishment.

Maldistribution between the guilty and the innocent is, by definition, unjust. But the injustice does not lie in the nature of the punishment. Because of the finality of the death penalty, the most grievous maldistribution occurs when it is imposed upon the innocent. However, the frequent allegations of discrimination and capriciousness refer to maldistribution among the guilty and not to the punishment of the innocent.

Maldistribution of any punishment among those who deserve it is irrelevant to its justice or morality. Even if poor or black convicts guilty of capital offenses suffer capital punishment, and other convicts equally guilty of the same crimes do not, a more equal distribution, however desirable, would merely be more equal. It would not be more just to the convicts under sentence of death.

Punishments are imposed on persons, not on racial or economic groups. Guilt is personal. The only relevant question is: does the person to be executed deserve the punishment? Whether or not others who deserved the same punishment, whatever their economic or racial group, have avoided execution is irrelevant. If they have, the guilt of the executed convicts would not be diminished, nor would their punishment be less deserved. To put the issue starkly, if the death penalty were imposed on guilty blacks, but not on guilty whites, or, if it were imposed by a lottery among the guilty, this irrationally discriminatory or capricious distribution would neither make the penalty unjust, nor cause anyone to be unjustly punished, despite the undue impunity bestowed on others.[†]

---

*Some writers, for example, Cesare Bonesana Marchese di Beccaria, have thought that life imprisonment is more severe. . . . More recently, Jacques Barzun has expressed this view. . . . However, the overwhelming majority of both abolitionists and of convicts under death sentence prefer life imprisonment to execution.

[†]Justice Douglas, concurring in *Furman* v. *Georgia*, 408 U.S. 238 (1972), wrote that "a law which . . . reaches that [discriminatory] result in practice has no more sanctity than a law which in terms provides the same." . . . Indeed, a law legislating this result "in terms" would be inconsistent with the "equal protection of the laws" provided by the fourteenth amendment, as would the discriminatory result reached in practice. But that result could be changed by changing the distributional practice. Thus, Justice Douglas notwithstanding, a discriminatory result does not make the death penalty unconstitutional, unless the penalty ineluctably must produce that result to an unconstitutional degree.

Equality, in short, seems morally less important than justice. And justice is independent of distributional inequalities. The ideal of equal justice demands that justice be equally distributed, not that it be replaced by equality. Justice requires that as many of the guilty as possible be punished, regardless of whether others have avoided punishment. To let these others escape the deserved punishment does not do justice to them, or to society. But it is not unjust to those who could not escape.

These moral considerations are not meant to deny that irrational discrimination, or capriciousness, would be inconsistent with constitutional requirements. But I am satisfied that the Supreme Court has in fact provided for adherence to the constitutional requirement of equality as much as is possible. Some inequality is indeed unavoidable as a practical matter in any system.* But, *ultra posse nemo obligatur.* (Nobody is bound beyond ability.)

Recent data reveal little direct racial discrimination in the sentencing of those arrested and convicted of murder.[2] The abrogation of the death penalty for rape has eliminated a major source of racial discrimination. Concededly, some discrimination based on the race of murder victims may exist; yet, this discrimination affects criminal victimizers in an unexpected way. Murderers of whites are thought more likely to be executed than murderers of blacks. Black victims, then, are less fully vindicated than white ones. However, because most black murderers kill blacks, black murderers are spared the death penalty more often than are white murderers. They fare better than most white murderers.[†] The motivation behind unequal

distribution of the death penalty may well have been to discriminate against blacks, but the result has favored them. Maldistribution is thus a straw man for empirical as well as analytical reasons.

II. Miscarriages of Justice

In a recent survey Professors Hugo Adam Bedau and Michael Radelet found that 7000 persons were executed in the United States between 1900 and 1985 and that 25 were innocent of capital crimes.[3] Among the innocents they list Sacco and Vanzetti as well as Ethel and Julius Rosenberg. Although their data may be questionable, I do not doubt that, over a long enough period, miscarriages of justice will occur even in capital cases.

Despite precautions, nearly all human activities, such as trucking, lighting, or construction, cost the lives of some innocent bystanders. We do not give up these activities, because the advantages, moral or material, outweigh the unintended losses. Analogously, for those who think the death penalty just, miscarriages of justice are offset by the moral benefits and the usefulness of doing justice. For those who think the death penalty unjust even when it does not miscarry, miscarriages can hardly be decisive.

III. Deterrence

Despite much recent work, there has been no conclusive statistical demonstration that the death penalty is a better deterrent than are alternative punishments.[4] However, deterrence is less than decisive for either side. Most abolitionists acknowledge that they would continue to favor abolition even if the death penalty were shown to deter more murders than alternatives could deter.

---

*The ideal of equality, unlike the ideal of retributive justice (which can be approximated separately in each instance), is clearly unattainable unless all guilty persons are apprehended, and thereafter tried, convicted and sentenced by the same court, at the same time. Unequal justice is the best we can do; it is still better than the injustice, equal or unequal, which occurs if, for the sake of equality, we deliberately allow some who could be punished to escape.

[†]It barely need be said that any discrimination *against* (for example, black murderers of whites) must also be discrimination *for* (for example, black murderers of blacks).

Abolitionists appear to value the life of a convicted murderer or, at least, his nonexecution, more highly than they value the lives of the innocent victims who might be spared by deterring prospective murderers.

Deterrence is not altogether decisive for me either. I would favor retention of the death penalty as retribution even if it were shown that the threat of execution could not deter prospective murderers not already deterred by the threat of imprisonment.* Still, I believe the death penalty, because of its finality, is more feared than imprisonment, and deters some prospective murderers not deterred by the threat of imprisonment. Sparing the lives of even a few prospective victims by deterring their murderers is more important than preserving the lives of convicted murderers because of the possibility, or even the probability, that executing them would not deter others. Whereas the lives of the victims who might be saved are valuable, that of the murderer has only negative value, because of his crime. Surely the criminal law is meant to protect the lives of potential victims in preference to those of actual murderers.

Murder rates are determined by many factors; neither the severity nor the probability of the threatened sanction is always decisive. However, for the long run, I share the view of Sir James Fitzjames Stephen: "Some men, probably, abstain from murder because they fear that if they committed murder they would be hanged. Hundreds of thousands abstain from it because they regard it with horror. One great reason why they regard it with horror is that murderers are hanged."[5] Penal sanctions are useful in the long run for the formation of the internal restraints so necessary to control crime.

The severity and finality of the death penalty is appropriate to the seriousness and the finality of murder.[†]

IV. Incidental Issues: Cost, Relative Suffering, Brutalization

Many nondecisive issues are associated with capital punishment. Some believe that the monetary cost of appealing a capital sentence is excessive. Yet most comparisons of the cost of life imprisonment with the cost of execution, apart from their dubious relevance, are flawed at least by the implied assumption that life prisoners will generate no judicial costs during their imprisonment. At any rate, the actual monetary costs are trumped by the importance of doing justice.

Others insist that a person sentenced to death suffers more than his victim suffered, and that this (excess) suffering is undue according to the *lex talionis* (rule of retaliation).[6] We cannot know whether the murderer on death row suffers more than his victim suffered; however, unlike the murderer, the victim deserved none of the suffering inflicted. Further, the limitations of the *lex talionis* were meant to restrain private vengeance, not the social retribution that has taken its place. Punishment—regardless of the motivation—is not intended to revenge, offset, or compensate for the victim's suffering, or to be measured by it. Punishment is to vindicate the law and the social order undermined by the crime. This is why a kidnapper's penal confinement is not limited to the period for which he imprisoned his victim; nor is a burglar's confinement meant merely to offset

---

*If executions were shown to increase the murder rate in the long run, I would favor abolition. Sparing the innocent victims who would be spared, *ex hypothesi*, by the nonexecution of murderers would be more important to me than the execution, however just, of murderers. But although there is a lively discussion of the subject, no serious evidence exists to support the hypothesis that executions produce a higher murder rate. . . .

[†]*Weems* v. *United States*, 217 U.S. 349 (1910), suggests that penalties be proportionate to the seriousness of the crime—a common theme of the criminal law. Murder, therefore, demands more than life imprisonment, if, as I believe, it is a more serious crime than other crimes punished by life imprisonment. In modern times, our sensibility requires that the range of punishments be narrower than the range of crimes—but not so narrow as to exclude the death penalty.

the suffering or the harm he caused his victim; nor is it meant only to offset the advantage he gained.*

Another argument heard at least since Beccaria is that, by killing a murderer, we encourage, endorse, or legitimize unlawful killing. Yet, although all punishments are meant to be unpleasant, it is seldom argued that they legitimize the unlawful imposition of identical unpleasantness. Imprisonment is not thought to legitimize kidnapping; neither are fines thought to legitimize robbery. The difference between murder and execution, or between kidnapping and imprisonment, is that the first is unlawful and undeserved, the second a lawful and deserved punishment for an unlawful act. The physical similarities of the punishment to the crime are irrelevant. The relevant difference is not physical, but social.[†]

V. Justice, Excess, Degradation

We threaten punishments in order to deter crime. We impose them not only to make the threats credible but also as retribution (justice) for the crimes that were not deterred. Threats and punishments are necessary to deter and deterrence is a sufficient practical justification for them. Retribution is an independent moral justification. Although penalties can be unwise, repulsive, or inappropriate, and those punished can be pitiable, in a sense the infliction of legal punishment on a guilty person cannot be unjust. By committing the crime, the criminal volunteered to assume the risk of receiving a legal punishment that he could have avoided by not committing the crime. The punishment he suffers is the punishment he voluntarily risked suffering and, therefore, it is no more unjust to him than any other event for which one knowingly volunteers to assume the risk. Thus, the death penalty cannot be unjust to the guilty criminal.[‡]

There remain, however, two moral objections. The penalty may be regarded as always excessive as retribution and always morally degrading. To regard the death penalty as always excessive, one must believe that no crime—no matter how heinous—could possibly justify capital punishment. Such a belief can be neither corroborated nor refuted; it is an article of faith.

Alternatively, or concurrently, one may believe that everybody, the murderer no less than the victim, has an imprescriptible (natural?) right to life. The law therefore should not deprive anyone of life. I share Jeremy Bentham's view that any

---

*Thus restitution (a civil liability) cannot satisfy the punitive purpose of penal sanctions, whether the purpose be retributive or deterrent.

[†]Some abolitionists challenge: if the death penalty is just and serves as a deterrent, why not televise executions? The answer is simple. The death even of a murderer, however well-deserved, should not serve as public entertainment. It so served in earlier centuries. But in this respect our sensibility has changed for the better, I believe. Further, television unavoidably would trivialize executions, wedged in, as they would be, between game shows, situation comedies, and the like. Finally, because televised executions would focus on the physical aspects of the punishment, rather than the nature of the crime and the suffering of the victim, a televised execution would present the murderer as the victim of the state. Far from communicating the moral significance of the execution, television would shift the focus to the pitiable fear of the murderer. We no longer place in cages those sentenced to imprisonment to expose them to public view. Why should we so expose those sentenced to execution?

[‡]An explicit threat of punitive action is necessary to the justification of any legal punishment: *nulla poena sine lege* (no punishment without [preexisting] law). To be sufficiently justified, the threat must in turn have a rational and legitimate purpose. "Your money or your life" does not qualify; nor does the threat of an unjust law; nor, finally, does a threat that is altogether disproportionate to the importance of its purpose. In short, preannouncement legitimizes the threatened punishment only if the threat is warranted. But this leaves a very wide range of justified threats. Furthermore, the punished person is aware of the penalty for his actions and thus volunteers to take the risk even of an unjust punishment. His victim, however, did not volunteer to risk anything. The question whether any self-inflicted injury—such as a legal punishment—ever can be unjust to a person who knowingly risked it is a matter that requires more analysis than is possible here.

such "natural and imprescriptible rights" are "nonsense upon stilts."*

Justice Brennan has insisted that the death penalty is "uncivilized," "inhuman," inconsistent with "human dignity" and with "the sanctity of life," that it "treats members of the human race as nonhumans, as objects to be toyed with and discarded," that it is "uniquely degrading to human dignity" and "by its very nature, [involves] a denial of the executed person's humanity."[7] Justice Brennan does not say why he thinks execution "uncivilized." Hitherto most civilizations have had the death penalty, although it has been discarded in Western Europe, where it is currently unfashionable probably because of its abuse by totalitarian regimes.

By "degrading," Justice Brennan seems to mean that execution degrades the executed convicts. Yet philosophers, such as Immanuel Kant and G. W. F. Hegel, have insisted that, when deserved, execution, far from degrading the executed convict, affirms his humanity by affirming his rationality and his responsibility for his actions. They thought that execution, when deserved, is required for the sake of the convict's dignity. (Does not life imprisonment violate human dignity more than execution, by keeping alive a prisoner deprived of all autonomy?)

Common sense indicates that it cannot be death—our common fate—that is inhuman. Therefore, Justice Brennan must mean that death degrades when it comes not as a natural or accidental event, but as a deliberate social imposition. The murderer learns through his punishment that his fellow men have found him unworthy of living; that because he has murdered, he is being expelled from the community of the living. This degradation is self-inflicted. By murdering, the murderer has so dehumanized himself that he

cannot remain among the living. The social recognition of his self-degradation is the punitive essence of execution. To believe, as Justice Brennan appears to, that the degradation is inflicted by the execution reverses the direction of causality.

Execution of those who have committed heinous murders may deter only one murder per year. If it does, it seems quite warranted. It is also the only fitting retribution for murder I can think of.

NOTES

1. For a discussion of the sources of opposition to corporal punishment, see E. van den Haag, *Punishing Criminals* 196–206 (1975).

2. *See* Bureau of Justice Statistics, U.S. Dept. of Justice, Bulletin No. NCJ-98, 399, *Capital Punishment 1984*, at 9 (1985); Johnson, "The Executioner's Bias," *Nat'l Rev.*, Nov. 15, 1985, at 44.

3. Bedau & Radelet, "Miscarriages of Justice in Potentially Capital Cases," (1st draft, Oct. 1985) (on file at Harvard Law School Library).

4. For a sample of conflicting views on the subject, see Baldus & Cole, "A Comparison of the Work of Thorsten Sellin and Isaac Ehrlich on the Deterrent Effect of Capital Punishment," 85 *Yale L. J.* 170 (1975); Bowers & Pierce, "Deterrence or Brutalization: What Is the Effect of Executions?," 26 *Crime & Delinq.* 453 (1980); Bowers & Pierce, "The Illusion of Deterrence in Isaac Ehrlich's Research on Capital Punishment," 85 *Yale L. J.* 187 (1975); Ehrlich, "Fear of Deterrence: A Critical Evaluation of the 'Report of the Panel on Research on Deterrent and Incapacitative Effects,'" 6 *J. Legal Stud.* 293 (1977); Ehrlich, "The Deterrent Effect of Capital Punishment: A Question of Life and Death," 65 *Am. Econ. Rev.* 397, 415–16 (1975); Ehrlich & Gibbons, "On the Measurement of the Deterrent Effect of Capital Punishment and the Theory of Deterrence," 6 *J. Legal Stud.* 35 (1977).

5. H. Gross, *A Theory of Criminal Justice* 489 (1979) (attributing this passage to Sir James Fitzjames Stephen).

6. For an example of this view, see A. Camus, *Reflections on the Guillotine* 24–30 (1959). On the limitations allegedly imposed by the *lex talionis*, see Reiman, "Justice, Civilization, and the Death Penalty: Answering van den Haag," 14 *Phil. & Pub. Aff.* 115, 119–34 (1985).

7. *Furman* v. *Georgia*, 408 U.S. 238 (1972) (Brennan, J., concurring).

The Works of Jeremy Bentham 105 (J. Bowring ed. 1972). However, I would be more polite about prescriptible natural rights, which Bentham described as "simple nonsense." *Id.* (It does not matter whether natural rights are called "moral" or "human" rights as they currently are by most writers.)

Review and Discussion Questions

1. Suppose, as many people believe, that murderers who are black or poor are more likely to be executed than other murderers. How would this situation affect your assessment of capital punishment?

2. How satisfactory do you find van den Haag's response to the fact, so troubling to critics of capital punishment, that over the years a number of innocent people have been executed?

3. Van den Haag believes that the death penalty is a better deterrent than alternative punishments, even though no statistical evidence supports this proposition. Do you agree? Explain why or why not.

4. Critics argue that the death penalty should be abandoned if it cannot clearly be shown to be a better deterrent than imprisonment. Van den Haag, on the other hand, contends that the death penalty should be maintained even if it is not a more effective deterrent. Which position is right?

5. Has van den Haag ignored or failed to answer adequately any arguments against capital punishment?

Justice, Civilization, and the Death Penalty

JEFFREY H. REIMAN

Jeffrey H. Reiman, professor of philosophy at American University in Washington, D.C., argues for the abolition of capital punishment. Although Reiman believes on retributive grounds that the death penalty is a just punishment for murder, he argues that, simply because something is deserved, it does not follow that it should be done. Torturers, for example, may deserve to be tortured, but it would be incompatible with the advance of civilization for society to punish them in this way. Likewise, Reiman contends, capital punishment is too horrible to do even to those who deserve it—unless execution were clearly proven a better deterrent to murder than life imprisonment, which he argues it has not been.

Study Questions

1. What's the difference between the *lex talionis* and "proportional retributivism"? How is there an affinity between the *lex talionis* and the Golden Rule?

2. How do the Hegelian and Kantian approaches to punishment lead to the "retributivist principle" and, thus, to the *lex talionis*?

3. Even if the *lex talionis* is just, Reiman argues, the question of what punishment we should administer is not settled. Why not?

From Philosophy & Public Affairs, *vol. 14, no. 2 (Spring 1985). Copyright © 1985 by Princeton University Press. Reprinted by permission of Princeton University Press. Some notes omitted.*

4. According to Reiman, in what ways is execution analogous to torture?

5. What is Ernest van den Haag's commonsense argument for the deterrent value of the death penalty? What four reasons does Reiman give for doubting van den Haag's argument?

O N THE ISSUE OF CAPITAL PUNISHMENT, there is as clear a clash of moral intuitions as we are likely to see. Some (now a majority of Americans) feel deeply that justice requires payment in kind and thus that murderers should die; and others (once, but no longer, nearly a majority of Americans) feel deeply that the state ought not be in the business of putting people to death. Arguments for either side that do not do justice to the intuitions of the other are unlikely to persuade anyone not already convinced. And, since, as I shall suggest, there is truth on both sides, such arguments are easily refutable, leaving us with nothing but conflicting intuitions and no guidance from reason in distinguishing the better from the worse. In this context, I shall try to make an argument for the abolition of the death penalty that does justice to the intuitions on both sides. I shall sketch out a conception of retributive justice that accounts for the justice of executing murderers, and then I shall argue that *though the death penalty is a just punishment for murder,* abolition of the death penalty is part of the civilizing mission of modern states. . . .

I. Just Deserts and Just Punishments

In my view, the death penalty is a just punishment for murder because the *lex talionis,* an eye for an eye, and so on, is just, although, as I shall suggest at the end of this section, it can only be rightly applied when its implied preconditions are satisfied. The *lex talionis* is a version of retributivism. Retributivism—as the word itself suggests—is the doctrine that the offender should be *paid back* with suffering he deserves because of the evil he has done, and the *lex talionis* asserts that injury equivalent to that he

imposed is what the offender deserves. But the *lex talionis* is not the only version of retributivism. Another, which I shall call "proportional retributivism," holds that what retribution requires is not equality of injury between crimes and punishments, but "fit" or proportionality, such that the worst crime is punished with the society's worst penalty, and so on, though the society's worst punishment need not duplicate the injury of the worst crime.* Later, I shall try to show how a form of proportional retributivism is compatible with acknowledging the justice of the *lex talionis.* Indeed, since I shall defend the justice of the *lex talionis,* I take such compatibility as a necessary condition of the validity of any form of retributivism.

There is nothing self-evident about the justice of the *lex talionis* nor, for that matter, of retributivism.[†] The standard problem confronting those who would justify retributivism is that of overcoming the suspicion that it does no more than

*"The most extreme form of retributivism is the law of retaliation: 'an eye for an eye'" (Stanley I. Benn, "Punishment," *The Encyclopedia of Philosophy* 7, ed. Paul Edwards [New York: Macmillan, 1967], p. 32). Hugo Bedau writes: "retributive justice need not be thought to consist of *lex talionis.* One may reject that principle as too crude and still embrace the retributive principle that the severity of punishments should be graded according to the gravity of the offense" (Hugo Bedau, "Capital Punishment," in *Matters of Life and Death,* ed. Tom Regan [New York: Random House, 1980], p. 177). See also, Andrew von Hirsch, "Doing Justice: The Principle of Commensurate Deserts," and Hyman Gross, "Proportional Punishment and Justifiable Sentences," in *Sentencing,* eds. H. Gross and A. von Hirsch (New York: Oxford University Press, 1981), pp. 243–56 and 272–83, respectively.

[†]Stanley Benn writes: "to say 'it is fitting' or 'justice demands' that the guilty should suffer is only to affirm that punishment is right, not to give grounds for thinking so" (Benn, "Punishment," p. 30).

sanctify the victim's desire to hurt the offender back. Since serving that desire amounts to hurting the offender simply for the satisfaction that the victim derives from seeing the offender suffer, and since deriving satisfaction from the suffering of others seems primitive, the policy of imposing suffering on the offender for no other purpose than giving satisfaction to his victim seems primitive as well. Consequently, defending retributivism requires showing that the suffering imposed on the wrongdoer has some worthy point beyond the satisfaction of victims. In what follows, I shall try to identify a proposition—which I call the *retributivist principle*—that I take to be the nerve of retributivism. I think this principle accounts for the justice of the *lex talionis* and indicates the point of the suffering demanded by retributivism. . . .

I think that we can see the justice of the *lex talionis* by focusing on the striking affinity between it and the *golden rule*. The *golden rule* mandates "Do unto others as you would have others do unto you," while the *lex talionis* counsels "Do unto others as they have done unto you." It would not be too far-fetched to say that the *lex talionis* is the law enforcement arm of the golden rule, at least in the sense that if people were actually treated as they treated others, then everyone would necessarily follow the golden rule because then people could only willingly act toward others as they were willing to have others act toward them. This is not to suggest that the *lex talionis* follows from the golden rule, but rather that the two share a common moral inspiration: the equality of persons. Treating others as you *would* have them treat you means treating others as equal to you, because adopting the golden rule as one's guiding principle implies that one counts the suffering of others to be as great a calamity as one's own suffering, that one counts one's right to impose suffering on others as no greater than their right to impose suffering on one, and so on. This leads to the *lex talionis* by two approaches [the "Hegelian" and the "Kantian"] that start from different points and converge. . . .

The "Hegelian" and "Kantian" approaches arrive at the same destination from opposite sides.

The "Hegelian" approach starts from the victim's equality with the criminal, and infers from it the victim's right to do to the criminal what the criminal has done to the victim. The "Kantian" approach starts from the criminal's rationality, and infers from it the criminal's authorization of the victim's right to do to the criminal what the criminal has done to the victim. Taken together, these approaches support the following proposition: The equality and rationality of persons implies that an offender deserves and his victim has the right to impose suffering on the offender equal to that which he imposed on the victim. This is the proposition I call the *retributivist principle,* and I shall assume henceforth that it is true. This principle provides that the *lex talionis* is the criminal's just desert and the victim's (or as his representative, the state's) right. Moreover, the principle also indicates the point of retributive punishment, namely, it affirms the equality and rationality of persons, victims and offenders alike.* And the point of this affirmation is, like any moral affirmation, to make a statement, to the criminal, to impress upon him his equality with his victim (which earns him a like fate) and his rationality (by which his actions are held to authorize his fate), and to the society, so that recognition of the equality and rationality of persons becomes a visible part of our shared moral environment that none can ignore in justifying their actions to one another. . . .

The truth of the retributivist principle establishes the justice of the *lex talionis,* but, since it establishes this as a right of the victim rather than a duty, it does not settle the question of whether or to what extent the victim or the state should exercise this right and exact the *lex talionis.* This is a separate moral question because strict adherence to the *lex talionis* amounts to allowing criminals,

---

*Herbert Morris defends retributivism on parallel grounds. See his "Persons and Punishment," *The Monist* 52, no. 4 (October 1968): 475–501. Isn't what Morris calls "the right to be treated as a person" essentially the right of a rational being to be treated only as he has authorized, implicitly or explicitly, by his own free choices?

even the most barbaric of them, to dictate our punishing behavior. It seems certain that there are at least some crimes, such as rape or torture, that we ought not try to match. And this is not merely a matter of imposing an alternative punishment that produces an equivalent amount of suffering, as, say, some number of years in prison that might "add up" to the harm caused by a rapist or a torturer. Even if no amount of time in prison would add up to the harm caused by a torturer, it still seems that we ought not torture him even if this were the only way of making him suffer as much as he has made his victim suffer. Or, consider someone who has committed several murders in cold blood. On the *lex talionis,* it would seem that such a criminal might justly be brought to within an inch of death and then revived (or to within a moment of execution and then reprieved) as many times as he has killed (minus one), and then finally executed. But surely this is a degree of cruelty that would be monstrous.*. . .

I suspect that it will be widely agreed that the state ought not administer punishments of the sort described above even if required by the letter of the *lex talionis,* and thus, even granting the justice of *lex talionis,* there are occasions on which it is morally appropriate to diverge from its requirements. . . .

This way of understanding just punishment enables us to formulate proportional retributivism so that it is compatible with acknowledging the justice of the *lex talionis:* If we take the *lex talionis* as spelling out the offender's just deserts, and if other moral considerations require us to refrain from matching the injury caused by the offender while still allowing us to punish justly, then surely

we impose just punishment if we impose the closest morally acceptable approximation to the *lex talionis.* Proportional retributivism, then, in requiring that the worst crime be punished by the society's worst punishment and so on, could be understood as translating the offender's just desert into its nearest equivalent in the society's table of morally acceptable punishments. Then the two versions of retributivism (*lex talionis* and proportional) are related in that the first states what just punishment would be if nothing but the offender's just desert mattered, and the second locates just punishment at the meeting point of the offender's just deserts and the society's moral scruples. And since this second version only modifies the requirements of the *lex talionis* in light of other moral considerations, it is compatible with believing that the *lex talionis* spells out the offender's just deserts, much in the way that modifying the obligations of promisers in light of other moral considerations is compatible with believing in the binding nature of promises. . . .

II. Civilization, Pain, and Justice

As I have already suggested, from the fact that something is justly deserved, it does not automatically follow that it should be done, since there may be other moral reasons for not doing it such that, all told, the weight of moral reasons swings the balance against proceeding. The same argument that I have given for the justice of the death penalty for murderers proves the justice of beating assaulters, raping rapists, and torturing torturers. Nonetheless, I believe, and suspect that most would agree, that it would not be right for us to beat assaulters, rape rapists, or torture torturers, *even though it were their just deserts*—and even if this were the only way to make them suffer as much as they had made their victims suffer. Calling for the abolition of the death penalty, though it be just, then, amounts to urging that as a society we place execution in the same category of sanction as beating, raping, and torturing, and treat it as something it would also not be right for us to do to offenders, *even if it were their just deserts.* . . .

*Bedau writes: "Where criminals set the limits of just methods of punishment, as they will do if we attempt to give exact and literal implementation to *lex talionis,* society will find itself descending to the cruelties and savagery that criminals employ. But society would be deliberately authorizing such acts, in the cool light of reason, and not (as is often true of vicious criminals) impulsively or in hatred and anger or with an insane or unbalanced mind. Moral restraints, in short, prohibit us from trying to make executions perfectly retributive" (Bedau, "Capital Punishment," p. 176).

Progress in civilization is characterized by a lower tolerance for one's own pain and that suffered by others. And this is appropriate, since, via growth in knowledge, civilization brings increased power to prevent or reduce pain and, via growth in the ability to communicate and interact with more and more people, civilization extends the circle of people with whom we empathize.* If civilization is characterized by lower tolerance for our own pain and that of others, then publicly refusing to do horrible things to our fellows both signals the level of our civilization *and, by our example, continues the work of civilizing*. And this gesture is all the more powerful if we refuse to do horrible things to those who deserve them. I contend then that the more things we are able to include in this category, the more civilized we are and the more civiliz*ing*. Thus we gain from including torture in this category, and if execution is especially horrible, we gain still more by including it. . . .

I accept that if some horrible punishment is necessary to deter equally or more horrible acts, then we may have to impose the punishment. Thus my claim is that reduction in the horrible things we do to our fellows is an advance in civilization *as long as our lives are not thereby made more dangerous,* and that it is only then that we are called upon to extend that reduction as part of the work of civilization. Assuming then, for the moment, that we suffer no increased danger by refraining from doing horrible things to our fellows when they justly deserve them, . . . such refraining to do what is just is not doing what is unjust. . . . Otherwise, it would be unjust to refrain from torturing torturers, raping rapists, or beating assaulters. . . .

To complete the argument, however, I must show that execution is horrible enough to warrant its inclusion alongside torture. Against this it will be said that execution is not especially horrible since it only hastens a fate that is inevitable for us. I think that this view overlooks important differences in the manner in which people reach their inevitable ends. I contend that execution is especially horrible, and it is so in a way similar to (though not identical with) the way in which torture is especially horrible. I believe we view torture as especially awful because of two of its features, which also characterize execution: intense pain and the spectacle of one human being completely subject to the power of another. . . .

In addition to the spectacle of subjugation, execution, even by physically painless means, is also characterized by a special and intense psychological pain that distinguishes it from the loss of life that awaits us all. Interesting in this regard is the fact that although we are not terribly squeamish about the loss of life itself, allowing it in war, self-defense, as a necessary cost of progress, and so on, we are, as the extraordinary hesitance of our courts testifies, quite reluctant to execute. I think this is because execution involves the most psychologically painful features of deaths. We normally regard death from human causes as worse than death from natural causes, since a humanly caused shortening of life lacks the consolation of unavoidability. And we normally regard death whose coming is foreseen by its victim as worse than sudden death, because a foreseen death adds to the loss of life the terrible consciousness of that impending loss.[†] As a humanly caused death whose advent is foreseen by its victim, an execution combines the worst of both.

---

*Van den Haag writes that our ancestors "were not as repulsed by physical pain as we are. The change has to do not with our greater smartness or moral superiority but with a new outlook pioneered by the French and American revolutions [namely, the assertion of human equality and with it 'universal identification'], and by such mundane things as the invention of anesthetics, which make pain much less of an everyday experience" (Ernest van den Haag and John P. Conrad, *The Death Penalty: A Debate* [New York: Plenum Press, 1983], p. 215; cf. van den Haag's *Punishing Criminals* [New York: Basic Books, 1975], pp. 196–206).

[†]This is no doubt partly due to modern skepticism about an afterlife. Earlier peoples regarded a foreseen death as a blessing allowing time to make one's peace with God. Writing of the early Middle Ages, Phillippe Aries says, "In this world that was so familiar with death, sudden death was a vile and ugly death; it was frightening; it seemed a strange and monstrous thing that nobody dared talk about" (Phillippe Aries, *The Hour of Our Death* [New York: Vintage, 1982], p. 11).

Thus far, by analogy with torture, I have argued that execution should be avoided because of how horrible it is to the one executed. But there are reasons of another sort that follow from the analogy with torture. Torture is to be avoided not only because of what it says about *what* we are willing to do to our fellows, but also because of what it says about *us* who are willing to do it. To torture someone is an awful spectacle not only because of the intensity of pain imposed, but because of what is required to be able to impose such pain on one's fellows. The tortured body cringes, using its full exertion to escape the pain imposed upon it—it literally begs for relief with its muscles as it does with its cries. To torture someone is to demonstrate a capacity to resist this begging, and that in turn demonstrates a kind of hardheartedness that a society ought not parade.

And this is true not only of torture, but of all severe corporal punishment. Indeed, I think this constitutes part of the answer to the puzzling question of why we refrain from punishments like whipping, even when the alternative (some months in jail versus some lashes) seems more costly to the offender. Imprisonment is painful to be sure, but it is a reflective pain, one that comes with comparing what is to what might have been, and that can be temporarily ignored by thinking about other things. But physical pain has an urgency that holds body and mind in a fierce grip. . . .

By placing execution alongside torture in the category of things we will not do to our fellow human beings even when they deserve them, we broadcast the message that totally subjugating a person to the power of others *and* confronting him with the advent of his own humanly administered demise is too horrible to be done by civilized human beings to their fellows even when they have earned it: too horrible to do, and too horrible to be capable of doing. And I contend that broadcasting this message loud and clear would in the long run contribute to the general detestation of murder and be, to the extent to which it worked itself into the hearts and minds of the populace, a

deterrent. In short, refusing to execute murderers though they deserve it both reflects and continues the taming of the human species that we call civilization. Thus, I take it that the abolition of the death penalty, though it is a just punishment for murder, is part of the civilizing mission of modern states.

III. Civilization, Safety, and Deterrence

Earlier I said that judging a practice too horrible to do even to those who deserve it does not exclude the possibility that it could be justified if necessary to avoid even worse consequences. Thus, were the death penalty clearly proven a better deterrent to the murder of innocent people than life in prison, we might have to admit that we had not yet reached a level of civilization at which we could protect ourselves without imposing this horrible fate on murderers, and thus we might have to grant the necessity of instituting the death penalty.* But this is far from proven. The available research by no means clearly indicates that the death penalty reduces the incidence of homicide more than life imprisonment does. . . .

Conceding that it has not been proven that the death penalty deters more murders than life imprisonment, van den Haag has argued that neither has it been proven that the death penalty does *not* deter more murders, and thus we must follow common sense which teaches that the higher the cost of something, the fewer people will choose it, and therefore at least some potential murderers who would not be deterred by life

---

*I say "might" here to avoid the sticky question of just how effective a deterrent the death penalty would have to be to justify overcoming our scruples about executing. It is here that the other considerations often urged against capital punishment—discrimination, irrevocability, the possibility of mistake, and so on—would play a role. Omitting such qualifications, however, my position might crudely be stated as follows: *Just desert limits what a civilized society may do to deter crime, and deterrence limits what a civilized society may do to give criminals their just deserts.*

imprisonment will be deterred by the death penalty. Van den Haag writes:

> . . . our experience shows that the greater the threatened penalty, the more it deters.
>
> . . . Life in prison is still life, however unpleasant. In contrast, the death penalty does not just threaten to make life unpleasant—it threatens to take life altogether. This difference is perceived by those affected. We find that when they have the choice between life in prison and execution, 99% of all prisoners under sentence of death prefer life in prison. . . .
>
> From this unquestioned fact a reasonable conclusion can be drawn in favor of the superior deterrent effect of the death penalty. Those who have the choice in practice . . . fear death more than they fear life in prison. . . . If they do, it follows that the threat of the death penalty, all other things equal, is likely to deter more than the threat of life in prison. One is most deterred by what one fears most. From which it follows that whatever statistics fail, or do not fail, to show, the death penalty is likely to be more deterrent than any other. [pp. 68–69]

Those of us who recognize how common-sensical it was, and still is, to believe that the sun moves around the earth, will be less willing than Professor van den Haag to follow common sense here, especially when it comes to doing something awful to our fellows. Moreover, there are good reasons for doubting common sense on this matter. Here are four:

1. From the fact that one penalty is more feared than another, it does not follow that the more feared penalty will deter more than the less feared, unless we know that the less feared penalty is not fearful enough to deter everyone who can be deterred—and this is just what we don't know with regard to the death penalty. Though I fear the death penalty more than life in prison, I can't think of any act that the death penalty would deter me from that an equal likelihood of spending my life in prison wouldn't deter me from as well. Since it seems to me that whoever would be deterred by a given likelihood of death would be deterred by an *equal*

likelihood of life behind bars, I suspect that the common-sense argument only seems plausible because we evaluate it unconsciously assuming that potential criminals will face larger likelihoods of death sentences than of life sentences. If the likelihoods were equal, it seems to me that where life imprisonment was improbable enough to make it too distant a possibility to worry much about, a similar low probability of death would have the same effect. After all, we are undeterred by small likelihoods of death every time we walk the streets. And if life imprisonment were sufficiently probable to pose a real deterrent threat, it would pose as much of a deterrent threat as death. And this is just what most of the research we have on the comparative deterrent impact of execution versus life imprisonment suggests.

2. In light of the fact that roughly 500 to 700 suspected felons are killed by the police in the line of duty every year, and the fact that the number of privately owned guns in America is substantially larger than the number of households in America, it must be granted that anyone contemplating committing a crime *already* faces a substantial risk of ending up dead as a result. It's hard to see why anyone *who is not already deterred by this* would be deterred by the addition of the more distant risk of death after apprehension, conviction, and appeal. Indeed, this suggests that people consider risks in a much cruder way than van den Haag's appeal to common sense suggests—which should be evident to anyone who contemplates how few people use seatbelts (14% of drivers, on some estimates), when it is widely known that wearing them can spell the difference between life (outside prison) and death.

3. Van den Haag has maintained that deterrence doesn't work only by means of cost-benefit calculations made by potential criminals. It works also by the lesson about the wrongfulness of murder that is slowly learned in a society that subjects murderers to the ultimate punishment (p. 63). But if I am correct in claiming that the refusal to execute even those who deserve it has a civilizing effect, then the refusal to execute also teaches a lesson about the wrongfulness of murder. My claim here is admittedly speculative, but no more so than van den Haag's to the contrary. And my view has the added virtue of accounting for the failure of research to show an increased deterrent effect from executions *without having to deny the plausibility of van den Haag's common-sense argument that at least some additional potential murderers will be deterred by the prospect of the death penalty.* If there is a deterrent effect from *not executing*, then it is understandable that while executions will deter some murderers, this effect will be balanced out by the weakening of the deterrent effect of not executing, such that no net reduction in murders will result.* And this, by the way, also disposes of van den Haag's argument that, in the absence of knowledge one way or the other on the deterrent effect of executions, we should execute murderers rather than risk the lives of innocent people whose murders might have been deterred if we had. If there is a deterrent effect of not executing, it follows that we risk innocent lives either way. And if this is so, it seems that the only reasonable course of action is to refrain from imposing what we know is a horrible fate.†

4. Those who still think that van den Haag's common-sense argument for executing murderers is valid will find that the argument proves more than they bargained for. Van den Haag maintains that, in the absence of conclusive evidence on the relative deterrent impact of the death penalty versus life imprisonment, we must follow common sense and assume that if one punishment is more fearful than another, it will deter some potential criminals not deterred by the less fearful punishment. Since people sentenced to death will almost universally try to get their sentences changed to life in prison, it follows that death is more fearful than life imprisonment, and thus that it will deter some additional murderers. Consequently, we should institute the death penalty to save the lives these additional murderers would have taken. But, since people sentenced to be tortured to death would surely try to get their sentences changed to simple execution, the same argument proves that death-by-torture will deter still more potential murderers. Consequently, we should institute death-by-torture to save the lives these additional murderers would have taken.

*A related claim has been made by those who defend the so-called brutalization hypothesis by presenting evidence to show that murders *increase* following an execution. See, for example, William J. Bowers and Glenn L. Pierce, "Deterrence or Brutalization: What Is the Effect of Executions?" *Crime & Delinquency* 26, no. 4 (October 1980): 453–84. They conclude that each execution gives rise to two additional homicides in the month following and that these are real additions, not just a change in timing of the homicides (ibid., p. 481). My claim, it should be noted, is not identical to this, since, as I indicate in the text, what I call "the deterrence effect of not executing" is not something whose impact is to be seen immediately following executions but over the long haul, and, further, my claim is compatible with finding no net increase in murders due to executions. Nonetheless, should the brutalization hypothesis be borne out by further studies, it would certainly lend support to the notion that there is a deterrent effect of not executing.

†Van den Haag writes: "If we were quite ignorant about the marginal deterrent effects of execution, we would have to choose—like it or not—between the certainty of the convicted murderer's death by execution and the likelihood of the survival of future victims of other murderers on the one hand, and on the other his certain survival and the likelihood of the death of new victims. I'd rather execute a man convicted of having murdered others than put the lives of innocents at risk. I find it hard to understand the opposite choice" (p. 69). Conway was able to counter this argument earlier by pointing out that the research on the marginal deterrent effects of execution was not *inconclusive* in the sense of *tending to point both ways*, but rather in the sense of *giving us no reason to believe that capital punishment saves more lives than life imprisonment*. He could then answer van den Haag by saying that the choice is not between risking the lives of murderers and risking the lives of innocents, but between killing a murderer with no reason to believe lives will be saved and sparing a murderer with no reason to believe lives will be lost (Conway, "Capital Punishment and Deterrence," [*Philosophy & Public Affairs* 3, no. 4], pp. 442–43). This, of course, makes the choice to spare the murderer more understandable than van den Haag allows. . . .

Anyone who accepts van den Haag's argument is then confronted with a dilemma: Until we have conclusive evidence that capital punishment is a greater deterrent to murder than life imprisonment, he must grant *either* that we should not follow common sense and not impose the death penalty; *or* we should follow common sense and torture murderers to death. In short, either we must abolish the electric chair or reinstitute the rack. Surely, this is the *reductio ad absurdum* of van den Haag's common-sense argument.

Conclusion

I believe that, taken together, these arguments prove that we should abolish the death penalty though it is a just punishment for murder.

Review and Discussion Questions

1. Is the *lex talionis* an acceptable principle of justice? Explain. How compelling do you find the Hegelian and Kantian cases for the retributivist principle? How would a utilitarian assess this principle?

2. Can something be a just punishment and yet be wrong? Why or why not?

3. Why has modern society stopped using torture and severe corporal punishments? Should execution be placed in the category of things we do not do to our fellow human beings even when they deserve them? Is abolition of the death penalty a sign of increased civilization?

4. Van den Haag upholds, and Reiman challenges, the deterrent value of capital punishment. With whom do you side and why? Is this an issue about which reasonable people can reach agreement? Suppose the deterrent value of the death penalty remains in dispute and the evidence inconclusive. What are the implications for the morality of capital punishment? Do proponents of capital punishment have an obligation to prove that it has deterrent value, or is the burden on critics of the death penalty to show that it is not effective?

Atkins v. *Virginia*

U.S. SUPREME COURT

Should the death penalty ever be imposed on mentally retarded persons? Writing for the majority of the Court, Justice Stevens argues that doing so violates the Eighth Amendment's prohibition of "cruel and unusual punishments." As proof that such executions violate "society's evolving standards of decency," the Court points to recent federal and state laws banning such executions as evidence of an emerging national moral consensus. Moreover, it is doubtful whether the two rationales for capital punishment, namely, retribution and deterrence, support executing the mentally retarded. And their impairments can jeopardize the reliability and fairness of capital proceedings against them. In a vigorous dissent, Justice Scalia denies that there is a

536 U.S. 304 (2002)

national consensus against the execution of the mentally retarded and argues that such executions can be squared with the death penalty's legitimate social purposes.

Study Questions

1. Summarize the facts of this case. What issue does the Eighth Amendment raise?
2. What evidence does Justice Stevens advance for the conclusion that a national consensus has developed against the execution of mentally retarded murderers? What is Scalia's response to this evidence?
3. Explain why the Court believes that the mentally retarded are not exempt from punishment, yet have diminished culpability.
4. What are the two justifications for capital punishment? Why does Scalia believe that the majority errs in thinking that executing mentally retarded criminals is incompatible with these justifications?
5. The majority believes that "mentally retarded defendants . . . face a special risk of wrongful execution." Why?

JUSTICE STEVENS *delivered the opinion of the Court:*

Those mentally retarded persons who meet the law's requirements for criminal responsibility should be tried and punished when they commit crimes. Because of their disabilities in areas of reasoning, judgment, and control of their impulses, however, they do not act with the level of moral culpability that characterizes the most serious adult criminal conduct. Moreover, their impairments can jeopardize the reliability and fairness of capital proceedings against mentally retarded defendants. . . . The American public, legislators, scholars, and judges have deliberated over the question whether the death penalty should ever be imposed on a mentally retarded criminal. The consensus reflected in those deliberations informs our answer to the question presented by this case: whether such executions are "cruel and unusual punishments" prohibited by the Eighth Amendment to the Federal Constitution.

I

Petitioner, Daryl Renard Atkins, was convicted of abduction, armed robbery, and capital murder,

and sentenced to death. At approximately midnight on August 16, 1996, Atkins and William Jones, armed with a semiautomatic handgun, abducted Eric Nesbitt, robbed him of the money on his person, drove him to an automated teller machine in his pickup truck where cameras recorded their withdrawal of additional cash, then took him to an isolated location where he was shot eight times and killed.

Jones and Atkins both testified in the guilt phase of Atkins' trial. Each confirmed most of the details in the other's account of the incident, with the important exception that each stated that the other had actually shot and killed Nesbitt. Jones' testimony, which was both more coherent and credible than Atkins', was obviously credited by the jury and was sufficient to establish Atkins' guilt. At the penalty phase of the trial, the State introduced victim impact evidence and proved two aggravating circumstances: future dangerousness and "vileness of the offense." To prove future dangerousness, the State relied on Atkins' prior felony convictions as well as the testimony of four victims of earlier robberies and assaults. To prove the second aggravator, the prosecution relied upon the trial record, including pictures of the deceased's body and the autopsy report.

In the penalty phase, the defense relied on one witness, Dr. Evan Nelson, a forensic psychologist who had evaluated Atkins before trial and concluded that he was "mildly mentally retarded." His conclusion was based on interviews with people who knew Atkins, a review of school and court records, and the administration of a standard intelligence test which indicated that Atkins had a full scale IQ of 59.

The jury sentenced Atkins to death, but the Virginia Supreme Court ordered a second sentencing hearing because the trial court had used a misleading verdict form. At the resentencing, Dr. Nelson again testified. The State presented an expert rebuttal witness, Dr. Stanton Samenow, who expressed the opinion that Atkins was not mentally retarded, but rather was of "average intelligence, at least," and diagnosable as having antisocial personality disorder. The jury again sentenced Atkins to death.

The Supreme Court of Virginia affirmed the imposition of the death penalty. Atkins did not argue before the Virginia Supreme Court that his sentence was disproportionate to penalties imposed for similar crimes in Virginia, but he did contend "that he is mentally retarded and thus cannot be sentenced to death." The majority of the state court rejected this contention. . . . The Court was "not willing to commute Atkins' sentence of death to life imprisonment merely because of his IQ score." . . .

II

The Eighth Amendment succinctly prohibits "excessive" sanctions. It provides: "Excessive bail shall not be required, nor excessive fines imposed, nor cruel and unusual punishments inflicted." . . . A claim that punishment is excessive is judged not by the standards that prevailed. . . . when the Bill of Rights was adopted, but rather by those that currently prevail. As Chief Justice Warren explained. . . . "The basic concept underlying the Eighth Amendment is nothing less than the dig-

nity of man. . . . The Amendment must draw its meaning from the evolving standards of decency that mark the progress of a maturing society." . . .

III

The parties have not called our attention to any state legislative consideration of the suitability of imposing the death penalty on mentally retarded offenders prior to 1986. In that year, the public reaction to the execution of a mentally retarded murderer in Georgia apparently led to the enactment of the first state statute prohibiting such executions. In 1988, when Congress enacted legislation reinstating the federal death penalty, it expressly provided that a "sentence of death shall not be carried out upon a person who is mentally retarded." In 1989, Maryland enacted a similar prohibition. It was in that year that we decided *Penry,* and concluded that those two state enactments, "even when added to the 14 States that have rejected capital punishment completely, do not provide sufficient evidence at present of a national consensus."

Much has changed since then. Responding to the national attention received by the Bowden execution and our decision in *Penry,* state legislatures across the country began to address the issue. In 1990 Kentucky and Tennessee enacted statutes similar to those in Georgia and Maryland, as did New Mexico in 1991, and Arkansas, Colorado, Washington, Indiana, and Kansas in 1993 and 1994. In 1995, when New York reinstated its death penalty, it emulated the Federal Government by expressly exempting the mentally retarded. Nebraska followed suit in 1998. There appear to have been no similar enactments during the next two years, but in 2000 and 2001 six more States—South Dakota, Arizona, Connecticut, Florida, Missouri, and North Carolina—joined the procession. The Texas Legislature unanimously adopted a similar bill, and bills have passed at least one house in other States, including Virginia and Nevada.

It is not so much the number of these States that is significant, but the consistency of the direction of change. . . . Moreover, even in those States that allow the execution of mentally retarded offenders, the practice is uncommon. Some States, for example New Hampshire and New Jersey, continue to authorize executions, but none have been carried out in decades. Thus there is little need to pursue legislation barring the execution of the mentally retarded in those States. And it appears that even among those States that regularly execute offenders and that have no prohibition with regard to the mentally retarded, only five have executed offenders possessing a known IQ less than 70 since we decided *Penry*. The practice, therefore, has become truly unusual, and it is fair to say that a national consensus has developed against it. . . .

IV

This consensus unquestionably reflects widespread judgment about the relative culpability of mentally retarded offenders, and the relationship between mental retardation and the penological purposes served by the death penalty. Additionally, it suggests that some characteristics of mental retardation undermine the strength of the procedural protections that our capital jurisprudence steadfastly guards.

. . . Mentally retarded persons frequently know the difference between right and wrong and are competent to stand trial. Because of their impairments, however, by definition they have diminished capacities to understand and process information, to communicate, to abstract from mistakes and learn from experience, to engage in logical reasoning, to control impulses, and to understand the reactions of others. There is no evidence that they are more likely to engage in criminal conduct than others, but there is abundant evidence that they often act on impulse rather than pursuant to a premeditated plan, and that in group settings they are followers rather than leaders. Their deficiencies do not warrant an exemption from criminal sanctions, but they do diminish their personal culpability.

In light of these deficiencies, our death penalty jurisprudence provides two reasons consistent with the legislative consensus that the mentally retarded should be categorically excluded from execution. First, there is a serious question as to whether either justification that we have recognized as a basis for the death penalty applies to mentally retarded offenders. *Gregg* v. *Georgia* (1976) identified "retribution and deterrence of capital crimes by prospective offenders" as the social purposes served by the death penalty. Unless the imposition of the death penalty on a mentally retarded person "measurably contributes to one or both of these goals, it 'is nothing more than the purposeless and needless imposition of pain and suffering,' and hence an unconstitutional punishment." . . .

The reduced capacity of mentally retarded offenders provides a second justification for a categorical rule making such offenders ineligible for the death penalty. The risk "that the death penalty will be imposed in spite of factors which may call for a less severe penalty" is enhanced, not only by the possibility of false confessions, but also by the lesser ability of mentally retarded defendants to make a persuasive showing of mitigation in the face of prosecutorial evidence of one or more aggravating factors. Mentally retarded defendants may be less able to give meaningful assistance to their counsel and are typically poor witnesses, and their demeanor may create an unwarranted impression of lack of remorse for their crimes. . . . Moreover, reliance on mental retardation as a mitigating factor can be a two-edged sword that may enhance the likelihood that the aggravating factor of future dangerousness will be found by the jury. Mentally retarded defendants in the aggregate face a special risk of wrongful execution.

Our independent evaluation of the issue reveals no reason to disagree with the judgment of "the legislatures that have recently addressed the matter" and concluded that death is not a suitable punishment for a mentally retarded criminal. We are not persuaded that the execution of mentally retarded criminals will measurably advance the deterrent or the retributive purpose of the death penalty. Construing and applying the Eighth Amendment in the light of our "evolving standards of decency," we therefore conclude that such punishment is excessive and that the Constitution "places a substantive restriction on the State's power to take the life" of a mentally retarded offender.

The judgment of the Virginia Supreme Court is reversed and the case is remanded for further proceedings not inconsistent with this opinion.

It is so ordered.

JUSTICE SCALIA, *dissenting:*

Today's decision is the pinnacle of our Eighth Amendment death-is-different jurisprudence. Not only does it, like all of that jurisprudence, find no support in the text or history of the Eighth Amendment; it does not even have support in current social attitudes regarding the conditions that render an otherwise just death penalty inappropriate. Seldom has an opinion of this Court rested so obviously upon nothing but the personal views of its members.

I

I begin with a brief restatement of facts that are abridged by the Court but important to understanding this case. After spending the day drinking alcohol and smoking marijuana, petitioner Daryl Renard Atkins and a partner in crime drove to a convenience store, intending to rob a customer. Their victim was Eric Nesbitt, an airman from Langley Air Force Base, whom they abducted, drove to a nearby automated teller machine, and forced to withdraw $200. They then drove him to a deserted area, ignoring his pleas to leave him unharmed. According to the co-conspirator, whose testimony the jury evidently credited, Atkins ordered Nesbitt out of the vehicle and, after he had taken only a few steps, shot him one, two, three, four, five, six, seven, eight times in the thorax, chest, abdomen, arms, and legs.

The jury convicted Atkins of capital murder. At resentencing . . . the jury heard extensive evidence of petitioner's alleged mental retardation. . . . The State contested the evidence of retardation. . . .

The jury also heard testimony about petitioner's 16 prior felony convictions for robbery, attempted robbery, abduction, use of a firearm, and maiming. . . . The jury sentenced petitioner to death. The Supreme Court of Virginia affirmed petitioner's sentence.

II

As the foregoing history demonstrates, petitioner's mental retardation was a *central issue* at sentencing. The jury concluded, however, that his alleged retardation was not a compelling reason to exempt him from the death penalty in light of the brutality of his crime and his long demonstrated propensity for violence. . . .

Under our Eighth Amendment jurisprudence, a punishment is "cruel and unusual" if it falls within one of two categories: "those modes or acts of punishment that had been considered cruel and unusual at the time that the Bill of Rights was adopted," and modes of punishment that are inconsistent with modern "standards of decency," as evinced by objective indicia, the most important of which is "legislation enacted by the country's legislatures."

The Court makes no pretense that execution of the mildly mentally retarded would have been considered "cruel and unusual" in 1791. . . . The Court is left to argue, therefore, that execution of the mildly retarded is inconsistent with the "evolving standards of decency that mark the progress of a maturing society." Before today, our opinions consistently emphasized that Eighth Amendment judgments regarding the existence of social "standards" "should be informed by objective factors to the maximum possible extent" and "should not be, or appear to be, merely the subjective views of individual Justices." . . . The Court pays lipservice to these precedents as it miraculously extracts a "national consensus" forbidding execution of the mentally retarded from the fact that 18 States—less than *half* (47%) of the 38 States that permit capital punishment (for whom the issue exists)—have very recently enacted legislation barring execution of the mentally retarded. Even that 47% figure is a distorted one. . . . Kansas apparently permits execution of all except the *severely* mentally retarded; New York permits execution of the mentally retarded who commit murder in a correctional facility.

But let us accept, for the sake of argument, the Court's faulty count. That bare number of States alone—*18*—should be enough to convince any reasonable person that no "national consensus" exists. How is it possible that agreement among 47% of the death penalty jurisdictions amounts to "consensus"? Our prior cases have generally required a much higher degree of agreement before finding a punishment cruel and unusual on "evolving standards" grounds. . . .

III

. . . The genuinely operative portion of the opinion, then, is the Court's statement of the reasons why it agrees with the contrived consensus it has found, that the "diminished capacities" of the mentally retarded render the death penalty excessive. . . . The Court gives two reasons why the death penalty is an excessive punishment for all mentally retarded offenders. First, the "diminished capacities" of the mentally retarded raise a "serious question" whether their execution contributes to the "social purposes" of the death penalty, viz., retribution and deterrence. (The Court conveniently ignores a third "social purpose" of the death penalty—"incapacitation of dangerous criminals and the consequent prevention of crimes that they may otherwise commit in the future," *Gregg* v. *Georgia*, . . .).

. . . Surely culpability, and deservedness of the most severe retribution, depends not merely (if at all) upon the mental capacity of the criminal (above the level where he is able to distinguish right from wrong) but also upon the depravity of the crime—which is precisely why this sort of question has traditionally been thought answerable not by a categorical rule of the sort the Court today imposes upon all trials, but rather by the sentencer's weighing of the circumstances (both degree of retardation and depravity of crime) in the particular case. The fact that juries continue to sentence mentally retarded offenders to death for extreme crimes shows that society's moral outrage sometimes demands execution of retarded offenders. By what principle of law, science, or logic can the Court pronounce that this is wrong? There is none. Once the Court admits (as it does) that mental retardation does not render the offender morally *blameless,* there is no basis for saying that the death penalty is *never* appropriate retribution, no matter *how* heinous the crime. As long as a mentally retarded offender knows "the difference between right and wrong," only the sentencer can assess whether his retardation reduces his culpability enough to exempt him from the death penalty for the particular murder in question.

As for the other social purpose of the death penalty that the Court discusses, deterrence: That is not advanced, the Court tells us, because the mentally retarded are "less likely" than their non-retarded counterparts to "process the information of the possibility of execution as a penalty and . . . control their conduct based upon that information." . . . The Court does not say that *all* mentally retarded individuals cannot "process the information of the possibility of execution as a penalty and . . . control their conduct based upon that information"; it merely asserts that they are "less likely" to be able to do so. But surely the deterrent effect of a penalty is adequately vindicated if it successfully deters many, but not all, of the target class. Virginia's death penalty, for example, does not fail of its deterrent effect simply because *some* criminals are unaware that Virginia *has* the death penalty. . . .

The Court throws one last factor into its grab bag of reasons why execution of the retarded is "excessive" in all cases: Mentally retarded offenders "face a special risk of wrongful execution" because they are less able "to make a persuasive showing of mitigation," "to give meaningful assistance to their counsel," and to be effective witnesses. . . . If this unsupported claim has any substance to it (which I doubt) it might support a due process claim in all criminal prosecutions of the mentally retarded; but it is hard to see how it has anything to do with an *Eighth Amendment* claim that execution of the mentally retarded is cruel and unusual. We have never before held it to be cruel and unusual punishment to impose a sentence in violation of some *other* constitutional imperative.

. . .

Today's opinion adds one more to the long list of substantive and procedural requirements impeding imposition of the death penalty imposed under this Court's assumed power to invent a death-is-different jurisprudence. None of those requirements existed when the Eighth Amendment was adopted, and some of them were not even supported by current moral consensus. They include prohibition of the death penalty for "ordinary" murder, for rape of an adult woman, and for felony murder absent a showing that the defendant possessed a sufficiently culpable state of mind; prohibition of the death penalty for any person under the age of 16 at the time of the crime; prohibition of the death penalty as the mandatory punishment for any crime; a requirement that the sentencer not be given unguided discretion, a requirement that the sentencer be empowered to take into account all mitigating circumstances, and a requirement that the accused receive a judicial evaluation of his claim of insanity before the sentence can be executed. There is something to be said for popular abolition of the death penalty; there is nothing to be said for its incremental abolition by this Court.

This newest invention promises to be more effective than any of the others in turning the process of capital trial into a game. One need only read the definitions of mental retardation adopted by the American Association of Mental Retardation and the American Psychiatric Association to realize that the symptoms of this condition can readily be feigned. . . .

I respectfully dissent.

Review and Discussion Questions

1. Has a national consensus emerged that it is wrong to execute mentally retarded murderers? Who is right about this—Justice Stevens or Justice Scalia? Does it matter whether there is such a consensus or not?

2. Assuming that we can in general justify executing murderers on the basis of either deterrence or retribution, does either consideration ever justify executing a murderer who is mentally retarded?

3. Are mentally retarded persons less culpable for their crimes that those who are not retarded? If so, does this always rule out capital punishment? The Supreme Court does not appear to distinguish between mild and severe mental retardation. Does the degree of the defendant's retardation matter?

4. How is your view of this case affected by the fact that the prosecution contested the defense's claim that defendant Atkins was mentally retarded? Will a defendant's mental retardation always be subject to dispute? Is Scalia right to contend that it is easy for a defendant to feign mental retardation?

5. The Court believes that mentally retarded persons generally know the difference between right and wrong, that they can be competent to stand trial, and that they are not exempt from punishment. Do you agree? If it is wrong to execute people who are mentally retarded, why isn't it also wrong to imprison them?

6. Do you agree that mentally retarded persons accused of murder are less likely to receive the same procedural protections as other defendants and that they face a "special risk of wrongful execution"? If so, does this imply that we should never execute mentally retarded murderers? Could the "special risk" problem be satisfactorily addressed by the courts' taking special precautions when dealing with mentally retarded defendants?

7. Should Daryl Renard Atkins be executed?

8. Justice Scalia complains that over the years the Supreme Court has placed various limits on capital punishment. Review each of the restrictions he mentions. Are they reasonable? Are they restrictions that supporters of capital punishment should be willing to accept, or do they reflect an anti–capital punishment bias on the part of the Court?

12

WAR AND TERRORISM

Terrorism, Innocence, and War

ROBERT K. FULLINWIDER

The events of September 11, 2001, left the world stunned, and trying to explain that day and grasp its full significance is a daunting task. One reason the whole world condemned the perpetrators of the attacks is that international law categorically outlaws terrorism and violence by non-state actors. However, it is too simple to see such violence as always wrong, argues Robert K. Fullinwider, Senior Research Scholar at the Center for Philosophy and Public Policy at the University of Maryland. We sometimes find ourselves sympathizing with individuals or groups that fight against oppression, even outside the scope of international law. After all, America itself was born from illegal rebellion. What is scary about terrorists, Fullinwider argues, is that "they appeal to morality without appealing to law." Terrorists like Osama bin Laden are not throwbacks to a prehistoric time before morality, but to a time when morality was not under the control of law. That is, they treat the world as if it were a "state of nature," where, in the absence of law, each person acts on his or her own private judgment of what justice requires. And the terrorists believe their own judgment is infallible.

Study Questions

1. How does the meaning of *innocence* with respect to moral wrongdoing and just punishment differ from its meaning during wartime? Explain why the perpetrators of September 11 are guilty from either perspective.

2. What does the U.N. International Convention for the Suppression of Terrorist Bombing state? What is the Arab League's position on terrorism? What did Thomas Jefferson say about violence?

3. Explain what Fullinwider means when he writes that terrorists "appeal to morality without appealing to law"?

Reprinted by permission from "Terrorism, Innocence, and War" by Robert K. Fullinwider as it appears in War After September 11, *edited by Verna V. Gehring, published by Rowman & Littlefield. References omitted.*

4. What is the distinctive feature of the "state of nature"? Why is "private judgment" a menace? Give an example of the exercise of private judgment by a state.

5. What point does Fullinwider draw from the remarks of Jerry Falwell?

T HE EVENTS OF SEPTEMBER 11, 2001 defy the power of words to describe, console, or even explain. Nevertheless, because the United States must respond in one way or another, and because people must give or withhold their support to any national course of action, words necessarily come into play, words to formulate goals and words to justify the means to achieve them. "Terrorism" is one of the words ubiquitous in the aftermath of September 11, "war" another.

Carlin Romano, a philosopher and critic, writes in the *Chronicle of Higher Education* that a third word, "innocence," should get more attention than it has received. The "clarification and defense of innocence" by intellectuals, social commentators, and public officials, Romano believes, could add an important element to the fight against terrorism.

Innocence

"Innocence" links "war" and "terrorism." Terrorists are counted as murderers because they kill the innocent. Similarly, in war, military forces are prohibited by common custom and international law from targeting civilians. This prohibition "assumes innocence at its core," notes Romano. Perhaps so, but not "innocence" in the sense that underwrites Romano's initial condemnation of terrorists.

Romano insists that terrorism cannot be justified morally, no matter what its political aims, because terrorists select their victims haphazardly, without concern for innocence or guilt. Here, he construes "innocence" under a model of crime and punishment. On that model, punishment should fall on the guilty, not the innocent, on the wrongdoer, not the mere bystander. Just punishment, accordingly, must allow for some sort of antecedent "due process," in which individuals are found guilty according to evidence and only then subjected to penalties in proper proportion to their wrongs. Since the terrorist kills "haphazardly," he doesn't fulfill this minimal demand of just punishment.

In war, however, the notion of "innocence" has nothing to do with lack of blameworthiness. Rather, it divides individuals into two classes: those who may be directly targeted by military force and those who may not. The former includes uniformed armed forces (combatants), the latter ordinary civilians (noncombatants). This division derives not from the imperatives of crime and punishment but from the imperatives of self-defense. In resisting aggression, a state may direct lethal force against the agency endangering it, and that agency is the military force of the aggressor.

From the point of view of moral-wrongdoing and just punishment, many of the aggressor's military personnel may be innocent; they may be reluctant conscripts with no sympathy for their nation's actions. Likewise, among ordinary civilians, many may actively support and favor their country's criminal aggression. They are not innocent. But *from the point of view of self-defense,* the moral quality of the conscript's reluctance and the civilian's enthusiasm is not relevant. What matters is that the former is a combatant, the latter not.

Consequently, war must be prosecuted by means that discriminate between the two classes. Specifying membership in the two classes is, of course, a difficult and somewhat arbitrary affair. Combatants are first of all those in a warring country's military service. They wear uniforms, bear arms, and are trained to be on guard. Because they wield the means of violence and destruction directed at a defending nation, such soldiers are fair targets of lethal response by that nation, even when they are in areas to the rear of active fighting and even when they are sleeping. However, not all enemy soldiers may be attacked. Those rendered *hors de combat** through injury, capture, or some other means possess the same immunities from being killed as civilian noncombatants. Conversely, individuals not in uniform but actively participating in the war effort, such as civilian leaders and managers directing overall military policy, are fair targets of attack. They count as combatants. The operative language in the Geneva Convention of 1949 and in the U.N. Resolution on Human Rights of 1968—two legal protocols governing the prosecution of war—confers immunity on those "not taking part in hostilities." Obviously, there is plenty of room to construe this phrase in very different ways. Even so, some people—the very old and the very young, for example—clearly qualify for noncombatant immunity on any construal.

While the two points of view—of crime and punishment, on the one hand, and self-defense, on the other—understand "innocence" in different ways, either of them seems clearly to indict the perpetrators of the September 11 attacks. First, those who used hijacked passenger planes as bombs targeted civilians as such, at least in their attack on the World Trade Center. If the attackers considered themselves at war, they violated one of war's laws. Second, the attackers provided no advance notice of their plan to exact punishment from the occupants of the World Trade Center and no forum for the occupants to answer any accusations or charges. If the attackers thought of themselves as avenging angels, they violated due process.

Terrorism

That Osama bin Laden and his network stepped across a clear line marking right from wrong seems signaled by the universal condemnation of

the events of September 11. Even the League of Arab States expressed its "revulsion, horror, and shock over the terrorist attacks" against America. Nevertheless, matters may not be as simple as the foregoing account suggests.

First of all, the laws of war and the distinctions they draw are creatures of *states* and *state interests*. Individuals and groups who have no states to represent their grievances, or who stand at odds to the arrangements of power imposed by the prevailing state system, are barred from using violence to vindicate their just demands (as they may see them). Indeed, whatever their cause, they are condemned as criminals if they resort to violence. The U.N. International Convention for the Suppression of Terrorist Bombings (1997), for example, makes it a crime to explode a lethal device "in a public place" or even to attack a government facility such as an embassy. These acts, it goes on to say, constitute terrorism and "are under no circumstances justifiable by considerations of a political, philosophical, ideological, racial, ethnic, [or] religious . . . nature." No cause however good warrants violent response if the actor is an individual or group, not a state.

Since the United States is a country founded on violent rebellion against lawful authority, we can hardly endorse a blanket disavowal of the right by others violently to rebel against their own oppressors. Indeed, Thomas Jefferson offered a small paean to political violence in letters he sent to Abigail Adams, James Madison, and William Smith in 1787. "I hold that a little rebellion now and then is a good thing," Jefferson wrote, "& as necessary in the political world as storms in the physical . . . . What signify a few lives lost in a century or two? The tree of liberty must be refreshed from time to time with the blood of patriots & tyrants. It is its natural manure." The occasion of Jefferson's letters was the just-suppressed Shay's Rebellion, the violent resistance by desperate farmers in western Massachusetts against the due process of law that, in a time of economic distress, was grinding them into dust. Only a handful of lives were lost in the short affair, but it lent

*Out of combat; disabled.—ED.

a degree of urgency to delegates from various states scurrying off to Philadelphia to replace the Articles of Confederation.

Nor is Jefferson alone in looking favorably at a "little rebellion" by people who resort to violence in the name of a great cause. John Brown remains for many Americans a martyr in the fight against slavery, though his actions would count as terrorism under contemporary definitions and international conventions. While leading a gang of anti-slavery guerilla fighters in eastern Kansas in 1855, Brown took revenge for an assault by slavers on the town of Lawrence by dragging five men out of the small proslavery settlement of Pottawatomie Creek one night and hacking them to death. In 1859, in his ill-fated attempt to seize the United States armory at Harper's Ferry, and precipitate (he fancied) a vast slave rebellion, Brown seized sixty hostages from the neighboring precincts.

Killing "innocents"—Brown's victims at Pottawatomie Creek were not accorded any due process, nor were they combatants in uniform—and taking civilian hostages: these are the very deeds deplored and condemned by U.N. resolutions and conventions.

They make Brown a quintessential terrorist. Yet many people refuse to view Brown this way because they don't accept the uncompromising U.N. position that "irregular" violence—violence initiated by individuals and groups—is "under no circumstances justifiable by considerations of a political, philosophical, ideological, racial, ethnic, [or] religious . . . nature." They believe that in some circumstances a cause *may be* sufficiently weighty to justify shedding blood, even "innocent" blood.

So, too, believes the League of Arab States. Though it condemned the September 11 attack as "terrorism," it refuses to accept an unqualified version of the U.N.'s view that, for example, exploding a lethal device "in a public place" counts always as terrorism. In its 1998 Convention for the Suppression of Terrorism, the League starts with a definition pretty much in line with the United Nation's. Terrorism is

[a]ny act of violence, whatever its motives or purposes, that occurs in the advancement of an individual or collective criminal agenda and seeking to sow panic among people, causing fear by harming them, or placing their lives, liberty or security in danger . . . .

A "terrorist offense" is any act in furtherance of a terrorist objective.

So far, so good (though we may wonder about the force of the modifier "criminal" in reference to the terrorist's "agenda"). But the Convention then adds:

All cases of struggle by whatever means, including armed struggle, against foreign occupation and aggression for liberation and self-determination, in accordance with the principles of international law, *shall not be regarded as an offense.*

What does this added qualification mean? Read one way (putting emphasis on the clause "in accordance with the principles of international law"), it can be taken as proscribing the same deeds outlawed by U.N. conventions. Read another way (taking account of the fact that the definition of "terrorism" is prefaced by an initial affirmation of "the right of peoples to combat foreign occupation and aggression by whatever means, in order to liberate their territories and secure their right to self determination"), it can be taken as licensing some irregular violence (that directed against foreign "occupation" and promoting Arab "self-determination") while precluding other violence (that on behalf of a "criminal agenda"). Moreover, the matter is muddied further by the fact that the U.N. itself recognizes a fundamental right to self-determination, a right to resist "colonial, foreign and alien domination." Through Osama bin Laden's eyes, the attack of September 11 fell upon an alien dominator of Arabia and bespoke a campaign that would not end "before all infidel armies leave the land of Muhammed." What could the right to self-determination mean if it tied one's hands against the very source of "humiliation and degradation" imposed upon the Islamic world from the outside for eighty years?

Carlin Romano writes that it probably never occurred to bin Laden "how awful it is to kill innocent people." But bin Laden's own self-justification indicates the contrary. "Millions of innocent children are being killed as I speak," he declared, children who are dying in Iraq as a putative consequence of the economic embargo imposed on that state by an American-led coalition. Osama bin Laden purported to act on behalf of innocence. Why should he not calculate, as Jefferson implied, that shedding the blood of a few now may save the lives and liberty of many others in the long run?

Moreover, why should he feel restrained by the conventional views of innocence? Isn't it arbitrary to immunize from attack people who may be causally implicated in the oppression one is resisting? By convention, the civilians of an aggressor nation who buy their country's war bonds are noncombatants and immune from attack. But without those war bonds, the aggressor nation would not be able to buy the guns and planes and bombs that enable it to prosecute its aggression. Why should those citizens be counted as "innocent" or made immune? . . .

Terrorists, writes Romano, must believe in some "philosophy of innocence, however pinched." They assume the guilt of their victims, but on "transparently flimsy grounds." Obviously, their grounds won't line up with the considerations operative in the conventions of international law, but those conventions weren't endorsed by the terrorists in the first place and don't take their perspectives to heart.

Consider the infamous massacre of Israeli athletes at the 1972 Munich Olympics by Black September, a Palestinian terrorist organization. Weren't those athletes uncontrovertibly innocent? From the point of view of Black September, they were not. They were the knowing and willing representatives of Israel to an international affair where their presence would lend further international credibility and legitimacy to their state. From the point of view of their attackers, the athletes were active and informed accessories to a continuing "crime"—the support of the "criminal" state of Israel. These are not flimsy grounds for charges of "guilt," although they are grounds thoroughly

contestable and clearly lying outside the scope of considerations allowed by international law.

The Rule of Law

It is too easy to dismiss the terrorist as evil incarnate, as a demon beyond the human pale. "The terrorist," claims one writer, "represents a new breed of man which takes humanity back to prehistoric times, to the times when morality was not yet born." But this characterization seems wrong. If anything, terrorists are throwbacks to a "prehistoric time" when morality was not yet under control. What is scary about terrorists is that they appeal to morality without appealing to law. They act as a law unto themselves. Let me explain.

Political theorists tell a story about the "State of Nature" to explain and defend government. The State of Nature proves to be intolerable for its inhabitants, whose lives are "solitary, poore, nasty, brutish, and short" (according to Thomas Hobbes). Contrary to common impressions, however, the problem in the State of Nature is not that people are so immoral, so lacking in any sense of justice or decency, that they prey wantonly upon one another. The problem is that people are *so moral*, so determined to vindicate rights or uphold honor at any cost that they become a menace to each other.

The distinctive feature of the State of Nature, as John Locke points out, is not the absence of morality but the absence of *law*. It is a circumstance in which the "law of nature"—the moral law—must be enforced by each individual. Each is responsible for vindicating her own rights and the rights of others. All prosecution of crime and injustice in the State of Nature is free-lance. Such a situation is the spawning ground of the never-ending chain of retaliation and counter-retaliation of the blood feud. "For every one in that state being both Judge and Executioner of the Law of Nature, Men being partial to themselves, Passion and Revenge is very apt to carry them too far, and with too much heat, in their own Cases; as well as negligence, and unconcernedness, to make them too remiss, in other Men's."

Even if persons were not biased in their own favor, the problems of enforcing justice in the State of Nature would remain deadly. How would crime be defined? How would evidence for its commission be gathered and validated? Who would be punished, and in what manner? What would constitute legitimate self-defense? Who would calculate the rectification due from unjust aggression? Nothing in the State of Nature ensures any common understanding about these questions. The contrary is the case. Private understanding pitted against private understanding produces an escalation of response and counter-response that lets violence erupt and feed on itself.

The solution, of course, is, as Locke proposed, "an establish'd, settled, known Law, received and allowed by common consent to be the Standard of Right and Wrong, and the common measure to decide all Controversies," and "a known and indifferent Judge, with Authority to determine all differences according to the established Law." This solution prevails, more or less, in the domestic case. In most states, a common law tolerably resolves disputes, even if that law is not always the product of common consent. The law does not always work well enough, however, and rebellious violence against its inflexibilities and oppressions as often elicits our sympathy as it invokes our fear and antipathy. "Irregular justice"—or vigilantism—can redirect the law toward a more just course. Moreover, sometimes the existing regime of law is so oppressive that outright revolution seems in order. At the end of the eighteenth century, a great many Americans, newly born of their own "revolution," sympathized with the revolution in France that destroyed a decadent monarchy and substituted republicanism; a great many others recoiled in horror at the revolution's excesses as it tumbled into tyranny. In the years since, Americans have both supported and resisted revolutions abroad. Our ambivalence is rooted in twin impulses: to warm to the oppressed in their liberation struggles and to fear the disorder of Private Judgment substituting for law.

At the international level, the rule of law likewise rescues the community of states from intolerable anarchy, though unlike domestic law, international law is a patchwork of treaties, conventions, and understandings among independent actors, each jealous of its sovereignty. Few tribunals exist where "a known and indifferent Judge" possesses full "Authority to determine all differences" among nations; nor is there a common agent of coercion to enforce the judge's rulings on recalcitrant parties. Still, laws and conventions bring some order to international affairs, including the laws of war and the conventions against terrorism referred to earlier. Admittedly, these laws and conventions stack the deck against non-state actors. And—as the posture of the League of Arab States indicates—some people and some states will want to support non-state actors in violent response to perceived wrongs and oppressions. But even behind such sympathizing and support lies the worrisome specter of Private Judgment. Osama bin Laden, in his isolated redoubts in the Afghan mountains, elects himself as the vindicator of Islamic honor and rights. He answers to no one or no community but to his own sense of justice. Self-elected vigilantes on the international scene may be tolerated—or even supported—by states when their vigilantism remains a mere thorn in the sides of enemies; but when the vigilantes hold in their hands the power to destroy people by the scores and hundreds of thousands, the face of Private Judgment is hideous even to those who join in its chosen cause. When the League of Arab States proffered its condemnation of the September 11 attacks, it had not suddenly forgotten the experience of eighty years of "humiliation and degradation" noted by bin Laden, it had not suddenly abandoned the cause of Palestinian justice, it had not suddenly converted to non-violence. Rather, it had suddenly lost its taste for Private Judgment. Osama bin Laden is beholden to no one, not even to the Arab states themselves. Consequently, he is a peril to all.

Private Judgment is not only a menace when exercised by individuals but when exercised by states as well. Countries undermine the efficacy of international law by reserving to themselves

Private Judgment about its application. For example, in 1928, Western powers agreed in the Kellogg-Briand Pact to outlaw war as a tool of national policy. They determined that armed aggression was henceforth a crime. But each of the Pact's signatories reserved to itself final judgment about when its acts were proper self-defense and when improper aggression against a neighbor. As a consequence, the Kellogg-Briand Pact inhibited war the way matches inhibit fire.

In the aftermath of World War II, when Nazi leaders were put on trial for war crimes, they interposed a potentially fatal objection: the Nuremberg tribunal before which they appeared had no standing to judge Germany's war policy since the Kellogg-Briand Pact reserved to each country final judgment about whether it was acting lawfully. In rebuttal, the United States joined Great Britain in arguing that although a state may be free in the first instance to decide whether it is acting in self-defense, its exercise of the right of self-defense is nevertheless ultimately subject to review by the international community. Whether this was an ingenious construction of the Kellogg-Briand Pact or an invention from whole cloth, the argument won the day and established an important principle of international law: that no state can take complete refuge in Private Judgment. Ultimately, states must face the bar of collective judgment and justify their violent conduct in terms acceptable to the common moral sense of mankind.

This new principle was an important step for international law, since a system of law in which each party can veto the application of the law to itself is no system of law at all. So long as each party remains the sole judge of its own case, the State of Nature remains in place.

Having struck a notable blow for the principle of law at Nuremberg, the United States has not always honored its own vital handiwork. For example, in 1985, when Nicaragua alleged in the World Court that we were guilty of aggression for supporting the Contras, we did not defend our support by arguing that it constituted collective self-defense. We argued instead an interpretation of the United Nations charter that made the question of whether we were acting in self-defense nonjusticiable. We argued that our actions could be reviewed only by the Security Council of the U.N., where, of course, we have a veto. In effect, the United States argued that only it could judge whether its actions were aggression or self-defense. Having so argued, our subsequent insistence that other, smaller states—states without a veto in the Security Council—must submit to the bar of collective judgment looks self-serving rather than principled. Private Judgment—whether manifested in the person of a terrorist like Osama bin Laden or in the agency of a rogue state like Iraq—increasingly reveals itself for the hazard it is. Our own interests as well as our principles demand that we put a stake through its heart. We must not claim it as our special prerogative.

Innocence Revisited

Suppose that the ideas of due process and noncombatant immunity referred to by Carlin Romano are nothing but conventions accepted within and among states. Still, they are precious ideas, hard-won in their application. They require that legitimate institutions resort to violence in ways that discriminate between those adjudicated guilty and those not, between those taking part in hostilities and those not. These are the rules fallible humans have fashioned to keep us out of the State of Nature. They issue, in part, from our collective recognition that the partiality toward our own interests and the unconcern we feel for the interests of others—those two facets of human nature remarked on by Locke—invariably distort Private Judgment and make it unreliable.

But what if you were assured of reliable judgment? What if you were assured of infallibility? Then you would need no conventions of innocence to guide you. No conventional limitations withstand the conceit that God is on your side, since whatever God does must be right. If God orders you to war against, and to "save alive nothing that breatheth" among, an enemy; if He commands you utterly to destroy the Hittites and the Amorites, the Canaanites and the Perizzites, the Hivites and the Jebusites; then you destroy without compunction and without distinction.

When Christians, who from the Middle Ages on have developed a profoundly influential doctrine of just war that puts special emphasis on noncombatant immunity and on the innocence, particularly, of those too young, too old, and too ill to be "taking part in hostilities"—when Christians, I say, read Deuteronomy 20, they must feel a considerable indigestion. Still, the text says what it says, and if "God by revelation made the Israelites . . . the executioners of His supernatural sentence" then the "penalty was within God's right to assign, and within the Israelites' communicated right to enforce"—so reads a passage from the *Catholic Encyclopedia*. As "Sovereign Arbiter of life and death," God can take or give as he pleases, and it must be just. But we who are without God's eyes "cannot argue natural right" from these Biblical cases of wholesale slaughter, the *Encyclopedia* passage goes on to say. Indeed we cannot. We must hew to those distinctions and discriminations embedded in the conventions on war and terrorism and we must wholeheartedly strive to see them everywhere honored.

The delusion that he and God act in concert is what makes Osama bin Laden's self-election as avenging angel a special threat to humanity. Had he the power, he would not hesitate to kill all that breathes among his "enemy." He would not hesitate to destroy whole cities, entire populations. America was "hit by God," declares bin Laden in his taped message after the September 11 attacks. God has made America the enemy and bin Laden merely executes His will.

Two days after the September 11 horrors, an unnerved Jerry Falwell intemperately offered his own version of bin Laden's delirium. God, announced Falwell, had lifted the curtain of protection around America, angered by the ACLU, gays and lesbians, abortionists, pagans, secularists, and the Federal court system. "God will not be mocked," he declared. But Falwell quickly repudiated his remarks in the face of widespread criticism. He apologized for his words, pleading weariness for his thoughtlessness. "[My] September 13 comments were a complete misstatement of what I believe and what I've preached for nearly 50 years," Falwell said in an interview. "Namely, I do not believe that any mortal person knows when God is judging or not judging someone or a nation." He repeated the point: "I have no way of knowing when or if God would lift the curtain of protection" around America. "My misstatement included assuming that I or any mortal would know when God is judging or not judging a nation."

In his recantation, Falwell is surely on the mark. He does not know God's will or God's plan. Neither he, nor you, nor I know, nor does Osama bin Laden.

In limning the salutary effects of a little political violence, Thomas Jefferson posed a standard against which to reckon its justification. "What signify a few lives lost in a century or two?" he asked. He meant: the favorable course of events will let us look back from afar and tolerate the violence that set it in motion. If this is the right standard, then the United States has it within its power now, by prudent and measured action, to make sure that in a century or two the lives lost on September 11 continue to signify something—a profound and everlasting wrong.

Review and Discussion Questions

1. Explain the distinction between combatants and noncombatants. Who may, and who may not, be legitimately killed during a war? To what extent are guilt and innocence relevant to the answer to the previous question?

2. How would you define "terrorism"? Is it always wrong? Explain why or why not. Was John Brown a terrorist?

3. When non-state groups fight what they perceive to be oppression or injustice, should they be bound by international law, which was designed by and for states?

4. What motivates terrorists like Osama bin Laden? Critically assess Fullinwider's argument that their actions take us back to a time when morality was not restrained by law.

5. Has the United States been guilty of damaging the system of international law by exercising its private judgment?

Human Rights, the Laws of War, and Terrorism

MICHAEL IGNATIEFF

Michael Ignatieff, Director of the Carr Center for Human Rights at Harvard University, begins this essay by examining the nature of human rights during terrorist emergencies. Abridging rights in exceptional circumstances is not necessarily wrong, he argues; the question is whether the institutions of a free society continue to do their job, holding the executive accountable for its actions. After discussing the interplay between human rights and the laws of war as two different systems of ethical constraints, Ignatieff goes on to probe the complex relationship between terror and human rights. Although human rights do not motivate terror, terrorists frequently justify their actions by appeal to human rights, in particular, to the right of self-determination. Human rights principles, however, require that any struggle for self-determination must be nonviolent and committed to negotiation and deliberation. Violence may be justified as a last resort, but in moving outside human rights, one must obey the laws of war relating to civilian immunity. Even the weak and oppressed are not permitted to fight dirty.

Study Questions

1. How does the ancient Roman legal adage, "the safety of the people is the ultimate law," conflict with the view of rights as unconditional? What is Dworkin's point about the trade-off between our liberty and our security in times of terrorist threat?

2. Ignatieff endorses the position taken by Abraham Lincoln during the Civil War. What was it? What point does the example of Japanese internment make?

3. Ignatieff says that human rights and the laws of war are closely related, but also contradictory. Explain.

4. How are human rights used to justify terrorism? What ethical limits do human rights principles in fact impose on struggles for self-determination?

5. According to Ignatieff, is the right of revolution a human right? Explain.

Reprinted by permission from Michael Ignatieff, "Human Rights, the Laws of War, and Terrorism," in Social Research, *vol. 69, no. 4 (Winter 2002).*

I

THE TWO TERMS—human rights and terror—look like a simple antithesis: human rights good, terror bad. My thesis is that the antithesis is not so simple. Of course, human rights and terror stand opposed to each other. Terrorist acts violate the right to life, along with many other rights. But equally, human rights—notably the right to self-determination—have constituted a major justification for the resort to political violence, including acts of terror, in the twentieth century. In this article I will consider the relation between these concepts from two sides: from the limitations that human rights impose on counterterrorism, and from the justifications that human rights accord terror. My purpose is to put pressure on human rights as a moral system, and to show its strengths and its weaknesses.

Let us begin with human rights as the chief set of principles that limit the types of ethically permissible action in a war on terror. Human rights both define what we are supposed to stand for and tie our hands when we seek to defend ourselves. Tying our hands behind our own backs is neither popular nor easy; but fundamental to the idea of all rights doctrines is the idea of precommitment. To believe in rights is to say we will not do certain things to fellow citizens or fellow human beings, no matter what.

Human rights are the rights we have as human beings, and therefore are the ones we cannot lose. They are not connected to political or civil status, moral worth or conduct. Even if you are a very bad human being you still have human rights. If this is so, it has to be true that terrorists have human rights. Why not? Once rights are distinguished from deserving and moral worth, they are the entitlement of even those who despise the very idea of rights.

Like Ulysses tying himself to the mast so that he will not be tempted by the Sirens' song, democratic states pre-commit themselves to respect rights even when they are sorely tempted to abridge, even abolish them. Terrorism is one of the biggest tests of a society's willingness to abide

by these precommitments. To the degree that terrorists exploit the freedoms of a free society to circulate, to evade detection and to plan attacks, they tempt societies to jettison these freedoms. This temptation is not new. Indeed, it is as old as law itself. The Romans had an adage, *salus populi primus lex*—the safety of the people is the ultimate law—that justified emergency measures for emergency circumstances. In these circumstances, law itself should be no barrier to the ultimate safety of the people. In the name of that principle, modern societies faced with terrorist threats—Italy, Spain, Great Britain, for example—have curtailed rights to political participation. Groups that do not dissociate themselves from terrorist activity are not allowed to compete for votes or hold office. People suspected of association with terrorist organizations may be interned or held without trial. These abridgements of rights may appear justified by *salus populi primus lex*, but they conflict with the idea that rights are either unconditional or they are worthless.

Terrorist states of emergency illuminate a neglected aspect of the supposed universality of human rights. Most discussions of universality focus on the issue of whether rights are universal across *cultures*. But there is an equally important sense in which human rights should be universal as between *persons* and as between normal *times* and times of emergency. Terrorist emergencies put these universalist commitments under strain. The reason is not just that terror causes fear and fearful majorities have it in their power to oppress minorities; it is also that they can do so with little direct cost to their own liberties and rights. As Ronald Dworkin has pointed out, there is no general tradeoff between *our* liberty and *our* security in times of terrorist threat, but between *our* supposed security and the liberty of small suspect groups, like adult male Arabs and particularly the subset of these groups that are in violation of immigration regulations. These abridgements of the rights of a few are easy to justify politically when the threat of terrorism appears to endanger the majority. Rights exist, however, precisely to set limits to what fearful majorities can do.

The idea of rights as precommitments presupposes the idea that when we face the choice between our security and their liberty, we start from a predisposition against the amendment of principle. We do so principally because of the value to the majority of rights remaining as invariant and universal as possible. Rights will not have much value to us if they are easily taken away from others. So we all have an interest in making as few exceptions as possible.

Some civil libertarians believe that the rule of law implies that there should be no exceptions at all, no emergencies and no derogations. In fact, most constitutions and most international human rights covenants accept that temporary suspensions of rights can become necessary to the preservation of the constitutional fabric itself. So exceptions, emergencies, and derogations are necessary to constitutional survival. What the rule of law requires . . . is not invariance, but public justification. International human rights law is not committed to absolute nonderogation of rights, but rather to limitation of derogation through an obligation to provide justification to accountable public bodies, especially the judiciary and elected legislatures.

The International Covenant on Civil and Political Rights allows states to derogate or suspend rights of political participation, habeas corpus, free assembly, immunity from arbitrary search and seizure, and freedom from detention before trial, but not absolute nonderogable rights such as immunity from torture, cruel and unusual punishment, the infliction of death, or free belief. Nations that sign the covenant are required to publicly announce and justify their derogations to UN treaty bodies. Similar obligations to publicly justify derogation are written into the European Convention on Human Rights. This seeks to save what can be saved from the idea of absolute precommitment by focusing those precommitments on preserving terrorist suspects from absolute violations of personal integrity like torture and by insisting on accountability and public justification. . . .

How should we think about emergency suspensions of rights? Do exceptions leave rules in ruins, or do they enable rules to survive? Are derogations of rights a lesser evil or a fatal compromise that jeopardizes their status in normal times? I will argue in favor of a lesser evil position, one that countenances democratically authorized abridgements of the liberties of some to preserve the liberties of all. In the wake of September 11, when no one knew how many cells Al Qaeda had in operation in the United States, it was legitimate to arrest and hold in administrative detention 1,200 people who had violated the terms of their immigration visas. But it was also incumbent on the authorities to process these people through public administrative hearings as quickly as possible and to afford them legal counsel and contact with their families. The hearings have not been open and they have not been expeditious, but they have been subject to judicial review, and the Supreme Court will probably examine their final constitutionality. In these circumstances, the abridgement of the rights of these 1,200 people could be justified. But the justification becomes less compelling with each passing day that the executive fails to prove that the detainees constitute an actual or possible danger.

Abraham Lincoln's abridgement of habeas corpus during the Civil War would be a further example of a necessary derogation in time of emergency. These exceptions need not fatally compromise the rule of law. To maintain that they do is to assume that rights suspended in emergency are never restored in peacetime. All constitutions assume a distinction between the rules that apply in emergencies and those that apply in times of safety, and seek a way to manage emergencies so that they do not become permanent or permanently damaging. The position I take is essentially that of Abraham Lincoln in his justification of the suspension of habeas corpus during the Civil War. Lincoln's position, set out in his letter to Erastus Corning, was that suspension of habeas corpus in wartime did not jeopardize its status in peacetime. Exceptions, he argued, did not erode the status of rules. Without exceptions, he insisted, the rule could not be preserved.

The problem with emergencies, as Lincoln saw, was not that they constitute a threat to constitutional principles in general. The problem with emergencies is whether they are justified in the specific circumstances. The problem is to identify what level of actual or apprehended threat constitutes a genuine emergency and to prove that the suspensions or abridgements of liberty are necessary to meet the threat, rather than simply offer a sop to public opinion. . . . The real danger is the manipulation of opinion, the manufacture of danger by executive authorities who are seeking more power. The rule of law is not compromised by emergencies per se, but by politicized construal of risk to justify emergency measures that are not actually necessary to meet the threat at hand.

The test of whether state power can be held to account when it makes these decisions is not so much what the emergency or antiterrorist laws say but rather whether the institutions of a free society do their jobs. It is, of course, the function of a legislature, a free press, a well-organized civil society and an independent judiciary to keep the executive under scrutiny. There have been few national emergencies where executives did not overstep the bounds, the internment of the Japanese by Roosevelt being the most egregious modern example. What this example seems to show is that institutions failed to do their proper job: the press kept silent, dissenting voices within the executive were stilled, and most important, the judiciary explicitly supported the executive.

The example of the Japanese internment suggests that civil liberties are most at risk when a popular president, facing a genuine threat, uses his formidable power to manipulate both popular and congressional opinion. In the case of the Japanese internment, it appears that race played a malign part in undermining the ability of both the president and the judiciary to understand that a fundamental violation of the rights of Americans had occurred. . . .

II

If we are at war with terror—and this seems more than a metaphor, for the reason that *they* are at war with *us*—then an additional question is not simply whether exceptional deviations from pre-commitments destroy the very idea of precommitments, but which precommitments—human rights or the laws of war—should apply in the circumstances. These two ethical systems are closely related, but they are also contradictory, and one way to understand the ethical complexity of a war against terror is to understand the differences between them. . . .

Sometimes—as in the case of torture—human rights and the laws of war impose the same ethical limitation on counterterror strategies. But at other points they diverge. In combat operations, using the armed forces of a state, you can shoot to kill; if you are conducting police operations only, you cannot or at least should not. In the case of Al Qaeda, which was a full-scale military formation with extensive training camps, munitions, stocks, and supplies, a military response to its threat was unavoidable. In other forms of terrorism, police operations may be sufficient and the appropriate ethical and operational limitations on deadly force should apply.

The larger point here is that human rights cannot serve as a complete guide for action when terrorists wage war against a state. Because of its fundamental commitment to the right to life, human rights is inherently a pacifist doctrine, and were societies to pre-commit to pacifist limitations, they would disarm themselves against mortal threat.

Moving beyond the limitations imposed by human rights does not mean passing from ethical limitation to barbarism. It simply means passing from one strategy of precommitment—human rights—to another: the laws of war. The laws of war seek to save, for conditions where combat is necessary, those ethical restraints that are built into human rights.

More complicated is the relation between the laws of war and standard criminal law. The laws of war hold that it is unlawful to kill a disarmed combatant taken prisoner. Further, prisoners must be released upon conclusion of hostilities. American criminal law sees the same situation very differently. A terrorist transferred to an

American criminal court and tried as a civilian defendant may face the death penalty or substantial periods of imprisonment. The Bush administration's handling of terrorist prisoners suggests that it picks its ethical restraints according to convenience. It abides by some of the laws of war for detainees at Guantánamo, respecting their religious rights, for example. But it will not grant them formal prisoner of war status, since that would require posthostilities release. So the Guantánamo detainees are in a legal limbo.

. . . The American position is that the executive should be accountable only to American courts and the American Congress. Yet it is holding prisoners while reserving the right to decide which of its international obligations under the Geneva Conventions do or do not apply. This makes the United States judge and jury in a matter affecting the human rights of detainees and this is precisely what the Geneva Convention regime is designed to prevent. This position more or less guarantees that the reciprocity on which the regime depends will break down when Americans are taken prisoner.

Since Al Qaeda has the characteristics of a criminal cell and a military formation, it is inevitable that the moral principles governing the combat against it should conflict. Where the action against Al Qaeda is primarily a civilian police operation, the rules regarding search and seizure, arrest, use of deadly force, and the civil liberties protections regarding detention and trial should be in force as much as possible. Where derogations or exceptions are required, they must be publicly justified and approved by court order. Where the actions are primarily military, the laws of war should apply—and since these are international instruments, the United States should accept international accountability for its actions, especially with noncitizen detainees.

III

Thus far, I have looked at human rights and the laws of war as precommitment strategies designed to restrain our conduct in a war on terror and

keep it within the confines of justice. Now I want to look at human rights and terror from a less familiar standpoint: the point of view of terrorists. It is not sufficiently appreciated that human rights—in particular the right to self-determination—also serve as an important justification for terror. Wherever subject or oppressed peoples seeking self-rule turn to terror, they do so in the name of this human right. The entire anticolonial resistance to imperial rule—in India, Algeria, Vietnam, to name only the epochal examples—was justified by the human right to self-determination. In some cases, notably Algeria, the anticolonial struggle turned to terror and justified the means as a necessity in the battle for freedom. The Palestinian struggle is a struggle for human rights, and acts of terror find justification in the claim to self-determination.

Human rights do not *motivate* terror—it is hard to see how they could motivate since they expressly enjoin us against taking human life—but this does not prevent them from serving as an important *justification* for acts of terror. For ordinary terrorists, terror is a way of life, a business, a means of exercising, consolidating, and increasing power in their own communities. Terrorism, by and large, is a career rather than a moral commitment, and it is generally motivated, as a daily matter, by the same matters that motivate criminality: hope of profit, love of violence for its own sake, and the glamour of the underworld life. Yet terrorism is not just criminality, since it seeks to attract civilian support and it does so by making political claims that are grounded in moral principles. So if human rights do not often feature as a direct motivation, they do figure as a justification, in the form of the claim, among the Irish terrorists, for example, that the people of Ireland should rule themselves free of British occupation. . . .

The complex relationship between human rights and terror is even better illuminated by the events of September 11. The apocalyptic nihilists who attacked on September 11 did not leave behind demands or justifications. But their acts have been interpreted by their supporters to have been in the name of the rights of the Palestinians and the rights of believers to worship in holy places free of foreign—that is, American—occupation. To be sure, it would be political idiocy to regard Al Qaeda as a human rights organization. The so-called martyrs defended their actions in the language of Islamic eschatology, not in the language of rights. Moreover, their intentions were apocalyptic, not political: to humiliate the archenemy of Islam and secure martyrdom in the process. Yet the enduring impact of September 11 depends not just on its shattering violence, but also on the degree to which the event was justified by millions of Palestinians and others in the Muslim world as an act in defense of a pair of linked rights claims.

What are we to make of the uses of human rights as a justification for terror? Obviously, the contradiction between the two is flagrant, and it would be easy to conclude the whole matter by saying that human rights must never be paired with violence of any kind as a vocabulary of justification. If believing in human rights means anything, it means believing that killing civilians for political purposes can never be justified. In short, there are no—and there cannot be—deserving victims of political violence. Terror justifies itself through a belief in the idea that victims deserve their fate, or at least if they do not deserve their fate, then that their fate is a secondary matter. Thus for a committed terrorist, there are no innocent civilians. Civilians who benefit from or collaborate with occupation or oppression are just as guilty as the agents of the state directly responsible for the oppression. For a human rights believer, this violates the bedrock of human rights, the Kantian idea that human beings are ends in themselves, never to be sacrificed, coerced, or destroyed for the sake of even the noblest end.

If this is so, how can we reconcile this prohibition against the instrumental use of human beings for political purposes with the equal commitment within human rights to a collective right to self-determination? The obvious answer—and it leads to problems we will deal with later—is that human

rights endorse collective self-determination as a goal without at the same time endorsing any and all means of struggle. Indeed, a consistent belief in human rights would only endorse nonviolent means of civil disobedience as an appropriate tactic for securing self-determination.

But that, of course, is not how the human right to self-determination is commonly understood (that is, as a right to self-government that can only be met, consistent with human rights principles, through peaceful negotiation and, if that fails, through nonviolent protest). Instead, when human rights language is used, it figures as a moral trump, as a table-clearing, game-winning claim to moral entitlement. In this more indirect sense, as a language of closed self-righteousness, human rights can pass from justification to actual motivation for terror.

Palestinians frequently argue as if their self-determination claim was a trump when, both as a matter of practical politics and as a matter of ethics, the real issue is to reconcile their justified claims with other equally justified claims held by Israelis. The same type of trumping argument is used by Irish Republicans in the face of Loyalist claims. All too frequently two or more claims to self-determination are competing for the same political space. Human rights principles—since they enjoin respect and observance of the right to life—would imply that the two or more claims must be reconciled through peaceful negotiation, not through war or terror.

Human rights principles thus justify self-determination struggles but also specify two practical ethical limits on waging a struggle for self-determination. The first is an injunction against violence, and the second is an injunction to respect the self-determination claims of others, through negotiation and deliberation.

. . . Historical analogies . . . suggest that those who follow the dual counsel of nonviolence and deliberation are not always condemned to morally honorable defeat. Sometimes they even win. Strict adherence to nonviolence and deliberation have won historic victories—consider the success of Gandhi against the British or Martin Luther King against the southern segregationists. These victories, it might be added, were all the more heroic since they were achieved in the face of almost constant provocations to repay violence with violence. But we can hardly address the claims of the oppressed with the comforting thought that in the end right will prevail. All too often it does not. And we must consider seriously the claim that for the weak to observe human rights is to deliver them up, defenseless, to the ruthlessness of the strong. This argument from weakness is a fundamental part of the ethical justification of acts of terror in pursuit of a self-determination claim. Where a state or occupying power possesses overwhelming military force, people fighting for freedom often argue that they will go down to defeat if they confine their struggle to nonviolent protest or if they seek to directly challenge the military might of the other side. The only tactic that converts weakness into strength is terrorism—hitting the enemy where it is most vulnerable, its civilian population. This is more than a tactical argument in favor of "asymmetrical" methods. It has a moral element. The weak must have the right to fight dirty; otherwise the strong will always win. . . .

We cannot resolve this problem with the piety that the weak are best served by not surrendering the high moral ground. This is sometimes true historically, but it is a council of perfection, which the weak have reason to reject when it is argued by the strong. Moreover, human rights principles themselves are not an ethics of resignation, but a call to struggle. To claim that human rights never justify the violation of the rights of others is to associate human rights with political quietism, with submission to oppression. But human rights are not an ethics of quietism. The European liberal political tradition incubated the idea of human rights, yet Locke and Jefferson explicitly reserve a right for the oppressed—the weak—to rise up in revolt against intolerable conditions: against the strong. What is Jefferson's Declaration of Independence but a reasoned defense of the necessity of political violence to overthrow imperial oppression?

The right of revolution, enshrined in Enlightenment liberal political theory, implies that political freedom is so valuable, so much the precondition for the safe enjoyment of any rights at all, that its defense can justify acts of armed resistance that, of necessity, will violate the rights of others. . . .

But let us be clear. The right of revolution is not a human right. It is contained within the liberal tradition that gave birth to human rights, but revolution itself—its justification, morality and a mode of action—is not articulated within the human rights tradition. The 1948 Universal Declaration of Human Rights confines the right of revolution to its preamble: "Whereas it is essential, if man is not to be compelled to have recourse, as a last resource, to rebellion against tyranny and oppression, that human rights should be protected by the rule of law." But the meaning of this reference is clearly a message of warning to states: they must entrench human rights or risk rebellion. It is not an endorsement of a right to rebellion as such, but rather the statement that rebellion becomes inevitable when essential rights are repeatedly denied.

The ambiguous place of revolution in the antechamber of the founding rights document exposes the limitations of human rights as a system of ultimate commitments. For these ultimate commitments—to respect, preserve, and defend human life and the exercise of human freedom—do not tell us what we are entitled to do when these values are denied, when oppression and tyranny crush the essential human aspirations defined in the human rights lexicon.

Indeed, if we seek answers to the question—what is permitted when rising up against oppression and tyranny?—we need to pass out of the rubric of human rights altogether and consider the body of reflection and codification known as the laws of war. The two systems of moral reflection are linked. The laws of war seek to protect the essential commitments of human rights; that is, to maintain the dignity and inviolability of combatants and noncombatants. But they are written for the situation that arises when the primary human right—to life—has been abrogated by a state of war, when states or parties to a conflict have declared their right to take up arms and to kill. This is the situation in which the question of revolution is posed—when a state has declared war on its own citizens and they take up arms to resist. The laws of war essentially seek to save what can be saved of the humanitarian impulse of human rights once violence has begun. The laws of war do not define when the resort to violence is justified, but they seek to regulate conduct once violence is chosen as a method of struggle. . . .

The very idea of civilian immunity illustrates the difference between the universalistic framework of human rights and the particularistic framework of the laws of war. Laws of war distinguish minutely between the moral status of various human actors—combatants, noncombatants, civilians, military, prisoners, medical staff—while human rights principles explicitly reject moral discriminations based on status. From a human rights perspective, civilian immunity is an incoherent moral principle, inconsistent with the equal respect due all human beings. From a law of war perspective, it is the principle that pre-serves some measure of ethical discrimination in the midst of combat.

Thus, if we view national liberation struggles exclusively through a human rights lens, we are forced to conclude that they must discipline themselves to follow the two rules of nonviolence and deliberation. This may condemn them to political failure. If we believe that their oppression is such that it justifies turning to violence as a last resort, then the ethics of their struggle passes out of human rights and into the rules of the laws of war. These rules expressly forbid the targeting of civilians.

If we sum up at this point, I am saying that there is an ethical way to defend the use of violence in support of a self-determination claim: as a last resort, when nonviolent, deliberative means have been exhausted, and provided that violence obeys the rules of war relating to civilian immunity. To be sure, this limits the struggle for freedom. You cannot fight dirty, you must take on military targets, not civilian ones, but at least you are not required to turn the other cheek when you are faced with assault and oppression. Those who observe such rules deserve the name of freedom fighters. Those who do not, deserve the name of terrorist.

Review and Discussion Questions

1. Under what, if any, circumstances is it permissible for a government to abridge or suspend the rights of its citizens? Respond to the argument that it contradicts the very idea of rights to ever permit their abrogation. If we grant that emergencies can sometimes justify suspending rights, doesn't this increase the likelihood that governments will exploit this idea to suspend rights unnecessarily?

2. Ignatieff claims that the real danger is not emergencies per se, but the manipulation of public opinion. Is it possible to guard against this danger? If so, how?

3. Do you agree with Igantieff's criticism of America's handling of detainees at Guantánamo? Explain why or why not.

4. Ignatieff believes that the laws of war conflict with human rights principles. If so, how can they be justified? Does it make sense to restrict warfare by laws or rules?

5. Is there a right to revolution? If so, what are the limits on this right? Assess Ignatieff's argument that revolution involves leaving the system of human rights for the laws of war.

6. Assess the following argument: "The weak and oppressed have a right to fight dirty against tyranny; otherwise they will always lose."

The Dark Art of Interrogation

MARK BOWDEN

In this essay, Mark Bowden, author of *Black Hawk Down* (1999) and *Killing Pablo* (2001), explores the use of coercion and torture in the interrogation of terrorists. Although the United States and the rest of the civilized world condemn torture, many believe that methods of coercion that fall short of outright torture—for example, sleep deprivation, exposure to heat or cold, and rough treatment—are justified because they help interrogators extract valuable information from terrorists, information that can save lives. Although raw pain and threats of death are unreliable techniques, skillful interrogators often succeed in using fear, disorientation, drugs, harsh conditions, and psychological manipulation to get prisoners to talk. Is the use of such means morally justified? Bowden believes that it can be, but there is still the problem of controlling the practice of coercion and ensuring that it doesn't become commonplace.

Study Questions

1. Describe the conditions under which Sheik Mohammed is probably being kept.
2. Give examples illustrating the difference between "torture" and "coercion," as Bowden uses these terms.
3. Why does Bowden believe that interrogation is more of an art than a science?
4. What's the difference between the "civilian sensibility" and the "warrior sensibility"?
5. Explain the change in Israeli policy. According to Jessica Montell, what should an interrogator do when the information he or she seeks can prevent a catastrophe?

SHEIKH MOHAMMED is considered the architect of two attempts on the World Trade Center: the one that failed, in 1993, and the one that succeeded so catastrophically, eight years later. He is also believed to have been behind the attacks on the U.S. embassies in Kenya and Tanzania in 1998, and on the USS *Cole* two years later, and behind the slaughter last year of the *Wall Street Journal* reporter Daniel Pearl, among other things. An intimate of Osama bin Laden's, Sheikh Mohammed has been called the operations chief of al-Qaeda. . . . Whenever, wherever, and however it happened, nearly everyone now agrees that Sheikh Mohammed is in U.S. custody, and has been for some time. In the first hours of his captivity . . . a picture was taken. It shows a bleary-eyed, heavy, hairy, swarthy man with a full black moustache. . . .

Intelligence and military officials would talk about Sheikh Mohammed's state only indirectly, and conditionally. But by the time he arrived at a more permanent facility, he would already have been bone-tired, hungry, sore, uncomfortable, and afraid—if not for himself, then for his wife and children, who had been arrested either with him or some months before, depending on which story you believe. He would have been warned that lack of cooperation might mean being turned over to the more direct and brutal interrogators of some third nation. He would most likely have been locked naked in a cell with no trace of daylight. The space would be filled night and day with harsh light and noise, and would be so small that he would be unable to stand upright, to sit comfortably, or to recline fully. He would be kept awake, cold, and probably wet. If he managed to doze, he would be roughly awakened. He would be fed infrequently and irregularly, and then only with thin, tasteless meals. Sometimes days would go by between periods of questioning, sometimes only hours or minutes. The human mind craves routine, and can adjust to almost anything in the presence of it, so his jailers would take care that no semblance of routine developed.

Questioning would be intense—sometimes loud and rough, sometimes quiet and friendly, with no apparent reason for either. He would be questioned sometimes by one person, sometimes by two or three. The session might last for days, with interrogators taking turns, or it might last only a few minutes. He would be asked the same questions again and again, and then suddenly be presented with something completely unexpected—a detail or a secret that he would be shocked to find they knew. He would be offered the opportunity to earn freedom or better treatment for his wife and children. Whenever he was helpful and the information he gave proved true, his harsh conditions would ease. If the information proved false, his treatment would worsen. On occasion he might be given a drug to elevate his mood prior to interrogation; marijuana, heroin, and sodium pentothal have been shown to overcome a reluctance to speak, and methamphetamine can unleash a torrent of talk in the stubbornest subjects, the very urgency of the chatter making a complex lie impossible to sustain. These drugs could be administered surreptitiously with food or drink, and given the bleakness of his existence, they might even offer a brief period of relief and pleasure, thereby creating a whole new category of longing—and new leverage for his interrogators.

Deprived of any outside information, Sheikh Mohammed would grow more and more vulnerable to manipulation. For instance, intelligence gleaned after successful al-Qaeda attacks in Kuwait and Saudi Arabia might be fed to him, in bits and pieces, so as to suggest foiled operations. During questioning he would be startled regularly by details about his secret organization—details drawn from ongoing intelligence operations, new arrests, or the interrogation of other captive al-Qaeda members. Some of the information fed to him would be true, some of it false. Key associates might be said to be cooperating, or to have completely recanted their allegiance to *jihad*. As time went by, his knowledge would decay while that of his questioners improved. He might come to see once-vital plans as insignificant, or already known. The importance of certain secrets would gradually erode.

Isolated, confused, weary, hungry, frightened, and tormented, Sheikh Mohammed would gradually be reduced to a seething collection of simple needs, all of them controlled by his interrogators.

The key to filling all those needs would be the same: *to talk*.

Smacky-Face

We hear a lot these days about America's overpowering military technology; about the professionalism of its warriors; about the sophistication of its weaponry, eavesdropping, and telemetry; but right now the most vital weapon in its arsenal may well be the art of interrogation. To counter an enemy who relies on stealth and surprise, the most valuable tool is information, and often the only source of that information is the enemy himself. Men like Sheikh Mohammed who have been taken alive in this war are classic candidates for the most cunning practices of this dark art. Intellectual, sophisticated, deeply religious, and well trained, they present a perfect challenge for the interrogator. Getting at the information they possess could allow us to thwart major attacks, unravel their organization, and save thousands of lives. They and their situation pose one of the strongest arguments in modern times for the use of torture.

Torture is repulsive. It is deliberate cruelty, a crude and ancient tool of political oppression. It is commonly used to terrorize people, or to wring confessions out of suspected criminals who may or may not be guilty. It is the classic shortcut for a lazy or incompetent investigator. Horrifying examples of torturers' handiwork are catalogued and publicized annually by Amnesty International, Human Rights Watch, and other organizations that battle such abuses worldwide. One cannot help sympathizing with the innocent, powerless victims showcased in their literature. But professional terrorists pose a harder question. They are lockboxes containing potentially life-saving information. Sheikh Mohammed has his own political and religious reasons for plotting mass murder, and there are those who would applaud his principled defiance in captivity. But we pay for his silence in blood.

The word "torture" comes from the Latin verb *torquere*, "to twist." *Webster's New World Dictionary* offers the following primary definition: "The inflicting of severe pain to force information and confession, get revenge, etc." Note the adjective "severe," which summons up images of the rack, thumbscrews, gouges, branding irons, burning pits, impaling devices, electric shock, and all the other devilish tools devised by human beings to mutilate and inflict pain on others. All manner of innovative cruelty is still commonplace, particularly in Central and South America, Africa, and the Middle East. . . . Governments around the world continue to employ rape and mutilation, and to harm family members, including children, in order to extort confessions or information from those in captivity. Civilized people everywhere readily condemn these things.

Then there are methods that, some people argue, fall short of torture. Called "torture lite,"

these include sleep deprivation, exposure to heat or cold, the use of drugs to cause confusion, rough treatment (slapping, shoving, or shaking), forcing a prisoner to stand for days at a time or to sit in uncomfortable positions, and playing on his fears for himself and his family. Although excruciating for the victim, these tactics generally leave no permanent marks and do no lasting physical harm.

The Geneva Convention makes no distinction: it bans any mistreatment of prisoners. But some nations that are otherwise committed to ending brutality have employed torture lite under what they feel are justifiable circumstances. In 1987 Israel attempted to codify a distinction between torture, which was banned, and "moderate physical pressure," which was permitted in special cases. Indeed, some police officers, soldiers, and intelligence agents who abhor "severe" methods believe that banning all forms of physical pressure would be dangerously naive. Few support the use of physical pressure to extract confessions, especially because victims will often say anything (to the point of falsely incriminating themselves) to put an end to pain. But many veteran interrogators believe that the use of such methods to extract information is justified if it could save lives—whether by forcing an enemy soldier to reveal his army's battlefield positions or forcing terrorists to betray the details of ongoing plots. As these interrogators see it, the well-being of the captive must be weighed against the lives that might be saved by forcing him to talk. A method that produces life-saving information without doing lasting harm to anyone is not just preferable; it appears to be morally sound. Hereafter I will use "torture" to mean the more severe traditional outrages, and "coercion" to refer to torture lite, or moderate physical pressure.

There is no clear count of suspected terrorists now in U.S. custody. About 680 were detained at Camp X-Ray, the specially constructed prison at Guantánamo, on the southeastern tip of Cuba. Most of these are now considered mere foot soldiers in the Islamist movement, swept up in

Afghanistan during the swift rout of the Taliban. They come from forty-two different nations. Scores of other detainees, considered leaders, have been or are being held at various locations around the world: in Pakistan, Saudi Arabia, Egypt, Sudan, Syria, Jordan, Morocco, Yemen, Singapore, the Philippines, Thailand, and Iraq. . . .

All these suspects are questioned rigorously, but those in the top ranks get the full coercive treatment. And if official and unofficial government reports are to be believed, the methods work. In report after report hard-core terrorist leaders are said to be either cooperating or, at the very least, providing some information—not just vague statements but detailed, verifiable, useful intelligence. . . . To some, all this jailhouse cooperation smells concocted. "I doubt we're getting very much out of them, despite what you read in the press," says a former CIA agent with experience in South America. "Everybody in the world knows that if you are arrested by the United States, nothing bad will happen to you."

Bill Cowan, a retired Marine lieutenant colonel who conducted interrogations in Vietnam, says, "I don't see the proof in the pudding. If you had a top leader like Mohammed talking, someone who could presumably lay out the whole organization for you, I think we'd be seeing sweeping arrests in several different countries at the same time. Instead what we see is an arrest here, then a few months later an arrest there."

These complaints are all from people who have no qualms about using torture to get information from men like Sheikh Mohammed. Their concern is that merely using coercion amounts to handling terrorists with kid gloves. But the busts of al-Qaeda cells worldwide, and the continuing roundup of al-Qaeda leaders, suggest that some of those in custody are being made to talk. This worries people who campaign against all forms of torture. They believe that the rules are being ignored. Responding to rumors of mistreatment at Bagram and Guantánamo, Amnesty International and Human Rights Watch have written letters and met with Bush Administration officials. They haven't been able to learn much.

Is the United States torturing prisoners? Three inmates have died in U.S. custody in Afghanistan, and reportedly eighteen prisoners at Guantánamo have attempted suicide; one prisoner there survived after hanging himself but remains unconscious and is not expected to revive. . . . Public comments by Administration officials have fueled further suspicion. An unnamed intelligence official told *The Wall Street Journal*, "What's needed is a little bit of smacky-face. Some al-Qaeda just need some extra encouragement." Then there was the bravado of Cofer Black, the counterterrorism coordinator, in his congressional testimony. . . .

Describing the clandestine war, Black said, "This is a highly classified area. All I want to say is that there was 'before 9/11' and 'after 9/11.' After 9/11 the gloves came off." He was referring to the overall counterterrorism effort, but in the context of detained captives the line was suggestive. A story in December of 2002 by the *Washington Post* reporters Dana Priest and Barton Gellman described the use of "stress and duress" techniques at Bagram [in Afghanistan], and an article in *The New York Times* in March described the mistreatment of prisoners there. . . .

In June [2003], at the urging of Amnesty and other groups, President Bush reaffirmed America's opposition to torture, saying, "I call on all governments to join with the United States and the community of law-abiding nations in prohibiting, investigating, and prosecuting all acts of torture . . . and we are leading this fight by example." A slightly more detailed response had been prepared two months earlier by the Pentagon's top lawyer, William J. Haynes II, in a letter to Kenneth Roth, the executive director of Human Rights Watch. . . . Haynes wrote,

> The United States questions enemy combatants to elicit information they may possess that could help the coalition win the war and forestall further terrorist attacks upon the citizens of the United States and other countries. As the President reaffirmed recently to the United Nations High Commissioner for Human Rights, United States policy condemns and prohibits torture.

When questioning enemy combatants, US personnel are required to follow this policy and applicable laws prohibiting torture.

As we will see, Haynes's choice of words was careful—and telling. The human-rights groups and the Administration are defining terms differently. Yet few would argue that getting Sheikh Mohammed to talk doesn't serve the larger interests of mankind. So before tackling the moral and legal questions raised by interrogation, perhaps the first question should be, What works?

What Works?

The quest for surefire methods in the art of interrogation has been long, ugly, and generally fruitless. Nazi scientists experimented on concentration-camp inmates, subjecting them to extremes of hot and cold, to drugs, and to raw pain in an effort to see what combination of horrors would induce cooperation. The effort produced a long list of dead and maimed, but no reliable ways of getting people to talk. . . .

Better results seemed to come from sensory deprivation and solitary confinement. For most people severe sensory deprivation quickly becomes misery; the effects were documented in the notorious 1963 CIA manual on interrogation, called the *Kubark Manual*. It remains the most comprehensive and detailed explanation in print of coercive methods of questioning—given the official reluctance to discuss these matters or put them in writing because such things tend to be both politically embarrassing and secret. . . .

The one constant in effective interrogation, it seems, is the interrogator. And some interrogators are just better at it than others.

"You want a good interrogator?" Jerry Giorgio, the New York Police Department's legendary third-degree man, asks. "Give me somebody who people like, and who likes people. Give me somebody who knows how to put people at ease. Because the more comfortable they are, the more they talk, and the more they talk, the more trouble they're in—the harder it is to sustain a lie."

Though science has made contributions, interrogation remains more art than science. Like any other subject, Sheikh Mohammed presented his interrogators with a unique problem. The critical hub of a worldwide secret network, he had a potential road map in his head to the whole shadow world of *jihad*. If he could be made to talk, to reveal even a few secrets, what an intelligence bonanza that would be! Here was a man who lived to further his cause by whatever means, who saw himself as morally, spiritually, and intellectually superior to the entire infidel Western world, a man for whom capitulation meant betraying not just his friends and his cherished cause but his very soul.

What makes a man like that decide to talk?

Alligator Clips

Bill Cowan spent three and a half years fighting the war in Vietnam. . . . So when he captured a Vietcong soldier who could warn of ambushes and lead them to hidden troops but who refused to speak, wires were attached to the man's scrotum with alligator clips and electricity was cranked out of a 110-volt generator.

"It worked like a charm," Cowan told me. "The minute the crank started to turn, he was ready to talk. We never had to do more than make it clear we could deliver a jolt. It was the fear more than the pain that made them talk."

Fear works. It is more effective than any drug, tactic, or torture device. According to unnamed scientific studies cited by the *Kubark Manual* (it is frightening to think what these experiments might have been), most people cope with pain better than they think they will. As people become more familiar with pain, they become conditioned to it. Those who have suffered more physical pain than others—from being beaten frequently as a child, for example, or suffering a painful illness—may adapt to it and come to fear it less. So once interrogators resort to actual torture, they are apt to lose ground. . . .

By similar logic, the manual discourages threatening a prisoner with death. As a tactic "it is often found to be worse than useless," the manual says, because the sense of despair it induces can make the prisoner withdraw into depression—or, in some cases, see an honorable way out of his predicament.

Others disagree.

"I'll tell you how to make a man talk," a retired Special Forces officer says. "You shoot the man to his left and the man to his right. Then you can't shut him up."

John Dunn found the truth to be a little more complicated. In his case the threat of execution forced him to bend but not break. He was a U.S. Army intelligence officer in the Lam Dong Province of Vietnam, in March of 1968, when he was captured by the Vietcong. . . . Again and again he refused to make a public statement. Starved, sore, and . . . frightened, Dunn was told, "You will be executed. After dark."

When the sun set, the interrogator, his aide, and the camp commander came for Dunn with a group of soldiers. They unlocked his chain, and he carried it as they led him away from the encampment into the jungle. They stopped in front of a pit they had dug for his grave and put a gun to his head. The interrogator gave him one more chance to agree to make a statement.

"No," Dunn said. He had gone as far as he was willing to go.

"Why do you want to die?" he was asked.

"If I must, I must," Dunn said. He felt resigned. He waited to be killed.

"You will not be executed," the camp commander said abruptly, and that was that.

Judging by Dunn's experience, the threat of death may be valuable to an interrogator as a way of loosening up a determined subject. But, as with pain, the most important factor is fear. An unfrightened prisoner makes an unlikely informer.

Civilians vs. Warriors

On a spring morning in the offices of Amnesty International, in Washington, D.C., Alistair Hodgett and Alexandra Arriaga were briefing me on their organization's noble efforts to combat torture wherever in the world it is found. They are bright, pleasant, smart, committed, attractive young people, filled with righteous purpose. Decent people everywhere agree on this: torture is evil and indefensible.

But is it always?

I showed the two an article I had torn from that day's *New York Times*, which described the controversy over a tragic kidnapping case in Frankfurt, Germany. On September 27 of last year a Frankfurt law student kidnapped an eleven-year-old boy named Jakob von Metzler, whose smiling face appeared in a box alongside the story. The kidnapper had covered Jakob's mouth and nose with duct tape, wrapped the boy in plastic, and hidden him in a wooded area near a lake. The police captured the suspect when he tried to pick up ransom money, but the suspect wouldn't reveal where he had left the boy, who the police thought might still be alive. So the deputy police chief of Frankfurt, Wolfgang Daschner, told his subordinates to threaten the suspect with torture. According to the suspect, he was told that a "specialist" was being flown in who would "inflict pain on me of the sort I had never experienced." The suspect promptly told the police where he'd hidden Jakob, who, sadly, was found dead. The newspaper said that Daschner was under fire from Amnesty International, among other groups, for threatening torture.

"Under these circumstances," I asked, "do you honestly think it was wrong to even *threaten* torture?"

Hodgett and Arriaga squirmed in their chairs. "We recognize that there are difficult situations," said Arriaga, who is the group's director of government relations. "But we are opposed to torture under any and all circumstances, and threatening torture is inflicting mental pain. So we would be against it."

Few moral imperatives make such sense on a large scale but break down so dramatically in the particular. A way of sorting this one out is to consider two clashing sensibilities: the warrior and the civilian.

The civilian sensibility prizes above all else the rule of law. Whatever the difficulties posed by a particular situation, such as trying to find poor Jakob von Metzler before he suffocated, it sees abusive government power as a greater danger to society. Allowing an exception in one case (saving Jakob) would open the door to a greater evil.

The warrior sensibility requires doing what must be done to complete a mission. By definition, war exists because civil means have failed. What counts is winning, and preserving one's own troops. To a field commander in a combat zone, the life of an uncooperative enemy captive weighs very lightly against the lives of his own men. There are very few who, faced with a reluctant captive, would not in certain circumstances reach for the alligator clips, or something else.

"It isn't about getting mad, or payback," says Bill Cowan, the Vietnam interrogator. "It's strictly business. Torturing people doesn't fit my moral compass at all. But I don't think there's much of a gray area. Either the guy has information you need or not. Either it's vital or it's not You know which guys you need to twist."

The official statements by President Bush and William Haynes reaffirming the U.S. government's opposition to torture have been applauded by human-rights groups—but again, the language in them is carefully chosen. What does the Bush Administration mean by "torture"? Does it really share the activists' all-inclusive definition of the word? In his letter to the director of Human Rights Watch, Haynes used the term "enemy combatants" to describe those in custody. Calling detainees "prisoners of war" would entitle them to the protections of the Geneva Convention, which prohibits the "physical or mental torture" of POWs, and "any other form of coercion," even to the extent of "unpleasant or disadvantageous treatment of any kind.". . . Detainees who are American citizens have the advantage of constitutional protections against being held without charges, and have the right to legal counsel. They would also be protected from the worst abuses by the Eighth Amendment, which prohibits "cruel and unusual punishment." The one detainee at

Guantánomo who was discovered to have been born in the United States has been transferred to a different facility, and legal battles rage over his status. But if the rest of the thousands of detainees are neither POWs (even though the bulk of them were captured during the fighting in Afghanistan) nor American citizens, they are fair game. They are protected only by this country's international promises—which are, in effect, unenforceable.

What are those promises? The most venerable are those in the Geneva Convention, but the United States has sidestepped this agreement in the case of those captured in the war on terror. The next most important would be those in the Universal Declaration of Human Rights, which asserts, in Article 5, "No one shall be subjected to torture or to cruel, inhuman or degrading treatment or punishment." There is also the Convention Against Torture, the agreement cited by Bush in June, which would seem to rule out any of the more aggressive methods of interrogation. It states, in Article I, "For the purposes of this Convention, torture means any act by which severe pain or suffering, whether physical or mental, is intentionally inflicted on a person." Again, note the word "severe." The United States is avoiding the brand "torturer" only by sleight of word.

The history of interrogation by U.S. armed forces and spy agencies is one of giving lip service to international agreements while vigorously using coercion whenever circumstances seem to warrant it. However, both the Army and the CIA have been frank in their publications about the use of coercive methods. The *Kubark Manual* offers only a few nods in its 128 pages to qualms over what are referred to, in a rare euphemism, as "external techniques": "Moral considerations aside, the imposition of external techniques of manipulating people carries with it the grave risk of later lawsuits, adverse publicity, or other attempts to strike back." The use of the term "strike back" here is significant; it implies that criticism of such unseemly methods, whether legal, moral, or journalistic, would have no inherent validity but would be viewed as an enemy counterattack.

. . . The full-scale U.S. retreat from the uglier side of espionage is well documented—but has, by all accounts, been sharply reversed in the aftermath of 9/11.

"People are being very careful, very legal, and very sensible," one former top intelligence official says. "We are not inflicting intense pain, or doing anything damaging or life-threatening. We are once again asking, 'How do you take people down a series of steps in such a way that it has an impact?' That's the only game in town."

Despite the hue and cry over mistreatment of prisoners at Guantánamo, two former Pakistani inmates there—Shah Muhammad and Sahibzada Osman Ali—told me that except for some roughing up immediately after they were captured, they were not badly treated at Camp X-Ray. They both felt bored, lonely, frustrated, angry, and helpless (enough for Shah Muhammad to attempt suicide), but neither believed that he would be harmed by his American captors. . . .

The perfect model of an interrogation center would be a place where prisoners lived in fear and uncertainty, a place where they could be isolated or allowed to mingle freely, as the jailer wished, and where conversations anywhere could be overheard. Interrogators would be able to control the experience of their subjects completely, shutting down access to other people, or even to normal sensation and experience, or opening that access up. Subjects' lives could be made a misery of discomfort and confusion, or restored to an almost normal level of comfort and social interaction within the limitations of confinement. Hope could be dangled or removed. Cooperation would be rewarded, stubbornness punished. Interrogators would have ever growing files on their subjects, with each new fact or revelation yielding new leads and more information—drawn from field investigations (agents in the real world verifying and exploring facts gathered on the inside), the testimony of other subjects, collaborators spying inside the prison, and surreptitious recordings. . . .

Serious interrogation is clearly being reserved for only the most dangerous men, like Sheikh Mohammed. So why not lift the fig leaf covering the use of coercion? Why not eschew hypocrisy, clearly define what is meant by the word "severe," and amend bans on torture to allow interrogators to coerce information from would-be terrorists?

This is the crux of the problem. It may be clear that coercion is sometimes the right choice, but how does one allow it yet still control it? Sadism is deeply rooted in the human psyche. Every army has its share of soldiers who delight in kicking and beating bound captives. Men in authority tend to abuse it—not all men, but many. As a mass, they should be assumed to lean toward abuse. How does a country best regulate behavior in its dark and distant corners, in prisons, on battlefields, and in interrogation rooms, particularly when its forces number in the millions and are spread all over the globe? In considering a change in national policy, one is obliged to anticipate the practical consequences. So if we formally lift the ban on torture, even if only partially and in rare, specific cases (the attorney and author Alan Dershowitz has proposed issuing "torture warrants"), the question will be, How can we ensure that the practice does not become commonplace—not just a tool for extracting vital, life-saving information in rare cases but a routine tool of oppression?

As it happens, a pertinent case study exists. Israel has been a target of terror attacks for many years, and has wrestled openly with the dilemmas they pose for a democracy. In 1987 a commission led by the retired Israeli Supreme Court justice Moshe Landau wrote a series of recommendations . . . allowing . . . "moderate physical pressure" and "nonviolent psychological pressure" in interrogating prisoners who had information that could prevent impending terror attacks. The commission sought to allow such coercion only in "ticking-bomb scenarios"—that is, in cases like the kidnapping of Jakob von Metzler, when the information withheld by the suspect could save lives.

Twelve years later the Israeli Supreme Court effectively revoked this permission, banning the use of any and all forms of torture. In the years following the Landau Commission recommendations, the use of coercive methods had become widespread in the Occupied Territories. It was estimated that more than two thirds of the Palestinians taken into custody were subjected to them. . . . In the abstract it was easy to imagine a ticking-bomb situation, and a suspect who clearly warranted rough treatment. But in real life where was the line to be drawn? Should coercive methods be applied only to someone who knows of an immediately pending attack? What about one who might know of attacks planned for months or years in the future?

"Assuming you get useful information from torture, then why not always use torture?" asks Jessica Montell, the executive director of B'Tselem, a human-rights advocacy group in Jerusalem. "Why stop at the bomb that's already been planted and at people who know where the explosives are? Why not people who are building the explosives, or people who are donating money, or transferring the funds for the explosives? Why stop at the victim himself? Why not torture the victims' families, their relatives, their neighbors? If the end justifies the means, then where would you draw the line?"

And how does one define "coercion," as opposed to "torture"? If making a man sit in a tiny chair that forces him to hang painfully by his bound hands when he slides forward is okay, then what about applying a little pressure to the base of his neck to aggravate that pain? When does shaking or pushing a prisoner, which can become violent enough to kill or seriously injure a man, cross the line from coercion to torture?

Montell has thought about these question a lot. . . . Although Montell and her organization have steadfastly opposed the use of coercion (which she considers torture), she recognizes that the moral issue involved is not a simple one.

She knows that the use of coercion in interrogation did not end completely when the Israeli Supreme Court banned it in 1999. The difference is that when interrogators use "aggressive methods" now, they know they are breaking the law and could potentially be held responsible for doing so. This acts as a deterrent, and tends to limit the use of coercion to only the most defensible situations.

"If I as an interrogator feel that the person in front of me has information that can prevent a catastrophe from happening," she says, "I imagine that I would do what I would have to do in order to prevent that catastrophe from happening. The state's obligation is then to put me on trial, for breaking the law. Then I come and say these are the facts that I had at my disposal. This is what I believed at the time. This is what I thought necessary to do. I can evoke the defense of necessity, and then the court decides whether or not it's reasonable that I broke the law in order to avert this catastrophe. But it has to be that I broke the law. It can't be that there's some prior license for me to abuse people."

In other words, when the ban is lifted, there is no restraining lazy, incompetent, or sadistic interrogators. As long as it remains illegal to torture, the interrogator who employs coercion must accept the risk. He must be prepared to stand up in court, if necessary, and defend his actions. Interrogators will still use coercion because in some cases they will deem it worth the consequences. This does not mean they will necessarily be punished. In any nation the decision to prosecute a crime is an executive one. A prosecutor, a grand jury, or a judge must decide to press charges, and the chances that an interrogator in a genuine ticking-bomb case would be prosecuted, much less convicted, is very small. As of this writing, Wolfgang Daschner, the Frankfurt deputy police chief, has not been prosecuted for threatening to torture Jakob von Metzler's kidnapper, even though he clearly broke the law.

The Bush Administration has adopted exactly the right posture on the matter. Candor and consistency are not always public virtues. Torture is a crime against humanity, but coercion is an issue that is rightly handled with a wink, or even a touch of hypocrisy; it should be banned but also quietly practiced. Those who protest coercive methods will exaggerate their horrors, which is good: it generates a useful climate of fear. It is wise of the President to reiterate U.S. support for international agreements banning torture, and it is wise for American interrogators to employ whatever coercive methods work. It is also smart not to discuss the matter with anyone.

If interrogators step over the line from coercion to outright torture, they should be held personally responsible. But no interrogator is ever going to be prosecuted for keeping Khalid Sheikh Mohammed awake, cold, alone, and uncomfortable. Nor should he be.

Review and Discussion Questions

1. Bearing in mind that he has not been convicted of a crime or appeared before any legal tribunal, is the treatment of Sheik Mohammed morally justified?

2. Do you agree with Bowden that coercion (or "torture lite") is not torture, or is Amnesty International right not to distinguish between the two? Do you believe that the United States uses either coercion or torture against those it believes to be terrorists?

3. Is it is permissible for interrogators to use coercive techniques like sleep deprivation, heat and cold, harsh treatment, and discomfort to compel prisoners to talk? Explain the moral principles that underlie your answer. Is torture ever permissible? In your view, which means would be moral, and which means immoral, for interrogators to use to elicit information from suspected terrorists?

4. Bowden believes that fear is the most important factor in inducing a prisoner to talk. Is inducing fear a form of torture? Was it wrong of the police to threaten the kidnapper of eleven-year-old Jakob von Metzler with torture?

5. Bowden describes the "perfect model of an interrogation center." Is it in fact a system of torture? Would it violate the rights of prisoners? Under what conditions, if any, would such a system be justified? Assuming that coercion is sometime permissible, what are the risks of permitting the practice?

6. Is the approach suggested by Jessica Montell and apparently endorsed by Bowden viable? Does it make sense to outlaw a technique that an interrogator might be morally justified in using?

7. If coercion or even torture of prisoners is sometimes morally justified, shouldn't the government be candid about what it is doing? Should the United States continue to support the Geneva Convention, which bans all mistreatment of prisoners?

Loyalty and Obedience

R. M. HARE

When is loyalty a virtue and when do we have a duty to obey? These are questions that military service during wartime can raise in a dramatic fashion. In addressing them in a lecture at the U.S. Military Academy at West Point, R. M. Hare, who was professor of philosophy at Oxford University and later at the University of Florida, focuses on a

From Objective Prescriptions and Other Essays (1999) *by R. M. Hare, pp. 168–178. Reprinted by permission of Oxford University Press.*

specific historical example from World War II, in which a submarine commander ordered the sinking of a ship with fifty women and children on board. Was he right to have done so, and were his subordinates right to have obeyed his order? According to Hare, to begin answering questions like these, one must understand that moral thinking can take place on two different levels. People need to have certain virtues of character, which govern their actions, and they must have moral principles that they stick to. However, in exceptional cases, in particular when two of one's principles come into conflict, one must go beyond everyday moral reasoning and think at another level—by examining carefully the consequences in the given circumstances of the alternative courses of action open to one.

Study Questions

1. Why does it appear that Lt. Anderson gave the order he did? Why did Mr. Hardman and the rest of the crew carry it out?

2. Soldiers and sailors are supposed to obey "lawful commands." What is ambiguous about "lawful" in this context? Hare writes that many people confuse legality with morality. Give an example.

3. Explain what Hare means when he writes that moral thinking takes place at two different levels.

4. What two virtues were in conflict in Mr. Hardman's situation? How does Hare respond to the point that Mr. Hardman would have been putting his own career at risk if he had disobeyed orders?

5. Hare writes that he is not saying "see what your moral convictions tell you." Why not? How should Anderson or Hardman decide what to do?

1

I HAD BETTER START with an example in which the problem arises of when we have a duty to obey, and when loyalty is a virtue. I choose a British example. . . . The British officer concerned came in the end to no harm, though there was an inquiry. He later had a successful career and obtained the Distinguished Service Cross and bar. . . .

Briefly, the story is this. On 25 November 1944 His Majesty's Submarine *Sturdy*, commander Lieutenant William St. George Anderson, was operating, under control of the U.S. fleet, against Japanese shipping in waters off Northern Australia. She encountered a 350-ton Indonesian coastal vessel, which Lieutenant Anderson suspected (rightly as it turned out) of being a supply ship for the Japanese. The vessel was stopped by

shell fire but did not sink. *Sturdy* was brought alongside and the vessel was boarded. Fifty crewmen had abandoned her in lifeboats, leaving behind the same number of women and children, possibly the families of the crew, or possibly being transported between islands. In the words of Lieutenant Anderson, 'Owing to the nature of the cargo (oil) and the use of this type of vessel to the enemy, I disregarded the humanitarian side of the question . . . Having no means at my disposal of saving the lives of the remaining passengers, I placed demolition charges which exploded four minutes later.'

They were actually laid, with the help of a torpedo petty officer and others, by a junior officer, Sub-Lieutenant Ronald Hardman, who said recently to *The Times*, 'There was no chance of anyone surviving. He knew what he was doing.' Captain Launcelot Shadwell, the British commander of the submarine flotilla at the time, who was later asked to examine the affair, said 'This was an inhuman action, utterly contrary to the traditional chivalry of the sea, as practised by the Royal Navy . . . The episode will be viewed with distaste and repugnance by the whole submarine service.' The American command took the same view. . . .

2

Two questions arise. First, ought Lieutenant Anderson to have ordered the sinking? Secondly, ought his subordinates to have obeyed his orders? The first is a very complex question which I shall come back to later, when I discuss loyalty. The problem is, just what does loyalty to my country or to the cause that it is fighting require me to do; and if it requires me to do *some* things, ought I to throw over the loyalty?

Mr. Hardman, who led the party that laid the demolition charges, when interviewed recently by *The Times*, confirmed that the coaster was being used as a Japanese supply boat. 'There was,' he said, 'a lot of strategic stuff, although I cannot remember specifically now.' But seeing the women and children he said he felt that they should have been left to take their chances on the holed vessel. 'We used,' he said, 'to fire on these ships and if it sank you might not know who was on board. I didn't want to do anything. We should have left the ship alone. I shouted to [Lieutenant Anderson] what the situation was, but he said, "Get on with it." I just had to obey orders or be up on a charge . . . The rest of the crew felt as I did. I was in charge of the boarding party and felt very bad about it. It was a blood-stained incident. I would agree with the view of Captain Shadwell that it was inhuman. I have tried to comfort myself over the years by saying that one has to obey orders. If one does not, you don't win the war.'

There is no doubt, then, that Mr. Hardman received explicit orders, and that he obeyed them only because they were orders, though he thought himself that the orders were ones that

morally ought not to have been given. The same plea was made by many of the accused at the German and Japanese war crimes trials after World War II. So is the plea ever justified, and if so, when?

3

All codes of military law have a section to the effect that it is an offence to disobey the command of a superior officer; but they vary in an important particular. The British Manual of Military Law puts before the word 'command' the word 'lawful.' That is, it is an offence to disobey a lawful command, but it is no offence to disobey an unlawful one. This was so in the edition used at the training unit I was in in 1939. I think that the corresponding U.S. manual now says the same, and that, curiously, the German manual in use in World War II also contained this qualification. . . . The qualification 'lawful command' does not really help very much, because it is ambiguous. It could be taken to mean 'morally legitimate.' Or it could be taken to mean just 'in accordance with the law of the state whose army you are in.' Whether it was lawful would then be decided by the courts of that state.

In the United States, treaties which have been signed and ratified are commonly treated as part of domestic law, having the status comparable to the constitution. This would make it easier for serving officers to determine what the law really is, and so alleviate the problem I have just raised, if only the treaties were framed in unambiguous terms. But unfortunately, as with the U.S. constitution itself, this is often not so. Just as a great many constitutional disputes have to be settled by going up to the Supreme Court, so cases will occur in which a serving officer or enlisted man will have to decide what he *thinks* the law requires, and may not know whether he was right till the lawyers have had their go at it, which may take years. However, in clear cases he ought to be in no doubt what it is; and in dubious cases he has to do the best he can to guess what it is, by looking at the case in hand and seeing how like it is to cases that are clear. I think that it really does help to have these treaties; they do set a standard, albeit sometimes rather a vague one. Those who want to bend the rules will always do so, but the standard is there for honourable people, and wars, if they have to happen, are much better for everybody if people are honourable. . . .

4

But none of this is going to help much with our main question, which is about the *morality* of acts done in obedience to orders, not their legality. The two need to be clearly distinguished, whether or not we think that one can be used in determining the other. Perhaps the people who operated the gas chambers were fulfilling their legal duty in obeying orders, according to the law then ruling in Germany; but it might have been morally wrong, all the same, for them to do it. There is a moral decision to be made, when the law is a morally bad one that requires one to do immoral things—a decision whether one morally ought to obey it.

Too many people confuse legality with morality. In Britain after World War II the Earl of Cork, a retired naval officer, used on occasion to get up in the House of Lords and say that officers had to learn that it was their *duty* to obey orders, and one could not then *condemn* them for obeying orders. But this confuses legality with morality. One can condemn someone morally for obeying an order, if it was a sufficiently immoral order, even though he was legally bound to obey it. The question needs much more discussion. Another British officer, the playwright William Douglas Home, brother of a former British Prime Minister, who was in tanks in the war, was put on a charge for disobeying orders. What he had done was refuse to gun down a lot of German troops during the campaign in Normandy, when the battle was already won and those troops were cut off and

were bound to surrender. He wrote letters to the papers thereafter, whenever the subject of the Nuremberg trials came up, saying that you could not consistently blame him for *disobeying* orders, and then blame the Germans for *obeying* orders. He was the victim of the same confusion. Perhaps nobody blamed him *morally* for disobeying; but pretty clearly he had committed an offence legally; and in the interests of discipline it was evidently (rightly or wrongly) thought expedient, or even morally right, to cashier (fire) him, which was what happened. Mr. Hardman in my original example might have been morally right if he had disobeyed, and his commanders might have been morally right if they disciplined him for it—though I should be surprised if they would have done anything serious to him. Anyway, *he* had a moral decision to make, because it was he who had to do the act in question.

You may think that I am getting us into an impasse by saying that one may be morally right to disobey an order, but that one's superiors may be morally right in disciplining one for it. So let us try to sort things out a bit more. It is a good thing to have strong and deep moral convictions, like the conviction that one ought not to run away in battle if the cause for which one is fighting is just. The conviction that one ought to obey orders, and indeed the conviction that one ought to obey the law, is like this. What is called in the British code 'good order and military discipline' will break down unless soldiers and officers have this well drummed into them. The same applies even in civilian life. If everybody thought it was all right to disobey the law whenever it suited him, the whole fabric of society would break down, because legal sanctions, operated by the police and the courts, would never be enough by themselves to enforce the law. Its enforcement depends on its acceptance, without question, by a vast majority of the citizens. Then the police can spend what time they have in catching the few delinquents. The same applies to armies. Unless everyone thinks it a prime duty (a moral duty) to obey orders, 'you don't win the war,' as Mr. Hardman put it.

5

The key to this whole problem lies in understanding that moral thinking takes place at at least two different levels. I did not invent this idea; it goes back in one form or another to Socrates, Plato, and Aristotle, and was used to good effect by the classical utilitarians in the nineteenth century. Plato in his dialogue *Meno* makes Socrates speak of a difference, to which he attaches great emphasis, between right opinion, and knowledge or understanding. In Plato's *Republic* the soldiers are supposed to have right opinion, and the rulers of the state to have understanding, which tells them that the opinions they have taught the soldiers are the right ones.

Aristotle similarly distinguishes between what he calls virtues of character and virtues of intellect. The virtues of character consist in having the right motivations and thus doing the right actions; the virtues of intellect, and especially what he calls practical wisdom, enable us to see *why* these motivations and actions are the right ones. Thus 'virtue is a habit of mind, governing our choices, which lies in a middle path, one determined by a reasoned principle, by which the wise man would determine it.'

We should probably agree with Aristotle, who, unlike Plato, did not ascribe wisdom to just one class in the state, and have all the rest obey its orders. For Aristotle, we all of us have to do our best to acquire wisdom, and this will guide us to right motivations and actions. But we should probably agree with him, also, that different people manage to acquire it to different degrees. He might have said that the officer's position demands more of it than the position of an enlisted man.

For most of the time, when we speak of the duty of obedience, we are talking at the level of right opinion and motivation—that is, about a virtue of character. Being ready to obey orders without question is one of the traits of character

that we expect good soldiers and officers to have. There are other traits of character, or virtues, that we expect all good people to have, in or out of the armed forces. For example, we expect them to be truthful, honest, considerate of other people, and so on. These are all virtues recognized at what I am going to call the intuitive level of moral thinking.

But all these virtues, and the principles of action that they impose, are rather general and unspecific. They tell us to obey orders in general, to tell the truth in general, to consider other people's interests in general. There is a reason why we have to insert the words 'in general' in each case. This is, that the principles are bound to conflict with one another in some cases, the world being like it is. For example, consideration for others may require me on rare occasions not to be truthful. If my wife asked me whether I liked her new dress, sometimes, in order not to hurt her feelings, I might, if my relations with my wife were not so stable as they are, be right to say that I did, when actually I did not. So at this intuitive level there are going to be conflicts of moral principles, in which, in order to display one virtue, we have to go light on another. Many of these conflicts are a great deal more serious—more agonizing—than the one I have just mentioned.

The case of Mr. Hardman is an example. The virtue of obedience, which all good officers have to have, required him to lay and fire the charges. The virtue of consideration for others (what Lieutenant Anderson called 'the humanitarian side of the question') required him not to. The question is then inescapable: how do we decide which of these virtues to practise or which of these duties to obey on the particular occasion?

6

Before I say what I think about this, I had better just mention one or two other considerations that might come in, but only in order to set them aside. First, it might be claimed that the original crew of the coaster had the duty of sticking by the women and children, who may have been their own families. Ought they to have put them into the lifeboats instead of taking to them themselves? Did they perhaps do what they did because they had heard that the British and American navies were run by humanitarian people who would not kill innocent civilians? Did they think that they could get away with their own lives and those of the women and children and the ship as well? And was it perhaps the duty of a good British officer, just this once, to teach them a lesson, not to presume too much on 'the traditional chivalry of the sea,' as Captain Shadwell called it? I do not myself find this suggestion very convincing; but I have no time to discuss it.

Another plea might be that Mr. Hardman would have been putting his own career at risk if he had disobeyed orders. He said he would be up on a charge. Did he then have a right to consider his own interests? Well, you might say he had a right to *consider* them. But when he had done that, were they as important before God as the lives of fifty women and children? From what Captain Shadwell said afterwards, I should guess that he would not have got into too much trouble. Some Germans and Japanese made such pleas in war crimes trials; but, given the sacrifices, including that of one's life, which in any case are the lot of serving officers and men, one way or another, I think that in most cases such pleas were rightly disregarded, even if it was true that they would suffer if they disobeyed.

Another and much more serious plea, which it is important to distinguish from this one, is that it was not Mr. Hardman's job to make the decision whether to blow up the coaster. That duty fell to his commanding officer. In armies and navies, we try to have the best, cleverest, most experienced, and therefore wisest people in the higher ranks. Notoriously we do not always succeed. But there is at least a presumption that our superiors know better than we do what ought to be done on a particular occasion. . . .

Of course it is not difficult to think of instances in which subordinates rightly disregarded orders—especially cases in which the subordinate had information which his superior lacked, and there

was no opportunity to communicate it. . . . Subordinates have to have *some* initiative, or the whole Army is in a straitjacket. The Duke of Wellington is said to have had two principles that he called 'regularity' and 'accommodation.' If people behave regularly nearly all the time, we all know what to expect and things go smoothly; but if we cannot accommodate exceptional cases, using our judgment, they do not go as well as they might.

The position then is that it is good and right for us to have the virtue of obedience and other virtues, and stick to the principles that they impose on us with a great deal of determination. But cases will very occasionally arise in which we ought to break one of these principles, usually because two sound principles conflict with one another. Then what we have to do is some thinking at a higher level, to which we may not be accustomed; and that is what causes the agony of these decisions. What we have to do then is to look at the individual case in the light of the consequences of the alternative actions, treating consequences to everybody affected as equally important: that is to say, treating their equal interests as of equal weight. I stress that it is only in extremely rare and difficult cases that we are driven to do this. It is very dangerous to do it under conditions of stress. That is the reason why we ought all, when *not* under conditions of stress, to forearm ourselves with good principles, arrived at by hard thinking when we have the leisure for it; and all institutions that train officers ought to provide opportunity for this. Then we shall not have to do so much thinking on our feet. But sometimes we will have to do it.

Ought Mr. Hardman to have obeyed his orders and sunk the coaster? It will depend on rather difficult predictions about what the consequences would have been. The consequences for the victims were obvious and cruel. The question is, were there other consequences of not obeying the order which were sufficiently bad and sufficiently important to make it right, all the same, to obey it? That is largely a matter for factual predictions—not easy, but an experienced naval officer, in the actual situation, might be better able to make them than I now am.

7

I come now to the even more tormenting question that faced Lieutenant Anderson, whether to give the order. I shall not have to deal with it at such length, because many of the relevant points are the same. We have a lot of sound principles which every officer should have absorbed through training and experience; and sometimes they come into conflict. One must, in general, do everything one can to help win the war, if it is a just one, as I assume it was. The coaster, if not destroyed, might have been of considerable use to the enemy. On the other hand, 'the traditional chivalry of the sea' is also extremely important. If it gets eroded, there will be no end to the unnecessary sinkings and loss of life. The same applies on land; if you really go out to win the war and think that absolutely *any* means are justified, you will have chemical warfare (which we were mercifully spared in World War II), murder of prisoners, and so on. Armies have often overstepped the limits of what is necessary and legitimate. I do not need to give you examples; we had plenty in the first Gulf War, that is the war between Iran and Iraq. It is still disputed whether the first two atom bombs were one of these examples. For myself, I think that at least the first of them saved more carnage than it caused. I am in much more doubt about the second; and I may be biased by being probably one of the lives that were saved.

Faced with such a decision, an officer cannot just appeal to his sound principles, because they are in conflict. What Lieutenant Anderson did was to appeal to just one of them and forget about the others. I suspect that the same was true of Lieutenant Calley, who is reported to have massacred a lot of innocent civilians in Vietnam, and possibly also of some high-up officers that have been in trouble recently in the United States. It is extremely difficult, under stress, to make balanced decisions about matters of tactics: if I order a withdrawal, shall I be sacrificing a crucial posi-

tion and lose the battle? But if I do not, shall I be sacrificing trained soldiers and equipment to no good end? Even if we leave morality out of it, the decision is horribly difficult. Admiral Jellicoe at the battle of Jutland in World War I decided not to engage the main German fleet, and it slipped back into harbour. He said afterwards that he was the only person who could have lost the war in a single day.

Lieutenant Anderson had to balance the competing considerations in the same way. He had to ask himself what would be the consequences of the alternative courses—what was likely to happen. And it was very difficult for him to know that. I want you to notice that I am not saying what intuitionists say: that when we have a conflict between duties we have to weigh them to see which is the most stringent. Intuitionists often give us no way of doing this weighing beyond yet another appeal to intuitions or moral convictions; but the trouble is that in such a situation the convictions have already had their say, and we are still in the dilemma.

What I am saying is not 'see what your moral convictions tell you'—which is no better than saying 'see how you feel.' I am saying 'think about what you are doing, and, so far as you can, find out what you *would* be doing if you took one or other of the two courses.' Lieutenant Anderson, if he sank the coaster, would be killing fifty women and children. He would also be depriving the Japanese of a useful ship. Without that ship, they might not be able to reinforce their forward positions, and a great many allied lives, perhaps many more than fifty, might be saved. The fact that these are speculations, and the immediate loss of life a certainty, is important. As the eighteenth-century philosopher Joseph Butler said, 'probability is the very guide of life' (*Analogy*, Introduction).

8

But now what about loyalty? After all, it may be said, the soldiers who would get killed taking those forward positions are our own people, and the women and children on the coaster are not. If they had been allied prisoners of war, it would have been different. We are fighting for our own countries and trying to win a war. It is important if it is a just war; but aside from that, have we not a duty of loyalty to our own country, even if we do not say 'my country right or wrong'? And there is not only loyalty to one's country. Colonel Oliver North said he did what he did out of loyalty to the President. When I joined the army I swore loyalty to our King. German officers swore loyalty to Hitler.

Loyalty *is* a virtue. It is a virtue, because without it states would fall to pieces. All over the world—in Sri Lanka, for example, or in Northern Ireland—we can see this happening. And if they do, we are all worse off. If the process goes far enough, we get anarchy, and only those who have not experienced anarchy become anarchists. Loyalty is one, but only one, of the virtues or principles that I mentioned just now. And, as I said, these principles can conflict. We must all pray to be spared these conflicts; but they do occur. Many people in Germany were torn between their loyalty to their government and what they thought to be more important moral duties. In the spring of 1939 there are said to have been Germans high up in the army and the foreign service who were prepared to depose the German government if Hitler marched into Czechoslovakia. If they had succeeded, there might not have been a World War II. Their required condition was that they received firm backing from the British and French; and this they did not get. Later, some other Germans including some of the same ones, notably Adam von Trott, tried to assassinate Hitler, putting their loyalty to their country above their loyalty to its government. These conflicts, as I said, do occur.

The way to handle them is the same as before, and it is not easy. We have, as before, to look at the consequences. . . . Sometimes, in other situations, it is very dangerous to start doing this, because, as I said earlier, we may deceive ourselves and get it wrong. Then it might have been better to stick to the sound principles. But when they conflict, one has to use all the wisdom one can command in resolving the conflict in favour of one or the other. Morally right action does not always come easy.

Review and Discussion Questions

1. Was Lt. Anderson right to order the sinking of the ship? What moral factors are relevant to answering this question? What alternatives might Anderson have had? If Anderson was wrong to do what he did, should the Navy have disciplined him?

2. Were the crew right to obey Anderson's order? Explain why or why not. What would you have done in their position?

3. Should we expect soldiers and sailors to think for themselves and hold them morally accountable for the orders they obey? Are they morally accountable if the war they are fighting in is unjust?

4. Explain and critically assess Hare's contention that "one may be morally right to disobey an order, but . . . one's superiors may be morally right in disciplining one for it."

5. Critically assess Hare's two-level view of morality. Do you find it plausible? How can you know when you should stick to your principles and when you should step back and act on the basis of the specific consequences of the alternatives before you?

6. Are loyalty and obedience virtues? If so, why?

13

AFFIRMATIVE ACTION

One Way to Understand and Defend Programs of Preferential Treatment

RICHARD A. WASSERSTROM

In this essay, Richard A. Wasserstrom, professor of philosophy at the University of California, Santa Cruz, defends programs that take race into account when considering an individual for admission, a job, or a promotion. By introducing blacks into careers and institutional positions from which they have been historically excluded, Wasserstrom argues, such programs help make society less racially oppressive and more just. He defends programs of preferential treatment against the charge that they violate the rights of individuals or treat them unfairly.

Study Questions

1. What is the point of Wasserstrom's thought experiment about choosing to be black or white?
2. In what ways, according to Wasserstrom, do affirmative action programs help to break down the existing system of racial disadvantage and oppression?
3. How does Wasserstrom answer the objection that, if it was wrong to take race into account in the past, then it is wrong to do so now?
4. Why is the arbitrariness of relying on an irrelevant characteristic not the main thing wrong with either slavery or racial segregation and discrimination?
5. How does Wasserstrom respond to the argument that one should take into account only an individual's qualifications when considering him or her for a job, for promotion, or for acceptance into a university?

From The Moral Foundations of Civil Rights *by Robert K. Fullinwider and Claudia Mills, eds. (Savage, Md.: Rowman and Littlefield Publishers, 1986). Reprinted by permission of the publisher. Section titles added.*

Pｒｏｇｒａｍｓ ｏｆ ｐｒｅｆｅｒｅｎｔｉａｌ ｔｒｅａｔｍｅｎｔ make relevant the race or sex of individuals in the sense that the race or sex of an applicant for admission, a job, or a promotion constitutes a relevant, although not a decisive, reason for preferring that applicant over others. In my discussion of these programs I will consider only preferential treatment programs concerned with preferring a person who is black over one who is white, but what I have to say will be illustrative of a way to approach and assess comparable programs in which members of other ethnic or minority groups, or women, are concerned.

My thesis is a twofold one. First, such programs can very plausibly be seen to be good programs for us to have in our society today because they help to make the social conditions of life less racially oppressive and thereby more just, and because they help to distribute important social goods and opportunities more equally and fairly. Second, these programs can be seen to help to realize these desirable aims without themselves being in any substantial respect unjust—without, that is, taking an impermissible characteristic into account, violating persons' rights, failing to give individuals what they deserve, or treating them in some other way that is unfair.

I. The Case for Programs of Preferential Treatment

The positive case for such programs begins with the following claim about our own society: we are still living in a society in which a person's race, his or her blackness rather than whiteness, is a socially significant and important category. Race is not, in our culture, like eye color. Eye color is an irrelevant category in that eye color is not an important social or cultural fact about individuals; nothing of substance turns on what eye color they have. To be black rather than white is not like that at all. To be black is to be at a disadvantage in terms of most of the measures of success or satisfaction—be they economic, vocational, political, or social. To see, in a very crude and rough way, that this is so one could conduct a thought experiment. If one wanted to imagine maximizing one's chances of being satisfied with one's employment or career, politically powerful rather than powerless, secure from arbitrary treatment within the social institutions, reasonably well off economically, and able to pursue one's own goals and develop one's own talents in ways that would be satisfying to oneself, and if one could choose whether to be born either white or black, wouldn't one choose to be born white rather than black?

If this claim about the existing social reality of race is correct, then two further claims seem plausible. The first is that there is in place what can correctly be described as a system of racial oppression. It is a racial system in that the positions of political, economic, and social power and advantage are concentrated and maintained largely in the hands of those who are white rather than black. It is an oppressive one in that some of these inequalities in social burdens and lessened opportunities are unjust because of the nature of the disadvantages themselves—they are among those that no one ought fairly be required to confront or combat in any decent society. And it is an oppressive one in that others of these inequalities are tied to race in contexts and ways that make such a connection itself manifestly unfair and unjust. But the primary and fundamental character of the oppression is in what results from these and related features and is not reducible to them. The oppression has to do, first, with the *systemic nature* of the unequal and maldistributed array of social benefits, opportunities, and burdens, and it has to do, as well, with *how* things are linked together to constitute an interlocking, mutually reinforcing system of social benefits and burdens, ideology, and the like which, when tied to race as they are, make it a system of *racial* disadvantage and oppression—and, for all of these reasons, a decidedly and distinctly unjust one.

Now, if this be granted, the next claim is that even if it is assumed that the intentions and motivations of those occupying positions of relative power and opportunity are wholly benign and proper with respect to the pursuit of the wrongful perpetuation of any unjust racial oppression toward blacks, it is likely that the system will perpetuate itself unless blacks come to occupy substantially more of the positions within the major social institutions than they have occupied in the past and now do. Thus, to have it occur that blacks do come to occupy more of these positions of power, authority, and the like is *a* way, if not *the* way, to bring about the weakening, if not the destruction, of that interlocking system of social practices, structures, and ideology that still plays a major if not fundamental role in preventing persons who are black from being able to live the kinds of lives that all persons ought to be able to live—lives free from the burdens of an existing, racially oppressive system.

If this is so, then the case for programs of preferential treatment can be seen to rest upon the truth of the claim that they are designed specifically to accomplish this end, and upon the truth of the claim that they do accomplish it. They do succeed in introducing more blacks into the kinds of vocations, careers, institutional positions, and the like than would have been present if these programs had not been in place. In this respect there is, I believe, little question but that the programs have worked and do work to produce, for example, black judges and lawyers where few if any existed before, and to produce, more generally, black employees in businesses and in places within the other major structures and hierarchies where few if any were present before. And this can be seen to be especially important and desirable because changes of this sort in the racial composition of these institutions have mutually reinforcing consequences that can reasonably be thought to play an important role in bringing about the dismantling of the existing system of racial disadvantage and oppression.

They do so, first, by creating role models for other black persons to identify with and thereby come to see as realizable in their own lives. They do so, second, by bringing members of this historically excluded and oppressed group into relationships of equality of power, authority, and status with members of the dominant group. This is important because when relationships of this kind are nonexistent or extremely infrequent, as they are in the system of racial oppression, the system tends most easily and regularly to sustain itself. Third, changes in the racial composition of the major social institutions work, as well, to make it possible for blacks, with their often different and distinctive but no less correct views of the nature of the complex social world in which we all live, to participate in such things as the shaping of academic programs and disciplines and to participate in the definition, focus, and direction of significant social, legal, economic, and related institutional policies, and in deliberations and debates concerning their supporting justifications. And they do so, finally, by making it more likely that there will be the more immediate and meaningful provision of important services and benefits to other members of that group who have up until now been denied fair and appropriate access to them.

Thus, the primary claim in support of these programs is that, in what they do and how they work, they can be seen to play a substantial role in weakening the system of racial oppression that is still in place and that makes a person's blackness have the kind of pervasively deleterious social meaning and significance that it ought not. The aim of these programs is to eliminate this system and to produce a society in which race will cease to matter in this way; and on this view of things it may be superficially paradoxical but is, nonetheless, more deeply plausible to believe that such can be significantly accomplished by taking race into account in the way these programs do.

What should be apparent is that, in some large measure, there are empirical claims involved here, and to the degree to which there are, disagreements about the justifiability of preferential treatment programs can be located and settled by attending to their truth or falsity. Thus, if such programs produce or exacerbate racial hostility, or if they lead to a reduced rather than an enhanced sense of self-respect on the part of blacks, then these are matters that count against the overall case for these programs. But I do not, myself, think the case against them can be rested very easily upon such grounds, and I do not think that, when it is, the evidence is very convincing and the arguments very plausible. Nor are such programs typically opposed on grounds of this sort. Instead, the main ground of principled opposition has to do with what is thought to be fundamentally wrong with them: with the fact that they are unjust, inconsistent with important ideals and principles, and violative of persons' basic rights. In what follows, I will seek very briefly to indicate why this is not so and how my way of understanding and justifying these programs can help to bring these matters, too, into a different and more proper focus.

II. Responses to Objections

The first argument that is both common and close to the core of the cluster of objections to these programs is this: if it was wrong to take race into account when blacks were the objects of racial policies of exclusion, then it is wrong to take race into account when the objects of the policies differ only in their race. Simple considerations of intellectual consistency—of what it means to have had a good reason for condemning those social policies and practices—require that what was a good reason then be a good reason now.

The right way to answer this objection is, I think, to agree that the practices of racial exclusion that were an integral part of the fabric of our culture, and which still are, to some degree, were and are pernicious. Yet, one can grant this and also believe that the kinds of racial preferences and quotas that are a part of contemporary preferential treatment programs are commendable and right. There is no inconsistency involved in holding both views. The reason why depends upon a further analysis of the social realities. A fundamental feature of programs that discriminated against blacks was that these programs were

a part of a larger social universe in which the network of social institutions concentrated power, authority, and goods in the hands of white individuals. This same social universe contained a complex ideology that buttressed this network of institutions and at the same time received support from it. Practices that prevented or limited the access of blacks to the desirable social institutions, places, and benefits were, therefore, wrong both because of their direct consequences on the individuals most affected by them, and because the system of racial superiority that was constituted by these institutions and practices was an immoral one, in that it severely and unjustifiably restricted the capacities, autonomy, and happiness of those who were members of the less favored category.

Whatever may be wrong with today's programs of preferential treatment, even those with quotas, it should be clear that the evil, if any, is simply not the same. Blacks do not constitute the dominant social group. Nor is the prevailing ideological conception of who is a fully developed member of the moral and social community one of an individual who is black rather than white. Programs that give a preference to blacks do not add to an already comparatively overabundant supply of resources and opportunities at the disposal of members of the dominant racial group in the way in which exclusionary practices of the past added to the already overabundant supply of resources and opportunities at the disposal of whites. Thus, if preferential treatment programs are to be condemned or abandoned, it cannot be either because they seek to perpetuate an unjust society in which the desirable options for living are husbanded by and for those who already have the most, or because they realize and maintain a morally corrupt ideal of distinct grades of political, social, and moral superiority and inferiority—in this case grades or classes of superiority and inferiority tied to and determined by one's race.

A related objection that fares no better, I believe, has to do with the identification of what exactly was wrong, say, with the system of racial discrimination in the South, or with what is wrong with any system of racial discrimination.

One very common way to think about the wrongness of racial discrimination is to see the essential wrongness as consisting in the use of an irrelevant characteristic, namely race, to allocate social benefits and burdens of various sorts, for, given this irrelevance, individuals end up being treated in an arbitrary manner. On this view, the chief defect of the system of racial segregation and discrimination that we had and still have is to be located in its systemic capriciousness. Hence, on this view, what is wrong and unjust about any practice or act of taking any individual's race into account is the irrational and arbitrary character of the interest in and concern with race.

I am far less certain that that is the central flaw at all—especially with our own historical system of racial segregation and discrimination. Consider, for instance, the most hideous of the practices, human slavery. The primary thing that was wrong, I think, with that institution was not that the particular individuals who were assigned the place of slaves were assigned there arbitrarily by virtue of an irrelevant characteristic, i.e., their race. Rather, the fundamental thing that was and is wrong with slavery is the practice itself—the fact that some human beings were able to own other human beings—and all that goes with the acceptance of that practice and that conception of permissible interpersonal relationships. A comparable criticism can be made of many of the other discrete practices and institutions that comprised the system of racial discrimination even after human slavery was abolished.

The fundamental wrongness in taking race into account in this way has to do, perhaps, with arbitrariness, but it is the special arbitrariness attendant upon using race in the constitution and maintenance of any system of oppression so as to make that system a system of racial oppression. The irrationality, arbitrariness, and deep injustice of taking race into account cannot, I think, be isolated or severed from the place of a racial criterion in the very constitution of that system which becomes both a system of *oppression* and a system of *racist* oppression in and through the regular systematic use of that criterion. Whatever may be

said about the appropriateness of regarding race as relevant in other contexts, the arbitrariness of taking race into account has a special and distinctive bite of injustice when race becomes the basis for fixing persons' unequal positions, opportunities, and status in this kind of systemically pervasive fashion. When viewed in the light of existing social realities and in the light of this conception of the wrongness of a racially oppressive system, the central consideration is that contemporary programs of preferential treatment, even when viewed as a system of programs, cannot plausibly be construed in either their design or effects as consigning whites to the kind of oppressed status systematically bestowed upon blacks by the dominant social institutions.

A third very common objection is that, when used in programs of preferential treatment, race is too broad a category for programs designed to promote, in a legitimate way in our present society, conditions of fair equality of opportunity and full equality with respect to political and social status. The objection presupposes that whatever the appropriate or relevant characteristic, it is not race. Instead, almost always it is taken to be disadvantaged socio-economic status.

This objection, too, helps to bring into focus the mistaken conception of the social realities upon which a number of the central objections to preferential treatment programs depend. While socio-economic status unquestionably affects in deep and pervasive ways the kinds of lives persons can and will be able to fashion and live, it is, I think, only a kind of implausible, vulgar Marxism, or socio-economic reductionism of some other type, that ultimately underlies the view that, in our society, socio-economic status is the sole, or even the primary, locus of systemic oppression. Given my analysis of the social realities, blackness is as much a primary locus of oppression as is socio-economic status. And if so, it is implausible to insist, as this objection does, that socio-economic status is central while race is not. Race is just the appropriate characteristic to make directly relevant if the aim is to alter the existing system of racial oppression and inequality, or otherwise to mitigate its effects. Socio-economic status is an indirect, imperfect, unduly narrow, and overly broad category with which to deal with the phenomena of *racial* oppression and disadvantage, in precisely the same way in which race is an indirect, imperfect, unduly narrow, and overly broad category to take on the phenomena of *socio-economic* oppression and disadvantage.

The final objection I wish to introduce concerns the claim that these programs are wrong because they take race into account rather than taking into account the only thing that does and should matter: an individual's qualifications. And qualifications, it is further claimed, have nothing whatsoever to do with race. Here, I can mention only very briefly some of the key issues that seem to me to be at stake in understanding and assessing such an objection.

First, it is important to establish what the argument is for making selections solely on the basis of who is the most qualified among the applicants, candidates, and the like. One such argument for the exclusive relevance of qualifications—although it is seldom stated explicitly—is that the most qualified persons should always be selected for a place or position because the tasks or activities connected with that place or position will then be done in the most economical and efficient manner. Now, there is nothing wrong in principle with an argument based upon the good results that will be produced by a social practice of selection based solely upon the qualifications of the applicant. But there is a serious problem that many opponents of preferential treatment programs must confront. The nature and magnitude of their problem is apparent if their objection to my way of justifying these programs is that any appeal to good and bad results is the wrong *kind* of justification to offer. For if that is the basis of their objection, then it is simply inconsistent for them to rest their case for an exclusive preoccupation with qualifications upon a wholly analogous appeal to the good results alleged to follow upon such a practice. In any event, what is central is that this reason for attending only to qualifications fails to shift inquiry to that different kind

of analysis having to do with justice that was originally claimed to be decisive.

Second, given the theses offered earlier concerning how the increased presence of blacks in the positions of the major social institutions changes the workings of those institutions, it is anything but obvious why a person's blackness cannot or should not appropriately be taken into account as one of the characteristics which, in any number of contexts, genuinely should count as an aspect of one's qualifications for many positions or places at this time in our social life. And preferential treatment programs can, therefore, often be plausibly construed as making just the judgment that a person's blackness is indeed one of the relevant characteristics helping to establish his or her overall qualifications.

Third, even if this way of looking at qualifications is rejected, a further question must still be addressed with respect to any or all of the characteristics of the more familiar sort that are thought to be the ones that legitimately establish who is the most qualified for a position: is the person who possesses these characteristics, and who is, hence, the most qualified, to be selected because that is what he or she deserves, or for some other reason? If persons do truly deserve to be selected by virtue of the possession of the characteristics that make them the most qualified, then to fail to select them is to treat them unjustly. But I am skeptical that a connection of the right sort can be established between being the most qualified in this sense and deserving to be selected. The confusion that so often arises in thinking about this issue comes about, I think, because of a failure to distinguish two very different ways in which the linkage between qualifications and desert might be thought to be a sound one.

The first way is this. If there is a system of selection in place with rules and criteria that specify how to determine who is the most qualified and therefore is to be selected, then there is, of course, a sense in which the most qualified, as defined by those criteria, do deserve to be selected by virtue of their relationship to those rules and criteria. But this sense of desert is a surface one, and any resulting desert claim is very weak because it derives its force and significance wholly from the existing criteria and rules for selection. In this same sense, once preferential treatment programs are established and in place, as many now are, these new programs can also be understood to establish alternative grounds and criteria for selection; as such, they stand on the same footing as more conventional systems of qualification and selection. In the identical manner, therefore, these new programs also give rise to surface claims of desert, founded now upon the respect in which those who best satisfy those criteria have a claim that they deserve to be selected because that is what the rules of these programs provide should happen.

What this suggests, I believe, is that the real and difficult question about the possible linkage between qualifications and desert has to be sought elsewhere, for that question has to do with whether those who possess certain characteristics deserve, in virtue of their possession of those characteristics, to have a selection procedure in place which makes selections turn on the possession of those characteristics. If they do, then those who possess those characteristics do deserve in a deep, nonsurface way to be selected because of their qualifications. But now the problem is that being the best at something, or being the most able in respect to some task or role, does not, by itself at least, seem readily convertible into a claim about what such persons thereby genuinely deserve in virtue of things such as these being true of them. Perhaps a theory of desert of the right sort can be developed and adequately defended to show how and why those who are most able deserve (in a deep sense) selection criteria that will make them deserving of selection (in a surface sense); however, given the difficulty of connecting in any uniform way the mere possession of abilities with things that the possessor can claim any credit or responsibility for, and given the alternative plausibility of claims of desert founded upon attributes such as effort or need, the intellectual task at hand is a formidable one,

and one that opponents of preferential treatment programs have not yet, I think, succeeded in coming to terms with in a convincing fashion.

Nonetheless, as was suggested earlier, there may be good reasons of other sorts for being interested in persons' qualifications—reasons which have to do, for example, with how well a predefined job or role will be performed and with the relative importance of having it done as well as possible. These reasons point directly to the good that will be promoted by selecting the most able. Still, a concern for having some predetermined job or role performed *only* by the person who will be *the best* at performing it is something that itself must be defended, given the good that is otherwise done by programs of preferential treatment (construed, as they must be within this objection, as programs which make race a relevant, but non-qualification-related criterion for selection). And the plausibility of that exclusive concern with performance will vary greatly with the position and its context. Sometimes this concern will be of decisive, or virtually decisive, importance; when it legitimately is, preferential treatment of the sort I have been defending should play a very minor or even nonexistent role in the selections to be made. But in many contexts, and most of them are the ones in which preferential treatment programs operate, no such exclusive concern seems defensible. In the case of admission to college or professional school, of selection to a faculty, or of selection for training or employment, the good that is secured in selecting the most qualified person, in this restricted sense, is at most only one of the goods to be realized and balanced against those other, quite substantial ones whose realization depends upon the implementation of such programs. In sum, therefore, preferential treatment programs are presumptively justifiable insofar as they work to dismantle the system of racial oppression that is still in place, although it should not be; and their justifiability is rendered more secure once it can be seen, as I think it should be, that they are not unjust either in themselves or as constitutive elements of any larger system of racial oppression.

Review and Discussion Questions

1. Is Wasserstrom correct to describe our social system as one of racial oppression? What would count as evidence for or against this claim?

2. To what extent can Wasserstrom's positive argument for preferential treatment be applied to other minorities? To women?

3. Does Wasserstrom dismiss too quickly the possibility that the programs he defends will exacerbate racial hostility or reduce rather than enhance blacks' sense of self-respect? How great a danger are these possibilities? To what extent do they undermine the good results of affirmative action? How would you evaluate programs of preferential treatment from a utilitarian point of view?

4. Are defenders of affirmative action guilty of inconsistency in opposing earlier discrimination on the basis of race while advocating programs of preferential treatment now? Do you agree with Wasserstrom that there are some basic and relevant differences between the historic discrimination that blacks have suffered and preferential treatment on the grounds of race today?

5. Some argue that, if we give preferential treatment at all, we should focus on disadvantaged socioeconomic status rather than race. Is Wasserstrom right to reject this position? How would Wasserstrom respond to the argument that African Americans from well-off families should not be given preferential treatment?

6. Does it make sense to say that race can be a relevant job qualification? Explain why or why not. Many people believe that the best-qualified person *deserves* the job. Wasserstrom challenges the linkage between qualifications and desert. Do you find his reasoning persuasive?

The Case Against Affirmative Action

LOUIS P. POJMAN

After distinguishing between modest and strong affirmative action, Louis P. Pojman, professor of philosophy at the U.S. Military Academy at West Point, argues that strong affirmative action is not morally justified. He first challenges four arguments often advanced in defense of strong affirmative action, namely, that it: (1) supplies a need for role models; (2) compensates blacks for injuries they have suffered; (3) is necessary for diversity; and (4) is not unjust because the better qualified person, who is passed over, does not have a right to the job or position in question. Professor Pojman then presses two arguments *against* affirmative action: it requires discrimination against white males and violates the principle of merit.

Study Questions

1. What is the difference between modest affirmative action and strong affirmative action? What does Pojman mean when he contends that strong affirmative action implies that "two wrongs make a right"?
2. What is Pojman's response to the role-models argument?
3. Why does Pojman reject the compensation argument?
4. What is the point of the "no one deserves his talents" argument?
5. What is the relevance of the chart on page 412 to Pojman's argument?
6. What are the two pillars that support the case for meritocracy?

HARDLY A WEEK GOES BY but that the subject of affirmative action does not come up. Whether in the form of preferential hiring, non-traditional casting, quotas, "goals and time-tables," minority scholarships, race-norming, reverse discrimination, or employment of members of underutilized groups, this issue confronts us as a terribly perplexing problem. . . .

Let us agree that despite the evidences of a booming economy, the poor are suffering grievously, with children being born into desperate material and psychological poverty, for whom the ideal of "equal opportunity for all" is a cruel joke. Many feel that the federal government has abandoned its guarantee to provide the minimum necessities for each American, so that the pace of this tragedy seems to be worsening daily. Add to this the fact that in our country African Americans have a legacy of slavery and unjust discrimination to contend with, and we have the makings of an inferno, and, perhaps, in the worst-case scenario, the downfall of a nation. What is the answer to our national problem? Is it increased welfare? More job training? More support for education? Required licensing of parents to have children? Negative income tax? More support for families or for mothers with small children? All of these have merit and should be part of the national debate. But, my thesis is, however tragic the situation may be (and we may disagree on just how tragic it is), one policy is *not* a legitimate part of the solution

and that is *reverse, unjust discrimination* against young white males. Strong affirmative action, which implicitly advocates reverse discrimination, while, no doubt, well intentioned, is morally heinous, asserting, by implication, that *two wrongs make a right.*

The *two wrongs make a right* thesis goes like this: Because *some* whites once enslaved some blacks, the descendants of those slaves, some of whom may now enjoy high incomes and social status, have a right to opportunities and offices over better qualified whites who had nothing to do with either slavery or the oppression of blacks, and who may even have suffered hardship comparable to that of poor blacks. . . .

When I speak about civil rights or affirmative action, people usually ask for my credentials. What have I done to end racism and sexism? Briefly, I began working for racial integration in my teens, quixotically fighting windmills in trying to integrate my all-white town of Cicero, Illinois in the 1950s. I went into Chicago's black ghetto every Sunday and Monday after school to work with poor children, tutoring them and organizing activities. I was a civil rights activist. When I entered the ministry in the early 1960s I was selected by a predominantly black congregation in the Bedford-Stuyvesant neighborhood of Brooklyn as its minister. There my wife and I served for about four years until I went back to graduate school. Our children were born in this community: Paul and Ruth Freedom, named in hopes that we could create a world where all children, regardless of race or class, could grow up with equal opportunity for a fulfilled life. I engaged in nonviolent civil rights demonstrations, led workshops on racial integration, was a member of the Congress of Racial Equality, and was even arrested for my activities. I was also a Black Studies student in graduate school, writing my master's thesis on "A Philosophy of Negro Culture." My goals have not changed over the years, but I have been chastened by the harsh realities of life. I still strive to promote equal opportunity and to eliminate unjust discrimination. The irony is that I have gone from being a radical liberal to being a conservative without changing a single basic idea! For equal opportunity, once the hallmark of liberalism, is now sneered at by many modern liberals as a conservative fantasy. Such are the ironies of history.

Before analyzing arguments concerning affirmative action, I must define my terms.

By *modest affirmative action* I mean policies that will increase the opportunities of disadvantaged people to attain social goods and offices. It includes the dismantling of segregated institutions, widespread advertisement to groups not previously represented in certain privileged positions, special scholarships for the disadvantaged classes (e.g., the poor, regardless of race or gender), and even using diversity or underrepresentation of groups or history of past discrimination as a tiebreaker when candidates for these goods and offices are relatively equal. The goal of *modest affirmative action* is equal opportunity to compete, not equal results. There is no more moral requirement to guarantee that 12 percent of professors are black than to guarantee that 85 percent of the players in the National Basketball Association are white.

By *strong affirmative action* I mean preferential treatment on the basis of race, ethnicity, or gender (or some other morally irrelevant criterion), discriminating in favor of underrepresented groups against overrepresented groups,

aiming at roughly equal results. *Strong affirmative action* is reverse discrimination. It says it is right to do wrong to correct a wrong. It is the policy that is currently being promoted under the name of *affirmative action,* so I will use that term or "AA" for short throughout this essay to stand for this version of affirmative action. I will not argue for or against the principle of *modest affirmative action*. Indeed, I think it has some moral weight. *Strong affirmative action* has none, or so I will argue.

In what follows I will mainly concentrate on affirmative action policies with regard to race, but the arguments can be extended to cover ethnicity and gender. I think that if a case for affirmative action can be made it will be as a corrective to racial oppression. I will examine [six] arguments regarding affirmative action. The first [four] will be *negative*, attempting to show that the best arguments for affirmative action fail. The last [two] will be *positive* arguments for policies opposing affirmative action.

I. A Critique of Arguments for Affirmative Action

1. The need for role models

This argument is straightforward. We all need role models, and it helps to know that others like us can be successful. We learn and are encouraged to strive for excellence by emulating our heroes and "our kind of people" who have succeeded.

In the first place it's not clear that role models of one's own racial or sexual type are necessary (let alone sufficient) for success. One of my heroes was Gandhi, an Indian Hindu; another was my grade school science teacher, Miss DeVoe; and another Martin Luther King, behind whom I marched in civil rights demonstrations. More important than having role models of one's "own type" is having genuinely good people, of whatever race or gender, to emulate. Our common humanity should be a sufficient basis for us to see the possibility of success in people of virtue and merit. To yield to the demand, however tempting it may be to do so, for "role-models-just-like-us" is to treat people like means, not ends. It is to elevate morally irrelevant particularity over relevant traits, such as ability and integrity. We don't need people exactly like us to find inspiration. . . .

Furthermore, even if it helps people with low self-esteem to gain encouragement from seeing others of their particular kind in successful positions, it is doubtful whether this need is a sufficient reason to justify preferential hiring or reverse discrimination. What good is a role model who is inferior to other professors or physicians or business personnel? The best way to create role models is not to promote people because of race or gender but because they are the best qualified for the job. . . .

2. The compensation argument

The argument goes like this: Blacks have been wronged and severely harmed by whites. Therefore white society should compensate blacks for the injury caused them. Reverse discrimination in terms of preferential hiring, contracts, and scholarships is a fitting way to compensate for the past wrongs.

This argument actually involves a distorted notion of compensation. Normally, we think of compensation as owed by a specific person A to another person B whom A has wronged in a specific way C. . . . Sometimes compensation is extended to groups of people who have been unjustly harmed by the greater society. For example, the U.S. government has compensated the Japanese Americans who were imprisoned during the Second World War, and the West German government has paid reparations to the survivors of Nazi concentration camps. But here a specific people have been identified who were wronged in an identifiable way by the government of the nation in question.

On the face of it, demands by blacks for compensation do not fit the usual pattern. Perhaps

Southern states with Jim Crow laws could be accused of unjustly harming blacks, but it is hard to see that the U.S. government was involved in doing so. Much of the harm done to blacks was the result of private discrimination, not state action. So the Germany/U.S. analogy doesn't hold. Furthermore, it is not clear that all blacks were harmed in the same way or whether some were *unjustly* harmed or harmed more than poor whites and others (e.g., short people). Finally, even if identifiable blacks were harmed by identifiable social practices, it is not clear that most forms of affirmative action are appropriate to restore the situation. The usual practice of a financial payment seems more appropriate than giving a high-level job to someone unqualified or only minimally qualified, who, speculatively, might have been better qualified had he not been subject to racial discrimination. . . .

Still, there may be something intuitively compelling about compensating members of an oppressed group who are minimally qualified. Suppose that the Hatfields and the McCoys are enemy clans and some youths from the Hatfields go over and steal diamonds and gold from the McCoys, distributing it within the Hatfield economy. Even though we do not know which Hatfield youths did the stealing, we would want to restore the wealth, as far as possible, to the McCoys. One way might be to tax the Hatfields, but another might be to give preferential treatment in terms of scholarships and training programs and hiring to the McCoys.

This is perhaps the strongest argument for affirmative action, and it may well justify some weaker versions of AA, but it is doubtful whether it is sufficient to justify strong versions with quotas and goals and timetables in skilled positions. There are at least two reasons for this. First, we have no way of knowing how many people of any given group would have achieved some given level of competence had the world been different. . . . Secondly, the normal criterion of competence is a strong prima facie consideration when the most important positions are at stake. There are two reasons for this: (1) Society has given people expectations that if they attain certain levels of excellence they will be awarded appropriately, and (2) filling the most important positions with the best qualified is the best way to insure efficiency in job-related areas and in society in general. These reasons are not absolutes. They can be overridden. But there is a strong presumption in their favor so that a burden of proof rests with those who would override them.

At this point we get into the problem of whether innocent nonblacks should have to pay a penalty in terms of preferential hiring of blacks.

3. The diversity argument

It is important that we learn to live in a pluralistic world, learning to get along with those of other races and cultures, so we should have fully integrated schools and employment situations. Diversity is an important symbol and educative device. Thus preferential treatment is warranted to perform this role in society.

But, again, while we can admit the value of diversity, it hardly seems adequate to override considerations of merit and efficiency. *Diversity for diversity's sake is moral promiscuity,* since it obfuscates rational distinctions, undermines treating individuals as ends, treating them, instead as mere means (to the goals of social engineering), and, furthermore, unless those hired are highly qualified, the diversity factor threatens to become a fetish. At least at the higher levels of business and the professions, *competence* far outweighs considerations of diversity. I do not care whether the group of surgeons operating on me reflect racial or gender balance, but I do care that they are highly qualified. Neither do most football or basketball fans care whether their team reflects ethnic and gender diversity, but whether their team has the best combination of players available. And likewise with airplane pilots, military leaders, business executives, and, may I say it, teachers and university professors. Moreover,

there are other ways of learning about other cultures besides engaging in reverse discrimination.

4. The "no one deserves his talents" argument against meritocracy

According to this argument, the competent do not deserve their intelligence, their superior character, their industriousness, or their discipline; therefore they have no right to the best positions in society. Hence it is not unjust to give these positions to less (but still minimally) qualified blacks and women. In one form this argument holds that since no one deserves anything, society may use any criteria it pleases to distribute goods. The criterion most often designated is social utility. Versions of this argument are found in the writings of John Arthur, John Rawls, Bernard Boxill, Michael Kinsley, Ronald Dworkin, and Richard Wasserstrom. Rawls writes, "No one deserves his place in the distribution of native endowments, any more than one deserves one's initial starting place in society. The assertion that a man deserves the superior character that enables him to make the effort to cultivate his abilities is equally problematic; for his character depends in large part upon fortunate family and social circumstances for which he can claim no credit. The notion of desert seems not to apply to these cases."[1] Michael Kinsley is even more adamant:

> Opponents of affirmative action are hung up on a distinction that seems more profoundly irrelevant: treating individuals versus treating groups. What is the moral difference between dispensing favors to people on their "merits" as individuals and passing out society's benefits on the basis of group identification?
>
> Group identifications like race and sex are, of course, immutable. They have nothing to do with a person's moral worth. But the same is true of most of what comes under the label "merit." The tools you need for getting ahead in a meritocratic society—not all of them but most: talent, education, instilled cultural values such as ambition—are distributed just as arbitrarily as

skin color. They are fate. The notion that people somehow "deserve" the advantages of these characteristics in a way they don't "deserve" the advantage of their race is powerful, but illogical.[2]

It will help to enumerate the argument's steps:

1. Society may award jobs and positions as it sees fit as long as individuals have no claim to these positions.
2. To have a claim to something means that one has earned it or deserves it.
3. But no one has earned or deserves his intelligence, talent, education, or cultural values, which produce superior qualifications.
4. If a person does not deserve what produces something, he does not deserve its products.
5. Therefore, better qualified people do not deserve their qualifications.
6. Therefore, society may override their qualifications in awarding jobs and positions as it sees fit (for social utility or to compensate for previous wrongs).

So it is permissible if a minimally qualified black or woman is admitted to law or medical school ahead of a white male with excellent credentials, or if a less qualified person from an "underutilized" group gets a professorship ahead of an eminently better-qualified white male. Sufficiency and underutilization together outweigh excellence.

My response: Premise 4 is false. To see this, reflect that just because I do not deserve the money that I have been given as a gift (for instance) does not mean that I am not entitled to what I get with that money. If you and I both get a gift of $100 and I bury mine in the sand for five years while you invest yours wisely and double its value at the end of five years, I cannot complain that you should split the increase 50/50 since neither of us deserved the original gift. If we accept the notion of responsibility at all, we must hold that persons deserve the fruits of their labor and conscious choices. . . .

The attack on moral desert is perhaps the most radical move that egalitarians like Rawls and company have made against meritocracy, and the ramifications of their attack are far reaching. . . . Since no one deserves anything, we do not deserve pay for our labors or praise for a job well done or first prize in the race we win. The notion of moral responsibility vanishes in a system of leveling.

But there is no good reason to accept the argument against desert. We do act freely and, as such, we are responsible for our actions. We deserve the fruits of our labor, reward for our noble feats and punishment for our misbehavior.

We have considered [four] arguments for affirmative action and have found no compelling case for Strong AA and only one plausible argument (a version of the compensation argument) for Modest AA. We must now turn to the arguments against affirmative action to see whether they fare any better.

II. Arguments Against Affirmative Action

5. Affirmative action requires discrimination against a different group

Modest AA weakly discriminates against new minorities, mostly innocent young white males, and Strong AA strongly discriminates against these new minorities. . . . This discrimination is unwarranted, since, even if some compensation to blacks were indicated, it would be unfair to make innocent white males bear the whole brunt of the payments. . . . In fact, it is poor white youth who have become the new pariahs on the job market. The children of the wealthy have no trouble getting into the best private grammar schools and, on the basis of superior early education, into the best universities, graduate schools, managerial and professional positions. Affirmative action simply shifts injustice, setting blacks, Hispanics, Native Americans, Asians, and women against young white males, especially ethnic and poor white males. It makes no more sense to discriminate in favor of a rich black or a female who had the opportunity of the best family and education available against a poor white, than it does to discriminate in favor of white males against blacks or women. It does little to rectify the goal of providing equal opportunity to all.

At the end of his essay supporting affirmative action, Albert Mosley points out that other groups besides blacks have been benefited by affirmative action: "women, the disabled, the elderly."[3] He's correct in including the elderly, for through powerful lobbies such as the AARP, they do get special benefits including medicare and may sue on the grounds of being discriminated against due to *Ageism*, prejudice against older people. Might this not be a reason to reconsider affirmative action? Consider the sheer rough percentages of those who qualify for affirmative action programs.

Group	Percentage
1. Women	52%
2. Blacks	12%
3. Hispanics	8%
4. Native Americans	2%
5. Asians	4%
6. Physically disabled	10%
7. Welfare recipients	6%
8. The elderly	30%
9. Italians (in New York City)	3%
Totals	127%

. . . If our goal is the creation of a society where everyone has a fair chance, then it would be better to concentrate on support for families and early education and decide the matter of university admissions and job hiring on the basis of traditional standards of competence. . . .

6. An argument from the principle of merit

Traditionally, we have believed that the highest positions in society should be awarded to those who are best qualified. The Koran states that "A ruler who appoints any man to an office, when there is in his dominion another man better qualified for it, sins against God and against the State." Rewarding excellence both seems just to the individuals in the competition and makes for efficiency. Note that one of the most successful acts of racial integration, the Brooklyn Dodgers' recruitment of Jackie Robinson in the late 1940s, was done in just this way, according to merit. If Robinson had been brought into the major leagues as a mediocre player or had batted .200 he would have been scorned and sent back to the minors where he belonged.

As I mentioned earlier, merit is not an absolute value, but there are strong prima facie reasons for awarding positions on its basis, and it should enjoy a weighty presumption in our social practices.

. . . We generally want high achievers to have the best positions, the best-qualified candidate to win the political office, the most brilliant and competent scientist to be chosen for the most challenging research project, the best qualified pilots to become commercial pilots, only the best soldiers to become generals. Only when little is at stake do we weaken the standards and content ourselves with sufficiency (rather than excellence)—there are plenty of jobs where "sufficiency" rather than excellence is required. . . .

Note! No one is calling for quotas or proportional representation of *underutilized* groups in the National Basketball Association where blacks make up 80 percent of the players. But, surely, if merit and merit alone reigns in sports, should it not be valued at least as much in education and industry?

The case for meritocracy has two pillars. One pillar is a deontological argument that holds that we ought to treat people as ends and not merely means. By giving people what they deserve as *individuals,* rather than as members of *groups,* we show respect for their inherent worth. . . .

The second pillar for meritocracy is utilitarian. In the end, we will be better off by honoring excellence. We want the best leaders, teachers, policemen, physicians, generals, lawyers, and airplane pilots that we can possibly produce in society. So our program should be to promote equal opportunity, as much as is feasible in a free market economy, and reward people according to their individual merit.

Conclusion

Let me sum up my discussion. The goal of the civil rights movement and of moral people everywhere has been justice for all, including equal opportunity. The question is: How best to get there. Civil rights legislation removed the legal barriers, opening the way toward equal opportunity, but it did not tackle the deeper causes that produce differential results. Modest affirmative action aims at encouraging minorities in striving for the highest positions without unduly jeopardizing the rights of majorities. The problem of Modest AA is that it easily slides into Strong AA where quotas, "goals and timetables," "equal results,"—in a word—

reverse discrimination prevails and is forced onto groups, thus promoting mediocrity, inefficiency, and resentment. Furthermore, affirmative action aims at the higher levels of society—universities and skilled jobs—but if we want to improve our society, the best way to do it is to concentrate on families, children, early education, and the like, so all are prepared to avail themselves of opportunity. Affirmative action, on the one hand, is too much, too soon and on the other hand, too little, too late.

NOTES

1. John Rawls, *A Theory of Justice* (Harvard University Press, 1971), p. 104; see Bernard Boxill, "The Morality of Preferential Hiring," *Philosophy and Public Affairs,* vol. 7:3 (1983).

2. Michael Kinsley, "Equal Lack of Opportunity," *Harper's* (June 1983).

3. Albert Mosley, "Affirmative Action: Pro" in Albert Mosley and Nicholas Capaldi, *Affirmative Action: Social Justice or Unfair Preference?* (Lanham, Md.: Rowman & Littlefield, 1997), p. 53.

Review and Discussion Questions

1. Explain each of the four arguments for affirmative action that Pojman criticizes. How effective are his criticisms? Are there plausible rejoinders to any of his criticisms?

2. Are there arguments for affirmative action that Pojman has overlooked or failed to do justice to?

3. Pojman gives two arguments against affirmative action. How might a defender of affirmative action respond to each of them?

4. Pojman seems to assume that we live in a basically meritocratic society in which—if it were not for affirmative action—people would be rewarded strictly according to their merit and ability. Is this assumption sound?

5. Pojman believes in equal opportunity, but can there be meaningful equality of opportunity for African Americans without affirmative action? If Wasserstrom is right that our society is racially oppressive, what are the implications of this fact for Pojman's arguments?

6. Is it possible to eliminate the socioeconomic disparities between blacks and whites without some form of affirmative action? If so, how?

7. Wasserstrom concedes that affirmative action might exacerbate racial hostility, but he appears confident that the social benefits outweigh the costs. Pojman believes that affirmative action does more harm than good. Who is right about this issue? Is it a purely factual dispute? How could it be resolved?

A Case for Race-Consciousness

T. ALEXANDER ALEINIKOFF

Color blindness with regard to race is widely affirmed as a fundamental moral and social ideal. In the past, the principle of color blindness underlay legal strategies to eliminate racial segregation and discrimination. Today, many critics of affirmative action reject it because it violates the principle of color blindness. In this essay, Professor T. Alexander Aleinikoff of the University of Michigan School of Law criticizes the principle of color blindness and defends the legitimacy of racially conscious programs. He argues that color blindness actually supports racial domination and that programs premised on it can do little to influence social consciousness and end racism.

Study Questions

1. Besides affirmative action, what sort of racially conscious programs does Aleinikoff have in mind?
2. What point does Aleinikoff make using the example of IQ tests?
3. What's the difference between "strong colorblindness" and "weak colorblindness"?
4. What does Clifford Geertz mean by "local knowledge"?
5. Why is the viewpoint of subordinated groups likely to differ from that of the dominant majority?
6. How does Aleinikoff respond to the criticism that affirmative action reinforces racism?

I WANT, IN THIS ARTICLE, to consider and critique "colorblindness.". . .

Specifically, I will argue that we are not currently a colorblind society, and that race has a deep social significance that continues to disadvantage blacks and other Americans of color. While the legal strategy of colorblindness achieved great victories in the past, it has now become an impediment in the struggle to end racial inequality. At the base of racial injustice is a set of assumptions—a way of understanding the world—that so characterizes blacks as to make persistent inequality seem largely untroubling. A remedial regime predicated on colorblindness will have little influence at this deep level of social and legal consciousness because it cannot adequately challenge white attitudes or recognize a role for black self-definition. In the pages ahead I will explain and justify this somewhat paradoxical claim that a norm of colorblindness supports racial domination. I will conclude that in order to make progress in ending racial oppression and racism, our political and moral discourse must move from colorblindness to color-consciousness, from antidiscrimination to racial justice.

I. Colorblindness and Race-Consciousness: Clarifying the Categories

. . . In the colorblind world, race is an arbitrary factor—one upon which it is doubly unfair to allocate benefits and impose burdens: one's race is neither voluntarily assumed nor capable of change. For nearly all purposes, it is maintained, the race of a person tells us nothing about an individual's capabilities and certainly nothing about her moral worth. Race-consciousness, from this perspective, is disfavored because it assigns a value to what should be a meaningless variable. To categorize on the basis of race is to miss the individual.

Adhering to a strategy of colorblindness does not make race a prohibited classification. Violations of the colorblind principle cannot be recognized and remedied without "noticing" the race of the harmed individual or racial group. But, to be true to the model, race-conscious measures must be limited to identified instances of past discrimination.

The debate over colorblindness and race-consciousness has usually appeared in the cases and literature discussing programs that give preferences in employment or other opportunities to non-whites. In now familiar terms, advocates of color-blindness characterize affirmative action programs as unjustifiably altering meritocratic standards and requiring a distribution of social goods that reflects the proportionate representation of minority groups in the population as a whole. . . .

In this article, I will use the term "race-consciousness" to apply to more than just "affirmative action" programs intended to help bring about a colorblind world or remedy past discrimination. There are many other situations in which race *qua* race might be seen as relevant to the pursuit of a legitimate and important governmental goal. These include: ensuring the presence of persons of color on juries; taking race into account in allocating radio and television licenses; seeking nonwhites to fill positions in social service agencies that deal largely with minority populations; requiring voting rules and districts that improve the chances of electing minority representatives; fostering integration by adopting race-based school assignment plans and housing programs; taking measures to integrate police forces; adding the works of minority authors to the "literary canon" taught to college students; and giving weight to the race of applicants for teaching positions in higher education. In each of these situations, the race-consciousness of the program may be justified in other than remedial (and colorblind) terms.

II. The Difference That Race Makes

We live in a world of racial inequality. In almost every important category, blacks as a group are worse off than whites. Compared to whites, blacks have higher rates of unemployment, lower family incomes, lower life expectancy, higher rates of infant mortality, higher rates of crime victimization, and higher rates of teenage pregnancies and single-parent households. Blacks are less likely to go to college, and those who matriculate are less likely to graduate. Blacks are underrepresented in the professions, in the academy, and in the national government.

Of course there has been progress. Comparing the situation of blacks half a century ago to their situation today shows a difference that is startling, and even encouraging, although the last decade evidences a slowing progress and some backsliding. But when the comparison is made between whites and blacks today, it is impossible to ignore the deep and widening difference that race makes.[1]

To say that race makes a difference means more than simply identifying material disadvantages facing people of color in contemporary America. It also recognizes that race may have an influence on how members of society understand their worlds and each other, and how such understandings may serve to perpetuate racial inequalities in our society. The next two sections pursue these psychological and cultural claims.

A. Race and cognition

Race matters. Race is among the first things that one notices about another individual. To be born black is to know an unchangeable fact about one-self that matters every day. "[I]n my life," wrote W. E. B. Du Bois in his autobiography *Dusk of Dawn*, "the chief fact has been race—not so much scientific race, as that deep conviction of myriads of men that congenital differences among the main masses of human beings absolutely condition the individual destiny of every member of a group."[2] To be born white is to be free from confronting one's race on a daily, personal, interaction-by-interaction basis. Being white, it has been said, means not having to think about it. Understandably, white people have a hard time recognizing this difference.* Most blacks have to overcome, when meeting whites, a set of assumptions older than this nation about one's abilities, one's marriageability, one's sexual desires, and one's morality. Most whites, when they are being honest with themselves, know that these racial understandings are part of their consciousness.

Race matters with respect to the people we choose to spend time with or marry, the neighborhoods in which we choose to live, the houses of worship we join, our choice of schools for our children, the people for whom we vote, and the people we allow the state to execute. We make guesses about the race of telephone callers we do not know and about persons accused of crimes. While not every decision we make necessarily has a racial component, when race is present it almost invariably influences our judgments. We are intensely—even if subconsciously—race-conscious.

It is common to speak of racial attitudes as being based on "stereotypes"—an incorrect or unthinking generalization applied indiscriminately to individuals simply on the basis of group membership. From this perspective, stereotypes can

be overcome by supplying more information about an individual or the group to which that individual belongs.

But this explanation fails to recognize race-consciousness as an entrenched structure of thought that affects how we organize and process information. Social science research suggests that stereotypes serve as powerful heuristics, supplying explanations for events even when evidence supporting nonstereotypical explanations exists, and leading us to interpret situations and actions differently when the race of the actors varies. It is often more likely that our mental schema will influence how we understand new information than it is that the new information will alter our mental schema.

A troubling example can be found in *Larry P. by Lucille P. v. Riles*, a case challenging the use of IQ tests that disproportionately assigned black children to special classes for the "educable mentally retarded." In discussing the expert testimony presented on the adequacy of the tests, the court of appeals observed:

> Since the 1920s it has been generally known that black persons perform less well than white persons on the standardized intelligence tests. IQ tests had been standardized so that they yielded no bias because of sex. For example, when sample tests yielded different scores for boys and girls, the testing experts assumed such differences were unacceptable and modified the tests so that the curve in the standardization sample for boys and girls was identical. No such modification on racial grounds has ever been tried by the testing companies.[3]

The testing companies received two sets of data and chose to act on just one. Their assumptions made one set of data "surprising" and the other "expected" or "natural."

Because cognitive racial categories predispose us to select information that conforms to existing categories and to process information in such a way that it will fit into those categories, they are self-justifying and self-reinforcing. And because we adopt racial categories more through a process of cultural absorption than rational construction, we

---

*Much as men have a difficult time understanding the routine and ever-present fears that women have for their physical safety.

are likely to be unaware of the role that the categories play in the way we perceive the world. . . .

This deeply imbedded race-consciousness has a distressing effect on discourse between the races. In many ways, whites and blacks talk past each other. The stories that African-Americans tell about America—stories of racism and exclusion, brutality and mendacity—simply do not ring true to the white mind. Whites have not been trained to hear it, and to credit such accounts would be to ask whites to give up too much of what they "know" about the world. It would also argue in favor of social programs and an alteration in power relations that would fundamentally change the status quo. White versions of substantial progress on racial attitudes are also likely to ring hollow for many blacks. One might see an equality of missed communication here. But there is actually a great inequality because it is the white version that becomes the "official story" in the dominant culture.

B. *The power of definition*

In our society, race has not been a benign mode of classification. The designation of one's race has had a double function, both defining social categories and assigning characteristics to members of those categories. The predominant power of social and cultural definition has, from the start, been exercised by and for whites.

. . . Blacks are "invisible" not in the sense that whites do not see them; they are "invisible" in the sense that whites see primarily what a white dominant culture has trained them to see. In a curious yet powerful way, whites create and reflect a cultural understanding of blackness that requires little contribution from blacks. . . .

Continued white ignorance of blacks and lack of contact in daily life makes white understandings of race difficult to alter.* Whites are only dimly aware

---

*This is not to say that simply putting white and black folks together will end discrimination. As social science studies have suggested, such contacts may actually increase prejudice unless the contact occurs under particular conditions. . . .

of how blacks live or what it means to be black in America. Despite attempts to bring African-American history into the classroom, most whites do not understand the role of black slavery in the economic development of the United States, nor are they familiar with major trends in black political and social thought, or even the contributions of Frederick Douglass, W. E. B. Du Bois, and Malcolm X. Absence of knowledge is compounded by physical and social segregation. Blacks and whites rarely get to know each other in neighborhoods, schools, or churches; and interracial friendships remain surprisingly rare. As a result, most of what a white person in America knows about blacks is likely to have been learned from white family, friends, or the white-dominated media.

That the white-created image of African-Americans should remain largely unchallenged by black conceptions is troubling not only because the white version reflects stereotypes, myths, and half-truths, but also because of the role the white definition plays in explaining the historical treatment and current condition of blacks. Given strong incentives to absolve whites and blame blacks for existing social and economic inequalities, the white story about blacks has never been flattering. . . . It works this way:

> Believing both that Blacks are inferior and that the economy impartially rewards the superior over the inferior, whites see that most Blacks are indeed worse off than whites are, which reinforces their sense that the market is operating "fairly and impartially"; those who should logically be on the bottom are on the bottom. This strengthening of whites' belief in the system in turn reinforces their beliefs that Blacks are *indeed* inferior. After all, equal opportunity *is* the rule, and the market *is* an impartial judge; if Blacks are on the bottom, it must reflect their relative inferiority.[4]

In sum, racial inequality has many faces. Social and economic statistics paint a clear and distressing picture of the differences among racial groups. Yet other inequalities are less obvious, based on nearly inaccessible and usually unchallenged assumptions that hide power and explain away domination. The next section examines alternative legal responses to this complex web of inequalities based on race. . . .

III. From Colorblindness to Race-Consciousness

Colorblindness may seem to be a sensible strategy in a world in which race has unjustly mattered for so long. Yet the claim that colorblindness today is the most efficacious route to colorblindness tomorrow has always been controversial. Justice Blackmun's paradoxical aphorism in *Bakke* reflects the usual counterclaim: "In order to get beyond racism, we must first take account of race. There is no other way. And in order to treat some persons equally, we must treat them differently."[5] . . .

The claim I wish to press here is different from Blackmun's familiar stance in the affirmative action debate. I will argue in this section that a legal norm of colorblindness will not end race-consciousness; rather, it will simply make the unfortunate aspects and consequences of race-consciousness less accessible and thus less alterable. Furthermore, colorblind strategies are likely to deny or fail to appreciate the contribution that race-consciousness can make in creating new cultural narratives that would support serious efforts aimed at achieving racial justice.

Before these claims can be made, however, two varieties of colorblindness should be distinguished. The first, which I will call "strong colorblindness," argues that race should truly be an irrelevant, virtually unnoticed, human characteristic. Richard Wasserstrom has described this "assimilationist ideal":

> [A] nonracist society would be one in which the race of an individual would be the functional equivalent of the eye color of individuals in our society today. In our society no basic political rights and obligations are determined on the basis of eye color. No important institutional benefits and burdens are connected with eye color. Indeed, except for the mildest sort of aesthetic preferences, a person would be thought odd who even made private, social decisions by taking eye color into account.[6]

The second type, "weak colorblindness," would not outlaw all recognition of race, but would condemn the use of race as a basis for the distribution of scarce resources or opportunities and the imposition of burdens. Under "weak colorblindness," race might function like ethnicity: an attribute that could have significance for group members, and one that society as a whole could recognize, but not one upon which legal distinctions could be based. Furthermore, individuals would be able to choose how important a role race would play in their associations and identifications, but their race would not be used by others to limit their opportunities or define their identities. Thus, college courses on "African-American literature" might well be permissible under a weak colorblindness regime, but such a regime would not tolerate allocating places in the class based on race or allowing race to be used as a factor in the choice of an instructor. In the sections that follow, I will argue that strong colorblindness is impossible and undesirable, and that weak colorblindness—although perhaps able to be implemented as a legal strategy—is an inadequate response to current manifestations of racial inequality.

A. Masking race-consciousness

It is apparently important, as a matter of widespread cultural practice, for whites to assert that they are strongly colorblind, in the sense that they do not notice or act on the basis of race. One can see this at work in such statements as: "I judge each person as an individual." Of course, it cannot be that whites do not notice the race of others. Perhaps what is being said is that the speaker does not begin her evaluation with any preconceived notions. But this too is difficult to believe, given the deep and implicit ways in which our minds are color-coded. To be truly colorblind in this way, as David Strauss has shown, requires color-consciousness: one must notice race in order to tell oneself not to trigger the usual mental processes that take race into account.

The denial of race-consciousness occasioned by the desire to be strongly colorblind is described in a recent study of a desegregated junior high school by psychologist Janet Schofield. She reports that teachers, apparently concerned that acknowledging racial awareness would be viewed as a sign of prejudice, claimed not to notice the race of their students. In pursuit of colorblindness, teachers rarely used the words "white" or "black," and avoided racial topics and identifications in class. . . .

> [One] teacher included George Washington Carver on a list of great Americans from which students could pick individuals to learn about but specifically decided not to mention he was black for fear of raising racial issues. In the best of all worlds, there would be no need to make such mention, because children would have no preconceptions that famous people are generally white. However, in a school where one white child was surprised to learn from a member of our research team that Martin Luther King was black, not white[!], it would seem reasonable to argue that highlighting the accomplishments of black Americans and making sure that students do not assume famous figures are white is a reasonable practice.[7]

Certainly such conduct creates possibilities for serious miscommunication. There is significant evidence of cultural differences between whites and blacks. . . . When white teachers, unaware of such differences, ask questions in a way that conforms to white middle-class practice, they unwittingly disadvantage black school children.

But the problem runs deeper than the level of miscommunication. Whites believe that they can act in a colorblind fashion merely by acting as they always have. Colorblindness puts the burden on blacks to change; to receive "equal" treatment, they must be seen by whites as "white."* Hence, the "compliment" that some whites pay to blacks:

---

*James Baldwin commented on the "tone of warm congratulation with which so many [white] liberals address their Negro equals. It is the Negro, of course, who is presumed to have become equal—an achievement that not only proves the comforting fact that perseverance has no color but also overwhelmingly corroborates the white man's sense of his own value." J. Baldwin, *The Fire Next Time* 127 (1962).

"I don't think of you as black." Colorblindness is, in essence, not the absence of color, but rather monochromatism: whites can be colorblind when there is only one race—when blacks become white.

B. Local knowledge: race-consciousness as cultural critique

Strong colorblindness, I have argued, is unlikely to produce the result it promises—a world in which race does not matter. In this section, I want to make the case for race-consciousness more direct by focusing on the benefits of race-consciousness in undermining and shifting deep cultural assumptions and ultimately, perhaps, making progress in overcoming racism. In presenting these claims, I hope also to undermine the case for weak colorblindness. To be effective, strategies for attacking racism may well demand affirmative race-conscious governmental policies. Clifford Geertz, in a collection of his essays entitled *Local Knowledge,* has stated that:

> To see ourselves as others see us can be eye-opening. To see others as sharing a nature with ourselves is the merest decency. But it is from the far more difficult achievement of seeing ourselves amongst others, as a local example of the forms human life has locally taken, a case among cases, a world among worlds, that the largeness of mind, without which objectivity is self-congratulation and tolerance a sham, comes.[8]

Colorblindness operates at Geertz's level of "merest decency." It begins and ends with the observation that there is something, under the skin, common to all human beings. . . . But Geertz clearly seeks more than this; he would reorient the usual hierarchical relationship between dominant and subordinate cultures by rotating the axis through its center point, making the vertical horizontal. This shift requires two related transformations: the first is to appreciate the contingency, the nonuniversalism of one's own culture—to view it as an example of "local knowledge"; the second is to recognize and credit the "local knowledges" of other groups. . . .

My claim outlined in the pages that follow is that race-consciousness can aid in these cultural transformations. . . .

Rotating the axis helps us to be open to other accounts and perspectives, and in doing so it reminds us of the fictional or constructed nature of "local knowledges"—including our own. Once white Americans shed the false assumption that "they know all they need to know" about African-Americans, they will begin to learn as much about themselves as about others. . . .

"[T]he quickest way to bring the reason of the world face to face [with white racism]," Du Bois wrote, "is to listen to the complaint of those human beings today who are suffering most from white attitudes, from white habits, from the conscious and unconscious wrongs which white folk are today inflicting on their victims."[9] . . . Since dominant groups are not the direct victims of their acts toward dominated groups, they may underestimate the burdens suffered by the dominated groups. This problem is compounded if dominant and dominated groups inhabit separate geographical and social spaces, so that the extent and harms of domination remain largely hidden from the dominant groups. . . .

Finally, recognizing race validates the lives and experiences of those who have been burdened because of their race. White racism has made "blackness" a relevant category in our society. Yet colorblindness seeks to deny the continued social significance of the category, to tell blacks that they are no different from whites, even though blacks as blacks are persistently made to feel that difference. . . . Color-consciousness makes blacks subjects and not objects, undermining the durability of white definitions of "blackness." . . .

C. Weak colorblindness and its costs

It is common for advocates of affirmative action to point out that a legal strategy dedicated to "equality of opportunity" is likely to replicate deeply imbedded inequalities. The familiar metaphor is of a race between two runners, one of whom starts many yards back from the starting line, or is encumbered by ankle weights. Color-conscious policies are said to remove the advantage that has for several centuries been granted to whites. The simplicity of this argument should not disguise its soundness or moral power. . . .

Beyond this familiar terrain in the affirmative action debate, there are other advantages to race-conscious programs that also call into question the adequacy of weak colorblindness. As Justice Stevens has noted, there are a number of situations in which it seems eminently reasonable for government decision makers to take race into account. For example:

> in a city with a recent history of racial unrest, the superintendent of police might reasonably conclude that an integrated police force could develop a better relationship with the community and thereby do a more effective job of maintaining law and order than a force composed only of white officers.[10]

Similar claims could be made about integrated civil service and school administrations. That situations exist that could benefit from race-conscious policies should hardly be surprising, given the prominent role that race has played in allocating benefits and burdens throughout American history. . . . To the extent that weak colorblindness makes these forms of race-consciousness problematic, it is simply nearsighted social policy. . . .

D. An objection to race-consciousness

. . . [An] objection . . . that figures prominently in the attack on affirmative action is that race-consciousness is self-defeating to the extent that it reinforces rather than undermines racism. Affirmative action, it is argued, may have this effect because it inevitably creates the impression of a lowering of standards in order to benefit minorities. Furthermore, as Shelby Steele argues, the "implication of inferiority in racial preferences" has a demoralizing effect on blacks, contributing to "an enlargement of self doubt."[11]

One response is that we ought to run this claim by those who have been the victims of racism. Despite assertions by whites that race-conscious programs "stigmatize" beneficiaries, blacks remain overwhelmingly in favor of affirmative action. Would we not expect blacks to be the first to recognize such harms and therefore to oppose affirmative action if it produced serious stigmatic injury? . . . Furthermore, Randall Kennedy provides a convincing argument that affirmative action, on balance, is more likely to reduce stigma than to impose it:

> It is unrealistic to think . . . that affirmative action causes most white disparagement of the abilities of blacks. Such disparagement, buttressed for decades by the rigid exclusion of blacks from educational and employment opportunities, is precisely what engendered the explosive crisis to which affirmative action is a response. . . . In the end, the uncertain extent to which affirmative action diminishes the accomplishments of blacks must be balanced against the stigmatization that occurs when blacks are virtually absent from important institutions in the society.[12]

Confident measures of the costs and benefits of affirmative action do not exist. Given the material gains afforded minorities by race-conscious programs and the fact that these gains are likely, as Kennedy notes, to counteract "conventional stereotypes about the place of the Negro," I would put the burden of proof on those who claim that affirmative action contributes more to racism than it diminishes racism. Significantly, the case for race-consciousness suggested here would affect the evaluation of the costs and benefits because it would count as one of the benefits— as colorblindness cannot—the gains to white society of increased association with minorities and greater awareness of nondominant cultures. . . .

IV. From Antidiscrimination to Racial Justice

. . . The strategy of colorblindness follows from an understanding of discrimination law that views the use of racial classifications as morally and politically objectionable. In contrast, support for broad race-conscious policies is usually imbedded in a description of race discrimination law as aimed at ending the second-class citizenship of African-Americans and other subordinated minorities. . . .

The choice among race discrimination law principles is, in the deepest sense, moral and political. Arrayed on the side of the antidiscrimination-as-colorblindness model is the knowledge of the terrible wrongs that color-consciousness has wrought in our history, the ending of legal segregation effectuated by color-blindness, an ideology of individualism that stresses evaluation and rewards based on individual effort and personal characteristics over which a person has control, and the antagonisms that race-based preferences may breed. These, of course, are not trivial arguments, which suggests why color-blindness has had such significant appeal.

But the claim that race should be ignored would be far more persuasive if the difference that race had made in the past had been overcome. What cannot be denied—even if it is often ignored—is that blacks, as a class, have never attained economic or social equality with whites. . . .

There are strong reasons for continuing the struggle to fulfill the initial goals of race discrimination law. Whether phrased as "anti-caste," "anti-group disadvantage," or "anti-subjugation," the task remains where it began: the ending of second class status of an historically oppressed group and the achieving of racial justice.

There are two interrelated aspects to this agenda for race discrimination law. The first supports programs that would produce material improvements in the lives of black people: programs promoting jobs, medical care, and decent housing. Such programs, it should be noted, need not be race-based. A "racial justice" perspective need not entail explicitly race-conscious policies. It seems clear, however, that a racial justice perspective is friendly to race-conscious policies directed at overcoming the effects of past and present societal discrimination. . . . Set-aside programs . . . are modest examples of the kind of state intervention that is needed.

The second aspect of a racial justice perspective is an attack on the set of beliefs that makes existing inequalities untroubling. What must be addressed is not just old-fashioned racism, but also the deeply ingrained mental structures that categorize and define race to the disadvantage of blacks and other nonwhite groups. As suggested above, altering the image of blacks in the white mind requires paying attention to, and crediting, black voices, and to refashioning institutions in ways that will allow those voices to be heard. Here race-conscious programs may be crucial. . . .

V. Conclusion: Toward an Inclusive American Story

In the current political and social climate, a call for color-consciousness poses real risks. For several centuries of American history, noticing race provided the basis for a caste system that institutionalized second-class status for people of color. It was precisely this oppressive use of race that colorblindness sought to overcome. Furthermore, central to white opposition to affirmative action is the belief that blacks have attained equality of opportunity, and therefore any assistance directed to minorities qua minorities affords them an undeserved benefit and an unfair advantage. . . .

[But] race-neutral strategies simply postpone our society's inevitable rendezvous with its history of racism. . . . Race-conscious programs alone will not end racism. At best, they represent a small step toward changing social relations and structures of thought and perception. What is needed is direct, self-conscious scrutiny of the way we think and of the assumptions about race that each

of us holds and upon which we act. Attention to black constructions of reality can provide a counterbalance to the white construction of blacks in the white mind. . . .

Blacks as blacks have had a unique history in this country. It is a history that whites and blacks confront every day and will continue to confront into the indefinite future. In pretending to ignore race, this society denies itself the self-knowledge that is demanded for eradicating racism and achieving racial justice.

NOTES

1. For data to support the assertions in the preceding two paragraphs, see *A Common Destiny: Blacks & American Society* (G. Jaynes & R. Williams, Jr. eds. 1989) at 3–32, 122–23, 278, 280–81, 293, 295, 302–03, 399, 416–17, 465, 524, 530.

2. W. E. B. Du Bois, *Dusk of Dawn* 139 (1940).

3. 793 F. 2d 969 (9th Cir. 1984) at 975–76. . . .

4. Crenshaw, "Race, Reform, and Retrenchment," 101 *Harv. L. Rev.* 1331, at 1380 (footnote omitted).

5. *Regents of Univ. of Cal.* v. *Bakke*, 438 U.S. 265, 407 (1978) (Blackmun, J., dissenting).

6. R. Wasserstrom, *Philosophy and Social Issues* 24 (1980). . . .

7. Schofield, "Causes and Consequences of the Colorblind Perspective," in *Prejudice, Discrimination, and Racism* (J. Dovidio & S. Gaertner eds., 1986) at 249.

8. C. Geertz, *Local Knowledge: Further Essays in Interpretive Anthropology* 16 (1983).

9. W. E. B. Du Bois, supra note [2], at 172.

10. *Wygant*, 476 U.S. at 314 (Stevens, J., dissenting).

11. S. Steele, *The Content of Our Character* 116–17 (1990).

12. Kennedy, "Persuasion and Distrust: A Comment on the Affirmative Action Debate," 99 *Harv. L. Rev.* 1327, 1331 (1986) (footnotes omitted).

Review and Discussion Questions

1. What do you see as the strong and weak points of colorblindness, in comparison with race-consciousness, as a principle underlying social policy?

2. Aleinikoff writes that whites and blacks tend to talk past one another and that whites have little understanding of the black experience. Would you agree or disagree? What evidence is there for and against what Aleinikoff says?

3. "If the goal is to make our society fairer and less racially divided, then adopting racially conscious policies will only make things worse—it's like fighting fire with fire." Explain why you agree or disagree with this statement.

4. Aleinikoff writes that "race-neutral strategies simply postpone our society's inevitable rendezvous with its history of racism." What does this statement mean? Do you agree with it?

5. How would Louis Pojman respond to Aleinikoff's defense of race-consciousness? With whom do you side, and why?

6. Are there some programs, institutions, and situations in which race-consciousness is necessary and others in which colorblindness would be more appropriate? Give examples. Should race be a consideration in university admission? Why or why not?

The University of Michigan Affirmative Action Cases

U.S. SUPREME COURT

In June 2003 in two cases involving the University of Michigan, the Supreme Court took up the issue of affirmative action in higher education for the first time since the *Bakke* case of 1978. In *Grutter* v. *Bollinger,* the Court held that the University of Michigan Law School's use of race as a factor in student admission is constitutionally permissible. In delivering the majority opinion (excerpted below), Justice O'Connor explains that the law school has a compelling interest in attaining a diverse student body and that its flexible, individualized admissions process is narrowly tailored to further that interest. However, in a vigorous dissent (reprinted below), Justice Thomas responds that marginal improvements in legal education cannot justify racial discrimination, and he criticizes the law school for not seeking race-neutral ways to enhance diversity.

On the same day, the Court ruled in a companion case, *Gratz* v. *Bollinger,* that the University's use of race in its undergraduate admissions process was constitutionally flawed because it guaranteed members of underrepresented minorities 20 points on a 150-point scale. Reproduced below are the dissents of Justices Souter and Ginsburg to this decision. Justice Souter argues that the undergraduate admissions policy simply does with a numbered scale what the law school accomplishes with its "holistic" review. Justice Ginsburg points to the continuing legacy "of a system of racial caste only recently ended" and stresses the difference between using race to exclude and taking race into account for the purpose of promoting equality.

Study Questions

1. In Justice O'Connor's view, what are the benefits of diversity?
2. She writes that the law school's policy is not unfair to nonminorities. Explain.

Nos. 02-241 and 02-516 (2003)

3. Why can't affirmative action be permanent? How long should it last?

4. The University of Michigan is a highly selective, elitist institution. How, in the eyes of Justice Thomas, does this bear on the issue of affirmative action?

5. Justice Thomas disputes the contention that minorities benefit from the law school's racial policies. Explain.

6. Why does Justice Souter believe there is nothing wrong with granting minority undergraduate applicants 20 points?

7. Justice Ginsburg maintains that Michigan's fully disclosed affirmative action program is better than what is likely to happen if such programs are deemed unconstitutional. Explain.

Grutter v. *Bollinger*

JUSTICE O'CONNOR *delivered the opinion of the Court:*

This case requires us to decide whether the use of race as a factor in student admissions by the University of Michigan Law School (Law School) is unlawful.

I

The Law School ranks among the Nation's top law schools. . . . The Law School looks for individuals with "substantial promise for success in law school" and "a strong likelihood of succeeding in the practice of law and contributing in diverse ways to the well-being of others." More broadly, the Law School seeks "a mix of students with varying backgrounds and experiences who will respect and learn from each other.". . . . The hallmark of [its] policy is its focus on academic ability coupled with a flexible assessment of applicants' talents, experiences, and potential "to contribute to the learning of those around them." The policy requires admissions officials to evaluate each applicant based on all the information available in the file, including a personal statement, letters of recommendation, and an essay describing the ways in which the applicant will contribute to the life and diversity of the Law School. . . .

The policy aspires to "achieve that diversity which has the potential to enrich everyone's education and thus make a law school class stronger than the sum of its parts." The policy does not restrict the types of diversity contributions eligible for "substantial weight" in the admissions process, but instead recognizes "many possible bases for diversity admissions." The policy does, however, reaffirm the Law School's long-standing commitment to "one particular type of diversity," that is, "racial and ethnic diversity with special reference to the inclusion of students from groups which have been historically discriminated against, like African-Americans, Hispanics and Native Americans, who without this commitment might not be represented in our student body in meaningful numbers.". . .

II

. . . Today, we hold that the Law School has a compelling interest in attaining a diverse student body.

The Law School's educational judgment that such diversity is essential to its educational mission is one to which we defer. The Law School's assessment that diversity will, in fact, yield educational benefits is substantiated by respondents[*] and their *amici*[†]. . . .

As part of its goal of "assembling a class that is both exceptionally academically qualified and broadly diverse," the Law School seeks to "enroll a 'critical mass' of minority students." The Law School's interest is not simply "to assure within its student body some specified percentage of a particular group merely because of its race or ethnic origin." That would amount to outright racial

---

[*]I.e., the Law School—ED.

[†]I.e., those submitting legal briefs in support of the respondents—ED.

balancing, which is patently unconstitutional. Rather, the Law School's concept of critical mass is defined by reference to the educational benefits that diversity is designed to produce.

These benefits are substantial. As the District Court emphasized, the Law School's admissions policy promotes "cross-racial understanding," helps to break down racial stereotypes, and "enables [students] to better understand persons of different races." These benefits are "important and laudable," because "classroom discussion is livelier, more spirited, and simply more enlightening and interesting" when the students have "the greatest possible variety of backgrounds."

The Law School's claim of a compelling interest is further bolstered by its *amici,* who point to the educational benefits that flow from student body diversity. In addition to the expert studies and reports entered into evidence at trial, numerous studies show that student body diversity promotes learning outcomes, and "better prepares students for an increasingly diverse workforce and society, and better prepares them as professionals."

These benefits are not theoretical but real, as major American businesses have made clear that the skills needed in today's increasingly global marketplace can only be developed through exposure to widely diverse people, cultures, ideas, and viewpoints. What is more, high-ranking retired officers and civilian leaders of the United States military assert that, "[b]ased on [their] decades of experience," a "highly qualified, racially diverse officer corps . . . is essential to the military's ability to fulfill its principle mission to provide national security." The primary sources for the Nation's officer corps are the service academies and the Reserve Officers Training Corps (ROTC), the latter comprising students already admitted to participating colleges and universities. At present, "the military cannot achieve an officer corps that is *both* highly qualified *and* racially diverse unless the service academies and the ROTC used limited race-conscious recruiting and admissions policies.". . .

III

To be narrowly tailored, a race-conscious admissions program cannot use a quota system—it cannot "insulat[e] each category of applicants with certain desired qualifications from competition with all other applicants." Instead, a university may consider race or ethnicity only as a "'plus' in a particular applicant's file," without "insulat[ing] the individual from comparison with all other candidates for the available seats." In other words, an admissions program must be "flexible enough to consider all pertinent elements of diversity in light of the particular qualifications of each applicant, and to place them on the same footing for consideration, although not necessarily according them the same weight." . . .

That a race-conscious admissions program does not operate as a quota does not, by itself, satisfy the requirement of individualized consideration. When using race as a "plus" factor in university admissions, a university's admissions program must remain flexible enough to ensure that each applicant is evaluated as an individual and not in a way that makes an applicant's race or ethnicity the defining feature of his or her application. The importance of this individualized consideration in the context of a race-conscious admissions program is paramount.

Here, the Law School engages in a highly individualized, holistic review of each applicant's file, giving serious consideration to all the ways an applicant might contribute to a diverse educational environment. The Law School affords this individualized consideration to applicants of all races. There is no policy, either *de jure* or *de facto,* of automatic acceptance or rejection based on any single "soft" variable. Unlike the program at issue in *Gratz* v. *Bollinger,* the Law School awards no mechanical, predetermined diversity "bonuses" based on race or ethnicity. . . .

We also find that . . . the Law School's race-conscious admissions program adequately ensures that all factors that may contribute to student body diversity are meaningfully considered alongside race in admissions decisions. With respect to the use of race itself, all underrepresented minority students admitted by the Law School have been deemed qualified. By virtue of our Nation's struggle with racial inequality, such students are both likely to have experiences of particular importance to the Law School's mission, and less likely to be admitted in meaningful numbers on criteria that ignore those experiences. . . .

What is more, the Law School actually gives substantial weight to diversity factors besides race. The Law School frequently accepts nonminority applicants with grades and test scores lower than underrepresented minority applicants (and other nonminority applicants) who are rejected. This shows that the Law School seriously weighs many other diversity factors besides race that can make a real and dispositive difference for nonminority applicants as well. . . .

We acknowledge that "there are serious problems of justice connected with the idea of preference itself." Narrow tailoring, therefore, requires that a race-conscious admissions program not unduly harm members of any racial group. . . .

We are satisfied that the Law School's admissions program does not. Because the Law School considers "all pertinent elements of diversity," it can (and does) select nonminority applicants who have greater potential to enhance student body diversity over underrepresented minority applicants. . . .

We are mindful, however, that "[a] core purpose of the Fourteenth Amendment was to do away with all governmentally imposed discrimination based on race." Accordingly, race-conscious admissions policies must be limited in time. This requirement reflects that racial classifications, however compelling their goals, are potentially so dangerous that they may be employed no more broadly than the interest demands. Enshrining a permanent justification for racial preferences would offend this fundamental equal protection principle.

. . . It has been 25 years since Justice Powell first approved the use of race to further an interest in student body diversity in the context of public higher education. Since that time, the number of minority applicants with high grades and test scores has indeed increased. We expect that 25 years from now, the use of racial preferences will no longer be necessary to further the interest approved today.

IV

In summary, the Equal Protection Clause does not prohibit the Law School's narrowly tailored use of race in admissions decisions to further a compelling interest in obtaining the educational benefits that flow from a diverse student body. . . . The judgment of the Court of Appeals for the Sixth Circuit, accordingly, is affirmed.

It is so ordered.

JUSTICE THOMAS, *dissenting:*

Frederick Douglass, speaking to a group of abolitionists almost 140 years ago, delivered a message lost on today's majority:

> "In regard to the colored people, there is always more that is benevolent, I perceive, than just, manifested towards us. What I ask for the negro is not benevolence, not pity, not sympathy, but simply *justice*. The American people have always been anxious to know what they shall do with us.
> . . . I have had but one answer from the beginning. Do nothing with us! Your doing with us has already played the mischief with us. Do nothing with us! . . . If the negro cannot stand on his own legs, let him fall also. All I ask is, give him a chance to stand on his own legs! Let him alone! . . . Your interference is doing him positive injury."

Like Douglass, I believe blacks can achieve in every avenue of American life without the meddling of university administrators. Because I wish to see all students succeed whatever their color, I share, in some respect, the sympathies of those who sponsor the type of discrimination advanced by the University of Michigan Law School (Law School). The Constitution does not, however, tolerate institutional devotion to the status quo in admissions policies when such devotion ripens into racial discrimination. . . .

No one would argue that a university could set up a lower general admission standard and then impose heightened requirements only on black applicants. Similarly, a university may not maintain a high admission standard and grant exemptions to favored races. The Law School, of its own choosing, and for its own purposes, maintains an exclusionary admissions system that it knows produces racially disproportionate results. Racial discrimination is not a permissible solution to the self-inflicted wounds of this elitist admissions policy. . . .

I

One must also consider the Law School's refusal to entertain changes to its current admissions system that might produce the same educational benefits. The Law School adamantly disclaims any race-neutral alternative that would reduce "academic selectivity," which would in turn "require the Law School to become a very different institution, and to sacrifice a core part of its educational mission." In other words, the Law School seeks to improve marginally the education it offers without sacrificing too much of its exclusivity and elite status.

. . . The Court upholds the use of racial discrimination as a tool to advance the Law School's interest in offering a marginally superior education while maintaining an elite institution. . . . There is no pressing public necessity in maintaining a public law school at all and, it follows, certainly not an elite law school. Likewise, marginal improvements in legal education do not qualify as a compelling state interest. . . . Even if the Law School's racial tinkering produces tangible educational benefits, a mar-

ginal improvement in legal education cannot justify racial discrimination where the Law School has no compelling interest in either its existence or in its current educational and admissions policies. . . .

II

Putting aside the absence of any legal support for the majority's reflexive deference, there is much to be said for the view that the use of tests and other measures to "predict" academic performance is a poor substitute for a system that gives every applicant a chance to prove he can succeed in the study of law. The rallying cry that in the absence of racial discrimination in admissions there would be a true meritocracy ignores the fact that the entire process is poisoned by numerous exceptions to "merit." For example, in the national debate on racial discrimination in higher education admissions, much has been made of the fact that elite institutions utilize a so-called "legacy" preference to give the children of alumni an advantage in admissions. This, and other, exceptions to a "true" meritocracy give the lie to protestations that merit admissions are in fact the order of the day at the Nation's universities. The Equal Protection Clause does not, however, prohibit the use of unseemly legacy preferences or many other kinds of arbitrary admissions procedures. What the Equal Protection Clause does prohibit are classifications made on the basis of race.

. . . Since its inception, selective admissions has been the vehicle for racial, ethnic, and religious tinkering and experimentation by university administrators. The initial driving force for the relocation of the selective function from the high school to the universities was the same desire to select racial winners and losers that the Law School exhibits today. Columbia, Harvard, and others infamously determined that they had "too many" Jews, just as today the Law School argues it would have "too many" whites if it could not discriminate in its admissions process.

Columbia employed intelligence tests precisely because Jewish applicants, who were predominantly immigrants, scored worse on such tests. Thus, Columbia could claim (falsely) that "[w]e have not eliminated boys because they were Jews and do not propose to do so. We have honestly attempted to eliminate the lowest grade of applicant [through the use of intelligence testing] and it turns out that a good many of the low grade men are New York City Jews." In other words, the tests were adopted with full knowledge of their disparate impact.

Similarly no modern law school can claim ignorance of the poor performance of blacks, relatively speaking, on the Law School Admissions Test (LSAT). Nevertheless, law schools continue to use the test and then attempt to "correct" for black underperformance by using racial discrimination in admissions so as to obtain their aesthetic student body. The Law School's continued adherence to measures it knows produce racially skewed results is not entitled to deference by this Court. . . .

Having decided to use the LSAT, the Law School must accept the constitutional burdens that come with this decision. The Law School may freely continue to employ the LSAT and other allegedly merit-based standards in whatever fashion it likes. What the Equal Protection Clause forbids, but the Court today allows, is the use of these standards hand-in-hand with racial discrimination. An infinite variety of admissions methods are available to the Law School. . . .

The Court will not even deign to make the Law School try other methods, however, preferring instead to grant a 25-year license to violate the Constitution. And the same Court that had the courage to order the desegregation of all public schools in the South now fears, on the basis of platitudes rather than principle, to force the Law School to abandon a decidedly imperfect admissions regime that provides the basis for racial discrimination.

III

. . . I believe what lies beneath the Court's decision today are the benighted notions that one can tell when racial discrimination benefits (rather than hurts) minority groups, and that racial discrimination is necessary to remedy general societal ills.

. . . I must contest the notion that the Law School's discrimination benefits those admitted as a result of it. . . . Nowhere in any of the filings in this Court is any evidence that the purported "beneficiaries" of this racial discrimination prove themselves by performing at (or even near) the same level as those students who receive no preferences. . . .

The Law School tantalizes unprepared students with the promise of a University of Michigan degree and all of the opportunities that it offers. These overmatched students take the bait, only to find that they cannot succeed in the cauldron of competition. And this mismatch crisis is not restricted to elite institutions. . . .

It is uncontested that each year, the Law School admits a handful of blacks who would be admitted in the absence of racial discrimination. Who can differentiate between those who belong and those who do not? The majority of blacks are admitted to the Law School because of discrimination, and because of this policy all are tarred as undeserving. This problem of stigma does not depend on determinacy as to whether those stigmatized are actually the "beneficiaries" of racial discrimination. When blacks take positions in the highest places of government, industry, or academia, it is an open question today whether their skin color played a part in their advancement. The question itself is the stigma—because either racial discrimination did play a role, in which case the person may be deemed "otherwise unqualified," or it did not, in which case asking the question itself unfairly marks those blacks who would succeed without discrimination. . . .

. . .

For the immediate future . . . the majority has placed its *imprimatur* on a practice that can only weaken the principle of equality embodied in the Declaration of Independence and the Equal

Protection Clause. "Our Constitution is color-blind, and neither knows nor tolerates classes among citizens." It has been nearly 140 years since Frederick Douglass asked the intellectual ancestors of the Law School to "[d]o nothing with us!" and the Nation adopted the Fourteenth Amendment. Now we must wait another 25 years to see this principle of equality vindicated. I therefore respectfully dissent from the remainder of the Court's opinion and the judgment.

Gratz v. *Bollinger*

JUSTICE SOUTER, *dissenting*:

. . . .*Grutter* reaffirms the permissibility of individualized consideration of race to achieve a diversity of students, at least where race is not assigned a preordained value in all cases. On the other hand, Justice Powell's opinion in *Regents of Univ. of Cal.* v. *Bakke* rules out a racial quota or set-aside, in which race is the sole fact of eligibility for certain places in a class. Although the freshman admissions system here is subject to argument on the merits, I think it is closer to what *Grutter* approves than to what *Bakke* condemns, and should not be held unconstitutional on the current record.

. . . Membership in an underrepresented minority is given a weight of 20 points on the 150-point scale. On the face of things, however, this assignment of specific points does not set race apart from all other weighted considerations. Nonminority students may receive 20 points for athletic ability, socioeconomic disadvantage, attendance at a socioeconomically disadvantaged or predominantly minority high school, or at the Provost's discretion; they may also receive 10 points for being residents of Michigan, 6 for residence in an underrepresented Michigan county, 5 for leadership and service, and so on.

The Court nonetheless finds fault with a scheme that "automatically" distributes 20 points to minority applicants because "[t]he only consideration that accompanies this distribution of points is a factual review of an application to determine whether an individual is a member of one of these minority groups." The objection goes to the use of points to quantify and compare characteristics, or to the number of points awarded due to race, but on either reading the objection is mistaken.

The very nature of a college's permissible practice of awarding value to racial diversity means that race must be considered in a way that increases some applicants' chances for admission. Since college admission is not left entirely to inarticulate intuition, it is hard to see what is inappropriate in assigning some stated value to a relevant characteristic, whether it be reasoning ability, writing style, running speed, or minority race. The college simply does by a numbered scale what the law school accomplishes in its "holistic review"; the distinction does not imply that applicants to the undergraduate college are denied individualized consideration or a fair chance to compete on the basis of all the various merits their applications may disclose.

Nor is it possible to say that the 20 points convert race into a decisive factor comparable to reserving minority places as in *Bakke*. Of course we can conceive of a point system in which the "plus" factor given to minority applicants would be so extreme as to guarantee every minority applicant a higher rank than every nonminority applicant in the university's admissions system. But . . . the present record obviously shows that nonminority applicants may achieve higher selection point totals than minority applicants owing to characteristics other than race. . . . It suffices for me, as it did for the District Court, that there are no *Bakke*-like set-asides and that consideration of an applicant's whole spectrum of ability is no more ruled out by giving 20 points for race than by giving the same points for athletic ability or socioeconomic disadvantage.

J USTICE GINSBURG, *dissenting:*

I

Educational institutions, the Court acknowledges, are not barred from any and all consideration of race when making admissions decisions. But the Court once again maintains that the same standard of review controls judicial inspection of all official race classifications. This insistence on "consistency," would be fitting were our Nation free of the vestiges of rank discrimination long reinforced by law. But we are not far distant from an overtly discriminatory past, and the effects of centuries of law-sanctioned inequality remain painfully evident in our communities and schools.

In the wake "of a system of racial caste only recently ended," large disparities endure. Unemployment, poverty, and access to health care vary disproportionately by race. Neighborhoods and schools remain racially divided. African-American and Hispanic children are all too often educated in poverty-stricken and underperforming institutions. Adult African-Americans and Hispanics generally earn less than whites with equivalent levels of education. Equally credentialed job applicants receive different receptions depending on their race. Irrational prejudice is still encountered in real estate markets and consumer transactions. "Bias both conscious and unconscious, reflecting traditional and unexamined habits of thought, keeps up barriers that must come down if equal opportunity and nondiscrimination are ever genuinely to become this country's law and practice."

The Constitution instructs all who act for the government that they may not "deny to any person . . . the equal protection of the laws." In implementing this equality instruction, as I see it, government decision-makers may properly distinguish between policies of exclusion and inclusion. Actions designed to burden groups long denied full citizenship stature are not sensibly ranked with measures taken to hasten the day when entrenched discrimination and its after effects have been extirpated. . . . "To say that two centuries of struggle for the most basic of civil rights have been mostly about freedom from racial categorization rather than freedom from racial oppressio[n] is to trivialize the lives and deaths of those who have suffered under racism." . . .

Our jurisprudence ranks race a "suspect" category, "not because [race] is inevitably an impermissible classification, but because it is one which usually, to our national shame, has been drawn for the purpose of maintaining racial inequality." But where race is considered "for the purpose of achieving equality," no automatic proscription is in order. For, as insightfully explained, "[t]he Constitution is both color blind and color conscious. To avoid conflict with the equal protection clause, a classification that denies a benefit, causes harm, or imposes a burden must not be based on race. In that sense, the Constitution is color blind. But the Constitution is color conscious to prevent discrimination being perpetuated and to undo the effects of past discrimination.". . .

The mere assertion of a laudable governmental purpose, of course, should not immunize a race-conscious measure from careful judicial inspection. Close review is needed "to ferret out classifications in reality malign, but masquerading as benign," and to "ensure that preferences are not so large as to trammel unduly upon the opportunities of others or interfere too harshly with legitimate expectations of persons in once-preferred groups."

II

Examining in this light the admissions policy employed by the University of Michigan's College of Literature, Science, and the Arts (College), and for the reasons well stated by JUSTICE SOUTER, I see no constitutional infirmity. . . . Like other top-ranking institutions, the College has many more applicants for admission than it can accommodate in an entering class. Every applicant admitted under the current plan . . . is qualified to attend the College. The racial and ethnic groups to which the College accords special consideration (African-Americans, Hispanics, and Native-Americans) historically have been relegated to inferior status by law and social practice; their members continue to experience class-based discrimination to this day. There is no suggestion that the College adopted its current policy in order to limit or decrease enrollment by any particular racial or ethnic group, and no seats are reserved on the basis of race. Nor has there been any demonstration that the College's program unduly constricts admissions opportunities for students who do not receive special consideration based on race.

The stain of generations of racial oppression is still visible in our society, and the determination to hasten its removal remains vital. One can reasonably anticipate, therefore, that colleges and universities will seek to maintain their minority enrollment—and the networks and opportunities thereby opened to minority graduates—whether or not they can do so in full candor through adoption of affirmative action plans of the kind here at issue. Without recourse to such plans, institutions of higher education may resort to camouflage. For example, schools may encourage applicants to write of their cultural traditions in the essays they submit, or to indicate whether English is their second language. Seeking to improve their chances for admission, applicants may highlight the minority group associations to which they belong, or the Hispanic surnames of their mothers or grandparents. In turn, teachers' recommendations may emphasize who a student is as much as what he or she has accomplished. If honesty is the best policy, surely Michigan's accurately described, fully disclosed College affirmative action program is preferable to achieving similar numbers through winks, nods, and disguises.

Review and Discussion Questions

1. Review and assess the benefits of educational diversity as explained by Justice O'Connor. In your view, what constitutes "diversity"? How important is it in higher education, and why?

2. Does the law school's admissions process treat nonminority applicants unfairly? Does the undergraduate admissions process? Explain your answers.

3. Will affirmative action no longer be necessary twenty-five years from now, as the Court suggests? Assess the following argument: "If affirmative action will be wrong twenty-five years from now, then it's wrong now. We shouldn't suspend the Constitution for twenty-five years."

4. Justice Thomas suggests that at the root of the problem is the law school's effort to both be diverse and have a highly selective admissions process. Do you agree? What alternatives to affirmative action are open to the law school for increasing diversity?

5. Assess Justice Thomas's argument that there is no pressing public necessity for Michigan to have a public law school, especially an elite law school, and that therefore it can have no compelling interest in improving diversity in legal education.

6. Do you agree with Justice Thomas that affirmative action stigmatizes all blacks? If so, is this a sufficient reason for rejecting affirmative action? Are blacks better off being left alone, as he implies when he quotes Frederick Douglass ("Do nothing with us!")?

7. Are you persuaded by Justice Souter's argument that there is no significant difference between the law school's admissions process and the undergraduate admissions process?

8. Assess Justice Ginsburg's contention that there's a difference between using race to exclude and taking it into account in order to promote equality.

ECONOMIC JUSTICE

Rich and Poor

PETER SINGER

After reviewing the seriousness and extensiveness of world poverty, Professor Peter Singer argues that we have a duty to provide far more aid to those in need than we now give. The principle to which he appeals is one that, he argues, we already implicitly acknowledge in everyday life. Singer answers several objections to his position: that we have an obligation to take care of our own poor first, that his argument ignores property rights, and that we should simply write off certain countries as "hopeless" and allow famine, disease, and natural disaster to reduce their populations.

Study Questions

1. What is the difference between absolute and relative poverty?
2. What is the key moral premise in Singer's argument for an obligation to assist? What is the analogy he uses to support it?
3. What is Singer's response to the position that we should take care of our own poor before aiding people overseas?
4. Why does Singer object to an individualistic theory of property rights?
5. What is triage? What is the point of Garrett Hardin's lifeboat analogy?

Some Facts About Poverty

CONSIDER THESE FACTS: by the most cautious estimates, 400 million people lack the calories, protein, vitamins and minerals needed to sustain their bodies and minds in a healthy state. Millions are constantly hungry; others suffer from deficiency diseases and from infections they would be able to resist on a better diet. Children are the worst affected. According to one study, 14 million children under five die every year from the combined effects of malnutrition and infection. In some districts half the children born can be expected to die before their fifth birthday.

Nor is lack of food the only hardship of the poor. To give a broader picture, Robert McNamara, when president of the World Bank, suggested the term "absolute poverty." The poverty we are familiar with in industrialised nations is relative poverty—meaning that some citizens are poor, relative to the wealth enjoyed by their neighbours. People living in relative poverty in Australia might be quite comfortably off by comparison with pensioners in Britain, and British pensioners are not poor in comparison with the poverty that exists in Mali or Ethiopia. Absolute poverty, on the other hand, is poverty by any standard. In McNamara's words:

> Poverty at the absolute level . . . is life at the very margin of existence. The absolute poor are severely deprived human beings struggling to survive in a set of squalid and degraded circumstances almost beyond the power of our sophisticated imaginations and privileged circumstances to conceive.
>
> Compared to those fortunate enough to live in developed countries, individuals in the poorest nations have:
>
> An infant mortality rate eight times higher
> A life expectancy one-third lower
> An adult literacy rate 60 per cent less
> A nutritional level, for one out of every two in the population, below acceptable standards;
> And for millions of infants, less protein than is sufficient to permit optimum development of the brain.

McNamara has summed up absolute poverty as "a condition of life so characterised by malnutrition, illiteracy, disease, squalid surroundings, high infant mortality and low life expectancy as to be beneath any reasonable definition of human decency." . . .

Death and disease apart, absolute poverty remains a miserable condition of life, with inadequate food, shelter, clothing, sanitation, health services and education. The Worldwatch Institute estimates that as many as 1.2 billion people—or 23 percent of the world's population—live in absolute poverty. For the purposes of this estimate, absolute poverty is defined as "the lack of sufficient income in cash or kind to meet the most basic biological needs for food, clothing, and shelter." Absolute poverty is probably the principal cause of human misery today. . . .

The problem is not that the world cannot produce enough to feed and shelter its people. People in the poor countries consume, on average, 180 kilos of grain a year, while North Americans average around 900 kilos. The difference is caused by the fact that in the rich countries we feed most of our grain to animals, converting it into meat, milk, and eggs. Because this is a highly inefficient process, people in rich countries are responsible for the consumption of far more food than those in poor countries who eat few animal products. If we stopped feeding animals on grains and soybeans, the amount of food saved would—if distributed to those who need it—be more than enough to end hunger throughout the world.

These facts about animal food do not mean that we can easily solve the world food problem by cutting down on animal products, but they show that the problem is essentially one of distribution rather than production. The world does produce enough food. Moreover, the poorer nations themselves could produce far more if they made more use of improved agricultural techniques.

So why are people hungry? Poor people cannot afford to buy grain grown by farmers in the richer nations. Poor farmers cannot afford to buy improved seeds, or fertilisers, or the machinery needed for drilling wells and pumping water. Only by transferring some of the wealth of the rich nations to the poor can the situation be changed.

That this wealth exists is clear. Against the picture of absolute poverty that McNamara has painted, one might pose a picture of "absolute affluence." Those who are absolutely affluent are not necessarily affluent by comparison with their neighbours, but they are affluent by any reasonable definition of human needs. This means that they have more income than they need to provide themselves adequately with all the basic necessities of life. After buying (either directly or through their taxes) food, shelter, clothing, basic health services, and education, the absolutely affluent are still able to spend money on luxuries. The absolutely affluent choose their food for the pleasures of the palate, not to stop hunger; they buy new clothes to look good, not to keep warm; they move house to be in a better neighborhood or have a playroom for the children, not to keep out the rain; and after all this there is still money to spend on stereo systems, video-cameras, and overseas holidays.

At this stage I am making no ethical judgments about absolute affluence, merely pointing out that it exists. Its defining characteristic is a significant amount of income above the level necessary to provide for the basic human needs of oneself and one's dependents. By this standard, the majority of citizens of Western Europe, North America, Japan, Australia, New Zealand, and the oil-rich Middle Eastern states are all absolutely affluent. To quote McNamara once more:

> The average citizen of a developed country enjoys wealth beyond the wildest dreams of the one billion people in countries with per capita incomes under $200.

These, therefore, are the countries—and individuals—who have wealth that they could, without threatening their own basic welfare, transfer to the absolutely poor.

At present, very little is being transferred. Only Sweden, the Netherlands, Norway, and some of the oil-exporting Arab states have reached the modest target, set by the United Nations, of 0.7 per cent of gross national product (GNP). Britain gives 0.31 per cent of its GNP in official development assistance and a small additional amount in unofficial aid from voluntary organisations. The total comes to about £2 per month per person, and compares with 5.5 per cent of GNP spent on alcohol, and 3 per cent on tobacco. Other, even wealthier nations, give little

more: Germany gives 0.41 per cent and Japan 0.32 per cent. The United States gives a mere 0.15 per cent of its GNP. . . .

The Obligation to Assist

The argument for an obligation to assist

The path from the library at my university to the humanities lecture theatre passes a shallow ornamental pond. Suppose that on my way to give a lecture I notice that a small child has fallen in and is in danger of drowning. Would anyone deny that I ought to wade in and pull the child out? This will mean getting my clothes muddy and either cancelling my lecture or delaying it until I can find something dry to change into; but compared with the avoidable death of a child this is insignificant.

A plausible principle that would support the judgment that I ought to pull the child out is this: if it is in our power to prevent something very bad from happening, without thereby sacrificing anything of comparable moral significance, we ought to do it. This principle seems uncontroversial. It will obviously win the assent of consequentialists; but non-consequentialists should accept it too, because the injunction to prevent what is bad applies only when nothing comparably significant is at stake. Thus the principle cannot lead to the kinds of actions of which non-consequentialists strongly disapprove—serious violations of individual rights, injustice, broken promises, and so on. If non-consequentialists regard any of these as comparable in moral significance to the bad thing that is to be prevented, they will automatically regard the principle as not applying in those cases in which the bad thing can only be prevented by violating rights, doing injustice, breaking promises, or whatever else is at stake. Most non-consequentialists hold that we ought to prevent what is bad and promote what is good. Their dispute with consequentialists lies in their insistence that this is not the sole ultimate ethical principle: that it is an ethical principle is not denied by any plausible ethical theory.

Nevertheless the uncontroversial appearance of the principle that we ought to prevent what is bad when we can do so without sacrificing anything of comparable moral significance is deceptive. If it were taken seriously and acted upon, our lives and our world would be fundamentally changed. For the principle applies, not just to rare situations in which one can save a child from a pond, but to the everyday situation in which we can assist those living in absolute poverty. In saying this I assume that absolute poverty, with its hunger and malnutrition, lack of shelter, illiteracy, disease, high infant mortality, and low life expectancy, is a bad thing. And I assume that it is within the power of the affluent to reduce absolute poverty, without sacrificing anything of comparable moral significance. If these two assumptions and the principle we have been discussing are correct, we have an obligation to help those in absolute poverty that is no less strong than our obligation to rescue a drowning child from a pond. Not to help would be wrong, whether or not it is intrinsically equivalent to killing. Helping is not, as conventionally thought, a charitable act that it is praiseworthy to do, but not wrong to omit; it is something that everyone ought to do.

This is the argument for an obligation to assist. Set out more formally, it would look like this.

First premise: If we can prevent something bad without sacrificing anything of comparable significance, we ought to do it.

Second premise: Absolute poverty is bad.

Third premise: There is some absolute poverty we can prevent without sacrificing anything of comparable moral significance.

Conclusion: We ought to prevent some absolute poverty.

The first premise is the substantive moral premise on which the argument rests, and I have tried to show that it can be accepted by people who hold a variety of ethical positions.

The second premise is unlikely to be challenged. Absolute poverty is, as McNamara put it,

"beneath any reasonable definition of human decency" and it would be hard to find a plausible ethical view that did not regard it as a bad thing.

The third premise is more controversial, even though it is cautiously framed. It claims only that some absolute poverty can be prevented without the sacrifice of anything of comparable moral significance. It thus avoids the objection that any aid I can give is just "drops in the ocean" for the point is not whether my personal contribution will make any noticeable impression on world poverty as a whole (of course it won't) but whether it will prevent some poverty. This is all the argument needs to sustain its conclusion, since the second premise says that any absolute poverty is bad, and not merely the total amount of absolute poverty. If without sacrificing anything of comparable moral significance we can provide just one family with the means to raise itself out of absolute poverty, the third premise is vindicated.

I have left the notion of moral significance unexamined in order to show that the argument does not depend on any specific values or ethical principles. I think the third premise is true for most people living in industrialised nations, on any defensible view of what is morally significant. Our affluence means that we have income we can dispose of without giving up the basic necessities of life, and we can use this income to reduce absolute poverty. Just how much we will think ourselves obliged to give up will depend on what we consider to be of comparable moral significance to the poverty we could prevent: stylish clothes, expensive dinners, a sophisticated stereo system, overseas holidays, a (second?) car, a larger house, private schools for our children, and so on. For a utilitarian, none of these is likely to be of comparable significance to the reduction of absolute poverty; and those who are not utilitarians surely must, if they subscribe to the principle of universalisability, accept that at least some of these things are of far less moral significance than the absolute poverty that could be prevented by the money they cost. So the third premise seems to be true on any plausible ethical view—although the precise amount of absolute poverty that can be prevented before anything of moral significance is sacrificed will vary according to the ethical view one accepts.

Objections to the argument

Taking Care of Our Own. Anyone who has worked to increase overseas aid will have come across the argument that we should look after those near us, our families, and then the poor in our own country, before we think about poverty in distant places.

No doubt we do instinctively prefer to help those who are close to us. Few could stand by and watch a child drown; many can ignore a famine in Africa. But the question is not what we usually do, but what we ought to do, and it is difficult to see any sound moral justification for the view that distance, or community membership, makes a crucial difference to our obligations.

Consider, for instance, racial affinities. Should people of European origin help poor Europeans before helping poor Africans? Most of us would reject such a suggestion out of hand: . . . people's need for food has nothing to do with their race, and if Africans need food more than Europeans, it would be a violation of the principle of equal consideration to give preference to Europeans.

The same point applies to citizenship or nationhood. Every affluent nation has some relatively poor citizens, but absolute poverty is limited largely to the poor nations. Those living on the streets of Calcutta, or in the drought-prone Sahel region of Africa, are experiencing poverty unknown in the West. Under these circumstances it would be wrong to decide that only those fortunate enough to be citizens of our own community will share our abundance.

We feel obligations of kinship more strongly than those of citizenship. Which parents could give away their last bowl of rice if their own children were starving? To do so would seem unnatural, contrary to our nature as biologically evolved beings—although whether it would be wrong is

another question altogether. In any case, we are not faced with that situation, but with one in which our own children are well-fed, well-clothed, well-educated, and would now like new bikes, a stereo set, or their own car. In these circumstances any special obligations we might have to our children have been fulfilled, and the needs of strangers make a stronger claim upon us.

The element of truth in the view that we should first take care of our own, lies in the advantage of a recognised system of responsibilities. When families and local communities look after their own poorer members, ties of affection and personal relationships achieve ends that would otherwise require a large, impersonal bureaucracy. Hence it would be absurd to propose that from now on we all regard ourselves as equally responsible for the welfare of everyone in the world; but the argument for an obligation to assist does not propose that. It applies only when some are in absolute poverty, and others can help without sacrificing anything of comparable moral significance. To allow one's own kin to sink into absolute poverty would be to sacrifice something of comparable significance; and before that point had been reached, the breakdown of the system of family and community responsibility would be a factor to weigh the balance in favour of a small degree of preference for family and community. This small degree of preference is, however, decisively outweighed by existing discrepancies in wealth and property.

Property Rights. Do people have a right to private property, a right that contradicts the view that they are under an obligation to give some of their wealth away to those in absolute poverty? According to some theories of rights (for instance, Robert Nozick's), provided one has acquired one's property without the use of unjust means like force and fraud, one may be entitled to enormous wealth while others starve. This individualistic conception of rights is in contrast to other views, like the early Christian doctrine to be found in the works of Thomas Aquinas, which holds that since property exists for the satisfaction of human needs, "whatever a man has in superabundance is owed, of natural right, to the poor for their sustenance." A socialist would also, of course, see wealth as belonging to the community rather than the individual, while utilitarians, whether socialist or not, would be prepared to override property rights to prevent great evils.

Does the argument for an obligation to assist others therefore presuppose one of these other theories of property rights, and not an individualistic theory like Nozick's? Not necessarily. A theory of property rights can insist on our *right* to retain wealth without pronouncing on whether the rich *ought* to give to the poor. Nozick, for example, rejects the use of compulsory means like taxation to redistribute income, but suggests that we can achieve the ends we deem morally desirable by voluntary means. So Nozick would reject the claim that rich people have an "obligation" to give to the poor, in so far as this implies that the poor have a right to our aid, but might accept that giving is something we ought to do and failing to give, though within one's rights, is wrong—for there is more to an ethical life than respecting the rights of others.

The argument for an obligation to assist can survive, with only minor modifications, even if we accept an individualistic theory of property rights. In any case, however, I do not think we should accept such a theory. It leaves too much to chance to be an acceptable ethical view. For instance, those whose forefathers happened to inhabit some sandy wastes around the Persian Gulf are now fabulously wealthy, because oil lay under those sands; while those whose forefathers settled on better land south of the Sahara live in absolute poverty, because of drought and bad harvests. Can this distribution be acceptable from an impartial point of view? If we imagine ourselves about to begin life as a citizen of either Bahrein or Chad—but we do not know which—would we accept the principle that citizens of Bahrein are under no obligation to assist people living in Chad?

Population and the Ethics of Triage. Perhaps the most serious objection to the argument that we have an obligation to assist is that since the major cause of absolute poverty is overpopulation, helping those now in poverty will only ensure that yet more people are born to live in poverty in the future.

In its most extreme form, this objection is taken to show that we should adopt a policy of "triage." The term comes from medical policies adopted in wartime. With too few doctors to cope with all the casualties, the wounded were divided into three categories: those who would probably survive without medical assistance, those who might survive if they received assistance, but otherwise probably would not, and those who even with medical assistance probably would not survive. Only those in the middle category were given medical assistance. The idea, of course, was to use limited medical resources as effectively as possible. For those in the first category, medical treatment was not strictly necessary; for those in the third category, it was likely to be useless. It has been suggested that we should apply the same policies to countries, according to their prospects of becoming self-sustaining. We would not aid countries that even without our help will soon be able to feed their populations. We would not aid countries that, even with our help, will not be able to limit their population to a level they can feed. We would aid those countries where our help might make the difference between success and failure in bringing food and population into balance.

Advocates of this theory are understandably reluctant to give a complete list of the countries they would place into the "hopeless" category; Bangladesh has been cited as an example, and so have some of the countries of the Sahel region of Africa. Adopting the policy of triage would, then, mean cutting off assistance to these countries and allowing famine, disease, and natural disasters to reduce the population of those countries to the level at which they can provide adequately for all.

In support of this view Garrett Hardin has offered a metaphor: we in the rich nations are like the occupants of a crowded lifeboat adrift in a sea full of drowning people. If we try to save the drowning by bringing them aboard, our boat will be overloaded and we shall all drown. Since it is better that some survive than none, we should leave the others to drown. In the world today, according to Hardin, "lifeboat ethics" apply. The rich should leave the poor to starve, for otherwise the poor will drag the rich down with them. . . .

Anyone whose initial reaction to triage was not one of repugnance would be an unpleasant sort of person. Yet initial reactions based on strong feelings are not always reliable guides. Advocates of triage are rightly concerned with the long-term consequences of our actions. They say that helping the poor and starving now merely ensures more poor and starving in the future. When our capacity to help is finally unable to cope—as one day it must be—the suffering will be greater than it would be if we stopped helping now. If this is correct, there is nothing we can do to prevent absolute starvation and poverty, in the long run, and so we have no obligation to assist. Nor does it seem reasonable to hold that under these circumstances people have a right to our assistance. If we do accept such a right, irrespective of the consequences, we are saying that, in Hardin's metaphor, we should continue to haul the drowning into our lifeboat until the boat sinks and we all drown.

If triage is to be rejected it must be tackled on its own ground, within the framework of consequentialist ethics. Here it is vulnerable. Any consequentialist ethics must take probability of outcome into account. A course of action that will certainly produce some benefit is to be preferred to an alternative course that may lead to a slightly larger benefit, but is equally likely to result in no benefit at all. Only if the greater magnitude of the uncertain benefit outweighs its uncertainty should we choose it. Better one certain unit of benefit than a 10 per cent chance of five units; but better a 50 per cent chance of three units than a single certain unit. The same principle applies when we are trying to avoid evils.

The policy of triage involves a certain, very great evil: population control by famine and disease. Tens of millions would die slowly. Hundreds of millions would continue to live in absolute poverty, at the very margin of existence. Against this prospect,

advocates of the policy place a possible evil that is greater still: the same process of famine and disease, taking place in, say, fifty years' time, when the world's population may be three times its present level, and the number who will die from famine, or struggle on in absolute poverty, will be that much greater. The question is: how probable is this forecast that continued assistance now will lead to greater disasters in the future?

Forecasts of population growth are notoriously fallible, and theories about the factors that affect it remain speculative. One theory, at least as plausible as any other, is that countries pass through a "demographic transition" as their standard of living rises. When people are very poor and have no access to modern medicine their fertility is high, but population is kept in check by high death rates. The introduction of sanitation, modern medical techniques, and other improvements reduces the death rate, but initially has little effect on the birth-rate. Then population grows rapidly. Some poor countries, especially in sub-Saharan Africa, are now in this phase. If standards of living continue to rise, however, couples begin to realise that to have the same number of children surviving to maturity as in the past, they do not need to give birth to as many children as their parents did. The need for children to provide economic support in old age diminishes. Improved education and the emancipation and employment of women also reduce the birth-rate, and so population growth begins to level off. Most rich nations have reached this stage, and their populations are growing only very slowly, if at all.

If this theory is right, there is an alternative to the disasters accepted as inevitable by supporters of triage. We can assist poor countries to raise the living standards of the poorest members of their population. We can encourage the governments of these countries to enact land reform measures, improve education, and liberate women from a purely child-bearing role. We can also help other countries to make contraception and sterilisation widely available. There is a fair chance that these measures will hasten the onset of the demographic transition and bring population growth down to a manageable level. According to United Nations estimates, in 1965 the average woman in the third world gave birth to six children, and only 8 per cent were using some form of contraception; by 1991 the average number of children had dropped to just below four, and more than half the women in the third world were taking contraceptive measures. Notable successes in encouraging the use of contraception had occurred in Thailand, Indonesia, Mexico, Colombia, Brazil, and Bangladesh. This achievement reflected a relatively low expenditure in developing countries—considering the size and significance of the problem—of $3 billion annually, with only 20 percent of this sum coming from developed nations. So expenditure in this area seems likely to be highly cost-effective. Success cannot be guaranteed; but the evidence suggests that we can reduce population growth by improving economic security and education, and making contraceptives more widely available. This prospect makes triage ethically unacceptable. We cannot allow millions to die from starvation and disease when there is a reasonable probability that population can be brought under control without such horrors.

Population growth is therefore not a reason against giving overseas aid, although it should make us think about the kind of aid to give. Instead of food handouts, it may be better to give aid that leads to a slowing of population growth. This may mean agricultural assistance for the rural poor, or assistance with education, or the provision of contraceptive services. Whatever kind of aid proves most effective in specific circumstances, the obligation to assist is not reduced.

One awkward question remains. What should we do about a poor and already overpopulated country that, for religious or nationalistic reasons, restricts the use of contraceptives and refuses to slow its population growth? Should we nevertheless offer development assistance? Or should we make our offer conditional on effective steps being taken to reduce the birth-rate? To the latter course, some would object that putting conditions on aid is an attempt to impose our own ideas on independent sovereign nations. So it is—but is this imposition unjustifiable? If the argument for an obligation to assist is sound, we have an obligation to reduce absolute poverty; but we have no obligation to make sacrifices that, to the best of our knowledge, have no prospect of reducing poverty in the long run. Hence we have no obligation to assist countries whose governments have policies that will make our aid ineffective. This could be very harsh on poor citizens of these countries—for they may have no say in the government's policies—but we will help more people in the long run by using our resources where they are most effective. (The same principles may apply, incidentally, to countries that refuse to take other steps that could make assistance effective—like refusing to reform systems of land holding that impose intolerable burdens on poor tenant farmers.)

Review and Discussion Questions

1. Are any people in the United States in absolute, as opposed to relative, poverty?
2. Why do governments and individuals in affluent countries do so little to aid people in absolute poverty overseas?
3. Review each of the premises in Singer's argument. Are they as uncontroversial as he thinks? How large a sacrifice do you think Singer's principle would require of us? What is "of comparable moral significance" to the reduction of absolute poverty?
4. Singer rejects an individualistic conception of property rights, but he also thinks that, even if we accept such a conception, it does not necessarily undermine his position. Assess Singer's reasoning on both of these points.

5. Hardin and Singer disagree about the long-term consequences of giving aid. Whose position do you find the most plausible?

6. Do you see any possible objections to Singer's argument that he has overlooked or failed to answer satisfactorily? Do you agree with him that helping people in absolute poverty is not just charity, but a moral obligation?

World Hunger and the Extent of Our Positive Duties

ROBERT N. VAN WYK

Drawing his inspiration from Kant, Robert N. Van Wyk, professor of philosophy at the University of Pittsburgh, rejects Peter Singer's implicitly utilitarian approach to world hunger. Instead, Van Wyk argues that wealthy countries may owe reparations to poorer countries and that individuals have a duty to do their fair share to alleviate hunger and distress (although their personal ideals may lead them to do more than their fair share).

Study Questions

1. What is Peter Singer's ethical approach to world hunger and what questions or problems does Van Wyk raise concerning it?

2. What is Robert Nozick's position and what shortcomings does Van Wyk see in it?

3. What is the point of the example about Bengal?

4. What is Van Wyk's "fair share" position, and how is it a middle way between Singer and Nozick? How does it address the "overload problem"?

AMORAL PROBLEM that faces institutions— especially governments, as well as individuals, is the question of the extent of the duty to prevent harm to other people, and/or benefit them. This is not an academic problem but one that stares us in the face through the eyes of starving and malnourished people, and in particular, children. Estimates of the number of severely malnourished people in the world have ranged from seventy million, to 460 million, to one billion. What duties do individuals have to help?

I. Utilitarian/Consequentialist Approaches

A. The views of Peter Singer and Garrett Hardin

According to some moral theories the very fact of widespread hunger imposes a duty on each person to do whatever he or she is capable of doing to accomplish whatever is necessary to see to it that all people have enough to eat. Peter Singer, a utilitarian, writes:

Reprinted by permission from "Perspectives on World Hunger and the Extent of Our Positive Duties," Public Affairs Quarterly, *vol. 2, no. 2 (April 1988). Copyright © 1988* Public Affairs Quarterly. *Some notes omitted.*

I begin with the assumption that suffering and death from lack of food, shelter, and medical care are bad. . . . My next point is this: if it is in our power to prevent something bad from happening without thereby sacrificing anything of comparable moral importance, we ought, morally, to do it.[1]

Does this mean that governments of prosperous countries ought to call upon their citizens to sacrifice enough of the luxuries of life to pay taxes that will be used to see to it that everyone in the world has the basic necessities of life? Suppose that governments do not do this. Suppose I give a considerable amount to famine relief but the need remains great because many others have not given. Is this case parallel to the following one to which Singer compares it? I have saved the life of one drowning person. There is still another person who needs to be saved. Other people could have saved the second person while I was saving the first but no one did. Even though I have saved one, and even though other people have failed in their duty to try to save the other, it would seem reasonable to claim that I have a duty to try to do so. Would I similarly have a duty to keep on giving more to aid the hungry regardless of the personal sacrifice involved? Many objections raised against giving sacrificially have to do with whether certain kinds of assistance really do much good. But such objections do not really affect the question of how much one should sacrifice to help others, but only have to do with the best way of using what is given (for example, for food assistance, development assistance, family planning, encouraging political change, supporting education, and so on). But if we reach the conclusion that we have a duty to do all we can, just as in the case of the drowning people, we are faced with the problem . . . of being overwhelmed with obligations in a way that expands the area of moral duty to the point of obliterating both the area of the morally indifferent and the area of the morally supererogatory.

There are, however, other considerations. What are the long range consequences of keeping people alive? "Neo-malthusians" and "crisis environmentalists" argue that population growth is outstripping food production and also leading both to the depletion of the world's natural resources and the pollution of the environment, so that the more people who are saved the more misery there will be in the long run. Garrett Hardin compares rich nations to lifeboats and the poor of the world to drowning people trying to get into the lifeboats. To allow them in would be to risk sinking the lifeboats and so to risk bringing disaster on everyone. The high rate of population growth among the poor nations insures that even if there is enough room at the moment, eventually the lifeboats will be swamped.[2] The lifeboat ethic is an application of what Hardin calls the logic of the commons. If a pasture is held as common property each herdsman is tempted to overgraze it for the sake of short-term profits. Even the individual who wants to preserve the land for the future has no reason to stop as long as there are others who will continue to overgraze it. Similarly, if we regard the food production of the world as a "commons" to which everyone is entitled we undermine any incentive among the poor of the world to increase production and limit population growth. The increasing population will continually reduce the amount available for each individual while at the same time increasing pollution and putting other strains on the environment.[3] So Hardin writes that "for posterity's sake we should never send food to any population that is beyond the realistic carrying capacity of its land."[4] This view that certain countries should be left to have "massive diebacks of population,"[5] while others should perhaps be helped, has been called "triage."

B. Questions about these approaches

One way of responding to Hardin's argument is to raise questions about the choice of metaphors and their applicability. Why speak of lifeboats rather than of luxury liners? Why should the Asian or African people be compared to the "sheep" who are the greatest threat to the commons when the average American uses up thirty times the amount of the earth's resources as does the average Asian or African,[6] and when the developed nations import more protein from the developing nations than they export to them?[7] How are the lifeboat metaphors applicable when apart from special famine conditions almost every country in the world has the resources necessary to feed its people if they were used primarily for that purpose?

The focus here, however, will be on moral theory. In spite of their very different conclusions, Singer and Hardin both presuppose a utilitarian position that says that what we ought to do depends completely on the anticipated consequences of our choices. . . .

II. Hunger, Respect for Persons, and Negative Duties

Many philosophers, especially those emphasizing the stringency of negative duties, subscribe to Kant's principle of respect for persons, whether or not they are supporters of Kant's moral philosophy taken as a whole. Robert Nozick uses the principle of respect for persons to defend absolute duties to do no harm while at the same time denying the existence of any duties to benefit others. Kant himself, however, maintained that we have imperfect duties to help others. One might still claim that government may not collect taxes for the sake of aiding others, since one ought not to force people (taxpayers) to fulfill imperfect duties when doing so violates the perfect duty to respect the right of citizens to use their resources as they themselves choose to do so. Kant himself did not reach such a conclusion, but Nozick does, arguing that since "individuals are ends and not merely means, they may not be sacrificed, or used for the achieving of other ends without their consent."[8]

Nozick's views can be attacked at many points. Even if they were correct, however, it would not follow that governments would have no right to tax citizens to aid people in distress. This is because individuals, corporations (to which individuals are related as stockholders and employees), and governments would still have duties not to harm, and thus also duties to take corrective action in response to past harms. So wealthy countries and their citizens could still have many responsibilities of compensatory justice with respect to the world's poor. Some countries face poverty because their economies are heavily dependent on a single export material or crop (for example, copper in Chile), the prices of which are subject to great fluctuations. If the original situation, or the subsequent fluctuations, were brought about by policies of wealthy nations or their corporations, then suffering does not just happen but is caused by the actions of people in developed nations. If corporations can strangle economies of developing nations and choose to do so if they do not get special tax advantages, or unfairly advantageous contracts, then poverty and hunger are harms caused by the decisions of the wealthy.[9] If, furthermore, government officials are bribed to keep taxes down, as was done in Honduras by the banana companies, then poverty is directly caused by human actions. If a developed nation overthrows the government of a poor nation which tries to correct some past injustice (as was done when the C.I.A. helped overthrow the democratically elected government of Guatemala in 1954 in order to protect the interests of the United Fruit Company), then poverty is a harm caused by human actions. The decisions of the Soviet Union to import large amounts of grain from the United States during the Nixon administration led to a dramatic and unexpected rise in the price of grain on the world market, which in turn caused hunger. Americans' use of energy at twice the rate of Western Europeans must raise energy prices for the poor. Dramatic price increases by oil exporting nations no doubt meant that people went without petroleum-based fertilizers, or energy to transport food or pump water for irrigation, and so led to additional people dying of hunger. When petroleum prices fall the poverty of people in some oil-exporting countries is aggravated because of the difficulty their governments have financing their debts—debts which were acquired partially due to the encouragement of the banks in the wealthy countries.

What duties do the wealthy countries have to the poor and hungry of the world? The first duty is not to harm them. While seldom are the hungry intentionally killed, they are often killed in the same way that someone is killed by a reckless driver who just does not take into consideration what his actions might do to other vulnerable human beings, and there is no doubt that reckless drivers are to be held accountable for what they do.[10] In some cases it may be morally justifiable to endanger the lives of people in order to work toward some desirable goal, as it may be morally justifiable to risk people's lives in order to rush a critically ill person to the hospital. But a person who is speeding for good reason, or who benefits from that speeding, is not thereby relieved of responsibility for someone who is thereby injured, for otherwise the endangered or harmed would be treated only as means to the ends of others. Similarly, those who make or benefit from economic and political decisions are not relieved of responsibility for those who are thereby harmed or endangered. So even if we were to accept the view that no individual or government has any duty to aid those in distress simply because they are in distress, there would still be few people of more than adequate means in the real world who would not have an obligation to aid those in need. As Onora Nell writes:

> Only if we knew that we were not part of any system of activities causing unjustifiable deaths could we have no duties to support policies which seek to avoid such deaths. Modern economic causal chains are so complex that it is likely that only those who are economically isolated and self-sufficient could know that they are part of no such system of activities.[11]

With respect to compensating those who have been harmed we do not have to be part of the causal chain that causes harm in order to have an obligation to those who still bear the effects of past harm. If A stole B's money yesterday and gave the money to C today, C obviously has a duty to return it. While in some cases mentioned above decisions were made by companies, individuals and governments still were beneficiaries of such decisions through lower prices and increased tax revenue. Furthermore, it would not make any difference if A stole B's money before C was born. Consider the following case:

> Bengal (today's Bangladesh and the West Bengal state of India), the first territory the British conquered in Asia, was a prosperous province with highly developed centers of manufacturing and trade, and an economy as advanced as any prior to the industrial revolution. The British reduced Bengal to poverty through plunder, heavy land taxes and trade restrictions that barred competitive Indian goods from England, but gave British goods free entry into India. India's late Prime Minister Nehru commented bitterly, "Bengal can take pride in the fact that she helped greatly in giving birth to the Industrial Revolution in England."[12]

Those who benefited from the Industrial Revolution in England, including those alive today, would still have duties to aid Bengal, just as those who inherited a fortune partially based on stolen money have a duty to return what was stolen, with interest, even though they themselves are in no way guilty of the theft. So it is with most citizens of the industrialized West with respect to the poor of some parts of the world. However, in the light of the complexity of both the causal chains of harm and the causal chains of benefit, we are again faced with a great deal of uncertainty as to the allocation of responsibility for correcting for past injustices.

III. Hunger, Positive Duties, and the Idea of a Fair Share

So there is no doubt that a Kantian ethic would include duties of reparation for harms done to people in the past and that this would be a basis of obligations to aid many of the underdeveloped countries in the world today, even though it would be difficult to specify the extent of obligation. But is there a duty to help those in severe need even if the causes of the need are not due to any past injustice or are unknown, as may also be true about parts of the world today? Kant does not always treat duties to aid others as fully binding, but whether or not, as one Kantian argues, "it is impermissible not to promote the well-being of others,"[13] it can be argued that it is impermissible not to relieve others in distress and provide them with the basic necessities of life, for this is to fail to treat them as having any value as ends in themselves. . . .

To what extent do individuals and nations have a duty to relieve those in distress? Is there a middle way between Singer and Nozick? Perhaps the following line of reasoning would provide a guideline. An estimate can be made of what resources would be needed to feed the hungry, bring about political and economic change, promote development, limit population growth, and to do whatever is necessary to see that all people have a minimally decent standard of living (or that their basic rights are met). Some formula based on ability to help could determine what a fair share would be for each citizen of a developed country to contribute to the needs of those in distress in that country and to that country's share of helping the people of other nations. To the extent that nations adopt this procedure and make it part of their tax structure a person could fulfill the duty of doing her share by paying her taxes. The ideal would be for nations to do this so that the responsibilities would be carried out and the burden would be distributed fairly. To the extent that nations have not done this (and it is unlikely that any have) what duties do citizens have to contribute through private or religious agencies? . . . In the absence of adequate government action each individual could still make some sort of estimate of what a fair share would be and give that amount (or what remains of that amount after taking into consideration that part of her taxes that are used for appropriate purposes) through private or religious agencies. I am claiming that it is a strict duty or duty of perfect obligation for an individual to give at least her fair share, according to some plausible formula, toward seeing that all human beings are

treated as ends in themselves, which involves seeing that they have the basic necessities of life in so far as that can depend on the actions of others. This conclusion can also be supported by a generalization argument. If everyone contributed at least a fair share the subsistence rights of human beings would cease to be violated (since that would be one of the criteria for deciding on a fair share). There is a problem about the applicability of generalization arguments where the efforts of one individual accomplishes nothing if most other people do not also do their fair share. (It is, for example, probably pointless to be the only person who refrains from taking a short cut across the grass; the grass will not grow.) In such cases the failure of some to fulfill their duties may relieve others of theirs. The duty to contribute to the cause of combatting hunger, however, is not of this sort, since one individual's contributions still accomplish some good whether or not other people are giving their fair share.

On the other hand there is the problem of whether the failure of some people to fulfill their duties increases the duties of others. If many are not giving a fair share, does the individual who is already giving a fair share have a duty to give more? The example of the two drowning people suggests that the individual who has done his fair share does have a duty to do more. But there is a major difference between the two cases. Saving people from drowning, in so far as the chances of losing one's own life are not great, is something that takes a minimal amount of time out of the rescuer's life and does not threaten his ability to live a life of pursuing goals he sets for himself. A similar duty to keep on giving of one's resources, even after one has done his fair share, would threaten to eclipse everything else a person might choose to do with his life, for example, develop his talents, raise a family, send his children to college, and so on, so that that person would become nothing but a means to meeting the needs of others. The idea of a strict duty to do at least one's fair share seems to avoid the problem of overload (unless the total need is overwhelming) and draws a line at a plausible point somewhere between doing nothing and sacrificing one's whole life to the cause of relieving the distress of others. . . . Of course a person might choose to make the rescuing of those in distress her special vocation, and it may be noble for her to do so, but to claim that if the needs of others are great enough she has a duty to surrender any choice about the direction of her own life is to claim that a person has a duty to be purely the means to meeting the needs of others, and so in fact a duty to love others not as oneself, but instead of oneself. On the other hand, not to recognize a duty to give a fair share is to indicate that one believes either that it is not important that the needs of those in distress should be met (perhaps because they do not have subsistence rights) or that others should do more than their fair share. . . .

IV. Considerations Beyond a Fair Share

If redistribution of wealth were in fact the major need of the most vulnerable in the world, and if in fact government foreign aid programs could be modified so that they could be trusted to meet that need, then . . . I would claim that for the sake of fairness both to those in need and those willing to help, it would be better if everyone did his or her fair share and it would be legitimate to coerce people through the tax system to do so. In the absence of such taxation and in the absence of any official calculation of such a share, individuals generally do not have the information on which to assess their own fair share, and if they did they would probably tend to underestimate it. What most people tend to think of as their fair share depends much less on any informed calculation than on what they think their neighbors, fellow citizens, or fellow church members, are contributing, consoling themselves with the thought that it cannot really be their duty to do more than others. But since most people who do something probably tend to think that they are doing more with respect to their resources than others, the idea of a duty to do a fair share is in danger of succumbing to a downward pressure to require less

and less. If the vulnerable are to be protected then perhaps doing one's fair share to meet their needs is not the only duty. Rather there must also be a duty to put upward pressure on the prevailing idea of a fair share. This can be done only by those who do considerably more than what is perceived of as a fair share, and often more than an actual fair share. This is embodied in Christian ethics in the ideal of being a light to witness to a higher and more demanding way of life and in the ideal of being the salt of the earth that preserves it from decay, perhaps primarily the decay brought about by downward pressure on prevailing standards.[14] Probably a secular counterpart to these ideals would be accepted by others.

There are doubts about whether redistribution of wealth is the major need, as opposed to various changes in policies, including trade policies. There are also grave doubts concerning the degree to which government aid in the past has really benefited the most vulnerable and about its prospects of doing so in the future. That raises the possibility that the major duty individuals have is that of exerting pressure on government to make sure that policies do protect the vulnerable. . . . Giving one's fair share to help those in need accomplishes some good whether or not others are cooperating by doing their share. In the matter of influencing legislation an insufficient number of people doing their fair share (with respect to all who might participate in the effort) may accomplish nothing. Does the failure of enough others to do their fair share release one from one's duty to work for change (as it may release one from the duty not to walk on the grass)? If so, the vulnerable are left without protection. Or does such a failure impose a duty on others to do as much as possible (as in the case of saving drowning people), so that we could again be faced with the problem of overload? . . . Perhaps there is no precise answer to the question of just how much more money or effort than prevailing standards require one "ought" to devote to the cause here being considered, since this may be a matter of living up to an ideal rather than fulfilling a perfect duty to a specific individual, or a perfect duty of doing a fair share. Even in the absence of any way of determining what a fair share might be one can attempt to live by this ideal by doing significantly more than the society as a whole generally thinks is required. . . .

V. Postscript: Additional Kantian Reflections on Duties to Others

There are still a number of things to be taken into consideration. Kant says that a person should "not push the expenditure of his means in beneficence . . . to the point where he would finally need the beneficence of others."[15] That could be regarded as treating others as a means to one's own end of trying to achieve some kind of sainthood. Secondly, help should not be given in a manner or to an extent that reduces the ability of the person (or group) that is helped to be self-reliant and self-determining. It is doubtful whether the wealthy have ever given too much help to the poor, but they have sometimes (perhaps frequently) given in a manner which made the recipients more dependent in the long run, for example, in a way that reduced the incentives of local farmers to increase production. Thirdly, according to Kant, every effort must be made to "carefully avoid any appearance of intending to obligate the other person, lest he (the giver) not render a true benefit, inasmuch as by his act he expresses that he wants to lay an obligation upon the receiver."[16] Presumably nations such as the United States can and do give aid for ulterior purposes, such as to get rid of agricultural surpluses, help farm prices, gain political influence, or to stimulate markets and/or a favorable climate of investment for U.S. companies, but then citizens of these nations ought not congratulate themselves on their generosity (as Americans often do). Such acts are not acts of beneficence and from Kant's point of view they have no moral worth since they are not done for the sake of duty, nor are they done from other motives that might be regarded as being other than morally neutral.

Fourthly, there are conditions under which it could be argued that a wealthy country has the right to refuse to give aid, other than emergency disaster aid, if it is not something that is owed as reparations. Suppose that achieving the goal of advancing the self-sufficiency and self-determination of a nation depends in part on the receiving nation's own effort to make necessary changes such as redistributing land, bringing population growth under control, and so on. It could be argued that if the receiving nation fails to make a good-faith effort to bring about these changes, and if it then asks for additional aid, the developed country may legitimately claim that it is being used, and its people are being used, solely as means to the ends of the underdeveloped country or its people. The major problem with using this line of argument is that the people who are facing hunger may have little to say about the decisions of their government. That problem, however, does not prevent the aid-giving country from legitimately making demands for reform in advance, from doing what it can to see to it that they are carried out, and from threatening sanctions other than those that would increase the deprivation of hungry people. Perhaps it has seldom, if ever, happened that a developed nation has given enough non-military aid to an underdeveloped nation to be in a position to dictate what steps the receiving nation should take to improve the ability of its people to be self-sufficient; or perhaps it has been in the interest of the political strategy, military effort, or business investment of the developed nations not to demand that specific remedial steps be taken on the part of the receiving country; but it would seem to be legitimate to make such demands.

NOTES

1. Peter Singer, "Famine, Affluence, and Morality," *Philosophy and Public Affairs*, vol. 1 (1972), p. 231.

2. Garrett Hardin, "Lifeboat Ethics: The Case Against Helping the Poor," *Psychology Today*, vol. 8 (1974), pp. 38–43, 123–126.

3. Garrett Hardin, "The Tragedy of the Commons," *Science,* vol. 102 (1968), pp. 1243–1248.

4. Garrett Hardin, "Carrying Capacity as an Ethical Concept," in George R. Lucas and Thomas W. Ogletree (eds.), *Lifeboat Ethics: The Moral Dilemmas of World Hunger* (New York: Harper and Row, 1976), p. 131.

5. Part of the title of an article by Garrett Hardin, "Another Face of Bioethics: The Case for Massive 'Diebacks' of Population," *Modern Medicine,* vol. 65 (March 1, 1975).

6. Paul Verghese, "Muddled Metaphors," in Lucas and Ogletree, *op. cit.,* p. 152. While changes in cattle production and eating habits may have brought some changes, at one time it was estimated that the average American citizen consumed 1,850 pounds of grain a year directly and through meat production, compared to 400 pounds in poor countries. . . . It was also estimated that the United States used as much energy for its air-conditioners as the billion people of China used for all purposes and that the United States wasted as much energy as Japan used.

7. U.N.'s *Handbook of International Trade and Development Statistics,* 1972; and U.N.'s *Monthly Bulletin of Statistics,* July 1975 and Feb. 1976; both cited by Ronald J. Sidor, *Rich Christians in an Age of Hunger* (Downers Grove, Ill.: Inter-varsity Press, 1977), p. 154; U.S. Bureau of the Census, *Statistical Abstract of the U.S.,* 1976, pp. 818, 820, cited by Sidor, p. 156. Protein is imported in the form of oilseed, oilseed products, and fish meal while grain is exported.

8. Robert Nozick, *Anarchy, State, and Utopia* (New York: Basic Books, Inc., 1974), p. 31

9. As occurred in Panama, Honduras, and Costa Rica at the hands of the fruit and banana import companies, United Brands, Castle and Cooke, and Del Monte.

10. There are, of course, still problems with the moral relevance of different sorts of causal relationships between past actions and harm to others. Have Western nations incurred special obligations to do something about poverty and hunger because they encouraged population growth by providing medicine and sanitation without dealing with the birth rate? If advantages to some countries and disadvantages to others are a byproduct of chance conditions and the operation of the free market system, do those who have benefited from these conditions have duties to those who were harmed? (For example, in 1968 it cost Brazil 45 bags of coffee to buy one U.S. jeep as compared to 14 in 1954. [Pierre Ghedo, *Why Is the Third World Poor?* (Maryknoll, N.Y.: Orbis Books, 1973), p. 64.])

11. Onora Nell, "Lifeboat Earth," *Philosophy and Public Affairs,* vol. 4 (1975), p. 286.

12. Arthur Simon, *Bread for the World* (New York: Paulist Press, 1975), p. 41.

13. Alan Donagan, *Theory of Morality* (Chicago: University of Chicago Press, 1977), p. 85.

14. See *Matthew* 5:6, 13–18, 20, 46–48.

15. Immanuel Kant, *Metaphysics of Morals,* tr. by John Ladd (Indianapolis: Bobbs-Merrill Co., 1965), p. 118 (454).

16. *Ibid.* (453).

Review and Discussion Questions

1. Should the moral problem of world hunger be approached from a utilitarian/consequentialist perspective? What is Kantian about Van Wyk's ethical orientation? How does his approach differ from Singer's?

2. Robert Nozick uses Kant's principle of moral respect to defend his own position. What is Nozick's position, and is it true to Kant's moral philosophy?

3. Can a country today owe reparation to another country because of wrongs done in the past?

4. Assess Van Wyk's claim that we have a strict duty to do our fair share to alleviate hunger. What does this imply in practice? What exactly is our fair share? What if others are not doing their fair share?

5. Van Wyk writes that we also have "a duty to put upward pressure on the prevailing idea of a fair share." What does this statement mean, and what are its implications? Should one do more than his or her fair share? Would a morally good person do so?

6. When, if ever, does a wealthy country have a right to refuse to aid a poorer country?

In Defense of International Sweatshops

IAN MAITLAND

These days, contractors in Third World countries like Indonesia and China manufacture most of the shoes, shirts, and other clothing that large American footwear and apparel companies sell. Because working conditions in these factories are poor and the wages they pay are exceedingly low, critics call them "sweatshops" and condemn American companies like Nike and Levi Strauss for using them. Although these critics believe that international sweatshops represent capitalism at its worse, Ian Maitland, a management professor at the University of Minnesota, defends them against the charge of exploitation on both factual and ethical grounds. He examines and rejects the idea that sweatshops pay unconscionable wages, that they impoverish local workers and widen the gap between rich and poor, and that American companies collude with repressive regimes that stifle dissent and repress workers. Arguing that interfering with the market can have terrible results, he concludes not only that paying market wages in developing countries is morally permissible, but also that it may be morally wrong for companies to pay wages that exceed market levels.

Study Questions

1. Explain the four different standards that have been proposed for setting wages and labor conditions in international sweatshops.
2. Why do Donaldson and De George reject the classical liberal standard?
3. Critics press four charges or arguments against international sweatshops. What are they?
4. Explain how Maitland responds to each of the four charges.
5. What negative results does Maitland see coming from attempts to improve upon market wages and working conditions in international sweatshops? What does he see as the ethical course of conduct for an American company to adopt?

IN RECENT YEARS, there has been a dramatic growth in the contracting out of production by companies in the industrialized countries to suppliers in developing countries. This globalization of production has led to an emerging international division of labor in footwear and apparel in which companies like Nike and Reebok concentrate on product design and marketing but rely on a network of contractors in Indonesia, China, Central America, etc., to build shoes or sew shirts according to exact specifications and deliver a high quality good according to precise delivery schedules. As Nike's vice president for Asia has put it, "We don't know the

Reprinted by permission of the author from "The Great Non-Debate Over International Sweatshops," British Academy of Management Annual Conference Proceedings, September 1997. Some notes omitted.

first thing about manufacturing. We are marketers and designers."

The contracting arrangements have drawn intense fire from critics—usually labor and human rights activists. The "critics" (as I will refer to them) have charged that the companies are (by proxy) exploiting workers in the plants (which I will call "international sweatshops") of their suppliers. Specifically, the companies stand accused of chasing cheap labor around the globe, failing to pay their workers living wages, using child labor, turning a blind eye to abuses of human rights, and being complicit with repressive regimes in denying workers the right to join unions and failing to enforce minimum labor standards in the workplace, and so on.

The campaign against international sweatshops has largely unfolded on television and, to a lesser extent, in the print media. What seems like no more than a handful of critics has mounted an aggressive, media-savvy campaign that has put the publicity-shy retail giants on the defensive. The critics have orchestrated a series of sensational "disclosures" on prime time television exposing the terrible pay and working conditions in factories making jeans for Levi's or sneakers for Nike or Pocahontas shirts for Disney. . . .

Objective of This Essay

In this confrontation between the companies and their critics, neither side seems to have judged it to be in its interest to seriously engage the issue at the heart of this controversy, namely: What are appropriate wages and labor standards in international sweatshops? . . . The companies have treated the charges about sweatshops as a public relations problem to be managed so as to minimize harm to their public images. The critics have apparently judged that the best way to keep public indignation at boiling point is to oversimplify the issue and treat it as a morality play featuring heartless exploiters and victimized third world workers. . . .

This essay takes up the issue of what are appropriate wages and labor standards in international sweatshops. Critics charge that the present arrangements are exploitative. I proceed by examining the specific charges of exploitation from the standpoints of both (a) their factual and (b) their ethical sufficiency. . . .

What Are Ethically Appropriate Labor Standards in International Sweatshops?

What are ethically acceptable or appropriate levels of wages and labor standards in international sweatshops? The following four possibilities just about run the gamut of standards or principles that have been seriously proposed to regulate such policies.

1. *Home-country standards*: It might be argued (and in rare cases has been) that international corporations have an ethical duty to pay the same wages and provide the same labor standards regardless of where they operate. However, the view that home-country standards should apply in host countries is rejected by most business ethicists and (officially at least) by the critics of international sweatshops. Thus, . . . Richard De George makes . . . the . . . argument: If there were a rule that said "that American MNCs [multinational corporations] that wish to be ethical must pay the same wages abroad as they do at home. . . . [then] MNCs would have little incentive to move their manufacturing abroad; and if they did move abroad they would disrupt the local labor market with artificially high wages that bore no relation to the local standard or cost of living."[1]

2. *"Living wage" standard*: It has been proposed that an international corporation should, at a minimum, pay a "living wage." Thus, De George says that corporations should pay a living wage "even when this is not paid by local firms."[2] However, it is hard to pin down what this means operationally. According to De George, a living wage should "allow the worker to live in dignity as a human being." In order to respect the human rights of its workers, he says, a corporation must pay "at least subsistence wages and as much above that as workers and their dependents need to live with reasonable dignity, given the general state of development of the society." As we shall see, the living wage standard has become a rallying cry of the critics of international sweatshops. Apparently, De George believes that it is preferable for a corporation to provide no job at all than to offer one that pays less than a living wage.

3. *Donaldson's test*: Thomas Donaldson believes that "it is irrelevant whether the standards of the host country comply or fail to comply with home country standards; what is relevant is whether they meet a universal, objective minimum." He tries to specify "a moral minimum for the behavior of all international economic agents." However, he concedes . . . that "many rights . . . are dependent for their specification on the level of economic development of the country in question." Accordingly, he proposes a test to determine when deviations from home-country standards are unethical. That test provides as follows: "The practice is permissible if and only if the members of the home country would, under conditions of economic development relevantly similar to those of the host country, regard the practice as permissible."[3] Donaldson's test is vulnerable to Bernard Shaw's objection to the Golden Rule, namely that we should not do unto others as we would they do unto us, because their tastes may be different. The test also complicates matters by introducing counterfactuals and hypotheticals (if I were in their place [which I'm not] what would I want?). This indeterminacy is a serious weakness in an ethical code: It is likely to confuse managers who want to act ethically and to provide loopholes for those who don't.

4. *Classical liberal standard:* Finally, there is what I will call the classical liberal standard. According to this standard a practice (wage or labor practice) is ethically acceptable if it is freely chosen by informed workers. For example, in a recent report the World Bank invoked this standard in connection with workplace safety. It said: "The appropriate level is therefore that at which the costs are commensurate with the value that informed workers place on improved working conditions and reduced risk."[4] Most business ethicists reject this standard on the grounds that there is some sort of market failure or the "background conditions" are lacking for markets to work effectively. Thus, for Donaldson full (or near-full) employment is a prerequisite if workers are to make sound choices regarding workplace safety: "The average level of unemployment in the developing countries today exceeds 40 percent, a figure that has frustrated the application of neoclassical economic principles to the international economy on a score of issues. With full employment, and all other things being equal, market forces will encourage workers to make tradeoffs between job opportunities using safety as a variable. But with massive unemployment, market forces in developing countries drive the unemployed to the jobs they are lucky enough to land, regardless of the safety."[5] . . . De George, too, believes that the necessary conditions are lacking for market forces to operate benignly. Without what he calls "background institutions" to protect the workers and the resources of the developing country (e.g., enforceable minimum wages) and/or greater equality of bargaining power, exploitation is the most likely result.[6] . . .

The Case Against International Sweatshops

To many of their critics, international sweatshops exemplify the way in which the greater openness of the world economy is hurting workers. According to one critic, "as it is now constituted, the world trading system discriminates against workers, especially those in the Third World." Globalization means a transition from (more or less) regulated domestic economies to an unregulated world economy. The superior mobility of capital, and the essentially fixed, immobile nature of world labor, means a fundamental shift in bargaining power in favor of large international corporations. Their global reach permits them to shift production almost costlessly from one location to another. As a consequence, instead of being able to exercise some degree of control over companies operating within their borders, governments are now locked in a bidding war with one another to attract and retain the business of large multinational companies.

The critics allege that international companies are using the threat of withdrawal or withholding of investment to pressure governments and workers to grant concessions. "Today [multinational companies] choose between workers in developing countries that compete against each other to depress wages to attract foreign investment." The result is a race for the bottom—a "destructive downward bidding spiral of the labor conditions and wages of workers throughout the world. . . ." Thus, critics charge that in Indonesia wages are deliberately held below the poverty level or subsistence in order to make the country a desirable location. The results of this competitive dismantling of worker protections, living standards and worker rights are predictable: deteriorating work conditions, declining real incomes for workers, and a widening gap between rich and poor in developing countries. I turn next to the specific charges made by the critics of international sweatshops.

Unconscionable wages

Critics charge that the companies, by their proxies, are paying "starvation wages" and "slave wages." They are far from clear about what wage level they consider to be appropriate. But they generally demand that companies pay a "living wage." . . . According to Tim Smith, wage levels should be "fair, decent or a living wage for an employee and his or her family." He has said that wages in the maquiladoras of Mexico averaged $35 to $55 a week (in or near 1993) which he calls a "shockingly substandard wage," apparently on the grounds that it "clearly does not allow an employee to feed and care for a family adequately."[7] In 1992, Nike came in for harsh criticism when a magazine published the pay stub of a worker at one of its Indonesian suppliers. It showed that the worker was paid at the rate of $1.03 per day which was reportedly less than the Indonesian government's figure for "minimum physical need."

Immiserization thesis

Former Labor Secretary Robert Reich has proposed as a test of the fairness of development policies that "[l]ow-wage workers should become better off, not worse off, as trade and investment boost national income." He has written that "[i]f a country pursues policies that . . . limit to a narrow elite the benefits of trade, the promise of open commerce is perverted and drained of its rationale.[8] A key claim of the activists is that companies actually impoverish or immiserize developing country workers. They experience an absolute decline in living standards. This thesis follows from the claim that the bidding war among developing countries is depressing wages. . . .

Widening gap between rich and poor

A related charge is that international sweatshops are contributing to the increasing gap between rich and poor. Not only are the poor being absolutely impoverished, but trade is generating greater inequality within developing countries. Another test that Reich has proposed to establish the fairness of international trade is that "the gap between rich and poor should tend to narrow with development, not widen." Critics charge that international sweatshops flunk that test. They say that the increasing GNPs of some developing countries simply mask a widening gap between rich and poor. "Across the world, both local and foreign elites are getting richer from the exploitation of the most vulnerable." And, "The major adverse consequence of quickening global economic integration has been widening income disparity within almost all nations. . . ." There appears to be a tacit alliance between the elites of both first and third world to exploit the most vulnerable, to regiment and control and conscript them so that they can create the material conditions for the elites' extravagant lifestyles.

Collusion with repressive regimes

Critics charge that, in their zeal to make their countries safe for foreign investment, third world regimes, notably China and Indonesia, have stepped up their repression. Not only have these countries failed to enforce even the minimal labor rules on the books, but they have also used their military and police to break strikes and repress independent unions. They have stifled political dissent, both to retain their hold on political power and to avoid any instability that might scare off foreign investors. Consequently, critics charge, companies such as Nike are profiting from political repression. "As unions spread in [Korea and Taiwan], Nike shifted its suppliers primarily to Indonesia, China and Thailand, where they could depend on governments to suppress independent union-organizing efforts."

Evaluation of the Charges Against International Sweatshops

The critics' charges are undoubtedly accurate on a number of points: (1) There is no doubt that international companies are chasing cheap labor. (2) The wages paid by the international sweatshops are—by American standards—shockingly low. (3) Some developing country governments have tightly controlled or repressed organized labor in order to prevent it from disturbing the flow of foreign investment. Thus, in Indonesia, independent unions have been suppressed. (4) It is not unusual in developing countries for minimum wage levels to be lower than the official poverty level. (5) Developing country govern-

ments have winked at violations of minimum wage laws and labor rules. However, most jobs are in the informal sector and so largely, outside the scope of government supervision. (6) Some suppliers have employed children or have subcontracted work to other producers who have done so. (7) Some developing country governments deny their people basic political rights. China is the obvious example; Indonesia's record is pretty horrible. . . . But on many of the other counts, the critics' charges appear to be seriously inaccurate. And, even where the charges are accurate, it is not self-evident that the practices in question are improper or unethical, as we see next.

Wages and conditions

Even the critics of international sweatshops do not dispute that the wages they pay are generally higher than—or at least equal to—comparable wages in the labor markets where they operate. According to the International Labor Organization (ILO), multinational companies often apply standards relating to wages, benefits, conditions of work, and occupational safety and health that both exceed statutory requirements and those practised by local firms. The ILO also says that wages and working conditions in so-called Export Processing Zones (EPZs) are often equal to or higher than jobs outside.[9] The World Bank says that the poorest workers in developing countries work in the informal sector where they often earn less than half what a formal sector employee earns. Moreover, "informal and rural workers often must work under more hazardous and insecure conditions than their formal sector counterparts."[10]

The same appears to hold true for the international sweatshops. In 1996, young women working in the plant of a Nike supplier in Serang, Indonesia, were earning the Indonesian legal minimum wage of 5,200 rupiahs or about $2.28 each day. As a report in the *Washington Post* pointed out, just earning the minimum wage put these workers among higher-paid Indonesians: "In Indonesia, less than half the working population earns the minimum wage, since about half of all adults here are in farming, and the typical farmer would make only about 2,000 rupiahs each day." . . . Also in 1996, a Nike spokeswoman estimated that an entry-level factory worker in the plant of a Nike supplier made five times what a farmer makes. Nike's chairman, Phil Knight, likes to teasingly remind critics that the average worker in one of Nike's Chinese factories is paid more than a professor at Beijing University. There is also plentiful anecdotal evidence from non-Nike sources. A worker at the Taiwanese-owned King Star Garment Assembly plant in Honduras told a reporter that he was earning seven times what he earned in the countryside.[11] In Bangladesh, the country's fledgling garment industry was paying women who had never worked before between $40 and $55 a month in 1991. That compared with a national per capital income of about $200 and the approximately $1 a day earned by many of these women's husbands as day laborers or richshaw drivers.[12] . . .

There is also the mute testimony of the lines of job applicants outside the sweatshops in Guatemala and Honduras. According to Lucy Martinez-Mont, in Guatemala the sweatshops are conspicuous for the long lines of young people waiting to be interviewed for a job.[13] Outside the gates of an industrial park in Honduras . . . "anxious onlookers are always waiting, hoping for a chance at least to fill out a job application [for employment at one of the apparel plants]."[14]

The critics of sweatshops acknowledge that workers have voluntarily taken their jobs, consider themselves lucky to have them, and want to keep them. . . . But they go on to discount the workers' views as the product of confusion or ignorance, and/or they just argue that the workers' views are beside the point. Thus, while "it is undoubtedly true" that Nike has given jobs to thousands of people who wouldn't be working otherwise, they say that "neatly skirts the fundamental human-rights issue raised by these production arrangements that are now spreading all across the world." Similarly, Charles Kernaghan says that "[w]hether workers think they are better

off in the assembly plants than elsewhere is not the real issue." Kernaghan, and Jeff Ballinger of the AFL-CIO, concede that the workers desperately need these jobs. But "[t]hey say they're not asking that U.S. companies stop operating in these countries. They're asking that workers be paid a living wage and treated like human beings."[15] Apparently these workers are victims of what Marx called false consciousness, or else they would grasp that they are being exploited. According to Barnet and Cavanagh, "For many workers . . . exploitation is not a concept easily comprehended because the alternative prospects for earning a living are so bleak."[16]

Immiserization and inequality

The critics' claim that the countries that host international sweatshops are marked by growing poverty and inequality is flatly contradicted by the record. In fact, many of those countries have experienced sharp increases in living standards—for all strata of society. In trying to attract investment in simple manufacturing, Malaysia and Indonesia and, now, Vietnam and China are retracing the industrialization path already successfully taken by East Asian countries such as Taiwan, Korea, Singapore, and Hong Kong. These four countries got their start by producing labor-intensive manufactured goods (often electrical and electronic components, shoes, and garments) for export markets. Over time they graduated to the export of higher value-added items that are skill-intensive and require a relatively developed industrial base.

As is well known, these East Asian countries have achieved growth rates exceeding eight percent for a quarter-century. . . . The workers in these economies were not impoverished by growth. The benefits of growth were widely diffused: These economies achieved essentially full employment in the 1960s. Real wages rose by as much as a factor of four. Absolute poverty fell. And income inequality remained at low to moderate levels. It is true that in the initial stages the rapid growth generated only moderate increases in wages. But once essentially full employment was reached, . . . the increased demand for labor resulted in the bidding up of wages as firms competed for a scarce labor supply.

Interestingly, given its historic mission as a watchdog for international labor standards, the ILO has embraced this development model. It recently noted that the most successful developing economies, in terms of output and employment growth, have been "those who best exploited emerging opportunities in the global economy."[17] An "export-oriented policy is vital in countries that are starting on the industrialization path and have large surpluses of cheap labour." Countries that have succeeded in attracting foreign direct investment (FDI) have experienced rapid growth in manufacturing output and exports. The successful attraction of foreign investment in plant and equipment "can be a powerful spur to rapid industrialization and employment creation.". . .

According to the World Bank, the rapidly growing Asian economies (including Indonesia) "have also been unusually successful at sharing the fruits of their growth."[18] In fact, while inequality in the West has been growing, it has been shrinking in the Asian economies. They are the only economies in the world to have experienced high growth *and* declining inequality, and they also show shrinking gender gaps in education. . . .

Profiting from repression?

What about the charge that international sweatshops are profiting from repression? It is undeniable that there is repression in many of the countries where sweatshops are located. But economic development appears to be relaxing that repression rather than strengthening its grip. The companies are supposed to benefit from government policies (e.g., repression of unions) that hold down labor costs. However, as we have seen, the wages paid by the international sweatshops already match or exceed the prevailing local wages. Not only that, but incomes in the East

Asian economies, and in Indonesia, have risen rapidly. Moreover, even the sweatshops' critics admit that the main factor restraining wages in countries like Indonesia is the state of the labor market. . . . The high rate of unemployment and underemployment acts as a brake on wages: Only about 55 percent of the Indonesian labor force can find more than thirty-five hours of work each week, and about two million workers are unemployed.

The critics, however, are right in saying that the Indonesian government has opposed independent unions in the sweatshops out of fear they would lead to higher wages and labor unrest. But the government's fear clearly is that unions might drive wages in the modern industrial sector *above* market-clearing levels—or, more exactly, farther above market. . . . I think we can safely take at face value its claims that its policies are genuinely intended to help the economy create jobs to absorb the massive numbers of unemployed and underemployed.

Labor Standards in International Sweatshops: Painful Trade-Offs

Who but the grinch could grudge paying a few additional pennies to some of the world's poorest workers? There is no doubt that the rhetorical force of the critics' case against international sweatshops rests on this apparently self-evident proposition. However, higher wages and improved labor standards are not free. After all, the critics themselves attack companies for chasing cheap labor. It follows that, if labor in developing countries is made more expensive (say, as the result of pressure by the critics), then those countries will receive less foreign investment, and fewer jobs will be created there. Imposing higher wages may deprive these countries of the one comparative advantage they enjoy, namely low-cost labor. . . .

By itself that may or may not be ethically objectionable. But these higher wages come at the expense of the incomes and the job opportunities of much poorer workers. As economists explain, higher wages in the formal sector reduce employment there and (by increasing the supply of labor) depress incomes in the informal sector. The case against requiring above-market wages for international sweatshop workers is essentially the same as the case against other measures that artificially raise labor costs, such as the minimum wage. In Jagdish Bhagwati's words: "Requiring a minimum wage in an overpopulated, developing country, as is done in a developed country, may actually be morally wicked. A minimum wage might help the unionized, industrial proletariat, while limiting the ability to save and invest rapidly which is necessary to draw more of the unemployed and nonunionized rural poor into gainful employment and income."[19] The World Bank makes the same point: "Minimum wages may help the most poverty-stricken workers in industrial countries, but they clearly do not in developing nations. . . . The workers whom minimum wage legislation tries to protect—urban formal workers—already earn much more than the less favored majority. . . . And inasmuch as minimum wage and other regulations discourage formal employment by increasing wage and nonwage costs, they hurt the poor who aspire to formal employment."[20]

The story is no different when it comes to labor standards other than wages. If standards are set too high they will hurt investment and employment. The World Bank report points out that "[r]educing hazards in the workplace is costly, and typically the greater the reduction the more it costs. Moreover, the costs of compliance often fall largely on employees through lower wages or reduced employment. As a result, setting standards too high can actually lower workers' welfare. . . ." Perversely, if the higher standards advocated by critics retard the growth of formal sector jobs, then that will trap more informal and rural workers in jobs that are far more hazardous and insecure than those of their formal sector counterparts. . . .

Of course it might be objected that trading off workers' rights for more jobs is unethical. But, so far as I can determine, the critics have not made this argument. Although they sometimes implicitly accept the existence of the trade-off (we saw that they attack Nike for chasing cheap labor), their public statements are silent on the lost or forgone jobs from higher wages and better labor standards. At other times, they imply or claim that improvements in workers' wages and conditions are essentially free: According to Kernaghan, "Companies could easily double their employees' wages, and it would be nothing."

In summary, the result of the ostensibly humanitarian changes urged by critics are likely to be (1) reduced employment in the formal or modern sector of the economy, (2) lower incomes in the informal sector, (3) less investment and so slower economic growth, (4) reduced exports, (5) greater inequality and poverty. . . .

Conclusion: The Case for Not Exceeding Market Standards

. . . The business ethicists whose views I summarized at the beginning of this essay—Thomas Donaldson and Richard De George—objected to letting the market alone determine wages and labor standards in multinational companies. Both of them proposed criteria for setting wages that might occasionally "improve" on the outcomes of the market.

Their reasons for rejecting market determination of wages were similar. They both cited conditions that allegedly prevent international markets from generating ethically acceptable results. Donaldson argued that neoclassical economic principles are not applicable to international business because of high unemployment rates in developing countries. And De George argued that, in an unregulated international market, the gross inequality of bargaining power between workers and companies would lead to exploitation.

But this essay has shown that attempts to improve on market outcomes may have unforeseen tragic consequences. We saw how raising the wages of workers in international sweatshops might wind up penalizing the most vulnerable workers (those in the informal sectors of developing countries) by depressing their wages and reducing their job opportunities in the formal sector. . . . As we have seen, above-market wages paid to sweatshop workers may discourage further investment and so perpetuate high unemployment. In turn, the higher unemployment may weaken the bargaining power of workers vis-à-vis employers. Thus, such market imperfections seem to call for more reliance on market forces rather than less. Likewise, the experience of the newly industrialized East Asian economies suggests that the best cure for the ills of sweatshops is more sweatshops. But most of the well-intentioned policies proposed by critics and business ethicists are likely to have the opposite effect.

. . . If the preceding analysis is correct, then it follows that it is ethically acceptable to pay market wage rates in developing countries (and to provide employment conditions appropriate for the level of development). That holds true even if the wages pay less than so-called living wages or subsistence or even (conceivably) the local minimum wage. The appropriate test is not whether the wage reaches some predetermined standard but whether it is freely accepted by (reasonably) informed workers. The workers themselves are in the best position to judge whether the wages offered are superior to their next-best alternatives. (The same logic applies *mutatis mutandis* to workplace labor standards.)

Indeed, not only is it ethically acceptable for a company to pay market wages, but it may be ethically unacceptable for it to pay wages that exceed market levels. That will be the case if the company's above-market wages set precedents for other international companies that raise labor costs to the point of discouraging foreign investment. Furthermore, companies may have a social responsibility to transcend their own narrow concern with protecting their brand image and to publicly defend a system that has improved the lot of millions of workers in developing countries.

NOTES

1. Richard De George, *Competing with Integrity in International Business* (New York: Oxford University Press, 1993), 79.

2. De George, *Competing with Integrity*, 356–57.

3. Donaldson, *Ethics of International Business* (New York: Oxford University Press, 1989), 101, 103, 145.

4. World Bank, *World Development Report 1995. "Workers in an Integrating World Economy"* (New York: Oxford University Press, 1995), 77.

5. Donaldson, *Ethics of International Business*, 115.

6. De George, *Competing with Integrity*, 48.

7. Tim Smith, "The power of business for human rights," *Business & Society Review* (January 1994): 36.

8. Robert B. Reich, "Escape from the global sweatshop: Capitalism's stake in uniting the workers of the world," *Washington Post*, May 22, 1994. Reich's test is intended to apply in developing countries "where democratic institutions are weak or absent."

9. International Labor Organization, *World Employment 1995* (Geneva: ILO, 1995), 73.

10. World Bank, *Workers in an Integrating World Economy*, 5.

11. Larry Rohter, "To U.S. critics, a sweatshop; for Hondurans, a better life," *New York Times*, July 18, 1996.

12. Marcus Brauchli, "Garment industry booms in Bangladesh," *Wall Street Journal*, August 6, 1991.

13. Lucy Martinez-Mont, "Sweatshops are better than no shops," *Wall Street Journal*, June 25, 1996.

14. Rohter, "To U.S. critics, a sweatshop."

15. William B. Falk, "Dirty little secrets," *Newsday*, June 16, 1996.

16. Richard J. Barnet and John Cavanagh, "Just undo it: Nike's exploited workers," *New York Times*, February 13, 1994.

17. ILO, *World Employment* 1995, 75.

18. World Bank, *The East Asian Miracle* (New York: Oxford University Press, 1993), 2.

19. Jagdish Bhagwati and Robert E. Hudec, eds., *Fair Trade and Harmonization* (Cambridge: MIT Press, 1996), vol. 1, p. 2.

20. World Bank, *Workers in an Integrating World Economy*, 75.

Review and Discussion Question

1. Critically assess each of the four different standards that have been proposed for setting wages and labor conditions in international sweatshops. Are you persuaded by Maitland's criticism of Donaldson's test? Explain why you agree or disagree with Donaldson's and De George's contention that the classical liberal standard is inapplicable to poor, developing countries?

2. By American standards, wages in international sweatshops are very low, and working conditions appear terrible. Does the fact that foreign workers are eager to take these jobs establish that those wages and conditions are morally acceptable?

3. Maitland appears to believe that with regard to the fairness of wages, "the appropriate test is … whether [the wage] is accepted by (reasonably) informed workers." Is this the only morally relevant test? Can wages be exploitative even if workers accept them?

4. Critics of international sweatshops believe that their wages and working conditions are morally inadequate, that international sweatshops impoverish local workers and increase inequality between rich and poor, and that the companies that use them end up colluding with repressive regimes. Maitland disputes each of these points. With regard to each point, with whom do you agree and why?

5. Business ethicists like Donaldson and De George believe that multinational companies operating in the Third World should not leave it to the market alone to determine wages and working conditions. Maitland, to the contrary, argues that interfering with the market may have tragic consequences. With whom do you agree and why?

6. Assess international sweatshops from a utilitarian point of view, taking into account their effect not just on foreign workers and countries, but also their consequences in terms of cheaper prices and lost jobs for Americans. What nonutilitarian moral considerations, if any, are also relevant to this issue?

7. Maitland believes that American companies act rightly by paying market wages in developing countries and that it may even be wrong for them to pay wages that exceed market levels. What would you do if you were an international manager of an American company?

The Ethics of Corporate Downsizing

JOHN ORLANDO

In recent years corporations have been downsizing their workforces at an unprecedented rate. Although this business trend may have benefited the economy overall, its human price has been high as hardworking employees suffer the emotional and financial repercussions of losing their jobs. In this essay John Orlando argues that downsizing is often morally wrong. He begins by challenging the assumption that the interests of shareholders take priority over those of employees, arguing instead for their moral equality. This equality implies that for downsizing to be permissible it must be justifiable from a utilitarian perspective, which takes into account the interests of both shareholders and workers. However, Orlando argues that the utilitarian case for it is unproved. Moreover, there are at least three moral arguments against downsizing. Although downsizing may be justified in extreme cases, for example, if it is necessary to save the corporation, Orlando concludes that downsizing merely to increase profit will usually be wrong.

Study Questions

1. Orlando discusses five arguments intended to show that the interests of shareholders take priority over those of other groups, such as workers who may be downsized. State each of these arguments in one or two sentences.

2. Give one of the reasons why Orlando believes that a utilitarian approach does not favor downsizing.

3. Explain the three arguments that Orlando gives against downsizing.

4. From Orlando's perspective, when might downsizing be morally justified? Give an example of when it would be clearly wrong.

I. The Issue

. . . MANY WORKERS, especially manufacturing workers, would place corporate downsizing—the closing of whole plants or divisions in order to increase profits—at the head of their list of ethically contentious business practices. Though the issue has provoked considerable debate in the popular press, the philosophical community has largely ignored it.

This oversight is curious given that downsizing is arguably the major business trend of our era. . . . The statistics on downsizing's human costs are sobering. One study found that 15 percent of downsized workers lost their homes, and another that the suicide rate among laid-off workers is thirty times the national average.[1] Despite the rosy picture of the economy painted by the popular media, where attention is constantly drawn to the growth of the stock market, evidence suggests that trends such as downsizing have led to a general decline in employee earnings, as well as a widening of the gulf between rich and poor in America.[2] Added to this is the fact that since the loss of jobs is concentrated in a relatively small geographic area, these closings affect the entire community. Businesses that rely upon work-

ers' spending will feel the pinch, often leading to secondary layoffs. Consequently, communities as a whole have been devastated by such closings. Downsizing also carries with it serious nonquantifiable harms. News of mass layoffs sends psychological tremors across the nation, leading to general worker apprehension about job security and less job satisfaction. Worse yet, the anxiety of unemployment often leads to psychological symptoms such as depression, or expresses itself through a variety of unpleasant behaviors: i.e., crime, domestic violence, child abuse, and alcohol and drug abuse.[3] . . .

I will argue that acts of downsizing are very often morally wrong. I will begin by demonstrating that the business ethics literature has yet to identify a morally relevant distinction between the situation of the shareholder and that of the worker in relation to the corporation. This means that the corporate manager has no naturally greater duty to shareholders than to workers. I will make my case by examining, and dismissing, the various arguments advanced for privileging the interests of shareholders above all other parties. I then advance arguments against the moral permissibility of acts of downsizing. I will finish with a few words about how the concerns I raise might [guide corporate managers and] provide direction for future investigations into the ethical status of [downsizing in particular business circumstances] . . .

II. The Moral Equality of Workers and Shareholders

Property rights

First, it must be understood that one cannot justify the position that shareholder concerns take precedence over all other groups simply by appeal to the fact that the shareholders are the legal owners of the corporation. In that case, all one has done is provide a definition of the term *shareholder*; one has yet to provide a morally relevant reason for privileging the interests of that group. . . .

The natural tack at this point is to assert that a legal owner has property rights that allow her to dispose of her property in any manner she sees fit. But this justification skews the issue in the shareholder's favor by appealing to a paradigm that does not apply in the case of corporate ownership. The term *property rights* conjures up images of property for personal *use*, not *profit*. For instance, property rights advocates normally worry about laws that place restrictions on the use of one's homestead, such as laws regulating the appearance of one's home. . . . We may harbor a deep-seated intuition that property is sacred, but that intuition is tied to property with which we are in some respect intimately connected, such as a home.

To avoid glossing over the distinction between property for private use and property for profit, we will need to narrow our inquiry to an example of property for profit. Imagine that I own an apartment which I have rented to a couple for ten or fifteen years (think Fred and Ethel from "I Love Lucy"). I discover that I can make more money by dividing up the apartment and renting it to college students. My intuition is that I have a responsibility to the people who rent from me. At the very least, I should assure the couple, who

might be frightened about the prospect of being thrown into the street, that I will not have them leave until they have procured similar housing elsewhere at a similar cost. I would also feel obligated to ensure that their transition is as easy as possible by, for instance, helping them move. Moreover, the purpose of the money will have a bearing on the moral status of the act. The act is far easier to justify if it is needed to pay for my wife's extended medical care, than if it merely allows me to buy a longer sailboat. Thus, the general appeal to property rights breaks down when the property in question is for profit, and when we turn to scenarios closer to the practice of downsizing itself.

Fiduciary duties

Many theorists and business managers defend the moral superiority of shareholders on grounds that corporate managers are bound by a fiduciary duty to their shareholders that trumps any competing duties. The burden of proof is then taken to fall on the shoulders of those arguing against this position to demonstrate that the manager has equally strong duties to others as well. . . .

But this characterization of the issue misconstrues the lines of justification for the duties of an agent in a fiduciary relationship. The fiduciary duty does not establish the obligations of the agent. . . . We must look to the particularities of the relationship to identify the contours of the manager's duty to her shareholders. The term *fiduciary duty* is merely a label for whatever obligations the manager owes to the shareholder; it does not create those duties, and thus cannot justify them. . . .

There is considerable evidence that the fiduciary duty of a corporate manager has been historically justified as a means of protecting the owner from that manager.

. . .The legal basis of fiduciary duties of corporate managers to shareholders has been construed as the obligation to not advance their own interests against those of the shareholders. Adopting this view of the fiduciary relationship would mean that when a corporate manager takes into account the interests of [other] stakeholders, even where that comes at the expense of profits, this does not conflict with a manager's fiduciary duty to shareholders.

Risk

Ian Maitland provides two justifications for the position that corporate managers have duties to shareholders over those to other parties. The first appeals to the fact that shareholders have invested capital in the corporation. Why is this fact morally relevant? According to Maitland, shareholders have taken a risk in placing their money in the hands of the corporation, and are thereby due compensation in the form of having their interests given privilege over those of other parties. Maitland states that:

> As a practical matter, no stakeholder is likely to agree to bear the risk associated with the corporation's activities unless it gets the commitment that the corporation will be managed for its benefit. That is logical because the stockholder alone stands to absorb any costs of mismanagement.[4]

It is strange, however, to think that the worker who loses his job has not absorbed any costs of mismanagement. Maitland's point must be that while workers stand to lose their jobs due to corporate mismanagement, they only lose future potential earnings, whereas shareholders lose something they have placed into the corporation. However, workers too have placed something at risk when accepting a job. At the very least, the worker has bypassed other possible job opportunities, opportunities that may have turned out to be financially more rewarding. Also, some have gone to school in the hopes of pursuing a career in the field, thereby investing substantial sums of money (or accruing substantial debt) in the process. Even more importantly, many workers have purchased homes in the expectation of a steady income, and in this manner have risked their homes on the corporation. We can also add to our list the various ways in which workers plant

roots in the community which are disrupted when they are forced to relocate, such as placing their children in local schools or having their spouses accept jobs. While the worker's investment in a corporation is not of the same sort as the shareholder's, it constitutes a risk nevertheless, and so the worker's position is not dissimilar to that of the shareholder. The only difference between the risks taken by the two parties is one of degree, and the degree of that risk will depend upon the particular situation of each individual.

Contracts

Maitland's second argument is that corporations are fundamentally a "freely chosen . . . nexus . . . of contracts" between its stakeholders, which establish both the "rights" and the "obligations" of each party.[5] These contracts stipulate that the worker will give the corporation her labor in return for a fixed wage, while the shareholder will receive all of the profits of the corporation in return for investing capital in it. When third parties tinker with that arrangement, they violate the right of self-determination of the members of the contract, who have determined the terms of the contracts under "free," "voluntary," and "uncoerced" bargaining circumstances. . . .

However, Maitland's picture of the corporation simply does not square with reality. It turns out that most shareholders expect corporate managers to take into account the interests of other constituencies when making decisions about the welfare of the corporation.[6] More importantly, shareholders tend to think of themselves not as owners of the corporation, but rather as investors in it. . . . For the vast majority of shareholders, dabbling in the stock market is thought of as one means among many of investing one's money, something chosen for its high rate of return, not in order to become a corporate owner. Thus, it is hard to understand how the investor can be acting under the assumption of an unstated contract between himself, management, and the company's employees. On the other side, employees have traditionally assumed that taking a job meant having it for life as long as they perform their duties well. Given these considerations, if we are basing such contracts on the implicit understandings and expectations of the parties involved, the evidence actually points in the very opposite direction to which Maitland argues.

Finally, one can raise serious doubts about the assertion that the worker/manager/shareholder relationship has been established under "free, voluntary, and uncoerced" circumstances. For one, the parties are by no means in an equal bargaining position. Despite Maitland's insistence that the disgruntled employee can always "fire his boss by resigning," employees often find that they have very few job options given their skills, the labor market, and the costs of moving to another area. Shareholders, however, have thousands of companies from which to choose, and a variety of mechanisms specifically designed to make movement in and out of the stock market as easy as possible. . . .

Other people's money

Milton Friedman also [argues] against the position that corporations have a responsibility to parties other than shareholders. Friedman's . . . objection is that "the corporation is an instrument of the stockholders who own it," meaning that the manager is acting with other people's money, and thus serving the public interest at the expense of profits is an impermissible use of that money.[7] Another way to put it is that any action that diminishes profits to aid other parties constitutes a "tax" on the shareholders' income.

However, such a use of the shareholders' income is only impermissible if it is unauthorized, and as I have noted, most shareholders expect managers to take into account considerations beyond maximizing profits. Moreover, shareholders in a modern corporation can withdraw their money from that corporation with a simple phone call, and thus the manager who announces his intention to act for the public good gives shareholders plenty of time to remove their money before such a "tax" is levied. More importantly, . . . an act of downsizing cannot be morally

justified in virtue of the fact that it is done in the interests of the shareholders of the corporation, since if it is wrong for the shareholder to perform that act, then it is equally wrong for the manager to do so for them. The fact that a manager is an agent of others cannot itself make the action morally right, and therefore the moral status of the act will turn on other considerations. . . .

I have argued that no philosophically sound argument has yet been advanced for privileging the interests of shareholders over those of workers simply by virtue of the fact that they are shareholders. This is not to say that no such argument may someday appear, but rather that in the absence of compelling reasons to the contrary, we must assume that the worker has an equal moral standing as the shareholder since they are, after all, both humans. Cast in this manner, the burden of proof in the debate runs contrary to what has been up to now believed by its participants. It has been tacitly assumed that it is the job of those arguing for the moral status of non-shareholders to establish their position, perhaps due to the earlier-mentioned view of fiduciary duties. But one of our most deeply felt convictions is that two human beings have equal moral status until morally relevant considerations can distinguish between them. Thus, it is really on the shoulders of those arguing for privileging the interests of the shareholders to make their case. This, I have argued, they have yet to do, leaving us to default to the presumption of equality.

The utilitarian argument

I now wish to examine the utilitarian defense of downsizing. It seems to me that once the moral equality of workers and shareholders has been granted, the only considerations that could justify acts of downsizing would be consequentialist in nature. At the very least, arguments currently advanced to justify acts of downsizing, when they do not rely upon the premise of a moral superiority of shareholders, have been utilitarian. Thus, if I can establish that the utilitarian case has yet to be made, I will have demonstrated that we have yet to find an adequate defense of downsizing.

. . . Utilitarianism is generally construed as the principle that the act that maximizes total utility is morally right. Thus, one could argue that downsizing benefits the majority of the population, and though it leaves some individuals by the wayside, the benefit to the whole outweighs the harm to the few. The entire economy, it might be argued, is becoming more efficient. Moreover, the stock market has skyrocketed, benefiting all those who have investments in mutual funds.

But there is reason to doubt whether downsizing has generated a net gain in utility. A group of researchers recently concluded a fifteen-year study which found that when acts of downsizing are not accompanied by careful restructuring of the corporation—in other words, when people are simply laid off in order to lower costs of production without thought of how the remaining employees will sustain levels of productivity—downsizing has always hurt the corporation in the long run.[8] Reich also notes that the downsizing trend has caused a general drop in employee loyalty in the United States.[9] Workers are far less likely to go the extra mile for firms who treat them as disposable cogs in the corporate machine. While loyalty is not easily quantifiable, and thus does not show up in a corporate ledger, it will affect the company's overall performance. . . .

But even if the case could be made that downsizing improves the overall health of the economy, there would still be a gap between this fact and the conclusion that overall utility has risen. If the argument were to terminate at this point, it would be assuming that one can equate well-being with financial gain; however, far more things go into determining one's well-being. For instance, it is indisputable that the anxiety from job loss has a profoundly negative influence upon one's psychic health. The harm of unemployment cannot simply be measured by the total loss of income; it produces fear for one's own well-being as well as the well-being of one's family, not to mention the anxiety experienced by those other groups themselves. When these factors are taken into account,

it becomes clear that utilitarian considerations do not clearly point in favor of downsizing. It might in fact be determined that downsizing improves net utility in the long run, but the empirical evidence is inconclusive. Our position on the issue, therefore, will need to be informed by other considerations.

III. Arguments Against Downsizing

Harming some to benefit others

Up to this point I have argued only that defenders of downsizing have failed to establish that downsizing is morally permissible. Here I will present reasons for thinking that downsizing is often morally wrong. The first argument appeals to the widely held intuition . . . that causing a great harm for a lesser benefit, even to a great number of people, cannot be morally justified. Most people would even consider it wrong to incur a great harm to a few in order to produce a great benefit to the many, such as removing the eyes from a sighted man and implanting them in two blind persons so that they can now see (with only a drop off in peripheral vision and depth perception distinguishing them from those with two eyes). There are even some who believe that no amount of harm to an individual can be justified on grounds that it will benefit others, since harms and benefits are incommensurable commodities. Given that statistics demonstrate that downsizing often leads to the loss of home and even suicide, it seems hard to deny that at least some downsized workers incur a significant harm from the practice. On the other side, since investors in a large corporation tend to diversify their assets, they incur only a minor benefit when any one stock price rises. Thus, if the act of downsizing is not done as a means of saving the corporation—preventing more workers from losing their jobs—but rather to increase profits, it involves causing a great harm for a minor benefit.

We can also draw a distinction within the practice of downsizing which will serve to amplify its wrongfulness in certain circumstances. Ask yourself if there is a difference in the moral status of the following two acts: First, a country involved in a just war bombs the other side's munitions factory in order to end the war, knowing that the bombing will also destroy a grade school bordering the factory and thus killing ten children. Second, a country in a just war bombs the school where the leaders of the opposing country send their kids in order to get them to end the war (accidentally destroying the neighboring munitions factory in the process). Most people would agree that the latter act is far worse than the former. The best way to explain this intuition is that in the latter act, the death of the children is a means to ending the war, while in the former it is an unfortunate byproduct of that means. The children in the second act are being *used* in a way that they are not being used in the former act.

Now consider the case where a CEO downsizes under the knowledge that the mere news of these layoffs will be greeted favorably by the stock market, and thus cause stock prices to rise . . . as opposed to the case where downsizing will improve profits by increasing productivity. Here the very act that harms the workers—the loss of their jobs—itself produces the benefit to shareholders. Harm is not a simple byproduct of an act which independently brings benefit, but rather is the means to that benefit. This grates even more deeply against our intuitions that it is wrong to use individuals for others' benefit.

Legitimate expectations

We might also approach the issue from the perspective of the legitimate expectations of the individuals involved. To illustrate this notion, consider the possibility that the federal government repeals the home interest tax break without any other modifications in the tax code. While I see no reason why homeowners, and not renters, deserve such a break, one could question the action on grounds that homeowners have made plans under the assumption that this break would continue. Those who lose their homes because of the change in the tax laws would have a legitimate complaint, even though there was never a written guarantee that current tax laws would remain forever unchanged. Similarly, workers have made plans under the assumption of a continued source of income. These are not simply plans for leisure activities such as vacations, but rather plans that impinge upon their fundamental well-being as well as the well-being of their families. There are, however, no similar expectations on the part of the shareholder. For one, shareholders know that stock prices are volatile and that they take a risk when entering the market. Thus, no reasonable investor backs her home on the future performance of her securities. Investors may expect a certain average rate of return, but this is over the long term and they budget accordingly. . . . Also, as mentioned earlier, shareholders tend to consider the companies in which they invest to have obligations to parties other than themselves. Hence, one cannot plead that shareholders entered the market expecting that the company would be run solely for their own benefit.

Fairness

. . . The idea here is that the individual does not deserve the rewards or punishments that come via things for which she is not responsible. At the very least, these factors include genetic endowments and the social institutions of the society in which she lives. . . .

To apply the principle here, we would first note that the worker who loses his job does so through no fault of his own. Someone fired due to incompetence is not downsized. Downsizing does not involve a surgical removal of all employees in a firm whose work is not up to snuff; instead, whole divisions are removed by virtue of their overall profitability, with no effort made to determine if individual members of those divisions are at fault. In fact, if a division or plant is unprofitable it is most likely due to mismanagement on the part of those running the corporation. This is perhaps one of the reasons why downsized workers feel betrayed, as no attempt is made by management to judge their actual job performance. Downsized workers find themselves harmed due to forces outside of their control. Moreover, these forces have conspired to selectively harm them since upper management tends to be insulated from these harms, by devices such as receiving a sizable "golden parachute" when dismissed. True, there are a variety of ways in which natural and social forces reward and punish arbitrarily but this does not make those harms permissible or release us from obligations to mitigate them.

On the other side, shareholders have done nothing to merit the sharp gains that downsizing produces. Perhaps they are owed good faith efforts at sound management by the corporation in virtue of their investment, but they cannot claim to deserve the special increases in the value of their investments due solely to laying off workers. The fact that we happen to live in a world where canning large numbers of workers is a quick means of increasing profits is not any of their doing. Note also that those shareholders who have invested through mutual funds have not themselves chosen to invest in this particular firm. These investors most likely have little idea as to which stocks their mutual funds actually hold, since one of the appeals of these funds is that they allow individuals to enter the market without the need to concern themselves with the intricacies of investing, or the day-to-day fluctuations of the market. . . .

IV. Applying the Results and Related Concerns

. . . Business managers will need to examine the actual situations of their shareholders and workers, as well as that of the company, in order to ascertain if a decision to downsize is morally permissible. While this grants that some acts of downsizing may be morally permissible, simply establishing that corporate managers cannot lay claim to a special duty to shareholders that trumps any competing duties cuts against the grain of much of corporate America's current philosophy. . . . While many business persons would agree

that corporations have some obligations to persons besides shareholders, all but the most socially conscious would likely consider anathema the position that these obligations stand on equal footing with obligations to shareholders. . . .

How might the corporate manager apply the insights gathered here to a particular situation? First and foremost, an act of downsizing that prevents the collapse of the corporation can be justified on grounds that the organism is saved by amputating a limb. However, we must keep in mind that bankruptcy does not always mean the complete shutting down of shop. Bankruptcy courts make every effort to find a way of restructuring the debts of the corporation to keep it in business. . . . But an act of downsizing that merely increases profits, which seems increasingly the case, requires a careful analysis of the harms and benefits it will incur to the parties involved. For a small firm, such as a fast-food franchise with a single proprietor, the owner may be at greater risk than her employees. The owner most likely has a large percentage of her personal fortune wrapped up in the company, whereas the workers are usually (but not always) high school students just earning extra spending money. However, with a large corporation, the results are likely to be quite different. It bears mention that . . . the owner of a corporation is not personally liable for its debts; if IBM dissolves, shareholders need not fear that IBM's creditors will come knocking at their doors. Legal protection to the shareholder is built into the corporation's charter. More importantly, since investors tend not to risk money that is required for their sustenance, their losses do not normally affect their immediate well-being. By contrast, the worker who banks his home on his job places his immediate well-being, as well as the well-being of his family, in far greater peril. Finally, investors today diversify their assets through mutual funds which own shares in thousands of corporations. Thus, losses from one stock create only a minor shift in the fund's overall value. This means that acts of downsizing can cause great harm to a few for a minor benefit to the many, something that I have argued is not morally permissible. Also, one can argue that the sole proprietor who has nursed the business from the ground up merits greater consideration than the mutual fund investor who may not even know that he or she owns shares in the corporation. Moreover, the worker who has purchased a home, and started a family, based on the assumption of the continued source of income, is deserving of greater consideration than the investor who finds that unprecedented gains in the stock market allow him to extend his vacation to Aruba by a week.

NOTES

1. Richard L. Bunning, "The Dynamics of Downsizing," *Personnel Journal* 69, no. 9 (Sept. 1990): 69.

2. Interview with Secretary of Labor Robert Reich in *Challenge*, July/August 1996, 4. Reich notes that while the *average* wage is up, the *median* wage (the wage of the individual in the middle) is down. The discrepancy is due to the unprecedented rise in compensation for top executives during the 1980s and 1990s.

3. David Dooley, Ralph Catalano, and Karen S. Rook, "Personal and Aggregate Unemployment and Psychological Symptoms," *Journal of Social Issues* 44 (1988): 107–23; David Dooley, Ralph Catalano, and Georjeanna Wilson, "Depression and Unemployment: Panel Findings from the Epidemiologic Catchment Area Study," *American Journal of Community Health* 22 (1994): 745–65.

4. Ian Maitland, "The Morality of the Corporation: An Empirical or Normative Disagreement?" *Business Ethics Quarterly* 4, no. 4 (1994): 445–57.

5. Maitland, op. cit., 449.

6. Larry D. Sonderquist and Robert P. Vecchio, "Reconciling Shareholders' Rights and Corporate Responsibility: New Guidelines for Management," *Duke Law Journal* (1978): 840; reproduced in John R. Boatright, "Fiduciary Duties and the Shareholder-Management Relation: Or, What's So Special About Shareholders?" *Business Ethics Quarterly* 4, no. 4 (October 1994): 398.

7. Friedman, "The Social Responsibility of Business Is to Increase Its Profits," *New York Times Magazine,* September 1970, reprinted in *Ethical Theory and Business,* ed. Tom L. Beauchamp and Norman E. Bowie (Englewood Cliffs, NJ: Prentice-Hall, 1979), 136–38.

8. Wayne F. Cascio, interview on National Public Radio, November 14, 1997.

9. Reich, op. cit.

Review and Discussion Questions

1. Orlando distinguishes property for private use and property for profit, using the example of a landlord renting an apartment. Do you find the example persuasive? Explain why or why not.

2. Critically assess each of the five arguments supporting the proposition that shareholders take priority over workers. Which of the arguments are strongest? Which do you see as the weakest? How convincing are Orlando's responses?

3. Do you agree that there is moral equality between workers and shareholders? If so, what does this imply?

4. Can downsizing be supported on utilitarian grounds? Explain why or why not.

5. Is downsizing wrong because it is instance of "harming some to benefit others," as Orlando argues?

6. Orlando's "legitimate expectations" argument against downsizing rests on the premise that "workers have made plans under the assumption of a continued source of income." Is that premise true and, if so, was it reasonable for workers to make this assumption?

7. Orlando argues that downsizing is unfair by appealing to the principle that people do not deserve rewards or punishments for things for which they are not responsible. Do you accept Orlando's principle? If so, does it show that downsizing is wrong?

8. In your view, when, if ever, is downsizing morally justifiable?

9. Assess the argument that Orlando's critique of downsizing ends up challenging the free market system itself. What are the implications of Orlando's essay for the issue of international sweatshops, discussed in the previous essay?

Welfare and Social Justice

JOHN ISBISTER

The United States stands out from other advanced capitalist countries in one unfortunate respect: its high rate of poverty. John Isbister, professor of economics at the University of California, Santa Cruz, maintains that in countries that can afford to do so (like the U.S.), there's no excuse for not eliminating poverty; the norms of equality and freedom require it. Even if some adults are responsible for their poverty, children never deserve this fate and yet they are twice as likely to be poor as adults are. Isbister goes beyond this, however, to argue that even those who are voluntarily unemployed should be guaranteed sufficient income to raise them out of poverty. He criticizes the welfare reforms of the 1990s as unjust. Besides demeaning recipients and violating their right to privacy, the reforms fail to promote equality and restrict people's freedom to make certain important life choices. In place of the current system, Isbister proposes a negative income tax that would give people an incentive to work while preserving their basic freedoms.

Study Questions

1. According to Isbister, why does justice require that rich countries eliminate poverty? What is special about the situation of children?

2. On what grounds does Isbister support welfare even for those who are voluntarily poor? What is Elster's objection to Isbister's position?

3. What were the main changes brought about by reform of the welfare laws in the 1990s?

4. On what grounds does Isbister reject the claim that a democratically elected government can impose whatever conditions it wants on recipients of financial assistance?

5. What is the "doctrine of moral hazard"?

6. Why does Isbister believe that the new welfare system is unjust?

7. Describe the three variants of a negative income system discussed by Isbister.

THE GREATEST INJUSTICE of unregulated, free-market capitalism is that it provides for only some of the people and excludes others. Some get rich, some do reasonably well, and others are left in poverty by the market. Consequently, governments of advanced capitalist countries intervene— in different ways and to different extents—to rescue those for whom the market system does not provide.

The United States Census Bureau estimates that in 1999, 17 percent of the population fell below the poverty line, set at just under $20,000 for a family of four. The poverty rates in the other advanced capitalist countries are at most half the

American rate, and in many countries they are far lower than half. Robert M. Solow, citing studies by L. Kenworthy, has shown that the high poverty rate in the United States is the consequence not of anything unusual about American labor markets but rather of a welfare system that does much less to support poor people than do the welfare systems in comparable countries. "What really distinguishes the U.S.," he writes, "is the equanimity with which the majority contemplates the poverty of a minority."[1] . . .

Any assessment of the welfare system is complicated by the fact that there are many different reasons for poverty. Some adults are poor even though they are working for pay part or full time; their wages are insufficient to pull them above the poverty line. Others are in the labor force but unemployed; they are willing and able to work but they cannot find a job. Still others are unable or unwilling to work. In this latter group are found the elderly, the sick, and the physically and mentally disabled, people who simply cannot work, as well as single parents of young children.

One overwhelming fact stands out among all the descriptive facts about poverty, a fact that can guide us through the conflicts of justice and give us a clue to the best sort of welfare programs: all categories of poor adults, no matter what the reasons for their poverty, have children. Children in the United States are twice as likely to be poor as adults. The children are victims of poverty, not its creators. Their parents may or may not be responsible for the poverty in which they live—no doubt some parents are and some are not, some to a greater extent and some to a lesser extent—but not a single child is responsible for her poverty. We can say with certainty, therefore, that programs that punish parents for their alleged irresponsibility do an injustice to their innocent dependent children, none of whom deserve to be impoverished.

Is Poverty Permissible?

The first question is whether it is permissible to have poor people at all in an affluent country.

According to the Gospel of Matthew, Jesus said, "For ye have the poor always with you," but first-century Palestine was not a rich society by today's standards, at least in material terms. Jesus' words may still be applicable in today's poor countries, but in a country like the United States where the average family income is close to $90,000,* it is not a requirement of nature that some families subsist on less than $20,000. Poverty could be eliminated simply by taxing those who are better off and transferring enough income to the poor to raise them above the poverty line.

It is difficult to argue against the proposition that since poverty could be eliminated in rich countries, justice requires that it be eliminated. The norms of equality and freedom demand it, and efficiency does not stand in its way. At the very least, . . . equality means equality of opportunity, and equality of opportunity is not available to children who are born into poverty. They lack the opportunities for intellectual and physical development that more affluent children have, and they find it harder to compete as adults. The true meaning of freedom . . . is that people have both the means and the absence of restrictions to pursue their goals. Poverty denies people the means to pursue their goals and therefore restricts their freedom. . . .

There is no excuse for working people to be in poverty. The minimum wage should be sufficient to raise a working person to the poverty level, rather than to just half that level, as it is now. Better programs than currently exist should be available to help people upgrade their skills and be more productive. Community development programs of all sorts can bring businesses and jobs to low-income neighborhoods. Similarly, the unemployed should not fall into poverty. They are looking for work, and it is not their fault that jobs are lacking. Neither should people be poor who are out of the labor force through no fault of their own, whether they are elderly or disabled or responsible for the care of young children or

*This is the mean family income. Elsewhere Isbister states that the median family income is approximately $45,000. —ED.

for some other reason. They are equally worthy as everyone else and therefore deserve some of society's bounty, and furthermore their children deserve the chance to start life on an even footing. There is no moral case that is even slightly plausible for allowing such people to live in poverty is an affluent country.

The tricky moral question comes with the voluntarily unemployed.

The Voluntarily Unemployed

Philippe Van Parijs asks whether surfers should be fed.[2] Do people who could work and voluntarily choose not to, for any reason at all, perhaps because they are lazy, have the right to be supported by the income-earning taxpayers? . . .

People who have followed the acrimonious debate over welfare may reasonably object to posing such a question, because it seems to malign poor people as undeserving parasites who have chosen to live off others. My purpose is the opposite. It is well documented that most poor people want to support themselves and get out of poverty.[3] Among those who appear not to want to do so are many who are psychologically incapable of sustained work, so their poverty is not really voluntary. Under the current welfare system, it is not clear that an able-bodied person who voluntarily chose a life of poverty could qualify for any welfare support at all. The current welfare system is, however, terribly unjust; later in this chapter I will propose reforms that would lift every person in the country out of poverty, irrespective of his or her motivations. Even though the proposed new welfare system would contain incentives to work, still I expect that under its provisions some people would choose not to work but to live off a grant that would leave them just at the margin of poverty. Unless this can be morally justified, the case for completely eliminating poverty collapses.

Under a welfare system such as I will propose, the voluntary poor would no doubt be a varied group. They might be Van Parijs's surfers; they might be contemplatives, scholars, artists, or wanderers. They might work hard at tasks that produced no income, or they might take it easy. They might hope to earn an income by their activities—like Vincent Van Gogh, creating a masterpiece every day but finding no market for his work—or they might be consciously disengaged from income-producing work. What they did with their time might be useful to other people, or not. They might move in and out of income-earning work. Would they have the right to an income sufficient to raise them out of poverty? Another way to put the question is this. Since they would need some income in order to survive, would they have the right to pursue their non-income-producing goals, or would they be forced into income-producing work that they preferred not to do?

Many people would argue that if they can work for pay they must and that any exemption from work constitutes exploitation of the taxpayers. Political scientist John Elster writes, "People who chose to work for an income . . . would have to pay higher taxes in order to support those who took the other option. They would think, correctly in my opinion, that they were being exploited by the other group."[4]

Against this is the argument from freedom. We have the right to pursue our goals and to have the means that are necessary to pursue them. If our goal is art or contemplation, we have the right to pursue our goal just as much as does the person whose goal is to be an investment banker. This cannot be an absolute right, and in this respect the right to pursue the goal of not working for pay is the same as most other freedoms, few of which are absolute. This particular freedom depends upon the existence of enough total income that the support of a few non-earners is not overly burdensome. It depends upon the number of voluntary non-earners being relatively small and their demands for subsistence being relatively low. It is a right that can be met more easily in the United States or Switzerland than in India or Zimbabwe. Surely it is a good thing, however, not a bad thing, to allow people to pursue the goals they really wish to pursue and not force them into a cookie-cutter life for which they have neither desire nor perhaps aptitude. . . .

The poverty cutoff is a good state-supported income for such people. It is low enough to keep the burden on the taxpayers from being onerous and to ensure that people not be attracted to this lifestyle just for the money. It is high enough that people can survive on it and pursue at least some of their goals.

Elster finds this sort of argument unpersuasive. He is less concerned with the freedom of the surfers and the scholars than with the freedom of the taxpayers. Just because people prefer work to nonwork, he says, is no reason to tax them for support of the nonworkers. "They might well prefer the forty-hour week over the fifty-hour week they had to work because of the high taxes imposed on them by those who chose to live on the grant. Hence the argument from freedom of choice fails, because the workers would be forced by the nonworkers to work harder than they wished."[5]

Elster's is a serious objection. It is not as extreme as the objection to taxation made by libertarians like Robert Nozick, who deny that there is any reason for the state to take away people's legitimately earned income without their individual consent. Elster simply argues that the freedom of people to pursue a life of nonpaid work or leisure conflicts with the freedom of working folk to pursue their goals, and he chooses the latter over the former. He is not alone.

He is wrong in this choice, however. Of course people who work for pay find that their life choices are constrained by the fact that they have to pay taxes. Taxation restricts our individual freedom. Virtually no working person has to change his or her way of life fundamentally because of taxes, however. Taxes limit our choices, but they do not eliminate them. The failure to provide a minimum income to a contemplative, however, is likely to make that entire way of life unattainable. The sorts of restrictions on our freedom imposed by taxes are significantly less severe, it seems obvious to me, than the dictate that one cannot pursue one's life goal. If taxes had to be so high as to be confiscatory, that would be an unacceptable violation of people's freedom to be secure in their property. If the transfer payment were so high as to attract a large number of otherwise working people to the nonworking life, the criterion of efficiency would be violated. Where overall national income is high enough, however, and the transfer payment fairly low, justice requires that even voluntary nonworkers receive financial support from the state.

If even voluntary nonworkers deserve support, there is no question but that the involuntary poor, the great majority, should be rescued from poverty.

Welfare Reform of the 1990s

Prior to the 1990s, most poor people in the United States qualified for some financial support—although usually not enough to raise them above the poverty line—simply because of their low income. Depending upon the category into which they fell, their grant might be higher or lower; for example, people with dependent children typically received more than people without. In either case, however, the welfare support continued for as long as the person remained in poverty. In the 1990s a new philosophy was imposed, first in several states and then nationally with the passage of the Parental Responsibility and Work Opportunity Act in 1996. Among other provisions, the law replaced the old AFDC (Aid to Families with Dependent Children) with the new TANF (Temporary Assistance to Needy Families):

- The entitlement of poor people to support was replaced by block grants, limited to a certain amount of money, to the states. If and when the grants run out, the people who depend upon them may be out of luck, since the states are not required to make additional expenditures.

- Welfare recipients can be required by the states to work for pay or to enroll in a training program, as a condition of support. They must work after two years on assistance.
- Support is limited to a lifetime maximum of five years, and this period may be shortened by the states. A recipient who has not successfully made the transition to self-sufficiency can be cut off.

The federal law is supplemented by welfare-to-work laws in the states, plus individual county plans. Taken together, it has been a controversial shift in policy, reversing decades of movement in the opposite direction. As it happened, it coincided with a significant decline in the number of people receiving welfare payments. The reasons for this decline are not clear. They may include an improving economy that offered more opportunities to the previously unemployed, and they may also include the success of the new approach in encouraging people to make themselves employable. Critics worry, however, that the decline in welfare rolls may partly be an indication of people being denied welfare support without having yet developed the skills to take care of themselves. Administrative data in most states do not reveal whether people who leave welfare are better off or if they are leaving welfare for work. A survey of New York State residents dropped from welfare under the new law found that only 29 percent had found employment—when employment was defined as earning at least $100 over three months. Other studies have found better results, but this may be because they added together people who voluntarily left welfare because they found a job with those who were involuntarily dropped.

The new time-limited welfare philosophy grew out of a concern that the previous approach to welfare had failed. The old approach had created, it was alleged, a dependent class of people who were encouraged to be unproductive because they were supported by the state. The new approach would require them to become productive, and this would have benefits both for the taxpayers and for the poor people themselves. The taxpayers would be relieved of much of their burden, and the previously poor would have the satisfaction of entering mainstream society.

The Injustice of the New Welfare System

The state does not have the moral right to impose the conditions on welfare recipients that it currently does, conditions relating to marital status, work requirements, and time limits.

It might be claimed that a democratically elected government has the right to impose these sorts of conditions, in return for offering financial support. To reason by analogy, if you pay money to the launderer, you have every right to impose conditions on him: you expect him to starch these shirts, leave those shirts unstarched, patch a rip in your jacket, and have everything washed and ironed by Wednesday morning. No one's rights or freedoms are violated by such an understanding. Why then is it not justified for the state to impose any condition a majority of the people want on welfare recipients?

The difference between the two cases is that you have no obligation to give money to the launderer, whereas people with means have an obligation to poor people. No one would criticize you if you washed your own shirts or if you took your laundry to a different establishment. You have a purely voluntary contract with the launderer: if you do not want to take your shirts to him you do not have to, and if he does not want to wash them he does not have to.

The obligation of middle-class and rich people to the poor is not like this commercial relationship. I do not owe the launderer anything unless he washes my shirts, but I owe poor people at least enough support that they not be destitute. The poor are owed support not because of the services they provide to the nonpoor but because they are human beings of equal moral standing with the nonpoor, human beings who share the same social space. The state does not, therefore, have an unconditional moral right to impose conditions on welfare recipients. It may impose some conditions, but the conditions should be defensible in terms of justice.

The conditions imposed on welfare recipients in the 1990s moved away from justice, not toward it. The first thing to say about them is that they severely restrict the freedom of the recipients. Most importantly, single mothers who would prefer to work in the home with even their very young children or babies have lost this right. They must be out of the house, either working for pay or getting trained. . . . The law will allow women to stay at home only if they are living with their husband or the father of their children. Authorities are entitled to the most personal of information pertaining to sexual habits, in order to identify absent fathers and collect child-support payments. These conditions are demeaning, and they violate the norms of privacy.

Liberty is not the only component of justice, however. Can the new approach to welfare be justified on efficiency grounds? This is how it is usually defended, as a kind of tough-love approach that gets recipients off their duffs and into the world of work so that they can be self-sufficient. It may well have this effect for some poor people, but it does not for others. The issue of efficiency is complex. The most obvious rejoinder for people who think the new system is efficient is to point out that it is based on the bizarre assumption that the raising of young children is not work. The truth is that child care is demanding and that it is just about the most valuable work that exists in our society. For the most part it is not paid work, but that is irrelevant to its true value. It is hard to think of anything more important than giving children a good foundation in life, but this is foreclosed by the new laws.

Beyond this obvious point, economic theory provides two conflicting perspectives on the relationship of efficiency to the welfare system. The first is that individuals know best what is best for them; the second is that insurance creates what is called a "moral hazard." The individuals-know-best doctrine leads to an argument against the imposition of any conditions on welfare recipients. . . . Efficiency . . . means getting the best out of a given set of resources: not the most, in a crude sense of accumulation, but the best. Who is better situated to decide what is best for a person than that person herself? If she is facing the difficult decision to work outside the home or to stay with her young children, is it likely that a social worker or a bureaucrat or a legislator can make the decision better than she can? This is what the current welfare reform assumes, and it is a patronizing assumption. If the conditions imposed by the state are different from the choices the poor person would have made herself, the doctrine of individuals-know-best tells us that the result will be inefficient.

The doctrine of moral hazard, however, gives one pause. The doctrine asserts that the existence of insurance is likely to induce people to make decisions that may be in their own self-interest but that are harmful to society as a whole, decisions they would not make in the absence of insurance. If you have fire insurance on your house, for example, you may be careless with matches, since you will not bear the cost of a fire. There is a real social cost to your house burning down, however, a cost that will be paid by all the purchasers of fire insurance in the form of higher premiums. If you have health insurance, you may go to the doctor more often than is really necessary, since the visits are free to you. They are not free to society, however, and we all pay for excessive medical use through higher health insurance premiums.

Does the welfare system, which can be thought of as insurance protecting against the possibility of being poor, create a moral hazard? It may. Even though the benefits are very low, some people may be induced into staying dependent, not becoming self-sufficient even though they could. This is the reason that the Congress decided to abandon the old entitlement approach to welfare and replace it with the personally intrusive, time-limited, workfare system. The new system can be thought of as an attempt to eliminate the moral hazard attendant upon welfare payments.

CHAPTER FOURTEEN: ECONOMIC JUSTICE

We must be careful, though. Just because we are likely safe in thinking that some people fall into the moral-hazard trap, it does not follow that every welfare recipient under the old system became dependent or even that most did. At the time of the debate over welfare reform, a pervasive image existed of the slothful, unmotivated, excessively fecund poor single mother, but no actual evidence existed that the image was accurate for a large number of people. . . .

Some people may be helped by the new system, in the sense of being forced to become self-sufficient when they could have done so all along but were discouraged or demoralized. It is clear, however, that others are hurt, because they are not able to measure up to the demands of the new system and will eventually be dropped from the welfare rolls.

The report card on the new system is therefore this: without question it violates people's freedom to choose their marital arrangements and to choose between caring for children or working outside the home. In terms of efficiency, it may help some become more efficient, but it hurts others by denying them the ability to make choices that they are competent to make. In terms of equality, it certainly harms those—and their children—who are unable in the long run to get a job. Overall, the welfare reform of the 1990s earns a failing grade: it is unjust.

A Welfare System Based on Justice

A way exists to preserve the positive effect of the new system, namely, encouragement of some people to develop labor market skills, while avoiding the negative effects—the facts that it leaves some people still in poverty and worse off than they were before and that it severely limits the freedom of choice of the recipients. It is a system that has sometimes been called the negative income tax.[6] It can be structured in such a way as to meet the goals of pulling everyone out of poverty, giving people an incentive to work and preserving basic freedoms. The current earned-income tax credit

goes a small distance in the direction of the negative income tax.

A normal income tax takes money away from people, the amount of the tax depending upon the person's income. A negative income tax gives money to people, the amount of the grant depending upon the person's income. Just as the normal income tax is adjusted by deductions—for example, people can claim deductions for their children and thereby reduce their tax liability—in the same way the negative income tax can be adjusted according to the number of dependents and perhaps other factors. Given these adjustments, the amount of the grant depends only on the person's adjusted income, not upon such factors as marital status, presence of a man in the house, length of time in poverty, participation in training programs, or success in finding a job. In the same way that taxpayers now file a form documenting their income and paying taxes that are based on that income, under the negative income tax poor people would file a form documenting their income and receiving a grant on that basis.

The first and most obvious advantage of the negative income tax over the current or previous welfare system is that it increases the recipients' freedom. They would be free to marry or not to marry, to stay home with the children or not, to get a job or not, to stay in a grant-receiving status for a long time or not. The amount of their grant would be affected by such choices, because the choices would affect their incomes, but their options would not be foreclosed to them by the law. On grounds of liberty, the negative income tax is easily preferable.

The more difficult questions about the negative income tax have to do with equality and efficiency, and here the devil is in the details. The precise terms of the negative income tax make a big difference. Suppose the tax is structured in such a way as to eliminate poverty and nothing more. With zero earned income over the year, a person receives a grant of $20,000. With $10,000 earned income, the grant is $10,000, and with $20,000 earned income, the grant is zero. Above an earned income of $20,000, people begin to pay positive taxes. The consequence is that poverty is eliminated. People who would otherwise be poor are raised to the poverty line. It sounds good, and from the perspective of equality, it certainly is good. It is bad for efficiency, however, since it contains a strong incentive not to work. A negative income tax structured this way has a 100 percent, confiscatory marginal tax rate. Think about a person earning nothing and contemplating whether to get a job and start earning money. Why should she do such a thing when she knows that, until she reaches an income of $20,000, her grant will be reduced by a dollar for every dollar she earns? Her take-home income will be $20,000, no matter how much she works.

The problem can be solved, although not easily. Suppose the negative income tax is set up in the following way. A person earning nothing receives a grant of $10,000. For every dollar he earns above zero, his grant is cut back by 50 cents. So, for example, if he earns $10,000, his grant is cut back from $10,000 to $5,000, and he nets $15,000. When he earns $20,000, the poverty line, his grant is cut back by the full $10,000, and he breaks even. This system solves the efficiency problem. The marginal tax rate is just 50 percent, not 100 percent. People get to keep 50 cents out of every extra dollar they earn, so they have an incentive to work. The problem with this second scheme is that it is not very good for equality. In fact, it raises no one out of poverty. It puts money in the hands of the poor, but the gap between their earnings and the poverty line is cut only in half, not completely.

So far, it seems, the negative income tax is good for freedom, but it contains an inherent conflict between equality and efficiency. A solution to this conflict exists, a solution that most observers have rejected out of hand, but which I think makes sense. Why not set the base income at $20,000, the poverty line, rather than $10,000, and impose something like a 50 percent marginal tax rate on all earned income? Here is how it would work. A person earning nothing would get a grant of $20,000, sufficient to pull her out of poverty. With $10,000 earned income, the grant would be

cut back to $15,000, for a net income of $25,000. With earned income of $20,000, the grant would be cut back to $10,000, for a net income of $30,000, and so forth. At an earned income of $40,000, the grant would be eliminated completely, and beyond that level people would pay positive taxes. This scheme would resolve both our problems. It would be good for equality, because it would raise everyone out of poverty. It would be good for efficiency, because people could keep half of every extra dollar they earned.

One may usefully compare this scheme with the current philosophy of time-limited welfare. Both embody incentives to get people off welfare and into the labor market, but the negative income tax uses the carrot while the time-limited scheme uses the stick. The difference is dramatic for those who do not or cannot respond to the stick. With the negative income tax, they are assured of a basic income that will keep them out of poverty, while in the time-limited scheme they are left penniless.

The third variant of the negative income tax is, however, very expensive, imposing a heavier burden on the taxpayers than the first two. In the first two, all the transfer payments from the government go to poor people, while people earning more than the poverty-level income begin to pay taxes at a moderate rate. In the third variant, people earning an income up to twice the poverty level receive a subsidy from the taxpayers. The overall distribution of the disbursed funds depends upon the number of people at each income level, but it is easily possible that more money will be transferred to the nonpoor than to the poor. Since so much money would have to be transferred, the positive tax rates on people earning more than $40,000 would have to be significantly higher than in the first two schemes.

One of the ways of understanding why the third variant is so expensive is to see that it is equivalent to what has sometimes been called the unconditional basic income, the basic grant or the demogrant.[7] The basic grant is a flat subsidy, the same amount of money paid to everyone regardless of their earned income. It is untaxed, but all earned income is taxed heavily in order to pay for the grant. The third variant can therefore be thought of as a basic grant of $20,000, with earned income between zero and $40,000 taxed at a 50 percent rate and earned income above that level taxed perhaps at a higher rate.

Neither the negative income tax nor the basic grant is in use in any country, but the structure of both programs reveals the problems and contradictions inherent in most programs of transfers to the poor. The American system of welfare subsidies, while more complex than the negative income tax, faces the same contradictions. If a welfare program is restricted to grants to the poor, it can honor the virtue of equality while violating efficiency (like the first scheme) or it can honor efficiency while violating equality (like the second). If a welfare program is to honor both, in the way that the third scheme does, it will transfer significant resources to the nonpoor and will impose a much higher burden on the taxpayers.

It is important, therefore, to decide whether something like the third plan can be justified. Most analysts of welfare programs have concluded that it is completely out of the question; they think it impossible because it imposes too high a tax burden and unjustified because it transfers resources to the nonpoor. I, on the other hand, think it is exactly what justice calls for. From the perspective of justice, the fact that it does not focus only on the poor is a merit. It narrows the dispersal of take-home incomes in the entire population and hence moves the population closer to a just overall income distribution. . . . All earning less than $40,000 receive some sort of subsidy, helping to push them toward the middle range of incomes. . . . The taxes necessary to finance this transfer are high but not confiscatory.

They allow high-income earners to retain some of their incomes, as freedom requires, but they can be structured in such a way as to reduce high incomes significantly and hence reduce the overall dispersion of incomes.

Among these various possibilities, therefore, the third is the best. It eliminates poverty and compresses the range of incomes in the society, while retaining incentives to work and allowing people to keep a portion of their earnings. It is certainly better than the time-limited approach to welfare, an approach that is designed to allow people to fall between the cracks and remain desperately poor.

NOTES

1. Robert M. Solow, "Welfare: The Cheapest Country," *New York Review of Books* 47 (March 23, 2000): 20–23.

2. Philippe Van Parijs, "Why Surfers Should Be Fed: The Liberal Case for an Unconditional Basic Income," *Philosophy and Public Affairs* 20 (1991): 101–31.

3. Robert M. Solow has collected evidence to support this statement in *Work and Welfare* (Princeton, N.J.: Princeton University Press, 1998).

4. Jon Elster, *Solomonic Judgements: Studies in the Limitations of Rationality* (Cambridge: Cambridge University Press, 1989), 215.

5. Elster, *Solomonic Judgements*, 216.

6. The negative income tax was proposed by Milton Friedman in 1962 and has received wide discussion since that time. See Milton Friedman, *Capitalism and Freedom* (Chicago: University of Chicago Press, 1962).

7. Van Parijs, "Why Surfers Should Be Fed," and Philippe Van Parijs, *Real Freedom for All: What (If Anything) Can Justify Capitalism?* (Oxford: Clarendon Press, 1995). For a proposal showing how the basic grant would work in practice, see S. Lerner, C. M. A. Clark, and W. R. Needham, *Basic Income: Economic Security for All Canadians* (Toronto: Between the Lines, 1999).

Review and Discussion Questions

1. Why does poverty continue to exist in a wealthy country like the U.S.? Have you known people who receive welfare or live below the poverty line? In your experience, did they have the same desire to work as other people? Was it their fault they were poor?

2. Do you agree that justice requires rich countries to eliminate poverty? Explain why or why not. If they are required to eliminate poverty, how should they do it?

3. State and critically assess the arguments for and against the proposition that justice requires us to support those who would rather surf than work. Do you agree that we have an obligation to preserve the voluntarily unemployed from poverty? If we do, how much support should they receive?

4. Assess the welfare reforms discussed by Isbister. Did they make the welfare system fairer? Did they make it more efficient? Do you agree with Isbister that "overall, the welfare reform of the 1990s earns a failing grade"? Are there considerations in favor of the present welfare system that he has overlooked or failed to do justice to?

5. Would a negative income tax be better—in particular, with respect to freedom, equality, and efficiency—than the present welfare system? Would it be more just? Which of the three negative income tax systems discussed by Isbister would be best? Is the system Isbister favors practicable? Is it worth pursuing as a goal even if politically unrealistic?

Is Inheritance Justified?

D. W. HASLETT

Many people support inheritance and believe it to be just because they believe it is an essential and necessary feature of capitalism. After reviewing some facts about wealth distribution and inheritance in the United States today, D. W. Haslett, a philosophy professor at the University of Delaware, argues against this view. He contends not only that inheritance is not essential to capitalism but that it is inconsistent with the fundamental values underlying capitalism. In particular, inheritance violates the capitalistic ideals of "distribution according to productivity," "equal opportunity," and "freedom." Haslett maintains, accordingly, that the practice of inheritance as it exists today should be abolished.

Study Questions

1. Do inheritance taxes do much to reduce inequalities in the distribution of wealth today?
2. How does inheritance contravene the ideal of distribution according to productivity?
3. Why does equal opportunity promote productivity and a more just distribution of income?
4. What is the difference between freedom in the narrow sense and freedom in the broad sense?
5. How would abolishing inheritance enhance freedom in the broad sense?
6. What exactly is Haslett's proposal for abolishing inheritance, and what are the three exceptions to it?
7. How does Haslett respond to the objection that without inheritance people will lose their incentive to work hard?

I. Background Information

FAMILY INCOME IN THE UNITED STATES today is not distributed very evenly. The top fifth of American families receives 57.3 percent of all family income, while the bottom fifth receives only 7.2 percent.

But, for obvious reasons, a family's financial well-being does not depend upon its income nearly as much as it does upon its wealth, just as the strength of an army does not depend upon how many people joined it during the year as much as it does upon how many people are in it altogether. So if we really want to know how unevenly economic well-being is distributed in the United States today, we must look at the distribution not of income, but of wealth.

Although—quite surprisingly—the government does not regularly collect information on the distribution of wealth, it has occasionally done so. The results are startling. One to two percent of American families own from around 20 to 30 percent of the (net) family wealth in the United States; 5 to 10 percent own from around 40 to 60 percent. The top fifth owns almost 80 percent of the wealth, while the bottom fifth owns only 0.2 percent. So while the top fifth has, as we saw, about eight times the income of the bottom fifth, it has about 400 times the wealth. Whether deliberately or not, by regularly gathering monumental amounts of information on the distribution of income, but not on the distribution of wealth, the government succeeds in directing attention away from how enormously unequal the distribution of wealth is, and directing it instead upon the less unequal distribution of income. But two things are clear: wealth is distributed far more unequally in the United States today than is income, and this inequality in the distribution of wealth is enormous. These are the first two things to keep in mind throughout our discussion of inheritance.

The next thing to keep in mind is that, although estate and gift taxes in the United States are supposed to redistribute wealth, and thereby lessen this inequality, they do not do so. Before 1981 estates were taxed, on an average, at a rate of only 0.2 percent—0.8 percent for estates over $500,000—hardly an amount sufficient to cause any significant redistribution of wealth. And, incredibly, the Economic Recovery Act of 1981 *lowered* estate and gift taxes.

Of course the top rate at which estates and gifts are *allegedly* taxed is far greater than the 0.2 percent rate, on the average, at which they are *really* taxed. Prior to 1981, the top rate was 70 percent, which in 1981 was lowered to 50 percent. Because of this relatively high top rate, the average person is led to believe that estate and gift taxes succeed in breaking up the huge financial empires of the very rich, thereby distributing wealth more evenly. What the average person fails to realize is that what the government takes with one hand, through high nominal rates, it gives back with the other hand, through loopholes in the law. . . . Indeed, as George Cooper shows, estate and gift taxes can, with the help of a good attorney, be avoided so easily they amount to little more than "voluntary" taxes.[1] As such, it is not surprising that, contrary to popular opinion, these taxes do virtually nothing to reduce the vast inequality in the distribution of wealth that exists today.

Once we know that estate and gift taxes do virtually nothing to reduce this vast inequality, what I am about to say next should come as no surprise. This vast inequality in the distribution of wealth is (according to the best estimates) due at least as much to inheritance as to any other factor. Once again, because of the surprising lack of information about these matters, the extent to which this inequality is due to inheritance is not known exactly. One estimate, based upon a series of articles appearing in *Fortune* magazine, is that 50 percent of the large fortunes in the United States were derived basically from inheritance. But by far the most careful and thorough study of this matter to date is that of John A. Brittain. Brittain shows that the estimate based upon the *Fortune* articles actually is too low;[2] that a more accurate estimate of the amount contributed by inheritance to the wealth of "ultra-rich" males is 67 percent.[3] In any case, it is clear that, in the

United States today, inheritance plays a large role indeed in perpetuating a vastly unequal distribution of wealth. This is the final thing to keep in mind throughout the discussion which follows.

II. Inheritance and Capitalism

Capitalism (roughly speaking) is an economic system where (1) what to produce, and in what quantities, is determined essentially by supply and demand—that is, by people's "dollar votes"—rather than by central planning, and (2) capital goods are, for the most part, privately owned. In the minds of many today, capitalism goes hand in hand with the practice of inheritance; capitalism without inheritance, they would say, is absurd. But, if I am right, the exact opposite is closer to the truth. Since, as I shall try to show in this section, the practice of inheritance is incompatible with basic values or ideals that underlie capitalism, what is absurd, if anything, is capitalism *with* inheritance. . . .

I do not try to show here that the ideals underlying capitalism are worthy of support; I only try to show that inheritance is contrary to these ideals. And if it is, then from this it follows that, *if* these ideals are worthy of support (as, incidentally, I think they are), then we have prima facie reason for concluding that inheritance is unjustified. What then are these ideals? For an answer, we can do no better than turn to one of capitalism's most eloquent and uncompromising defenders: Milton Friedman.

Distribution according to productivity

The point of any economic system is, of course, to produce goods and services. But, as Friedman tells us, society cannot very well *compel* people to be productive and, even if it could, out of respect for personal freedom, probably it should not do so. Therefore, he concludes, in order to get people to be productive, society needs instead to *entice* them to produce, and the most effective way of enticing people to produce is to distribute income and wealth according to productivity. Thus we arrive at the first ideal underlying capitalism: "To each according to what he and the instruments he owns produces."[4]

Obviously, inheritance contravenes this ideal. For certain purposes, this ideal would require further interpretation; we would need to know more about what was meant by "productivity." For our purposes, no further clarification is necessary. According to *any* reasonable interpretation of "productivity," the wealth people get through inheritance has nothing to do with their productivity. And one need not be an adherent of this ideal of distribution to be moved by the apparent injustice of one person working eight hours a day all his life at a miserable job, and accumulating nothing, while another person does little more all his life than enjoy his parents' wealth, and inherits a fortune.

Equal opportunity

But for people to be productive it is necessary not just that they be *motivated* to be productive, but that they have the *opportunity* to be productive. This brings us to the second ideal underlying capitalism: equal opportunity—that is, equal opportunity for all to pursue, successfully, the occupation of their choice. According to capitalist ethic, it is OK if, in the economic game, there are winners and losers, provided everyone has an "equal start." As Friedman puts it, the ideal of equality compatible with capitalism is not equality of outcome, which would *discourage* people from realizing their full productive potential, but equality of opportunity, which *encourages* people to do so.[5]

Naturally this ideal, like the others we are considering, neither could, nor should, be realized fully; to do so would require, among other things, no less than abolishing the family and engaging in extensive genetic engineering. But the fact that this ideal cannot and should not be realized fully in no way detracts from its importance. Not only is equal opportunity itself an elementary requirement of justice but, significantly, progress in realizing this ideal could bring with it progress in at least two other crucial areas as well: those of productivity and income distribution. First, the closer we come to equal opportunity for all, the more people there will be who, as a result of increased opportunity, will come to realize their productive potential. And, of course, the more people there are who come to realize their productive potential, the greater overall productivity will be. Second, the closer we come to equal opportunity for all, the more people there will be with an excellent opportunity to become something other than an ordinary worker, to become a professional or an entrepreneur of sorts. And the more people there are with an excellent opportunity to become something other than an ordinary worker, the more people there will be who in fact become something other than an ordinary worker or, in other words, the less people there will be available for doing ordinary work. As elementary economic theory tells us, with a decrease in the supply of something comes an increase in the demand for it, and with an increase in the demand for it comes an increase in the price paid for it. An increase in the price paid for it would, in this case, mean an increase in the income of the ordinary worker vis-à-vis that of the professional and the entrepreneur, which, surely, would be a step in the direction of income being distributed more justly.

And here I mean "more justly" even according to the ideals of capitalism itself. As we have seen, the capitalist ideal of distributive justice is "to each according to his or her productivity." But, under capitalism, we can say a person's income from some occupation reflects his or her productivity only to the extent there are no unnecessary limitations upon people's opportunity to pursue, successfully, this occupation—and by "unnecessary limitations" I mean ones that either *cannot* or (because doing so would cause more harm than good) *should not* be removed. According to the law of supply and demand, the more limited the supply of people in some occupation, then (assuming a healthy demand to begin with) the higher will be the income of those pur-

suing the occupation. Now if the limited supply of people in some high-paying occupation . . . is the result of unnecessary limitations upon people's opportunity to pursue that occupation, then the scarcity is an "artificial" one, and the high pay can by no means be said to reflect productivity. The remedy is to remove these limitations; in other words, to increase equality of opportunity. To what extent the relative scarcity of professions and entrepreneurs in capitalist countries today is due to natural scarcity, and to what extent to artificial scarcity, no one really knows. I strongly suspect, however, that a dramatic increase in equality of opportunity will reveal that the scarcity is far more artificial than most professionals and entrepreneurs today care to think—*far* more artificial. . . .

That inheritance violates the (crucial) second ideal of capitalism, equal opportunity, is, once again, obvious. Wealth *is* opportunity, and inheritance distributes it very unevenly indeed. Wealth is opportunity for realizing one's potential, for a career, for success, for income. There are few, if any, desirable occupations that great wealth does not, in one way or another, increase—sometimes dramatically—one's chances of being able to pursue, and to pursue successfully. And to the extent that one's success is to be measured in terms of one's income, nothing else, neither intelligence, nor education, nor skills, provides a more secure opportunity for "success" than does wealth. Say one inherits a million dollars. All one then need do is purchase long-term bonds yielding a guaranteed interest of 10 percent and (presto!) one has a yearly income of $100,000, an income far greater than anyone who toils eight hours a day in a factory will probably ever have. If working in the factory pays, relatively, so little, then why, it might be asked, do not all these workers become big-time investors themselves? The answer is that they are, their entire lives, barred from doing so by a lack of initial capital which others, through inheritance, are simply handed. With inheritance, the old adage is only too true: "The rich get richer, and the poor get poorer." Without inheritance, the vast fortunes in

America today, these enormous concentrations of economic power, would be broken up, allowing wealth, and therefore opportunity, to become distributed far more evenly.

Freedom

But so far I have not mentioned what many, including no doubt Friedman himself, consider to be the most important ideal underlying capitalism: that of liberty, or, in other words, freedom. This ideal, however, takes different forms. One form it takes for Friedman is that of being able to engage in economic transactions free from governmental or other types of human coercion. The rationale for this conception of freedom—let us call it freedom in the "narrow" sense—is clear. As Friedman explains it, assuming only that people are informed about what is good for them, this form of freedom guarantees that ". . . no exchange will take place unless both parties benefit from it."[6] If at least the parties themselves benefit from the transaction, and it does not harm anyone, then, it is fair to say, the transaction has been socially valuable. So people with freedom of exchange will, in doing what is in their own best interests, generally be doing what is socially valuable as well. In other words, with this form of freedom, the fabled "invisible hand" actually works.

All of this is a great oversimplification. For one thing, a transaction that benefits both parties may have side effects, such as pollution, which harm others and, therefore, the transaction may not be socially valuable after all. So freedom, in the narrow sense, should certainly not be absolute. But the fact that freedom, in this sense, should not be absolute does not prevent it from serving as a useful ideal. . . .

There are [those] whose conception of freedom is that of not being subject to any governmental coercion (or other forms of human coercion) for any purposes whatsoever—a conception sometimes referred to as "negative" freedom. It is true that governmental (or other) coercion for purposes of enforcing the abolition of

inheritance violates this ideal, but then, of course, so does any such coercion for purposes of *maintaining* inheritance. So this "anticoercion" ideal . . . neither supports nor opposes the practice of inheritance, and therefore this conception of freedom need not concern us further here. . . .

A very popular variation of the anticoercion conception of freedom is one where freedom is, once again, the absence of all governmental (or other human) coercion, *except for any coercion necessary for enforcing our fundamental rights.* Prominent among our fundamental rights, most of those who espouse such a conception of freedom will tell us, is our right to property. So whether this conception of freedom supports the practice of inheritance depends entirely upon whether our "right to property" should be viewed as incorporating the practice of inheritance. But whether our right to property should be viewed as incorporating the practice of inheritance is just another way of stating the very point at issue in this investigation. . . . Consequently, this popular conception of freedom cannot be used here in support of the practice of inheritance without begging the question.

But there is still another conception of freedom espoused by many: that which we might call freedom in the "broad" sense. According to this conception of freedom, to be free means to have the ability, or the opportunity, to do what one wants. For example, according to this conception of freedom, rich people are, other things being equal, freer than poor people, since their wealth provides them with opportunities to do things that the poor can only dream about. . . .

Let us now see whether inheritance and freedom are inconsistent. Consider, first, freedom in the narrow sense. Although inheritance may not be inconsistent with this ideal, neither is the *abolishment* of inheritance. This ideal forbids governmental interference with free exchanges between people; it does not necessarily forbid governmental interference with *gifts* or *bequests* (which, of course, are not *exchanges*). Remember, Friedman's rationale for this ideal is, as we saw, that free exchange promotes the "invisible hand"; that is, it promotes the healthy functioning of supply and demand, which is at the very heart of capitalism. Supply and demand hardly require gifts, as opposed to exchanges, in order to function well.

If anything, gifts and bequests, and the enormous concentrations of economic power resulting from them, hinder the healthy functioning of supply and demand. First of all, gifts and bequests, and the enormous concentrations of economic power resulting from them, create such great differences in people's "dollar votes" that the economy's demand curves do not accurately reflect the needs of the population as a whole, but are distorted in favor of the "votes" of the rich. And inheritance hinders the healthy functioning of supply and demand even more, perhaps, by interfering with supply. As we have seen, inheritance (which, as I am using the term, encompasses large gifts) is responsible for some starting out in life with a vast advantage over others; it is, in other words, a major source of unequal opportunity. As we have also seen, the further we are from equal opportunity, the less people there will be who come to realize their productive potential. And, of course, the less people there are who come to realize their productive potential, the less overall productivity there will be or, in other words, the less healthy will be the economy's *supply* curves. So, while inheritance may not be *literally* inconsistent with freedom in the narrow sense, it does, by hindering indirectly both supply and demand, appear to be inconsistent with the "spirit" of this ideal. . . .

So we may conclude that, at best, inheritance receives no support from freedom in the narrow sense. But it remains for us to consider whether inheritance receives any support from the other relevant ideal of freedom, an ideal many, including myself, would consider to be the more fundamental of the two: freedom in the broad sense—being able to do, or having the opportunity to do, what one wants. So we must now ask whether, everything considered, there is more overall opportunity throughout the country for people to do what they want with inheritance, or without it.

On the one hand, without inheritance people are no longer free to leave their fortunes to whomever they want and, of course, those who otherwise would have received these fortunes are, without them, less free to do what they want also.

But to offset these losses in freedom are at least the following gains in freedom. First, as is well known, wealth has, generally speaking, a diminishing marginal utility. What this means is that, generally speaking, the more wealth one already has, the less urgent are the needs which any given increment of wealth will go to satisfy and, therefore, the less utility the additional wealth will have for one. This, in turn, means that the more evenly wealth is distributed, the more overall utility it will have.* And since we may assume that, generally speaking, the more utility some amount of wealth has for someone, the more freedom in the broad sense it allows that person to enjoy, we may conclude that the more evenly wealth is distributed, the more overall freedom to which it will give rise. Now assuming that abolishing inheritance would not lessen *overall* wealth . . . and that it would indeed distribute wealth more evenly, it follows that, by abolishing inheritance, there would be some gain in freedom in the broad sense attributable to the diminishing marginal utility of wealth. Next, abolishing inheritance would also increase freedom by increasing equality of opportunity. Certainly those who do not start life having inherited significant funds (through either gift or bequest) start life, relative to those who do, with what amounts to a significant handicap. Abolishing inheritance, and thereby starting everyone at a more equal level, would obviously leave those who otherwise would have suffered this handicap (which would be the great majority of people) more free in the broad sense.

---

*The more evenly wealth is distributed, the more overall utility it will have since any wealth that "goes" from the rich to the poor, thereby making the distribution more even, will (given the diminishing marginal utility of wealth) have more utility for these poor than it would have had for the rich, thus increasing overall utility.

I, for one, believe these gains in freedom—that is, those attributable to the diminishing marginal utility of wealth and more equality of opportunity—would *more* than offset the loss in freedom resulting from the inability to give one's fortune to whom one wants. Abolishing inheritance is, I suggest, analogous to abolishing discrimination against blacks in restaurants and other commercial establishments. By abolishing discrimination, the owners of these establishments lose the freedom to choose the skin color of the people they do business with, but the gain in freedom for blacks is obviously greater and more significant than this loss. Likewise, by abolishing inheritance the gain in freedom for the poor is greater and more significant than the loss in freedom for the rich. So to the list of ideals that inheritance is inconsistent with, we can, if I am right, add freedom in the broad sense.

To recapitulate: three ideals that underlie capitalism are "distribution according to productivity," "equal opportunity," and "freedom," the latter being, for our purposes, subject to either a narrow or a broad interpretation. I do not claim these are the *only* ideals that may be said to underlie capitalism; I do claim, however, that they are among the most important. Inheritance is inconsistent with both "distribution according to productivity," and "equal opportunity." Perhaps it is not, strictly speaking, inconsistent with the ideal of freedom in the narrow sense, but neither is the abolishment of inheritance. On the other hand, it probably *is* inconsistent with what many would take to be the more fundamental of the two relevant ideals of freedom: freedom in the broad sense. Since these are among the most important ideals that underlie capitalism, I conclude that inheritance not only is not essential to capitalism, but is probably inconsistent with it. . . .

III. A Proposal for Abolishing Inheritance

First, my proposal for abolishing inheritance includes the abolishment of all large gifts as well—gifts of the sort, that is, which might serve as alternatives to bequests. Obviously, if such gifts were not abolished as well, any law abolishing inheritance could be avoided all too easily.

Of course we would not want to abolish along with these large gifts such harmless gifts as ordinary birthday and Christmas presents. This, however, raises the problem of where to draw the line. I do not know the best solution to this problem. The amount that current law allows a person to give each year tax free ($10,000) is too large a figure at which to draw the line for purposes of a law abolishing inheritance. We might experiment with drawing the line, in part at least, by means of the distinction between, on the one hand, consumer goods that can be expected to be, within ten years, either consumed or worth less than half their current value and, on the other hand, all other goods. We can be more lenient in allowing gifts of goods falling within the former category since, as they are consumed or quickly lose their value, they cannot, themselves, become part of a large, unearned fortune. The same can be said about gifts of services. But we need not pursue these technicalities further here. The general point is simply that, so as to avoid an obvious loophole, gifts (other than ordinary birthday presents, etc.) are to be abolished along with bequests.

Next, according to my proposal, a person's estate would pass to the government, to be used for the general welfare. If, however, the government were to take over people's property upon their death then, obviously, after just a few generations the government would own virtually everything—which would certainly not be very compatible with capitalism. Since this proposal for abolishing inheritance *is* supposed to be compatible with capitalism, it must therefore include a requirement that the government sell on the open market, to the highest bidder, any real property, including any shares in a corporation, that it receives from anyone's estate, and that it do so within a certain period of time, within, say, one year from the decedent's death. This requirement is, however, to be subject to one qualification: any person specified by the decedent in his will shall be given a chance to *buy* any property specified by the decedent in his will before it is put on the market (a qualification designed to alleviate slightly the family heirloom/business/farm problem discussed elsewhere). The price to be paid by this person shall be whatever the property is worth (as determined by governmental appraisers, subject to appeal) and any credit terms shall be rather lenient (perhaps 10 percent down, with the balance, plus interest, due over the next 30 years).

Finally, the abolishment of inheritance proposed here is to be subject to three important exceptions. First, there shall be no limitations at all upon the amount a person can leave to his or her spouse. A marriage, it seems to me, should be viewed as a joint venture in which both members, whether or not one stays home tending to children while the other earns money, have an *equally* important role to play; and neither, therefore, should be deprived of enjoying fully any of the material rewards of this venture by having them taken away at the spouse's death. And unlimited inheritance between spouses eliminates one serious objection to abolishing inheritance: namely, that it is not right for a person suddenly to be deprived, not only of his or her spouse, but also of most of the wealth upon which he or she has come to depend—especially in those cases where the spouse has, for the sake of the marriage, given up, once and for all, any realistic prospects of a career.

The second exception to be built into this proposal is one for children who are orphaned, and any other people who have been genuinely dependent upon the decedent, such as any who are mentally incompetent, or too elderly to have any significant earning power of their own. A person shall be able to leave funds (perhaps in the form of a trust) sufficient to take care of such dependents. These funds should be used only for the dependent's living expenses, which would include any educational or institutional expenses no matter how much. They should not, of course, be used to provide children with a "nest egg" of the sort others are prohibited from leaving their children. And at a certain age, say twenty-one (if the child's formal education has been completed), or upon removal of whatever disability has caused dependency, the funds should cease. This exception eliminates another objection to abolishing inheritance—the objection that it would leave orphaned children, and other dependents, without the support they needed.

The third and final exception to be built into this proposal is one for charitable organizations—ones created not for purposes of making a profit, but for charitable, religious, scientific, or educational purposes. And, in order to prevent these organizations from eventually controlling the economy, they must, generally, be under the same constraint as is the government with respect to any real property they are given, such as an operating factory: they must, generally, sell it on the open market within a year. . . .

IV. An Objection

We turn next to what is, I suppose, the most common objection to abolishing inheritance: the objection that, if people were not allowed to leave their wealth to their children, they would lose their incentive to continue working hard, and national productivity would therefore fall. In spite of the popularity of this objection, all the available evidence seems to indicate the contrary. For example, people who do not intend to have children, and therefore are obviously not motivated by the desire to leave their children a fortune, do not seem to work any less hard than anyone else. And evidence of a more technical nature leads to the same conclusion: people, typically, do not need to be motivated by a desire to leave their children (or someone else) great wealth in order to be motivated to work hard.[7]

Common sense tells us the same thing. The prospect of being able to leave one's fortune to one's children is, no doubt, for some people one factor motivating them to be productive. But even for these people, this is only *one* factor; there are usually other factors motivating them as well, and motivating them to such an extent that, even if inheritance were abolished, their productivity would be unaffected. Take, for example, professional athletes. If inheritance were abolished, would they try any less hard to win? I doubt it. For one thing, abolishing inheritance would not, in any way, affect the amount of money they would be able to earn for use during their lives. So they would still have the prospect of a large income to motivate them. But there is something else which motivates them to do their best that is, I think, even more important, and is not dependent on money: the desire to win or, in other words, to achieve that which entitles them to the respect of their colleagues, the general public, and themselves. Because of the desire to win, amateur athletes compete just as fiercely as professionals. Abolishing inheritance would in no way affect this reason for doing one's best either. Athletes would still have the prospect of winning to motivate them. Businessmen, doctors, lawyers, engineers, artists, researchers—in general, those who contribute most to society—are not, with respect to what in the most general sense motivates them, really very different from professional athletes. Without inheritance, these people would

still be motivated by the prospect of a sizable income for themselves and, probably even more so, by the prospect of "winning"; that is, by the prospect of achieving, or continuing to achieve, that which entitles them to the respect of their colleagues, the general public, and themselves.

NOTES

1. George A. Cooper, *A Voluntary Tax? New Perspectives on Sophisticated Estate Tax Avoidance* (Washington, D.C.: Brookings Institution, 1979).

2. John A. Brittain, *Inheritance and the Inequality of National Wealth* (Washington, D.C.: Brookings Institution, 1978), pp. 14–16.

3. *Ibid.*, p. 99.

4. Milton Friedman, *Capitalism & Freedom* (Chicago: University of Chicago Press, 1962), pp. 161–162.

5. Milton & Rose Friedman, *Freedom to Choose* (New York: Harcourt Brace Jovanovich, 1979), pp. 131–140. . . .

6. Friedman, *Capitalism & Freedom*, p. 13.

7. See, for example, D. C. McClelland, *The Achieving Society* (Princeton: Van Nostrand, 1961), pp. 234–235; and Seymour Fiekowsky, *On the Economic Effects of Death Taxation in the United States* (unpublished doctoral dissertation, Harvard University, 1959), pp. 370–371.

Review and Discussion Questions

1. Has Haslett correctly identified the fundamental ideals underlying capitalism? Would you agree that inheritance is contrary to capitalism's fundamental values?

2. Do you agree that inheritance violates the principle of equality of opportunity and that abolishing it would promote productivity and a distribution of income that is fairer even by capitalist standards?

3. Explain and assess Haslett's argument that abolishing inheritance would not violate capitalism's commitment to freedom in the narrow sense and would actually enhance people's freedom in the broad sense.

4. How feasible do you find Haslett's proposal for abolishing inheritance? Would you modify it in any way?

5. Has Haslett overlooked any arguments in favor of inheritance? How would a utilitarian look at Haslett's proposal? Would abolishing inheritance violate anyone's moral rights?

ETHICS IN BUSINESS

The Inconclusive Ethical Case Against Manipulative Advertising

MICHAEL J. PHILLIPS

Critics of advertising maintain that it manipulates our needs and fears, increasing our propensity to consume and swaying our individual purchasing decisions. Granting for the sake of argument that the critics of advertising are correct about its effectiveness, Michael J. Phillips, professor emeritus of business administration at Indiana University, assesses four possible attacks on manipulative advertising, each from a different ethical perspective: (1) that manipulative advertising has negative consequences for utility, (2) that it undermines personal autonomy, (3) that it violates Kant's categorical imperative, and (4) that it weakens the personal virtue of its practitioners and victims. After considering one final, partial defense of manipulative advertising, he concludes that although the practice is morally problematic, there is room for doubt about its badness and no completely definite basis for condemning it.

Study Questions

1. What is "manipulative advertising"? What are the two distinct ways in which it manipulates people? What is "associative advertising"?
2. Galbraith's "dependence effect" refers to the relationship between production and consumer wants. What exactly is the dependence effect?
3. Explain Theodore Levitt's view of advertising. How does it improve our lives?
4. What is the autonomy-related objection to manipulative advertising?
5. Hare makes two Kantian arguments against manipulative advertising (based on two ways of formulating Kant's categorical imperative). What are they?
6. In the eyes of its critics, how does manipulative advertising undermine the virtue of its practioners and its targets?
7. What is manipulative advertising's "last defense"?

From Business and Professional Ethics Journal *13 (Winter 1994). Reprinted by permission of the author.*

THIS ESSAY EXPLORES the ethical implications of [the] perception that advertisers successfully "exploit and manipulate the vast range of human fears and needs." It begins by defining its sense of the term *manipulative advertising*. Then the essay asserts for purposes of argument that manipulative advertising actually works. Specifically, I make two controversial assumptions about such advertising: (1) that it plays a major role in increasing the general propensity to consume, and (2) that it powerfully influences individual consumer purchase decisions. With the deck thus stacked against manipulative advertising, the essay goes on to inquire whether either assumption justifies its condemnation, by considering four ethical criticisms of manipulative advertising. Ethically, I conclude, manipulative advertising is a most problematic practice. If probabilistic assertions are valid in ethics, then the odds strongly favor the conclusion that manipulative advertising is wrong. Nevertheless, there still is room for doubt about its badness. Like the apparently easy kill that continually slips out of the hunter's sights, manipulative advertising evades the clean strike that would justify its condemnation for once and all.

What Is Manipulative Advertising?

. . . What, then, is manipulative advertising? . . . I define "manipulative advertising" as advertising that tries to favorably alter consumers' perceptions of the advertised product by appeals to factors other than the product's physical attributes and functional performance. There is no sharp line between such advertising and advertising that is nonmanipulative; even purely informative ads are unlikely to feature unattractive people and depressing surroundings. Nor is it clear what proportion of American advertising can fairly be classed as manipulative. Suffice it to say that that proportion almost certainly is significant. As we will see, advertising's critics sometimes seem to think that all of it is manipulative.

Perhaps the most common example of manipulative advertising is a technique John Waide (1987, 73–74) calls "associative advertising." Advertisers using this technique try to favorably influence consumer perceptions of a product by associating it with a nonmarket good (e.g., contentment, sex, vigor, power, status, friendship, or family) that the product ordinarily cannot supply on its own. By purchasing the product, their ads suggest, the consumer somehow will get the nonmarket good. Michael Schudson describes this familiar form of advertising as follows: "The ads say, typically, 'buy me and you will overcome the anxieties I have just reminded you about' or 'buy me and you will enjoy life' or 'buy me and be recognized as a successful person' or 'buy me and everything will be easier for you' or 'come spend a few dollars and share in this society of freedom, choice, novelty, and abundance'" (1986, 6). Through such linkages between product and nonmarket good, associative advertising seeks to increase the product's perceived value and thus to induce its purchase. Because these linkages (e.g., the connection between beer and attractive women) generally make little sense, such advertising is far removed from rational persuasion.

The Effects of Manipulative Advertising: What the Critics Think

In the previous section, I tried to describe manipulative advertising in terms of sellers' *efforts*, rather than their actual accomplishments. But does manipulative advertising successfully influence consumers? As might be expected, advertising's critics generally answer this question in the affirmative. Perhaps the best-known example is chapter XI of John Kenneth Galbraith's *The Affluent Society*, where he described his well-known dependence effect.

Galbraith's dependence effect might be described as the way the process of consumer goods production creates and satisfies consumer wants (1958, 158). "That wants are, in fact, the fruit of production," he intoned, "will now be denied by few serious scholars" (154). In part, these wants result from emulation, as increased production means increased consumption for some, followed by even more consumption as others follow suit (154–55). But advertising and salesmanship provide an even more direct link between production and consumer wants. Those practices, Galbraith says:

> [C]annot be reconciled with the notion of independently determined desires, for their central function is to create desires. . . . This is accomplished by the producer of goods or at his behest. A broad empirical relationship exists between what is spent on production of consumers' goods and what is spent in synthesizing the desires for that production. A new consumer product must be introduced with a suitable advertising campaign to arouse an interest in it. The path for an expansion of output must be paved by a suitable expansion in the advertising budget. Outlays for the manufacturing of a product are not more important in the strategy of modern business enterprise than outlays for the manufacturing of demand for the product. (155–56)

. . . To Galbraith, therefore, advertising in general is manipulative. In *The Affluent Society*, it apparently worked mainly to promote aggregate demand, rather than to shift demand from one brand to another. Many of advertising's critics follow Galbraith's lead by stressing how it socializes people to embrace consumerist values. . . .

From all this, it is a short step to the notion that advertising plays a major role in shaping and sustaining the modern society of material abundance. Implicitly, at least, some accounts of this kind liken society to a huge machine whose aim is the conversion of natural resources into consumer products. For the machine to work properly, its human components must be motivated to play their role in producing those products. This can be accomplished by: (1) implanting in people an intense desire for consumer goods, and (2) requiring that they do productive work to get the money to buy those goods. . . . Galbraith suggested that these social imperatives of production and consumption make the worker/consumer resemble a squirrel who races full-tilt to keep abreast of a wheel propelled by his own efforts (1958, 154, 159).

Although they naturally evaluate the matter differently, business leaders often second the argument that advertising is essential to prosperity. In . . . an exchange on advertising expenditures by the fast-food industry, William H. Genge, the chairman of Ketchum Communications' board, wrote:

> I regard the many millions of dollars spent by fast-food companies (and other retailers as well) as healthy and necessary stimulation of the consumption that makes our economy the most dynamic and productive in the world.
> Some people talk as though large advertising budgets are wasteful and nonproductive. It just takes one simple question to put that down. The question is: Where does the money go? The answer is: It provides jobs and livelihoods for hundreds of thousands of people—not only in the advertising and communications sector but for all the people employed by fast-food companies and, indeed, all marketing organizations. (1985, 58–59)

"So," Genge concluded, "large advertising expenditures are not a misallocation of economic resources. They are, in fact, an essential allocation and the driving force behind consumption, job creation, and prosperity" (59).

Advertising that is sufficiently manipulative to create a consumer society also might be able to determine consumers' individual purchase decisions. Most often, I suppose, these would be brand choices within a particular product category, although advertising might also steer people toward certain products and away from others. . . .

Assumptions and Plan of Attack

As we have just seen, many critics of advertising say that it socializes people to a life of consumption. And some regard it as a strong influence on individual brand or product decisions. However, these beliefs are not universally shared. Some students of advertising doubt that ads do much to dictate individual brand choices. And even if advertising strongly influences consumer decisions, it does not follow that any specific ad invariably compels the purchase of the product it touts. The reason is that a particular product advertisement is only one of many factors—especially competing advertisements—influencing consumers (Hayek 1961, 347). For the same general reason, it is difficult to assess advertising's role in making people lifetime consumers. . . .

Despite such difficulties, this essay assumes for the sake of argument that manipulative advertising really works. Thus, I assume that such advertising strongly influences individual purchase decisions, and that it plays a major role in producing consumerist attitudes among the populace. In neither case, however, do I wish to specify all the links in the causal chain through which manipulative advertising does its work. In particular, I make no assumptions about the personal traits that render consumers responsive to manipulative advertising. Later in the essay, for example, I consider the possibility that manipulative advertising succeeds because consumers want and need it.

Operating under the assumptions just stated, I now consider four possible ethical attacks on manipulative advertising. These are the claims that such advertising: (1) has negative consequences for utility, (2) undermines personal autonomy, (3) violates Kant's categorical imperative, and (4) weakens the personal virtue of its practitioners and its victims. I also consider one qualified defense of manipulative advertising: that even though no moral person would choose it were he writing on a clean slate, by now its elimination would be worse than its continuance.

For each attack on manipulative advertising, I assume the validity of the relevant moral value or ethical theory, thus precluding defenses of manipulative advertising that attack the value or theory itself. . . .

Utilitarianism

As just stated, this essay assumes that advertising can manipulate people in two distinct ways: (1) by socializing them to embrace consumerist values, and (2) by dictating individual purchase decisions. One important utilitarian criticism of manipulative advertising seems mainly to involve the first of these effects. Another implicates the second effect. . . . I now discuss each of these utilitarian attacks in turn. Throughout, I explicitly or implicitly compare my assumed world in which manipulative advertising exists and is effective with a world in which all advertising is merely informative.

The implications of the dependence effect

The Affluent Society marked Galbraith's arrival as a critic of consumer society and its works. For his critique to be persuasive, he had to counter the argument that America's enormous production of consumer goods is justified because people want, enjoy, and demand them. This required that he undermine at least two widespread beliefs: (1) that consumer desires are genuinely autonomous, and (2) that they produce significant satisfactions. As we saw earlier, he attacked the first assumption by maintaining that consumer wants are created by the productive process through which they are satisfied, with advertising serving as the main generator of those wants. This argument would have enabled Galbraith to contend that advertising is bad because it denies autonomy, but he seemed not to emphasize that point. Instead, he maintained that the satisfaction of advertising-induced desires generates little additional utility. His argument was that if advertising is needed to arouse consumer wants, they cannot be too strong. "The fact that wants can be synthesized by advertising, catalyzed by salesmanship, and shaped by the discreet manipulations of the persuaders shows that they are not very urgent. A man who is hungry need never be told of his need for food" (1958, 158).

As a result, Galbraith continued, one cannot assume that the increased production characterizing the modern affluent society generates corresponding increases in utility. Instead, as he summarizes the matter:

[O]ur concern for goods . . . does not arise in spontaneous consumer need. Rather, the dependence effect means that it grows out of the process of production itself. If production is to increase, the wants must be effectively contrived. In the absence of the contrivance the increase would not occur. This is not true of all goods, but that it is true of a substantial part is sufficient. It means that since the demand for this part would not exist, were it not contrived, its utility or urgency, ex contrivance, is zero. If we regard this production as marginal, we may say that the marginal utility of present aggregate output, ex advertising and salesmanship, is zero. (160)

Because wants must be contrived for production to increase, on Galbraith's assumptions production would be lower were advertising completely informative. Since on those assumptions that contrived production generates little additional utility, however, the loss would not be much felt. Indeed, with resources shifted away from advertising and consumption and toward activities that improve the quality of our lives, overall utility might well grow in manipulative advertising's absence.

Galbraith's basic argument was that because consumer wants are contrived, they are not urgent; and that because they are not urgent, their satisfaction does not generate much utility. One way to attack his argument is to maintain that consumer desires really do arise from within the individual, but my two assumptions foreclose that possibility here. Another is to follow the lead established by Friedrich Hayek's 1961 critique of Galbraith's dependence effect. To Hayek, Galbraith's argument involves a massive non sequitur: the attempt to reason from a desire's origin outside the individual to its unimportance (1961, 346–47). If that assertion were valid, he thought, it would follow that "the whole cultural achievement of man is not important" (346).

Surely an individual's want for literature is not original with himself in the sense that he would experience it if literature were not produced. Does this mean that the production of literature cannot be defended as satisfying a want because

it is only the production which provokes the demand? In this, as in the case of all cultural needs, it is unquestionably, in Professor Galbraith's words, "the process of satisfying the wants that creates the wants." (347)

Presumably, the same general point applies to utility-maximization. Just because product desire A originated within Cal Consumer while product desire B came his way through manipulative advertising, it does not follow that satisfying desire A would give him more utility than satisfying desire B. Indeed, as we will see presently, the opposite may be true.

The frustration of rational interbrand choices

The second major utilitarian objection to manipulative advertising concerns its power to distort consumer choices among brands and products. As R. M. Hare once observed:

[T]he market economy is only defensible if it really does . . . lead to the maximum satisfaction of the preferences of the public. And it will not do this if it is distorted by various well-known undesirable practices. . . . By bringing it about that people decide on their purchases . . . after being deceived or in other ways manipulated, fraudulent advertisers impair the wisdom of the choices that the public makes and so distort the market in such a way that it does not function to maximize preference-satisfactions. (Hare 1984, 27–28)

For example, now suppose that Cal Consumer's preferences would find their optimum satisfaction in Product A. Intoxicated by Product B's manipulative advertising, Cal instead buys that product, which satisfies his original preferences less well than Product A. If Cal would have bought Product A in a regime where advertising is purely informative, presumably B's manipulative advertising cost him some utility.

The previous argument, however, might fail if manipulative advertising gives consumers satisfactions that they would not otherwise obtain from their purchases. In that event, the utility lost when manipulative advertising causes consumers to choose the wrong product for their needs must be weighed against the utility consumers gain from such advertising. Due to the inherent uncertainty of utility calculations, it may be unclear which effect would predominate. Sometimes, though, the gains could outweigh the losses: that is, manipulative advertising could generate more utility than purely informative advertising.

But how can "manipulated" desires and purchases generate more utility than their "rational" counterparts? One answer emerges from the dark masterpiece of the literature on manipulative advertising—Theodore Levitt's 1970 contribution to the *Harvard Business Review.* Levitt's main thesis is that "embellishment and distortion are among advertising's legitimate and socially desirable purposes" (Levitt 1970, 85). His determinedly nonlinear argument for that conclusion may be regarded as proceeding through several steps. The first is his assertion that when seen without illusions, human life is a poor thing. Natural reality, Levitt insists, is "crudely fashioned"; "crude, drab, and generally oppressive"; and "drab, dull, [and] anguished" (86, 90). For this reason, people try to transcend it whenever they can. "Everyone everywhere wants to modify, transform, embellish, enrich, and reconstruct the world around him—to introduce into an otherwise harsh or bland existence some sort of purposeful and distorting alleviation" (87). People do so mainly through artistic endeavor, but also through advertising. "[W]e use art, architecture, literature, and the rest, and advertising as well, to shield ourselves, in advance of experience, from the stark and plain reality in which we are fated to live" (90). Thus, "[m]any of the so-called distortions of advertising, product design, and packaging may be viewed as a paradigm of the many responses that man makes to the conditions of survival in the environment" (90).

From all this, it follows that consumers demand more than "pure operating functionality" from the products they buy (89). As Charles Revson of Revlon, Inc. once said: "In the factory we make cosmetics; in the store we sell hope" (85). Thus, "[i]t is not cosmetic chemicals women want, but the seductive charm promised by the alluring symbols with which these chemicals have been surrounded—hence the rich and exotic packages in which they are sold, and the suggestive advertising with which they are promoted" (85). In other words, consumers demand an expanded notion of functionality which includes "'non-mechanical' utilities," and do so to "help . . . solve a problem of life" (89). Therefore, "the product" they buy includes not only narrowly functional attributes, but also the emotional or affective content produced by its packaging and advertising. "The promises and images which imaginative ads and sculptured packages induce in us are as much the product as the physical materials themselves. . . . [T]hese ads and packagings describe the product's fullness for us; in our minds, the product becomes a complex abstraction which is . . . the conception of a perfection which has not yet been experienced" (89–90). . . .

To Levitt, therefore, we do not merely buy a physical product, but also a set of positive feelings connected with it by advertising. If his argument is sound, those feelings give us extra utility above and beyond the utility we get from the product's performance of its functions. This extra utility might well outweigh the utility we lose because manipulative advertising has made us buy a product that is suboptimum in purely functional terms and that we would not have bought were advertising only informative.

Is Levitt's argument sound? Although his description may not apply to all people, or even to most, it hardly seems ridiculous. People who object to Levitt's contention that human life is crude, drab, and dull should recall that he is speaking of a human life we infrequently experience—human life absent the embellishments all civilizations try to give it. If his contention is correct, the need to transcend our natural condition is an obvious motive for those embellishments. John Waide, however, insists that our need for embellishment can be satisfied without manipulative advertising—through, for example, ideals, fantasies, heroes, and dreams (Waide 1987, 76). But why assume this? If the need for comforting illusions is strong and pervasive, why should embellishment not extend to the products people buy?

Bigger problems, however, arise from Levitt's assumption that consumers are aware of advertising's illusions. If people know that advertising lies, how can they derive much psychic benefit—i.e., much utility—from its embellishments? Worse yet, products tend not to deliver on manipulative advertising's promises of sex, status, security, and the like. When this is so, how can such advertising deliver much utility to the consumers it controls (cf. Waide 1987, 75)? Indeed, the gap between manipulative advertising's implicit promises and its actual performance may lead to frustrated expectations and significant *disutility*.

Recall, however, that for Levitt consumers want and need to be manipulated because life without advertising's illusions is too much to bear. If so, it is unlikely that everyone would be *continuously* aware of advertising's illusions and the low chance of their realization. Only intermittently, in other words, would people assume a tough-minded, rational-actor mentality toward advertising. On other occasions, some would effectively suspend disbelief in advertising's embellishments. Although they might retain latent knowledge of those illusions, that knowledge would not be constantly present to their consciousness. And when the illusions rule, they could generate real satisfactions.

Are these assumptions about consumers realistic ones? To me, they are plausible as applied to some people some of the time. . . . There . . . is nothing ridiculous in assuming that people gain utility by accepting advertising's illusions, while retaining some latent and/or intermittent knowledge of their condition. . . .

Autonomy

All things considered, the utilitarian arguments against manipulative advertising are unimpressive. Indeed, utilitarianism might even support that practice. Galbraith claimed that little utility is generated when we satisfy contrived wants. But the connection between a desire's origin outside the individual and the low utility resulting from its satisfaction is unclear. At first glance, it appears that manipulative advertising robs consumers of utility by inducing them to buy functionally suboptimal products. But while this may be true, the resulting utility losses arguably are counterbalanced by the utility people gain from manipulative advertising. . . .

The autonomy-related objection to manipulative advertising

To some people, however, the preceding points may say more about utilitarianism's deficiencies than about manipulative advertising's worth. One standard criticism of utilitarianism emphasizes its indifference to the moral quality of the means by which utility is maximized. Thus, even if manipulative advertising increases consumers' utility, it is bad because it does so by suppressing their ability to make intelligent, self-directed product choices on the basis of their own values and interests. In a word, manipulative advertising now seems objectionable because it denies personal *autonomy*.

Among the many strands within the notion of autonomy, one of the most common equates it with self-government or self-determination. According to Steven Lukes, for example, autonomy is "self-direction"; the autonomous person's "thought and action are his own, and [are] not determined by agencies or causes outside his control" (Lukes 1973, 52). At the social level, Lukes adds, an individual is autonomous "to the degree to which he subjects the pressures and norms with which he is confronted to conscious and critical evaluation, and forms intentions and reaches practical decisions as the result of independent and rational reflection" (52).

If manipulative advertising has the effects this essay assumes, it apparently denies autonomy to the individuals it successfully controls. On this essay's assumptions, people become consumers and make product choices precisely through "agencies and causes outside [their] control," and not through "conscious and critical evaluation" or "independent and rational reflection." To Lippke [1990], moreover, advertising also has an "implicit content" that further suppresses autonomy. Among other things, this implicit content causes people to accept emotionalized, superficial, and oversimplified claims; desire ease and gratification rather than austerity and self-restraint; let advertisers dictate the meaning of the good life; defer to their peers; and think that consumer products are a means for acquiring life's nonmaterial goods (44–47). People so constituted are unlikely to be independent, self-governing agents who subject all social pressures to an internal critique. Nor is it likely that they would have much resistance to manipulative appeals to buy particular products.

*Are consumers autonomous on
Levitt's assumptions?*

On Levitt's assumptions, however, perhaps consumers do act autonomously when they submit to manipulative advertising. If Levitt is correct: (1) manipulative advertising works much as its critics say that it works; because (2) consumers suspend disbelief in its claims and embrace its illusions; because (3) they want, need, and demand those illusions to cope with human existence; while (4) nonetheless knowing on some level that those illusions indeed are illusions. In sum, one might say, advertising manipulates consumers because they knowingly and rationally want to be manipulated. That is, they half-consciously sacrifice their autonomy for reasons that make some sense on Levitt's assumptions about human life. In still other words, they more or less autonomously relinquish their autonomy. . . .

Levitt's argument, however, appears to concern only individual purchase decisions, and not advertising's assumed ability to socialize people to accept consumerism and reject autonomy. But his argument is broad enough to explain this second process. On Levitt's assumptions, people would more or less knowingly embrace consumerism because unfiltered reality is too much to bear, and would reject autonomy in favor of Lippke's "implicit content" because autonomy offers too little payoff at too much cost. If those assumptions are accurate, moreover, people arguably have sound reasons for behaving in these ways. . . .

The Categorical Imperative

One problem with some of the claims discussed thus far is that they present difficult empirical issues. This is plainly true of Levitt's claims. It also is true of Galbraith's assertion that because advertising-induced wants originate outside the individual, they have low urgency and therefore generate little utility when they are satisfied. The same can be said of Hayek's response to Galbraith. Given these problems, maybe manipulative advertising is best addressed by ethical theories whose conclusions do not depend on empirical matters such as consumer psychology, or on manipulation's consequences for utility. Kant's categorical imperative is an obvious candidate.

R. M. Hare made two Kantian arguments against manipulative advertising. "Kantians will say . . . that to manipulate people is not to treat them as ends—certainly not as autonomous legislating members of a kingdom of ends. . . . But even apart from that it is something that we prefer not to happen to us and therefore shall not will it as a universal maxim" (Hare 1984, 28). His reference, of course, was to the two major formulations of Kant's categorical imperative. The first, which comes in several versions, underlies Hare's second argument. The version employed here goes as follows: "Act only on that maxim through which you can at the same time will that it should become a universal law" (Kant 1964, 88). According to the second major formulation of the imperative, one must "[a]ct in such a way that you always treat humanity, whether in your own person or in the person of any other, never simply as a means, but always at the same time as an end" (96).

Under either formulation of the imperative, it seems, manipulative advertising stands condemned. Under the first formulation, it seems difficult to identify a maxim that would: (1) clearly justify manipulative advertising, and (2) be universalized by any advertiser. Consider, for example, the following possibility: "In order to induce purchases and make money, business people can use advertising tactics that undermine the rational evaluation and choice of products by associating them with desired states to which they have little or no real relation." Presumably, no one would will the maxim's universalization, because to do so is to waive any moral objection to manipulative advertising aimed at oneself. Manipulative advertising apparently fares even worse under the second statement of the categorical imperative. As James Rachels has noted, under this formulation "we may never *manipulate* people, or *use* people, to achieve our purposes" (Rachels 1993, 129). Instead, we should respect their rational nature by giving them the information that will enable them to make informed, autonomous decisions (Rachels 1993, 129–30). As the term *manipulative advertising* suggests, businesses that employ it to generate sales obviously try to use people as means to their own ends, and do so precisely by undermining their rationality and their ability to make informed, autonomous decisions.

Even in the Kantian realm, however, empirical concerns intrude. Suppose again that Levitt is right in claiming that people want and need manipulative advertising. Given this assumption, the relevant maxim becomes something like the following: "In order to induce purchases and make money, people can use manipulative advertising tactics that undermine the rational evaluation and choice of products and services, but only when such advertising tactics liberate consumers from their dark, stark, and depressing natural existence." Although I cannot speak for everyone (or for Kant), I might will this maxim's universalization if I found Levitt's conception of the human condition at all plausible. This illustrates a common criticism of the first formulation of the

categorical imperative: that one can manipulate the imperative to get the results one wishes by framing the maxim appropriately.

Even if Levitt's account is perfectly accurate, however, the second major statement of the imperative still creates problems for manipulative advertising. Here, the question seems to boil down to the following: are firms that employ manipulative advertising using a consumer merely as a means to their own ends and therefore violating the imperative if the consumer, in effect, needs and wants to be manipulated? If, as I suggested earlier, the suspension of disbelief required for one to accept manipulative advertising may be more or less reasonable, then advertisers conceivably *are* respecting consumers' rationality by providing them with product-related illusions. . . .

Virtue Ethics

Earlier I depicted Galbraith as a utilitarian, but other moral aspirations probably were at work within *The Affluent Society*. The book opened with the following quotation from Alfred Marshall: "The economist, like everyone else, must concern himself with the ultimate aims of man." Galbraith's conviction that consumerism does not rank high among those aims pervades much of his writing, and almost certainly informed his critique of advertising. However, the ethical values and theories previously considered in this essay do not state and enjoin the desirable substantive conditions of human life. . . .

Waide's alternative to such approaches is to examine "the virtues and vices at stake" in manipulative advertising (1987, 73), and to see "what kind of lives are sustained" by it (77). Stanley Benn sounds the same note when he suggests that the key question about advertising is whether it promotes "a valuable kind of life," with this determination depending on "some objective assessment of what constitutes excellence in human beings" (1967, 273). Because manipulative advertising encourages advertisers to ignore the well-being of their targets and encourages those targets to neglect the cultivation of nonmarket goods, Waide concludes that it makes us less virtuous persons and therefore is morally objectionable (1987, 74–75). Many other critics of advertising make the same general point. . . . Heilbroner called advertising "perhaps the single most value-destroying activity of a business civilization," due to the "subversive influence of the relentless effort to persuade people to change their lifeways, not out of any knowledge of, or deeply held convictions about, the 'good life,' but merely to sell whatever article or service is being pandered" (1976, 113–14). His main specific complaint is that by offering a constant stream of half-truths and deceptions, advertising makes "cynics of us all" (114). Virginia Held makes a related point when she criticizes advertising for undermining intellectual and artistic integrity (1984, 64–66).

To Christopher Lasch, on the other hand, advertising's greatest evil may be its tendency to leave consumers "perpetually unsatisfied, restless, anxious, and bored" (1978, 72). . . . One suspects that Lasch might reject advertising's consequences as inherently bad even if they did mark an increase in utility. The same probably holds for most of advertising's cultural critics. As a group, Michael Schudson remarks, they see "the emergence of a consumer culture as a devolution of manners, morals and even manhood, from a work-oriented production ethic of the past to the consumption, 'lifestyle'-obsessed, ethic-less pursuits of the present" (1986, 6–7).

Uniting all these varied criticisms of advertising is the notion that it promotes substantive behaviors, experiences, and states of character which are inherently undesirable, and that it is morally objectionable for this reason. . . . This essay assumes that manipulative advertising both creates a consumer culture and strongly influences individual purchase decisions. Its main means for accomplishing the second aim (and perhaps the first) is to associate the product with such nonmarket goods as sex, status, and power. On those assumptions, manipulative advertising almost certainly undermines such standard virtues as honesty and benevolence in its practi-

tioners, and arguably dilutes its targets' moderation, reasonableness, self-control, self-discipline, and self-reliance (Rachels 1993, 163 [listing these virtues]). . . .

Manipulative Advertising's Last Defense

All things considered, virtue ethics appears to be the best basis for attacking manipulative advertising. In particular, it seems to dispose of a defense that has plagued our other three attacks on such advertising: Levitt's claim that people want and need advertising's illusions and therefore more or less knowingly and willingly embrace it. Like our other bases for attacking manipulative advertising, however, virtue ethics is not assumed to be an absolute. This might mean that the claims of virtue would have to give way if human beings simply could not endure without advertising's illusions or if its psychic satisfactions give people enormous amounts of utility.

In any event, there is yet another possible defense of manipulative advertising. This defense is mainly utilitarian, but it also implicates my other three ethical criteria to some degree. It arises because by hypothesis all my criteria must be weighed against competing moral claims. The defense does not so much challenge the assertion that manipulative advertising is bad, as argue that it is the lesser of two evils.

Throughout this essay, I have assumed for the sake of argument that manipulative advertising's critics are correct in their assessment of its effects. As we have seen, these people usually maintain that manipulative advertising plays an important role in socializing people to consume. This means that on the critics' view of things, manipulative advertising is central to the functioning of modern consumer society. But if manipulative advertising is central to the system's operation, how safely can it be condemned? Assuming that the condemnation is effective, manipulative advertising disappears, and all advertising becomes informative, people gradually would be weaned from their consumerist ways. This is likely to create social instability, with a more authoritarian form of government the likely end result. That, in turn, could well mean an environment in which aggregate utility is lower than it is today, human autonomy and rational nature are less respected, and/or the virtues less recognized.

One set of reasons for these conclusions is largely economic. If people become less consumerist as manipulative advertising leaves the scene, aggregate demand and economic output should decline. At first glance, this would seem to be of little consequence because by hypothesis people would value material things less. The problem is that the economic losses probably will be unevenly distributed: for example, some businesses will fail and some will not, and some people will lose their jobs while others stay employed. These inequalities are a potential source of social instability. Both to redress them and to preserve order, government is likely to intervene. This may involve a significant increase in outright governmental coercion. . . .

To my knowledge, Waide is the only business ethicist to raise these kinds of problems, and he finds himself without a solution to them. Because "[i]t seems unlikely that [manipulative] advertising will end suddenly," however, Waide is "confident that we will have the time and the imagination to adapt our economy to do without it" (1987, 77). Although I suspect that Waide is too optimistic, I have no solution to the dilemma either. Thus, I am left with the unsatisfactory conclusion that while various moral arguments may provide sound bases for attacking manipulative advertising, prudential considerations dictate that none of them be pressed too vigorously. Manipulative advertising's ultimate justification, in other words, may be its status as a necessary evil.

Concluding Remarks

For all the preceding reasons, it seems that there is no completely definitive basis for con-

demning manipulative advertising. But this obviously is not to say that the practice is morally unproblematic. Of my four suggested attacks on the practice, virtue ethics seems the strongest, with Kantianism a close second, autonomy third, and utilitarianism last. Indeed, utilitarianism may even support manipulative advertising. The main reason is that the practice's three most important defenses—Levitt's argument, the assertion that there is little connection between a want's origin outside the individual and the benefit resulting from its satisfaction, and manipulative advertising's centrality to our economic system—are more or less utilitarian in nature.

Except perhaps for hard-core utilitarians, therefore, manipulative advertising actually works. Specifically, I assumed that such advertising is a morally dubious practice. However, this conclusion may depend heavily on a critical assumption made earlier: that manipulative advertising: (1) socializes people to adopt a consumerist lifestyle, and (2) strongly influences individual purchase decisions. But what happens if, by and large, each assumption is untrue?

On first impressions, at least, it appears that if manipulative advertising is inefficacious, utilitarianism, autonomy, and virtue ethics largely cease to be bases for criticizing it. . . .

However, Kantian objections to manipulative advertising might well remain even if it is inefficacious. On that assumption, admittedly, perhaps one would will the universalization of a maxim permitting such advertising. If manipulative advertising simply fails to work, moreover, maybe it does not treat consumers merely as means to advertisers' ends. But such arguments ignore the strong anti-consequentialism of Kant's ethics, which arguably renders advertising's ineffectiveness irrelevant. More importantly, those arguments ignore Kant's stress on the motives with which people should act. The only thing that is unqualifiedly good, Kant says, is a good will; and the good will is good not because of what it accomplishes, but simply because it wills the good (Kant 1964, 61–62).

Even if manipulative advertising is unsuccessful, advertisers presumably try to make it work. Unless they believe that their efforts would benefit consumers in the end, it is unlikely that they are acting with a good will when they devise and employ their stratagems.

At a first cut, therefore, it seems that if manipulative advertising is ineffective, the only significant ethical objections to it are Kantian. (To these we might add the money wasted on the practice, as well as its effect on the virtue of its practitioners.) For those inclined to ignore Kantian objections, therefore, it seems that manipulative advertising's rightness or wrongness depends less on ethical theory than on empirical questions within the purview of the social sciences. . . . As the preceding discussion suggests, the most important such question is the extent to which manipulative advertising actually affects purchase decisions and socializes people to consume. Even if manipulative advertising actually has those effects, other more or less empirical issues would remain. These include the validity of Levitt's arguments, Galbraith's asserted connection between a desire's origin outside the individual and the low utility resulting from its satisfaction, and manipulative advertising's contribution to gross domestic product. All these questions, I submit, are unlikely to be answered any time soon.

REFERENCES

Benn, S. (1967) "Freedom and persuasion." *The Australasian Journal of Philosophy* 45: 259–75.

Galbraith, J. K. (1958) *The Affluent Society* (Boston: Houghton Mifflin).

Genge, W. (1985) "Ads stimulate the economy." *Business and Society Review* 1, no. 55: 58–59.

Hare, R. M. (1984) "Commentary." *Business and Professional Ethics Journal* 3, nos. 3 & 4: 23–28.

Hayek, F. A. (1961) "The *non sequitur* of the 'dependence effect.'" *Southern Economic Journal* 27: 346–48.

Heilbroner, R. (1976) *Business Civilization in Decline* (New York: W. W. Norton).

Held, V. (1984) "Advertising and program content." *Business and Professional Ethics Journal* 3, nos. 3 & 4: 61–76.

Kant, I. (1964) *Groundwork of the Metaphysic of Morals* (New York: Harper Torchbook, H. J. Paton tr.).

Lasch, C. (1978) *The Culture of Narcissism: American Life in An Age of Diminishing Expectations* (New York: W. W. Norton).

Levitt, T. (1970). "The morality (?) of advertising." *Harvard Business Review* (July-August): 84–92.

Lippke, R. (1990) "Advertising and the social conditions of autonomy." *Business and Professional Ethics Journal* 8, no. 4: 35–58.

Lukes, S. (1973) *Individualism* (Oxford: Basil Blackwell).

Rachels, J. (1993) *The Elements of Moral Philosophy* (New York: McGraw-Hill, 2nd ed.).

Schudson, M. (1986). *Advertising, the Uneasy Persuasion: Its Dubious Impact on American Society* (New York: Basic Books, 2nd ed.).

Waide, J. (1987) "The making of self and world in advertising." *Journal of Business Ethics* 6, no. 2: 73–79.

Review and Discussion Questions

1. Give examples of advertisements that you consider manipulative. Does advertising socialize people to a life of consumption? To what extent does it influence or even dictate our individual brand and product choices?

2. Assess Galbraith's contention that because advertising induces or creates consumer wants, those wants are not urgent and their satisfaction does not generate much utility.

3. Is Levitt correct that consumers need and want the illusions of advertising? Is it true that as consumers we are buying not only a physical product, but also a set of positive feelings connected with it by advertising? Do you agree with Levitt that "embellishment and distortion are among advertising's legitimate and socially desirable purposes"? Do the promises and images of advertising bring us genuine satisfaction?

4. Does Kant's categorical imperative forbid manipulative advertising? Explain why or why not.

5. Assuming that manipulative advertising is effective, does it undermine one's autonomy? Does it promote undesirable behaviors and character traits, as the virtue-ethics critique alleges?

6. Assess the argument that manipulative advertising is a necessary evil because it is central to the continued functioning of our socioeconomic system. In your view, does advertising play a positive or negative role in our society?

7. Is manipulative advertising wrong? What do you see as the strongest ethical argument against it? Suppose manipulative advertising doesn't work. Would it still be wrong?

The Ethics of Sales

THOMAS L. CARSON

In this essay, Thomas L. Carson, professor of philosophy at Loyola University of Chicago, examines the moral obligations of salespeople. After explaining and criticizing David Holley's well-known account of the ethics of sales, Carson puts forward his own theory, which identifies four moral duties of salespeople. Carson contends that his theory provides intuitively plausible results in concrete cases, that it avoids the weaknesses of Holley's approach, and that it explains why different kinds of salespeople have different kinds of duties to their customers. He goes on to argue that the most plausible version of the Golden Rule supports his theory. He concludes by discussing several examples that illustrate and clarify his theory.

Study Questions

1. What is the difference between lying and deception? According to Carson, does withholding information constitute deception? What about concealing information?

2. What is the principle of *caveat emptor*? What legal duty do sellers now have?

3. Holley writes that salespersons are required to avoid undermining the conditions of an acceptable exchange. What three conditions are necessary for an "acceptable exchange"?

4. What are Carson's three criticisms of Holley?

5. According to Carson, what four duties do salespersons have?

6. What is the Golden Rule, as stated by Carson, and how does it support the four duties of salespersons? Explain the argument that Carson gives in defense of the Golden Rule.

Sales

THE ETHICS OF SALES is an important, but neglected, topic in business ethics. Approximately 10 percent of the U.S. work force is involved in sales. In addition, most of us occasionally sell major holdings such as used cars and real estate. Because sales were long governed by the principle of *caveat emptor*, discussions of the ethics of sales usually focus on the ethics of withholding information and the question "What sort of information is a salesperson obligated to reveal to customers?"

One of the best treatments of this topic is David Holley's paper "A Moral Evaluation of Sales Practices." In this essay, I explain Holley's theory, propose several criticisms, and formulate what I take to be a more plausible theory about the duties of salespeople. My theory avoids the objections I raise against Holley and yields intuitively plausible results when applied to cases. I also defend my theory by appeal to the golden rule and offer a defense of the version of the golden rule to which I appeal.

Preliminaries: A Conceptual Roadmap

We need to distinguish between lying, deception, withholding information, and concealing information. Roughly, deception is intentionally causing someone to have false beliefs. Standard dictionary definitions of lying say that a lie is a false statement intended to deceive others. The *Oxford English Dictionary* (1989) defines a lie as: "a false statement made with the intent to deceive." *Webster's* (1963) gives the following definition of the verb *lie:* "to make an untrue statement with intent to deceive." (We might want to add a third condition to this definition and say that in order for a false statement to be a lie, the person who makes it must know or believe that it is false. The third condition makes a difference in cases in which someone attempts to deceive another person by means of a false statement that he mistakenly believes to be true. Nothing in the present essay turns on this issue.) Lying arguably requires the intent to deceive others—I express my doubts about this in Carson (1988)—but lies that don't succeed in causing others to have false beliefs are not instances of deception. The word *deception* implies success in causing others to have false beliefs, but lying is often unsuccessful in causing deception. A further difference between lying and deception is that, while a lie must be a false statement, deception needn't involve false statements; true statements can be deceptive and many forms of deception do not involve making statements of any sort. Thus, many instances of deception do not constitute lying. Withholding information does not constitute deception. It is not a case of *causing* someone to have false beliefs; it is merely a case of failing to correct false beliefs or incomplete information. On the other hand, actively concealing information usually constitutes deception.

The Common Law Principle of *Caveat Emptor*

According to the common law principle of *caveat emptor,* sellers are not required to inform prospective buyers about the properties of the goods they sell. Under *caveat emptor,* sales and contracts to sell are legally enforceable even if the seller fails to inform the buyer of serious defects in the goods that are sold. Buyers themselves are responsible for determining the quality of the goods they purchase. In addition, English common law sometimes called for the enforcement of sales in cases in which sellers made false or misleading statements about the goods they sold (Atiyah 464–65).

Currently, all U.S. states operate under the Uniform Commercial Code of 1968. Section 2-313 of the code defines the notion of sellers' warranties (Preston 52). The code provides that all factual affirmations or statements about the goods being sold are warranties. This means that sales are not valid or legally enforceable if the seller makes false statements about the goods s/he is selling. . . . Many local ordinances require that people who sell real estate inform buyers about all known serious defects of the property they sell. These ordinances are also a significant limitation on the traditional principle of *caveat emptor.*

Deceptive sales practices also fall under the purview of the Federal Trade Commission (FTC). The FTC prohibits deceptive sales practices—practices likely to materially mislead reasonable consumers (FTC Statement 1983).

Many salespeople take complying with the law to be an acceptable moral standard for their conduct and claim that they have no moral duty to provide buyers with information about the goods they sell, except for that information which the law requires for an enforceable sale.

Holley's Theory

Holley's theory is based on his concept of a "voluntary" or "mutually beneficial" market exchange (Holley uses the terms *voluntary exchange* and *mutually beneficial exchange* interchangeably). He says that a voluntary exchange occurs "only if" the following conditions are met (Holley takes his conditions to be *necessary* conditions for an acceptable exchange):

1. Both buyer and seller understand what they are giving up and what they are receiving in return.

2. Neither buyer nor seller is compelled to enter into the exchange as a result of coercion, severely restricted alternatives, or other constraints on the ability to choose.

3. Both buyer and seller are able at the time of the exchange to make rational judgments about its costs and benefits. (Holley 463)

These three conditions admit of degrees of satisfaction. An ideal exchange is an exchange involving people who are fully informed, fully rational, and "enter into the exchange entirely of their own volition" (Holley 464). The conditions for an ideal exchange are seldom, if ever, met in practice. However, Holley claims that it is still possible to have an "acceptable exchange" if the parties are "adequately informed, rational, and free from compulsion."

According to Holley, "the primary duty of salespeople to customers is to avoid undermining the conditions of an acceptable exchange." He makes it clear that, on his view, acts of omission (as well as acts of commission) can undermine the conditions of an acceptable exchange (Holley 464).

Because of the complexity of many goods and services, customers often lack information necessary for an acceptable exchange. Careful examination of products will not necessarily reveal problems or defects. According to Holley, *caveat emptor* is not acceptable as a moral principle, because customers often lack information necessary for an acceptable exchange. In such cases, salespeople are morally obligated to give information to the buyer. The question then is: *What kind of information* do salespeople need to provide buyers in order to ensure that the buyer is adequately informed? Holley attempts to answer this question in the following passage in which he appeals to the golden rule:

> Determining exactly how much information needs to be provided is not always clear-cut. We must in general rely on our assessments of what a reasonable person would want to know. As a practical guide, a salesperson might consider, "What would I want to know, if I were considering buying this product?" (Holley 467)

This principle is very demanding, perhaps more demanding than Holley realizes. Presumably, most reasonable people would *want* to know *a great deal* about the things they are thinking of buying. They might want to know *everything* relevant to the decision whether or not to buy something (more on this point shortly).

Criticisms of Holley

First, when time does not permit it, a salesperson cannot be morally obligated to provide all information necessary to ensure that the customer is adequately informed (all the information that a reasonable person would *want* to know if she were in the buyer's position). In many cases, reasonable customers would *want* to know a great deal of information. Often salespeople simply don't have the time to give all customers all the information Holley deems necessary for an acceptable exchange. Salespeople don't always know all the information that the buyer needs for an acceptable exchange. It cannot be a person's duty to do what is impossible—the statement that someone *ought* to do a certain act implies that she *can* do that act. Further, in many cases, salespeople don't know enough about the buyer's state of knowledge to know what information the buyer needs in order to be adequately informed. A salesperson might know that the buyer needs certain information in order to be adequately informed but not know whether or not the buyer possesses that information. One might reply that salespeople *should* know all the information necessary for an adequate exchange. However, on examination, this is not a plausible view. A salesperson in a large retail store cannot be expected to be knowledgeable about every product he sells. Often, it is impossible for realtors and used car salesmen to know much about the condition of the houses and cars they sell or the likelihood that they will need expensive repairs.

Second, Holley's theory implies that a salesperson in a store would be obligated to inform customers that a particular piece of merchandise in her store sells for less at a competing store if she knows this to be the case. (Presumably, she would *want* to know where she can get it for the lowest price, were she herself considering buying the product.) Not only do salespeople have no duty to provide this kind of information, (ordinarily) it would be wrong for them to do so.

Third, Holley's theory seems to yield unacceptable consequences in cases in which the buyer's alternatives are severely constrained. Suppose that a person with a very modest income attempts to buy a house in a small town. Her options are severely constrained, since there is only one house for sale in her price range. According to Holley, there can't be an acceptable exchange in such cases, because condition number 2 is not satisfied. However, it's not clear what he thinks sellers ought to do in such cases. The seller can't be expected to remove these constraints by giving the buyer money or building more homes in town. Holley's view seems to imply that it would be wrong for anyone to sell or rent housing to such a person. This result is unacceptable.

Toward a More Plausible Theory About the Ethics of Sales

I believe that salespeople have the following moral duties regarding the disclosure of information when dealing with *rational adult consumers* (cases involving children or adults who are not fully rational raise special problems that I will not try to deal with here):

1. Salespeople should provide buyers with safety warnings and precautions about the goods they sell. (Sometimes it is enough for salespeople to call attention to written warnings and precautions that come with the goods and services in question. These warnings are unnecessary if the buyers already understand the dangers or precautions in question.)

2. Salespeople should refrain from lying and deception in their dealings with customers.

3. As much as their knowledge and time constraints permit, salespeople should fully answer questions about the products and services they sell. They should answer questions forthrightly and not evade questions or withhold information that has been asked for (even if this makes it less likely that they will make a successful sale). Salespeople are obligated to answer questions about the goods and services they sell. However, they are justified in refusing to answer questions that would require them to reveal information about what their competitors are selling. They are not obligated to answer questions about competing goods and services or give information about other sellers.

4. Salespeople should not try to "steer" customers toward purchases that they have reason to think will prove to be harmful to customers (financial harm counts) or that customers will come to regret.

These are *prima facie* duties that can conflict with other duties and are sometimes overridden by other duties. A *prima facie* duty is one's actual duty, other things being equal; it is an actual duty in the absence of conflicting duties of greater or equal importance. For example, my *prima facie* duty to keep promises is my actual duty in the absence of conflicting duties of equal or greater importance. The above is a *minimal list* of the duties of salespeople concerning the disclosure of information. I believe that the following are also *prima facie* duties of salespeople, but I am much less certain that these principles can be justified:

5. Salespeople should not sell customers goods or services they have reason to think will prove to be harmful to customers or that the customers will come to regret later, without giving the customers their reasons for thinking that this is the case. (This duty does not hold if the seller has good reasons to think that the customer already possesses the information in question.)

6. Salespeople should not sell items they know to be defective or of poor quality without alerting customers to this. (This duty does not hold if the buyer can be reasonably expected to know about the poor quality of what he is buying.)

I have what I take to be strong arguments for 1–4, but I'm not so sure that I can justify 5 and 6. I believe that reasonable people can disagree about 5 and 6. (I have very little to say about 5 and 6 in the present essay. See Carson [2001] for a discussion of arguments for 5 and 6.)

There are some important connections between duties 2, 4, and 6. Lying and deception in sales are not confined to lying to or deceiving customers about the goods one sells. Many salespeople misrepresent their own motives to customers/clients. Almost all salespeople invite the trust of customers/clients and claim, implicitly or explicitly, to be acting in the interests of customers/clients. Salespeople often ask customers to defer to their judgment about what is best for them. For most salespeople, gaining the trust of customers or clients is essential for success. Many

salespeople are *not* interested in helping customers in the way they represent themselves as being. A salesperson who misrepresents her motives, and intentions to customers violates rule 2. This simultaneous inviting and betrayal of trust is a kind of treachery. In ordinary cases, rules against lying and deception alone prohibit salespeople from steering customers toward goods or services they have reason to think will be bad for them. It is difficult to steer someone in this way without lying or deception, e.g., saying that you believe that a certain product is best for someone when you don't believe this to be the case. Similar remarks apply to selling defective goods. Often, it is impossible to do this without lying to or deceiving customers. In practice, most or many violations of rules 4 and 6 are also violations of rule 2.

A Justification for My Theory

Rules 1–4 yield intuitively plausible results in concrete cases and avoid all of the objections I raised against Holley. They can also be justified by appeal to the golden rule.

Taken together, rules 1–4 give us an intuitively plausible theory about the duties of salespeople regarding the disclosure of information; they give more acceptable results in actual cases than Holley's theory. They can account for cases in which the conduct of salespeople seems clearly wrong, e.g., cases of lying, deception, and steering customers into harmful decisions. Unlike Holley's theory, rules 1–4 do not make unreasonable demands on salespeople. They don't require that salespeople provide information that they don't have or spend more time with customers than they can spend. Nor do they require salespeople to divulge information about the virtues of what their competitors are selling.

In addition, my theory explains why different kinds of salespeople have different kinds of duties to their customers. For example, ordinarily, realtors have a duty to provide much more information to customers than sales clerks who sell inexpensive items in gift stores. My theory explains this difference in terms of the following:

1. the realtor's greater knowledge and expertise;

2. the much greater amount of time the realtor can devote to the customer;

3. the greater importance of the purchase of a home than the purchase of a small gift and the greater potential for harm or benefit to the buyer; and (in some cases)

4. implicit or explicit claims by the realtor to be acting on behalf of prospective home buyers (clerks in stores rarely make such claims).

The golden rule

I think that the golden rule is most plausibly construed as a consistency principle (those who violate the golden rule are guilty of inconsistency). The following version of the golden rule can be justified.

> **GR:** Consistency requires that if you think that it would be morally permissible for someone to do a certain act to another person, then you must consent to someone else doing the same act to you in relevantly similar circumstances.

How the golden rule supports my theory

Given this version of the golden rule, any rational and consistent moral judge who makes judgments about the moral obligations of salespeople will have to accept rules 1–4 as *prima facie* duties. Consider each duty in turn:

1. All of us have reason to fear the hazards about us in the world; we depend on others to warn us of those hazards. Few people would survive to adulthood were it not for the warnings of others about such things as oncoming cars, live electric wires, and approaching tornadoes. No one who values her own life can honestly say that she is willing to have others fail to warn her of dangers.

2. Like everyone else, a salesperson needs correct information in order to act effectively to achieve her goals and advance her interests. She is not willing to act on the basis of false beliefs. Consequently, she is not willing to have others deceive her or lie to her about matters relevant to her decisions in the marketplace. She is not willing to have members of other professions (such as law and medicine) make it a policy to deceive her or lie to her whenever they can gain financially from doing so.

3. Salespeople have questions about the goods and services they themselves buy. They can't say that they are willing to have others evade or refuse to answer those questions. We want our questions to be answered by salespeople or else we wouldn't ask them. We are not willing to have salespeople evade or refrain from answering our questions. (Digression: Rule 3 permits salespeople to refuse to answer questions that would force them to provide information about their competitors. Why should we say *this*? Why not say instead that salespeople are obligated to answer *all questions* that customers ask? The answer is as follows: A salesperson's actions affect *both* her customers and her employer. In applying the golden rule to this issue she can't simply ask what kind of information she would want were she in the customer's position [Holley poses the question in just this way]. Rule 3 can probably be improved upon, but it is a decent first approximation. A disinterested person who was not trying to give preference to the interests of salespeople, employers, or customers could endorse 3 as a policy for salespeople to follow. We can and must recognize the legitimacy of employers' demands for loyalty. The role of being an advocate or agent for someone who is selling things is legitimate within certain

bounds—almost all of us are willing to have real estate agents work for us. A rational person could consent to the idea that everyone follow principles such as rule 3.)

4. All of us are capable of being manipulated by others into doing things that harm us, especially in cases in which others are more knowledgeable than we are. No one can consent to the idea that other people (or salespeople) should manipulate us into doing things that harm us whenever doing so is to their own advantage. Salespeople who claim that it would be permissible for them to make it a policy to deceive customers, fail to warn them about dangers, evade their questions, or manipulate them into doing things that are harmful to them whenever doing so is advantageous to them are inconsistent because they are not willing to have others do the same to them. They must allow that 1–4 are *prima facie* moral duties.

Rules 1–4 are only *prima facie* duties. The golden rule can account for the cases in which 1–4 are overridden by other more important duties. For example, we would be willing to have other people violate rules 1–4 if doing so were necessary in order to save the life of an innocent person. In practice, violating 1, 2, 3, or 4 is permissible only in very rare cases. The financial interests of salespeople seldom justify violations of 1, 2, 3, or 4. The fact that a salesperson can make more money by violating 1, 2, 3, or 4 would not justify her in violating any of these unless she has very pressing financial obligations that she cannot meet otherwise. Often, salespeople need to meet certain minimum sales quotas to avoid being fired. Suppose that a salesperson needs to make it a policy to violate 1–4 in order to meet her sales quotas and keep her job. Would this justify her in violating 1–4? *Possibly.* But, in order for this to be the case, the following conditions would have to be met: (a) she has important moral obligations such as feeding and housing her family that require her to be employed (needing money to keep one's family in an expen-

sive house or take them to Disney World wouldn't justify violating 1–4); and (b) she can't find another job that would enable her to meet her obligations without violating 1–4 (or other equally important duties). Those salespeople who can't keep their jobs or make an adequate income without violating 1–4 should seek other lines of employment.

A Defense of the Version of the Golden Rule Employed Earlier

My argument is as follows:

1. Consistency requires that if you think that it would be morally permissible for someone to do a certain act to another person, then you must grant that it would be morally permissible for someone to do that same act to you in relevantly similar circumstances.

2. Consistency requires that if you think that it would be morally permissible for someone to do a certain act to you in certain circumstances, then you must *consent* to him/her doing that act to you in those circumstances.

Therefore,

GR: Consistency requires that if you think that it would be morally permissible for someone to do a certain act to another person, then you must consent (not object to) someone doing the same act to you in relevantly similar circumstances. (You are inconsistent if you think that it would be morally permissible for someone to do a certain act to another person, but do not consent to someone doing the same act to you in relevantly similar circumstances.) (This argument follows the argument given by Gensler 89–90.)

This argument is valid, i.e., the conclusion follows from the premises, and both its premises are true. Both premises are consistency requirements. Premise 1 addresses questions about the consistency of a person's different moral beliefs. Premise 2 addresses questions about whether a person's moral beliefs are consistent with her attitudes and actions. Our attitudes and actions can be either consistent or inconsistent with the moral judgments we accept.

Premise 1

Premise 1 follows from, or is a narrower version of, the universalizability principle (UP). The UP can be stated as follows:

> Consistency requires that, if one makes a moral judgment about a particular case, then one must make the same moral judgment about any similar case, unless there is a morally relevant difference between the cases.

Premise 1 is a principle of consistency for judgments about the moral permissibility of actions. The UP, by contrast, is a principle of consistency for *any kind of moral judgment,* including judgments about what things are good and bad.

Premise 2

How shall we understand what is meant by "consenting to" something? For our present purposes, we should not take consenting to something to be the same as desiring it or trying to bring it about. My thinking that it is morally permissible for you to beat me at chess does not commit me to desiring that you beat me, nor does it commit me to playing so as to allow you to beat me. Consenting to an action is more like not objecting to it, not criticizing, or not resenting the other person for doing it. If I think that it is permissible for you to beat me at chess then I cannot object to your beating me. I am inconsistent if I object to your doing something that I take to be morally permissible. If I claim that it is permissible for someone to do something to another person, then, on pain of inconsistency, I cannot object if someone else does the same thing to me in relevantly similar circumstances. The gist of my application of the golden rule to sales is that since we *do object* to salespeople doing such things as lying to us, deceiving us, and failing to answer our questions, we cannot consistently say that it is morally permissible for them to *do* these things.

Examples

I will discuss several cases to illustrate and clarify my theory.

Example A

I am selling a used car that I know has bad brakes; this is one of the reasons I am selling the car. You don't ask me any questions about the car, and I sell it to you without informing you of the problem with the brakes.

Example B

I am selling a used car that starts poorly in cold weather. You arrange to look at the car early in the morning on a very cold day. I don't own a garage so the car is out in the cold. With difficulty, I start it up and drive it for thirty minutes shortly before you look at it and then cover the car with snow to make it seem as if it hasn't been driven. The engine is still hot when you come and the car starts up immediately. You then purchase the car, remarking that you need a car that starts well in the cold to get to work, since you don't have a garage.

Example C

While working as a salesperson, I feign a friendly concern for a customer's interests. I say, "I will try to help you find the product that is best suited for your needs. I don't want you to spend any more money than you need to. Take as much time as you need." The customer believes me, but she is deceived. In fact, I couldn't care less about her welfare. I only want to sell her the highest priced item I can as quickly as I can. I don't like the customer; indeed, I am contemptuous of her.

In example A, I violate rule 1 and put the buyer and other motorists, passengers, and pedestrians at risk. In example B, I violate rules 2 and 5. In example C, I violate rule 2. In the absence of conflicting obligations that are at least as important as the rules I violate, my actions in cases A–C are morally wrong.

Example D: a longer case (an actual case)

In 1980, I received a one-year fellowship from The National Endowment for the Humanities. The fellowship paid for my salary, but not my fringe benefits. Someone in the benefits office of my university told me that I had the option of continuing my health insurance through the university if I paid for the premiums out of my own pocket. I told the benefits person that this was a lousy deal and that I could do better by going to a private insurance company. I went to the office of Prudential Insurance agent Mr. A. O. "Ed" Mokarem. I told him that I was looking for a one-year medical insurance policy to cover me during the period of the fellowship and that I planned to resume my university policy when I returned to teaching. (The university provided this policy free of charge to all faculty who were teaching.) He showed me a comparable Prudential policy that cost about half as much as the university's policy. He explained the policy to me. I asked him to fill out the forms so that I could purchase the policy. He then told me that there was a potential problem I should consider. He said roughly the following:

> You will want to return to your free university policy next year when you return to teaching. The Prudential policy is a one-year terminal policy. If you develop any serious medical problems during the next year, Prudential will probably consider you "uninsurable" and will not be willing to sell you health insurance in the future. If you buy the Prudential policy, you may encounter the same problems with your university policy. Since you will be dropping this policy *voluntarily*, they will have the right to underwrite your application for re-enrollment. If you develop a serious health problem during the next year, their underwriting decision could be "Total Rejection," imposing some waivers and/or exclusions, or (at best) subjecting your coverage to the "pre-existing conditions clause," which would not cover any pre-existing conditions until you have been covered under the new policy for at least a year.

If I left my current health insurance for a year, I risked developing a costly medical condition for which no one would be willing to insure me. That would have been a very foolish risk to take. So, I thanked him very much and, swallowing my pride, went back to renew my health insurance coverage through the university. I never bought any insurance from Mr. Mokarem and never had occasion to send him any business.

I have discussed this case with numerous classes through the years. It usually generates a lively discussion. Most of my students do not think that Mr. Mokarem was morally obligated to do what he did, but they don't think that what he did was wrong either—they regard his actions as supererogatory or above and beyond the call of duty.

My View About Example D. On my theory, this is a difficult case to assess. If rules 1–4 are a salesperson's only duties concerning the disclosure of information, then Mr. Mokarem was not obligated to inform me as he did. (In this case, the information in question was information about a *competing product*—the university's health insurance policy.) If rule 5 is a *prima facie* duty of salespeople, then (assuming that he had no conflicting moral duties of greater or equal importance) it was his duty, all things considered, to inform me as he did. Since I am uncertain that 5 can be justified, I'm not sure whether or not Mr. Mokarem was obligated to do what he did or whether his actions were supererogatory. This case illustrates part of what is at stake in the question of whether rule 5 is a *prima facie* duty of salespeople.

ACKNOWLEDGMENTS

This essay is a revised and abridged version of material from two earlier essays, "Deception and Withholding Information in Sales," *Business Ethics Quarterly* 11 (2001): 275–306, and "Ethical Issues in Selling and Advertising," *The Blackwell Guide to Business Ethics,* ed. Norman Bowie (Oxford: Blackwell, 2002), 186–205. Many thanks to Ivan Preston for his very generous and helpful advice and criticisms. Everyone interested in these topics should read his work.

REFERENCES

Atiyah, P. S. (1979) *The Rise and Fall of Freedom of Contract.* Oxford: The Clarendon Press.

Carson, Thomas. (1988) "On the definition of lying: a reply to Jones and revisions." *Journal of Business Ethics,* 7: 509–14.

Carson, Thomas. (2001) "Deception and withholding information in sales." *Business Ethics Quarterly* 11: 275–306.

FTC policy statement on deception. (1983—still current) Available on the Web at: http://www.ftc.gov/bcp/guides/guides.htm then click on FTC Policy Statement on Deception.

Gensler, Harry. (1986) "A Kantian argument against abortion." *Philosophical Studies* 49: 83–98.

Holley, David. (1993) "A moral evaluation of sales practices." In Tom Beauchamp and Norman Bowie, eds., *Ethical Theory and Business,* fourth edition, 462–72. Englewood Cliffs, NJ: Prentice Hall.

Preston, Ivan. (1975) *The Great American Blow-Up: Puffery in Advertising and Selling.* Madison: University of Wisconsin Press, 1975.

Review and Discussion Questions

1. Do sellers have a moral duty to buyers that goes beyond merely complying with the law? Restate Holley's theory and assess the three criticisms that Carson makes of it. Do you find them persuasive?

2. Is Carson's interpretation of the Golden Rule the best way of understanding it? In your view, is the Golden Rule a basic principle of ethics? Explain why or why not. What implications does the Golden Rule have for salespeople?

3. Do Carson's duties 1 through 4 provide a more plausible account of the ethics of sales than Holley's theory does? Explain why or why not. Do you agree that the actions in examples A, B, and C are morally wrong?

4. Carson believes that he makes a strong case for duties 1 through 4, but that reasonable people can disagree about duties 5 and 6. In your view, do salespeople have duties 5 and 6? In example D, was Mr. Mokarem morally obligated to do what he did?

5. Do salespeople ever face ethical issues that Carson's theory doesn't answer? If so, give an example.

6. Have you encountered unethical conduct by a salesperson? Is such conduct widespread, or do most salespeople try to behave ethically? When salespeople do act unethically, what explains this, and what can be done about it?

Some Paradoxes of Whistleblowing

MICHAEL DAVIS

When is whistleblowing morally justified? In this essay, Michael Davis, professor of philosophy at the Illinois Institute of Technology, challenges the standard theory of justified whistleblowing, arguing that it gives rise to three paradoxes—the paradox of burden, the paradox of missing harm, and the paradox of failure. In its place he advocates what he calls the *complicity theory.* In contrast to the standard theory, which focuses on the whistleblower's obligation to prevent harm, the complicity theory justifies whistleblowing on the

From Business and Professional Ethics Journal *15 (Spring 1996). Reprinted by permission of the author. Some notes omitted.*

basis of the whistleblower's obligation to avoid complicity in wrongdoing. Davis tests his theory against a classic case of whistleblowing, Roger Boisjoly's testimony before the commission investigating the *Challenger* disaster. (A senior engineer at Morton-Thiokol, Boisjoly had recommended that the space shuttle *Challenger* not be launched because the temperature at the launch site had fallen below the safety range for the O-ring seals in the rocket boosters. Top management overrode the recommendation, and the next day, shortly after being launched, the *Challenger* exploded, killing its seven crew members.)

Study Questions

1. What are the three senses, distinguished by Davis, in which an act may be morally "justified"?

2. According to Davis, the police officer, the criminal informant, and the clerk who happens upon evidence of wrongdoing in another department are not whistleblowers. Why not?

3. According to the standard theory, when is whistleblowing morally permissible? When is it morally required?

4. Explain the paradox of burden, the paradox of missing harm, and the paradox of failure.

5. What two advantages does Davis say that his complicity theory has over the standard theory? What four differences does he highlight between the two theories?

Introduction

BY "PARADOX" I mean an apparent—and, in this case, real—inconsistency between theory (our systematic understanding of whistleblowing) and the facts (what we actually know, or think we know, about whistleblowing). What concerns me is not a few anomalies, the exceptions that test a rule, but a flood of exceptions that seems to swamp the rule.

This essay has four parts. The first states the standard theory of whistleblowing. The second argues that the standard theory is paradoxical, that it is inconsistent with what we know about whistleblowers. The third part sketches what seems to me a less paradoxical theory of whistleblowing. The fourth tests the new theory against one classic case of whistleblowing, Roger Boisjoly's testimony before the presidential commission investigating the *Challenger* disaster ("the Rogers Commission"). I use that case because the chief facts are both uncontroversial enough and well-known enough to make detailed exposition unnecessary. For the same reason, I also use that case to illustrate various claims about whistleblowing throughout the essay.

Justification and Whistleblowing

The standard theory is not about whistleblowing, as such, but about justified whistleblowing—and rightly so. Whether this or that is, or is not, whistleblowing is a question for lexicographers. For the rest of us, mere moral agents, the question is—when, if ever, is whistleblowing justified?

We may distinguish three (related) senses in which an act may be "justified." First, an act may be something morality permits. Many acts, for example, eating fruit at lunch, are morally justified in this weak sense. They are (all things considered) morally all right, though some of the alternatives are morally all right too. Second, acts may be morally justified in a stronger sense. Not only is doing them morally all right, but doing anything else instead is morally wrong. These acts are *morally* required. Third, some acts, though only morally justified in the weaker sense, are still required all things considered. That is, they are mandatory because of some non-moral consideration. They are *rationally* (but not morally) required.

I shall be concerned here only with *moral* justification, that is, with what morality permits or requires. I shall have nothing to say about when other considerations, for example, individual prudence or social policy, make (morally permissible) whistleblowing something reason requires.

Generally, we do not *need* to justify an act unless we have reason to think it wrong (whether morally wrong or wrong in some other way). So, for example, I do not need to justify eating fruit for lunch today, though I would if I were allergic to fruit or had been keeping a fast. We also do not need a justification if we believe the act in question wrong. We do not need a justification because, insofar as an act is wrong, justification is impossible. The point of justification is to show to be right an act the rightness of which has been put in (reasonable) doubt. Insofar as we believe the act wrong, we can only condemn or excuse it. To condemn it is simply to declare it wrong. To excuse it is to show that, while the act was wrong, the doer had good reason to do it, could not help doing it, or for some other reason should not suffer the response otherwise reserved for such a wrongdoer.

Most acts, though permitted or required by morality, need no justification. There is no reason to think them wrong. Their justification is too plain for words. Why then is whistleblowing so problematic that we need *theories* of its justification? What reason do we have to think whistleblowing might be morally wrong?

Whistleblowing always involves revealing information that would not ordinarily be revealed. But there is nothing morally problematic about that; after all, revealing information not ordinarily revealed is one function of science. Whistleblowing always involves, in addition, an actual (or at least declared) intention to prevent something bad that would otherwise occur. There is nothing morally problematic in that either. That may well be the chief use of information.

What seems to make whistleblowing morally problematic is its organizational context. A mere individual cannot blow the whistle (in any interesting sense); only a member of an organization, whether a current or a former member, can do so. Indeed, he can only blow the whistle on his own organization (or some part of it). So, for example, a police officer who makes public information about a burglary ring, though a member of an organization, does not blow the whistle on the burglary ring (in any interesting sense). He simply alerts the public. Even if he came by the information working undercover in the ring, his revelation could not be whistleblowing. While secret agents, spies, and other infiltrators need a moral justification for what they do, the justification they need differs from that which whistleblowers need. Infiltrators gain their information under false pretenses. They need a justification for that deception. Whistleblowers generally do not gain their information under false pretenses.

What if, instead of being a police officer, the revealer of information about the burglary ring were an ordinary member of the ring? Would such an informer be a (justified) whistleblower? I think not. The burglary ring is a criminal organization. The whistleblower's organization never is, though it may occasionally engage in criminal activity (knowingly or inadvertently). So, even a burglar, who, having a change of heart, volunteers information about his ring to the police or the newspaper, does not need to justify his act in the way the whistleblower does. Helping to destroy a criminal organization by revealing its secrets is morally much less problematic than whistleblowing.

What then is morally problematic about the whistleblower's organizational context? The whistleblower cannot blow the whistle using just any information obtained in virtue of membership in the organization. A clerk in Accounts who, happening upon evidence of serious wrongdoing while visiting a friend in Quality Control, is not a whistleblower just because she passes the information to a friend at the *Tribune*. She is more like a self-appointed spy. She seems to differ from the whistleblower, or at least from clear cases of the whistleblower, precisely in her relation to the information in question. To be a whistleblower is to reveal information with which one is *entrusted*.

But it is more than that. The whistleblower does not reveal the information to save his own skin (for example, to avoid perjury under oath). He has no excuse for revealing what his organization does not want revealed. Instead, he claims to be doing what he should be doing. If he cannot honestly make that claim—if, that is, he does not have that intention—his revelation is not whistleblowing (and so, not justified as whistleblowing), but something analogous, much as pulling a child from the water is not a rescue, even if it saves the child's life, when the "rescuer" merely believes herself to be salvaging old clothes. What makes whistleblowing morally problematic, if anything does, is this high-minded but unexcused misuse of one's position in a generally law-abiding, morally decent organization, an organization that *prima facie* deserves the whistleblower's loyalty (as a burglary ring does not).

The whistleblower must reveal information the organization does not want revealed. But, in any actual organization, "what the organization wants" will be contested, with various individuals or groups asking to be taken as speaking for the organization. Who, for example, did what Thiokol wanted the night before the *Challenger* exploded? In retrospect, it is obvious that the three vice presidents, Lund, Kilminster, and Mason, did not do what Thiokol wanted—or, at least, what it would have wanted. At the time, however, they had authority to speak for the company—the conglomerate Morton-Thiokol headquartered in Chicago—while the protesting engineers, including Boisjoly, did not. Yet, even before the explosion, was it obvious that the three were doing what the company wanted? To be a whistleblower, one must, I think, at least temporarily lose an argument about what the organization wants. The whistleblower is disloyal only in a sense—the sense the winners of the internal argument get to dictate. What can justify such disloyalty?

The Standard Theory

According to the theory now more or less standard,[1] such disloyalty is morally permissible when:

(S1) The organization to which the would-be whistleblower belongs will, through its product or policy, do serious considerable harm to the public (whether to users of its product, to innocent bystanders, or to the public at large);

(S2) The would-be whistleblower has identified that threat of harm, reported it to her immediate superior, making clear both the threat itself and the objection to it, and concluded that the superior will do nothing effective; and

(S3) The would-be whistleblower has exhausted other internal procedures within the organization (for example, by going up the organizational ladder as far as allowed)—or at least made use of as many internal procedures as the danger to others and her own safety make reasonable.

Whistleblowing is morally required (according to the standard theory) when, in addition:

(S4) The would-be whistleblower has (or has accessible) evidence that would convince a reasonable, impartial observer that her view of the threat is correct; and

(S5) The would-be whistleblower has good reason to believe that revealing the threat will (probably) prevent the harm at reasonable cost (all things considered).

Why is whistleblowing morally required when these five conditions are met? According to the standard theory, whistleblowing is morally required, when it is required at all, because "people have a moral obligation to prevent serious harm to others if they can do so with little cost to themselves."[2] In other words, whistleblowing meeting all five conditions is a form of "minimally decent Samaritanism" (a doing of what morality requires) rather than "good Samaritanism" (going well beyond the moral minimum). . . .

Three Paradoxes

That's the standard theory—where are the paradoxes? The first paradox I want to call attention to concerns a commonplace of the whistleblowing literature. Whistleblowers are not minimally decent Samaritans. If they are Samaritans at all, they are good Samaritans. They always act at considerable risk to career, and generally, at considerable risk to their financial security and personal relations.

In this respect, as in many others, Roger Boisjoly is typical. Boisjoly blew the whistle on his employer, Thiokol; he volunteered information, in public testimony before the Rogers Commission, that Thiokol did not want him to volunteer. As often happens, both his employer and many who relied on it for employment reacted hostilely. Boisjoly had to say goodbye to the company town, to old friends and neighbors, and to building rockets; he had to start a new career at an age when most people are preparing for retirement.

Since whistleblowing is generally costly to the whistleblower in some large way as this, the standard theory's minimally decent Samaritanism provides *no* justification for the central cases of whistleblowing.[3] That is the first paradox, what we might call "the paradox of burden."

The second paradox concerns the prevention of "harm." On the standard theory, the would-be whistleblower must seek to prevent "serious and considerable harm" in order for the whistleblowing to be even morally permissible. There seems to be a good deal of play in the term *harm*. The harm in question can be physical (such as death or disease), financial (such as loss of or damage to property), and perhaps even psychological (such as fear or mental illness). But there is a limit to how much the standard theory can stretch "harm." Beyond that limit are "harms" like injustice, deception, and waste. As morally important as injustice, deception, and waste can be, they do not seem to constitute the "serious and considerable harm" that can require someone to become even a minimally decent Samaritan.

Yet, many cases of whistleblowing, perhaps most, are not about preventing serious and considerable physical, financial, or psychological harm. For example, when Boisjoly spoke up the evening before the *Challenger* exploded, the lives of seven astronauts sat in the balance. Speaking up then was about preventing serious and considerable physical, financial, and psychological harm—but it was not whistleblowing. Boisjoly was then serving his employer, not betraying a trust (even on the employer's understanding of that trust); he was calling his superiors' attention to what he thought they should take into account in their decision and not publicly revealing confidential information. The whistleblowing came after the explosion, in testimony before the Rogers Commission. By then, the seven astronauts were beyond help, the shuttle program was suspended, and any further threat of physical, financial, or psychological harm to the "public" was—after discounting for time—negligible. Boisjoly had little reason to believe his testimony would make a significant difference in the booster's redesign, in safety procedures in the shuttle program, or even in reawakening concern for safety among NASA employees and contractors. The *Challenger's* explosion was much more likely to do that than anything Boisjoly could do. What Boisjoly could do in his testimony, what I think he tried to do, was prevent falsification of the record.

Falsification of the record is, of course, harm in a sense, especially a record as historically important as that which the Rogers Commission was to produce. But falsification is harm only in a sense that almost empties "harm" of its distinctive meaning, leaving it more or less equivalent to "moral wrong." The proponents of the standard theory mean more by "harm" than that. De George, for example, explicitly says that a threat justifying whistleblowing must be to "life or health."[4] The standard theory is strikingly more narrow in its grounds of justification than many examples of justified whistleblowing suggest it should be. That is the second paradox, the "paradox of missing harm."

The third paradox is related to the second. Insofar as whistleblowers are understood as people out to prevent harm, not just to prevent moral wrong, their chances of success are not good. Whistleblowers generally do not prevent much harm. In this too, Boisjoly is typical. As he has said many times, the situation at Thiokol is now much as it was before the disaster. Insofar as we can identify cause and effect, even now we have little reason to believe that—whatever his actual intention—Boisjoly's testimony actually prevented any harm (beyond the moral harm of falsification). So, if whistleblowers must have, as the standard theory says (S5), (beyond the moral wrong of falsification) "good reason to believe that revealing the threat will (probably) prevent the harm," then the history of whistleblowing virtually rules out the moral justification of whistleblowing. That is certainly paradoxical in a theory purporting to state sufficient conditions for the central cases of justified whistleblowing. Let us call this "the paradox of failure."

A Complicity Theory

As I look down the roll of whistleblowers, I do not see anyone who, like the clerk from Accounts, just happened upon key documents in a cover-up.[5] Few, if any, whistleblowers are mere third-parties like the good Samaritan. They are generally deeply involved in the activity they reveal. This involvement suggests that we might better understand what justifies (most) whistleblowing if we understand the whistleblower's obligation to derive from *complicity* in wrongdoing rather than from the ability to prevent harm.

Any complicity theory of justified whistleblowing has two obvious advantages over the standard theory. One is that (moral) complicity itself presupposes (moral) wrongdoing, not harm. So, a complicity justification automatically avoids the paradox of missing harm, fitting the facts of whistleblowing better than a theory which, like the standard one, emphasizes prevention of harm.

That is one obvious advantage of a complicity theory. The second advantage is that complicity invokes a more demanding obligation than the ability to prevent harm does. We are

morally obliged to avoid doing moral wrongs. When, despite our best efforts, we nonetheless find ourselves engaged in some wrong, we have an obligation to do what we reasonably can to set things right. If, for example, I cause a traffic accident, I have a moral (and legal) obligation to call help, stay at the scene until help arrives, and render first aid (if I know how), even at substantial cost to myself and those to whom I owe my time, and even with little likelihood that anything I do will help much. Just as a complicity theory avoids the paradox of missing harm, it also avoids the paradox of burden.

What about the third paradox, the paradox of failure? I shall come to that, but only after remedying one disadvantage of the complicity theory. That disadvantage is obvious—we do not yet have such a theory, not even a sketch. Here, then, is the place to offer a sketch of such a theory.

Complicity Theory. You are morally required to reveal what you know to the public (or to a suitable agent or representative of it) when:

(C1) what you will reveal derives from your work for an organization;

(C2) you are a voluntary member of that organization;

(C3) you believe that the organization, though legitimate, is engaged in serious moral wrongdoing;

(C4) you believe that your work for that organization will contribute (more or less directly) to the wrong if (but *not* only if) you do not publicly reveal what you know;

(C5) you are justified in beliefs C3 and C4; and

(C6) beliefs C3 and C4 are true.

The complicity theory differs from the standard theory in several ways worth pointing out here. The first is that, according to C1, what the whistleblower reveals must derive from his work for the organization. This condition distinguishes the whistleblower from the spy (and the clerk in Accounts). The spy seeks out information in order to reveal it; the whistleblower learns it as a proper part of doing the job the organization has assigned him. The standard theory, in contrast, has nothing to say about how the whistleblower comes to know of the threat she reveals (S2). For the standard theory, spies are just another kind of whistleblower.

A second way in which the complicity theory differs from the standard theory is that the complicity theory (C2) explicitly requires the whistleblower to be a *voluntary* participant in the organization in question. Whistleblowing is not—according to the complicity theory—an activity in which slaves, prisoners, or other involuntary participants in an organization engage. In this way, the complicity theory makes explicit something implicit in the standard theory. The whistleblowers of the standard theory are generally "employees." Employees are voluntary participants in the organization employing them.

What explains this difference in explicitness? For the Samaritanism of the standard theory, the voluntariness of employment is extrinsic. What is crucial is the ability to prevent harm. For the complicity theory, however, the voluntariness is crucial. The obligations deriving from complicity seem to vary with the voluntariness of our participation in the wrongdoing. Consider, for example, a teller who helps a gang rob her bank because they have threatened to kill her if she does not; she does not have the same obligation to break off her association with the gang as someone who has freely joined it. The voluntariness of employment means that the would-be whistleblower's complicity will be more like that of one of the gang than like that of the conscripted teller.

A third way in which the complicity theory differs from the standard theory is that the complicity theory (C3) requires moral wrong, not harm, for justification. The wrong need not be a new event (as a harm must be if it is to be *pre-*

vented). It might, for example, consist in no more than silence about facts necessary to correct a serious injustice.

The complicity theory (C3) does, however, follow the standard theory in requiring that the predicate of whistleblowing be "serious." Under the complicity theory, minor wrongdoing can no more justify whistleblowing than can minor harm under the standard theory. While organizational loyalty cannot forbid whistleblowing, it does forbid "tattling," that is, revealing minor wrongdoing.

A fourth way in which the complicity theory differs from the standard theory, the most important, is that the complicity theory (C4) requires that the whistleblower believe that her work will have contributed to the wrong in question if she does nothing, but it does *not* require that she believe that her revelation will prevent (or undo) the wrong. The complicity theory does not require any belief about what the whistleblowing can accomplish (beyond ending complicity in the wrong in question). The whistleblower reveals what she knows in order to prevent complicity in the wrong, not to prevent the wrong as such. She can prevent complicity (if there is any to prevent) simply by publicly revealing what she knows. The revelation itself breaks the bond of complicity, the secret partnership in wrongdoing, that makes her an accomplice in her organization's wrongdoing. The complicity theory thus avoids the third paradox, the paradox of failure, just as it avoided the other two.

The fifth difference between the complicity theory and the standard theory is closely related to the fourth. Because publicly revealing what one knows breaks the bond of complicity, the complicity theory does not require the whistleblower to have enough evidence to convince others of the wrong in question. Convincing others, or just being able to convince them, is not, as such, an element in the justification of whistleblowing.

The complicity theory does, however, require (C5) that the whistleblower be (epistemically) justified in believing both that his organization is engaged in wrongdoing and that he will contribute to that wrong unless he blows the whistle. Such (epistemic) justification may require substantial physical evidence (as the standard theory says) or just a good sense of how things work. The complicity theory does not share the standard theory's substantial evidential demand (S4).

In one respect, however, the complicity theory clearly requires more of the whistleblower than the standard theory does. The complicity theory's C6—combined with C5—requires not only that the whistleblower be *justified* in her beliefs about the organization's wrongdoing and her part in it, but also that she be *right* about them. If she is wrong about either the wrongdoing or her complicity, her revelation will not be justified whistleblowing. This consequence of C6 is, I think, not as surprising as it may seem. If the would-be whistleblower is wrong only about her own complicity, her revelation of actual wrongdoing will, being otherwise justified, merely fail to be justified *as whistleblowing* (much as a failed rescue, though justified as an attempt, cannot be justified as a rescue). If, however, she is wrong about the wrongdoing itself, her situation is more serious. Her belief that wrong is being done, though fully justified on the evidence available to her, cannot justify her disloyalty. All her justified belief can do is *excuse* her disloyalty. Insofar as she acted with good intentions and while exercising reasonable care, she is a victim of bad luck. Such bad luck will leave her with an obligation to apologize, to correct the record (for example, by publicly recanting the charges she publicly made), and otherwise to set things right.

The complicity theory says nothing on at least one matter about which the standard theory says much—going through channels before publicly revealing what one knows. But the two theories do not differ as much as this difference in emphasis suggests. If going through channels would suffice to prevent (or undo) the wrong, then it cannot be true (as C4 and C6 together require) that the would-be whistleblower's work will contribute to the wrong if she does not publicly reveal what she knows. Where, however, going through channels would *not* prevent (or undo) the wrong, there is no need to go through channels. Condition C4's if-clause will be satisfied. For the complicity theory, going through channels is a way of finding out what the organization will do, not an independent requirement of justification. . . .

A last difference between the two theories worth mention here is that the complicity theory is only a theory of morally required whistleblowing while the standard theory claims as well to define circumstances when whistleblowing is morally permissible but not morally required. This difference is another advantage that the complicity theory has over the standard theory. The standard theory, as we saw, has trouble making good on its claim to explain how whistleblowing can be morally permissible without being morally required.

Testing the Theory

Let us now test the theory against Boisjoly's testimony before the Rogers Commission. Recall that under the standard theory any justification of that testimony seemed to fail for at least three reasons: First, Boisjoly could not testify without substantial cost to himself and Thiokol (to whom he owed loyalty). Second, there was no serious and substantial harm his testimony could prevent. And, third, he had little reason to believe that, even if he could identify a serious and considerable harm to prevent, his testimony had a significant chance of preventing it.

Since few doubt that Boisjoly's testimony before the Rogers Commission constitutes justified whistleblowing, if anything does, we should welcome a theory that—unlike the standard one—justifies that testimony as whistleblowing. The complicity theory sketched above does that:

(C1) Boisjoly's testimony consisted almost entirely of information derived from his work on booster rockets at Thiokol.

(C2) Boisjoly was a voluntary member of Thiokol.

(C3) Boisjoly believed Thiokol, a legitimate organization, was attempting to mislead its client, the government, about the causes of a deadly accident. Attempting to do that certainly seems a serious moral wrong.

(C4) On the evening before the *Challenger* exploded, Boisjoly gave up objecting to the launch once his superiors, including the three Thiokol vice presidents, had made it clear that they were no longer willing to listen to him. He also had a part in preparing those superiors to testify intelligently before the Rogers Commission concerning the booster's fatal field joint. Boisjoly believed that Thiokol would use his failure to offer his own interpretation of his retreat into silence the night before the launch, and the knowledge that he had imparted to his superiors, to contribute to the attempt to mislead Thiokol's client.

(C5) The evidence justifying beliefs C3 and C4 consisted of comments of various officers of Thiokol, what Boisjoly had seen at Thiokol over the years, and what he learned about the rocket business over a long career. I find this evidence sufficient to justify his belief both that his organization was engaged in wrongdoing and that his work was implicated.

(C6) Here we reach a paradox of *knowledge*. Since belief is knowledge if, but only if, it is *both* justified *and* true, we cannot *show* that we know anything. All we can show is that a belief is now justified and that we have no reason to expect anything to turn up later to prove it false. The evidence now available still justifies Boisjoly's belief both about what Thiokol was attempting and about what would have been his part in the attempt. Since new evidence is unlikely, his testimony seems to satisfy C6 just as it satisfied the complicity theory's other five conditions.

Since the complicity theory explains why Boisjoly's testimony before the Rogers Commission was morally required whistleblowing, it has passed its first test, a test the standard theory failed.

NOTES

1. Throughout this essay, I take the standard theory to be Richard T. De George's version in *Business Ethics*, 3rd Edition (New York: Macmillan, 1990), pp. 200–214 (amended only insofar as necessary to include non-businesses as well as businesses). Why treat De George's theory as standard? There are two reasons: first, it seems the most commonly cited; and second, people offering alternatives generally treat it as the one to be replaced. The only obvious competitor, Norman Bowie's account, is distinguishable from De George's on no point relevant here. See Bowie's *Business Ethics* (Englewood Cliffs, NJ: Prentice Hall, 1982), p. 143.

2. De George, *op. cit.* . . .

3. Indeed, I am tempted to go further and claim that, where an informant takes little or no risk, we are unlikely to describe her as a whistleblower at all. So, for example, I would say that using an internal or external "hot-line" is whistleblowing only when it is risky. We are, in other words, likely to consider using a hot-line as disloyalty (that is, as "going out of channels") only if the organization (or some part of it) is likely to respond with considerable hostility to its use.

4. De George, p. 210: "The notion of *serious* harm might be expanded to include serious financial harm, and kinds of harm other than death and serious threats to health and body. But as we noted earlier, we shall restrict ourselves here to products and practices that produce or threaten serious harm or danger to life and health."

5. See Myron Peretz Glazer and Penina Migdal Glazer, *The Whistleblowers: Exposing Corruption in Government and Industry* (New York: Basic Books, 1989) for a good list of whistleblowers (with detailed description of each); for an older list (with descriptions), see Alan F. Westin, *Whistleblowing! Loyalty and Dissent in the Corporation* (New York: McGraw-Hill, 1981).

Review and Discussion Questions

1. Most things we do require no justification. What, if anything, makes whistleblowing morally problematic—that is, why does it require justification in the first place?

2. Critically examine conditions S1 through S5 of the standard theory. Do you see any problems with them?

3. Davis argues that the standard theory gives rise to three paradoxes. Do they pose serious problems for the standard theory? For each of the alleged paradoxes, is there some way for a defender of the standard theory to respond to Davis's argument?

4. Explain Davis's complicity theory. What do you see as the most important differences between it and the standard theory? Is Davis's theory an improvement over the standard theory? Explain why or why not.

5. Does the example of Roger Boisjoly fit the complicity theory better then it does the standard theory? If it does, is that a good argument for the complicity theory? Can you think of any examples of whistleblowing that favor the standard theory over the complicity theory?

6. Are there any aspects of whistleblowing that Davis's theory neglects or fails to do full justice to?

Drug Testing in Employment

JOSEPH R. DESJARDINS AND RONALD DUSKA

According to philosophy professors Joseph R. DesJardins (College of St. Benedict) and Ronald Duska (American College), privacy is an employee right, and drug testing is compatible with this right only if the information it seeks is relevant to the employment contract. DesJardins and Duska then critically assess two arguments intended to establish that knowledge of drug use is job-relevant information: first, that drug use adversely affects employee performance and, second, that it can harm the employer, other employees, and the public. Although they reject the first argument, they grant that, in certain limited circumstances, the second argument can justify drug testing. But even in these cases, strict procedural limitations should be placed on drug testing—despite the fact that drug use is illegal. They conclude by asking whether employee consent to drug testing is voluntary.

Study Questions

1. According to DesJardins and Duska, when or under what circumstances does it violate an employee's right to privacy for an employer to request, collect, or use personal information?

2. The authors examine two arguments used to establish that knowledge of drug use is job-relevant information. What is the first argument, and what are their reasons for rejecting it?

Reprinted by permission of the authors from Joseph R. DesJardins and John J. McCall, eds., Contemporary Issuess in Business Ethics, *4th ed. (Belmont, Calif.: Wadsworth, 2000). Originally published in* Business and Professional Ethics Journal, *Vol. 6, No. 3. Notes abridged.*

3. The authors agree that drug testing can prevent harm and, thus, that knowledge of it is job relevant. Nevertheless, they believe that there are limits to this defense of drug testing. What are they?

4. How do the authors respond to the argument that employers are justified in testing employees because drug use is illegal?

5. Why is there a problem about the voluntariness of drug testing?

WE TAKE PRIVACY TO BE an "employee right," by which we mean a presumptive moral entitlement to receive certain goods or be protected from certain harms in the workplace.[1] Such a right creates a prima facie obligation on the part of the employer to provide the relevant goods or, as in this case, refrain from the relevant harmful treatment. These rights prevent employees from being placed in the fundamentally coercive position where they must choose between their jobs and other basic human goods.

Further, we view the employer-employee relationship as essentially contractual. The employer-employee relationship is an economic one and, unlike relationships such as those between a government and its citizens or a parent and a child, exists primarily as a means for satisfying the economic interests of the contracting parties. The obligations that each party incurs are only those that it voluntarily takes on. Given such a contractual relationship, certain areas of the employee's life remain his or her own private concern, and no employer has a right to invade them. On these presumptions we maintain that certain information about an employee is rightfully private, in other words, that the employee has a right to privacy.

The Right to Privacy

George Brenkert has described the right to privacy as involving a three-place relation between a person A, some information X, and another person B. The right to privacy is violated only when B deliberately comes to possess information X about A and no relationship between A and B exists that would justify B's coming to know X about A.[2] Thus, for example, the relationship one has with a mortgage company would justify that company's coming to know about one's salary, but the relationship one has with a neighbor does not justify the neighbor's coming to know that information.

Hence, an employee's right to privacy is violated whenever personal information is requested, collected, or used by an employer in a way or for any purpose that is *irrelevant to* or *in violation of* the contractual relationship that exists between employer and employee.

Since drug testing is a means for obtaining information, the information sought must be relevant to the contract if the drug testing is not to violate privacy. Hence, we must first decide whether knowledge of drug use obtained by drug testing is job relevant. In cases in which the knowledge of drug use is *not* relevant, there appears to be no justification for subjecting employees to drug tests. In cases in which information of drug use is job relevant, we need to consider if, when, and under what conditions using a means such as drug testing to obtain that knowledge is justified.

Is Knowledge of Drug Use Job-Relevant Information?

Two arguments are used to establish that knowledge of drug use is job-relevant information. The first argument claims that drug use adversely affects job performance, thereby leading to lower productivity, higher costs, and consequently lower profits. Drug testing is seen as a way of avoiding these adverse effects. According to some estimates

$25 billion are lost each year in the United States through loss in productivity, theft, higher rates in health and liability insurance, and similar costs incurred because of drug use. Since employers are contracting with an employee for the performance of specific tasks, employers seem to have a legitimate claim upon whatever personal information is relevant to an employee's ability to do the job.

The second argument claims that drug use has been and can be responsible for considerable harm to individual employees, to their fellow employees, and to the employer, and third parties, including consumers. In this case, drug testing is defended because it is seen as a way of preventing possible harm. Further, since employers can be held liable for harms done to employees and customers, knowledge of employee drug use is needed so that employers can protect themselves from risks related to such liability. But how good are these arguments?

The First Argument: Job Performance and Knowledge of Drug Use

The first argument holds that drug use lowers productivity and that, consequently, an awareness of drug use obtained through drug testing will allow an employer to maintain or increase productivity. It is generally assumed that the performance of people using certain drugs is detrimentally affected by such use, and any use of drugs that reduces productivity is consequently job relevant. If knowledge of such drug use allows the employer to eliminate production losses, such knowledge is job relevant.

On the surface this argument seems reasonable. Obviously some drug use, in lowering the level of performance, can decrease productivity. Since the employer is entitled to a certain level of performance and drug use adversely affects performance, knowledge of that use seems job relevant.

But this formulation of the argument leaves an important question unanswered. To what level of performance are employers entitled? Optimal

performance, or some lower level? If some lower level, what? Employers have a valid claim upon some *certain level* of performance, such that a failure to perform at this level would give the employer a justification for disciplining, firing, or at least finding fault with the employee. But that does not necessarily mean that the employer has a right to a maximum or optimal level of performance, a level above and beyond a certain level of acceptability. It might be nice if the employee gives an employer a maximum effort or optimal performance, but that is above and beyond the call of the employee's duty and the employer can hardly claim a right at all times to the highest level of performance of which an employee is capable. . . .

If the person is producing what is expected, knowledge of drug use on the grounds of production is irrelevant since, by this hypothesis, the production is satisfactory. If, on the other hand, the performance suffers, then to the extent that it slips below the level justifiably expected, the employer has preliminary grounds for warning, disciplining, or releasing the employee. But the justification for this action is the person's unsatisfactory performance, not the person's use of drugs. Accordingly, drug use information is either unnecessary or irrelevant and consequently there are not sufficient grounds to override the right of privacy. Thus, unless we can argue that an employer is entitled to optimal performance, the argument fails.

This counterargument should make it clear that the information that is job relevant, and consequently is not rightfully private, is information about an employee's level of performance and not information about the underlying causes of that level. The fallacy of the argument that promotes drug testing in the name of increased productivity is the assumption that each employee is obliged to perform at an optimal or at least quite high level. But this is required under few if any contracts. What is required contractually is meeting the normally expected levels of production or performing the tasks in the job description adequately (not optimally). If one can do that under the influence of drugs, then on the grounds of job performance at least, drug use is rightfully private. An employee who cannot perform the task adequately is not fulfilling the contract, and knowledge of the cause of the failure to perform is irrelevant on the contractual model.

Of course, if the employer suspects drug use or abuse as the cause of the unsatisfactory performance, then she might choose to help the person with counseling or rehabilitation. However, this does not seem to be something morally required of the employer. Rather, in the case of unsatisfactory performance, the employer has a prima facie justification for dismissing or disciplining the employee. . . .

The Second Argument: Harm and the Knowledge of Drug Use to Prevent Harm

The performance argument is inadequate, but there is an argument that seems somewhat stronger. This is an argument that takes into account the fact that drug use often leads to harm. Using a variant of the Millian argument, which allows interference with a person's rights in order to prevent harm, we could argue that drug testing might be justified if such testing led to knowledge that would enable an employer to prevent harm.

Drug use certainly can lead to harming others. Consequently, if knowledge of such drug use can prevent harm, then knowing whether or not an employee uses drugs might be a legitimate concern of an employer in certain circumstances. This second argument claims that knowledge of the employee's drug use is job relevant because employees who are under the influence of drugs can pose a threat to the health and safety of themselves and others, and an employer who knows of that drug use and the harm it can cause has a responsibility to prevent it.

Employers have both a general duty to prevent harm and the specific responsibility for harms done by their employees. Such responsibilities are

sufficient reason for any employer to claim that information about an employee's drug use is relevant if that knowledge can prevent harm by giving the employer grounds for dismissing the employee or not allowing him or her to perform potentially harmful tasks. Employers might even claim a right to reduce unreasonable risks, in this case the risks involving legal and economic liability for harms caused by employees under the influence of drugs, as further justification for knowing about employee drug use.

This second argument differs from the first, in which only a lowered job performance was relevant information. In this case, even to allow the performance is problematic, for the performance itself, more than being inadequate, can hurt people. We cannot be as sanguine about the prevention of harm as we can about inadequate production. Where drug use may cause serious harm, knowledge of that use becomes relevant if the knowledge of such use can lead to the prevention of harm and drug testing becomes justified as a means for obtaining that knowledge.

Jobs with potential to cause harm

In the first place, it is not clear that every job has a potential to cause harm—at least, not a potential to cause harm sufficient to override a prima facie right to privacy. To say that employers can use drug testing where that can prevent harm is not to say that every employer has the right to know about the drug use of every employee. Not every job poses a threat serious enough to justify an employer coming to know this information.

In deciding which jobs pose serious-enough threats, certain guidelines should be followed. First the potential for harm should be *clear* and *present*. Perhaps all jobs in some extended way pose potential threats to human well-being. We suppose an accountant's error could pose a threat of harm to someone somewhere. But some jobs—like those of airline pilots, school bus drivers, public transit drivers, and surgeons—are jobs in which unsatisfactory performance poses a clear and present danger to others. It would be much harder to make an argument that job perform-ances by auditors, secretaries, executive vice-pres-idents for public relations, college teachers, professional athletes, and the like could cause harm if those performances were carried on under the influence of drugs. They would cause harm only in exceptional cases.[3]

Not every person is to be tested

But, even if we can make a case that a particular job involves a clear and present danger for causing harm if performed under the influence of drugs, it is not appropriate to treat everyone holding such a job the same. Not every jobholder is equally threatening. There is less reason to investigate an airline pilot for drug use if that pilot has a twenty-year record of exceptional service than there is to investigate a pilot whose behavior has become erratic and unreliable recently, or one who reports to work smelling of alcohol and slurring his words. Presuming that every airline pilot is equally threat-ening is to deny individuals the respect that they deserve as autonomous, rational agents. It is to ignore their history and the significant differences between them. It is also probably inefficient and leads to the lowering of morale. It is the likelihood of causing harm, and not the fact of being an air-line pilot per se, that is relevant in deciding which employees in critical jobs to test.

So, even if knowledge of drug use is justifiable to prevent harm, we must be careful to limit this justification to a range of jobs and people where the potential for harm is clear and present. The jobs must be jobs that clearly can cause harm, and the specific employee should not be someone who has a history of reliability. Finally, the drugs being tested should be those drugs that have genuine potential for harm if used in the jobs in question.

Limitations on Drug-Testing Policies

Even when we identify those situations in which knowledge of drug use would be job relevant, we still need to examine whether some proce-dural limitations should not be placed upon the employer's testing for drugs. We have said when a real threat of harm exists and when evidence exists suggesting that a particular employee poses such a threat, an employer could be justified in knowing about drug use in order to prevent the potential harm. But we need to recognize that so long as the employer has the discretion for decid-ing when the potential for harm is clear and pres-ent, and for deciding which employees pose the threat of harm, the possibility of abuse is great. Thus, some policy limiting the employer's power is called for.

Just as criminal law imposes numerous restric-tions protecting individual dignity and liberty on the state's pursuit of its goals, so we should expect that some restrictions be placed on employers to protect innocent employees from harm (includ-ing loss of job and damage to one's personal and professional reputation). Thus, some system of checks upon an employer's discretion in these matters seems advisable.

A drug-testing policy that requires all employ-ees to submit to a drug test or to jeopardize their jobs would seem coercive and therefore unac-ceptable. Being placed in such a fundamentally coercive position of having to choose between one's job and one's privacy does not provide the conditions for a truly free consent. Policies that are unilaterally established by employers would likewise be unacceptable. Working with employ-ees to develop company policy seems the only way to ensure that the policy will be fair to both parties. Prior notice of testing would also be required in order to give employees the option of freely refraining from drug use. Preventing drug use is morally preferable to punishing users after the fact, because this approach treats employees as capable of making rational and informed decisions.

Further procedural limitations seem advisable as well. Employees should be notified of the results of the test, they should be entitled to appeal the results (perhaps through further tests by an inde-pendent laboratory), and the information obtained though tests ought to be kept confidential.

In summary, limitations upon employer discretion for administering drug tests can be derived from the nature of the employment contract and from the recognition that drug testing is justified by the desire to prevent harm, not the desire to punish wrongdoing.

The Illegality Contention

At this point critics might note that the behavior which testing would try to deter is, after all, illegal. Surely this excuses any responsible employer from being overprotective of an employee's rights. The fact that an employee is doing something illegal should give the employer a right to that information about his or her private life. Thus, it is not simply that drug use might pose a threat of harm to others, but that it is an *illegal* activity that threatens others. But again, we would argue that illegal activity itself is irrelevant to job performance. At best, *conviction* records might be relevant, but since drug tests are administered by private employers we are not only ignoring the question of conviction, we are also ignoring the fact that the employee has not even been arrested for the alleged illegal activity.

Further, even if the due process protections and the establishment of guilt are acknowledged, it still does not follow that employers have a claim to know about all illegal activity on the part of their employees.

Consider the following example: Suppose you were hiring an auditor whose job required certifying the integrity of your firm's tax and financial records. Certainly, the personal integrity of this employee is vital to adequate job performance. Would we allow the employer to conduct, with or without the employee's consent, an audit of the employee's own personal tax return? Certainly if we discover that this person has cheated on a personal tax return we will have evidence of illegal activity that is relevant to this person's ability to do the job. Given one's own legal liability for filing falsified statements, the employee's illegal activity also poses a threat to others. But surely, allowing private individuals to audit an employee's tax returns is too intrusive a means for discovering information about that employee's integrity. The government certainly would never allow this violation of an employee's privacy. It ought not to allow drug testing on the same grounds. Why tax returns should be protected in ways that urine, for example, is not, raises interesting questions of fairness. Unfortunately, this question would take us beyond the scope of this paper.

Voluntariness

A final problem that we also leave undeveloped concerns the voluntariness of employee consent. For most employees, being given the choice between submitting to a drug test and risking one's job by refusing an employer's request is not much of a decision at all. We believe that such decisions are less than voluntary and thereby hold that employers cannot escape our criticisms simply by including within the employment contract a drug-testing clause. Furthermore, there is reason to believe that those most in need of job security will be those most likely to be subjected to drug testing. Highly skilled, professional employees with high job mobility and security will be in a stronger position to resist such intrusions than will less skilled, easily replaced workers. This is why we should not anticipate surgeons and airline pilots being tested and should not be surprised when public transit and factory workers are. A serious question of fairness arises here as well.

Drug use and drug testing seem to be our most recent social "crisis." Politicians, the media, and employers expend a great deal of time and effort addressing this crisis. Yet, unquestionably, more lives, health, and money are lost each year to alcohol abuse than to marijuana, cocaine, and other controlled substances. We are well advised to be careful in considering issues that arise from such selective social concern. We will let other social commentators speculate on the reasons why drug use has received scrutiny while other white-collar crimes and alcohol abuse are ignored. Our only concern at this point is that such selective prosecution suggests an arbitrariness that should alert us to questions of fairness and justice.

In summary, then, we have seen that drug use is not always job relevant, and if drug use is not job relevant, information about it is certainly not job relevant. In the case of performance it may be a cause of some decreased performance, but it is the performance itself that is relevant to an employee's position, not what prohibits or enables that employee to do the job. In the case of potential harm being done by an employee under the influence of drugs, the drug use seems job relevant, and in this case drug testing to prevent harm might be legitimate. But how this is practicable is another question. It would seem that standard motor dexterity or mental dexterity tests given immediately prior to job performance are more effective in preventing harm, unless one concludes that drug use invariably and necessarily leads to harm. One must trust the individuals in any system for that system to work. One cannot police everything. Random testing might enable an employer to find drug users and to weed out the few to forestall possible future harm, but are the harms prevented sufficient to override the rights of privacy of the people who are innocent and to overcome the possible abuses we have mentioned? It seems not.

Clearly, a better method is to develop safety checks immediately prior to the performance of a job. Have a surgeon or a pilot or a bus driver pass a few reasoning and motor-skill tests before work. The cause of the lack of a skill, which lack might lead to harm, is really a secondary issue.

NOTES

1. "A Defense of Employee Rights," Joseph DesJardins and John McCall, *Journal of Business Ethics* 4 (1985). We should emphasize that our concern is with the *moral* rights of privacy for employees and not with any specific or prospective *legal* rights. . . .

2. "Privacy, Polygraphs, and Work," George Brenkert, *Journal of Business and Professional Ethics,* vol. 1, no. 1 (Fall 1981). . . .

3. Obviously we are speaking here of harms that go beyond the simple economic harm that results from unsatisfactory job performance. These economic harms are discussed in the first argument above. Further, we ignore such "harms" as providing bad role models for adolescents, harms often used to justify drug tests for professional athletes. We think it unreasonable to hold an individual responsible for the image he or she provides to others.

Review and Discussion Questions

1. Is the employer-employee relationship "essentially contractual"? If it is, what are the implications of this for business ethics?

2. Is privacy an employee right? Explain why or why not. If it is a right, give examples of employer actions or policies that would violate this right.

3. Do you agree that the central question regarding drug testing in employment is whether the information sought is job relevant? Are there other reasons for drug testing that don't turn on this issue?

4. Are you persuaded by DesJardins and Duska's reasons for rejecting the job-performance argument for drug testing? Explain why or why not.

5. How serious is the danger posed by employee drug use? Do you agree that there are important limits to the "prevention of harm" argument for drug testing?

6. Assuming that drug testing is justified in the particular circumstances, what procedural restrictions, if any, should be placed on it, and why?

7. Are DesJardins and Duska correct to maintain that the illegality of drug use is irrelevant?

8. How voluntary do you think employee consent to drug testing really is? Is the voluntariness of consent an important moral issue?

9. What steps do you think employers should take to deal with the problem of employee drug use?

FOR FURTHER READING

Ethical Theory

Christina Hoff Sommers, ed., *Right and Wrong: Basic Readings in Ethics* (New York: Harcourt Brace Jovanovich, 1986) and Mark Timmons, ed., *Conduct and Character: Readings in Moral Theory*, 4th ed. (Belmont, Calif.: Wadsworth, 2003) contain important, accessible essays on Kantianism, utilitarianism, relativism, egoism, and other topics. James Rachels, *The Elements of Moral Philosophy*, 4th ed. (New York: McGraw-Hill, 2003) is an excellent, succinct introduction to the major ideas and theories of ethics. Tom L. Beauchamp, *Philosophical Ethics*, 2nd ed. (New York: McGraw-Hill, 1991) is also an excellent introduction to ethics, combining text and readings on the nature of morality, on classical ethical theories, and on rights, liberty, and justice. A good, but more advanced text is Stephen Darwall, *Philosophical Ethics* (Boulder, Colo.: Westview, 1998). William H. Shaw, *Contemporary Ethics: Taking Account of Utilitarianism* (Oxford: Blackwell, 1999) sympathetically examines the utilitarian approach to ethics. Peter Singer, ed., *A Companion to Ethics* (Cambridge, Mass.: Blackwell, 1991) is a comprehensive reference work with survey essays by many individual authors on both theoretical and applied issues. Hugh LaFollette, ed., *The Blackwell Guide to Ethical Theory* (Oxford: Blackwell, 2000) is a useful, but advanced reference work. Three large collections of more difficult essays on a variety of theoretical topics in ethics that have engaged contemporary philosophers are George Sher, ed., *Moral Philosophy: Selected Readings*, 2nd ed. (New York: Harcourt Brace Jovanovich, 1998), Louis P. Pojman, ed., *Ethical Theory: Classical and Contemporary Readings*, 4th ed. (Belmont, Calif.: Wadsworth, 2002), and Thomas L. Carson and Paul K. Moser, eds., *Morality and the Good Life* (New York: Oxford University Press, 1997). For more on ethical relativism see, Michael Wren, "How Tolerant Must a Relativist Be?" *Public Affairs Quarterly*, vol. 15, no. 4 (October 2001).

Suicide, Euthanasia, and Abortion

The following six collections are a good place to start; they contain intelligent but accessible essays on both sides of these controversial issues, along with further references: John Donnelly, ed., *Suicide: Right or Wrong?*, 2nd ed. (Buffalo, N.Y.: Prometheus, 1998);

Margaret P. Battin, ed, *The Death Debate: Ethical Issues in Suicide* (Englewood Cliffs, N. J.: Prentice-Hall, 1996); Margaret P. Battin, Rosamond Rhodes, and Anita Silvers, eds., *Physician-Assisted Suicide: Expanding the Debate* (London: Routledge, 1998); Robert M. Baird and Stuart E. Rosenbaum, eds., *Euthanasia: The Moral Issues* (Buffalo, N.Y.: Prometheus, 1989) and *The Ethics of Abortion: Pro-Life vs. Pro-Choice*, 3rd ed. (Buffalo, N.Y.: Prometheus, 2001); Joel Feinberg, ed., *The Problem of Abortion*, 2nd ed. (Belmont, Calif.: Wadsworth, 1984). For a collection of advanced essays on physician-assisted suicide, see the special issue of *Ethics* devoted to it (vol. 109, no. 3, April 1999).

L. W. Sumner defends a moderate position on abortion from a basically utilitarian perspective in *Abortion and Moral Theory* (Princeton, N.J.: Princeton University Press, 1981), as does D. W. Haslett in "On Life, Death, and Abortion," *Utilitas*, vol. 8., no. 2 (July 1996). Another good essay is Elizabeth Harman, "Creation Ethics: The Moral Status of Early Fetuses and the Ethics of Abortion," *Philosophy & Public Affairs*, vol. 28, no. 4 (Fall 1999). Jeffrey Reiman and Don Marquis debate the morality of abortion in the *Journal of Social Philosophy*, vol. 27, no. 3 (Winter 1996); vol. 29, no. 1 (Spring 1998); and vol. 29, no. 2 (Fall 1998). Judith Jarvis Thomson revisits the abortion issue in "Abortion," *Boston Review*, vol. 20, no. 3 (Summer 1995). David B. Hershenov assesses Thomson's original thought experiments in "Abortions and Distortions," *Social Theory and Practice*, vol. 27, no. 1 (January 2001). Keith Allen Korcz, "Two Moral Strategies Regarding Abortion," *Journal of Social Philosophy*, vol. 33, no. 4 (Winter 2002) critically examines Thomson's arguments and those of Don Marquis.

Animals and Environmental Ethics

Peter Singer, *Animal Liberation*, 2nd ed. (New York: Random House, 1990) is a seminal work advocating a radical change in our treatment of animals. Gary L. Francione, *Introduction to Animal Rights: Your Child or the Dog?* (Philadelphia: Temple University Press, 2000) is a well-written and provocative critique of our treatment of animals. An excellent recent collection of essays, with an emphasis on law and policy, is Cass R. Sunstein and Martha C. Nussbaum, eds., *Animal Rights: Current Debates and New Directions* (Oxford: Oxford University Press, 2004). Susan Armstrong and Richard Botzler, eds., *The Animal Ethics Reader* (New York: Routledge, 2003), is a large, comprehensive collection, offering a range of perspectives. Older but still valuable collections of good philosophical essays debating our obligations to animals are Harlan B. Miller and William H. Williams, eds., *Ethics and Animals* (Clifton, N.J.: Humana Press, 1983) and Peter Singer and Tom Regan, eds., *Animal Rights and Human Obligations*, 2nd ed. (Englewood Cliffs, N.J.: Prentice-Hall, 1989). *The Monist*, vol. 70, no. 1 (January 1989) focuses on animal rights, with several essays discussing Tom Regan's influential book *The Case for Animal Rights* (Berkeley: University of California Press, 1983). David Paterson and Richard D. Ryder, eds., *Animals' Rights—a Symposium* (London: Centaur Press, 1979) and Peter Singer, ed., *In Defence of Animals* (Oxford: Blackwell, 1985) are interesting and readable collections of essays favorable to animal rights, with contributions from a number of leading animal-rights activists. R. G. Frey ably defends meat eating in *Rights, Killing, and Suffering* (Oxford: Blackwell, 1983). On vegetarianism, see Jeff Jordan, "Why Friends Shouldn't Let Friends Be Eaten," *Social Theory and Practice*, vol. 27, no. 2 (April 2001). Robert M. Baird and

Stuart E. Rosenbaum, eds., *Animal Experimentation: The Moral Issues* (Buffalo, N.Y.: Prometheus, 1991) offers accessible essays, both pro and con. See also T. Ryan Gregory, "The Failure of the Traditional Arguments in the Vivisection Debate," *Public Affairs Quarterly*, vol. 14, no. 2 (April 2000).

On environmental ethics, the following collections are a good place to begin: Tom Regan, ed., *Earthbound: Introductory Essays in Environmental Ethics* (Prospect Heights, Ill.: Waveland, 1984); James Sterba, *Earth Ethics: Introductory Readings on Animal Rights and Environmental Ethics*, 2nd ed. (Upper Saddle River, N. J.: Prentice-Hall, 2000); Louis P. Pojman, *Environmental Ethics: Readings in Theory and Practice*, 3rd ed. (Belmont, Calif.: Wadsworth, 2001); Dale Jamieson, ed., *A Companion to Environmental Philosophy* (Oxford: Blackwell, 2001); and Andrew Light and Holmes Rolston III, eds., *Environmental Ethics: An Anthology* (Oxford: Blackwell, 2003). A brief, but solid introduction to the subject is Joseph R. DesJardins, *Environmental Ethics: An Invitation to Environmental Philosophy*, 3rd ed. (Belmont, Calif.: Wadsworth, 2001), and the journal *Environmental Ethics* is a good source of more advanced work in the field.

Pornography and Sexual Morality

Susan Dwyer, ed., *The Problem of Pornography* (Belmont, Calif.: Wadsworth, 1995), and David Copp and Susan Wendel, eds., *Pornography and Censorship* (Buffalo, N.Y.: Prometheus, 1983) are very useful collections, as are Robert M. Baird and Katherine M. Baird, eds., *Homosexuality* (Buffalo, N.Y.: Prometheus, 1995); Robert M. Baird and Stuart E. Rosenbaum, eds., *Same-Sex Marriage* (Buffalo, N.Y.: Prometheus, 1997); John Corvino, ed., *Same Sex: Debating the Ethics, Science, and Culture of Homosexuality* (Lanham, Md.: Rowman and Littlefield, 1997); and Alan Soble, ed., *The Philosophy of Sex* (Lanham, Md.: Rowman and Littlefield, 2002). For a stimulating but advanced discussion of various themes pertinent to sexual morality, see Martha C. Nussabaum, *Sex and Social Justice* (Oxford: Oxford University Press, 1999). On date rape, see Lois Pineau's influential essay, "Date Rape: A Feminist Analysis," *Law and Philosophy*, vol. 8 (1989), and Leslie Francis, ed., *Date Rape* (University Park, Penn: Penn State Press, 1996), which contains critical discussions of Pineau's analysis. On adultery, Richard Wasserstrom's "Is adultery Immoral?" *Philosophical Forum*, vol. 5 (1974) is a classic. See also Eric M. Cave, "Marital Pluralism: Making Marriage Safer for Love," *Journal of Social Philosophy*, vol. 34, no. 3 (Fall 2003).

Liberty, Paternalism, and Freedom of Expression

Richard A. Wasserstrom, ed., *Morality and the Law* (Belmont, Calif.: Wadsworth, 1971) contains some classic essays on John Stuart Mill's principle and the legal enforcement of morality. Also recommended are Robert M. Baird and Stuart E. Rosenbaum, eds., *Morality and the Law* (Buffalo, N.Y.: Prometheus, 1988) and—for rather more advanced reading—Rolf Sartorius, ed., *Paternalism* (Minneapolis: University of Minnesota Press, 1983), which contains Gerald Dworkin's later essay, "Paternalism: Some Second Thoughts." C. L. Ten, *Mill on Liberty* (Oxford: Oxford University Press, 1980) and John C. Rees, *John Stuart Mill's On Liberty* (Oxford: Oxford University Press, 1985) are very good for further scholarly study of Mill's classic essay. Daniel Shapiro, "Smoking Tobacco:

Irrationality, Addiction, and Paternalism," *Public Affairs Quarterly*, vol. 8, no. 2 (April 1994) is a response to Goodin. Fred Berger, ed., *Freedom of Expression* (Belmont, Calif.: Wadsworth, 1980) is a good source of some important essays on the topic. On drug policy, a good accessible essay is Paul Smith, "Drugs, Morality, and the Law," *Journal of Applied Philosophy*, vol. 19, no. 1 (2002). See also Jeffrey A. Schaler, ed., *Drugs: Should We Legalize, Decriminalize, or Deregulate?* (Buffalo, N.Y.: Prometheus, 1998), and the symposium on "Drug Legalization" in *Criminal Justice Ethics*, vol. 22, no. 1 (Winter/Spring 2003). On free speech and racial harassment, with special reference to Stanford University's policy, see Thomas C. Grey, "Civil Rights Versus Civil Liberties: The Case of Discriminatory Verbal Harassment," *Social Philosophy & Policy*, vol. 8, no. 2 (Spring 1991). On provocative speech, see Randall Kennedy, *Nigger: The Strange Career of a Troublesome Word* (New York: Random House, 2002).

The Responsibilities of Citizens

Plato's famous *Apology* is an account of the trial of Socrates, which sets the immediate historical backdrop to *Crito*. For further background, see Thomas C. Brickhouse and Nicholas D. Smith, eds., *The Trial and Execution of Socrates: Sources and Controversies* (New York: Oxford University Press, 2002). For a survey of the literature on political obligation, see M. B. E. Smith, "The Duty to Obey the Law," in D. Patterson, ed., *Companion to the Philosophy of Law* (Oxford: Blackwell, 1996). Also useful is Mark Tunick, "The Moral Obligation to Obey the Law," *Journal of Social Philosophy*, vol. 33, no. 3 (Fall 2002). Despite its age, Peter Singer's *Democracy and Disobedience* (Oxford: Oxford University Press, 1974) remains an excellent, very readable analysis of political obligation in a democracy. For more on the obligation to vote, see David T. Risser, "The Moral Problem of Nonvoting," *Journal of Social Philosophy*, vol. 34, no. 3 (Fall 2003). Robert K. Fullinwider responds to Galston in "Conscription—No," *Philosophy & Public Policy Quarterly*, vol. 23, no. 1 (Summer 2003).

Gun Control and Capital Punishment

For essays both for and against gun control, see Tamara Roleff, ed., *Gun Control: Opposing Viewpoints* (San Diego: Greenhaven, 1997), and Lee Nisbet, ed., *The Gun Control Debate: You Decide*, 2nd ed (Buffalo, N.Y.: Prometheus, 2000). Hugh LaFollette, "Gun Control," *Ethics*, vol. 110, no. 2 (January 2000), provides a cool, thoughtful discussion of this controversial topic. Also useful is Todd C. Hughes and Lester H. Hunt, "The Liberal Basis of the Right to Bear Arms," *Public Affairs Quarterly*, vol. 14, no. 1 (January 2000).

Hugo Adam Bedau is a long-time critic of the death penalty. His "Capital Punishment" in Tom Regan, ed., *Matters of Life and Death* (New York: Random House, 1980) is a very useful introduction; also recommended is his book *Death Is Different: Studies in the Morality, Law, and Politics of Capital Punishment* (Boston: Northeastern University Press, 1987). Ernest van den Haag and John P. Conrad debate capital punishment in *The Death Penalty: A Debate* (New York: Plenum, 1983). Tom Sorell, *Moral Theory and Capital Punishment* (Oxford: Blackwell, 1988) draws the links between normative theory and the debate over capital punishment in a clear and accessible way. Some influential essays on both capital punishment and the justification of punishment in general are reprinted in Robert M. Baird and Stuart E. Rosenbaum, eds., *Punishment and the Death Penalty* (Buffalo, N.Y.: Prometheus, 1995). For some good recent essays, see "Symposium: The Death Penalty," *Criminal Justice Ethics*, vol. 21, no. 2 (Summer/Fall 2002), with contributions from Hugo Adam, Tom Sorell, Michael Davis, and others.

War and Terrorism

A good, readable introduction to the ethics of war is Douglas P. Lackey, *The Ethics of War and Peace* (Englewood Cliffs, N.J.: Prentice-Hall, 1989). A classic in the field is Michael Walzer's very rich study, *Just and Unjust Wars: A Moral Argument with Historical Illustrations*, 3rd ed. (New York: Basic Books, 2000). One older essay that still repays study is Richard A. Wasserstrom, "On the Morality of War: A Preliminary Inquiry," *Stanford Law Review*, vol. 21, no. 6 (June 1969). Also older, but still very valuable is Marshall Cohen's, ed., *War and Moral Responsibility* (Princeton: Princeton University Press, 1974). Very recent and very readable is Verna V. Gehring, ed., *War After September 11* (Lanham, Md.: Rowman & Littlefield, 2003). Martha C. Nussbaum, "Compassion and Terror," *Daedalus*, vol. 132, no. 1 (Winter 2003) is a pertinent, thought-provoking essay. A clear, succinct presentation of Kant's thinking about the morality of war is Lawrence Masek, "All's Not Fair in War: How Kant's Just War Theory Refutes War Realism," *Public Affairs Quarterly*, vol. 16, no. 2 (April 2002). Aleksandar Jokic and Burleigh Wilkins, eds., *Humanitarian Intervention: Moral and Philosophical Issues* (Petersborough, Ontario: Broadview, 2003) is a collection of new, but advanced essays on military intervention for humanitarian reasons. The major statement of R. M. Hare's moral philosophy is *Moral Thinking: Its Levels, Method, and Point* (Oxford: Oxford University Press, 1981). Essays 1, 2, 5, and 13 from Hare's *Objective Prescriptions and Other Essays* (Oxford: Oxford University Press, 1999) provide a good introduction to his moral philosophy.

Affirmative Action

Steven M. Cahn, ed., *The Affirmative Action Debate*, 2nd ed. (New York: Routledge, 2002); Francis Beckwith and Todd E. Jones, eds., *Affirmative Action: Social Justice or Reverse Discrimination?* (Buffalo, N.Y.: Prometheus, 1997); Marshall Cohen, Thomas Nagel, and Thomas Scanlon, eds., *Equality and Preferential Treatment* (Princeton, N.J.: Princeton University Press, 1977); and *Social Philosophy & Policy*, vol. 5, no. 1 (Autumn 1987), "Equal Opportunity," and vol. 8, no. 2 (Spring 1991), "Reassessing Civil Rights," provide useful selections of philosophical essays both for and against affirmative action. Gertude Ezorsky, *Racism and Justice: The Case for Affirmative Action* (Ithaca, N.Y.: Cornell University Press, 1991) is a short, clear defense. Carl Cohen and James P. Sterba take opposing sides of the debate in *Affirmative Action and Racial Preferences* (New York: Oxford University Press, 2003). Also valuable are K. Anthony Appiah and Amy Gutman, *Color Consciousness: The Political Morality of Race* (Princeton, N.J.: Princeton University Press, 1996) and Robert Post, *Prejudicial Appearances: The Logic of American Antidiscrimination Law* (Durham, N.C.: Duke University Press, 2001), which contains replies by four writers to Post's cover essay. Luke Charles Harris and Uma Narayan offer a fresh perspective in "Affirmative Action as Equalizing Opportunity:

Challenging the Myth of 'Preferential Treatment,'" *National Black Law Journal*, vol. 16, no. 2 (1999). James P. Sterba and Terence J. Pell debate the University of Michigan cases in four essays in the *Journal of Social Philosophy*, vol. 34, no. 2 (Summer 2003). See also Stephen Kershnar, "Experiential Diversity and *Grutter*," *Public Affairs Quarterly*, vol. 17, no. 2 (April 2003). For a good but challenging critique of the diversity argument for affirmative action, see George Sher, "Diversity," *Philosophy & Public Affairs*, vol. 28, no. 2 (Spring 1999).

Economic Justice

John Arthur and William H. Shaw, eds., *Justice and Economic Distribution*, 2nd ed. (Englewood Cliffs, N.J.: Prentice-Hall, 1991) contains representative extracts from the major contemporary theories of justice along with recent essays discussing the topic. Will Kymlicka, *Contemporary Political Philosophy*, 2nd ed. (Oxford: Oxford University Press, 2002) covers today's major schools of political thought and their competing views of justice and community. On world hunger, Will Aiken and Hugh LaFollette, eds., *World Hunger and Morality*, 2nd ed. (Englewood Cliffs, N.J.: Prentice-Hall, 1996), and Henry Shue, *Basic Rights: Subsistence, Affluence, and U.S. Foreign Policy*, 2nd ed. (Princeton, N.J.: Princeton University Press, 1996) are recommended. Jean Drèze and Amartya Sen, *Hunger and Public Action* (Oxford: Oxford University Press, 1989) brings economic theory and empirical data to bear on the analysis of world hunger. A useful, recent discussion of Singer is James R. Otteson, "Limits of Our Obligation to Give," *Public Affairs Quarterly*, vol. 14, no. 3 (July 2000). Insightful, but more difficult is Garrett Cullity, "International Aid and the Scope of Kindness," *Ethics*, vol. 105, no. 1 (October 1994). For more of Peter Singer's thinking, see his essay "The Singer Solution," *New York Times Magazine* (September 5, 1999). A good, but difficult non-Singerian defense of a strong obligation to give is Peter Unger, *Living High and Letting Die* (Oxford: Oxford University Press, 1996). For a viewpoint opposed to Ian Maitland, see Liza Featherstone, *Students Against Sweatshops* (London: Verso, 2002). For more on welfare, see the *Social Philosophy & Policy* issue on "The Welfare State," vol. 14, no. 2 (Summer 1997). Also pertinent is Liam Murphy and Thomas Nagel, "Taxes, Redistribution, and Public Provision," *Philosophy & Public Affairs*, vol. 30, no. 1 (Winter 2001). Mark L. Ascher, "Curtailing Inherited Wealth," *Michigan Law Review* (October 1990) is a long, extensively documented critique of our inheritance system. For further development of Haslett's views, see his essay "Distributive Justice and Inheritance," in Guido Erreygers and Toon Vandevelde, eds., *Is Inheritance Legitimate? Ethical and Economic Aspects of Wealth Transfers* (Heidelberg: Springer, 1997).

Ethics in Business

General introductions to business ethics are provided by Richard T. De George, *Business Ethics*, 5th ed. (Upper Saddle River, N.J.: Prentice Hall 1999), Manual Velasquez, *Business Ethics*, 5th ed. (Upper Saddle River, N.J.: Prentice Hall 2001), and William H. Shaw, *Business Ethics*, 5th ed. (Belmont, Calif.: Wadsworth 2005). Three good sources of advanced work in business ethics are the *Business and Professional Ethics Journal*, *Business Ethics Quarterly*, and the *Journal of Business Ethics*.

Two early and influential contributions to the debate over advertising are John Kenneth Galbraith, *The Affluent Society* (New York: Houghton Mifflin, 1959), and Theodore Levitt, "The Morality (?) of Advertising," *Harvard Business Review* 48 (July–August 1970). Other important discussions are Robert L. Arrington, "Advertising and Behavior Control," *Journal of Business Ethics* 1 (February 1982); John Waide, "The Making of Self and World in Advertising," *Journal of Business Ethics* 6 (February 1987); Roger Crisp, "Persuasive Advertising, Autonomy, and the Creation of Desire," *Journal of Business Ethics* 6 (July 1987); Richard L. Lippke, "Advertising and the Social Conditions of Autonomy," *Business and Professional Ethics Journal* 8 (Winter 1989); and Andrew Gustafson, "Advertising's Impact on Morality in Society: Influencing Habits and Desires of Consumers," *Business and Society Review* 106 (Fall 2001).

David M. Holley's essay, "A Moral Evaluation of Sales Practices," originally appeared in *Business and Professional Ethics Journal* 5 (Fall 1987). Holley revisits the issue in "Information Disclosure in Sales," *Journal of Business Ethics* 17 (April 1998), and replies to Carson in "Alternative Approaches to Applied Ethics: A Response to Carson's Critique," *Business Ethics Quarterly* 12 (January 2002). For further discussion of the ethics of sales, see James M. Ebejer and Michael J. Morden, "Paternalism in the Marketplace: Should a Salesman Be His Buyer's Keeper?" *Journal of Business Ethics* 7 (May 1988); Kerry S. Walters, "Limited Paternalism and the Pontius Pilate Plight," *Journal of Business Ethics* 8 (December 1989), and George Brockway, "Limited Paternalism and the Salesperson: A Reconsideration," *Journal of Business Ethics* 12 (April 1993).

Richard T. De George originally presented his criteria for assessing whistleblowing in "Ethical Responsibilities of Engineers in Large Organizations," *Business and Professional Ethics Journal* 1 (Fall 1981). Subsequent versions can be found in the different editions of his book *Business Ethics*. Gene G. James discusses De George's theory in "Whistle Blowing: Its Moral Justification," in W. Michael Hoffman, Robert E. Frederick, and Mark S. Schwartz, eds., *Business Ethics: Readings and Cases in Corporate Morality*, 4th ed. (New York: McGraw-Hill, 2001). Other good studies of the moral complexity of whistleblowing are Michael Davis, "Avoiding the Tragedy of Whistleblowing," *Business and Professional Ethics Journal* 8 (Winter 1989); Natalie Dandekar, "Can Whistleblowing Be Fully Legitimated?" *Business and Professional Ethics Journal* 10 (Fall 1990); Mike W. Martin, "Whistleblowing: Professionalism, Personal Life, and Shared Responsibility for Safety in Engineering," *Business and Professional Ethics Journal* 11 (Summer 1992); and C. Fred Alford, "Whistleblowing: Professionalism, Personal Life, and Shared Responsibility," *Journal of Social Philosophy* 32 (Fall 2001).

Two good, recent essays—one defending drug testing, the other arguing against it—are Michael Crawford, "Drug Testing and the Right to Privacy: Arguing the Ethics of Workplace Drug Testing," *Journal of Business Ethics* 17 (November 1998), and John R. Rowan, "Limitations on the Moral Permissibility of Employee Drug Testing," *Business and Professional Ethics Journal* 19 (Summer 2001). Also useful are Douglas Birsch, "The Universal Drug Testing of Employees," *Business and Professional Ethics Journal* 14 (Fall 1995), and Nicholas J. Caste, "Drug Testing and Productivity," *Journal of Business Ethics* 11 (April 1992).